EGYPT
Tropic of Cancer
RED SEA
ERITREA
SUDAN
Nile River
DJIBOUTI
SOMALIA
ETHIOPIA
RAL
EPUBLIC
Lake Turkana
Lake Albert
UGANDA
KENYA
INDIAN OCEAN
RWANDA
Lake Victoria
RE
BURUNDI
SEYCHELLES
Lake Tanganyika
TANZANIA
Aldabra (SEYCHELLES)
COMOROS
Lake Malawi
Mayotte
(FRANCE)
ZAMBIA
Lake
Kariba
MALAWI
ZIMBABWE
Zambezi River
MAURITIUS
OTSWANA
MOZAMBIQUE
Réunion
(FRANCE)
Rodriguez
(MAURITIUS)
SWAZILAND
MADAGASCAR
LESOTHO
H AFRICA

Collins Guide to African Wildlife

Peter C. Alden

Richard D. Estes
Duane Schlitter
Bunny McBride

HarperCollins*Publishers*

Published by HarperCollins*Publishers*
77-85 Fulham Palace Road
London
W6 8JB
UK

Prepared and produced by Chanticleer Press, Inc., New York.

Printed and bound by Toppan Printing Co., Ltd., Tokyo, Japan.

Published 1996
Third Printing, September 2004

A British Library CIP data for this book is available

ISBN 0-00-719811-6

CONTENTS

THE AUTHORS

Peter C. Alden, who wrote most of the essays in Part I as well as the birds, reptiles, and insects accounts, is a freelance safari leader, cruise lecturer, and wildlife tour leader. He has designed and led bird and nature tours to 27 countries in Africa and more than 100 countries on seven continents. These have been sponsored by Friends of the Harvard Museum of Natural History, the Massachusetts and National Audubon Societies, Overseas Adventure Travel, Lindblad Travel, and a variety of cruise lines. A graduate of the University of Arizona, he is the author of several books, including *Finding the Birds in Western Mexico* (University of Arizona Press), *Finding Birds Around the World* (Houghton Mifflin), and National Audubon Society field guides to California, Florida, New England, the Pacific Northwest, and the Mid-Atlantic, Rocky Mountain, southeastern, and southwestern states. He also organizes biodiversity days for the Massachusetts Executive Office of Environmental Affairs. Alden lives in Concord, Massachusetts.

Richard D. Estes, Ph.D., author of the large mammals species accounts (ungulates through primates), has spent more than three decades studying, observing, and writing and lecturing about African mammals. He began eight years of field studies in 1962 by living for two and a half years in Tanzania's Ngorongoro Crater, researching wildebeest territorial behavior. He spent another two years (1968–1970) studying the sable antelope, followed by a year in Angola observing the giant sable; from 1979 to 1981 he studied antelopes in Serengeti National Park. As a member of the World Conservation Union's (IUCN) Species Survival Commission and as chairman of the Antelope Specialists Group, Estes is working for conservation of African mammals and their habitats. He is the author of two books on animal behavior: *The Behavior Guide to African Mammals* (University of California Press) and *The Safari Companion* (Chelsea Green). Estes lives in Peterborough, New Hampshire.

Duane Schlitter, Ph.D., who contributed the small mammals species accounts (insectivores through rodents), has a doctorate in zoology from the University of Maryland and is curator of mammals at the Carnegie Museum of Natural History in Pittsburgh, Pennsylvania. He is a specialist in the small mammals of Africa, especially bats, rodents, and insectivores. Since 1967 Schlitter has conducted research in 22 African countries and has spent nearly nine years living in tents in the bush. He has published more than 100 professional papers and edited two books on his research. In addition to basic systematic research, he also studies mammals as agricultural pests and reservoirs of human diseases, and conducts biotic inventories to help establish new parks and reserves. Schlitter resides in Pittsburgh.

Bunny McBride, a free-lance writer with a masters degree in anthropology from Columbia University, co-authored the "Countries and Reserves" section of the guide. McBride writes most often on cultural survival and wildlife conservation topics, and her work has appeared in a wide variety of publications, in particular *The Christian Science Monitor,* for whom she worked as a stringer (1978–1988). Her books include *Our Lives in Our Hands: Micmac Indian Basketmakers* (Tilbury House, 1990) and *Molly Spotted Elk: A Penobscot in Paris* (University of Oklahoma Press, 1995). She lives in Manhattan, Kansas.

ACKNOWLEDGMENTS

The authors would like to thank our many African resident hosts and colleagues who have shown us their countries and wildlife. We wish we could list all the expert naturalist guides, national park staff members, driver-guides, pilots, camp staff members, game lodge staff members, travel industry professionals, and rural people who have extended so many courtesies to us in Africa. We also owe a debt of gratitude to the many explorers, conservationists, zoologists, authors, artists, photographers and film-makers who have published works on this fascinating continent.

Peter Alden would like to thank Gabrielle Whitehouse, Alfred Alcorn, José Rosada, Van Wallach (who vetted the reptiles section), and the library staff of Harvard University's Museum of Comparative Zoology; James Baird, Gerard Bertrand, Chris Leahy, and Simon Perkins of the Massachusetts Audubon Society; and Judi Wineland, Kathryn Cooney, Chris Bensley, and Alan Lewis of Overseas Adventure Travel. In addition, he wishes to thank Eddie Brewer (Gambia), Alec Forbes-Watson (Kenya and Madagascar), Richard Forster (help with the birds accounts), Ted and Florence Glass (research grants), Stuart Keith (author of *The Birds of Africa* and birds consultant for this volume), Jorie Butler Kent (Abercrombie & Kent), Michel Kleinbaum, Oliver Komar (typing and computers), the late Lars-Eric Lindblad (Lindblad Travel and Polaris cruises of West Africa), Lysa Leland (Uganda and primates), Lynne Leakey (Kenya), Roger Tory and Virginia Peterson, Russell Peterson (National Audubon Society), Leif Stahl (Senegal), Peter Steyn (southern Africa), Rick Thomson and the superb Tanzanian staff of Thomson Safaris, Guy Tudor, Don and Steve Turner (East African Ornithological Safaris), and William Weber (countries consultant for this volume), John Gwynne, and Amy Vedder of the New York Zoological Society. Alden wishes he could list individually the many hundreds of individuals and couples with whom he has traveled on many wildlife safaris, tours, and cruises to Africa since 1970.

Richard Estes would like to thank the following: for permission to conduct research in Ngorongoro Crater, the Chief Conservator, Ngorongoro Conservation Area Authority; in Serengeti National Park, the Director of the Serengeti Wildlife Research Institute and the Director of Tanzania National Parks; in Nairobi National Park, the Director of the Kenya Wildlife Service; in Kruger National Park, the Chief Warden and the National Parks Board of South Africa; in Mkuzi Game Reserve, the Natal Parks Board; in Willem Pretorius Reserve, the Director of Nature and Environmental Conservation, Orange Free State; in Etosha National Park, the Director of Nature Conservation. The following organizations provided research grants: the Conservation Foundation, the National Geographic Society (Committee for Research and Exploration), the National Science

Foundation, the Harvard Travellers Club, the Explorers Club, and the African Safari Club of Philadelphia. The following colleagues and friends helped in carrying out field work: Bill Baker, Ron Benninger, Marina Botje, Runi Estes, George Frame, Jeannette Hanby, Jack Ingram, Karen Nielsen, Ranka Sekulic, David Van Vleck, Savvas Vrahimas, and Jessie Williams. Too many people have extended hospitality and assistance over the years to be listed individually, but the following were especially forthcoming: Peter Beard, Henry Fosbrooke, Richard Jeffery, Andreas von Nagy, and Vivian Wilson.

Duane Schlitter would like to thank the late Professor J. Knox Jones, Jr., University of Kansas and Texas Tech University, and the late Dr. Henry W. Setzer, Smithsonian Institution, both of whom provided considerable support in his early career. Although the friends and colleagues in Africa who have contributed their time, efforts, and knowledge over the years are too numerous to mention, some must be singled out for special thanks: Naas and Kobie Rautenbach, Gary Bronner, Gerrie De Graaff, Nico Dippenaar, the late Reay Smithers, the late Waldo Meester, Pierre Swanepoel, Jan Nel, Hennie Erasmus, Jennifer Jarvis, and Wynand and Annatjie Theron (South Africa); Chris Chimimba (Malawi and South Africa); Neels and Marianna Coetzee (Namibia); the late Harry Hoogstraal and Ibrahim Helmy (Egypt); Richard Leakey, Issa Aggundey, Mohamed Isahakia, and Paul Kabochie (Kenya); Afework Bekele (Ethiopia); Abdulcadir Nur, Abdullahi Karani, Omar Haji, Abdulwahab Josuf, Mohamed Ali, John and Jonquil Ash, Bill and Sally Smythe, John and Sahara Miskall, and Tony and Lynette Johnston

(Somalia); Jonathan Baranga (Uganda); Kim Howell (Tanzania); Frank Ansell (Zambia); Bremah Mosi, Luri Kanton, and Christian Briandt (Ghana); and Clement Njeti, James Powell, Evelyne Laurent, Paul Rodewald, Philip Agbor, and Felix Inyangi (Cameroon). The personnel of the various national wildlife agencies and parks and reserves have always been very helpful. Also due thanks are Rodney Honeycutt, Steve Williams, Lynn Robbins, Laurie Robbins, Mazin Qumsiyeh, Marc Allard, Kim Nelson, Carl Phillips, Caroline Plazek, Mike Smolen, Ron Ruiz, Deanna Tolliver, Jan and Laurel Decher, Mike Hearst, John Gruwell, Brian Robbins, Ralph and Judy Vaden, John Herbert, Dick Davis, the late Jack McCoy, Tom McIntyre, and Abdu Farhang-Azad. Robert Traub, University of Maryland and Smithsonian Institution, must be acknowledged as a special friend and mentor. Finally, the love and support of Judy, Tammy, and Tanya Schlitter have made the many days and nights in the African bush worthwhile.

Bunny McBride would like to thank David and Petal Allen (Allen Safaris, Nairobi), Katie Beaver and Lindsay Chongseng (Seychelles Tourist Board), Heidi and Sigi Ernst-Luseno (Nairobi), Sandy Evans and David Markham (Abercrombie & Kent), Karl Jahn (Rufigi River Camp, Tanzania), Peter and Sarah Jenkins (Kenya Wildlife Service), John Lampl (British Airways), Robert and Betty Press (*Christian Science Monitor,* Nairobi Bureau), Dr. Herbert Prins, Monique Rodriguez (Cortez Travel), Craig Sholley (Mountain Gorilla Project, Rwanda), Edwin and Gail Sadd and Joseph Mutua (Bushbuck Travel, Nairobi), Adrian Skerrett (Victoria, Seychelles), Mark Stanley-Price (African Wildlife Foundation), and Bill and Ruth Woodley (Kenya Wildlife Service).

The authors have enjoyed working with the personnel of Chanticleer Press: Andrew Stewart, whose vision made this book a reality; Edie Locke, managing editor; Patricia Fogarty, project editor; Amy K. Hughes, senior editor; Lisa Leventer, copy editor; Peggy Grohskopf, fact checker; Kristina Lucenko, editorial assistant; Giema Tsakuginow and Tiffany Lee, photo editors; designers Areta Buk and Drew Stevens; design assistant Taruna Singh; typesetter Barbara Sturman; and production manager Susan Schoenfeld. The fine drawings by Barry Van Dusen and Kim Honda and the exacting maps generated to the authors' specifications by Paul Singer and Acme Design complement the text superbly. We appreciate the many hours spent by hundreds of amateur and professional photographers gathering the photographs that we reviewed. We wish we could have printed dozens more of the stunning pictures submitted.

The authors and the staff of Chanticleer Press would like to especially thank wildlife experts George Walter Frame and Lory Herbison Frame for the extensive assistance they provided as consultants for many segments and phases of this project, particularly with the mammals. Their work was always thorough and meticulous, and the project has benefited enormously from their involvement.

INTRODUCTION

This portable field guide introduces the reader to the wildlife and nature reserves of Africa, the second-largest continent and the only one centered on the equator. The premier continent for wildlife-oriented eco-tourism, Africa has roughly 70 of the world's top 100 parks for observing large numbers of mammals and birds.

The greatest diversity and numbers of large land mammals on the planet survive in Africa, chiefly in the savannas and swamplands of the south and east. A major factor in the survival of large mammals has been the enlightened creation of reserves by both colonial and African governments over the years. Strange as it may seem, tsetse flies have also played an important role in creating sanctuaries for these animals, as the diseases the flies spread have kept humans and domestic cattle out of these regions for many centuries (the wild animals are immune to the diseases).

Most mammals, birds, and reptiles that live south of the Sahara are endemic (restricted) to Africa. They are not found in similar habitats in South America or tropical Asia, because there has not been any recent land connection to either continent. Conversely, the wildlife of North Africa (the Sahara and

Mediterranean regions) is very much like that of similar habitats in southern Europe and southwestern Asia, due to current and recent land connections between the continents.
The unique fauna of Africa is of universal value, and conservation efforts there have worldwide importance. African wildlife also has great economic value in attracting international travelers who want to see the great herds and fascinating species.

Geographical Scope

This guide covers wildlife of the African continent, which extends from the Mediterranean Sea south to the Cape of Good Hope, and of many island groups off the Atlantic Ocean and Indian Ocean coasts. The continent's physical geography, climate, and vegetation are introduced in the section "Biogeography of Africa." Africa's countries and the surrounding islands are covered in the "Countries and Reserves" section. Two maps of Africa are provided in the end papers of the guide: One shows the countries and chief rivers and lakes of Africa; the other graphically depicts the principal vegetation zones.

Wildlife Coverage

The species of wildlife selected for this guide come from all over the African continent, from the Sahara to the West African rain forests to Madagascar to the Cape of Good Hope. Most heavily represented are the wide-ranging, common species of the savannas of western, eastern, and southern Africa, including the Serengeti Plains, which attract most of Africa's visitors. Many of the species seen among the great migrating herds, including wildebeests, zebras, antelopes, giraffes, elephants, lions, hyenas, and a vast array of birds, are covered. The rain forests of Africa, which attract fewer visitors, are represented by some of the characteristic species of these lush habitats. Likewise, we highlight a few regional endemic

species and subspecies (or races) that visitors may encounter in the field in various parts of the continent.
In addition to the wide variety of common birds and land mammals, the guide covers a few of the thousands of reptile and insect species of Africa. Included are representatives from each of the three main orders of reptiles (tortoises, crocodiles, and scaled reptiles), with an emphasis on species that are common or of special interest. The insect groups covered are three of the most prominent in Africa: tsetse flies, dung beetles, and termites.

Organization of the Guide

The Collins Guide to African Wildlife is composed of four sections: introductory essays on the African continent; color photographs of African habitats and geographical features and of common mammals, birds, reptiles, and insects; written descriptions of the mammal, bird, and reptile species, and of the insect groups; and appendices.

The African Continent

Part I of the guide opens with an essay on the biogeography of Africa that explains the continent's physical geography and climate and vegetation zones.
The section "Countries and Reserves: Where to See Wildlife" provides concise descriptions of 47 African countries, plus Madagascar and ten island groups. These essays focus on a selection of the most important nature reserves and wild areas (with brief listings of their wildlife), and include basic information on the geography and climate of each country. Because of limitations of space, some animals mentioned in the country overviews are not covered in the species accounts in this guide. Maps of the countries are provided.

The Photographs

The color plates section (Part II) presents 577 photographs: 50 of key African landforms and habitats, 200

of mammals, 300 of birds, and 27 of reptiles and insects. Most of the photographs show adult males, or adults when the sexes are alike. For some species a female (♀), subspecies (race), or color phase is pictured, when these differ significantly from the typical male or adult. For birds that acquire a special plumage during the breeding season, breeding individuals are shown; exceptions are noted as "nonbreeding." The page number of the text description of the species is given in the photograph's caption.
The guide includes some important species that are difficult to photograph in the wild because of their habitats, such as rain forests, or their habits, such as shyness or a nocturnal activity pattern. Some of these are depicted in photographs known or presumed to have been taken in captivity; in these cases, the photo caption includes the abbreviation "cap." About a dozen others are illustrated in black-and-white drawings that appear in the margin of the species description.
The photographs of African habitats illustrate some of the vegetation zones and geological features of the continent. The page numbers in each caption refer to the pages of text on which that feature, vegetation type, or place is discussed in the "Biogeography of Africa" and the "Countries and Reserves" sections.

The Animals This book is designed as an introduction to African wildlife rather than a comprehensive guide to every animal species represented on the continent. Because of the limited space afforded by a single volume, the authors and editors have had to be selective, choosing the mammals, birds, and reptiles that are the most important representatives of their genus or family. The focus throughout is on animals that are most likely to be seen (or asked about) by visitors. Part III presents approximately 250 words each on 169 mammals, 284 birds, 24 reptiles, and 3 insect groups, for a total of 480 full species accounts. In addition, a special section within each account presents brief descriptions of species that are similar to or related to the main subject; these "Similar Species" sections bring the total coverage to more than 850 species. Because that number represents only about one-fifth of Africa's mammal, bird, and reptile species, we have attempted to include representative species of nearly all orders and most families. When a genus had several members in different areas of Africa, we often chose the eastern or south-central representative, as these are the most-visited areas. Given the space limitations, the whales and dolphins of the order Cetacea, which range over the oceans of the world, have been omitted. The guide does not include amphibians, fish, or invertebrates, except for three insect groups.

At the beginning of the mammals and the birds sections, schematic black-and-white drawings of an antelope and a bird indicate the names of key features of the animals' external anatomy. Many of these terms are explained in the Glossary.

Appendices Part IV consists of an essay on conservation, a Glossary of terms relating to the geography, vegetation, and animals of Africa, and two indexes. The Species Index includes the main common (English) name, alternate common names, and the scientific name for each bird, mammal, reptile, and insect discussed, including subspecies and similar species. The Geographical Index includes countries, islands, and parks and reserves. The indexes give both page numbers and color plate numbers.

Sequence of Photographs and Text The species accounts and photographs of the birds, reptiles, and insects are arranged in a traditional sequence that reflects taxonomic order, which, in biology, is the systematic categorization of organisms according to presumed natural relationships. The orders of mammals have been placed in a sequence created for the convenience of the reader; within the orders (e.g., carnivores, primates) the mammals are arranged in the traditional taxonomic sequence.

Animal Classification Animals are classified in taxonomic categories that proceed from large to small. The categorization of the Blue Monkey *(Cercopithecus mitis)* is as follows: kingdom Animal; phylum or division Chordata; class Mammalia; order Primates; family Cercopithecidae; genus *Cercopithecus;* species *mitis.* This guide contains brief text descriptions of the classes, orders, and families represented; these provide basic information about the species these larger groups contain. Species accounts follow the family descriptions in the text sequence. When reading about a particular animal, readers should review the order and family accounts that precede the species account.

The Species Accounts

The species accounts, which follow the color plates, provide basic information for each animal covered:

Animal Names Each species account opens with the animal's common name. Important alternative names for the animal—often regional names, subspecies names, or former names—may appear on the following line. Below the common name(s) is the scientific name, which consists of two parts (genus and species); the scientific name provides an internationally recognized designation for the animal. Scientific names continue to be modified as our knowledge and understanding of the relationships among animals expands. To allow for easy reference to both old and new sources, we have provided alternative scientific names in parentheses.

Description This section presents the basic characteristics that permit identification of an animal, including shape, color, distinctive markings, and anatomical features. The key distinguishing characteristics appear in italic type. For a few birds, the plumage of immatures or nonbreeders is described. Mammal newborns and young, usually identifiable by their similarity and proximity to adults, generally are not described. The description section concludes with measurement statistics. For *mammals,* length (L) is the distance from the tip of the nose, with head and neck extended, to the base of the tail. A separate length measure (T) is provided for the tail. Height (Ht) is measured from the ground to the shoulder. A range of recorded lengths, heights, and weights (Wt) includes male and female measurements; when male and female sizes differ greatly, separate statistics are provided. Horns are measured along the curves. For *birds and reptiles,* length is measured from the tip of the bill or snout to the end of the tail; when a single figure is given, it reflects the larger end of a range of recorded measurements. The wingspan (W) is provided for most large birds.

Similar Species This section briefly describes either an animal that is similar in appearance to the main species or another important species that is not similar in appearance but bears mention for another reason. When a similar species is covered with a full account elsewhere in this guide, only its common name is given, along with a brief note on its comparative field marks. When the similar species is not given a full account, we give important alternative names, the scientific name, a note on comparative field marks, and a range description.

Subspecies Many widespread species have (sometimes numerous) subspecies, or races—geographical populations that differ in appearance from other populations of that species but that freely interbreed at their points of overlap. In a number of the mammals accounts, and a few of the birds, a separate section is devoted to discussion of the most important subspecies. Space constraints make it impossible in most cases to include mention of all subspecies.

Voice Most bird species have characteristic songs and calls. A song, generally more complex than a call, is employed to advertise ownership of a nesting or feeding territory, and in most species is sung only by males. Calls are usually shorter and simpler, and generally express some emotion, such as alarm or anger. A brief description or a simple phonetic rendering of the song or the call (sometimes both) is given.

Habitat This section lists the habitats in which the animal may be found, in order of preference, beginning with those most favored.

Nesting/ Breeding In this section, information is given on a variety of topics, including, for birds, the number of eggs and the type of nest; for mammals, the number of young, the period of gestation, and the time of year when births take place; for reptiles, the number of young and the method of reproduction. For all groups, interesting courtship and parenting behaviors are described.

Range This section states the geographical limits of normal occurrence of a species. This is sometimes supplemented with data on elevations and specific sites where the animal lives. We generally give the range from west to east and from north to south. The term "local" is used when animals occur at widely scattered localities, usually because of very specific habitat requirements. A range map is provided in the margin beside each species account. The map shows the areas in which the species may be found. Please note that ranges are plastic; species constantly expand and decrease their ranges, and reintroductions of species can also alter ranges. Migrating birds may be at a specific site for only a short period during the year.

Comments Each species account concludes with coverage of a variety of behavioral themes, which may include the animal's diet, social and mating habits, and survival strategies; other significant or interesting facts; and tips on the best places and times for seeing the animal.

Margin Art In addition to the range maps and the drawings of a dozen animals for which suitable photographs could not be found, black-and-white illustrations are provided in the following categories:

Tracks Accompanying the species accounts of selected animals is a drawing of a typical footprint or track. The print represents an impression made in firm mud.

Antelope Heads The size and formation of the horns are key features in the identification of antelope species. For 24 members of the various antelope tribes, drawings of the head and horns appear in the margins of the species accounts. These drawings also appear together at the beginning of the antelopes section of the text in a two-page spread that gives an indication of the relative sizes of the different antelope species. (While the proportions of the different heads indicate relative sizes, they are not drawn to a precise scale.)

Bird Illustrations Various margin illustrations accompany some of the birds species accounts. Overhead flight drawings are provided for certain birds that are likely to be spotted in flight. Nests and behavioral drawings are also supplied for selected birds.

Conventions and Abbreviations In the species accounts—in which the focus is on a single animal, often in comparison with another—we follow zoological preference and capitalize the species name: Greater Kudu. In the Part I essays, however, where many animals are mentioned, we follow most nonscientific texts in foregoing capital letters: greater kudu. We also omit some modifiers in Part I, calling African Elephants simply elephants, for example.

To conserve space, in the species accounts we have used the following abbreviations: "n" for northern, "s" for southern, "e" for eastern, "w" for western, and "c" for central. For the same reason, shortened designations are used for parks and reserves: Serengeti NP for Serengeti National Park (names on the country maps in Part I are likewise abbreviated). The full name can be found in the geographical index and in the "Countries and Reserves" essay. Abbreviations used in the color-plate captions are explained in the Key to the Color Plates.

HOW TO USE THIS GUIDE

The photographs and species accounts present the animals in an identical sequence. (See the section "Sequence of Photographs and Text" in the Introduction for a discussion of the sequencing.) Mammals are presented first, followed by birds and reptiles. A glimpse into the class Insecta completes the wildlife coverage. Preceding the animals plates are 50 color photographs of African habitats and geological formations. The text for these can be found in Part I, The African Continent.
For detailed information on the different sections of the book, see the Introduction.

Key to the Color Plates For help in identifying an animal you have seen, consult the Key to the Color Plates, which follows the African Habitats and Geography color plates. There you will find silhouette drawings of 45 animal groups that reflect the orders or families into which the animals fall: 17 for mammals (usually an animal with hair), 23 for birds (whose bodies are covered with feathers), 4 for reptiles (covered with scales or plates), and 1 for insects. Listed below each silhouette are the animal groups that make up each order or family, and the plate numbers on which they are pictured. To make it easy to locate the larger groups, the 46 silhouettes are used as thumb tabs on the color plate pages (a few thumb tabs show more than one order).

If you see an animal and don't know the group to which it belongs, find the shape (or shapes) in the silhouette key that most resembles it, and review the photographs on the plates listed for that group. If you know the family or group name of an animal, review the list provided below each silhouette. The index can also be used to locate text or photographs. Remember that only a selection of African animal species is covered in this guide.

Cross-references

The caption for each photograph carries the page number of the text discussion of the animal or landscape depicted. The heading for each species account in the text provides the plate number(s) for that animal. Plate numbers for the habitat photos are provided within the text of Part I, The African Continent.

Indexes

The guide contains two indexes. Use the Species Index of animal names to find the text descriptions or photographs of animals. Use the Geographical Index of place names for the location of text on countries, cities, islands, nature reserves, and other areas of natural interest.

Part I
The African Continent

BIOGEOGRAPHY OF AFRICA

The following essay provides a brief discussion of the physical geography, climate, vegetation, and major animal migrations of the African continent. Many of the vegetation types and geographical features discussed here are pictured in the African Habitats and Geography section of the color plates. Corresponding plate numbers appear at the head of each section.

Physical Geography

Africa, the second-largest continent (after Asia), extends from 37° N to 35° S of the equator. Bordered by the Atlantic Ocean on the west, the Mediterranean Sea on the north, and the Red Sea and Indian Ocean on the east, it is connected by land only to Asia at the Sinai Peninsula of Egypt.

Highlands PLATES 1, 3, 5–9

Africa has the highest average land elevation of any continent. While it lacks the splendid long mountain ranges found on other continents, it has relatively little land at or near sea level. Much of eastern, central, and southern Africa lies above 5,000′ (1,500 m) elevation. In the north, a wall of mountains dominated by the *Atlas range* stretches from Morocco east to northern Tunisia. The Sahara desert is peppered with massive mountain ranges that culminate in Chad's *Tibesti Mountains,* which peak at 11,204′ (3,415 m) elevation. In West Africa, which has the lowest percentage of highland area, the Guinea highlands reach up to 6,069′ (1,850 m) at *Mount Nimba,* in Ivory Coast. The highlands of Cameroon, which stretch to the Gulf of Guinea islands, are crowned by *Mount Cameroon,* at 13,353′ (4,070 m). Ethiopia has the highest average elevation of any large African country, with extensive mountain ranges and high plateaus on both sides of its rift valley (see section below). The high point is Ras Dashan, at 15,158′ (4,620 m), in the *Simen Mountains.* There are numerous isolated volcanic peaks along the eastern rift valley, such as *Mount Kenya* (17,058′/5,199 m) and *Mount Elgon* (14,178′/4,321 m) in Kenya, and *Mount Kilimanjaro* (Africa's tallest, at 19,340′/ 5,895 m), *Mount Meru* (14,979′/4,566 m), and the highlands surrounding *Ngorongoro Crater* (see "Volcanoes," below) in Tanzania. Along the western arm of the rift valley there are both volcanic peaks, such as the recently active *Nyiragongo,* in Zaire, and nonvolcanic ranges such as the *Ruwenzori,* on the Uganda-Zaire boundary, which peaks at 16,763′ (5,109 m) on Mount Stanley. Most of southern Africa, as far north as Angola, Zambia, and Malawi, sits on vast plateaus of over 3,300′ (1,000 m) elevation. The south's highest peaks are in eastern Zimbabwe and in the *Drakensberg Mountains* of South Africa and Lesotho, which reach 11,425′ (3,482 m).

Coasts and Coastal Plains PLATES 24, 28, 29, 31

Africa's highlands give way to coastal plains of varying widths. Wide coastal plains are a feature chiefly in the Mauritania/Senegal/Gambia/Guinea-Bissau area; from Ivory Coast east to Nigeria (and inland along the Niger Valley); in southern Somalia; and from southern Tanzania to Mozambique. Coastal plains in most of eastern and southern Africa are relatively narrow. Africa's coastline is rarely broken up by peninsulas or inshore archipelagos. Coral reefs flank much of the Red Sea and Indian Ocean shores but are absent on the Atlantic side. Inland of the beaches in much of tropical Africa there are strings of small lagoons flanked with mangrove swamps.

Rift Valley PLATE 2

The most dramatic geological feature of the African continent is the rift valley system of eastern Africa known as the Great Rift Valley. "Temporary" features in geological time, rift valleys form when a landmass is splitting apart due to the divergent movements of tectonic plates. When the plates separate, the land in between drops, forming a rift in the earth's crust. Africa's rift valley is a long strip of land extending from the Dead Sea area of Israel and Jordan south to Mozambique that is gradually dropping in elevation, causing the areas on either side to rise. The resulting friction has spawned volcanoes on the sides of the valley in certain areas. Some of the valley has been filled in by saline or freshwater lakes. The Red Sea covers most of the northern third of the valley floor. Between southern Ethiopia and Malawi, the rift valley splits into eastern and western branches. The *eastern rift valley* slices through Kenya and Tanzania. The *western rift valley* runs through eastern Zaire and the western borders of Uganda, Rwanda, Burundi, and Tanzania. The two rejoin in Malawi (under Lake Malawi), and the single rift extends to Mozambique and will probably one day reach the Indian Ocean.

Volcanoes PLATES 1, 4, 8, 36
Formerly active volcanic zones are scattered about Africa. In the northwestern half these include the *Canary* and *Cape Verde islands,* in the Atlantic Ocean off Morocco and Senegal, respectively; several ranges in the *central Sahara;* and the *Cameroon line of volcanoes,* which extends into the Gulf of Guinea islands. In the southeastern half the major areas are along the *western rift valley* in eastern Zaire and Rwanda; flanking the *eastern rift valley* in Kenya and northern Tanzania; and an arc in the *Indian Ocean* from Grand Comoro island east to Mauritius and Réunion islands. *Ngorongoro Crater,* along the rift valley in northern Tanzania, was once a mountain—perhaps as tall as Kilimanjaro—whose cone collapsed inward, forming a *caldera,* a great basin ringed by slopes.

Rivers and Marshes PLATES 32, 33, 41–46
Of the four great river systems of Africa, only the *Congo River* (called the *Zaire River* in Zaire) has a relatively constant flow. The highly seasonal rainfall distribution away from the equator causes great variability in the flow of the *Nile River* in northeastern Africa, the *Niger River* in West Africa, and the *Zambezi River* in the south. While Africa's four major rivers flow into the sea, forming large deltas, other continental rivers are land-locked, flowing into lakes such as Lake Chad. The *Okavango Delta* of Botswana is an inland delta without a lake that is fed by rivers draining the Angola highlands. Seasonally flooded *marshes,* important for wildlife, particularly birds, are found along the Nile in the Sudd area of Sudan, along the Niger in Mali, and near the Zambezi in Zambia and northern Botswana.

Lakes and Pans PLATES 34–40
The largest lake on the continent is shallow *Lake Victoria* in East Africa, a source of the Nile River. Several long, very deep lakes fill parts of the rift valleys, including *Lake Tanganyika* and *Lake Malawi*. A variety of freshwater and soda or alkaline lakes, some very important for waterbirds, dot other areas of the rift valleys. Soda lakes, such as *Lake Natron,* in Tanzania, a breeding ground for flamingos, form in interior drainage lakes (with no outlets to the sea) in dry

areas that become subject to intense evaporation. Their waters become saltier in dry periods and turn highly alkaline. Some may dry out completely, leaving a wasteland crusted over with minerals.

The gradual drying out of the Sahara has eliminated many former lakes, and has contributed to the reduction in size of *Lake Chad* to its south. The water level in Lake Chad rises and falls drastically with variable multiannual cycles of wet and dry. In dry areas many lake beds have no water at all for long periods; these are called *chotts* in northern Africa and pans in southern Africa. During exceptionally wet periods, fresh water may cover these lake beds.

Water Holes PLATES 47–50

Many of Africa's parks and reserves have natural or man-made water holes that attract many types of animals, which come to drink and in some cases bathe. Some water holes are fed by natural springs or rainwater; others are remnant ponds in dried-out riverbeds, becoming part of the river in the wet season. Some water holes under dry streambeds reach the depth of the water table and are dug out by thirsty animals.

Islands PLATES 4, 13, 30

Islands of varying sizes and origins are scattered around continental Africa. Generally islands have fewer species of wildlife than nearby continents, and those near the mainland have few or no endemic wildlife species (species not found anywhere else). Africa's largest island, *Madagascar,* was joined with Africa for part of the Age of Mammals (both were part of the supercontinent of Gondwanaland, along with India, Australia, South America, and Antarctica). After Madagascar became an island it lost contact with (and ceased to be invaded by) newer land mammal groups, and its mix of wildlife evolved on its own. Today Madagascar is home to a fascinating range of chiefly endemic species. Volcanic islands that rise from the sea and were never a part of a continent have many fewer species than would be found in similar vegetation on a continent. (The same can be said of coralline islands or atolls, which build up over submerged volcanoes.) The chance arrivals of wildlife to such islands often lead to rapid evolution of new species. This has occurred on *São Tomé* and *Príncipe,* in the Gulf of Guinea; the *Comoro Islands* in the Indian Ocean; and in the *Canary* and *Cape Verde islands* in the Atlantic.

Climate

The climatic zones of Africa are quite predictable, except where disrupted by mountain ranges and unusual ocean currents. In general, areas along the equator are warm and humid with rain all year (with two peaks). Proceeding northward and southward from the equator, rainfall totals gradually decrease; near the Tropics of Cancer and Capricorn, there is a single *high-sun* (summer) rainy season. The northwestern and southwestern extremes of the continent have *low-sun* (winter) rainfall. Temperatures are highest in much of Africa in the late dry season before the rains cool things down.

Rainfall Patterns

In most of Africa, rainfall patterns are greatly influenced by the height of the midday sun in the sky. Because of the tilt of the earth on its axis (at an angle of 23.4°), the sun is directly overhead at the Tropic of Cancer (23.4° N) on or around June 21, the first day of the Northern Hemisphere summer, and is directly overhead at the Tropic of Capricorn (23.4° S) on or around December 21, the first day of the Southern Hemisphere summer. At the equator the sun is directly overhead in March and September. The time at which the sun is directly overhead at a particular place is referred to as that region's *high-sun season.* Between December and June, the sun appears to move northward in the sky as it approaches its highest point over the Tropic of Cancer in June. Having reached this point it then proceeds southward, arriving overhead at the Tropic of Capricorn on December 21. Areas between the Tropics, including the equator, experience high sun twice: once when the sun is moving northward and again when it is returning southward. The higher the sun the more it warms the air, thereby pulling up from the earth moisture that forms clouds and then falls as rain. Generally, areas with a single high-sun season have one rainy season, while those with two high-sun seasons have two periods of peak rainfall. Rainfall amounts generally decrease with increased distance from the equator. In the vast swath of Africa from Senegal to Sudan, the number of months with reliable rainfall decreases from five in southerly areas to two months in the more northerly Sahara.

In *summer rainfall zones* north of the equator, from Senegal east to Ethiopia, most of the rain falls from May through October, while to the south, from inland Namibia east to Mozambique, most of the rain falls from November through April. These areas experience a long, very dry season in the lower-sun months. Closer to the equator there are generally two rainy seasons. These occur roughly from March through May and September through November. In much of eastern Africa, the former period is called the *long rains,* the latter the *short rains.* Rainfall is relatively constant year-round only in parts of the Congo (Zaire) Basin and in the coastal strip of Natal in South Africa. *Winter rainfall zones,* which have hot dry summers and get their rains during *low sun,* are found in Africa's northern and southern extremes: Morocco and eastward along the Mediterranean Sea in the north, and in the Cape area of South Africa. During the winter months, cyclonic storms from the west, which bring rain to Europe or subantarctic regions, stray into these edges of Africa that are farthest from the equator. During the summer, these regions see little or no rain for many months.

Other factors can affect an area's rainfall totals. *Mountains* often have increased rainfall on higher elevations and windward slopes, and decreased rainfall on the highest summits, leeward slopes, and in lowlands in the downwind rain shadow. Warm offshore currents bring higher rainfall accumulations as air masses over them come ashore. In southeastern Africa, the southward-flowing *Mozambique Current* sweeps down along eastern South Africa, past Natal to southeastern Cape Province. With the much higher rainfall, humidity, and temperatures brought by this current, a wide variety of savanna and forest wildlife are able to extend their ranges southward to Natal.

Desert Climates PLATES 22–25

The *Sahara* region, centered on the Tropic of Cancer, is the largest desert in the world. Stretching from Mauritania in the west to Egypt in the east, the Sahara covers about one-sixth of Africa. Most years it receives little or no rain. With rare exceptions, neither the cyclonic storms to the north nor the summer monsoon rains of the tropics to the south penetrate the region. Heat can be intense in the late dry season in areas near the deserts. The Sahara is very dry and hot in summer but can be cold in winter and at night.

Dry desert climates are rare near the equator. The equatorial deserts of the Horn of Africa, sometimes called the *Somali-Masai arid zone,* blanket much of Somalia, eastern Ethiopia, Djibouti, Eritrea, and northern Kenya. Two of the factors that created this desert are the rain-shadow effect of the Ethiopian highlands and the cold currents off Somalia.

Along the western coast of southern Africa, the cold, north-flowing *Benguela Current* is responsible for the *Namib Desert,* a long strip of foggy, yet nearly rain-free land that extends along the Namibia and Angola coastline, almost as far north as the equator. Inland, the *Kalahari Desert* of

South Africa and Botswana, which gets light summer rains, blends into the *Karroo,* arid scrublands of interior Cape Province. During the southern winter, nighttime temperatures in these desert regions dip to freezing.

Vegetation

The annual and seasonal distribution of rainfall and latitudinal and elevational temperature gradients largely determine the vegetation of an area. The vegetation of Africa can be categorized in several distinct zones, but much of the landscape is transitional or a mosaic of types; in places it has been greatly altered by the activities of humans, including farming, logging, and grazing of domestic animals. Here we provide a simple breakdown of the continent's plant geography. An equatorial belt of *rain forest* runs along the Gulf of Guinea coast of West Africa, expanding into a broader zone from Gabon through much of Zaire. Extending away from the rain forest to the north, east, and south are belts of gradually drier vegetation. The *forest/savanna mosaic* belt ranges from rain forest in the better-watered soils to forest mixed with wooded savanna in better-drained soils. Next is a zone of *savanna woodland and grassland.* Beyond this are regions of *subdesert,* which has scattered small bushes, and *steppe,* sparse grassland without trees. These zones give way in some areas to true *desert,* which is nearly devoid of vegetation. Far from the equator, in the winter rainfall areas near the Mediterranean and Cape Town, *macchia scrub,* typical Mediterranean-type vegetation, dominates. Mountainous areas, scattered throughout the continent, are complicated in vegetation. Many have high forests *(montane forests)* and are topped with specialized flora and alpine grasslands and deserts.

Tropical Rain Forest PLATES 12, 13

These lowland forests receive more than 60″ (1,500 mm) of rain, well distributed year-round. They can be subdivided into *tropical rain forests,* with no dry season, and *tropical evergreen forests,* which have most of the characteristics of rain forests but experience three or so drier months. Unlike temperate-zone forests, tropical rain forests have many dozens, sometimes more than 100, species of trees. The interlocking canopy of branches—which may be 65–100′ (20–30 m) high, with scattered emergent giant trees reaching 200′ (60 m)—allows very little light to reach the forest floor. Most rain-forest trees have smooth trunks with few branches at lower and middle levels; their branches typically support a rich array of *epiphytic plants,* including orchids. Lengthy climbing woody vines called *lianas* snake from tree to tree. In uncut primary (virgin) rain forest there is little undergrowth, and it is relatively easy to walk about. In forest that has been partly cut, and around clearings in forests, a dense tangle of undergrowth forms. These areas have quick-growing but short-lived trees and are often rich in fruiting and flowering species of interest to birds and mammals. While significant blocks of rain forest, known as *Congolese forest,* survive in Gabon, Congo, and Zaire, very little forest remains west of Cameroon. Great conservation efforts are needed to save the small remnants in Sierra Leone, Liberia, and Ivory Coast.

There is a great diversity of species in the African rain forests, which are little visited by tourists. Most birds, mammals, and reptiles of the rain forest are hard to see because of the dense foliage and their innate shyness, nocturnal habits, and low population densities. The few large mammals, such as small antelopes and treetop monkeys, are heavily persecuted by bushmeat gatherers. Photography is difficult, due to the dark forest interior and the distance to the treetop haunts of the animals.

Forest-Savanna Mosaic

A hybrid vegetation zone, the forest-savanna mosaic forms a transition between the rain forest and the savanna. It receives somewhat less rainfall than the rain forest, but rain forest survives along its rivers and floodplain swamps and in some hilly areas. There may be patches or strips of forest penetrating into and among neighboring areas of wooded savanna and luxuriant grassland. *Derived savanna,* poor, shrubby grassland, occurs in areas of moist forest that have been cleared or eroded. The forest-savanna mosaic is expanding in area as humans clear more and more of the rain forest. For characteristics of the components of this mosaic, see the tropical rain forest section, above, or savanna woodland and grassland, below.

Savanna Woodland and Grassland PLATES 14–21

There is an enormous variety of savanna habitats, which together cover about 40 percent of the African landscape. The savannas are divided by the equator into *northern savanna* and *southern savanna.* With annual rainfall accumulations ranging from 12 to 60″ (300–1,500 mm), savannas are often subdivided into moister and drier types. *Moist savanna,* usually covered with broad-leafed deciduous woodland, receives 35–60″ (900–1,500 mm) of rainfall yearly, with one very dry season (two near the equator). Fires sweep through in the dry season, but they rarely kill the thick-barked trees. The moist savanna north of the equator in higher-rainfall areas, called the *Guinea savanna,* has broad-leafed deciduous woodlands (*Isoberlinia* is a dominant tree genus) with tall (10′/3 m) coarse grasses. In south-central Africa, the wooded moist savanna is called *miombo woodland.* Dominated by trees of the *Brachystegia* genus, which often form a canopy overhead, miombo woodland covers vast areas of Zambia and Zimbabwe. Wildlife is fairly conspicuous in these habitats, particularly in the drier months. In the wetter months, access and visibility are restricted by muddy roads and the high grasses, which may grow to 12′ (3.5 m) tall.

The *drier savannas,* characterized by scattered thorny trees and bushes, typically have a yearly rainfall of 12–35″ (300–900 mm), with a long dry season. These savannas extend in a broad belt from Senegal to southern Somalia, southward through Tanzania, and from Angola and western Zambia south to South Africa. North of the equator this zone is called *Sudan savanna.* Dry woodland, grassland with bushes, and open grassland steppe predominate. Feather-leafed acacias are common; various deciduous broad-leafed trees and enormous-trunked baobabs predominate in certain areas. The thin strip of these drier savannas and steppe habitats extending across the continent at the southern boundary of the expanding Sahara is called the *Sahel.* This greatly degraded zone is subject to long periodic droughts and suffers from severe overgrazing by domestic animals. In south-central Africa, the drier savanna is covered with a leguminous, open woodland called *mopane woodland,* which has fewer species of shorter, thinner trees than miombo woodland. Mopane woodland occurs in badly drained clay soils from central Zambia south to Transvaal and west to southwestern Angola.

During wet seasons in drier savannas, both north and south of the equator, the grass may grow several feet tall; grass fires here are less severe than those in the moist savanna. Many of the great eastern and southern wildlife reserves are located in drier savanna regions, where nutritious grasses, leaves, and the seedpods of trees attract wildlife. The good visibility in the drier savannas makes them excellent areas for viewing and photographing wildlife.

Subdesert and Steppe PLATES 26, 27

Between the savanna and the true desert are areas that receive 6–12″ (150–300 mm) of rain a year (on average). This scant rain usually is concentrated in one or two months, followed by ten or more dry months. Plant life in subdesert—also called *semi-desert* or *semi-arid desert*—usually consists of scattered dwarf shrubs, irregular growths of short grasses (depending on rains), and a sparse line of trees along the intermittent streambeds. This habitat extends along the southern edge of the Sahara, making up much of the area known as the *Sahel,* and is the dominant vegetation in the subdeserts of the Horn of Africa, which are known as the *Somali-Masai arid zone* and cover the lowlands of Somalia, Djibouti, Eritrea, eastern Ethiopia, northern Kenya, and northeastern Uganda, with fingers reaching south into Tanzania. The *Kalahari Desert* of much of Botswana, eastern Namibia, and South Africa, along with the *Karroo* region of interior Cape Province, South Africa, are of similar vegetational structure. *Steppe* is a term for dry grasslands neighboring true deserts. There is a swath of steppe on the northern edge of the Sahara, south of the Atlas and other mountain ranges of North Africa.

True Desert PLATES 22–25

In *true desert,* most of the land is devoid of plant life of any kind, and annual rainfall ranges from none to 6″ (0–150 mm). African deserts occur in three main areas: the vast *Sahara,* in the north from Mauritania east to the Red Sea; some of the *Horn of Africa* in Somalia, Djibouti, and neighboring Ethiopia; and the coastal *Namib Desert* of Namibia. Plants are scarce in such places, but seeds, lying dormant for years, do sprout when erratic rains soak the ground. Barren sand dunes, gravel, and rocks blanket vast areas of true deserts. The Sahara has been getting drier and expanding in size steadily since the time of the Roman Empire. In this century the misuse by humans (and their domestic animals) of the fragile ecosystems of the subdeserts and steppes is causing more rapid expansion of the desert in a process termed *desertification.*

Macchia Scrub PLATE 31

Macchia scrub is a term applied to the common vegetation associated with Mediterranean regions. It covers areas poleward from either tropic (Cancer or Capricorn) that have a single rainy season in winter. Globally it occurs only on the western sides of continents, in southern Europe, southwestern Australia, central Chile, California, and two areas of Africa: along the Mediterranean from Morocco east to Tunisia, and in the southern Cape Province of South Africa. The cool wet winters are followed by long, hot, rainless summers. The dominant vegetation consists of dense evergreen shrubs, stunted trees, and superb spring wildflowers. The isolated macchia scrub vegetation zone in South Africa's Cape Province is so rich in endemic plant species that it is called the "Cape floral kingdom."

Montane Vegetation PLATES 10, 11

In Africa the forests above 5,000′ (1,500 m) elevation are often called *montane forests* (in Latin America these would be called subtropical and temperate-zone cloud forests). Africa's montane forests thrive in cool, moist areas with frequent cloud cover or fog. They are usually not as tall as lowland rain forests, and have a smaller average leaf size. Those on a mountain's windward side tend to be evergreen, while those on the leeward side, in the rain shadow, tend to be deciduous. Long strands of *Usnea lichensii* (similar to Spanish moss of the Americas) hang from the limbs on moister ridges. Above the tree line *afro-alpine vegetation* occurs, including giant lobelias and senecio plants in moister areas of the equatorial mountains and *alpine grassland* in some drier areas. *Coniferous* and *oak forests* cover moister areas of the Atlas Mountains in northwestern Africa. Patches of *broad-leafed forest* extend from East Africa down through Malawi, eastern Zimbabwe, and the Drakensberg Mountains of South Africa, to the coast of Cape Province near Knysna. Because montane forests tend to occur in isolated pockets interrupted by intervening lowland forests or savannas, they have given rise to a large number of endemic plant and animal species with restricted ranges. Such species need careful protection if they are to survive. The isolated relict montane forests of the Guinea highlands, Cameroon, Angola, and various islands are of particular concern to conservationists.

Waterside Habitats PLATE 29

Although most vegetation zones are at the mercy of rainfall, Africa also has several important habitats that have little dependence on rainfall. *Riverine (or gallery) forests* grow along most rivers and streambeds. Their trees and undergrowth, whose roots have access to water levels normally found in much wetter regions, are much more luxuriant than would be found in the surrounding area away from the watercourses. These conditions allow many plant and animal species usually found in wetter areas to survive in relatively arid regions. Among the permanent vegetation found in marshy areas in both wet and dry regions is *papyrus,* a marsh plant with large clumps of fine tassels at the top. Along the coasts of tropical Africa *mangrove swamps* are common. Unlike other trees, mangroves, with their tangles of stilted roots, thrive in brackish and salty water. They provide an important habitat for wildlife.

Migration Patterns

For millions of years there have been annual migrations of large numbers of mammals—herds of herbivores and some of the carnivores that fed on them—in drier zones of Africa. The herds take advantage of temporary good grazing in one area part of the year and move to other areas the rest of the year. Excessive hunting, fencing, grainfield production, and competition with domestic livestock have eliminated some of Africa's migrations, but significant migrations of large grazing mammals still occur in the Sudd region and Boma National Park of southern Sudan; between the Okavango Delta and Chobe National Park in Botswana; and in the Kalahari Desert. The present-day wildebeest and zebra migration of Tanzania's Serengeti and Kenya's Masai Mara reserves is a unique circular migration pattern. The animals move clockwise, grazing in the short-grass plains of the southeast from December to April, in the wooded savanna of the west from May to July, and in the taller grass hills to the north from August to October. This migration has not been interrupted by human activity and has increased in recent years to more than a million animals.

Bird Migration

Bird migration takes place over all of Africa and its islands. Vast numbers of birds that breed in Europe and Asia fly to Africa to spend the fall, winter, and spring. The Sahara is an enormous barrier, yet a number of birds store up body fat and cross it twice a year in a broad front. Soaring birds that ride thermal air currents over land avoid crossing large expanses of water as they would use up too much energy flapping their wings. These larger birds enter and leave Africa at four sites: the Tangier area of Morocco; Cap Bon, Tunisia; the Sinai area of Egypt; and the Ras Siyan Peninsula, Djibouti. Shorebirds are found widely around the continent, while most ducks from Eurasia winter north of the equator. The grassland parks of eastern Africa are winter home to impressive numbers of wheatears, yellow wagtails, and Caspian plovers. Eagles (especially steppe eagles), common buzzards, and various falcons follow the rains southward to southern Africa, returning northward with the rains in the spring. Many intra-African migrants breed during the rains north of the equator and then winter south of the equator during the southern summer rains.

COUNTRIES AND RESERVES: WHERE TO SEE WILDLIFE

The sections that follow discuss the geography, climate, vegetation, and parks and reserves of each of 47 African countries, plus Madagascar and 10 offshore island groups, arranged alphabetically. Within the text on each country the parks, reserves, and other areas of wildlife or natural interest are highlighted in bold-face type. Because of the space limitations inherent in a book of this size, we are able to describe only the most prominent or noteworthy parks and reserves. We give the acreage, with the conversion in hectares (ha), for most reserves. Climate and weather notes, including average daily high temperatures, are given for most capitals and points of entry and some interior locales. Many African places have variant names and/or spellings. We have used the traditional names for most places. Some alternate place names are given in parentheses. In some areas the names and boundaries of provinces and regions may be in flux, as in South Africa, where provinces have recently been subdivided. When such new divisions have not been definitively settled, we have used the traditional names and boundaries.

Country Maps

The essays are illustrated by regional maps covering one to four countries that show key cities, rivers, mountains, and major reserves. Each map accompanies a section on one of the countries it represents, usually the most prominent in terms of wildlife viewing. The essays on the other countries covered by the map begin with a note on the map's location. The maps use shortened designations for parks and reserves (Serengeti NP for Serengeti National Park, for example). The full name is given in the text as well as in the geographical index.

The Wildlife

Significant animals, usually more common large mammals and interesting birds, are noted in the reserve descriptions. Most of these are featured in the photographs and species accounts later in the book, but some animals mentioned here are not described or depicted elsewhere in this guide. Usually these are animals that are not common over a large enough area to have been selected for a book of this nature, but often they are of local importance, or they may be the focus of study and conservation efforts by zoologists. Specialized books are available on specific countries and their wildlife.

The status of animals and natural reserves is sometimes uncertain due to poorly managed or poorly funded conservation programs or because of temporary or ongoing civil unrest. When the status of an area and its facilities and wildlife is uncertain, we describe the recent historical distribution of species; for example, in Angola we say that the Bikuar and Mupa national parks "have been home to the elephant, black rhino," etc. It is hoped that threatened parks can be reestablished, that missing components of the ecosystem can be healed, and that vanished species can be reintroduced.

Classification of Reserves

Legal protection of habitats and wildlife, the stability of funding, and the staffing vary widely among the various classes of parks and reserves and from country to country. Parks and reserves are designated as such by national governments. A *national park* has a high level of protection, with patrolled borders and anti-poaching teams, if needed. Hunting, logging, mining, farming, and grazing of domestic animals are prohibited. Tourism is usually both permitted and encouraged.

Below the national park level most countries have created a number of other classes of reserves with varying degrees of protection for habitats and wildlife. Some have large populations of wildlife or have been set up to partly protect special ecosystems and/or locally rare species. Depending on the laws within each country, some activities such as hunting, logging, mining, farming, and grazing of domestic animals may be allowed or tolerated. Among these classifications are *total faunal reserves,* in the confines of which all wildlife is protected, and *partial faunal reserves,* which protect certain species. A few countries have *strict nature reserves,* set up for the protection of highly endangered species. Access to these is usually denied to all but a few scientists and researchers. There are also private reserves, usually dubbed *game reserves,* where corporations and

individuals have set aside rich habitats for wildlife, often with lodgings and wildlife-viewing safaris.
A number of important reserves have been recognized as World Heritage Sites and/or Biosphere Reserves by the United Nations Educational, Scientific, and Cultural Organization (UNESCO). *World Heritage Sites* are natural sites or natural sites with cultural aspects of outstanding value. These may have extraordinary physical features, large areas of intact ecosystems, or encompass the last viable habitats of certain endangered species. *Biosphere Reserves* protect wildlife and their habitats and facilitate research, monitoring, training, and educational objectives.

ALGERIA PLATE 22

For map, see Tunisia.

Algeria, in northwestern Africa, is the third-largest country (896,588 sq mi/2,322,163 sq km) on the continent, after Sudan and Zaire. It extends southward from the Mediterranean Sea over several mountain ranges and deep into the Sahara desert.

The North

The northern quarter of Algeria is relatively humid, with an average of 16–32″ (400–800 mm) of rain annually, falling mainly from October through April. Algiers, the capital city, is located on the central coast. Between the northeastern city of Annaba and Tunisia, **Lake Kala National Park and Biosphere Reserve** (188,802 acres/76,438 ha) and two nearby wetlands of note, **Lake Oubeira** and **Lake Tonga,** attract waterbirds. Inland there are many mountain ranges running east–west, dominated by the **Tell Atlas.** Elevations reach 7,600′ (2,300 m), and snow is common in winter above 3,000′ (900 m). The native flora here is Mediterranean: macchia scrub, oaks, and cedars and other conifers. The Barbary macaque and Kabylie nuthatch live in the Grande and Petite Kabylie ranges, east of Algiers, and can be seen in **Djurdjura National Park** (45,820 acres/18,550 ha) and **Babor Natural Reserve** (4,200 acres/1,700 ha). South of the Tell Atlas, a plateau stretches south to the Saharan Atlas Mountains. This vast steppe, dotted with lake beds called *chotts,* is home to a few gazelles and small carnivores.

The Sahara

The southern three-quarters of Algeria are in the Sahara desert. The terrain consists of sand dunes and gravel or hardpan (compacted soil), with occasional freshwater oases with palms. Average highs are 113°F (45°C) in July, 70°F (21°C) in January; nighttime temperatures in winter are near or below freezing. Rainfall in some areas is less than 1″ (25 mm) a year. The **Tassili N'Ajjer National Park/World Heritage Site/Biosphere Reserve** (19,760,000 acres/8,000,000 ha), north of the town of Djanet, has fascinating stone towers, glacial debris, deep canyons, arches, and rounded mountains up to 7,100′ (2,150 m) high. It protects some desert wildlife and has rock paintings from much wetter times after the last ice age, depicting hippos, giraffes, and antelopes. Tamanrasset, the largest town in the south, has an airport and lodgings. It serves as a base for visits to **Ahaggar National Park** (11,115,000 acres/4,500,000 ha), which has fabulous domed mountains. One trail leads to a hermitage on top of Assekram Peak (9,500′/2,900 m).

ANGOLA

For map, see Zaire.

Angola, the largest country in southern Africa (481,350 sq mi/1,246,697 sq km), is located on a high plateau on the Atlantic coast between the equator and the Tropic of Capricorn. It has a single wet season, October through April, and otherwise is pleasantly dry and cool. With 26 permanent rivers flowing into the Atlantic, along with major tributaries of the Congo, Zambezi, and Okavango rivers, it is well watered (except in the southwest). About 90 percent of the country is covered with miombo woodland and savanna, and national parks and nature reserves have covered 6.6 percent of the country. However, after years of civil war, the status of wildlife and the integrity of the parks is uncertain at this writing. The wildlife listings below reflect the status in 1975. Lost species may be reintroduced when protection improves.

The Southern and Central Coasts

The north-flowing Benguela Current brings cold water from the direction of Antarctica nearly to the equator. The very arid coastal Namib Desert enters Angola south of the port of Namibe (formerly Mossamedes). There is no rainy season here, yet it is often foggy, with low clouds and low temperatures. Average highs range from 68°F to 84°F (20–29°C). South of Namibe lie **Namibe Nature Reserve** (about 1,235,000 acres/500,000 ha) and **Iona National Park** (3,742,100 acres/1,515,000 ha). The scant vegetation includes the welwitschia, a primitive conifer with two long, coiled leaves. The gravel desert and valley of the Cunene River to the east host herds of springboks and ostriches, and lesser numbers of elephants, black rhinos, Hartmann's mountain zebras, and gemsboks.

Angola's central shoreline, which receives only 13″ (330 mm) of rain per year, is lined with beaches, mangroves, and salt marshes. Cape gannets, sea terns, and cormorants are common at **Luanda,** the capital. South of Luanda, on the southern side of the Cuanza River, **Kisama (Quicama) National Park** (2,346,500 acres/950,000 ha) has tracks and lodging. It comprises coast, floodplain, savanna, woodland, and hill forest. Wildlife includes the bushbuck, forest buffalo, roan, eland, elephant, lion, cheetah, leopard, wild dog, manatee, talapoin monkey, palm-nut vulture, crocodile, and sea turtles. Baobab and euphorbia trees dot the grassy savanna south to **Lobito,** where flamingos and wading birds flock to the many salt pans.

The Mountains and Plateau

Inland, a transition zone leads up to a north–south range of mountains *(serras).* In the north this is a series of gentle steps, but in the south steep cliffs, up to 3,000′ (900 m) high, rise to the edge of a great tilted plateau. Isolated patches of humid montane forest, with rare flora and endemic birds, occur in Huambo, Benguela, and Huíla provinces. The mountain city of Huambo (formerly Nova Lisboa) lies at 5,600′ (1,700 m) elevation near a lake and coffee plantations. It enjoys 57″ (1,425 mm) of annual rainfall, with average highs of 82–90°F (28–32°C). **Lubango,** to the south, is near the great rounded peaks of the Serra da Chela. Nearby live the Muila people, who create impressive beadwork, and the Mucubau, known for their fabulous headgear.

East of the mountains lies the Angolan plateau, with average elevations of 4,000–6,100′ (1,200–1,850 m). Temperatures are relatively cool, and frost occurs in winter above 5,000′ (1,500 m). **Malange,** a city 220 mi (360 km) east of Luanda, is the base for visiting the multi-channel Duque de Bragança Falls. To the south are **Kangandala (Cangandala) National Park** (155,600 acres/63,000 ha) and **Luando Integral Reserve** (2,045,200 acres/828,000 ha), both of which were set up to protect the last herds of the giant sable. The hilly miombo woodland and grassland also support buffalos, elands, roans, sitatungas, and hippos.

The Southern Interior

In southern Angola, southeast of Lubango, there are two parks of open woodland, grassland, and thickets along the upper Cunene River: **Bikuar (Bicuari) National Park** (1,951,300 acres/790,000 ha) and **Mupa National Park** (1,630,200 acres/660,000 ha). Both have been home to the elephant, black rhino, zebra, eland, buffalo, black-faced impala, blue wildebeest, giraffe, roan, and greater kudu. The top safari area in the southeast, a vast area of undulating plains over deep Kalahari sand, is **Kameia (Cameia) National Park** (3,569,200 acres/1,445,000 ha), near the Zambia border, flanking the Zambezi and Luena rivers. It has camps, and hosts the lion, elephant, giraffe, and ostrich.

The North

Northern Angola is mainly savanna with grassland and miombo woodland, and patches of evergreen forest. The northern border runs along the south bank of the Congo River. To the north of the Congo is the oil-rich enclave of **Cabinda,** which has had tall unprotected rain forest with lowland gorillas, chimpanzees, elephants, and more than 400 species of birds, including great blue turacos and large hornbills.

BENIN

For map, see Nigeria.

This narrow country (43,483 sq mi/112,621 sq km) in West Africa extends from the Gulf of Guinea 420 mi (675 km) north to the Niger River.

The South

The shoreline on the Gulf of Guinea is backed by beaches, a sandy coastal plain, and coastal lagoons and marshes. Cotonou, the largest city, and nearby Porto-Novo, the capital, have average highs of 90–95°F (32–35°C) and receive 52″ (1,300 mm) of rain annually. Remnants of lowland rain forest survive in the east, but none is well protected. Palm plantations and man-made savanna now blanket most of the area. Inland the land rises gradually to a fertile plateau at 660–1,000′ (200–300 m).

The North

The **Atakora Mountains** run northeastward from neighboring Togo, peaking at 2,100′ (640 m). This is a scenic area with deep gorges, towering quartzite cliffs, forests, and waterfalls. **Natitingou,** at 1,450′ (440 m) elevation, is the chief town and the base for visits to the Tanagou waterfall and the parks. The land slopes downhill to the Pendjari River, a tributary of the Volta, at 500′ (150 m), and down to the plains along the Niger River. The annual rainfall of 40″ (1,000 mm) falls from June through October, but its volume is declining. Average highs hover at 100°F (38°C) late in the dry season. The two national parks in Benin, along with reserves in neighboring countries, protect the largest remaining expanse of West African savanna ecosystems and contain the most important concentrations of wildlife in Benin. **Boucle de la Pendjari National Park** (679,300 acres/ 275,000 ha) has lodging, a road network, and hippo lakes. To the northeast, **W du Benin National Park** (1,403,000 acres/568,000 ha), operated cooperatively by Benin, Niger, and Burkina Faso, is named for a W-shaped series of bends in the Niger River; it is less developed. Both parks contain savanna woodlands (with many acacias), wide grassy plains, gallery forests, rivers (with multi-trunked borassus palms), and seasonal marshes. The parks have similar animal populations, including warthogs, hippos, three types of duikers, red-fronted gazelles, reedbucks, kobs, roans, hartebeests, topis, bushbucks, buffalos, elephants, spotted hyenas, lions, leopards, cheetahs, baboons, and patas monkeys. Among the birds and reptiles are many seasonal waterbirds, hawks, scissor-tailed kites, secretarybirds, crowned cranes, ground-hornbills, crocodiles, and pythons.

BOTSWANA PLATES 15, 27, 46, 48

Much of Botswana, in southern Africa (219,916 sq mi/ 569,582 sq km), is a flat plateau averaging 3,300′ (1,000 m) elevation. The single rainy season produces 20″ (500 mm) or more of annual rain in the north and east from November through March. The Kalahari Desert, stretching across the southern half of Botswana, receives about 8″ (200 mm) annually, but the rains fail some years. Parks protect 17 percent of the land. The Okavango Delta and Chobe National Park are among the finest wildlife areas in Africa.

The East

Near **Gaborone,** the capital, the rare Cape vulture has several breeding hills. Along the Limpopo River to the north are isolated hills in relatively wet savanna with a number of private game reserves (with lodging), including the vast **Mashutu Private Game Reserve.** Large mammals have been reintroduced here to join the abundant small

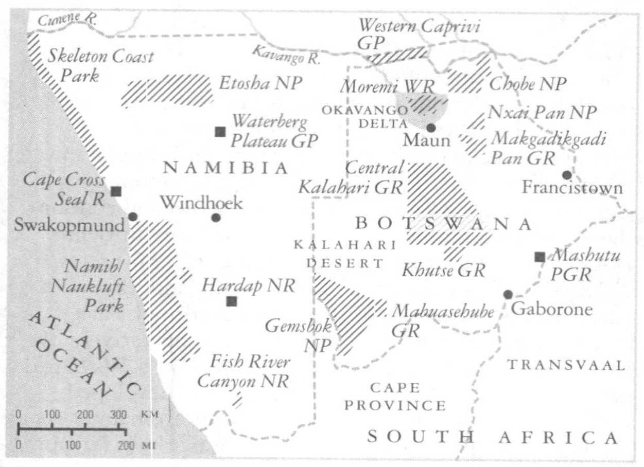

BOTSWANA AND NAMIBIA

animal and bird life. Francistown, near the Zimbabwe border, is the starting point for roads west to the pans (vast salt flats), the Okavango Delta, and Chobe National Park.

The Kalahari Desert

This desert of semi-arid acacia steppes, grassland, thickets along dry streambeds, and flat pans is home to the last groups of San Bushmen. While temperatures exceed 100°F (38°C) on summer days, in winter (May through September) days are warm and nights near freezing. Safari outfitters with four-wheel-drive vehicles, fuel, camping gear, food, and water are essential, because there are no paved roads or lodgings in this area. **Gemsbok National Park** (5,928,000 acres/2,400,000 ha) and adjacent **Mabuasehube Game Reserve** (442,600 acres/179,200 ha) are in the southwest, while **Central Kalahari (Kgalagdi) Game Reserve** (12,794,600 acres/5,180,000 ha) and nearby **Khutse (Kutse) Game Reserve** (602,700 acres/244,000 ha) are in central Botswana. Mammals in these parks include the gemsbok, red hartebeest, blue wildebeest, greater kudu, springbok, steenbok, lion, leopard, wild dog, cheetah, and brown hyena. The larger ungulates migrate from summer to winter ranges, and to wherever sporadic rains have fallen.

The Pans

Makgadikgadi Pan Game Reserve (1,020,110 acres/413,000 ha) protects the northwestern edge of a vast pan (a salt flat that collects erratic rainfall). Some years it gets overflow water from the Okavango Delta (see below) and hosts flamingos and many other waterbirds. It is a dry-season (May through October) grazing area for tens of thousands of zebras, blue wildebeests, gemsboks, elands, and springboks. In the wet season (November through April) the animals move north to **Nxai Pan National Park** (370,500 acres/150,000 ha), a lake bed covered with grass and fringed with baobab trees and palms. Giraffes, lions, cheetahs, bat-eared foxes, and aardwolves are also present. **Lake Ngami,** 47 mi (75 km) southwest of the town of Maun, attracts numerous waterbirds during years when it gets overflow water from the Okavango.

Okavango Delta

Maun is the chief town near this famous wildlife area; its airport is the connection point for charter aircraft to remote camps and lodges. The Okavango is an inland delta that receives rainwater from the highlands of Angola via the Cubango River. The flood reaches the southeastern delta in June and July, during the dry season. This influx evaporates, and the delta's own rainy season begins in November, so water levels are always fluctuating. There is a maze of channels, papyrus swamps, seasonally wet swales, grasslands, gallery forests, and mopane woodlands. Temperatures are near freezing at night from June through August, but the days are warm and there are few or no mosquitoes. Although the delta is not a national park, much of it is protected in the **Moremi Wildlife Reserve** (963,300 acres/390,000 ha). There are many small camps hereabouts, including one that specializes in elephant-back safaris, plus a few medium-size lodges. Nighttime game drives are permitted, increasing visitors' chances to sight leopards, bushbabies, porcupines, springhares, and small carnivores. Mokoros (small, hand-poled boats) and canoes take visitors through shallow reedy marshes. Among the birds in the region are the wattled crane, saddle-billed stork, slaty egret, pygmy goose, fish-eagle, and Pel's fishing owl. Gray go-away-birds, hornbills, and barbets come to feeders at many camps. The red lechwe, tsessebe, greater kudu, and waterbuck are common in the delta, while the sable, roan, lion, and wild dog occur in fewer numbers. Buffalos, zebras, and elephants are often plentiful, but many migrate out to the pans or to Chobe. Some species are distrustful of humans and vehicles, due to the checkerboard of hunting areas in this region.

Chobe National Park

Located at the northern tip of Botswana, the park covers 2,610,800 acres (1,057,000 ha). It is watered by Angola's Kuando River and is adjacent to Namibia's panhandle, the

Caprivi Strip. The waters fill the Linyanti Swamp and then flow northeastward, forming the Chobe River, which flows into the Zambezi. Kasane, just east of the park, has an airport and is 53 mi (85 km) via paved road from Victoria Falls, Zimbabwe. There are lodges and camps on the river, from which boats depart to view hippos, waterbirds, fish-eagles, and carmine bee-eaters. Dirt tracks allow access to shoreline points, grassland, thickets, and woodland. Elephants number up to 73,000, while buffalos occur in herds of hundreds. Other mammals include the puku, impala, Chobe bushbuck, greater kudu, giraffe, lion, and chacma baboon. The camps of the Savuti Marsh area in the southwest are good bases for seeing lions, waterbirds, and great migratory herds of elephants and buffalos.

BRITISH INDIAN OCEAN TERRITORY (UNITED KINGDOM)

The **Chagos Archipelago** (76 sq mi/197 sq km) lies about 2,000 mi (2,720 km) off the coast of Tanzania and 980 mi (1,090 km) east of Seychelles. Diego Garcia serves as a naval communications facility, and the other islands are now uninhabited. Hardwood forest covers some islands that get 100″ (2,500 mm) of rain per year. Chagos has the largest undisturbed reef in the Indian Ocean. The **Three Brothers** islets and the northern atolls are major breeding areas for sea turtles, shearwaters, tropicbirds, boobies, lesser frigatebirds, and terns.

BURKINA FASO

This inland country, formerly called Upper Volta, lies to the south of the big bend in the Niger River, which doesn't enter Burkina Faso's borders, and occupies an area of 105,869 sq mi (274,200 sq km). Most of the land is on the southward-tilting Mossi Plateau at 660–1,650′ (200–500 m) elevation.

The Southwest

The most pleasant area is the hill country in the far west, which reaches 2,405′ (733 m) in elevation. There are a number of waterfalls hereabouts during the rainy season (June through September). **Lake Tangrela,** just west of Banfora, has hippos. The Black Volta River area in the far south gets 40″ (1,000 mm) of rain each summer; its open

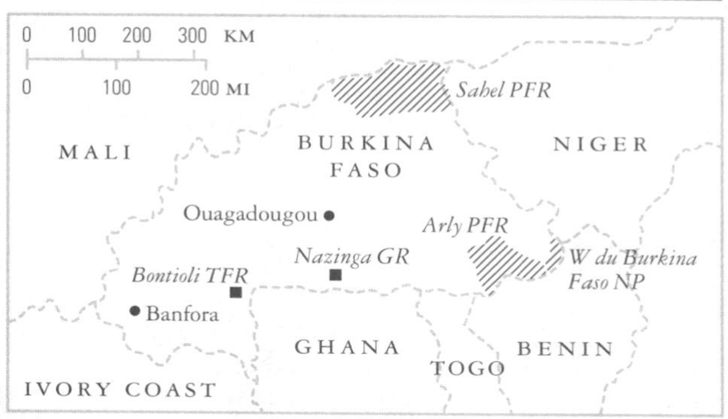

BURKINA FASO

forests are taller and have more species of trees than areas to the north. Along the river, **Deux Bales Classified Forest** (139,800 acres/56,600 ha) and **Bontioli Total Faunal Reserve** (60,500 acres/24,500 ha) have been subject to heavy poaching and have few larger animals remaining.

The Center

Ouagadougou, the capital, receives 35″ (875 mm) of rain each year, mainly in the summer. Temperatures are high year-round, with average highs over 100°F (38°C) from March through May. The vegetation in the central region is of the dry Sudan savanna type, with open grassland and deciduous trees. **Sahel Partial Faunal Reserve** (2,865,200 acres/1,160,000 ha) in the northeast is now degraded due to the influx of poor nomads and their domestic animals, but the Seno-Mango area to the west has intact Sahel vegetation. **Kabore-Tambi National Park** (599,500 acres/242,700 ha), south of the capital, is not developed for tourism. Visitors are allowed at the nearby private **Nazinga Game Ranch,** west of Po. Wooded savanna and grassland in the region support elephants, lions, buffalos, waterbucks, kobs, reedbucks, roans, oribis, bushbucks, baboons, and patas and vervet monkeys.

The Southeastern Parks

Located where Burkina Faso meets Benin and Niger, **W du Burkina Faso National Park** (469,300 acres/190,000 ha) was named for a series of bends in the nearby Niger River. Not developed for tourism, it protects open and wooded savanna that is home to many large mammals. **Arly (Arli) Partial Faunal Reserve** (187,700 acres/76,000 ha), on the north bank of the Pendjari River, and a series of flanking faunal reserves offer some protection for animals and have facilities for visitors. There are permanent ponds along the

Pendjari, as well as temporary ponds in the wet season. These parks have crocodiles, lions, leopards, cheetahs, elephants, hippos, buffalos, waterbucks, kobs, roans, hartebeests, topis, bushbucks, and red-flanked duikers.

BURUNDI

For map, see Uganda.

This small highland country (10,759 sq mi/27,866 sq km) on Lake Tanganyika encompasses part of the western rift valley, a mountain chain, and wooded savanna in the east. Annual rainfall is 33″ (825 mm) on the lake, almost double that in the mountains. June through September are the drier months. Average highs are 82–88°F (28–31°C) on the lake, lower inland.

The West

The capital, Bujumbura, at the northern tip of **Lake Tanganyika,** at 2,525′ (770 m) elevation, has boat connections to Kigoma, Tanzania. The lakeshore is lined with coconut palms and hippos. Tanganyika's waters support 270 endemic fish, chiefly cichlids, with an immense variety of color and behavioral characteristics. From the Bujumbura area there are fine views west to Zaire's Itombwe Mountains. **Rusizi Managed Nature Reserve** (3,700 acres/1,500 ha) protects part of the Imbo Plain northwest of Bujumbura. The Rusizi Delta has marshes and lagoons that host saddle-billed storks and nesting skimmers. Another sector has dry palm forest and riverine habitats, with hippos, bushbucks, and sitatungas. Elephants, common in the delta area before 1953, may be reintroduced in the future.

The Mountains

A backbone of mountains that peak at 8,800′ (2,680 m), the Congo-Nile Divide runs north–south. Lush montane forest, with vast areas of bamboo, is protected in **Kibira National Park** (93,540 acres/37,870 ha) in the north. Chimpanzees, gray-cheeked mangabeys, red-tailed monkeys, black-and-white colobus monkeys, duikers, and more than 150 birds live here. In the south only a fragment of montane forest remains, protected in **Bururi Natural Forest Reserve** (3,700 acres/1,500 ha).

The East

While rivers west of the mountains drop steeply, those in the east drop gradually in a northeasterly direction down to

5,000′ (1,500 m). **Ruvubu National Park** (107,766 acres/43,630 ha) protects grassland and riverine forest along the Ruvubu River. Hippos, bushbucks, waterbucks, buffalos, lions, leopards, servals, spotted hyenas, and crocodiles live here. There is some miombo woodland, evergreen bushland, and acacia savanna in the southeast. The **Lake Rwihinda Managed Nature Reserve** (1,050 acres/425 ha) is located in the Busoni area of northeastern Burundi in an area of freshwater lakes with vast papyrus swamps and great nesting colonies of herons, ibises, and storks.

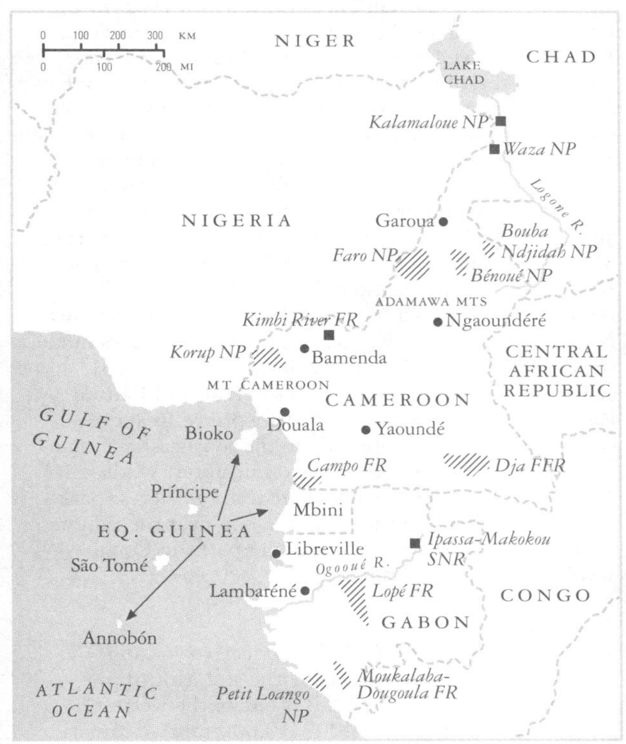

CAMEROON, GABON, AND EQUATORIAL GUINEA

CAMEROON PLATE 12

Cameroon (183,591 sq mi/475,500 sq km), on the Gulf of Guinea, extends from 2° to 12° north of the equator. It has bands of most West African ecological zones, from rain forest in the south to near-desert in the north, as well as spectacular mountain scenery. It has the best park and reserve system in West Africa, but the montane forests and lowland rain forests need more protection.

The South

Douala is Cameroon's largest city and port, and has the main airport. It is one of the world's rainiest cities, receiving 154″ (3,850 mm) a year; the drier season is December through February. Average highs are in the high 80s and low 90s F (low 30s C) year-round. The 360-mi (590-km) coastline is highly indented and encompasses rocky areas, beaches, rivers, and mangrove and swamp forests. Limbe, a beach resort on the Gulf of Guinea below Mount Cameroon, has a good botanical garden. **Douala-Edea Faunal Reserve** (395,200 acres/160,000 ha) protects lagoons and rain forest near the mouth of the Sanaga River, 54 mi (90 km) south of Douala. Its wildlife includes the elephant, hippo, manatee, sitatunga, blue duiker, and giant pangolin, and such primates as De Brazza's and greater spot-nosed monkeys, black and red colobus monkeys, white-collared and gray-cheeked mangabeys, mandrills, and chimpanzees. **Campo Faunal Reserve** (74,100 acres/ 30,000 ha), south of the beach-resort town of Kribi near Equatorial Guinea, is also rich in primates, but both reserves have suffered from poaching. Inland the country is a hilly plateau that was once heavily forested. Yaoundé, the capital, at 2,500′ (770 m) elevation, receives 61″ (1,525 mm) of rain annually. **Dja Forest and Faunal Reserve/World Heritage Site/Biosphere Reserve** (1,299,200 acres/526,000 ha), to the southeast, is home to traditional Pygmy peoples and rain-forest wildlife. There is a plan to create a three-nation rain-forest park in the southeastern corner of Cameroon near the Sangha River, linking the area with existing parks in Congo and Central African Republic.

The Mountains

West of Douala, West Africa's only active volcano and tallest mountain rises above the sea: **Mount Cameroon** (13,353′/4,070 m) is one of the wettest places in the world, with 400″ (10,000 mm) of rain a year. Buea is a town on its southeastern flank, 3,000′ (900 m) above the beach resort of Limbe. Visitors must hire guides to explore the montane forest or to do the three-day climb to the peak. The forest gives way to high grassland at 9,000′ (2,700 m). The Mount Cameroon francolin is found only here, and other birds with small ranges, such as the gray-necked rockfowl and green-breasted bush-shrike, also occur. There are 22 species of birds restricted to the Cameroon montane forest, with several dozen more shared only with the Gulf of Guinea islands.

Korup National Park (311,000 acres/125,900 ha), located to the north of Mount Cameroon on the border with Nigeria, has a great variety of endangered primates and birds in a pristine area of exceptionally diverse rain forest. Bamenda is a hill town in the center of the southern end of the largest arc of mountains in West Africa. These cool, formerly forested highlands with many lakes, gorges, and steep escarpments have been turned into grazing lands. **Mount Oku** (9,900′/3,000 m high), north of Bamenda, has tall podocarpus forest and is home to such rarities as Bannermann's turaco, the banded wattle-eye, and Preuss's monkey. Small **Kimbi River Faunal Reserve** (13,894 acres/5,625 ha) is home to the mona monkey, buffalo, kob, and waterbuck.

The center of the country is a plateau with a mosaic of farms, secondary grassland, and patches of forest. Just north of the town of Ngaoundéré, the Adamawa Mountains run east–west, topping elevations of 6,600′ (2,000 m), with volcanic craters, lakes, and lava flows.

The North

North of the Adamawa Mountains the climate is much drier, with a single wet season from April through September. Rainfall decreases northward, ranging from 70″ to 40″ (1,750–1,000 mm) annually. Most parks are open only from mid-November through mid-May or June due to flooded areas and muddy roads in the wet season. South of the town of Garoua, site of a wildlife institute, the Benue River drains west to the Niger River. There are three national parks here that were established for the protection of the black rhino and the Derby eland. **Faro National Park** (815,100 acres/330,000 ha), **Bénoué National Park/Biosphere Reserve** (444,600 acres/180,000 ha), and **Bouba Ndjidah National Park** (543,400 acres/220,000 ha) are located in wet Guinea savanna with rocky outcrops, plains, woodlands, and hills inhabited by elephants, hippos, red-flanked duikers, oribis, kobs, lelwel hartebeests, waterbucks, reedbucks, roans, bushbucks, topis, warthogs, lions, leopards, cheetahs, caracals, and spotted hyenas.

Farther north the woodlands are drier, and there are areas of dry Sahel acacia savanna. The rivers overflow in the wet season and pour into Lake Chad. **Waza National Park** (419,900 acres/170,000 ha) has lodging, tracks, and blinds at water holes. Animals feed in western woodlands until mid-March, then move out into the grassy plains until the rains come. This is one of the last places in West Africa to see giraffes. The park's other highlights are 50,000 antelopes—chiefly kobs, reedbucks, roans, and topis—and fewer numbers of elephants, striped hyenas, sand foxes, cats, and red-fronted gazelles. Birds include the ostrich, bateleur, crowned crane, and Arabian bustard. Walking is permitted in **Kalamaloue National Park** (11,100 acres/4,500 ha) on the Logone River near N'Djamena, Chad. Within the park are hippos, elephants, and many antelopes, as well as the Abyssinian roller and nesting colonies of carmine and red-throated bee-eaters.

CANARY ISLANDS (SPAIN) PLATE 4

The Canaries consist of seven main volcanic islands in the Atlantic Ocean, the closest of which is 60 mi (100 km) west of the southwestern coast of Morocco. They have relatively warm winters and cool summers for their latitude. Rainfall, occurring chiefly in winter, is heaviest in the western islands and the highlands of the central islands; the eastern islands are low and arid. The chain supports 470 endemic plant species. Vegetation of the higher islands begins with semi-desert on the coast and rises through juniper scrub, tree heath, and evergreen laurel forest to pine savanna and montane scrub. Most of the islands have endemic lizards, but there are no large land mammals and only six endemic birds, including the "original" canary. Most resident birds are subspecies of European species. La Palma, the northwesternmost island, is dominated by **Caldera de Taburiente National Park** (11,584 acres/4,690 ha), a desolate crater whose outer slopes support mist forest with rare species of pigeons and woodcocks. In the highlands of Gomera, **Garajonay National Park** (9,840 acres/3,984 ha) has tall laurel forests with many songbirds as well as laurel and long-toed pigeons. Tenerife's **Pico de Teide National Park** (33,520 acres/13,571 ha) encompasses the highest peak (often snowcapped) in the Atlantic Ocean, at 12,198′ (3,718 m), reachable by cable car. The endemic blue chaffinch lives in pine forests on the slopes. Grand Canary has remnant laurel forest in the **Canal y Los Tiles Biosphere Reserve** (1,262 acres/511 ha), north of Cruz de Tejada peak, at 4,760′ (1,450 m). Fuerteventura is a dry island with an endemic chat. Lanzarote, with 5″ (125 mm) of annual rain, is home to **Timanfaya National Park** (12,614 acres/5,107 ha), a moonscape with pipe-like lava tubes that form as the edges of lava rivers cool.

CAPE VERDE ISLANDS

This archipelago consists of ten large and eight small islands in the Atlantic Ocean, 370 mi (600 km) west of Dakar, Senegal. These arid volcanic islands rose from the sea in the same manner as the Galápagos did. The sea here is usually warmer than the relatively cool air above (average highs are 72–81°F/22–27°C). The scant rainfall comes between August and October, but some years there is none. The higher western islands have a green zone of irrigated cropland. The island of **Fogo** has an active volcano 9,281′ (2,829 m) tall. The eastern islands are very arid. There are no native land mammals, though vervet monkeys have been introduced on **São Tiago.** Forty-four bird species breed on the islands; four of these (a swift, lark, warbler, and sparrow) are endemic. Important colonies of shearwaters and storm-petrels can be found on uninhabited islets. **Raso** (only home of the Raso lark), **Branco,** and **Cima** islets, all good candidates to become sanctuaries, are home to several sea turtles, lizards, geckos, and skinks.

CENTRAL AFRICAN REPUBLIC

For map, see Sudan.

This nation of 240,376 sq mi (622,573 sq km) has wet rain forest in the southwest, wetter Guinea savanna in the center, and drier Sudan savanna in the north. From the sandstone Ubangi Plateau, waters flow south to the Congo and north to basins in Chad and to Lake Chad. Vast areas of the country are open to hunters. There are still large numbers of animals inside and outside parks, but the elephant, black rhino, lowland gorilla, and leopard have been hit hard by poachers.

The Southwest

Bangui, the capital, is located on the Ubangi River, which affords access via riverboats to Congo and Zaire. It gets 60″ (1,500 mm) of rain, chiefly from March through November. Average highs are 84–93°F (29–34°C), with highest temperatures February through April. The south is a mosaic of farms, secondary grasslands, and rain forests. In the far southwest, on the Central African Republic border with Congo and Cameroon, there is rain forest and swamp forest along the Sangha River, where annual rainfall exceeds 80″ (2,000 mm). **Dzanga-Ndoki National Park** (301,300 acres/ 122,000 ha) and adjacent faunal reserves are part of a three-nation park project with Cameroon and Congo. Core areas are restricted to research and tourism, while buffer areas are managed for traditional hunting and gathering activities by resident Pygmies and other locals. Primates found here include the lowland gorilla, chimpanzee, mustached and greater spot-nosed monkeys, gray-cheeked mangabey, and red colobus. Among other wildlife are forest races of the elephant and buffalo, the bongo, sitatunga, giant forest hog, Gabon adder, python, and many birds.

The Northeast

The Bongo Massif of the northeast culminates at 4,600′ (1,400 m), forming the divide between the Nile, Chad, and Congo river basins. Annual rainfall is about 40″ (1,000 mm). The area has dense woodlands, vast grassy floodplains, tall termite mounds, and rich gallery forests along the many northwest-flowing rivers. There are three major national parks, each surrounded by faunal reserves. Until recently these parks had the largest concentration of black rhinos anywhere. **Manovo-Gounda–Saint Floris National Park/World Heritage Site** (4,297,800 acres/ 1,740,000 ha), on the Chad border, is home to the 265′ (80-m) Matakil waterfall, and is reachable by charter aircraft from Bangui; there are lodgings at Koumbala and Gounda and a good network of roads. The park is home to ten species of primates, such hoofed mammals as hippos, pigs, giraffes, giant elands, roans, oribis, red-fronted gazelles, reedbucks, topis, hartebeests, buffalos, and kobs, and the forest and savanna races of elephant. Lions, leopards, cheetahs, golden cats, spotted hyenas, and wild dogs represent the carnivores. Nile perch, tilapia, and catfish become trapped in the receding waters of the floodplains, attracting a spectacular variety of large wading birds, including shoebills. More than 400 species of birds have been recorded here. **Bamingui-Bangoran National Park/World Heritage Site** (2,642,900 acres/ 1,070,000 ha) is to the west; to the east is **André Félix National Park** (419,900 acres/170,000 ha). The dry season (November through May) is the best time to visit the three parks.

CHAD

For map, see Sudan.

This land-locked country stretches 1,090 mi (1,760 km) from the swampy savannas of the south to the heart of the Sahara desert in the north; its total area is 495,752 sq mi

(1,283,998 sq km). Its two national parks and seven faunal reserves cover 9 percent of the country.

The South

With 40″ (1,000 mm) of rain annually, this area is the greenest in the country. Sudanese woodland, acacia savanna, and tall grassland flank the floodplains of the rivers that drain northwest to Lake Chad. Elephants were widespread in many uninhabited zones until recently. **Zakouma National Park** (741,000 acres/300,000 ha) protects an immense floodplain, two rivers, woodland, and rocky outcrops southwest of Am Timan. There are an airstrip and lodging at Bahr Tinga just outside the park. Zakouma used to have—and may still have—the elephant, black rhino, greater kudu, and Derby eland. Other animals that can be found here are giraffes, buffalos, oribis, waterbucks, bushbucks, roans, topis, kobs, hartebeests, red-fronted gazelles, warthogs, baboons, vervet and patas monkeys, crocodiles, and many bird species. Carnivores include the lion, leopard, cheetah, caracal, serval, and spotted hyena. **Manda National Park** (281,600 acres/ 114,000 ha), along the Chari River northwest of Sarh, lacks lodging; its bushy savanna hosts elephants, hippos, Derby elands, roans, buffalos, and lions.

The Center

N'Djamena, the capital, lies beside the wide Chari River. It gets 30″ (750 mm) of rain, chiefly between June and September. Average highs are 88°F (31°F) in August, but reach 108°F (42°C) in April, late in the dry season. **Lake Chad** once covered 115,800 sq mi (300,000 sq km), but had shrunk to 10,800 sq mi (28,000 sq km) by the 1950s. With drought and water diversion, it is down to about 4,000 sq mi (10,000 sq km) and is only 16.5′ (5 m) at its deepest. Flanked by papyrus swamp and marsh, it has been home to elephants, hippos, sitatungas, crocodiles, and myriad resident and wintering birds. There is a wetland reserve at **Lake Fitri** (481,700 acres/195,000 ha), a permanent lake east of Lake Chad that is fed by the seasonal Batha River. To the north, **Ouadi Rimé–Ouadi Achim Faunal Reserve** (19,760,000 acres/8,000,000 ha) once was the largest in Africa but has suffered from massive overgrazing by domestic animals and uncontrolled shooting. This had been a stronghold of the scimitar-horned oryx (formerly seen in herds of thousands) and the addax. Other highlights are dorcas, dama, and red-fronted gazelles, the cheetah, and the ostrich.

The Sahara

Northern Chad is a land of sandy desert and camel caravans. The **Ennedi Mountains** have spectacular gorges and receive 8″ (200 mm) of rain annually. Aoudads live in the hills, while Nile crocodiles survive in remnant water holes. The oasis town of Faya to the north receives 0.7″ (18 mm) of rain a year. Average highs exceed 100°F (38°C) from April through October, but drop to 82°F (28°C) in December. Just to Faya's north are the vast, spectacularly scenic **Tibesti Mountains.** This is a recent volcanic massif, as evidenced by the Trou au Natron caldera, southwest of the town of Bardaï; it is 5 mi (8 km) wide, with black craters, steaming vents, and white soda deposits. The Tibesti feature ancient rock carvings, steep cliffs, narrow gorges, and pink sandstone mountains, as well as the highest peak in the Sahara, Mount Koussi, which reaches 11,204′ (3,415 m). Palm groves grow in canyons, while the somewhat cooler and wetter mountain slopes have a unique Saharan montane flora. The Tibesti range would make a fascinating national park.

COMORO ISLANDS

This archipelago consists of four mountainous volcanic islands in the southwestern Indian Ocean. The three westernmost islands make up the republic of the Comoros; the fourth, Mayotte, elected to remain part of France (see also Mayotte). The islands are hot and rainy from November through April, drier and cooler between May and October. Thirteen species of birds are restricted to the Comoros and Mayotte, including a blue pigeon, bulbul, thrush, warbler, flycatcher, and fody, plus several white-eyes and sunbirds. Sea turtles and huge Comoros fruit bats are found on all the islands.

Grand Comoro, the largest (367 sq mi/950 sq km), is located 174 mi (280 km) east of Mozambique. Moroni, the capital, is connected by paved road to various resorts along the northern coast. The island is dominated by **Mount Karthala,** an active volcano rising to 7,874′ (2,400 m), with 288″ (7,200 mm) of annual rainfall. Its desolate crater, 2 mi (3 km) wide, can be reached via a difficult trail; it has been proposed as a national park. The island of **Mohéli** (83 sq mi/216 sq km) is known for its forests, its mongoose lemurs, and superb diving around its fringing coral reefs. The ancient coelacanth fish occurs here in deep water. A marine park has been proposed to protect the reefs and sea turtle nesting beaches.

Anjouan (146 sq mi/378 sq km) is full of perfume-plant plantations and has attractive Arab-style villages with mosques and narrow alleyways.

CONGO

For map, see Zaire.

West of Zaire and the Congo River, and east of Cameroon and Gabon, Congo (formerly the Moyen-Congo sector of French Equatorial Africa) has 10 percent of the remaining rain forest in Africa, but only 4 percent of the country's total area (132,000 sq mi/342,000 sq km) is protected in parks and reserves.

The South

Brazzaville, the capital, is located on the west bank of the Congo River below Stanley Pool and above the Congo Rapids. It receives 58″ (1,450 mm) of rain annually, chiefly between September and May. Average highs are 90–99°F (32–37°C). The environs west into the Niari Valley and north onto the Bateke Plateau (1,600–2,100′/500–650 m) feature cultivated land, secondary grassland, and patches of forest. **Lefini Faunal Reserve** (1,556,100 acres/630,000 ha), 90 mi (150 km) north of Brazzaville, has buffalos and waterbucks. The port/resort of Pointe-Noire, on the Atlantic, has a cool and dry climate for its latitude. **Conkouati Faunal Reserve** (741,000 acres/300,000 ha), to the north of Pointe-Noire, has fine white-sand beaches, several lagoons with manatees, grassland with waterbucks, and steep forested hills with elephants, gorillas, and chimpanzees. The jagged Mayombe Mountains, which reach 3,050′ (930 m) on the Gabon border, are home to several small reserves. **Mont Fouari Faunal Reserve** (38,500 acres/15,600 ha) is home to buffalos, waterbucks, bushbucks, bush pigs, gorillas, and chimpanzees. Nearby **Nyanga Nord Faunal Reserve** (19,000 acres/7,700 ha) protects forest remnants and a river with hippos.

The North

Reachable chiefly by air and boat, this region's vast areas of rain forest are home to Ba Aka Pygmies. It receives 72″ (1,800 mm) of rain annually, and is somewhat drier in January and from June through August. On the remote lakes and rivers, and in the swamp forests of Likouala province, between the Sangha and Ubangi rivers, there have been numerous reported sightings of a long-necked swamp dinosaur, the *mokele-mbembe.* **Nouabale-Ndoki National Park,** northeast of the town of Ouésso, is located in an area of forest and clearings on the Central African Republic border that shelters thousands of relatively tame elephants and swamp-dwelling lowland gorillas, as well as bongos, forest buffalos, and leopards. **Odzala National Park/Biosphere Reserve** (311,220 acres/126,000 ha), southwest of Ouésso, adjoins **Lekoli-Pandaka Faunal Reserve** (168,500 acres/68,200 ha). Habitats include rain forest, marshes, Lake Moba, man-made savanna (poor grassland), and natural salt pans. Among the wildlife are isolated lions and spotted hyenas in the savanna, and elephants, forest buffalos, giant forest hogs, bongos, sitatungas, duikers, and many primates, including gorillas and chimpanzees, elsewhere.

DJIBOUTI

For map, see Ethiopia.

A small country (8,880 sq mi/23,000 sq km), Djibouti is located 25 mi (40 km) southwest of Yemen, where the Red Sea meets the Gulf of Aden. Djibouti, the capital, is a refueling port and French naval base; it receives 5″ (125 mm) of rain per year, and has average highs of 84°F (29°C) in January, 106°F (41°C) in July. There are superb coral reefs just north of the capital in the offshore **Musha (Mouscha) Islands Marine National Park.** Migrant raptors cross to and from Yemen over the Ras Siyan Peninsula and the **Sept Frères Islands** in northeastern Djibouti. In southern Djibouti the rift valley meets the sea; volcanoes, multi-colored soda lakes, and low plains occur at the southern end of the Danakil Depression, an arid valley that in places is below sea level. **Lake Abbe,** on the Ethiopia border, has limestone needles 40′ (12 m) tall and colorful hot springs of steam and sulfur. Much of Djibouti is lowland plains of rock or sand sparsely covered with small thorny trees and short grasses. Sandgrouse and small birds are common, while Waller's and Soemmerring's gazelles, cheetahs, and ostriches are rare.

Annual rainfall increases to 20″ (500 mm) in **Day Forest National Park** (24,700 acres/10,000 ha), which protects juniper trees, wild olives, and montane evergreen thickets on the eastern face of the Goda Mountains. The hill town of Randa is located nearby, below a peak that reaches 5,774′ (1,760 m). The hamadryas baboon and the endemic Djibouti francolin occur here and in the Mabla Mountains, northeast of the port of Tadjoura.

EGYPT AND LIBYA

EGYPT PLATE 42

Located at the northeastern corner of Africa, Egypt (386,198 sq mi/1,004,115 sq km) is bordered by the Red Sea and the Mediterranean Sea. The very arid Sahara and Sinai deserts cover 95 percent of Egypt. **Cairo,** Egypt's capital and the largest city in Africa, is just east of the Great Pyramids and the Sphinx. Cairo and most of Egypt receive less than 2″ (50 mm) of rain a year. Cairo winters are pleasant, with average highs in the 60s F (18–21°C). Summers are extremely hot, with average highs of nearly 100°F (38°C) from May through September.

The Nile Valley

Rainwater from the highlands of Ethiopia and much of eastern Africa (south to Burundi) flows northward in the Nile River through Sudan and Egypt to the Mediterranean Sea. Most of the birds that migrate between Eurasia and tropical Africa use this corridor twice a year. **Qarun Lake,** 66 mi (110 km) southwest of Cairo in the El Faiyun oasis, hosts the little green bee-eater, Senegal coucal, and wintering waterfowl. Visitors who journey up the **Nile River** by felucca (a Nile sailboat) or river steamer or cover the Luxor, Aswan, and Abu Simbel touring circuit by road or rail have many opportunities to see birds, such as laughing doves, pied kingfishers, and crested hoopoes, but no large wild mammals. The **Kharga** and **Dakhla** oases, accessible by road west from Luxor, are home to desert birds, reptiles, and such mammals as the sand fox and fennec. East of Abu Simbel on Lake Nasser, **Gebel Elba** is a range of hills with relict stunted woodland and savanna, very unlike the barren hills elsewhere in Egypt, with a few sub-Saharan species of plants and animals. The area is administered by Sudan and is very difficult to visit.

The Coasts and Sinai Peninsula

Flamingos and large numbers of wintering geese and ducks frequent the Nile Delta and Egypt's coastal lagoons, despite excessive hunting and pollution in the area. In the northern Sinai, east of the Suez Canal, are **Bardawil Lake** and **Zaranikh Natural Protectorates** (each 150,000 acres/60,000 ha), both located between Port Said and El Arish. In the southern Sinai, visitors can make a four-hour round-trip hike up **Mount Sinai** from St. Catherine's Monastery. The area is a natural protectorate with a very few Nubian ibexes, slender-horned gazelles, and leopards. There are many resorts along the Gulf of 'Aqaba on the eastern shore of the Sinai. A heavy concentration of migrating raptors and storks can be seen overhead from the southern tip of the Sinai. Just offshore, the clear waters of **Ras Mohammed National Marine Park** (48,700 acres/19,700 ha) protect a fabulous underwater shelf. The waters here and elsewhere on Egypt's Red Sea coast are a paradise of coral, colorful fish, sea turtles, and birds such as sooty and white-eyed gulls.

EQUATORIAL GUINEA

For map, see Cameroon.

This small, three-part country was formerly called Spanish Guinea. The mainland section (10,040 sq mi/ 26,000 sq km), situated between Cameroon and Gabon, is called **Mbini** (formerly Río Muni). The main city, Bata, is on the Gulf of Guinea. The coastal plain rises up in steps to an interior marked by granitic inselbergs and mountains rising to 3,900′ (1,200 m). The Spanish had established several good parks, but these have been abandoned. There are proposals to set up a number of reserves south of the Uolo River to protect gorillas, chimpanzees, buffalos, hippos, and gray-necked rockfowl.

Bioko (formerly Fernando Póo), a rugged island (779 sq mi/ 2,018 sq km) 20 mi (33 km) off Cameroon with three 10,000′ (3,000-m) volcanoes, is also part of Equatorial Guinea. The island's lowlands are covered with plantations and some lush rain forest. Higher up montane forest, tree ferns, and alpine meadows prevail. Many interesting birds and primates reside on Bioko. Reserves are proposed on

Basile volcano, in the southern part of the island, and at beaches where sea turtles are known to breed. Rainfall reaches an astounding 456″ (11,400 mm) annually in places (giving the island claim to some of the wettest land on earth); Malabo, the capital, receives 68″ (1,700 mm). The third part of Equatorial Guinea lies 325 mi (525 km) southwest of Mbini: the island of **Annobón** (or Pagalu; 7 sq mi/18 sq km), a jumble of volcanic peaks that is the only home of two birds, the Annobón white-eye and a race of rufous-bellied paradise-flycatcher.

ERITREA

For map, see Ethiopia.

This country (45,405 sq mi/117,599 sq km) regained its independence from neighboring Ethiopia in 1993. Asmara, the capital, is located in the relatively green central highlands, where the tallest peaks exceed 9,840′ (3,000 m). The highlands are subject to erratic summer rains, while hot temperatures prevail in the lowlands. December and January are the cooler months. Eritrea has no mainland reserves at this writing. The long **Red Sea coastline** has mangrove swamps, tidal mudflats, salt marshes, and beaches, which are important habitats for the Eurasian spoonbill, osprey, crabplover, white-eyed and sooty gulls, terns, wintering Eurasian waders, and breeding sea turtles. **Dahlak Islands Marine Park** protects marvelous coral formations off the 126 islands of an archipelago east of the port of Mits'iwa (Massawa).

ETHIOPIA PLATES 5, 6, 38

Often called the "roof" of Africa, this fascinating country (471,775 sq mi/1,221,897 sq km) has two vast areas of mountain and plateau split by the rift valley, and a great variety of vegetation and endemic wildlife. When making and confirming flight and hotel reservations, travelers should note that the months and years on the Ethiopian calendar differ from those used in most other countries.

The North and West

Addis Ababa, the capital, is located at 8,000′ (2,440 m) in the western highlands. It gets 48″ (1,200 mm) of rain, chiefly between April and September. Average highs are only 70–77°F (21–25°C), average lows 41–50°F (5–10°C).

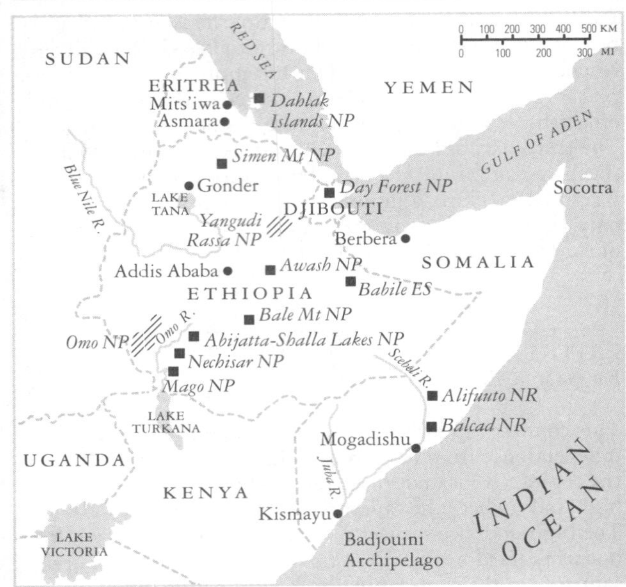

ETHIOPIA, SOMALIA, ERITREA, AND DJIBOUTI

The highlands were once covered with coniferous forest, but most of it has been cut down. A remnant podocarpus woodland, habitat of the white-cheeked turaco, is found in the **Menagesha Forest,** 42 mi (68 km) west of Addis Ababa. In the mountains of Kefa Province in the west are wet montane forests that receive 80″ (2,000 mm) of rain annually. **Lake Tana,** a large lake at 6,000′ (1,830 m) elevation in the northwest, is the source of the Blue Nile River. A grebe-like waterbird lives in the river between the lake and the impressive Blue Nile Falls to the southeast. **Simen (Simien) Mountain National Park/World Heritage Site** (44,200 acres/17,900 ha), in the Simen Mountains, is a wonderland of extremely deep gorges and grassy plateaus. Ras Dashan, at 15,158′ (4,620 m) the tallest mountain in Ethiopia, has frequent snowfall. Mammals in the area include the Ethiopian wolf (also called the Simien jackal), walia ibex, gelada and hamadryas baboons, and serval. Among the 400 species of birds are the wattled ibis, lammergeier, and thick-billed raven. Visitors to Simen park and Ras Dashan (just outside the park) must travel by foot or horseback. Safaris leave from the town of Debarek, reachable by road northeast of the city of Gonder.

The Rift Valley

Running northeast to southwest, the rift valley lowlands of Ethiopia are hot and dry. In the northeast, the valley is a wide arid plain dotted with volcanic cones and colorful alkaline lakes. **Yangudi Rassa National Park** (1,168,310 acres/473,000 ha), in the Danakil Desert, hosts the wild ass and the beisa oryx. **Awash National Park** (186,700 acres/75,600 ha), which lies along the Awash River, features waterfalls, hot springs, palm groves, grassy plains, and a semi-dormant volcano. It has lodging and is easily reached via paved road east from Addis Ababa. Mammals here include the beisa oryx, waterbuck, Soemmerring's gazelle, Swayne's hartebeest, lesser and greater kudus, dik-diks, Grevy's zebra, and hamadryas and savanna baboons. Among the 392 species of birds are the ostrich, carmine bee-eater, and Abyssinian roller.

To the south of Addis Ababa there is a string of eight lakes, many reached via good roads; some are salty, while others are fresh, fed by rivers and springs from the highlands. Freshwater **Lake Zwai** hosts the hippo and the saddle-billed stork. **Lake Langano** is a brown freshwater lake, with Hemprich's hornbill residing in nearby cliffs. **Abijatta-Shalla Lakes National Park** (219,100 acres/ 88,700 ha) is in a deep bowl flanked by tall cliffs. Abijatta provides rich feeding grounds for countless waterbirds, especially Eurasian migrants. Nearby Lake Shalla is a deep-water, blue salt lake with large nesting colonies of pelicans and flamingos. The freshwater **Lake Awasa,** south of the city of Awasa, has the goliath heron, wattled ibis, and pygmy goose. Swayne's hartebeests and zebras are protected in **Nechisar National Park** (127,000 acres/ 51,400 ha), east of Lake Chamo. West of the rift valley, the **Omo River,** whose waters and banks are home to crocodiles, hippos, and various antelopes, runs south into Lake Turkana (most of which is in Kenya). River-rafting excursions are offered in this wild area, which is served by a lodge. Visitors may encounter Surma women, who wear lip and ear plates. **Omo National Park** (1,004,800 acres/ 406,800 ha) and **Mago National Park** (534,000 acres/ 216,200 ha) protect plains, bushland, and gallery forest along the Omo. In addition to the many mammals here—among them elephants, giraffes, buffalos, elands, kudus, oryxes, lions, and leopards—early human fossils have been found. This is hot country, with rains from April through July.

The East

East of the rift valley are a number of towering green mountain ranges. A road from Shashamane in the rift valley winds up to the town of Goba on the northern edge of **Bale Mountain National Park** (610,300 acres/ 247,100 ha). Major efforts are being made to protect this tableland of alpine lakes, giant heath, bamboo forests, and woodland such as the Harenna Forest. The park's Mount Batu reaches an elevation of 14,130′ (4,307 m). This park is the chief protected home of the mountain nyala, an Ethiopian endemic. Other mammals include the Ethiopian wolf, leopard, caracal, and Menelik's race of bushbuck. Twelve of Ethiopia's 23 endemic bird species, including the blue-winged goose, live here. South of the city of Dire Dawa, isolated groups of elephants live in the **Babile Elephant Sanctuary** (1,724,100 acres/698,000 ha). The status of such ungulates as the beira antelope, dibatag, wild ass, and Speke's and Pelzeln's gazelles at Babile and in the Ogaden Desert to the east and south is unknown.

GABON

For map, see Cameroon.

Formerly part of French Equatorial Africa, Gabon lies on the equator where the Atlantic Ocean meets rain forest. The climate is hot, wet, and humid all year, but somewhat drier and cooler from June through August. Rainfall varies by locality from 50″ to 100″ (1,250–2,500 mm), while average high temperatures are 82–90°F (28–32°C). Rain forest, a third of it very pristine, covers 85 percent of the country's 103,089 sq mi (268,031 sq km).

The Coast

Northwest of Libreville, the capital, is **Cap Estérias,** a peninsula with nice beaches and roadside swamp forest that is home to birds such as the rosy bee-eater. Ferries and flights connect the capital with Port-Gentil, a major port to the south. The north-flowing currents offshore host humpback and sperm whales, tarpons, and swordfish. The vast **Wonga-Wongué National Park** (938,600 acres/ 380,000 ha), between the two cities, is well protected from poachers, but is open only to presidential parties hunting elephants, buffalos, sitatungas, and bongos.

Gabon has a coastal plain ranging from 30 mi to 90 mi (50–150 km) wide that has relict and man-made savannas, rain forest, lagoons, mangroves, and fine beaches. Recently enlarged **Petit Loango National Park** (1,185,600 acres/ 480,000 ha) is the only place in Africa where gorillas might be seen along a beach; it also harbors chimpanzees (among a dozen primates), forest elephants, manatees, various antelopes, and nesting leatherback sea turtles. There are a number of faunal and hunting reserves southward on the coast and inland, including **Moukalaba-Dougoula Faunal Reserve** (197,600 acres/80,000 ha) and the **Mont Fouari** area on the Congo border.

The Interior

The Ogooué River and its tributaries drain most of the country. Lambaréné is a river island city, reachable by air and road from Libreville. Albert Schweitzer's hospital, home, office, and library are still open on the north bank nearby. Pirogue (a canoe-like boat) trips of a few hours upriver to **Lac Zile** as well as overnight water safaris allow visitors to see hippos, forest-edge birds, and sandbank birds such as the white-crowned lapwing and gray pratincole. **Lopé Faunal Reserve** (1,235,000 acres/ 500,000 ha) and adjacent **Lopé-Okanda Hunting Reserve** extend from the river south to Mount Iboundji, Gabon's highest peak at 5,167′ (1,575 m). The parks have road and air access, as well as lodging. Buffalos, elephants, and mandrills inhabit the heavy forest and savanna. The wildest rain forests and swamp forests are in the northeast, where some mountaintops are covered with elfin (stunted) woodland. Gorillas, chimpanzees, numerous other primates, elephants, more than 400 bird species, and Gabon adders are widespread. **Ipassa-Makokou Strict Nature Reserve** (37,100 acres/15,000 ha), located in rain forest, has hosted a rich fauna but suffers from hunting and logging.

GAMBIA PLATE 29

For map, see Senegal.

This long narrow country (4,003 sq mi/10,367 sq km) lines the Gambia River for 195 mi (315 km). Its western border is on the Atlantic Ocean; otherwise it is surrounded by Senegal. Annual rainfall ranges from 40″ (1,000 mm) on the coast to 30″ (750 mm) inland. The rainy period (June through October) is followed by a long dry season. Average highs are 91–106°F (33–41°C).

The Coast

Banjul, the capital, is located just northeast of a string of Atlantic beach hotels. **Abuko Nature Reserve** (153 acres/ 62 ha), located 12 mi (20 km) south of Banjul, protects a small area of tall forest, savanna, and ponds. It is home to sitatungas, bushbucks, red colobus monkeys, vervet and patas monkeys, green mambas, and pythons, plus more than 200 species of birds, including the hammerkop, palm-nut vulture, and violet and green turacos. Chimpanzees are raised here before their release on islands upriver. **Gambia Saloum (Niumi/Sine) National Park** (12,200 acres/4,940 ha) on the north bank of the mouth of the Gambia River, adjacent to the Senegal border, protects coastal wetlands where many waterbirds breed.

Upriver

Much of the countryside is devoted to peanut and rice crops, while most villages have tall mango and baobab trees. The rest of the land is wooded savanna and bush. Birds are abundant everywhere, and such waterbirds as herons, hammerkops, and yellow-billed storks are common until the dry season progresses (they are best seen before January). Organized boat trips on the Gambia River visit the Fort James Island ruins, 22 mi (35 km) from Banjul, which are opposite Juffure village, of *Roots* fame. The river is lined with mudflats and vast mangrove forests in many areas. **Kiangs West National Park** (27,200 acres/11,000 ha) is located on the south bank of the river, 45 mi (75 km) east of Banjul and just west of Tendaba, which has lodging. **Gambia River National Park** (6,200 acres/2,500 ha), west of Georgetown, shelters hippos, baboons, and many birds. Several islands in the river are home to chimpanzees being reintroduced into the wild.

GHANA

Ghana (92,100 sq mi/238,539 sq km) is one of a string of countries on the Gulf of Guinea with a wetter green south merging into drier northern wooded savanna.

The South

Accra, the capital, is on the coast, where it is washed by a relatively cool current. It receives 28″ (700 mm) of rain annually, chiefly in two rainy seasons (a greater one April through June and a lesser one September through November). Average highs are 81–88°F (27–31°C). Ghana's coast has extensive lagoons, mangrove swamps, mudflats, and beaches (important wintering grounds for Eurasian waders), backed by scrub dotted with tall termite mounds.

The inland southwestern third of the country once was covered by humid, closed-canopy forest, with a yearly rainfall of up to 86″ (2,150 mm). Today there are 100

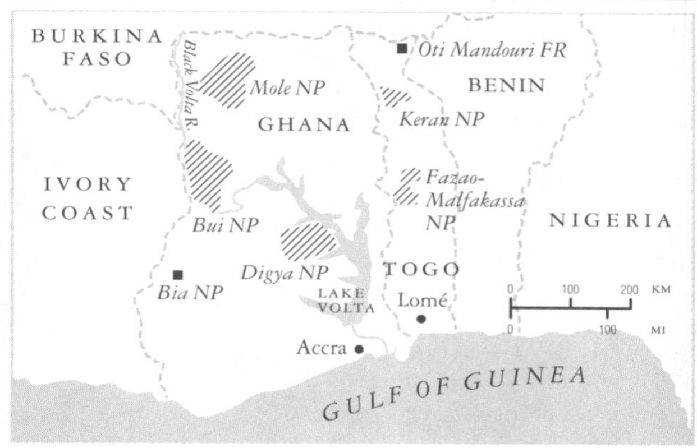

GHANA AND TOGO

scattered forest reserves, chiefly south and west of the city of Kumasi. The only extensive virgin rain forest is located in **Bia National Park/Biosphere Reserve** on the Ivory Coast border. It and an adjacent hunting reserve cover 75,300 acres (30,500 ha) that harbor forest elephants, bongos, buffalos, giant forest hogs, duikers, leopards, chimpanzees, diana and mona monkeys, collared mangabeys, black, red, and olive colobus monkeys, crowned eagles, and black- and yellow-casqued hornbills.

The North

Most of interior Ghana is in the drainage area of the Volta River. The Akwapim-Togo ranges start near Accra and rise to 2,900′ (885 m) on the Togo border. West of the mountains a huge dam has formed massive Lake Volta, which rises and falls with the rainfall cycles. **Digya National Park** (772,110 acres/312,595 ha) occupies a peninsula on the western side of the lake. It contains savanna woodland and gallery forest with elephants, hippos, buffalos, bushbucks, reedbucks, kobs, and black colobus and patas monkeys. **Bui National Park** (511,900 acres/207,250 ha), on the Black Volta River in the west, has hippos, roans, and other savanna wildlife. The finest wildlife viewing in the north can be had at **Mole National Park** (1,213,860 acres/491,440 ha), northwest of the town of Larabanga, which contains several lodges, miles of tracks, water holes, and a range of habitats from forest to grassland. It receives 48″ (1,200 mm) of rain in its June through September wet season. Wildlife is most visible late in the dry season. Mammals include the elephant, buffalo, roan, kob, waterbuck, bushbuck, hartebeest, oribi, red-flanked duiker, black colobus, baboon, lion, leopard, side-striped jackal, wild dog, and spotted hyena. More than 315 species of birds occur here, including the stone partridge, violet turaco, red-throated bee-eater, and double-toothed barbet.

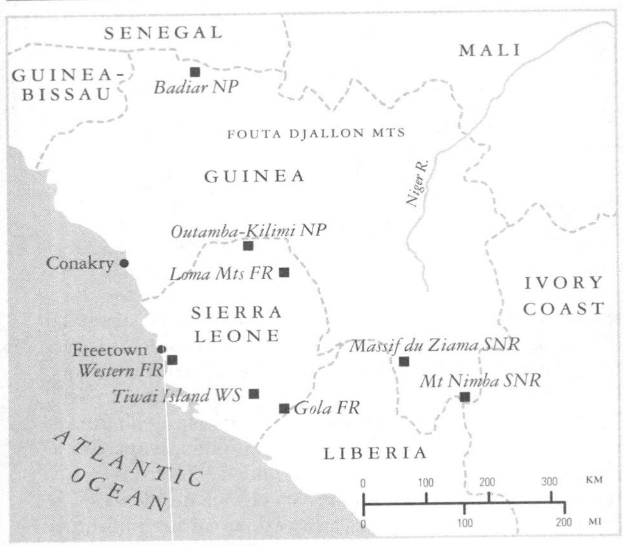

GUINEA AND SIERRA LEONE

GUINEA

Guinea, with an area of 94,925 sq mi (245,856 sq km), borders the Atlantic Ocean and has extensive mountains in the interior. Conakry, the capital, is located on the coast, opposite the Los Islands, home to the blue-breasted kingfisher. The city receives 165″ (4,125 mm) of rain yearly, chiefly from May through November. Average highs are 82–90°F (28–32°C). The coast is quite indented, with many estuaries and mangrove swamps important to wintering wading birds. Inland, the mountains of the **Fouta Djallon** rise steeply, culminating at Mount Laura at 4,970′ (1,515 m). Some 20 percent of Guinea is above 3,300′ (1,000 m) and was once covered with moist forest. As the headwater region for the Gambia, Senegal, and Niger rivers, the Fouta Djallon has many waterfalls. Its northwestern and northeastern slopes, in the rain shadow, are covered with dry Sudan savanna habitats dotted with baobab trees. **Badiar National Park** (94,400 acres/ 38,200 ha), adjacent to Senegal's Niokola-Koba National Park, is home to elephants, roans, kobs, leopards, spotted hyenas, and baboons. The mountainous spine runs southeastward into a forested region around the highland town of N'Zérékoré. Biosphere reserves have been declared at two strict nature reserves: **Massif du Ziama** (286,940 acres/116,170 ha) and **Mount Nimba** (42,311 acres/17,130 ha). The latter, which has a sister park in Ivory Coast, has primary montane forest and high-elevation grassland. Its wildlife highlights include chimpanzees and other primates, pygmy hippos, buffalos, duikers, dwarf otter-shrews, and montane birds.

GUINEA-BISSAU

For map, see Senegal.

This relatively small country (13,948 sq mi/36,125 sq km) is wedged between Senegal, Guinea, and the Atlantic Ocean. About 96″ (2,400 mm) of rain falls between June and November, followed by a long dry season that is very hot from March onward. Bissau, the capital, is on a wide estuary lined with mangrove forests and rice paddies. Inland there is a mosaic of forest and wooded savanna. In the southeast elevations rise to 660′ (200 m) in the foothills of Guinea's Fouta Djallon. There may soon be several reserves in selected forests, but the elephants, giraffes, and lions were eliminated by hunting long ago. The beautiful **Bijagós Archipelago,** 103 islands scattered southwest of Bissau, are lightly populated; some forests are home to the gray parrot. Sea turtles nest on the beaches, while vast numbers of wading birds winter on the islands. Many of these islands may become part of a proposed biosphere reserve.

IVORY COAST

This country, which faces the western end of the Gulf of Guinea, has three major regions: the rain forests of the south, with two rainy seasons; the western highlands; and the drier savanna woodland of the north, with a single summer rainy season. The center of the country is a transitional mosaic of the three. The total area of Ivory Coast is 124,503 sq mi (322,463 sq km).

The Southern Rain Forests

Abidjan, the capital, is located in a coastal plain among vast lagoons that lie behind a series of long sand bars. Its

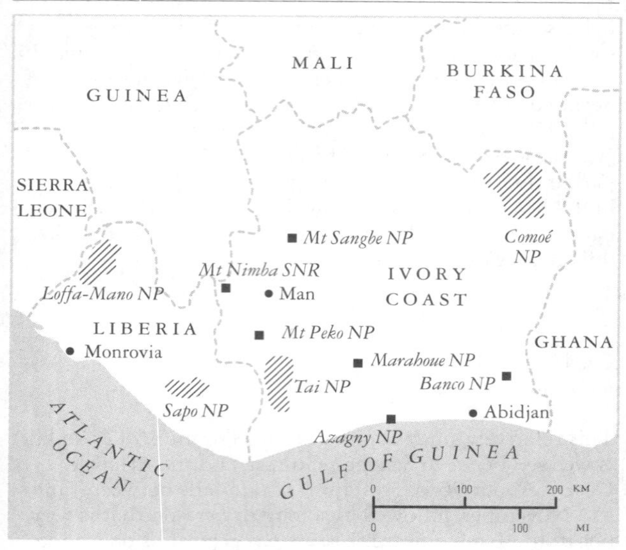

IVORY COAST AND LIBERIA

77" (1,925 mm) of annual rain is heaviest between April and July and in October and November. Average highs are 82–90°F (28–32°C). **Banco National Park** (7,400 acres/ 3,000 ha) is a small patch of rain forest just northeast of Abidjan. Bird-watching is good along its forest tracks, but most of the primates and antelopes have been poached. **Azagny National Park** (46,900 acres/19,000 ha), located on the coast near Grand-Lahou (west of Abidjan), has savanna and swamp forest with manatees, chimpanzees, elephants, and buffalos.

The largest remaining tract of lowland rain forest in western Africa is protected in **Tai National Park/World Heritage Site/Biosphere Reserve** (864,500 acres/ 350,000 ha), near the Liberia border. Massive towering trees rise above a rich ground flora. The wildlife here, much of it endangered, is often shy, nocturnal, or hard to see in the canopy. Tai has the last viable population of pygmy hippopotamuses, and is home to six duikers—banded, bay, black, Jentick's, Ogilby's, and yellow-backed—and such primates as the collared mangabey, diana monkey, chimpanzee, and three colobus species. Other mammals in residence include the tiny royal antelope, the water chevrotain, the bongo, the elephant, three pangolin species, and the golden cat. Among the birds of note are the white-breasted guineafowl and white-necked rockfowl.

The Western Highlands

Man, the chief highland town, is located in an area of beautiful forested mountains; it is a center of the Dan people, famous for their masks and stilt dances. A road climbs up 3,900′ (1,190-m) Mount Tonkoui past forests and waterfalls. Forest mammals and birds may be seen in **Mount Peko National Park** (84,000 acres/34,000 ha) to the south and **Mount Sangbe National Park** (234,700 acres/95,000 ha) to the northeast. The Odienne highlands continue north in ever-drier country. The **Mount Nimba Strict Nature Reserve/World Heritage Site** (12,400 acres/5,000 ha), on the border with Guinea and Liberia, is a massive granitic inselberg 25 mi (40 km) long and rich in iron ore. From 2,600′ (800 m) to its peak at 6,069′ (1,850 m), an area of mist forest and natural highland grassland, there is often heavy cloud. The reserve is most interesting for its endemic plants and smaller animals, but also has chimpanzees, bongos, and forest buffalos.

The Northern Savannas

In the southern portions of the country's savannas, **Marahoue National Park** (249,500 acres/101,000 ha), northwest of the town of Bouaflé, has dome-like hills bordering the Bandama River. Wildlife includes the elephant, hippo, buffalo, red river hog, warthog, waterbuck, hartebeest, kob, reedbuck, and chimpanzee. Ivory Coast's major savanna park is **Comoé National Park/Biosphere Reserve/World Heritage Site** (2,840,500 acres/ 1,150,000 ha), in the northeast, with lodging and a fine network of tracks. It is well forested in the south, with drier savanna woodland to the north and grassy floodplains and gallery forests by the Comoé River. Annual rainfall reaches 44″ (1,100 mm), followed by a long dry season in winter and spring. The park contains primates such as the black-and-white colobus, patas monkey, and baboon; many antelopes, including the roan, oribi, kob, hartebeest, waterbuck, and bushbuck; and elephants, hippos, buffalos, spotted hyenas, and lions. As for birds, 445 species have been recorded, and secretarybirds, bustards, and ground-hornbills walk the grasslands. Among the park's reptiles are all three African crocodile species, as well as monitor lizards and snakes.

KENYA PLATES 2, 7, 9, 10, 19, 20, 37, 44

Encompassing 224,960 sq mi (582,646 sq km), Kenya straddles the equator between Lake Victoria and the Indian

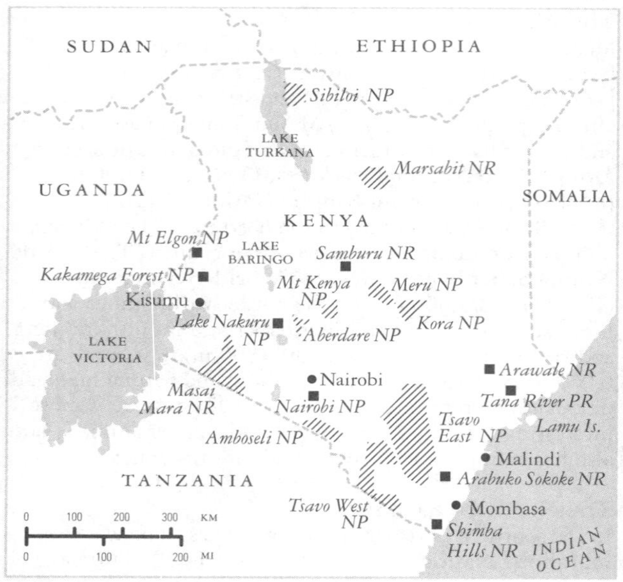

KENYA

Ocean. It harbors a rich diversity of habitats: grassy plains, rock-strewn deserts, fresh and saline lakes, forested mountains, palm-fringed beaches, and coral reefs. A green highland plateau, crowned by snow-capped Mount Kenya and cleaved by the arid eastern rift valley, covers much of the country. There are usually two rainy seasons, the long rains from March through May and the short rains in November and December. Temperatures in the highlands are pleasantly cool, despite their location on the equator. Kenya has done a remarkable job establishing wildlife sanctuaries. Its 18 national parks, 4 marine national parks, 4 nature reserves, 23 national reserves, and 5 marine national reserves are the focus of the greatest wildlife tourism industry in the world.

Nairobi

Nairobi, the capital, lies at the transition zone between the lower, drier plains to the south and east and the higher, greener highlands to the north and west. It receives 37″ (925 mm) of rain annually. The average high is 70°F (21°C) in July, 79°F (26°C) in February. **Nairobi National Park** (28,951 acres/11,721 ha), just south of the city, has many water holes and a network of tracks. Primarily rolling grassland, the park borders the forest-fringed Athi River, home to hippos and crocodiles. Heavily protected, black rhinos roam the park. Common grazers include zebras, giraffes, Thomson's and Grant's gazelles, hartebeests, wildebeests, bushbucks, elands, and ostriches. There are many lions, and fewer leopards and cheetahs.

The Highlands

The central highlands lie to the north and west of Nairobi. Rainfall averages 50″ (1,250 mm) a year and is much higher on some slopes. Often cold and drizzly between June and September, the area is sunniest from December through March. There are superb safari hotels between the Aberdare Mountains (west of the town of Nyeri) and Mount Kenya (east of the town of Nanyuki). Nearby highland grasslands have long-tailed widowbirds. Private ranches near Lewa Downs and at Sweetwaters, west of Nanyuki, offer camel and horseback safaris into animal-rich country. The region's other facilities include a mountain lodge on the southwestern slope of Mount Kenya, and two (Treetops and the Ark) in the eastern Aberdares. Each has a water hole and salt licks that attract elephants, buffalos, waterbucks, bushbucks, and sometimes bongos.
Mount Kenya National Park (177,245 acres/71,759 ha) protects most of the land above 10,500′ (3,200 m) on Africa's second-tallest mountain (after Tanzania's Mount Kilimanjaro). On clear days one can see the permanent snowfields on its twin glacial peaks, which reach 17,058′ (5,199 m). There are lodges at the base of the Naro Moru trail on the west and the Simiron trail on the drier northwestern side. The trails pass by deep gorges and cut through dense montane forest hosting black-fronted duikers, sunis, blue monkeys, giant forest hogs, black-and-white colobus monkeys, and Hartlaub's turacos. Above 11,000′ (3,340 m) the forest yields to open moorland with giant heather and tall columns of lobelia and groundsel where the rock hyrax, several raptors, and the scarlet-tufted malachite sunbird are found. **Aberdare National Park** (189,249 acres/76,619 ha) sits at the eastern edge of the rift valley. Soaring to 13,100′ (4,000 m) elevation, it has heavy montane forest and moorland. Wildlife, difficult to see in such lush vegetation, is plentiful. There are more than 200 bird species, plus elephants, buffalos, bongos, lions, and black rhinos. Armed ranger guides are required when hiking.

The North

To the north of verdant Mount Kenya lies an austere semi-desert of thornbush flats, dry grassland, open acacia woodland, and rugged ranges that averages only 14″

(350 mm) of rain a year. These hot, sun-baked landscapes, home to red-robed goat and camel herders, extend north to Ethiopia and east to Somalia. At the southern edge of this arid region stands a trio of contiguous national reserves with varied lodging and good access by road from Nairobi, 200 mi (325 km) to the south. **Samburu National Reserve** (40,800 acres/16,500 ha), **Shaba National Reserve** (59,058 acres/23,910 ha), and **Buffalo Springs National Reserve** (32,400 acres/13,100 ha) line the perennial Ewaso Ng'iro River, rimmed with towering river acacias and doum palms. The river and several springs attract much wildlife, especially in dry periods. Mammals restricted to the Somali-Masai arid zone are found here, such as Grevy's zebra, the reticulated giraffe, the beisa oryx, Guenther's dik-dik, and the gerenuk. Also present are lesser kudus, elephants, Grant's gazelles, lions, cheetahs, leopards, and 350 bird species, including the blue-flushed Somali ostrich and the bristle-crowned starling.

Meru National Park (214,999 acres/87,044 ha) lies southeast of Samburu and borders the Tana River, along with **Kora National Park** (441,587 acres/178,780 ha). Meru, well watered by streams flowing eastward from the Nyambeni Hills and Mount Kenya, hosts many mammals: elephants, buffalos, plains zebras, Grant's gazelles, leopards, servals, and hippos, plus arid-zone mammals, such as the beisa oryx, reticulated giraffe, and Guenther's dik-dik. Birds include the vulturine guineafowl, golden pipit, and golden-breasted starling.

North of Meru, in a scrubby and stony semi-desert, Marsabit Mountain rises to 5,594′ (1,705 m). Protected in the little-visited **Marsabit National Reserve** (515,700 acres/208,800 ha), this sky-high oasis is pocked with volcanic craters, including Paradise Lake, with its lush montane forest necklace. Marsabit's once abundant population of elephants, and its wildlife in general, has plummeted due to poaching and human encroachment. Still, more than 300 bird species and many mammals live here, including greater kudus.

The Rift Valley

Kenya's rift valley runs north–south and is generally hot and arid. It is bordered by tall cliffs in some areas and relatively shallow steps in others. Numerous lakes line the valley. Some are fresh and others alkaline, with salinity levels varying relative to rainfall. The most northerly, salty **Lake Turkana,** is the largest and lowest in elevation at 1,230′ (375 m). **Sibiloi National Park** (388,000 acres/157,085 ha), on its eastern shore, embraces a petrified forest and abuts fossil beds that harbor early hominid remains. Thousands of crocodiles breed on Central Island, west of the park.

In west-central Kenya, **Lake Baringo,** reached by paved road north of the town of Nakuru, is freshwater and has lodging and boat trips. Baringo is known for its density and variety of birds: Hundreds of species, including endemics, throng its shores and the surrounding woodlands and cliffs. **Lake Bogoria National Reserve** (26,441 acres/ 10,705 ha), east of the Baringo road, is a scenic soda lake with hot springs that erupt in boiling geysers. Its shores are often busy with flamingos. **Lake Nakuru National Park** (46,400 acres/18,800 ha) is a jewel in this chain of lakes, located south of the town of Nakuru on the main highway west from Nairobi. It is framed by tall cliffs and yellow fever trees, and encircled by a dirt track. The park is fenced to protect black and white rhinos that have been relocated here for sanctuary. Notable mammals include the Rothschild's giraffe, hippos, defassa waterbucks, bohor reedbucks, bushbucks, and leopards. Birds are the true highlight; birder Roger Tory Peterson proclaimed Nakuru "the most fabulous bird spectacle in the world." Most years its shores and shallow alkaline waters are jammed with birds: millions of lesser flamingos, thousands of greater flamingos, and vast numbers of pelicans, cormorants, herons, storks, ibises, ducks, geese, plovers, sandpipers, gulls, and terns.

Nearby **Lake Naivasha,** a freshwater lake fringed with papyrus, supports fish-eagles, little grebes, red-knobbed coots, malachite kingfishers, and an array of other birds. Black-and-white colobus monkeys live in lakeside woods, while hippos graze ashore at night. Shoreside lodging and boating are offered. **Hell's Gate National Park** (16,800 acres/ 6,800 ha), 8 mi (13 km) southeast of Naivasha, features a gorge with towering cliffs where Verreaux's eagles and Rüppell's griffon vultures nest.

The West

West of the rift valley Kenya is highly diverse, with hot semi-desert in the north, large areas of cool highlands, vast grasslands rich in game in the south, humid rain forest in the west, and papyrus beds on an inland sea. **Masai Mara National Reserve** (373,000 acres/151,000 ha) is the northern extension of Tanzania's famous Serengeti Plains and is usually called "the Mara." Reachable by road or air from Nairobi, the Mara is Kenya's premier place for seeing wildlife. It features many excellent game lodges and camps, and a wide network of dirt roads slice through its open rolling grassland and wooded savanna. Two sizable rivers, the Mara and Talek, wind through the landscape, flanked by gallery forests and seasonal marshes. The reserve is most extraordinary between July and October, when well over 1 million migrant herbivores (especially wildebeests and zebras) settle in for dry-season grazing. Besides migrants, the Mara hosts resident populations of elephants, hippos, topis, hartebeests, buffalos, giraffes, Thomson's and Grant's gazelles, impalas, Kirk's dik-diks, and a few black rhinos. Predators are plentiful, notably cheetahs, leopards, and unusually large prides of lions. Birding is excellent around the lodges and from vehicles; 450 species have been recorded, including 54 raptors. The gallery forests host primates and a number of birds usually found farther west. The pastoral Masai (Maasai) people lead a semi-nomadic life just outside the reserve.

Northward, Kisumu is the main Kenyan port on **Lake Victoria.** With an elevation of 3,725′ (1,135 m), Kisumu has rain all year, with the annual accumulation of 45″ (1,125 mm) mainly concentrated between March and May. Average highs are 81–84°F (27–29°C). The lake, not part of either the eastern or the western rift valley, is banked with papyrus beds that attract many waterbirds and a number of songbirds not found elsewhere in Kenya.

Kakamega Forest National Park (11,036 acres/4,468 ha) is located east of the town of Kakamega, 32 mi (51 km) north of Kisumu. It is a relict of a much larger tract of wet tropical forest that once covered the area. Some of its wildlife and many of its 125 species of trees are those of the Congo Basin and are not found farther east. Kenya's only true "jungle," this area is overlooked by most tourists. Mammals of note include the red-tailed monkey, blue monkey, and duikers by day, and the potto, tree pangolin, and giant flying squirrel at night. Highlights among the 320 bird species are the gray parrot, great blue turaco, Narina's trogon, black-and-white casqued hornbill, African broadbill, and many barbets, wattle-eyes, sunbirds, and weavers. There are fine walking trails and a rest camp.

Mount Elgon National Park (41,800 acres/16,923 ha) covers a flank of this 14,178′ (4,321-m) peak on the Uganda border northwest of the town of Kitale. It has a lodge and features a cave that elephants enter for mineral salts, plus trails through montane forest and moorlands dotted with giant groundels and lobelias. Tiny **Saiwa Swamp National Park** (470 acres/190 ha) is located 11 mi (18 km) southeast of Kitale. Sitatungas inhabit its marshes, while De Brazza's monkeys and Ross's turacos live in nearby woodland. Descending the highlands north over the Kongolai Escarpment takes one into dry woodland, home to the stone partridge, the yellow-billed shrike, and the curly-crested race of the white helmet-shrike.

The Southeast

Between Nairobi and the Kenya coast sprawl three superb national parks. Masai herders inhabit nearby grasslands studded with baobab trees and open acacia woodland. **Amboseli National Park** (96,838 acres/39,206 ha), reached via air or road 150 mi (240 km) south of Nairobi, is Kenya's most visited game park, offering fine lodging, abundant mammal and bird life, and the dramatic backdrop of snow-capped Mount Kilimanjaro, just across the Tanzania border. Its saline lake is usually dry, but the park embraces two large, spring-fed swamps that provide permanent water to a region that receives only 12″ (300 mm) of rain a year. This is a splendid place to view elephants. Some 55 other mammal species roam the land, including lions, leopards, cheetahs, impalas, Grant's gazelles, elands, fringe-eared oryxes, gerenuks, buffalos, and a few black rhinos. Many wildebeests, zebras, and Thomson's gazelles leave the park during the rains but return to be near the swamps in the dry months. More than 425 species of birds live here, with the Taveta golden weaver a highlight, and ostriches, vultures, eagles, bustards, sandgrouse, hornbills, and larks common in the grasslands. **Tsavo East National Park** (2,901,500 acres/1,174,700 ha) and **Tsavo West National Park** (2,239,100 acres/906,500 ha) flank both the highway and the railroad that link Nairobi to coastal Mombasa (roughly 200 mi/335 km southeast). There are excellent lodges, most with water holes to attract animals, and some (in Tsavo West) with views of Kilimanjaro. The Galena River, with its attendant gallery forests and seasonal swamps, snakes through both parks. Enormous baobabs provide nesting sites for many parrots, rollers, and barbets. Giraffes, buffalos, elands, gazelles, waterbucks, gerenuks, lesser kudus, and elephants browse the bushed terrain; lions are numerous. Tsavo West has recent volcanic craters and lava flows, as well as Mzima Springs, a lush oasis where hippos breed. More than 400 species of birds have been recorded, including Eurasian migrants and relatively local "east of the rift" species such as the vulturine guineafowl, golden pipit, and Fischer's and golden-breasted starlings. Freshwater **Lake Jipe,** on the Tanzania border, draws many waterbirds, including the black heron.

The Coast

At Mombasa, Kenya's chief port, the airport serves direct flights to and from Europe and Nairobi. The city gets 47″ (1,175 mm) of rain, spread throughout the year with a peak between April and June. Average highs are 81–88°F (27–31°C). Kenya's 300-mi (480-km) shoreline on the

Indian Ocean is endowed with sublime white sand beaches and a colorful chain of fringing coral. Onshore breezes temper the heat and humidity. Portions of the shore and coastal waters are protected as marine national parks and reserves, most with fine accommodations nearby, including Kiunga (in the north), Ras Tenewi, Malindi/Watamu, Mombasa, and Kisite/Mpunguti (in the south). Carmine bee-eaters roost on mangrove islands above the town of Kilifi, while crabplovers and myriad waders throng the flats of Mida Creek in Watamu reserve. Inland, **Shimba Hills National Reserve** (47,550 acres/19,251 ha), 35 mi (56 km) southwest of Mombasa, is home to sable and roan antelopes. Coastal woodlands such as Shimba Hills host birds not found elsewhere in Kenya, including Fischer's turaco. Many very rare birds and the yellow-rumped elephant-shrew live in the dense woodlands of **Arabuko Sokoke Nature Reserve** (10,700 acres/4,332 ha), between Kilifi and Watamu. **Tana River Primate Reserve** (41,700 acres/16,900 ha), which lies 74 mi (120 km) north of Malindi, protects the Tana crested mangabey and red colobus. The very local Hunter's antelope lives in **Arawale National Reserve** (131,710 acres/53,324 ha), 25 mi (40 km) farther north.

LESOTHO

For map, see Natal, South Africa.

The "roof" of southern Africa, this country is largely above 6,000′ (1,800 m) and is surrounded by South Africa. Its total area is 11,716 sq mi (30,344 sq km). Maseru, the capital, is in the somewhat lower and drier northwestern third. The rest is a mass of steep canyons, mountain ranges, and the inland plateau edge of the great escarpment of the Drakensberg range. The vegetation is chiefly grassland, with some scrub on hillsides and alpine heathland higher up. The highest point is the eastern Mount Thabana Ntlenyana at 11,425′ (3,482 m), source of the Orange River. Rainfall averages 28″ (700 mm) yearly, with fog, heavy thunderstorms, and hail in the summer, and frequent snow in the winter. Temperatures vary from 90°F (32°C) in summer to well below freezing in winter. There are organized foot and pony trips to many scenic areas. **Sehlabathebe National Park** (16,808 acres/6,805 ha), on the southeastern border, has lodging and trails. It is home to the gray rhebok, eland, baboon, bald ibis, lammergeier, ground woodpecker, and orange-breasted rockjumper.

LIBERIA

For map, see Ivory Coast.

Covering 43,000 sq mi (111,370 sq km), Liberia has a 300-mi (500-km) coastline on the Atlantic Ocean. Monrovia, the capital, on the western coast, gets 192″ (4,800 mm) of rain annually, with a lull from January through March. Average highs are 81–88°F (27–31°C), accompanied by high humidity. A series of large rivers flow into the sea from the even wetter highlands. The Wologizi Mountains in the north, Mount Nimba in the northeast, and the Putu range in the south have elevations well over 3,300′ (1,000 m). Half the country is still covered with closed-canopy rain forest, 30 percent of which is protected in ten national forests and one national park. **Sapo National Park** (322,945 acres/130,747 ha) in the southern interior has dense virgin rain forest populated by forest elephants, pygmy hippopotamuses, bongos, bushbucks, royal antelopes, duikers (Jentick's, banded, black, and others), chimpanzees, diana monkeys, and three colobines. More than 300 species of birds are known, including the white-breasted guineafowl and white-necked rockfowl. **Loffa-Mano National Park** (568,100 acres/230,000 ha), on the Sierra Leone border, has many rivers with rapids in heavy forest, supporting similar wildlife to that of Sapo. Other parks and reserves have been proposed along the Cavally and Cestos rivers, in the highlands, and around Cape Mount and Lake Piso.

LIBYA

For map, see Egypt.

This predominantly Saharan country (679,358 sq mi/ 1,759,537 sq km) has two somewhat cooler and greener areas in the north. Tripoli, the capital, located on the coast in the northwest, averages 15″ (375 mm) of annual rain, which falls between October and March. Average highs are 61°F (16°C) in January, 86°F (30°C) in July. The Jebel Nefusa Mountains to its south are wet enough to support olive groves. On the coast east of Tripoli are two areas with rare running streams and freshwater marshes that attract huge numbers of trans-Saharan bird migrants. One is the **Garabulli** protected area and **Wadi Turghat.** The other is **Wadi Kaam,** east of the great Roman ruins of Leptis Magna.

Benghazi is the main city of the northeastern Cyrenaica region. To the north lie wetlands with many wintering greater flamingos and other waders. To the west, the Gulf of Sidra has important sea-grass beds with marine life. To the east lies Jebel Akhdar, which rises to 2,300′ (700 m) and receives 24″ (600 mm) of annual rain. Popular **Kouf National Park** (86,500 acres/35,000 ha), just east of Benghazi, has relict Mediterranean woodland with waterfalls, resident blue tits, juniper trees, and more than 100 endemic plants.

In a band just to the north of the Sahara, there is a zone of hilly grassland steppes that is home to dorcas, dama, and slender-horned gazelles, aoudads, and cheetahs. The area has been overhunted and overgrazed by camels and sheep, but reintroductions offer hope. In the Sahara, which covers three-quarters of the country, winter nights can get cold, while summer temperatures often exceed 122°F (50°C) at midday. Landscapes here vary from giant mobile sand dunes to stony deserts and plateaus, volcanic peaks, and palm-lined oases. One protected area is **Zellaf Nature Reserve** (247,000 acres/100,000 ha), just northwest of Sebha oasis; the status of its fauna is unknown at this time.

MADAGASCAR PLATE 13

The fourth-largest island in the world (226,657 sq mi/ 587,042 sq km), Madagascar, formerly known as the Malagasy Republic, is 975 mi (1,570 km) long. It lies 185 mi (300 km) east of Mozambique in the southwestern Indian Ocean. It contains an amazing diversity of landforms, climates, soils, flora, and fauna. The eastern and northern coasts are hot and rainy, the central highlands cool and pleasant much of the year. The west is drier, with an exotic spiny desert in the south. The rainy season is November through March. Most of the flora and fauna are endemic, as Madagascar split off from India and Africa tens of millions of years ago. Mammals include tenrecs, bats, rodents, small carnivores, and "primitive" primates called lemurs. The 10′ (3-m) tall elephantbird, weighing 1,100 lb (500 kg), lived here until A.D. 1700. Of 250 bird species, 130 are endemic, and there are several endemic families. Madagascar hosts a high diversity of chameleons and geckos, and nearly all of its 150 amphibians and 270 reptiles are endemic. Three boa and seven iguana species live here, groups found elsewhere chiefly in Latin America. Flora (nearly 10,000 species) is about 80 percent endemic, and includes 1,000 species of orchids, 130 palms, 97 ebonies, and 9 baobabs (compared to only one in continental Africa). Some 85 percent of the native vegetation has been

MADAGASCAR

cleared, and only 2 percent of the country is in protected areas. With less and less habitat, wildlife is extremely endangered, and most experts view Madagascar as the number-one conservation priority in the world. Permits, obtainable in Tana (see below), are required to visit most parks and special reserves. Most strict nature reserves are open only to scientists.

The Central Highland Plateau

Antananarivo, the capital (commonly called **Tana**), sprawls over 12 hills in the middle of a vast plateau that runs the length of the island and is punctuated with extinct volcanoes. Average elevations on the plateau are 2,600–5,000′ (800–1,500 m). Tana receives 53″ (1,325 mm) of rain yearly, and has average highs of 68°F (20°C) in July and 81°F (27°C) in November. Nights may approach freezing in winter. Lemurs, reptiles, and a number of free-living native birds (including herons) can be seen around the gardens and the lake at the Tsimbazaza Zoo. **Lake Alaotra,** 110 miles (180 km) to the northeast, supports waterfowl and a lemur species.

Ranomafana National Park (102,708 acres/41,582 ha) lies on the central plateau 255 mi (410 km) south of Tana. It is located near the town of the same name (which has lodging), about two hours by road from the highland city of Fianarantsoa. High rainfall feeds churning rivers flanked by virgin rain forest on steep slopes. This forest is home to Madagascar's biggest carnivore, the cat-like fossa, and 11 lemur species, including the aye-aye, the red-bellied and red-fronted, all three bamboo-lemurs, and the diademed sifaka. Birds include the crested wood ibis, brown mesite, blue coua, velvet asity, and seven species of vanga shrikes.

The East Coast

The east coast has a long, narrow coastal plain backed by a chain of mountains that meets the edge of the central plateau. Moisture-laden northeastern winds are forced upward here, resulting in massive amounts of rainwater. Toamasina, the main port, gets 121″ (3,025 mm) of rain, which falls year-round. Average highs are 75°F (24°C) in June and 86°F (30°C) in January.

Mananara Nord National Park/Biosphere Reserve (56,800 acres/23,000 ha) is a new coastal and marine park on the western entrance to Antongil Bay, north of Toamasina. **Nosy Mangabe Special Reserve** (1,284 acres/ 520 ha) is a pristine island in Atongil Bay where the endangered nocturnal aye-aye and other lemurs are protected. Tourists can reach it via boat from Maroantsetra.

Masoala National Park (618,000 acres/250,000 ha) is located on the Masoala Peninsula east of Nosy Mangabe Island and Maroantsetra and south of Antalaha (both of which have lodging). Its primary lowland rain forest, coastal forest, and mangroves are home to such rarities as the red-ruffed lemur, helmetbird, and Madagascar serpent-eagle.

Perinet-Analamazaotra Special Reserve (2,000 acres/ 810 ha), 100 mi (160 km) east of Tana alongside the main Tana–Toamasina highway and railroad, has lodging. There are wide trails in tall rain forest with many lianas and palms. Among the nine lemur species that reside here is the indri, the largest lemur, which produces fabulous calls and is the main attraction. Among 70 species of birds are the Madagascar green pigeon, both black parrots, and the blue and the nuthatch vangas.

The Northwest

Beautiful beaches rim the bays at the northern tip of the island around the town of **Antsiranana** (Diego Suarez). Twenty-five miles (40 km) to the southwest, **Montagne d'Ambre National Park** (45,000 acres/18,200 ha) is reachable in the dry season by road. Its 19 mi (30 km) of sign-posted paths lead through a tall montane forest with an understory of palms and tree ferns. Beyond the marked trail, elevations reach 4,744′ (1,446 m), and several scenic crater lakes dot the landscape. Among the park's wildlife are Sanford's brown lemur, the crowned lemur, and 54 of the island's endemic birds. Just off the northwestern coast is the resort island of **Nosy Be.** At Hell-Ville, its main port, an airport, resorts, and a few cruise ships serve visitors. **Lokobe Integral Nature Reserve** (1,828 acres/ 740 ha), in southeastern Nosy Be, protects the last block of forest on this island and has three species of lemurs. Five miles (8 km) south is **Nosy Komba,** an idyllic island where black lemurs commonly greet visitors at its small north-end village. **Nosy Tanikely,** another nearby islet, has great snorkeling, tidal pools, and fruit bats.

The western coast of Madagascar has extensive reefs and mangrove forests. Mahajanga, located at the mouth of the Betsiboka River, is the main port city in the northwest. Sixty-six miles (106 km) southeast is **Ankarafantsika Integral Nature Reserve** (149,484 acres/60,520 ha). Much of this reserve is closed to tourists, but visitors may explore trails around the adjacent **Ampijora forest station.** The paths cut through dense deciduous forests inhabited by woolly, mongoose, and brown lemurs, plus Coquerel's race of Verreaux's sifaka. Bird species include the crested wood ibis, the white-breasted mesite, Schlegel's asity, and several couas (large cuckoos) and vangas. Madagascar herons, fish-eagles, and jacanas congregate near lakes and rice paddies between here and Ampijora. Grand baobab forests survive in spots to the southwest.

The South

Receiving about 16″ (400 mm) of rain annually, southern Madagascar is arid, with a long dry season. The native vegetation is of the spiny desert type, and includes water-storing plants like bottle trees (pygmy baobab), octopus trees, cactus-like euphorbias, and succulents. **Taolanaro** (Fort-Dauphin) is the main town on the southeastern coast. **Berenty Private Reserve** (618 acres/250 ha), located 54 mi (87 km) westward, has overnight lodging. It protects remnants of spiny and riverside gallery forests. Visitors to the riverine forest are greeted by friendly ring-tailed lemurs and are likely to spot members of the white race of Verreaux's sifaka. Birds include sickle-billed and hook-billed vangas and four species of couas: the giant, crested, running, and Verreaux's.

The coastal city of Toliara (Tulear) is located on the Tropic of Capricorn in the southwest. The long-tailed ground-roller and the sub-desert mesite live in spiny forest near the resort of **Ifaty,** 15 mi (24 km) to the north. Red-tailed tropicbirds nest on **Nosy Ve** islet off the town of Anakao, south of Toliara. **Beza-Mahafaly Special Reserve,** 80 mi (130 km) southeast of Toliara, protects 247 acres (100 ha) of riverine forest and 1,200 acres (500 ha) of spiny forest, home to the endangered radiated tortoise. The ring-tailed lemur and Verreaux's sifaka live here and at **Isalo National Park** (201,404 acres/81,540 ha), a hiker's wonderland 150 mi (240 km) northeast of Toliara on the main highway to Tana near the town of Ranohira. Reaching 4,300′ (1,300 m), the Isalo Massif has crystal-clear pools, waterfalls, deep gorges, caves, and rock-clinging plants.

MALAWI PLATE 35

For map, see Zambia.

Encompassing 45,193 sq mi (117,050 sq km), Malawi is a narrow country, 580 mi (935 km) long, located at the southern end of the rift valley. The centerpiece is Lake Malawi, the third-largest lake in Africa and third-deepest in the world. The country has a greater range of climates and elevation than most, and 9 percent of its area is national parks and wildlife reserves, covering all major vegetation types.

Central and North

Lilongwe, the capital, is located in the western plateau country. It receives 31″ (775 mm) of annual rainfall, chiefly between November and April. Average highs are 73°F (23°C) in June and 82°F (28°C) in December. East of Lilongwe lies **Lake Malawi National Park/World Heritage Site** (21,500 acres/8,700 ha), which protects some of a peninsula near the resort of Cape McLear and Monkey Bay, plus three islets. The site's wildlife includes hippos, crocodiles, and fish-eagles; many white-breasted cormorants and Nile monitor lizards reside on the islets. **Lake Malawi,** also called Lake Nyasa, is 364 mi (587 km) long and supports the most diverse fish population of any lake in the world, with 450 species; 90 percent are endemic, and of these 350 are in the Cichlidae family. It

sits at an elevation of 1,434′ (437 m). The shoreline varies from sandy beaches to swamps and cliffs.
Much of western Malawi is plateau country, with peaks reaching 8,000′ (2,400 m). **Kasungu National Park** (572,100 acres/231,600 ha) is a large area of rolling hills above 3,300′ (1,000 m) on the Zambia border. Covered with miombo woodland and grassland, it has lodging, tracks, and walking safaris. Mammals include the elephant, buffalo, sable, roan, Lichtenstein's hartebeest, eland, greater kudu, zebra, black rhino, and cheetah. The park is closed between January and May, when the roads are impassable due to rains. **Vwaza Marsh Game Reserve** (242,100 acres/98,000 ha) protects highland marshes west of Rumphi but is not developed for tourism.
Nyika National Park (774,100 acres/313,400 ha), north of Rumphi, is open all year, despite an annual rainfall that reaches 80″ (2,000 mm), heaviest in March and April. Elevations range from 5,250′ to 8,500′ (1,600–2,600 m), and frosts occur from June through August. This spectacular area of vast open grassland is dissected by deep valleys and waterfalls and topped by jagged peaks. The gorges support patches of montane evergreen forest where tall podocarpus and junipers meet seven species of proteas, which are typical of southern Africa. Mammals, which can be easy to spot in this open country, include the leopard, side-striped jackal, spotted hyena, reedbuck, roan, Lichtenstein's hartebeest, puku, klipspringer, bushbuck, and herds of elands and zebras. Water holes near the lodge at Chelinda attract waterbirds and mammals, while wattled cranes, Denham's bustards, and ground-hornbills walk the grasslands.

The South

Blantyre, the chief commercial city, lies in the much lower and hotter country of southern Malawi. The Shire River drains out from the southern end of Lake Malawi, descending to 230′ (70 m) elevation and joining the great Zambezi River just south of the Malawi-Mozambique border. There are extensive marshes and swamps along the river. **Liwonde National Park** (132,900 acres/53,800 ha) lies on the east bank of the river 87 mi (140 km) north of Blantyre. There is lodging nearby. Boat trips are available year-round, but park roads are closed in the wet season. Vegetation away from the river is mopane woodland, dotted with baobabs and candelabra euphorbias. Bird life is rich, and mammals are plentiful: many elephants, hippos, sables, waterbucks, greater kudus, and lions. **Lengwe National Park** (219,100 acres/88,700 ha), located 50 mi (80 km) southwest of Blantyre, is dry deciduous woodland, with several water holes featuring shaded blinds with seating. This is the northernmost range of the nyala. Other mammals include the lion, leopard, greater kudu, suni, Lichtenstein's hartebeest, Sharpe's grysbok, impala, and blue monkey. Birds range from the crested guineafowl and the trumpeter hornbill to the lilac-breasted roller. Thirty-five miles (56 km) southeast of Blantyre is **Mulanje Forest Reserve,** which protects part of the isolated Mount Mulanje, the tallest mountain in Malawi, reaching 9,843′ (3,000 m). This is trekking country, with a number of overnight huts. Habitats include open moorland, cliffs, and montane forest in the gullies, populated by a diverse avifauna.

MALI AND NIGER

MALI PLATE 41

A landlocked country on the southern edge of the Sahara, Mali has a total area of 478,652 sq mi (1,239,709 sq km). Its chief source of wealth is the Niger River, whose headwaters are in the rainy highlands of Guinea's Fouta Djallon mountains. Overhunting, overgrazing, fuel-wood gathering, and drought have eliminated most of Mali's wildlife.

The Southwest

Bamako, the capital, is located on the Niger River. It gets up to 44″ (1,100 mm) of rain annually, chiefly in July and August. Average high temperatures are lowest in the summer wet season, reaching 88°F (31°C) in August; they climb to 102°F (39°C) in April. In hilly western Mali there is an area of moist evergreen forest in the south near the Guinea–Ivory Coast border. The country's only national park is northwest of Bamako: **Boucle du Baoulé National Park** (864,500 acres/350,000 ha). The area has wooded grassland and dense riverine forest, but they have been severely degraded. Elephants, giraffes, hippos, roans, waterbucks, elands, hartebeests, warthogs, leopards, lions, cheetahs, baboons, and vervet and patas monkeys have resided here in the past.

Central Mali

The waters of the Niger River flow northeastward through Mali, forming the **Niger Inland Delta.** Mopti is a small city and transport hub in the heart of the delta. Summer and autumn rains cause flooding of vast areas of the delta each autumn, followed by the drying out of most areas during the increasing heat in the arid late winter and spring. Great herds of antelopes, associated predators, and countless waterbirds (including Eurasian winterers) formerly coexisted with humans here. These waters fueled the medieval riches of Timbuktu, a city at the northern end of the wetlands where the river begins to bend eastward and then southward. Timbuktu is near the northern limit of the summer rain belt and may get only 9″ (225 mm) a year. Its average high in May is 109°F (43°C). Decades of drought combined with water diversion and irrigation schemes have depleted the annual floods, causing great economic suffering and loss of most of the wildlife. **Gourma Elephant Faunal Reserve** (2,964,000 acres/1,200,000 ha), northeast of Mopti, may have the last elephants in Mali. **Falaise de Bandiagara World Heritage Site** (988,000 acres/400,000 ha), 45 mi (75 km) southeast of Mopti, is home to the classic hill villages of the Dogon people. North of the river port of Gao there is an area of stark hills, with slightly higher rainfall; this is **Adrar des Iforas,** an extension of the Ahaggar Mountains of southern Algeria. Northern Mali is covered with the bone-dry, shifting sand dunes of the Sahara desert.

MAURITANIA

For map, see Morocco.

The Atlantic Ocean meets the western edge of the Sahel and the Sahara in Mauritania, whose total area is 397,955 sq mi (1,030,703 sq km). Most of the country is pure Sahara desert, with rocky plains and sand dunes, broken in places by hills and oases. The scant summer rainfall supports grassland and light Sahel woodland in the south. About 330 species of birds occur in Mauritania, but most larger mammals have been eliminated.

The Coast

Mauritania's 505-mi (815-km) coastline is backed by a broad coastal plain. Nouakchott, the capital, sits on the coast. Rainfall in the region is erratic, averaging 6″ (150 mm), most of which falls in August. The port of Nouadhibou, on the Cap Blanc peninsula in the far north, receives only 2″ (50 mm) of rain yearly. Highs on the coast, tempered by sea breezes, average 84–93°F (29–34°C).

Baie du Levrier Integral Reserve (765,700 acres/ 310,000 ha), off Cap Blanc, protects the rare Mediterranean monk-seal. **Banc d'Arguin National Park** (2,897,300 acres/ 1,173,000 ha) lies to the east and south, where upwellings and a clash of cool and warm currents mix and flood over shallow waters with extensive sea-grass beds. Vast tidal mudflats are winter and/or migration homes for millions of shorebirds, especially the bar-tailed godwit, dunlin, knot, and curlew sandpiper. Offshore 14 islands host 40,000 pairs of breeding herons, cormorants, flamingos, pelicans, spoonbills, and terns. Green and loggerhead sea turtles and bottle-nosed and Atlantic hump-backed dolphins are regularly seen. The Imraguen fishermen take visitors out by boat from Iwik, a town that is a six-hour, four-wheel-drive trip from either Nouakchott or Nouadhibou.

The South

Southern Mauritania is greener, receiving up to 15″ (375 mm) of rain annually. Semi-desert shrubland blends into sparse acacia woodland in the far south near the Senegal and Mali borders. The Senegal River, the first river south of the Sahara, forms the Mauritania-Senegal border. Floods in the second half of the year fill wetlands at Aftout-es-Saheli, Lake Rkiz, and the new **Diawling (Diaouling) National Park** (32,100 acres/13,000 ha), all of which are located on the north bank of the river, just to the north of Senegal's Djoudj National Park in the delta region. African birds such as the hammerkop, fish-eagle, dark chanting-goshawk, double-spurred francolin, red-billed oxpecker, and red-cheeked cordonbleu are found here. Farther east, just north of where Senegal and Mali meet, is **El Agher Partial Faunal Reserve** (617,500 acres/250,000 ha), which has lost all of its elephants to guns.

MAURITIUS

This large volcanic island (720 sq mi/1,865 sq km) in the southwestern Indian Ocean lies east of Madagascar, south of Seychelles, and 95 miles (160 km) northeast of Réunion. It is 34 mi (55 km) long and reaches an elevation of 2,720′ (825 m) in the mountainous southwest. The capital of this heavily populated island is Port Louis, in the northwest. An international airport and numerous beach hotels serve travelers. The island is dotted with steep volcanic plugs and hilly ranges and was once clothed in lowland palm forests in dry areas and wet evergreen forests elsewhere. Nowadays sugarcane covers vast areas. The coastline is a mix of white-sand beaches and mangrove forests, encircled by fringing reefs. Annual rainfall varies from 31″ (775 mm) in drier coastal areas to 141″ (3,525 mm) in wetter mountains, falling chiefly between November and April. Once the home of the dodo, which was killed off by 1681, Mauritius retains nine of its 20-plus native land birds. Heroic efforts have been made to save the last pink pigeons, echo parakeets, and Mauritius kestrels around **Black River Gorge Fishing Reserve** (2,200 acres/900 ha) and **Macchabee Bel Ombre Nature Reserve/Biosphere Reserve** (8,919 acres/3,611 ha), both in a massive forested canyon in the southwest with a paved road that leads to viewing areas. Introduced crab-eating macaques raid the nests of native birds, while introduced plants, goats, and pigs are killing off native plants. Many smaller reserves have been established, fenced off, and weeded of non-native species.

A string of protected islands extends to the northeast of Mauritius. **Round Island Nature Reserve** (373 acres/151 ha), 12 mi (20 km) offshore, is home to rare palms, boas, geckos, and seabirds that are bouncing back now that goats and rabbits have been eliminated. **Rodriguez Island,** 352 mi (568 km) to the east and just 10.5 mi (17 km) long, has lost three tortoises, two giant lizards, and 11 birds, including the huge, dodo-like Rodriguez solitaire. A fruit bat, fody, brush warbler, and some endemic plants barely survive. Newly established **Grande Montagne Nature Reserve** (86 acres/35 ha) should help. Rodriguez has several small hotels and is connected to Mauritius by sea and air.

MAYOTTE (FRANCE)

The easternmost and oldest of the four Comoro islands (see also Comoro Islands), Mayotte (144 sq mi/373 sq km) is a volcanic island 200 mi (320 km) northwest of Madagascar that remained French when the Comoro Islands declared their independence in 1975. Mayotte's climate is hot and

rainy from November through April, with up to 80″ (2,000 mm) of rain falling in the mountains. The period between May and October is warm and drier. The capital, Dzaoudzi, is connected by causeway with Pamanzi islet, with its airport and a crater lake. Mamoudzou, located on the main island opposite Dzaoudzi, is the commercial center. Mayotte is a hilly, green, plantation island where perfume plants are grown. There are many patches of forest left, with the largest on the upper slopes of southern **Mount Outsongui** (3,000′/640 m), home of the brown lemur, which is unprotected. The island has three endemic birds—a drongo, white-eye, and sunbird—plus the cuckoo-roller, Comoro blue pigeon, and bulbul. Comoro fruit bats are common by day, even in towns.
Mayotte's shoreline is a mix of red and black volcanic rock, mangroves, beaches, and mudflats. An extensive **barrier reef** surrounds Mayotte, enclosing a pristine lagoon. Marine reserves have been established recently to the southeast of the town of Saziley and elsewhere.

MOROCCO PLATES 3, 23

This country comprises 2,170 mi (3,500 km) of Atlantic and Mediterranean coastline, four major mountain ranges, temperate forests, and Sahara desert. Its total area is 172,413 sq mi (446,500 sq km). The rainy season is November through March, and pleasant weather prevails in spring and fall. Summers are comfortable in the Atlas Mountains, but the lowlands are very hot. Most larger mammals and bustards have been eliminated by hunting, but the country offers excellent birding.

The Mediterranean Coast

Just 9 mi (15 km) south of Spain at the Strait of Gibraltar, the north coast has a Mediterranean climate. The northern tip, between the ports of Tangier and Spanish Ceuta, has huge migrations of raptors, storks, and songbirds from March through May and from September through November. The major nesting site of the rare Audouin's gull is on the Spanish **Chafarinas Islands,** 28 mi (45 km) east of the Spanish enclave of Melilla, along the Mediterranean coast of Morocco. **Bokkoyas Biological Reserve** (106,200 acres/43,000 ha) is a marine reserve on Morocco's northeastern coast, west of Al Hoceima, with common and bottle-nosed dolphins and the long-finned pilot whale.

MOROCCO AND MAURITANIA

The Atlantic Coast

The cool Canaries Current moderates temperatures on the western coast, which is backed by lagoons important for waterbirds. **Merdja Zerga Biological Reserve** (17,300 acres/7,000 ha), south of Moulay-Bousselham, is the largest lagoon, host to many wintering flamingos, spoonbills, ducks, coots, and waders, including a few slender-billed curlews. Farther south is Rabat, the capital of Morocco, which receives 16″ (400 mm) of annual rain and has average highs of 82°F (28°C) in August, 63°F (17°C) in January. Eleanora's falcons breed on the Salé cliffs nearby. **Lake Sidi Bouhaba,** 19 mi (30 km) north, hosts wintering ducks such as the marbled teal. The natural cork oak woodlands south of Rabat are home to the double-spurred francolin and the Barbary partridge. The **Mogador Islets** off Essaouira are a restricted reserve, home to a pair of peregrines and 90 pairs of Eleanora's falcons.

The mouth of the Sous River, south of the seaport of Agadir, attracts many waterbirds, while the fertile valley inland has the tawny eagle, the dark chanting-goshawk, the black-shouldered kite, the black-headed bush-shrike, and Moussier's redstart. The waldrapp ibis has had colonies here. **Sous-Massa National Park** (83,500 acres/ 33,800 ha), 25 mi (40 km) south of Agadir, protects another river-mouth lagoon with the plain sand martin, waldrapp ibis (at times), golden jackal, red fox, Egyptian cobra, and wintering European crane.

The Atlas Mountains

The Atlas Mountains comprise four ranges: the Mediterranean Rif between Tangier and Fez; the well-forested Middle Atlas south of Fez; the taller High Atlas southeast of Marrakech; and the drier Anti-Atlas between Agadir and the Sahara. There are still large tracts of pine, cedar, and evergreen oak in parts of these ranges. Ifrane, at 5,350′ (1,630 m) elevation, and nearby Azrou are resort towns in the **Middle Atlas** south of Fez. The tall cedar forests nearby are home to many Barbary macaques and a few leopards, as well as Levaillant's green woodpeckers and Moussier's redstarts. Red-knobbed coots and a few demoiselle cranes are found near small lakes east of Ifrane. The best time to visit is from April through July, after the snow has melted. Marrakech, which lies at the northern base of the **High Atlas,** gets only 9″ (225 mm) of rain yearly, while the mountains get considerably more, with snow lasting into summer. **Toubkal National Park** (88,900 acres/36,000 ha) is reachable via two roads south of the city. Those wishing to climb Morocco's tallest peak, Mount Toubkal (13,671′/4,167 m), drive to Imlil village. The other park road (to the southeast) passes through the Ourika Valley, which has the southernmost Barbary macaques. It rises through oak and juniper forest before reaching alpine scrub at the Oukaimeden ski resort. This area is home to the Barbary ground-squirrel, golden eagle, lammergeier, alpine accentor, and alpine chough.

The Sahara

There are superb views south and east into the Sahara from the Tizi-n-Tichka pass in the High Atlas between Marrakech and the town of **Ouarzazate,** the gateway to the desert. Desert birds may be seen en route to the ancient kasbah of **Ait Benhaddou,** 19 mi (30 km) northwest of Ouarzazate. The reservoir to the east of Ouarzazate has spotted and black-bellied sandgrouse, plus wintering ruddy shelducks. The **Dades Gorge,** 71 mi (115 km) to the east, and the **Todra Gorge,** 34 mi (55 km) farther east, are future parks, with many raptors, the crested hoopoe, and the crimson-winged finch. Near the town of **Erfoud**, 186 mi (310 km) from Ouarzazate, sand dunes, stony desert, and palm groves are habitats for small mammals, sandgrouse, larks, wheatears, and reptiles of the Sahara. Morocco now governs the former Spanish territory of Western Sahara, which is very arid desert stretching south to Mauritania. There may be a few surviving gazelles and ostriches inland. Whales, dolphins, seabirds, green sea turtles, and a few Mediterranean monk-seals live in the rich waters offshore.

MOZAMBIQUE

For map, see Zimbabwe.

On the Indian Ocean coast in southeastern Africa, directly west of Madagascar, Mozambique (297,846 sq mi/ 771,421 sq km) stretches from Tanzania south to the South African province of Natal. The entire country has a single high-sun rainy season from November through March. Mozambique once had the best national parks in southern Africa, but the status of the parks and wildlife has not been a priority in recent times. Below we describe wildlife present before the recent civil war. Reintroductions of animals might be possible when the parks are suitably protected again.

Maputo, the capital, located in the far south, gets 32″ (800 mm) of annual rainfall. Average highs are 75°F (24°C) in July and 88°F (31°C) in February. **Maputo Reserve** (222,300 acres/90,000 ha), on the Natal border, has an enormous mix of habitats. Some 337 species of birds have been recorded, and there are many hundreds of elephants. The island of Inhaca, a three-hour ferry ride east of the capital, has lodging. Part of the island is protected today in **Inhaca Faunal Reserve** (4,900 acres/ 2,000 ha), which has evergreen forest on dunes on the eastern shore. Local songbirds, crabplovers, and waders feed on the mudflats in summer, while yellow-nosed albatrosses cruise offshore in winter.

The dry savannas east of Transvaal's Kruger National Park and southeastern Zimbabwe's Gonarezhou National Park may be joined with Mozambique's **Banhine National Park** (1,729,000 acres/700,000 ha) and the former Pafuri Game Reserve, which flank the Limpopo River, forming a vast international park. The open grassland and wooded savanna of Pafuri have been home to many roans, sables, giraffes, brown hyenas, and cheetahs. **Zinave National**

Park (1,235,000 acres/500,000 ha) protects savanna on the south bank of the Save River and is rich in wildlife, including many nyalas.

Mozambique has 1,200 mi (1,900 km) of coastline, with a mix of mangroves, beaches, and vast coral reefs with sea-grass beds, which host seabird colonies, sea turtles, and fish. **Bazaruto National Park** (37,100 acres/15,000 ha), an archipelago off Vilanculos, is home to more than 100 individual dugongs, five species of nesting sea turtles, the Natal red duiker, and the blue monkey. Luxury lodgings here are reachable by air charter. The greatest concentration and variety of mammals and birds in southern Africa was once found in **Gorongoza National Park** (931,200 acres/377,000 ha), 100 mi (160 km) northwest of the seaport of Beira. It features vast swamps along the Púngoè and Urema rivers, palm savanna, riverine forest, grassland, and inselbergs. Major mammal species that have resided here include the elephant, buffalo, sable, greater kudu, nyala, Lichtenstein's hartebeest, blue wildebeest, reedbuck, oribi, eland, impala, hippo, zebra, black rhino, lion, and leopard. Nearby **Mount Gorongoza** (6,112′/1,863 m) gets 80″ (2,000 mm) of rain yearly. Its dense evergreen forests are home to rare birds, such as the green-headed oriole.

There is still some montane forest and grassland in the **Chimanimani**, mountains on the Zimbabwe border that reach 9,000′ (2,750 m). The Zambezi river valley and much of the north is covered with dry miombo woodland. Just above the Zambezi delta, 25,000 buffalos once lived in the **Marromeu Reserve** (2,470,000 acres/1,000,000 ha).

In far northern Mozambique is **Niassa Game Reserve** (3,705,000 acres/1,500,000 ha), on the Ruvuma River. No zoologist has visited this site in recent years; with protection and/or reintroductions it could be similar to Tanzania's Mikumi and Selous reserves. Part of the eastern shore of scenic **Lake Malawi** in the rift valley is in Mozambique's northwestern corner.

NAMIBIA PLATES 24, 25, 39, 40, 47

For map, see Botswana.

This vast arid country (317,887 sq mi/823,327 sq km) on the southern Atlantic Ocean has spectacular scenic attractions and great animal parks. There are generally three seasons: cool and dry, from April through August; hot and dry, from September through November; hot and wet, from December through March. Most visitors come between March and October. The coast is very arid, with less than 4″ (100 mm) of annual rainfall; much of the interior highlands gets between 4″ and 20″ (100–500 mm), while the northeast receives more than 20″ (500 mm) annually. Reserves cover 13 percent of the country.

The Plateau

Much of interior Namibia is elevated, averaging 3,300–5,000′ (1,000–1,500 m). Grasslands with scattered trees are punctuated by craggy mountains. The highest point is **Brandberg** (8,448′/2,575 m), an isolated, misty massif with Bushman rock paintings north of the resort town of Swakopmund. Windhoek, the capital, is located among hills at 5,645′ (1,720 m) elevation. Its average highs are 86°F (30°C) in December, but only 79°F (26°C) in winter, when nighttime temperatures drop to freezing. Walking is allowed in **Daan Viljoen Game Park** (9,764 acres/3,953 ha), 16 mi (25 km) west, which has roads and lodging. With wooded savanna and a lake, it harbors mountain zebras, klipspringers, springboks, and many other antelopes. Its 200 species of birds include Verreaux's eagle, Rüppell's parrot, Monteiro's hornbill, and the white-tailed shrike. **Hardap Nature Reserve** (62,187 acres/25,177 ha) is farther south, 9 mi (15 km) northwest of the town of Mariental. Visitors may walk among black rhinos, mountain zebras, and gemsboks. Its lake has nesting pelicans, cormorants, and fish-eagles. In far southern Namibia, **Fish River Canyon Nature Reserve** (854,909 acres/346,117 ha) has landscapes similar to those of North America's Grand Canyon. There are organized five-day hikes of 50 mi (85 km) along the canyon bottom during the cooler months of May through August. Wildlife here includes the mountain zebra, klipspringer, baboon, lanner falcon, white-backed mousebird, and Nile monitor lizard. North of Windhoek, **Waterberg Plateau Game Park** (100,160 acres/40,550 ha) is on a flat-topped escarpment rising above the plains. This lost world has relatively lush, broad-leafed woodlands, springs, and dinosaur tracks. Among the park's wildlife are black and white rhinos, sables, roans, buffalos, Cape vultures, Hartlaub's francolins, and rosy-faced lovebirds. Lodging, trails, and ranger-led wildlife-viewing drives are available.

The North

Etosha National Park (5,500,700 acres/2,227,000 ha) surrounds a vast, glaring salt pan set among grassland and mopane woodland, 250 mi (400 km) north of Windhoek. The pan temporarily fills with water during wetter summers, attracting breeding flamingos, pelicans, and other waterbirds. Gravel tracks connect natural and pump-fed water holes, where herds of animals come to drink in the dry season. The more common hoofed mammals are the springbok, blue wildebeest, gemsbok, red hartebeest, greater kudu, giraffe, steenbok, black-faced impala, and the Damara race of Kirk's dik-dik. These are joined by 300 black rhinos and 1,500 elephants, all well protected. Lions, leopards, cheetahs, black-backed jackals, and Cape foxes are the most visible predators. The ostrich, the blue crane, and the kori, crested, and black bustards head a list of 340 birds. There are three lodges in the park and a luxury lodge at Mokuti just to the east. Namutoni Lodge occupies an old German fort in the east near **Fischer's Pan,** which sometimes has water when Etosha Pan is dry in early winter. The lodge at Halali, located in hills in the southeast, has local bare-cheeked babblers. The lodge at Okaukuejo, in the south, features an adjacent water hole that attracts an ongoing procession of elephants, black rhinos, antelopes, and birds, such as the crimson boubou.

The **Caprivi Strip,** the panhandle of Namibia that reaches east to the Zambezi River just above Victoria Falls, is covered with woodland on Kalahari sand and has vast wetlands along the rivers. The Caprivi Strip has four reserves (listed here from west to east): **Mahango Game Park** (60,421 acres/24,462 ha), **Western Caprivi Game Park** (1,482,000 acres/600,000 ha), **Mudumu National Park** (205,500 acres/101,400 ha), and **Mamili National Park** (79,000 acres/32,000 ha). There are airstrips, lodging, and four-wheel-drive tours over the sandy roads in this complex of adjacent reserves. Hippos, otters, and crocodiles live in the rivers. The marshlands are host to the red lechwe, reedbuck, waterbuck, and sitatunga. Upland areas have elephants, buffalos, giraffes, greater kudus, bushbucks, impalas, pukus, wildebeests, zebras, lions, leopards, and wild dogs. The region is rich in bird life, with 430 species known; highlights are the slaty egret, saddle-billed stork, wattled crane, skimmer, and Pel's fishing owl.

The Coast

Cold waters from Antarctica flow north in the Benguela Current along Africa's southern Atlantic coast. Although these waters are rich in fish and support many seabirds and mammals, they are not conducive to creating rain. At the port of Walvis Bay and the resort of Swakopmund, on the central coast, rainfall averages 0.8″ (20 mm) a year despite frequent low fog between May and October. Temperatures are cool year-round, with average highs of 66–75°F (19–24°C). There is a guano-gathering platform north of

Walvis Bay with many Cape cormorants (scrapings from nesting and perching stations are used for fertilizer). To the south and east of Swakopmund stretches the enormous **Namib/Naukluft Park** (12,292,700 acres/4,976,800 ha). Among the park's wildlife are the gemsbok, springbok, bat-eared fox, ostrich, three elephant-shrews, three gerbils, Gray's lark, the herero chat, lizards, geckos, and the side-winding adder. The **Namib Desert** is the oldest in the world, and the park encompasses many of its different habitats. Sandwich harbor, reachable by four-wheel-drive south of Walvis Bay, has freshwater and saltwater lagoons, with flocks of waders, terns, and flamingos. Between the Swakop and Kuiseb rivers to the east there is stony desert with welwitschia (a conifer that looks like a giant, two-leafed agave) and some succulents. South of the Kuiseb River there is a sea of sand dunes; stunning orange dunes are found near the temporary lagoon of Sossusvlei, reached by road 36 mi (60 km) southwest of Sesriem, due west of Mariental (but not reachable from Swakopmund). From Lüderitz, an old German port to the south of Namib/Naukluft Park, visitors can take boat trips to islets and beaches with Cape fur seals and jackass penguins.
Cape Cross Seal Reserve (14,820 acres/6,000 ha), 74 mi (120 km) north of Swakopmund, is home to roughly 100,000 Cape fur seals; the bulls arrive in mid-October.
Skeleton Coast Park (3,952,000 acres/1,600,000 ha) protects a long strip of foggy coast up to the Cunene River on the Angola border. Brown hyenas and black-backed jackals scavenge washed-up seals, whales, and shipwrecks; lions were formerly among the scavengers. Small numbers of elephants, giraffes, and zebras wander the dune country inland. There are a few freshwater channels that attract springboks, gemsboks, and birds. One such source is the Uniab Delta, 21 mi (33 km) south of the camp at Terrace Bay. The only travel allowed on the northern coast is via licensed local operators. Restricted to existing tracks (to protect the fragile desert plant life), travel is undertaken in groups of two or more four-wheel-drive vehicles, as vehicles can get stranded easily.

NIGER PLATES 18, 41

For map, see Mali.

This country, which stretches from the Sahara desert south to the Niger River and Lake Chad, has a total area of 459,073 sq mi (1,188,999 sq km). It contains the interesting Aïr Mountains and several savanna reserves.

The South

Niamey, the capital, located on the Niger River, receives 22″ (560 mm) of annual rainfall, mainly between May and September. It is generally hot, with highs near or above 90°F (32°C), except in July and August, during the rains. Northward toward the Sahara from the Benin and Nigeria borders, the landscape changes from Sudan wooded savanna to a belt of semi-arid scrubland to degraded grassland before becoming true desert. These areas of scattered trees and wind-eroded fields south of the Sahara are known as the **Sahel**, an area suffering from the southward march of desertification.

W du Niger National Park (543,400 acres/220,000 ha) and **Tamou Nature Reserve** (192,020 acres/77,740 ha) are located 78 mi (125 km) south of Niamey. Adjacent to parks in Benin and Burkina Faso, they occupy the west bank of the Niger River. The Tapoa and Mekrou rivers join the Niger here with a series of beautiful gorges and rapids. An annual rainfall of 28″ (700 mm) supports dense woodland, gallery forest, and seasonal marshes; washed-out roads often make these parks inaccessible between June and December. Resident hoofed mammals include the buffalo, waterbuck, kob, topi, roan, hartebeest, bushbuck, reedbuck, and red-fronted gazelle. Elephants, lions, leopards, cheetahs, spotted hyenas, servals, caracals, baboons, and patas monkeys also live here. Hippos and crocodiles inhabit the waters. Birds are plentiful, among them martial eagles and ground-hornbills. East of the Niger River are areas with a few nomadic giraffes.

Gadabedji Faunal Reserve (187,700 acres/76,000 ha), 90 mi (150 km) north of the town of Maradi, is now a gazelle sanctuary, but it was set up to save the very rare scimitar-horned oryx, which was hunted out of this area.

The Sahara

Most of Niger is in the southern Sahara, and rainfall in some areas reaches only 0.2″ (5 mm) a year. Other areas, particularly in the mountains, get occasional summer storms and flash floods. There is a paved road to the ancient town of Agadez and north to the mines at Arlit. Tuareg people with herds of camels and goats live in the area. **Aïr and Ténéré National Strict Nature Reserve** (19,107,900 acres/7,736,000 ha) and, within it, the core **Addax Sanctuary Strict Nature Reserve** (3,162,800 acres/1,280,500 ha) were set up in 1988. The latter closed area protects the very rare addax from the mechanized vehicles of hunters and tourists that formerly chased them. The Aïr Mountains are a continuation of Algeria's Ahaggar Mountains that end northeast of Agadez at Mount Banguezane (6,234′/1,900 m); these granitic and volcanic peaks get 6″ (150 mm) of annual rain, and there are clumps of trees in the valleys and palm canyons, and little pools of water in the gorges. To the east lie the vast Ténéré sand dunes. The park's mammals include addaxes, cheetahs, aoudads, baboons, striped hyenas, and dorcas, Loder's, and dama gazelles. Lanner falcons feed on the many trans-Sahara songbird migrants attracted to the bits of greenery. The park is the last ostrich stronghold in West Africa, and the scimitar-horned oryx may be reintroduced. It is hoped that the numbers of the area's once-rich wildlife, now hunted down to a very few shy remnants, will return.

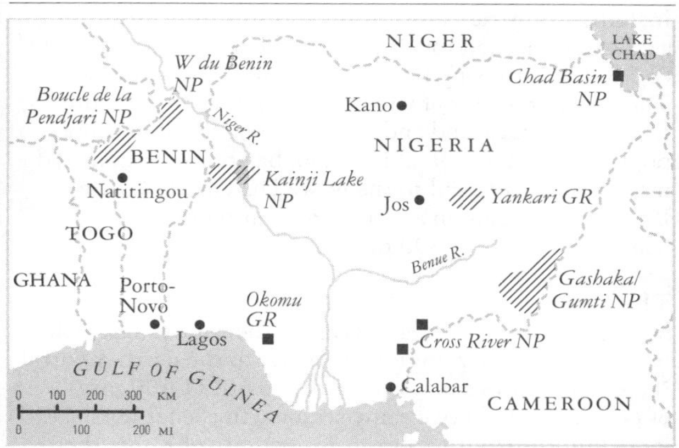

NIGERIA AND BENIN

NIGERIA

Africa's most heavily populated nation is located between the Gulf of Guinea and Lake Chad. The original vegetation of the south is wet rain forest merging northward into wooded savanna; there are some dry, Sahel-like, semi-arid areas in the northeast. The Niger River flows in from the northwest and is joined by the Benue River, which drains northeastern Nigeria. About 4.5 percent of the country's 356,669 sq mi (923,773 sq km) is protected in reserves. Poaching, logging, and illegal grazing plague all areas, so the surviving mammals are shy of humans.

The Wet South

Lagos, the capital, in the southwest, receives 72″ (1,800 mm) of annual rain, chiefly between March and November. Average highs of 82–90°F (28–32°C) are accompanied by high humidity. Nearby are large lagoons and marshlands with many birds. **Omo Strict Nature Reserve/Biosphere Reserve** (1,140 acres/460 ha), northeast of Lagos, protects elephants, duikers, and birds in a fragment of lowland rain forest near the Omo River. **Okomu Game Reserve** (305,800 acres/123,800 ha), west of Benin City, 120 mi (200 km) east of Lagos, is home to the mona monkey and the white-throated guenon. The delta of the Niger River and coastal areas to the east are a maze of waterways, mangroves, and swamp forests with no parks. North of Calabar, along the border with Cameroon, is **Cross River National Park** (1,044,039 acres/422,688 ha). The southern sector and nearby **Boshi-Okwango Game Reserve** protect lowland rain forest with many primates, including Nigeria's last lowland gorillas, and birds, such as the gray-necked rockfowl. Annual rainfall exceeds 100″ (2,500 mm), causing frequent mist in the mountains. The northern sector of Cross River park in the Obudu Plateau has grassland and rich montane forest on slopes populated by the emerald cuckoo, bar-tailed trogon, and many birds not found to the west. The Obudu Cattle Ranch has lodging in a scenic area south of Mount Sonkwala (6,200′/1,890 m).

The Interior

Stretching from the Niger River in the west to Lake Chad in the east, interior Nigeria dries out to the north. Central Nigerian localities may receive up to 60″ (1,500 mm) of rain annually in two rainy seasons. In the far north, including the environs of the ancient city of Kano, there is a single summer rainy season that brings only 24″ (600 mm). Average highs in Kano are 84°F (29°C) during the rains of August, and 100°F (38°C) late in the dry season in April. The main sector of **Kainji Lake National Park** (1,319,183 acres/534,082 ha) lies to the west of a huge reservoir on the Niger River near the Benin border. There is lodging, and many tracks cross the mosaic of wooded savanna, grassland, and riverine forest. The waters are home to manatees, hippos, and crocodiles. The park's land mammals include elephants, buffalos, kobs, roans, hartebeests, bushbucks, oribis, lions, leopards, side-striped jackals, wild dogs, and patas monkeys. The park is also home to 360 species of savanna birds.

The **Jos Plateau,** around the highland town of Jos, has the westernmost klipspringers. **Yankari Game Reserve** (554,300 acres/224,400 ha), 150 mi (240 km) east of Jos, has tracks crossing the swamp, woods, and grassland. Lodging is available at Wikki Warm Springs. The park's rivers have both Nile and long-snouted crocodiles as well as hippos. Among the park's mammals are lions, leopards, elephants, buffalos, roans, waterbucks, bushbucks, hartebeests, common duikers, warthogs, a few giraffes, and many baboons. There are more than 300 birds, including the white-headed vulture, bateleur, western gray plantain-eater, blue-breasted kingfisher, and piapiac. **Gashaka/ Gumti National Park** (1,571,700 acres/636,300 ha) is located on the Cameroon border, with a mix of savanna and montane fauna on the slopes of Mount Gotel (7,933′/ 2,418 m). **Chad Basin National Park** (112,869 acres/ 45,696 ha) protects marshy habitats around Lake Chad. Drought and water-diversion schemes are shrinking this lake, which formerly was lined with mammals and home to millions of birds.

REUNION (FRANCE)

Réunion's main island (969 sq mi/2,510 sq km) is 425 mi (685 km) east of Madagascar and 95 mi (160 km) southwest of Mauritius. Much of the coastline is steep cliffs; most beaches and a 6-mi (10-km) fringing reef are on the drier southwestern coast. Saint-Denis, the capital, is on the north coast. The rugged interior is dominated by great volcanoes, peaks, interior basins called cirques, waterfalls, and cliffs exceeding 3,300′ (1,000 m). Roads to the resorts of Hell-bourg and Cilaos provide access to high-country trails. At 10,069′ (3,070 m), **Piton des Neiges,** often snow-capped, is the tallest mountain in the Indian Ocean. Windward northeastern slopes receive 156″ (3,900 mm) of rain, chiefly from November through April. Once covered with forest, Réunion was home to the Réunion dodo and a host of now-extinct birds and reptiles, including tortoises. Some 200 of the 500 flowering plants are endemic, but many are threatened by the 1,000 species of introduced plants that are spreading throughout the island. Among the surviving endemic birds are a stonechat, bulbul, white-eye, and cuckoo-shrike (rare); Barau's petrel breeds high in the mountains.

Réunion also governs Ile Europa, Bassas da India, Juan de Nova, and the Iles Glorieuses west of Madagascar, plus Tromelin, north of Réunion; these are all coralline atolls, which are managed as reserves and host nesting seabirds and sea turtles.

RWANDA PLATE 8

For map, see Uganda.

In the heart of central Africa, this small highland country (10,169 sq mi/26,338 sq km) is dramatically beautiful. Most of its rolling land, punctuated by terraced hills and mountains, stands above 5,000′ (1,520 m). It is intensively cultivated, yet more than 10 percent of its land is protected. Kigali, the capital, which sits among farmed hills, receives about 50″ (1,250 mm) of annual rainfall. Rwanda has four seasons: the long wet, from mid-March through mid-May; the long dry, through mid-September; the short wet, through mid-December; and the short dry, through mid-March.

The West

The town of Ruhengiri, 60 mi (100 km) northwest of Kigali, has lodging for visitors setting out on gorilla treks in nearby **Volcanoes National Park/Biosphere Reserve** (37,100 acres/15,000 ha). The park protects the upper reaches (about 7,900′/2,400 m) of six dormant volcanoes rising in a row along the borders with Zaire and Uganda. It abuts sister reserves in those countries. The park's lower slopes—the gorilla's primary habitat—are covered with dense montane forest and bamboo, while moorland with giant heath, lobelia, and groundsel prevails higher up. Frequently shrouded in clouds, the area has heavy rainfall (80″/2,000 mm annually), with some snow up high. Visitors can take hikes, ranging from four hours to two days, up several volcanoes. Most visitors make a pilgrimage to visit with one of several groups of mountain gorillas that are habituated to humans. Limited to guided groups of eight, these require expensive permits. Hikes may involve scrambles up steep muddy slopes, often in the rain. Golden monkeys, yellow-backed duikers, and perhaps 200 species of birds (including the Ruwenzori turaco) also live here. Lake Kivu, a deep freshwater lake 56 mi (90 km) long, lies at the bottom of the western rift valley. The resort town of Gisenyi, at the northern end of the lake, is connected by road and ferry to Cyangugu at the southern end. The **Nyungwe Forest Reserve,** 33 mi (54 km) east of Cyangugu on the main road east to the town of Butare, is a conservation area covering a large (239,600 acres/97,000 ha) forest tract on the Congo-Nile divide. There is no lodging as of this writing, but campers are welcome. Living among the forest's enormous trees are 275 species of birds and 13 species of primates, including chimpanzees, black-and-white colobus monkeys, and L'Hoest's, red-tailed, and golden monkeys. Views from the ridges to the lakes and volcanoes can be spectacular.

The East

There are many waterbirds in the Mugesera-Rugwero lakes and swamps in the southeast, but no formal reserve exists to protect them. **Akagera National Park** (770,600 acres/ 312,000 ha) in the northeast is relatively low (4,265′/ 1,300 m) and dry, receiving 40″ (1,000 mm) of rain annually. Most of the park is a mix of grassland and wooded hills punctuated with tall, cactus-like euphorbia trees. Akagera's east side, bounded by the Kagera River, features vast swamplands, lakes, and islands, with sitatungas, hippos, shoebills, and crocodiles. The park's mammal population includes the elephant, roan, eland, bushbuck, lion, leopard, and black rhino, along with herds of topis, buffalos, impalas, and zebras. More than 500 birds, 50 mammals, and 80 reptiles have been recorded. Civil war has taken a toll on lodges at Lake Ihema in the park's southern portion and at Gabiro in the north.

SAINT HELENA (UNITED KINGDOM)

The British colony of Saint Helena includes three volcanic island groups in the southern Atlantic Ocean, on or near the mid-Atlantic Ridge.

Ascension

This barren volcanic island of 34 sq mi (88 sq km) is covered with lava flows and 17 black or red craters, and has clumps of euphorbia and grasses. It lies 720 mi (1,160 km) northwest of Saint Helena. While the lowlands get only 6″ (150 mm) of annual rain, 25″ (625 mm) fall on Green Mountain, which rises to 2,817′ (859 m). There are no endemic land birds or mammals on the island. The endemic Ascension frigatebird breeds only on **Boatswain Island,** a bird sanctuary, one of 14 inshore islets. About 100,000 seabirds breed around Ascension, including many sooty and white terns, boobies, and tropicbirds. The nearby seas have many dolphins, whales, sharks, and schools of 12″ (30-cm) piranha-like "blackfish." There is a military airport, but no tourist facilities.

Saint Helena

Great cliffs rise above the sea, interrupted by only two beaches, on this island of 47 sq mi (122 sq km), which lies 1,760 mi (2,840 km) northwest of Cape Town, South Africa. There is no airport, but ships call at Jamestown, the capital, which gets 8″ (200 mm) of annual rain. The island is home to doves, mynas, waxbills, and weavers, all introduced, as are most plants on the island. Its offshore rocks have nesting red-billed tropicbirds, sooty and white terns, and two noddies. The plateau grasslands are home to the wirebird, a race of Kittlitz's plover. The highlands enjoy a spring-like average temperature of 59°F (15°C) and receive up to 40″ (1,000 mm) of annual rain, at its heaviest between June and August. The only native forests, home to many of the 50 endemic plants, are found on Diana's Peak, High Peak, and Horse Ridge, where elevations reach 2,700′ (823 m).

Tristan da Cunha Islands

Tristan da Cunha (38 sq mi/98 sq km) is the only inhabited island in an archipelago of four main islands, isolated 1,550 mi (2,500 km) west of Cape Town. Edinburgh, the only settlement, is on a narrow plain backed by cliffs reaching up toward the main volcano, which at 7,086′ (2,160 m) elevation is snow-capped in winter (June through September). Annual rainfall is 50″ (1,250 mm) at the coast. Vegetation consists of dense tussock grass, sedges, mosses, ferns, and the now-rare native buckthorn tree. While rats have taken the local songbirds, yellow-nosed and sooty albatrosses nest in the highlands.

Nightingale Island, 20 mi (32 km) south of Tristan da Cunha, and **Inaccessible Island,** 11 mi (18 km) northwest of Nightingale, are home to such endemics as two buntings, a thrush, and a rail. Millions of greater shearwaters breed on the two islands, along with petrels, prions, and other seabirds. **Gough Island** is a rugged, heavily wooded island rising to 2,913′ (888 m), some 270 mi (435 km) southeast of Tristan da Cunha. Fur seals and southern elephant seals line the rocky beaches, while rockhopper penguins, wandering albatrosses, and giant petrels nest higher up. Gough has two endemic birds: a gallinule and a bunting.

SÃO TOME AND PRINCIPE

These are the middle pair of four islands formed by the Cameroon line of volcanoes, which bisects the Gulf of Guinea in the Atlantic Ocean (they lie between Equatorial Guinea's Bioko and Annobón islands). Their jagged peaks, lush vegetation, and beaches are reminiscent of Polynesia, minus the coral reefs. They lie 90 mi (150 km) apart: Príncipe is 130 mi (210 km) south-southwest of Bioko, while São Tomé is 136 mi (220 km) west of Gabon. Both islands have mean temperatures of 75–81°F (24–27°C) on the coast and are driest between June and August and during January and February. Moist southerly winds drop up to 200″ (5,000 mm) of rain yearly in the mountains, with only 40″ (1,000 mm) on the northern coasts. Plantations cover much of the former rain forests in the lowlands, while montane forest blankets the higher areas. Because of the rugged topography, one-third of each island still has virgin forest. Like the Galápagos, these islands never have been connected to a continent and are home to many endemic birds but no large land mammals. **São Tomé Island** (330 sq mi/855 sq km) has 14 endemic birds, some still common around the capital of São Tomé. Many of the others are easily seen on trails above the *pousada* (inn) in the highlands above Nova Moca. A proposed park south of that area surrounds Pico Gago Coutinho (6,640′/2,024 m). White-tailed tropicbirds with unusual yellow tails soar around the hills. Highly scenic **Príncipe Island** (42 sq mi/109 sq km) has six endemic birds and many gray parrots. There should be a park around the virgin forests flanking Pico Papagaio (3,110′/948 m) in the south. The underwater life around both islands is rich (whales frequent the waters), and marine reserves are needed.

SENEGAL

Located on the Atlantic Ocean at the western tip of Africa, Senegal surrounds Gambia. Generally flat or rolling country with hills in the southeast, Senegal has a total area of 76,124 sq mi (197,161 sq km). Most of it is covered with dry Sahel woodland, while the center and the southeast have taller deciduous woodlands, dotted with baobabs. The Casamance region in the south has some tall evergreen forest. Annual rainfall reaches only 12″ (300 mm) in the north, but increases to 40″ (1,000 mm) to the south, and even 60″ (1,500 mm) locally in the Casamance. Rain falls chiefly between June and September, longer in the south. Temperatures are cooler on the coast.

The North

Dakar, the capital, on the Cape Verde peninsula, gets 21″ (533 mm) of rain yearly and has average highs of 79–90°F (26–32°C). **Iles de la Madeleine National Park** (1,100 acres/450 ha) is a group of three volcanic rocks 2.5 mi (4 km) offshore, with dwarf baobabs, red-billed tropicbirds, cormorants, brown boobies, and bridled terns.

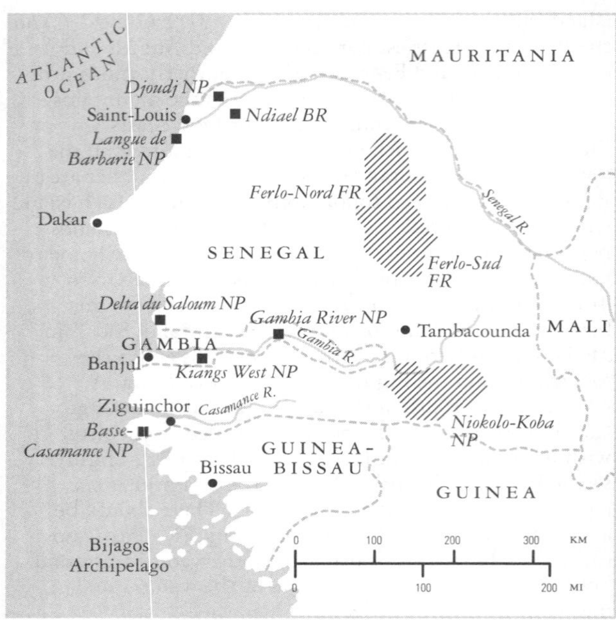

SENEGAL, GAMBIA, AND GUINEA-BISSAU

Many birds, including the splendid sunbird, live in the baobab forests northeast of Dakar.

Saint-Louis, on Senegal's northern coast, is an old city at the mouth of the Senegal River. The Senegal River's floodwaters are decreasing, due to drought and upstream dams. **Langue de Barbarie National Park** (4,900 acres/ 2,000 ha) is a long sand spit 11 mi (18 km) south of town, with boat access; it has nesting gulls, terns, and sea turtles. **Djoudj National Park/World Heritage Site** (39,500 acres/16,000 ha), about 34 mi (55 km) northeast of Saint-Louis, has lodging and tracks and boats that offer access to seasonal lakes, channels, grassland, and riverine woodland. It harbors a large nesting colony of great white pelicans and is a major wintering area for Eurasian ducks and waders. African ducks, geese, jacanas, and crowned cranes are among the 300 species that have been recorded. Mammals include the warthog, golden jackal, patas monkey, and reintroduced dorcas gazelle. **Ndiael Bird Reserve** (114,980 acres/46,550 ha) lies to the east, on the west bank of Lake Ndiael, an important seasonal wetland. The adjacent **Ferlo-Nord and Ferlo-Sud Faunal Reserve** (total combined area 2,766,400 acres/1,120,000 ha) in northeastern Senegal protect Sahelian wildlife.

The South

Delta du Saloum National Park (187,700 acres/76,000 ha), located on the coast just north of Gambia, has lodging at Keur Saloum near the mouths of the Sine and Saloum rivers. Its mangroves, mudflats, and sand spits (reachable by boat) have many waterbirds, a few manatees, and some nesting flamingos. Red colobus monkeys live in the upland Fathala forest sector. South of Gambia, the **Casamance River** is lined with mangroves and rice paddies. The port of Ziguinchor, on the Casamance, has storks, vultures, and pink-backed pelicans nesting in the city's shade trees. Thirty-seven miles (59 km) southwest, en route to the beach resort of Cap Skiring, **Basse-Casamance National Park** (12,400 acres/5,000 ha) has the last tall, moist tropical forest in Senegal, with mona and red colobus monkeys, duikers, bushbucks, buffalos, and a few sitatungas. There are many forest-undergrowth birds, as well as palm-nut vultures, crowned eagles, blue-bellied rollers, and yellow-casqued hornbills.

The East

The best park for wildlife viewing in Senegal is **Niokolo-Koba National Park/Biosphere Reserve/World Heritage Site** (2,255,100 acres/913,000 ha), on the Guinea border southeast of the town of Tambacounda. It has flat woodland, grassland, seasonally flooded wetlands, and gallery forest. The park receives 40″ (1,000 mm) of rain yearly and is open from December to May, in the dry season. Facilities include an airstrip, tracks, open-air game-viewing vehicles, and a river-bluff lodge at Simenti. The Gambia River, which passes through the park, is home to hippos, elephants, three crocodile species, the crocodilebird, and the Nile monitor lizard. The more common hoofed mammals in Niokolo-Koba are the kob, waterbuck, reedbuck, hartebeest, bushbuck, roan, and buffalo. There are also a few elusive herds of Derby elands. Predators include wild dogs, lions, and leopards. Chimpanzees live on remote Mount Assirik (1,020′/311 m) in the eastern part of the park. The 350 bird species include the goliath heron, bateleur, stone partridge, and violet turaco.

SEYCHELLES PLATE 30

This island republic in the western Indian Ocean lies roughly 1,000 mi (1,600 km) east of Tanzania. It is the world's only oceanic archipelago of continental granitic origin, consisting of fragments of an ancient land area

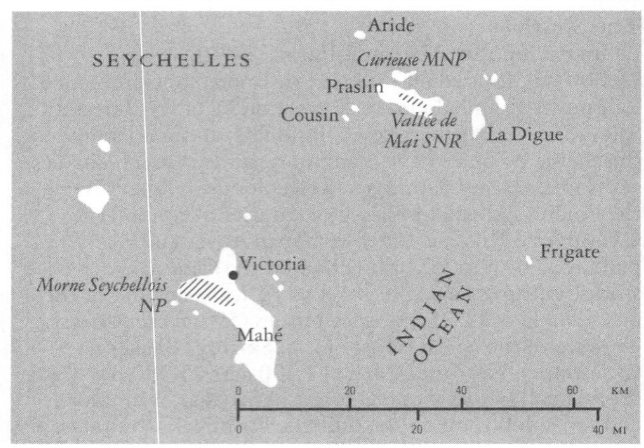

SEYCHELLES

called Gondwanaland, which included Africa, India, Australia, New Zealand, Antarctica, and South America. The climate is hot and humid between December and May, cooler and drier between June and November. Average highs range from 75° to 86°F (24–30°C). There are no large land mammals but vast numbers of birds. The few endemic birds and reptiles include some highly endangered species.

The Inner Granitic Islands

The 43 rugged granitic islands at the heart of Seychelles are encircled by beaches and headlands. Rain forests, rich in palms, have been cleared from most lowlands but survive in mountain gullies. Victoria, the capital, is located on **Mahé,** the largest island (58 sq mi/150 sq km). Mahé's annual rainfall reaches 92″ (2,300 mm). At the **botanical garden** in town one can see the local fruit bat, kestrel, and sunbird, and some endemic flora. Off the northeastern and northwestern coasts are three marine parks with coral reefs and snorkeling opportunities. **Morne Seychellois National Park** (7,521 acres/3,045 ha) protects the northern highlands, including mossy montane forest on the country's highest peak (2,993′/912 m). Almost all of Mahé's endemic plants inhabit this park, along with local species of scops-owl, blue pigeon, and white-eye. Ferries, light aircraft, and cruises connect Mahé with other islands.

Praslin, sitting amid a cluster of islets 25 mi (40 km) northeast of Mahé, is the next largest island (7 sq mi/ 18 sq km). **Vallée de Mai Strict Nature Reserve/World Heritage Site** (45 acres/18 ha), on the eastern side of

Praslin, harbors six endemic palm genera. The coco-de-mer boasts 40′ (12-m) leaves and a "double coconut" weighing up to 62 lb (28 kg), the world's largest seed. Wildlife includes the lesser black parrot, Seychelles blue pigeon, and Seychelles fruit bat. All of **Cousin Island,** just west of Praslin, is a special reserve (69 acres/28 ha). It seasonally hosts 250,000 breeding seabirds: white and bridled terns, brown and black noddies, the white-tailed tropicbird, and two shearwaters. The island's residents include the Seychelles brush warbler, Seychelles fody, giant tortoises, land crabs, sea turtles, skinks, and geckos. **Curieuse Marine National Park** (740 acres/300 ha), less than a mile off Praslin, protects **Curieuse Island** and its surrounding waters, mangrove swamps, and coral colonies. About 300 giant tortoises lumber about, and lesser black parrots fly to and fro. To the north, **Aride Island** is a special reserve of 150 acres (61 ha). Up to 1 million seabirds breed here between April and October; among them are 250,000 lesser noddies and six tern species, including rare roseate terns. The island is also a nesting spot for hawksbill turtles and the permanent home of Seychelles brush warblers. **La Digue,** just east of Praslin, is known for white-sand beaches framed by monumental boulders and for the **Black Paradise-flycatcher Reserve** (20 acres/8 ha). **Frigate Island** (500 acres/200 ha), 25 mi (40 km) southeast, is the last stronghold of a very rare magpie-robin.

The Outer Coralline Islands

Beyond the Seychelles granitic isles are 72 far-flung coralline islands, consisting of sandy cays, atolls, and raised limestone. Covered with scrub-forest or coconut plantations, some are important seabird and sea turtle nesting sites. **Bird Island,** 60 mi (97 km) northwest of Mahé, has an airstrip and lodge. White terns nest in the trees, while 1 million sooty terns breed in the dunes between May and November. Most of the rest of the outer islands lie along necklaces to the south. **Desnouefs,** 200 mi (325 km) southwest of Mahé, hosts masked boobies, brown noddies, and 2 million sooty terns. **Aldabra Atoll Strict Nature Reserve/World Heritage Site** (86,500 acres/35,000 ha) lies 600 mi (1,000 km) southwest of Mahé and 250 mi (400 km) northwest of Madagascar. One of the largest coral atolls in the world (22 mi/35 km long), it is formed of raised limestone isles fringed with mangroves, scrub forest, and grassland surrounding a large tidal lagoon. It is home to 150,000 Aldabra giant tortoises, endemic species of fruit bat, brush warbler, drongo, and green gecko, and endemic subspecies of the sacred ibis, flightless white-throated rail, and several

Madagascar birds. Among its vast colonies of nesting seabirds are the red-footed booby, red-tailed and white-tailed tropicbirds, and greater and lesser frigatebirds.

SIERRA LEONE

For map, see Guinea.

A humid country on the Atlantic Ocean, Sierra Leone (27,699 sq mi/71,740 sq km) has a high-sun rainy season from April through November, with a peak in July and August. Freetown, the capital, gets 134″ (3,345 mm) of annual rain; average highs vary from 82°F to 88°F (28–31°C). It sits at the northern end of the **Freetown Peninsula,** where 374 species of birds have been seen. **Western Forest Reserve** (43,689 acres/17,688 ha), on the peninsula, protects the most westerly large area of tall rain forest in Africa, situated in a coastal mountain range almost 3,000′ (900 m) high, with annual rainfall of 240″ (6,000 mm). A paved road through forest up to Guma Dam provides access to such birds as the white-crested and yellow-casqued hornbills. The coast of Sierra Leone has fine beaches, with extensive stands of mangroves at river mouths.

Outamba-Kilimi National Park (199,608 acres/80,813 ha) sits on the Guinea border between the Little Scarcies and Great Scarcies rivers in the far north. This inland hilly area is drier, receiving only 70″ (1,750 mm) of rain annually. The park's habitats—wooded savanna, grassland, forest, and swamp—support chimpanzees, forest elephants, buffalos, waterbucks, hippos, and crocodiles. There are three forest reserves in the northeast, including **Loma Mountains Forest Reserve** (82,006 acres/33,201 ha), which is topped by Mount Bintimani (6,390′/1,948 m) and home to the great blue turaco and the rare Cassin's hawk-eagle.

The far south gets 160″ (4,000 mm) of rain a year, but only 5 percent of the original rain forest remains. **Tiwai Island Wildlife Sanctuary** is a proposed biosphere reserve in the Moa River, 11 mi (18 km) southeast of Potoru, with 11 species of primates, plus pygmy hippos. **Gola Forest Reserve,** on the Liberia border, shrinks yearly as refugee, logging, and hunting problems mount. It has had the banded duiker, three colobines, the diana monkey, the white-breasted guineafowl, and the white-necked rockfowl.

SOMALIA

For map, see Ethiopia.

Somalia, which occupies most of the Horn of Africa, is the centerpiece of a vast area of arid country, known as the **Somali-Masai arid zone,** that stretches from southern Eritirea south to northeastern Tanzania. As one of the few dry areas on the equator, most of the country gets less than 10″ (250 mm) of rain annually, and vast areas are desert scrub. Somalia has perhaps the least spoiled coastline in Africa, hosting major nesting colonies of crabplovers. The country's total area is 246,154 sq mi (637,539 sq km). *Note:* Due to protracted periods of civil unrest and the lack of a centralized national government, the status of wildlife in Somalia's reserves is uncertain at this time.

The South

Mogadishu, the capital, gets 18″ (450 mm) of rain yearly, chiefly between April and November. The Scebeli River, which runs parallel to the coast inland from Mogadishu, is one of two rivers that enter Somalia from the Ethiopian highlands. **Balcad Nature Reserve** (470 acres/190 ha) protects an area of riverine forest and grassland 19 mi (30 km) north of the city. More than 200 birds occur, including the goliath heron, carmine bee-eater, golden weaver, and sulphur-breasted bush-shrike. **Alifuuto Nature Reserve** (444,600 acres/180,000 ha) is a swampy area along the river 110 mi (170 km) north of Mogadishu that has been home to the elephant, giraffe, hippo, buffalo, many antelopes, and the ostrich. The Juba River, farther south, has also had much wildlife in the past. **Bush Bush–Lake Badana Game Reserve** (825,000 acres/334,000 ha), in the far south, has a mix of habitats, including woodland, acacia savanna, seasonal lakes, and coastline. Native mammals here include the elephant, buffalo, lesser kudu, beisa oryx, reticulated giraffe, Peter's race of Grant's gazelle, Hunter's hartebeest, lion, cheetah, and leopard. Offshore, the **Badjouini (Bajuni) Archipelago** stretches from the city of Kismayu south to Kenya. The coral reefs and idyllic islands here support a rich variety of marine life, including dugongs.

The North

The Gulf of Aden coast is cooled by cold offshore currents in winter. Berbera, the main port city, gets 2″ (50 mm) of rain in its relatively cool winter, when highs average 88°F (31°C). In summer there is no rain, and highs average 106°F (41°C). Pelzeln's gazelles live on the coastal lowlands along the gulf. The Yemeni islands of Kuri and

Socotra, off the tip of the Horn, are rich in endemic species. Inland, a great range of mountains with peaks exceeding 7,000′ (2,100 m) runs east–west. The mountains, which receive more rain than lowland areas, have bushland and remnants of juniper forest; several proposed parks have endemic birds. To the south of the mountains, the stark landscape of the low plateau drained by the Nogal River is home to the wild ass and a number of rare antelopes, such as Speke's gazelle, the dibatag, and the beira.

SOUTH AFRICA PLATES 26, 28, 31

This southernmost country in Africa has 1,860 mi (3,000 km) of coastline and a total area of 471,445 sq mi (1,221,042 sq km). The Atlantic side features the cold Antarctic waters of the northward-flowing Benguela Current. Warm waters of the Agulhas Current flow southwestward along the Indian Ocean coast. The coastal plain is rather narrow. In the east, foothills of the Drakensberg Mountains lead up to a high plateau that tops 3,900′ (1,200 m). In the southwest, ancient series of mountains rise over 6,600′ (2,000 m) before yielding to a lower-elevation dry plateau called the Great Karroo. Southwestern Cape Province has a Mediterranean climate with cool winter rains and hot dry summers. The Indian Ocean coast has both winter and summer rains. Most of the plateau has rain in the high-sun summer months. *Note:* The names and boundaries of the provinces in South Africa are under review and likely to change. We use the traditional names here and in the species accounts.

The natural vegetation of South Africa can be divided into six types, with many transitional types: (1) The "Cape floral kingdom" of southern and southwestern Cape Province is highly diverse, with thousands of endemic plant species. Much of this vegetation is *fynbos*—shrubby, heath-like plants of many species. The region also has many showy flowering plants, such as the thick-leafed proteas. (2) The Karroo semi-arid scrub on the lower Karroo plateau has sparse shrubs and succulents. (3) Highveld grassland carpets the high plateau, with scattered trees in places. (4) Lowveld wooded savanna blankets lower elevations in northern and eastern Transvaal Province. (5) Moist savanna and dune forest mosaic occurs in northern Natal. (6) Subtropical evergreen forest patches grow in the high Drakensberg Mountains and along the sea on the southern coast.

South Africa has a superb system of national parks, provincial game reserves, and other protected areas numbering in the hundreds. Rather than focusing on the foreign tourist (as do parks elsewhere in Africa), its parks and reserves cater primarily to local residents who enjoy seeing and experiencing wildlife and wilderness. Superior lodging, camps, tracks, and wilderness trails are the norm. Protection has been excellent and poaching rare. In contrast to the local extinctions of species after species in parks in tropical Africa, here rhinos, large hoofed mammals, and predators are being restocked in many parks in their former ranges. Cape Province, Natal, Orange Free State, and Transvaal are treated in separate sections below.

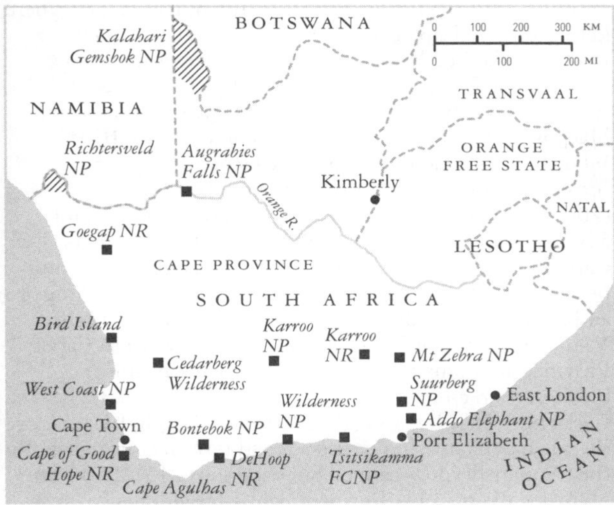

CAPE PROVINCE

Cape Province

The Southwest Cape

Cape Town is a scenic port city at the southwestern corner of Africa. It receives 21″ (525 mm) of rain yearly, chiefly in its low-sun winter, between April and October. Cable cars take visitors up to the flat-topped sandstone massif of **Table Mountain Nature Reserve** (7,173 acres/2,904 ha). Hiking trails lead through montane *fynbos* with the rock hyrax, speckled pigeon, and orange-breasted sunbird. **Cape of Good Hope Nature Reserve** (19,143 acres/ 7,750 ha) protects the tall cliffs of Cape Point and open flatlands with 1,200 plant species. The chacma baboon, Hartlaub's and kelp gulls, the red-winged starling, and the reintroduced bontebok are common. Southern right whales, Cape fur seals, and Cape cormorants feed in nearby waters. Jackass penguins burrow in mainland scrub above the beach just south of Simon's Town on the False Bay shore, north of the reserve. Above the vineyards and the old university town of Stellenbosch, 25 mi (40 km) east of Cape Town, lies **Hottentots Holland Mountain Catchment Area** (209,792 acres/84,936 ha), which protects the montane *fynbos* in a water catchment area of rugged mountains, cliffs, and forested gorges. Victoria Peak rises to 5,213′ (1,589 m), receiving 140″ (3,500 mm) of annual rain, and snow in winter.

West Coast National Park (49,400 acres/20,000 ha), 74 mi (120 km) northwest of Cape Town, has islands where kelp gulls and Cape gannets nest. The park's Langebaan Lagoon is flanked by marshlands that attract numerous waders. The Postberg sector has sandveld and coastal *fynbos* habitats with impressive spring wildflowers where black wildebeests, bonteboks, and elands roam. **Bird Island** can be reached on foot via a smooth-topped breakwater from the port of Lambert's Bay, 125 mi (200 km) north of Cape Town. There are pathways and a blind beside a colony of 5,000 pairs of Cape gannets. Cape and bank cormorants and jackass penguins also nest here, and southern right whales occur offshore. Flamingos and South African shelducks are often seen at **Waldrift Vlei** just to the south. Grainfields in southwestern Cape Province are home to the blue crane, black bustard, black harrier, and red bishop.

Cedarberg Wilderness (175,400 acres/71,000 ha), east of the town of Clanwilliam, has rugged terrain culminating in the frequently snow-capped Sneeuberg (8,215′/2,504 m). Many small antelopes live here, while larger ones, such as the black wildebeest and bontebok, have been reintroduced northeast of the town of Ceres at the private **Kagga Kamma** reserve, which has relocated Bushmen into ancestral areas. One of the highlights of the reserve, which has lodging, is a spectacular canyon.

The South Coast

South Africa claims the far-off **Prince Edward Islands,** 1,360 mi (2,200 km) to the southeast of Cape Agulhas, the southernmost point in Africa. These windy subantarctic islands of tussock grass have nesting seals, penguins, and albatrosses. **Bontebok National Park** (6,881 acres/ 2,786 ha), east of Cape Town, has low-growing *fynbos;* the last 22 bonteboks in the world were transferred here in 1931. Today, in addition to several hundred bonteboks, visitors may see the gray rhebok, Cape grysbok, common duiker, steenbok, Cape batis, and bokmakierie bush-shrike. Nearby **De Hoop Nature Reserve** (148,200 acres/ 60,000 ha) includes a marine reserve where dolphins and southern right whales are seen. De Hoop preserves the largest remaining tract of coastal *fynbos,* with 1,500 recorded plant species, including 50 restricted to this site. It has the world's largest herd of bonteboks, plus elands (reintroduced) and Cape mountain zebras.

The **Garden Route,** a scenic drive between Mossel Bay and Port Elizabeth, passes among east–west ranges and a wild coastline of cliffs, canyons, and beaches. **Wilderness National Park** (24,700 acres/10,000 ha), between the coast towns of George and Knysna, contains a series of reed-lined lakes with blinds, boardwalks, and many waterbirds. **Tsitsikamma Forest and Coastal National Park** (8,195 acres/3,318 ha) lines the coast east of the resort of Plettenberg Bay. Some tall patches of native forest remain, with giant yellowwoods and stinkwoods. The Knysna race of the green turaco lives in the forests, and the Cape clawless otter lives in the streams.

Port Elizabeth is a major coastal city that receives 23″ (575 mm) of rain evenly spread through the year. **Addo Elephant National Park** (22,200 acres/9,000 ha), 43 mi (70 km) northeast of Port Elizabeth, is fenced to keep its wildlife away from nearby farms. The vegetation is thick evergreen bush, making animal spotting difficult, except from hills and water holes. There are about 100 elephants, plus black rhinos, elands, buffalos, and some 160 species of birds. Just to the north, **Suurberg National Park** (59,621 acres/24,138 ha) has reintroduced the Cape mountain zebra. The park has rare cycads and pincushion plants in its rounded mountains covered in *fynbos* and evergreen forest.

The Interior

Mountain Zebra National Park (16,144 acres/6,536 ha), 125 mi (200 km) north of Port Elizabeth, is in the Bankberg Mountains, which rise to 6,421′ (1,957 m) and have frequent winter snow. Karroo scrub and grassland blanket the slopes. Several hundred Cape mountain zebras have been protected here, along with the eland, black wildebeest, blesbok, springbok, and mountain reedbuck. To the west, near the historic town of Graaff-Reinet, **Karroo Nature Reserve** (34,600 acres/14,000 ha) has many of the same mammals, plus the greater kudu. It has a reservoir, succulent veld, and a great chasm called the Valley of Desolation. **Karroo National Park** (69,884 acres/ 28,293 ha), west of Beaufort West on Karroo-scrub hillsides around the cliffs of the Nieuwveld Mountains, gets about 10″ (250 mm) of rain annually. The park has

180 species of birds and such mammals as the Cape mountain zebra, red hartebeest, black wildebeest, springbok, bat-eared and Cape foxes, and the caracal.

The Orange River, which forms much of the boundary between Namibia and Cape Province, flows through **Augrabies Falls National Park** (203,565 acres/82,415 ha), 79 mi (128 km) west of the town of Upington. It forms rapids, then a gorge, and finally tumbles over Bridal Falls (184′/56 m). This is a dry area dotted with aloes and euphorbias; many black rhinos, springboks, steenboks, klipspringers, rock hyraxes, and 161 species of birds live here. The river divides the Karroo scrub to the south from the Kalahari sandveld to the north. Remote **Kalahari Gemsbok National Park** (2,368,984 acres/959,103 ha) occupies the northern wedge of Cape Province; 220 mi (350 km) north of Upington, it is flanked by Namibia and Botswana. There are lodges at three sites, and gravel and sandy tracks through semi-desert savanna with sand ridges. This area has hot summers, cold winters, and 8″ (200 mm) of erratic rainfall. Rains bring forth flowers, wild melons and cucumbers, and fills the normally dry riverbeds. Bore holes provide water for the wildlife that migrates through here chiefly between February and May. Mammals of note include the gemsbok, eland, blue wildebeest, red hartebeest, springbok, suricate, lion, cheetah, leopard, and brown and spotted hyenas. Some 215 birds are known, including the ostrich, kori bustard, pygmy falcon, namaqua sandgrouse, and sociable weaver, with its huge communal nests.

In the northwestern corner of Cape Province, **Richtersveld National Park** (400,100 acres/162,000 ha) protects unique plant life in rugged mountains near the mouth of the Orange River. **Goegap Nature Reserve** (37,100 acres/ 15,000 ha), to the south, east of the village of Springbok, has kokerboom (tall aloe trees), succulents, and beautiful wildflowers after rare winter rains, plus Hartmann's race of the mountain zebra.

NATAL

Located between the Drakensberg Mountains and the Indian Ocean, Natal stretches from Cape Province northeast to Mozambique. Inland it borders land-locked Lesotho and Transvaal. Its major city is Durban, a port and resort on the warm waters of the Indian Ocean. It receives 40″ (1,000 mm) of rain spread evenly year-round. Average highs are 72°F (22°C) in July and 81°F (27°C) in January.

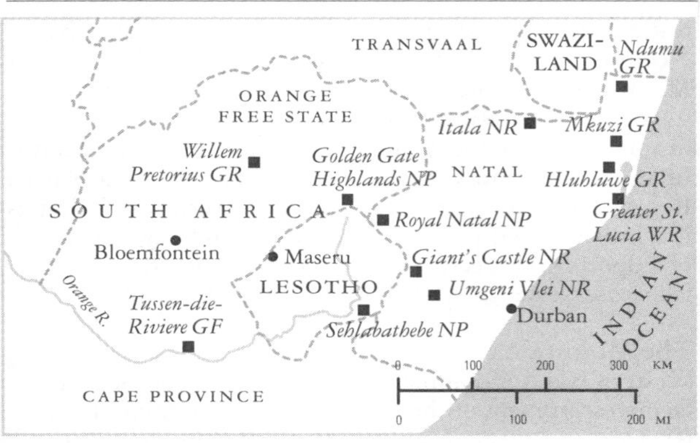

NATAL, ORANGE FREE STATE, AND LESOTHO

Zululand Area

There is a cluster of excellent wildlife reserves in the northeastern Zululand area, up the coast from Durban: **Umfolozi Game Reserve** (117,955 acres/47,755 ha), **Hluhluwe Game Reserve** (56,975 acres/23,067 ha), and **Mkuzi Game Reserve** (84,000 acres/34,000 ha). Each has lodging inside and nearby, tracks, water holes, rivers, and wilderness trails. Vegetation is a mix of hillside woodland, grassy flats, wooded savanna, and thickets. These reserves feature the best viewing and photography blinds in Africa. Visitors walk through avenues of tall canes along boardwalks to large, thatched-roof blinds built right in the middle of water holes and come face to face with drinking mammals and birds. For years Umfolozi was the secret stronghold of white rhinos, which were being hunted everywhere else; most relocations into protected areas have come from this stock. These parks are also a stronghold of the nyala and have elephants, hippos, giraffes, elands, blue wildebeests, greater kudus, waterbucks, impalas, buffalos, Natal red duikers, sunis, zebras, black rhinos, lions, cheetahs, and leopards. Many of the 450 species of birds are at the southern limit of their ranges.

Phinda Resource Reserve (37,100 acres/15,000 ha), located east of Hluhluwe, is a new eco-tourism reserve with most of the same species; it blends the needs of local people with luxury lodgings for visitors. **Greater Saint Lucia Wetland Reserve,** along the coast south of Mkuzi and Hluhluwe, will create the third-largest park in South Africa, incorporating a string of existing reserves along with new areas of lakes, lagoons, dune forest, beaches, and offshore reefs. The various areas are home to hippos, crocodiles, nesting pink-backed pelicans, many waterbirds, and nesting sea turtles, including leatherbacks. **Ndumu Game Reserve** (24,988 acres/10,117 ha), on the Mozambique border, has no great animal herds, but its forests have many localized songbirds, while Pel's fishing owl, waterbirds, and pythons inhabit its waterways. Inland on the Transvaal border at Louwsburg, **Itala Nature Reserve** (63,963 acres/25,896 ha) has a variety of lodgings in a hilly area with steep valleys along the Pongolo River; it supports 400 species of birds, both rhinos, cheetahs, leopards, tsessebes, reedbucks, impalas, and giraffes.

The Mountains

Western Natal is dominated by the tall wall of the east-facing escarpment of the Drakensberg Mountains. This long row of sandstone and basaltic lava cliffs along the Lesotho border is the highest range in southern Africa and is often dusted with snow in winter. Rainfall is highest in summer. There are colonies of the rare bald ibis near the Mooi River, northwest of Pietermaritzburg. Wattled cranes breed in **Umgeni Vlei Nature Reserve,** southwest of the Mooi River. The **Giant's Castle Nature Reserve** (85,556 acres/34,638 ha) is 40 mi (65 km) west of the Mooi River. While there is a road up to the rest camp, the network of trails beyond is accessible only by foot and horseback. Massive cliffs are pocked with caves where Bushman art is common. The slopes are chiefly grassland, with woodland along the rushing streams. Set aside for the eland, the reserve is also home to the blesbok, black wildebeest, red hartebeest, and 140 species of birds, including the lammergeier. **Royal Natal National Park** (21,874 acres/8,856 ha), on the Orange Free State–Lesotho border, has a range of lodging facilities. This is a scenic wonderland, with Mont aux Sources (10,822′/3,299 m), the crescent-shaped bowl (formed by an adjacent mountain and canyon) called the Amphitheatre, and three-tier Tugela Falls, which drops 3,110′ (948 m). The few mammals in the park include baboons, bushbucks, klipspringers, gray rheboks, and mountain reedbucks.

Orange Free State

For map, see Natal.

In the 1800s this interior state was an endless highveld grassland with vast herds of migratory animals, including the quagga, a partially striped zebra that is now extinct. Orange Free State is now a sea of fenced grainfields, and most of its animals have been reintroduced to various reserves near reservoirs. Bloemfontein, the provincial capital, at 4,660′ (1,420 m), receives 22″ (550 mm) of rain in the high-sun months of October through April. Average highs are 86°F (30°C) in January, 61°F (16°C) in July; frosts are common at night in winter. **Willem Pretorius Game Reserve** (29,652 acres/12,005 ha), 100 mi (161 km) northeast, has the world's largest herd of black wildebeests, and remnant herds of springboks, red hartebeests, blesboks, and elands. **Tussen-die-Riviere Game Farm** (54,300 acres/22,000 ha) also has those species, plus the white rhino, gemsbok, aardwolf, and bat-eared fox; it is located in the far south at the confluence of the Orange and Caledon rivers. Waterbirds and other birds such as the blue bustard occur at both reserves. **Golden Gate Highlands National Park** (15,415 acres/6,241 ha) is located on the Lesotho border, 37 mi (60 km) southeast of the Orange Free State town of Bethlehem. Golden sandstone cliffs rise above grassland and protea scrub at 6,000–9,100′ (1,825–2,770 m); the area receives 34″ (850 mm) of annual rain, chiefly in summer. There are wildlife-viewing roads here; mammals of interest are the black wildebeest, eland, red hartebeest, blesbok, and oribi. Bird life includes the lammergeier, Cape vulture, jackal buzzard, black eagle, ground woodpecker, and Gurney's sugarbird. **Qwaqwa Conservation Area** (74,100 acres/30,000 ha), located between Golden Gate and Royal Natal National Park, in Natal, is home to the bald ibis and the wattled crane.

Transvaal

The Highveld

Johannesburg, the largest city in southern Africa, is located at 5,460′ (1,665 m) elevation; it gets 28″ (700 mm) of annual rain, chiefly in summer. Average highs are 79°F (26°C) in January and 63°F (17°C) in June; frosts occur in winter. Pretoria, the administrative capital of South Africa, 35 mi (56 km) to the north, is slightly lower and warmer. **Pilanesberg National Park** (123,500 acres/50,000 ha), near the resort of Sun City, several hours northwest of both cities, shows how protection and reintroductions can restore an ecosystem. This is a huge volcanic crater rising above the plains, with tracks, trails, and blinds. It has an abundance of antelopes, plus elephants, both rhinos, giraffes, zebras, leopards, and cheetahs.

Barberspan Nature Reserve (7,622 acres/3,086 ha), located in western Transvaal, 12 mi (19 km) northeast of the town of Delareyville, is an important wetland, often

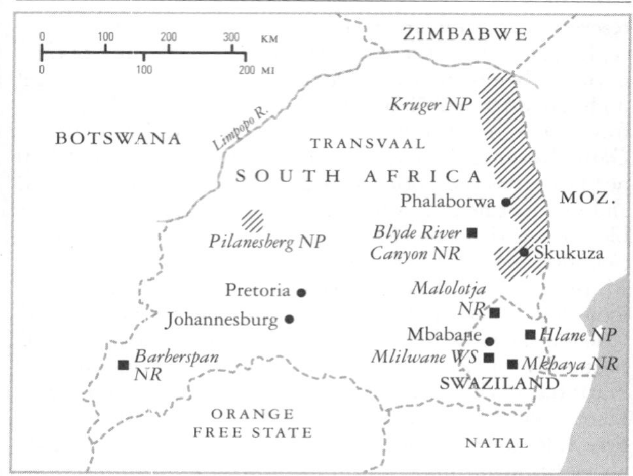

TRANSVAAL AND SWAZILAND

full of flamingos, herons, ducks, and waders, among 350 recorded bird species. In northeastern Transvaal, the highveld grasslands meet another sector of the Drakensberg escarpment. **Blyde River Canyon Nature Reserve** (55,980 acres/22,664 ha), which overlooks Kruger National Park (see below) to the east, has subtropical evergreen forest, protea shrubs, and grassland in a spectacular setting of rounded peaks, dramatic waterfalls, and rushing rivers. There are country hotels and trails, and visitors may see Bushman paintings, many small antelopes, five primates, and highland birds.

The Lowveld

Kruger National Park (4,812,864 acres/1,948,528 ha), one of the world's oldest and largest parks, is 217 mi (350 km) long. It lies along the Mozambique border, stretching from Zimbabwe south almost to Swaziland. There are an airport (at Skukuza), 24 lodges and camps, eight entrance gates, and a vast network of both gravel and paved roads. The remote northern sector is chiefly mopane woodland, with most of the park's elephants, roans, tsessebes, and elands. The drier southern sector has more grassland and acacias, with most of the giraffes, impalas, black rhinos, and lions. The higher, greener southwestern area has white rhinos and sables. Other mammals, such as the greater kudu, buffalo, waterbuck, warthog, leopard, and wild dog, are found widely. The rivers are trickles in the winter dry season, with pools where hippos and crocodiles congregate. Riverine woodlands with many fig trees harbor nyalas and bushbucks.

The 480 species of birds are chiefly widespread savanna species; the greatest variety is found in the rainy summer months when few tourists visit. The private wildlife reserves of Klaserie, Londolozi, Mala Mala, Sabi Sabi, Sabi Sand, and Timbavati lie between Skukuza and Phalaborwa on the western side of Kruger. Offering excellent protection, they have large numbers of wildlife, especially rhinos. Most have private airstrips and luxury lodging; they provide open-sided wildlife-viewing vehicles and encourage night drives.

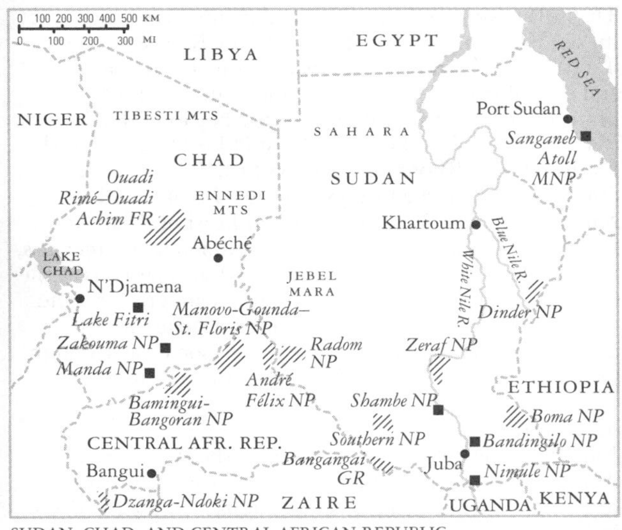

SUDAN, CHAD, AND CENTRAL AFRICAN REPUBLIC

SUDAN

The largest country in Africa (967,500 sq mi/2,505,825 sq km), Sudan contains much of the flat Nile basin and is flanked by peripheral highlands on some borders. With Sahara desert in the north, semi-arid Sahel in the center, and Sudan wooded savanna in the south, rainfall increases southward.

The North

Khartoum, the capital, lies at the confluence of the White Nile and the Blue Nile in an area that receives only 6″ (150 mm) of annual rain. Average highs range from 99°F (37°C) in January to 108°F (42°C) in May. Saharan sand dunes cover most of northwestern Sudan. The **Wadi**

Howar area near the Chad border is not protected but has harbored the addax, the scimitar-horned oryx, and several desert gazelles. The volcanic peak **Jebel Mara,** 80 mi (130 km) northwest of the town of Nyala in the Darfur region, at the southern end of the Sahara, deserves to be a park. Woodland and waterfalls flank this volcano, which reaches 10,073′ (3,070 m). **Radom National Park** (3,087,500 acres/1,250,000 ha), flanking two rivers, is on the Central African Republic border in wooded savanna. It has elephants, hippos, giraffes, and many antelopes. East of the Nile, the Nubian Desert rises gradually up into the Red Sea hills, where elevations reach 7,412′ (2,259 m). The hills have some vegetation and mammals such as ibexes, but no parks. Port Sudan, on the Red Sea, receives 4″ (100 mm) of rain yearly. The coastline has mangroves and coastal marshes in places. Some islands and reefs are protected in **Sanganeb Atoll Marine National Park** (64,200 acres/26,000 ha), southeast of Port Sudan. **Dinder National Park/Biosphere Reserve** (2,198,300 acres/ 890,000 ha) is on the Ethiopia border east of the Blue Nile and about 300 mi (500 km) southeast of Khartoum. It encompasses acacia savanna, seasonal floodplain marshes, and gallery forest, which have harbored such animals as the elephant, black rhino, giraffe, buffalo, roan, greater kudu, tora race of hartebeest, Soemmerring's gazelle, lion, and ostrich. The park is closed in the wet season (May through October), when it receives 28″ (700 mm) of rain.

The South

Juba, the chief city in the south, is on the White Nile. Annual rain, falling mainly from April through November, reaches 40″ (1,000 mm). Average highs are 100°F (38°C) in February and 88°F (31°C) in July. In **Nimule National Park** (101,300 acres/41,000 ha), south of Juba on the banks of the Nile at the Uganda border, smaller rivers run off the Ilingua Mountains through wooded savanna. The white rhino was the centerpiece here, along with the elephant, kob, hippo, buffalo, and Nile lechwe. **Bandingilo National Park** (4,075,500 acres/1,650,000 ha) and **Shambe National Park** (153,100 acres/62,000 ha) flank the Nile north of Juba. Both are home to Nile lechwes, giraffes, and elephants. The **Sudd marshes** (known as the Sudd) are vast, seasonally flooded wetlands along the Nile north of the two parks that even out the flood pulse of the great river. Varying water levels influence the movements of vast herds of mammals, including elephants, 500,000 topis (tiang race), 65,000 individuals of the mongalla race of Thomson's gazelle, reedbucks, Nile lechwes, and sitatungas. The waters and skies are full of waterbirds and raptors year-round. The Sudd is the main home of the shoebill (5,000 birds), the black crowned crane, and wintering Eurasian birds, including the ruff. **Zeraf Game Reserve** (2,395,900 acres/970,000 ha) protects (on paper) a large portion of the Sudd marshes east of the Nile. The massive Jonglei Canal project will channel much of the Nile's water away from the Sudd, its cattle-raising Dinka people, and the wildlife. The goal of this ambitious project is to tame the Nile, opening up the Sudd for agriculture and providing more water for irrigation downstream. **Southern National Park** (5,681,000 acres/2,300,000 ha) is a vast savanna park in the west, south of Wau. It has not been developed, but in the past the area has been home to the giant eland, giraffe, buffalo, lion, roan, wild dog, and white rhino. **Bangangai Game Reserve** (42,000 acres/ 17,000 ha) has dense tropical evergreen forest on the Zaire border, 50 mi (80 km) west-northwest of Yambio. It is home to nine primates, including the chimpanzee, four duikers, three pigs, the bongo, the forest elephant, and both Cape and forest races of buffalo. Bird life includes the long-tailed hawk, great blue turaco, and black-bellied seedcracker.

East of Juba, the **Imatong Mountains** rise to 10,456′ (3,187 m), with unprotected cool wet forests and many plants and animals found nowhere else in Sudan. **Boma National Park** (5,631,600 acres/2,280,000 ha), located on the Ethiopia border 180 mi (300 km) northeast of Juba, at a juncture of ecosystems at 1,300–3,600′ (400–1,100 m), has the richest diversity of fauna in Sudan and perhaps in Africa. It has montane forest on the Boma Plateau, arid Somali semi-desert, wooded savanna, and vast swamps. Like the Serengeti, it is home to seasonal migrations of hundreds of thousands of mammals. The herds spend January through April in the dry floodplains in the northeast, leaving the park for better-drained areas to the southwest in the wet season. These herds involve 870,000 of the local white-eared kob, plus topis (tiang race), elands, plains zebras, hartebeests, reedbucks, and Thomson's gazelles (mongalla race). Elephants, hippos, beisa oryxes, lesser kudus, dik-diks, Grant's gazelles, cheetahs, and shoebills also live in the park.

SWAZILAND

For map, see Transvaal, South Africa.

This small country (6,705 sq mi/17,433 sq km) lies between Mozambique and South Africa. Mbabane, the capital, receives 55″ (1,375 mm) of rain, chiefly between September and April. Average highs are 77°F (25°C) in January, 66°F (19°C) in June; some frost occurs in winter. Rising to 6,027′ (1,837 m), **Malolotja Nature Reserve** (44,892 acres/18,175 ha) is located in the northwest in the highveld grasslands of the Drakensberg escarpment. It has hiking trails and roads to caverns and to Malolotja Falls (330′/100 m). Montane evergreen forest and open hillsides with rare cycads, proteas, aloes, and orchids are home to mountain reedbucks, gray rheboks, oribis, klipspringers, and blesboks. The bald ibis, blue crane, and blue swallow breed here. **Mlilwane Wildlife Sanctuary** (11,226 acres/ 4,545 ha), 14 mi (22 km) south of Mbabane, has many hippos and has been restocked with white rhinos and 18 species of antelopes, including the sable. **Mkhaya Nature Reserve** (15,314 acres/6,200 ha), in the center of the lowveld, offers luxury tenting, open-sided animal-viewing vehicles, walking trails, and rafting. The savanna here has elephants, both rhinos, zebras, giraffes, nyalas, greater kudus, roans, and elands, plus many ostriches and eagles. In the northeastern corner of the country there are two adjacent reserves, **Hlane National Park** (74,100 acres/ 30,000 ha) and **Mlawula/Ndzindza Nature Reserve** (45,400 acres/18,400 ha). Among the parks' activities are walking, canoeing, and watching the vulture-feeding program. They are home to the white rhino, hippo, impala, blue wildebeest, giraffe, oribi, zebra, cheetah, leopard, and more than 300 species of birds.

TANZANIA PLATES 1, 7, 16, 17, 21, 34, 36, 43, 49, 50

The largest country in East Africa (364,943 sq mi/ 945,202 sq km), Tanzania lies just south of the equator, between the Indian Ocean and the great lakes of Victoria, Tanganyika, and Malawi. Westward from its narrow coastal plain the land rises steadily to the 3,000–5,000′ (900–1,500 m) plateau that comprises most of the country. The landscape is dramatically interrupted by the eastern and western rift valleys and fertile highlands punctuated with extinct volcanoes. The north is a mix of acacia savanna and open grassland, while the central and southern regions are chiefly miombo woodland. The cool highlands have montane forests; wet tropical forest patches occur in the northwest, and stunted coastal forests in the east. The north has two rainy seasons: the long rains between March and June, and the short rains from mid-October through December. The south has a single rainy season between

TANZANIA

November and April. More than one-quarter of the country is under some form of protection. Tanzania is the home of the world-famous Serengeti and Ngorongoro safari circuit.

The Arusha Area

Arusha, the main city and safari center of the north, is connected to Nairobi, Kenya, by paved road; it is an hour west of Kilimanjaro Airport. Visitors can choose from a number of hotels in town and lodges set among verdant plantations in the eastern outskirts. **Arusha National Park** (33,800 acres/13,700 ha) and **Mount Meru Game Reserve** (74,100 acres/30,000 ha) flank 14,979′ (4,566 m) Mount Meru, which rises north of Arusha. There is a lodge on the eastern slope of Mount Meru near the Momela lakes, which are surrounded by brushland with giraffes, bushbucks, and waterbucks. Visitors accompanied by a ranger-guide may walk along the lakes, which host flamingos, Cape teals, maccoa ducks, and waders. The forested rim of mile-wide Ngurdoto Crater overlooks a swampy crater floor well-trod by elephants, buffalos, and other mammals. The crater rim is home to silvery-cheeked hornbills, black-and-white colobus monkeys, and Natal red duikers. The mountain's annual rainfall of up to 96″ (2,400 mm) nourishes dense montane forest, which yields to moorland higher up. Those wishing to climb all or part of Mount Meru can hire guides and stay in modest huts overnight. Crowned eagles, bar-tailed trogons, and montane white-eyes may be spotted from the slopes. **Kilimanjaro National Park/World Heritage Site** (186,670 acres/75,575 ha) protects the upper reaches (above 8,860′/2,700 m) of Africa's tallest mountain (19,340′/5,895 m), an enormous, freestanding massif, with snowfields and small glaciers among its three volcanoes (Shira, Kibo, and Mawenzi). The park's lower slopes are cloaked in montane forest hosting Abbott's duikers and Hartlaub's turacos. Above this zone, moorland features giant lobelia plants, the four-striped grass mouse, the lammergeier, and the scarlet-tufted malachite sunbird. Organized five- to seven-day hikes (with nights in huts or tents) traverse cold alpine desert above 13,100′ (4,000 m), where annual rainfall is only 8″ (200 mm).

The Eastern Rift Valley

West of Arusha, the eastern side of the rift valley drops down gradually in a series of terraces, while the western wall is impressively steep. **Lake Natron,** a vast soda lake near the Kenya border, is a major nesting site for flamingos, while the very arid acacia savanna nearby hosts the fringe-eared oryx. Towering above the southern end of Lake Natron is the perfect volcanic cone of Ol Doinyo Lengai, which frequently shows a plume of smoke. **Lake Manyara National Park/Biosphere Reserve** (80,300 acres/32,500 ha), a slim sanctuary extending from the northern and western parts of Lake Manyara to the top of the western rift valley wall, is 75 mi (120 km) southwest of Arusha, just south of the main road to the Serengeti Plains. Verreaux's eagles, vultures, storks, swifts, and swallows wing by lodgings atop the spectacular cliffs overlooking the lake. Springs in the park's northern end support a dense groundwater forest of giant figs and mahogany, which shelters blue monkeys, baboons, bushbucks, common waterbucks, elephants, and silvery-cheeked hornbills. South of the groundwater forest, acacia woodland and open grassland are frequented by buffalos, wildebeests, impalas, giraffes, zebras, lions, and gray-backed fiscal-shrikes. Streams attract pythons, Nile monitor lizards, and mountain wagtails. Lake Manyara, at 3,150′ (960 m), varies in salinity levels with wetter and drier climate cycles. At times it is replete with flamingos, pelicans, storks, and cormorants. The hippo pool, where visitors may get out of their vehicles, is located on a freshwater stream that enters the lake at its northern tip. **Tarangire National Park** (642,200 acres/260,000 ha) lies near the end of a paved road, 70 mi (114 km) south of Arusha and southeast of Lake Manyara. Its tented lodge and several campsites are set in pretty rolling hills dotted with enormous baobab trees and umbrella acacias. Tarangire hosts many animals year-round, including elephant herds. During the June to October dry season these are joined by huge herds of zebras and wildebeests from the Masai Steppe, to the east, attracted to the Tarangire River's permanent water. Resident species include fringe-eared oryxes, impalas, hartebeests, giraffes, steenboks, lions, and leopards. More than 300 bird species have been recorded; among them, yellow-necked and red-necked spurfowls, orange-bellied parrots, yellow-collared lovebirds, bare-faced and white-bellied go-away-birds, magpie shrikes, and ashy starlings.

Ngorongoro Crater

On the main road to Ngorongoro Crater, just north of Karatu, **Gibb's Farm** lodge runs an excellent bird-feeding operation that attracts Reichenow's weavers, Cape robin-chats, and tropical boubous. **Ngorongoro Conservation Area/World Heritage Site** (2,045,200 acres/828,000 ha) protects wildlife habitat as well as the rights of local Masai who graze their livestock on about 75 percent of the area. **Ngorongoro Crater,** 12 mi (19 km) wide, is the world's largest intact caldera. Before the cataclysmic collapse of its cone 2 million years ago, this volcanic mountain may have been taller than Kilimanjaro. Its rim, which averages 7,600′ (2,316 m) elevation, is cloaked in moist montane forest and grassland, hosting elephants, golden-winged and eastern double-collared sunbirds, stonechats, and Jackson's widowbirds. From lodges and campsites on the rim, visitors are driven down to the crater floor for a day-long survey. At 5,600′ (1,700 m) elevation, the crater floor is primarily grassland, with patches of spring-fed marshes, freshwater ponds, a salt lake, and small forests. Harboring 20,000 large animals, it is a virtual Noah's Ark (without giraffes). Great effort has gone into saving the black rhino here, and several dozen are resident. Buffalos, wildebeests, zebras, gazelles, and hartebeests graze the grassland, while elephants roam the wooded areas, and hippos gather in marshes and ponds. Lions, spotted hyenas, and golden and black-backed jackals are easy to find, and servals and cheetahs are sighted rarely. Resident ostriches, crowned cranes, and kori bustards are joined seasonally by migrant flocks of white and Abdim's storks. The conservation area also includes two other voluminous craters, six peaks that top 10,000′ (3,000 m), and the southeastern corner of the vast Serengeti Plains. **Olduvai Gorge,** just north of the road to the Serengeti, has yielded hominid fossils key to the study of human evolution. Here sit a museum and shaded picnic sites. Red-and-yellow barbets join less colorful birds here for crumbs, while cheetahs sometimes roam nearby.

The Serengeti Plains

Serengeti National Park/World Heritage Site (3,646,500 acres/1,476,300 ha) lies between Ngorongoro and Lake Victoria and adjoins Kenya's Masai Mara. Isolated lodges dot its northern, southern, and western sectors, but the tourism center of the park is Seronera, with several lodges and camps, 197 mi (318 km) west of Arusha. To the east and south vast open grasslands are punctuated with occasional kopjes (rocky outcrops), while to the west and north grasslands are interspersed with hills and open woodland and sliced by rivers. Near Seronera, yellow fever trees and palm thickets line the Seronera River and its hippo pools. This is a superb area for seeing predators such as lions, leopards, and cheetahs, along with giraffes, topis, bohor reedbucks, defassa waterbucks, buffalos, and impalas. The kopjes host hyraxes, dwarf mongooses, and red-headed agamas. The open grassland to the east is home to large groups of Thomson's and Grant's gazelles, spotted hyenas, jackals, and such birds as the double-banded courser, yellow-throated sandgrouse, red-capped lark, Fischer's sparrow-lark, and capped wheatear. As part of their famous clockwise migration, more than 1 million wildebeests, accompanied by hundreds of thousands of other herbivores, descend upon the short-grass plains of the southeastern Serengeti at the start of the rainy season around December. After calving in January and February, they scatter over the southern and central plains. By May the rains end, the grass has been reduced to stubble, and the animals begin their long march to dry-season grazing grounds near the permanent waters of the Serengeti's northern woodlands and Kenya's Masai Mara. Reaching these destinations by July or so, they remain until October, when they head back to the southeastern Serengeti. The seasonally saline Ndutu Lake, in southeastern Serengeti, sits in arid thorny acacia country with a lodge nearby. The area's inhabitants include Kirk's dik-diks, giraffes, elephants, lions, pygmy falcons, gray-breasted spurfowls, Fischer's lovebirds, and rufous-tailed weavers.

The West

Lake Victoria, in northwestern Tanzania, is a huge freshwater lake shared with Uganda and Kenya. **Rubondo National Park** (112,900 acres/45,700 ha), on an island in the southwestern corner of the lake, is home to native sitatungas and hippos and introduced chimps, black rhinos, elephants, and roans. **Lake Tanganyika,** in the western rift valley opposite Zaire, is the longest lake in Africa. It is very deep, with its floor 1,000′ (305 m) below sea level, and hosts an extremely rich fish life.

Kigoma, on Lake Tanganyika, is the chief town and port in the west. It receives 37″ (925 mm) of rain, and has average highs of 79–84°F (26–29°C). **Gombe National Park** (12,800 acres/5,200 ha) is also on the lake, 10 mi (16 km) north of Kigoma. Accessible only by boat, it has huts for tourists and a research station. A long-term study of chimpanzees here has habituated them to humans; visitors (with guides) may see them at close range. There are trails in tropical evergreen forest in the valleys where baboons, monkeys, and such West African birds as the blue-breasted kingfisher and double-toothed barbet can be seen.

Mahale Mountains National Park (398,400 acres/161,300 ha), 74 mi (120 km) south of Kigoma on a peninsula in Lake Tanganyika, is a chimpanzee research site, with an airstrip and a seasonal luxury camp. The mountains exceed 8,000′ (2,400 m), draining 75″ (1,875 mm) of yearly rain onto evergreen and montane forest. The wet western slopes are home to 700 chimpanzees, while the miombo woodland of the drier eastern side is inhabited by giraffes, elephants, roans, and lions. **Katavi National Park** (556,500 acres/225,300 ha), 25 mi (40 km) south of Mpanda, is a floodplain with typically southern mammals such as the puku, common reedbuck, sable, and tsessebe, and 400 species of birds, including the gray go-away-bird, red-faced mousebird, and white-winged babbling-starling.

The South

The undervisited southern parks are best seen in the dry season (May through October), when the dirt tracks are passable. **Mikumi National Park** (797,800 acres/323,000 ha), located 180 mi (290 km) west of the coastal city of Dar es Salaam on the main highway to Zambia, has lodging and offers wildlife-viewing drives centered on the floodplain of the Mkata River. This scenic area of grassland, enormous baobabs, miombo woodland, palm thickets, and gallery forests is flanked by mountain ranges. Elephants, giraffes, buffalos, some black rhinos, Lichtenstein's hartebeests, sables, wildebeests, zebras, impalas, lions, leopards, and wild dogs roam the park. Among 370 bird species are the pale-billed hornbill, the racquet-tailed roller, and Dickinson's kestrel. The **Uluguru Mountains,** just east of Mikumi, are not yet protected. On these sharp-toothed peaks, which reach 8,200′ (2,500 m), the montane forests are home to two endemic bird species: a bush-shrike and a sunbird. The vast **Selous Game Reserve/World Heritage Site** (12,350,000 acres/5,000,000 ha) is Africa's largest wildlife sanctuary. It lies south of Mikumi and has airstrips and tracks connecting the lodges and camps. Lions and elephants live throughout Selous. Large numbers of zebras, impalas, and buffalos inhabit the savannas, while sables, greater kudus, and Sharpe's grysboks browse the miombo woodlands. In the northeast the Great Ruaha and Rufiji rivers create a vast inland delta, a maze of seasonal channels flanked by grassy plains, dunes, steep banks, and borassus palm forests. Hippos, crocodiles, and carmine bee-eaters are common. Hunting, encouraged in most of the Selous, is illegal in this sector. **Ruaha National Park** (3,198,700 acres/ 1,295,000 ha) sits 70 mi (112 km) west of the town of Iringa in southwestern Tanzania. An escarpment bisects this refuge, making a neat ecological divide between the Ruaha River valley and the high plateau covered with miombo woodland. The valley sector features spectacular gorges along the Ruaha River, baobabs and euphorbias, flooded grassland, acacia woodland, gallery forests, and graceful isolated hills. Thousands of elephants and many buffalos inhabit the park, along with all the major cats. The superb array of antelopes includes lesser and greater kudus, Lichtenstein's hartebeests, sables, roans, elands, steenboks, and oribis. Among the 370 bird species in the area are the purple-crested turaco, Pel's fishing owl, and the ashy starling. **Uzungwa Forest National Park,** south of Iringa, hosts the Sanje mangabey and montane forest birds with restricted ranges.

The Coast

Dar es Salaam, the capital, gets 42″ (1,050 mm) of annual rain, chiefly between November and May. It is humid, and has average highs of 82–88°F (28–31°C). Tanzania's coastline is a maze of beaches, cliffs, and mangroves, backed by a mosaic of short green forest and savanna. There are fine coral reefs and three large islands offshore. **Mafia Island,** 80 mi (130 km) southeast of Dar es Salaam, is a luxury fishing resort. The surrounding area has been proposed as a marine park; reef fish, spotted dolphins, humpback whales, and green and hawksbill sea turtles are found here. **Zanzibar,** 25 mi (40 km) off the coast, north of Dar es Salaam, is 53 mi (85 km) long. The **Jozani Forest** in the southeast shelters most of the island's remaining Zanzibar red colobus monkeys, blue monkeys, a fine-spotted race of leopard, Zanzibar duikers, sunis, and Fischer's turacos. Tiny, treeless **Latham Island,** 35 mi (56 km) southeast of Zanzibar, has many breeding terns and masked boobies. **Pemba Island,** east of the seaport of Tanga, hosts an endemic white-eye and scops-owl. Its forests have been heavily cut, and only the secondary Ngezi Forest remains standing.

There is a very rich avifauna in the unprotected patches of montane forests of the **Usambara Mountains,** west of Tanga. To the north, in a rain shadow of these wet slopes, lies the reopened **Mkomazi Game Reserve** (247,000 acres/100,000 ha). Adjacent to Tsavo National Park in southern Kenya, Mkomazi's thornbush savannas are home to the gerenuk, lesser kudu, vulturine guineafowl, and golden-breasted starling.

TOGO

For map, see Ghana.

Stretching 340 mi (550 km) from the Gulf of Guinea north to Burkina Faso, Togo averages only 60 mi (100 km) wide; its total area is 21,853 sq mi (56,599 sq km). The south has two wet seasons (April through July, and October and November), while the north has a single wet season, June through September. Lomé, the capital, is on the coast. It gets only 24″ (600 mm) of rain a year due to a cool current. Kpalime, 90 mi (147 km) northwest of Lomé, gets 70″ (1,750 mm) of rain annually. There is some forest around the nearby hill town of Kloto, where the white-crested hornbill, red-billed helmet-shrike, and black-winged oriole occur.

Fazao-Malfakassa National Park (474,200 acres/ 192,000 ha) is located on the Ghana border, 38 mi (61 km) southwest of the town of Sokodé. It features lines of cliffs 1,640′ (500 m) tall, gorges, tree savanna, and hill forest. There is good lodging, but illegal gold mining and poaching are rampant. It has the bongo, sitatunga, lion, golden cat, black colobus, and chimpanzee, as well as many of the mammals found in Togo's best-protected park, **Keran National Park** (404,191 acres/163,640 ha), 280 mi (450 km) north of Lomé. There is lodging at Naboulgou, plus wildlife-viewing vehicles and artificial water holes. The 52″ (1,300 mm) of annual rain supports floodplains on wooded Sudan savanna. Buffalos, hartebeests, kobs, roans, warthogs, waterbucks, reedbucks, and baboons are commonly seen. Less common are giraffes, elephants, topis, leopards, wild dogs, and patas monkeys. Black crowned cranes, secretarybirds, bustards, and ground-hornbills walk the plains, while hippos, crocodiles, and waterbirds line the waterways. **Fosse aux Lions Forest Reserve** (4,075 acres/ 1,650 ha), south of Dapaong in the northwest, has elephant herds, but no lions. **Oti Mandouri Faunal Reserve** (365,165 acres/147,840 ha) is an area of floodplains in the northeast; many hippos occur along the Oti River.

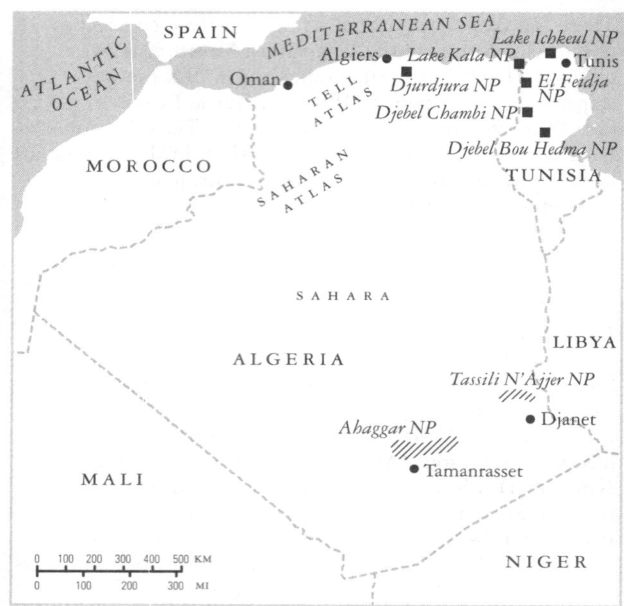

TUNISIA AND ALGERIA

TUNISIA

Located on the Mediterranean Sea, Tunisia (63,378 sq mi/ 164,149 sq km) has a mountainous north with winter rainfall, but it grades into true Sahara desert in the south. Its biological inventory includes 400 species of birds and 75 mammals. Most larger species, such as the ostrich, addax, scimitar-horned oryx, Barbary stag, and various gazelles have been eliminated, but some animals are being reintroduced. Tunisia's wetlands attract many wintering and migrant waterbirds. **Tunis,** the capital, which gets 16″ (400 mm) of annual rain, is flanked by lagoons that draw wintering shelducks, avocets, and flamingos. **Cap Bon,** a peninsula to the east, has impressive spring migrations of raptors, storks, and songbirds headed for Europe. **Zaghouan Mountain,** 30 mi (50 km) south of Tunis, has nesting long-legged buzzards, Barbary falcons, and Moussier's redstarts. **Lake Ichkeul National Park/ Biosphere Reserve/World Heritage Site** (31,100 acres/ 12,600 ha), 30 mi (50 km) northwest of Tunis, is flooded with fresh water in winter but becomes salty in late summer. It attracts many breeders, including the purple swamphen, stilt, pratincole, and great crested grebe. Greylag geese and many ducks and coots winter here. Egyptian vultures and lanner falcons breed on limestone hills to the south. Thickets along the inbound rivers host wild boars, golden jackals, and black-headed bush-shrikes.

El Feidja National Park (6,513 acres/2,637 ha) is located in green mountains near the Algeria border, west of Ain Draham at 3,300′ (1,000 m) elevation. The 32″ (800 mm) of rain (some in the form of snow, which falls an average of ten days each winter) support a rich growth of conifers, cork oak, and other oaks. Among the park's birds are the European cuckoo, nightingale, and green woodpecker.

The tallest peak in Tunisia, at 5,066′ (1,544 m), is in **Djebel Chambi National Park** (16,606 acres/6,723 ha), northwest of the village of Kasserine. Conifer woodlands here are home to the red crossbill and Tristram's warbler.

Djebel Bou Hedma National Park (40,725 acres/16,488 ha), northwest of the seaport town of Gabès, has steppe grasslands, with remnants of gum acacia and juniper in the hills. The park is home to a few dorcas gazelles and aoudads, and small mammals such as gundis, gerbils, and jerboas.

Jerba Island and the southern coast are warmer in winter and cooler in summer than the inland areas, where average highs in summer are 100°F (38°C). **Bibane Lagoon,** near the Libya border, has many waterbirds. **Chott Djerid** is the largest of the usually dry salt lakes west of Gabès. There are hotels in the palm oases in the towns of Tozeur and Nefta, on the shore of Chott Djerid. The surrounding area has few mammals beyond camels, fennecs, and rodents. The bird life is richer, with many desert hawks, falcons, sandgrouse, coursers, larks, wheatears, and warblers in residence.

UGANDA PLATES 11, 33

Uganda (91,134 sq mi/236,037 sq km) has a great mix of habitats among its many lakes and rivers. The Victoria Nile flows out of Lake Victoria, first over a dam that has created Lake Kioga, then over Murchison Falls; in the western rift valley it becomes the Albert Nile. Uplifted and volcanic mountains line Uganda's border with Zaire. Much of the country lies on a plateau at 3,300–4,600′ (1,000–1,400 m) elevation. It is mostly wooded savanna, but there are also papyrus swamps, montane forest, rain forest in the west, and semi-arid acacia savanna in the northeast. Despite the country's position on the equator, the climate is pleasant.

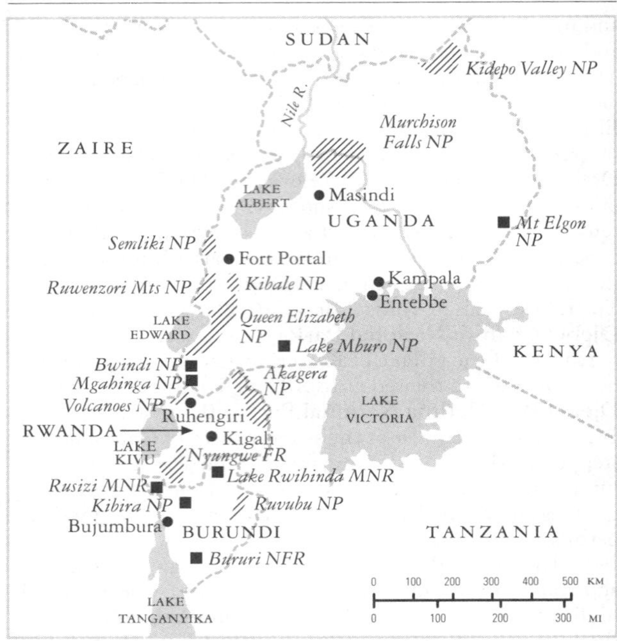

UGANDA, RWANDA, AND BURUNDI

The Southeast

Entebbe is located at an elevation of 3,878′ (1,182 m) on the shores of Lake Victoria, just south of the capital, Kampala. Entebbe's year-round rainfall of 60″ (1,500 mm) peaks in April and May; its average highs range from 77–81°F (25–27°C). **Entebbe Wildlife Education Center** (12,646 acres/5,120 ha) has wild sitatungas, gray parrots, Ross's turacos, and black-and-white casqued hornbills in residence. North of Lake Victoria, **Mount Elgon National Park,** on an isolated peak (shared with Kenya) that rises to 14,178′ (4,321 m), protects montane forest and heathland.

The Northwest

Murchison Falls (Kabalega) National Park (948,500 acres/384,000 ha), about 190 mi (304 km) northwest of Kampala, offers lodging, tracks, and boat trips along the Victoria Nile, which divides the park in two. The boats glide past hippos and crocodiles to the western base of the falls, which drop 130′ (40 m). Most of the land is rolling grassland, with patches of forest at elevations of 1,650′ (500 m) and higher. Among the mammals in residence are the elephant, buffalo, oribi, Jackson's hartebeest, bohor reedbuck, waterbuck, lion, and leopard. The 350 species of birds include the rare shoebill and open-billed stork, African skimmer, red-throated bee-eater, and piapiac. The **Budongo Forest,** west of the town of Masindi, is an eastern remnant of the rain-forest zone of the Congo Basin. Despite heavy logging, it is home to chimpanzees and a rich array of birds.

The Northeast

Kidepo Valley National Park (332,000 acres/134,400 ha) lies on the Sudan border in Karamoja province. It has a lodge, and there is an airstrip at Apoka at 2,950′ (900 m) elevation. The best time to visit is between December and April. Unlike other Ugandan parks, Kidepo is chiefly subdesert, with seasonal rivers lined with borassus palms and some gallery forest. It is enclosed by wild mountains that rise up to 9,022′ (2,750 m), with dry montane forest and grassland. It is the only Ugandan park with greater and lesser kudus, the beisa oryx, Bright's race of Grant's gazelle, Chanler's mountain reedbuck, Kirk's dik-dik, bat-eared fox, cheetah, and ostrich. These are joined by elephants, zebras, buffalos, roans, klipspringers, Rothschild's giraffes, and Jackson's hartebeests, as well as many birds: scissor-tailed kites, pygmy falcons, stone partridges, white-crested turacos, Abyssinian rollers, and Abyssinian ground-hornbills.

The South

Lake Mburo National Park (132,400 acres/53,600 ha), located near the Tanzania border 120 mi (200 km) southwest of Kampala, has several bungalows for visitors. Open undulating grasslands, dotted with acacias, flank papyrus-bordered lakes. Among the park's residents are Uganda's only impalas, along with elands, roans, oribis, reedbucks, buffalos, zebras, spotted hyenas, and leopards. The 400 birds include the rufous-bellied heron and southern red bishop.

Kabale, 240 mi (400 km) southwest of Kampala, is the chief town of Kigezi province, in the southwestern mountains. Average highs are only 72–75°F (22–24°C); nights are cool. **Mgahinga National Park** (6,039 acres/ 2,445 ha), west of Kabale, protects montane forest and bamboo on the north slopes of peaks whose southern slopes are in Rwanda's Volcanoes National Park. There are organized mountain gorilla treks here, and visitors may also see the golden monkey, Ruwenzori turaco, and regal sunbird. **Bwindi National Park,** which protects much of the Impenetrable Forest in western Kigezi, has both lowland and montane forest in a nonvolcanic mountain range. Gorillas, chimpanzees, L'Hoest's monkeys, and otter-shrews are among the mammalian highlights here, while the rich forest avifauna includes great blue and black-billed turacos. Mountain gorilla treks depart from the town of Buhoma, which has a luxury tent camp and lodge nearby.

The West

Ruwenzori Mountains National Park protects a spectacular range of nonvolcanic mountains rising over the western rift valley. Called the Mountains of the Moon, they are a jumble of glacier-flanked peaks, with Mount Stanley the highest at 16,763′ (5,109 m). Guided treks, lasting five to seven days and using huts, leave from Ibanda, northwest of the town of Kasese. Primates and many unusual birds live in the montane forests and in the zone of giant lobelias, giant groundsels, moss, and tree ferns above the tree line. The weather is usually cloudy, misty, and rainy, with somewhat drier periods in January and February and between June and August. **Queen Elizabeth National Park** (488,600 acres/197,800 ha) flanks both Lake George and Lake Edward, 260 mi (420 km) west of the city of Kampala. The lodge at Mweya lies on a peninsula in Lake Edward with spectacular views. Boat trips follow the Kazinga Channel between the two lakes past numerous hippos, pelicans, and kingfishers (among 542 species of birds). Wildlife-viewing drives cross euphorbia-dotted grassland, acacia savanna, and swamps, and pass 80 volcanic craters. There are many elephants, kobs, buffalos, and bushbucks, with fewer lions, leopards, and reedbucks. The lodge at Ishasha in the southern sector of the park is a good base for seeing topis and tree-climbing lions. Nearby Chambura Gorge has healthy populations of chimpanzees in the forest.

Kibale National Park (189,200 acres/76,600 ha) claims the world's highest density of primates and is one of Uganda's most popular tourist draws. Located north of Queen Elizabeth National Park and south of the town of Fort Portal, it receives 60″ (1,500 mm) of annual rain that supports dense forest, swamps, and grassland. Primates include bushbabies, pottos, chimpanzees, gray-cheeked mangabeys, and red colobus, black-and-white colobus, blue, L'Hoest's, and red-tailed monkeys. The reserve is also home to the elephant, the golden cat, the serval, many duikers, and more than 300 bird species. Facilities for visitors have been developed at Kanyanchu on the park's eastern border. **Semliki National Park** lies along the Semliki River, west of Fort Portal on the Zaire border. Its fauna resembles that of the Congo Basin, with the black mangabey, De Brazza's monkey, the giant forest squirrel, and 400 birds, including the white-crested hornbill and long-tailed hawk, in residence.

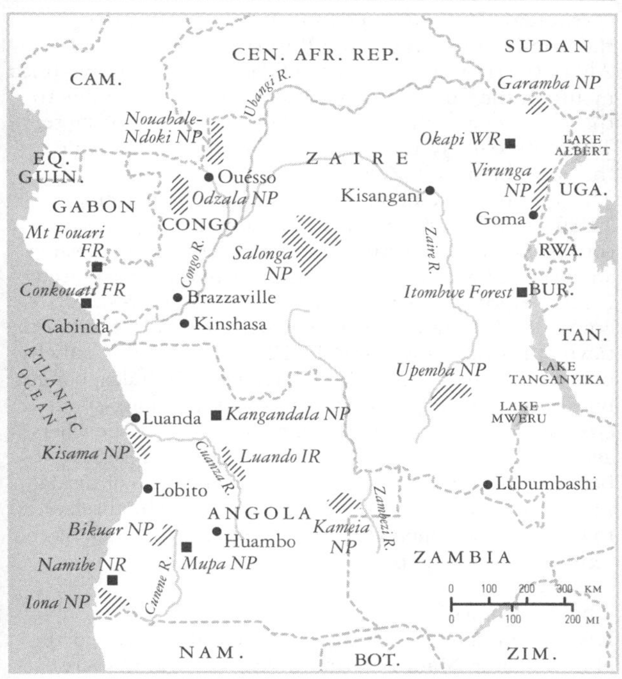

ZAIRE, CONGO, AND ANGOLA

ZAIRE PLATES 8, 11

The second-largest country on the continent (905,063 sq mi/2,344,113 sq km), extending from the Atlantic Ocean east to Uganda, Zaire is the Amazonia of Africa, but unlike the Amazon boasts no luxury cruises or comfortable eco-resorts. Zaire's borders enclose half of Africa's rain forest, and tropical forest covers half the country. The rest consists of wooded and open savanna, as well as some montane habitats along the western rift valley in the far east. Rainfall is heavy in most areas, with high-sun rain in areas well to the north or south of the equator.

The West

Kinshasa, the capital, is located on the Congo River, south of Stanley Pool and northwest of Livingstone Falls. It receives 53″ (1,325 mm) of annual rain, chiefly between October and May. Highs average 81–90°F (27–32°C) year-round. There are no national parks nearby, but the **Bombo-Lumene Game Reserve** (592,800 acres/ 240,000 ha) to the east is a candidate. The mangrove-lined mouth of the Congo is in a moderate-rainfall area due to the effects of a cool, northward-flowing current offshore. The south bank of the river mouth is in Angola, while the north bank is in Zaire.

The interior of the broad and flat Congo Basin averages 1,000–2,000′ (300–600 m) elevation; higher plateau country lies to the north and south. There are vast swamp and upland forests, with savannas where these have been logged. **Salonga National Park** (9,030,310 acres/ 3,656,000 ha), located in an area with no roads south of the town of Boende in west-central Zaire, is accessible only by boat and has no lodging. It has elephants, buffalos, bongos, bushbucks, sitatungas, Congo peacocks, and long-snouted crocodiles. The park is home to many bushmeat poachers and has virtually no visitors at this time. The forests between the Yekokora and Lomako rivers south of Lisala, in the northwest, shelter one of the closest animal relatives to humans, the bonobo (pygmy chimpanzee), which has no reserve anywhere to protect it.

The Northeast

Kisangani is a major port on the Congo River just north of the equator. **Maiko National Park** (2,675,000 acres/ 1,083,000 ha) lies in rain forest along the Maiko River about 150 mi (244 km) southeast of Kisangani, but it lacks access and facilities. It was created for the okapi and the Congo peacock, and also has Grauer's race of gorilla, the elephant, and the buffalo. The recently protected **Okapi Wildlife Reserve** is located at Epulu in the Ituri Forest, in the northeastern corner of the rain-forest zone. It is 264 mi (440 km) northeast of Kisangani on the road to the city of Bunia (west of Lake Albert). The tall forests here, which are home to Pygmy villages, have okapis, bongos, Bates's pygmy antelopes, elephants, chimpanzees, and the very local golden-naped and yellow-legged weavers.

Garamba National Park/World Heritage Site (1,215,200 acres/492,000 ha) is located in the northeast on the Sudan border. While it has some evergreen forest and gallery forest, it is a savanna park, with tall grassland and papyrus swamps. It is on the Nile-Congo divide at elevations that reach 3,500′ (1,060 m). This area is best visited between November and March, in the dry season. Valiant efforts are saving the last of the wild northern race of white rhinoceros. The rich mammal life here includes the chimpanzee, elephant, buffalo, giraffe, hippo, Derby eland, Jackson's hartebeest, kob, waterbuck, and roan. Predators include the lion, leopard, wild dog, golden cat, serval, five mongooses, and two otters.

The Highlands
Zaire's eastern border has a spectacular mix of rift valley lakes, high mountains, and a mosaic of wet forests and savannas. There are airports at the cities of Goma and Bukavu on Lake Kivu. **Virunga National Park/World Heritage Site** (1,951,300 acres/790,000 ha), one of Africa's best reserves, is an enormous park with a diverse mix of landscapes and wildlife. Here we discuss the highlights northward from Lake Kivu to Mount Hoyo. Just north of Goma is the recently active 11,400′ (3,475-m) Nyiragongo volcano. Visitors to this area have many opportunities to see primates, including the Djomba and Rumangabo groups of mountain gorillas on the volcanoes, which can be seen on an organized tour, and chimpanzees at a chimpanzee sanctuary near a lodge at Tongo, west of the town of Rutshuru. Golden, spot-nosed, blue, and red and black-and-white colobus monkeys may also be spotted. The Rwindi and Vitshumbi sector of the park, on the southern side of Lake Edward, is in a rain shadow, accumulating only 20″ (500 mm) annually. Its grasslands and lakeshores are home to abundant wildlife—elephants, buffalos, kobs, topis, waterbucks, lions, and black-backed jackals. The lakeshore has many hippos, yellow-billed storks, hammerkops, and pelicans. The park also incorporates the western flank of the snow-capped **Ruwenzori Mountains,** which get 120″ (3,000 mm) of yearly rain. Hikers need guides and must bring food to cook in primitive huts. The northern end of the park encompasses the slopes of Mount Hoyo, which are dotted with Pygmy villages. Among the area's sights are its waterfalls and large forest hornbills.
Kahuzi-Biega National Park/World Heritage Site (1,482,000 acres/600,000 ha), west of Goma, is home to eastern lowland gorillas, which are larger than mountain gorillas, with shorter hair and longer arms. Gorilla treks leave from Tshivanga, 20 mi (31 km) northwest of the town of Bukavu. This park has montane forest, bamboo thickets, and alpine heathland culminating on Mount Kahuzi at 10,853′ (3,308 m). The western sector near Irangi (2,600′/800 m elevation) has lowland forest that gets 76″ (1,900 mm) of annual rain, chiefly between September and May. Other wildlife includes the owl-faced monkey, both

black-and-white and red colobus monkeys, duikers, chimpanzees, and forest birds, including the rare African green broadbill. The unprotected **Itombwe Forest,** west of the town of Uvira, is opposite Burundi, overlooking the northern end of Lake Tanganyika. There are also lowland and montane forests south of Uvira on Mount Nyombe and Mount Mohi, which reaches 11,400′ (3,475 m). Gorillas and many endemic animals live in this isolated range.

The Southeast

Lubumbashi, the chief city in the south, sits at an elevation of 4,035′ (1,230 m) on a plateau of rolling grassland and wet miombo woodland. There is a long dry season between May and October; average highs reach only 79°F (26°C) in June at low sun. There are two national parks in the southeast where zebras, elands, roans, sables, leopards, and cheetahs live. **Kundelungu National Park** (1,877,200 acres/760,000 ha) is 93 mi (150 km) north of Lubumbashi at 3,900–5,600′ (1,200–1,700 m) elevation. Its western border is a long escarpment of cliffs over which the Lofoi Falls drop 1,122′ (342 m), one of the largest such drops in Africa. The park has the main Zaire population of the greater kudu, the klipspringer, and the wattled crane. **Upemba National Park** (2,897,300 acres/1,173,000 ha), 250 mi (400 km) northwest of Lubumbashi on the eastern bank of the Congo River, encompasses lakes, marshes, and acacia savanna flanked by plateau with miombo woodland. Formerly a black rhino stronghold, it is now home to elephants, hippos, buffalos, waterbucks, Lichtenstein's hartebeests, lions, spotted hyenas, wild dogs, six primates, and two crocodiles. Robert's lechwes live here and near Lake Mweru, east of Upemba on the Zambia border. Pukus roam the **Luama Valley Reserve** (839,800 acres/340,000 ha), northwest of the port of Kalemie on Lake Tanganyika.

ZAMBIA PLATES 32, 45

Located on the central African plateau, most of this country is above 3,300′ (1,000 m) elevation. Its total area is 290,585 sq mi (752,615 sq km). The natural vegetation is chiefly miombo woodland, with drier mopane woodland along the lower elevations of the Zambezi and Luangwa rivers. There are extensive seasonal marshes in the floodplains, several lakes, and small areas of evergreen and montane forests. There are three seasons: cool and dry, between May and August; hot and dry, September and October; and hot and wet, from November through April.

ZAMBIA AND MALAWI

Central

Lusaka, the capital, receives 33″ (825 mm) of annual rain and enjoys average highs of 73°F (23°C) in June and 88°F (31°C) in October. **Lower Zambezi National Park** (1,022,600 acres/414,000 ha), east of Lusaka, lies along the northern bank of the Zambezi between Kariba Dam and the Mozambique border. Canoe trips are offered (with camping ashore) that take visitors past elephants and hippos.

Lochinvar National Park (101,300 acres/41,000 ha), 155 mi (250 km) southwest of Lusaka on the southern bank of the Kafue River, has a lodge. Dirt tracks run through grassland dotted with euphorbia, termite mounds, and trees. The floodplains reach maximum water levels in May and dry up by November. There are 35,000 Kafue lechwes here, along with zebras, elands, blue wildebeests, impalas, oribis, greater kudus, and hippos. More than 400 birds have been recorded, including crowned and wattled cranes, the slaty egret, and Denham's bustard.

Blue Lagoon National Park (111,200 acres/45,000 ha), opposite Lochinvar on the north side of the Zambezi River 85 mi (135 km) west of Lusaka, lacks lodging at this writing, but has a causeway into the flats where 100,000 Kafue lechwes live, as well as wild dogs, roans, sables, buffalos, and the local Chaplin's barbet.

To the west, huge **Kafue National Park** (8,002,800 acres/ 3,240,000 ha) has several lodges and an airstrip. It is covered with miombo and mopane woodland and teak forest, and has clay-based floodplains in the north at Busanga Swamp. Much of the park is open only from July through December. It has a few Kafue lechwes and sitatungas, and many buffalos, hippos, waterbucks, pukus, reedbucks, impalas, and Lichtenstein's hartebeests. In addition there are lions, leopards, a few cheetahs, sables, roans, elephants, zebras, and black rhinos. Yellow baboons live in the north, and chacma baboons in the south. Remote **West Lunga National Park** (415,900 acres/ 168,400 ha), northwest of Kafue, requires camping and four-wheel-drive vehicles. It has dry evergreen forest, elephants, and a variety of antelopes and carnivores.

The Southwest

Victoria Falls is the centerpiece of **Mosi-Oa-Tunya National Park** (16,300 acres/6,600 ha), on the north bank of the Zambezi River near the city of Livingstone. The river drops 355′ (108 m) in a long sheet of water. A wide, lazy river above the falls, the Zambezi is a narrow raging torrent in the zigzag of canyons below. The maximum flow is in March and April, when the rising mist all but obscures the view. Birds of the area include the Taita falcon, bat hawk, white-collared pratincole, mocking cliff chat, and various swifts. **Sioma-Ngwezi National Park** (1,303,200 acres/527,600 ha) occupies the southwestern corner of Zambia on the Namibia border, west of the Zambezi. It is relatively arid Kalahari sandveld, with mopane and teak woodland. There are no lodges, and four-wheel-drive is a must. The park is home to one of Zambia's two giraffe populations, elephants, steenboks, sables, and dry-country birds such as Bradfield's hornbill and Burchell's starling. **Liuwa Plain National Park** (904,000 acres/366,000 ha), also undeveloped, is located near the Angola border. There are flat grassy plains with 20,000 blue wildebeests, plus red lechwes, tsessebes, zebras, lions, cheetahs, and wattled cranes.

The Luangwa Valley

In eastern Zambia, four national parks line the meandering Luangwa River, which follows the rift valley to the southwest before joining the Zambezi. The chief park is **South Luangwa National Park** (2,235,400 acres/ 905,000 ha); an hour by air from Lusaka, it is one of Africa's best in terms of wildlife abundance and variety of lodges and camps. Night wildlife-viewing drives are encouraged. It has wooded savanna beyond the ponds, seasonal floodplains, and gallery forests that line the river. The Thornicroft race of giraffe, the endangered black rhino, and large herds of elephants, zebras, buffalos, and impalas are features. Hippos, crocodiles, common waterbucks, many waterbirds, carmine bee-eaters, and Nile monitors reside along the river. The wooded areas host the greater kudu, puku, roan, eland, and Lichtenstein's hartebeest. There are good numbers of lions, leopards, and side-striped jackals. The local Lilian's lovebird is but one of 400 known species of birds. **North Luangwa National Park** (1,145,100 acres/463,600 ha), just to the north, is a wilderness trail area with no vehicle access. Hikers overnight in camps among wildlife similar to that in the southern park, with the addition of Cookson's race of wildebeest, but no giraffes. The undeveloped **Luambe National Park** (62,700 acres/25,400 ha), east of the river, is the main stronghold of Cookson's wildebeest and also has many elephants. **Lukusuzi National Park** (671,800 acres/ 272,000 ha), on a plateau east of the rift valley escarpment, has granite outcrops with klipspringers, miombo woodland with sables, and many mammals around its grassy floodplains. It lacks lodging and is visited in day trips from South Luangwa National Park.

The Northeast

Nyika National Park (19,760 acres/8,000 ha) is adjacent to the much larger Malawian park of the same name. Its high plateau grassland, steep cliffs, and relict patches of evergreen montane woodland are home to many small mammals and birds not found elsewhere in Zambia. Elevations reach 7,300′ (2,225 m). Between North Luangwa National Park and Lake Bangweulu, **Isangano National Park** (207,500 acres/84,000 ha) protects some of the flooded marshlands east of the lake, the main area for the highly local black lechwe. The rich bird life includes the shoebill, wattled crane, and pygmy-goose. There are no lodges or roads, so most visitation is by day aircraft from South Luangwa and by boat. Farther south, **Lavushi Manda National Park** (370,500 acres/150,000 ha), southwest of the town of Mpika, is a scenic park with roads reaching rugged hills, high cliffs, palm canyons, and riverine habitats. **Kasanka National Park** (96,300 acres/39,000 ha), to the west, requires four-wheel-drive vehicles and camping to visit. Its extensive swamp forest and wetlands are home to sitatungas, pukus, and hippos.

Sumbu (Nsumbu) National Park (498,900 acres/ 202,000 ha) is on the southwestern corner of Lake Tanganyika, the second-largest lake in Africa. The park has several lodges and an airstrip, as well as 60 mi (100 km) of shoreline, including a few beaches. Inland there are thickets in the valleys and rolling grassland on the plateau, where animals are easy to see. Elephants, buffalos, pukus, and bushbucks are common, while zebras, Lichtenstein's hartebeests, roans, sables, elands, and Sharpe's grysboks occur in lesser numbers. The

Tanganyika water cobra can be seen from jetties. **Mweru-Wantipa National Park** (774,100 acres/313,400 ha), just to the west, has vast marshes and grasslands with sitatungas, pukus, and shoebills, but no facilities. There are waterfalls along the Kalugwishi River and evergreen forest in **Lusenga Plain National Park** (217,400 acres/ 88,000 ha), east of Lake Mweru, where elephants, sables, elands, and leopards reside.

ZIMBABWE AND MOZAMBIQUE

ZIMBABWE PLATES 14, 32

Another plateau country mostly above 3,900′ (1,200 m) elevation, Zimbabwe has a total area of 150,820 sq mi (390,623 sq km). The Great Dyke, a broad, mineral-rich ridge 400 mi (650 km) long, runs through the center of the country on a southeast–northwest diagonal. The land slopes downward to the Zambezi Valley in the north and to the Sabi and Limpopo valleys in the south. The natural vegetation is mostly miombo woodland, along with drier mopane woodland at lower elevations, and montane forest, grassland, and heath in the eastern highlands. The climate is quite pleasant, except in the lowlands late in the dry season, when it is very hot. The high-sun rains fall from November through March. The low river valleys get an annual rainfall of 16–24″ (400–600 mm), the plateau 30–40″ (750–1,000 mm), and the eastern highlands 60–80″ (1,500–2,000 mm).

The Plateau

Harare, the capital, is at an altitude of 4,833′ (1,473 m). Between Harare and the southwestern city of Bulawayo there are a number of recreational and animal parks around artificial reservoirs; many birds and reintroduced mammals can be seen at such lakes as **McIlwaine, Ngezi, Sebakwe,** and **Kyle,** all of which are designated recreation areas, and **Mushandike,** which is a sanctuary. The **Great Zimbabwe National Monument/World Heritage Site** (1,843 acres/ 746 ha) is 181 mi (292 km) south of Harare near Masvingo. Greater kudus and steenboks graze near the walled ruins of a city-state that controlled trade over a vast area from Botswana to Mozambique, reaching its height from A.D. 1000 to 1400. **Matobo National Park** (105,000 acres/ 42,500 ha) lies 20 mi (32 km) south of Bulawayo in the Matobo Hills, which have many kopjes with giant boulders, Bushman paintings, and deep valleys. Tracks lead through wooded slopes, grassy vleis, and swamps. Native mammals include the impala, greater kudu, bushbuck, sable, klipspringer, leopard, and hyrax. The white rhino and other antelopes have been reintroduced. More than 300 species of birds are known, and many pairs of Verreaux's eagles are resident.

The East

Green highlands mark the Mozambique border. **Nyanga (Inyanga) National Park** (81,500 acres/33,000 ha) lies 125 mi (200 km) east of Harare. Very scenic, the park includes Mount Nyangani, the highest point in Zimbabwe at 8,517′ (2,596 m), and Mtarazi Falls, which drop 820′ (250 m). Habitats include montane woodland with some cedar and protea, grassland, and cliffs. There are few mammals, but birds of note include the rare wattled crane, crowned eagle, Gurney's sugarbird, and blue swallow. **Vumba Botanical Reserve** (500 acres/200 ha), 17 mi (28 km) southeast of the town of Mutare, is near many fine country hotels. The gardens and montane forest are home to the silvery-cheeked hornbill, rare bush-shrikes, and sunbirds. **Chimanimani National Park** (42,200 acres/ 17,100 ha) is 47 mi (75 km) south of Mutare. While there is lodging near the park, it has no roads, only hiking trails, which wind about rugged peaks, including Mount Binga at about 8,000′ (2,400 m), deep gorges, and waterfalls. There are many proteas, ferns, and orchids; the park should be enlarged to include nearby forests. Residents include elands, bushbucks, duikers, and klipspringers, and such highland birds as the malachite sunbird, chirinda apalis, and Cape robin-chat. **Gonarezou National Park** (1,248,100 acres/505,300 ha) is located in the southeastern corner of Zimbabwe, just north of Kruger National Park in South Africa's Transvaal Province. Visits are best made between May and October in the dry season. Gonarezhou features great walls of cliffs, three major river valleys with hippos and crocodiles, and extensive savanna woodland. It is the Zimbabwe stronghold for the nyala, the suni, and Lichtenstein's hartebeest. Elephants and small antelopes such as Sharpe's grysbok and the oribi live here. Fruit trees attract parrots, trumpeter hornbills, African green pigeons, purple-crested turacos, barbets, and starlings.

The Northwest

Mana Pools National Park/World Heritage Site (542,400 acres/219,600 ha) lies at an elevation of 1,650′ (500 m) on the eastward-flowing Zambezi River. Several very small lodges and camps are open between April and October. There are tall gallery forests, ponds, and grassland along the river, beginning about 60 mi (100 km) downstream from Kariba Dam, and thick mopane woodland on the escarpment above. The park has many elephants, buffalos, zebras, and hippos, but few black rhinos survive. Such antelopes as the nyala, eland, puku, waterbuck, and impala coexist with lions, leopards, and spotted hyenas. The 380 birds include the Nyasa lovebird and Livingstone's flycatcher. **Lake Kariba** on the Zambezi, up to 25 mi (40 km) wide at some points, was the scene of Operation Noah, which rescued animals trapped when the closing of Kariba Dam first filled the lake with water. There are lodges on the lake's southern side at Fothergill and Spurwing islands, and at Bumi Hills. These lodges flank **Matusadona National Park** (347,500 acres/140,700 ha), which has grassy flats by the lake and woodlands in the hills. The shores have good numbers of elephants, buffalos, waterbucks, hippos, and impalas, plus a rich array of birds, such as cormorants, herons, fish-eagles, Dickinson's kestrels, jacanas, and white-crowned lapwings. **Chizarira National Park** (471,800 acres/191,000 ha), in a hilly wilderness area to the southwest of Matusadona, is a sanctuary for black rhinos, elephants, roans, sables, tsessebes, and lions.

The Far West

Hwange National Park (3,618,800 acres/1,465,100 ha), southeast of Victoria Falls on the Botswana border, gets about 26″ (650 mm) of annual rain. It is most pleasant between May and August but has the largest concentration of animals in the very hot months of September and October, before the rains. There are many lodges and camps, a jet airstrip, and 280 mi (450 km) of tracks for animal drives. The 62 water holes are the focal points for visitors and wildlife. **Nyamandhlovu Pan,** 6 mi (10 km) from the main camp, has a shaded viewing platform from which visitors observe the procession of mammals and birds coming to drink. The northern half of the park is slightly wet woodland, while the south has more open and drier grassland. Recent counts tallied 15,000 elephants, 15,000 buffalos, 6,000 impalas, 5,000 greater kudus, and 2,000 sables. Both black and white rhinos have been reintroduced with good protection. Giraffes, blue wildebeests, elands, roans, tsessebes, lions, leopards, wild dogs, two hyenas, two jackals, and bat-eared foxes also occur. The more than 400 birds include the ostrich, dark chanting-goshawk, kori bustard, and yellow-billed hornbill.

At **Kazuma Pan National Park** (77,300 acres/31,300 ha), southwest of Victoria Falls, gemsboks visit the flat open grassland, where cheetahs, oribis, and tsessebes also live.

Zambezi National Park (139,100 acres/56,300 ha) protects the south bank of the river west of the falls. Hippos and crocodiles live in the river and can be seen from cruise boats. The mopane woodland and grassland inland are home to many sables, plus roans, greater kudus, giraffes, elephants, lions, and leopards. The town of Victoria Falls has a fine airport and an excellent range of lodgings. At **Victoria Falls National Park** (4,900 acres/2,000 ha), rising clouds of spray create a wonderful mist forest of ebony, mahogany, and fig trees on a carpet of ferns and mosses. This is home to bushbucks, Livingstone's green turacos, trumpeter hornbills, Heuglin's robins, and African paradise-flycatchers.

PART II
Color Plates

African Habitats and Geography

Plates 1–50 depict 50 African landforms and habitats. General habitat types are reflected in the headings at the top of each page. The habitats and areas pictured are described in detail in Part I. The "Biogeography of Africa" essay surveys landforms and habitat types. Within the "Countries and Reserves" section, the writeups for individual African countries provide information about specific pictured areas. In both essays, cross-references to related plate numbers are provided. The caption for each photograph provides the page number in Part I where that habitat type or area is discussed.

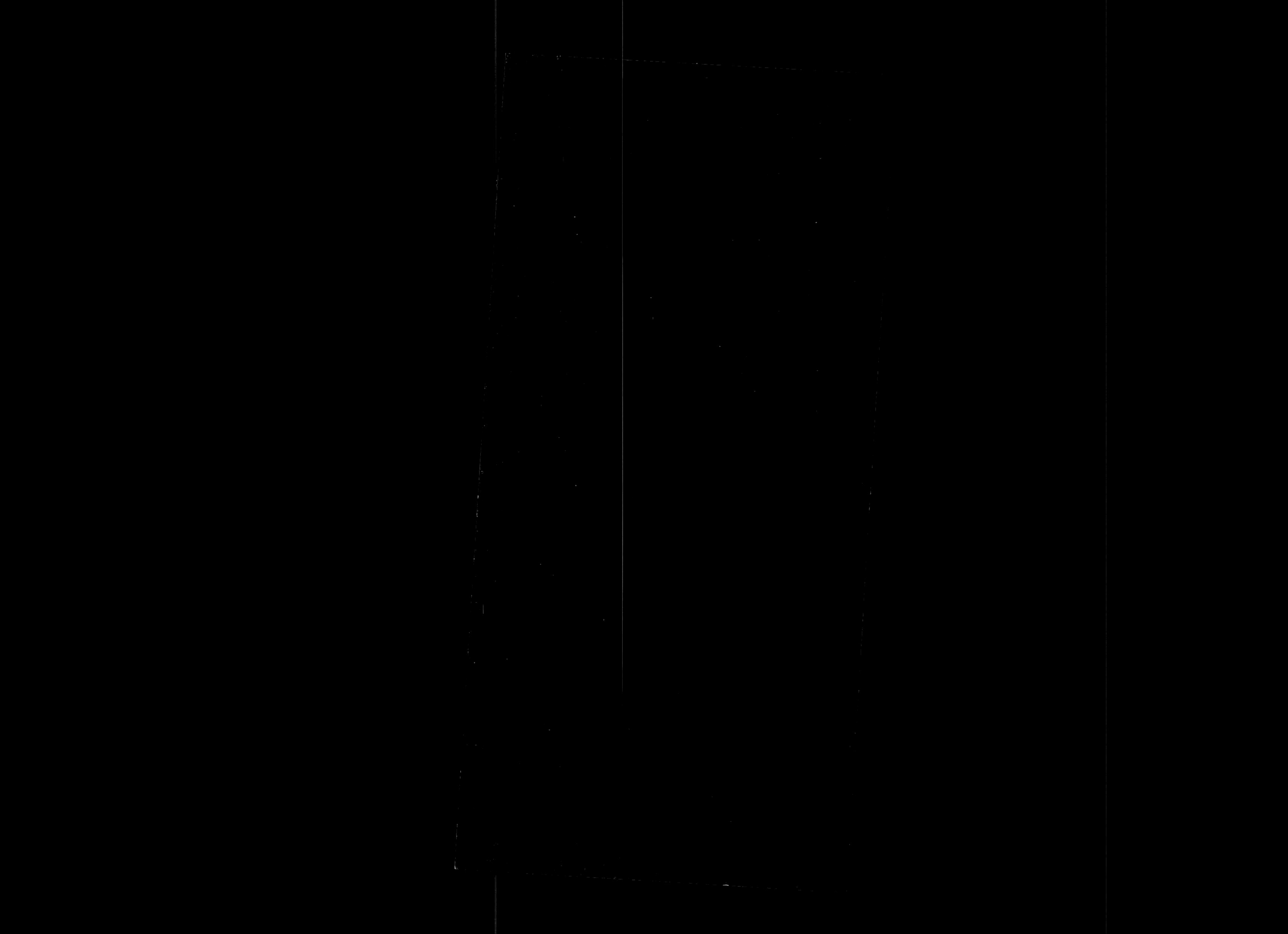

1 Caldera, Ngorongoro Crater, Tanzania, *pp. 29, 31, 131*

3 High Atlas Mountains, Morocco, *pp. 29, 96*

5 Central plateau, Ethiopia, *pp. 29, 65*

6 Bale Mountains, Ethiopia, *pp. 29, 68*

Amboseli National Park, Kenya, *pp. 29, 81, 129*

8 Volcanic caldera lake, Virunga Mountains, Rwanda-Zaire border, *pp. 29, 31, 106, 143*

9 Mount Kenya, Kenya, *pp. 29, 77*

10 Montane forest with podocarpus, Mount Kenya, Kenya, *pp. 39, 77*

11 High-elevation montane forest, Ruwenzori Mountains, Uganda-Zaire border, *pp. 39, 140, 143*

12 Tropical lowland rain forest, Mount Cameroon, Cameroon, *pp.* 35, 54

13 Tropical lowland rain forest, eastern Madagascar

14 Miombo woodland, Zimbabwe, *pp. 36, 148*

15 Mopane woodland, Botswana, *pp. 36, 47*

16 Wooded savanna in wet season, Tarangire National Park, Tanzania, *pp. 36, 130*

17 Baobabs and acacias in savanna, dry season, Tarangire National Park, Tanzania, *pp. 36, 130*

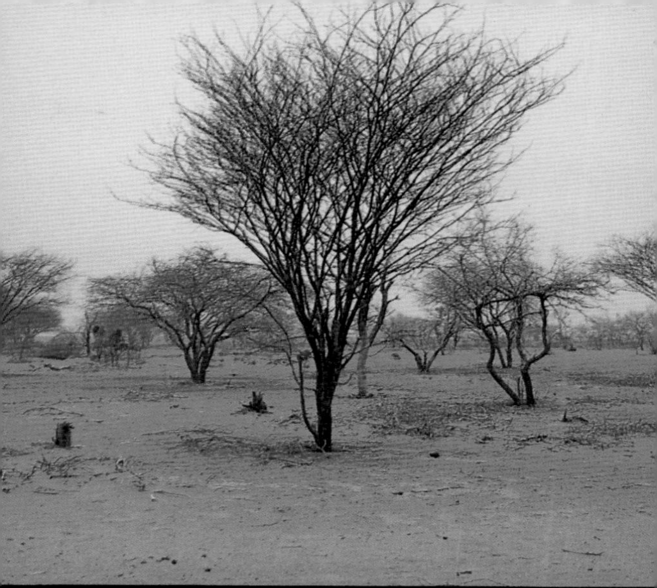

18 Sudan savanna (Sahel) in dry season, Niger, *pp. 36, 101*

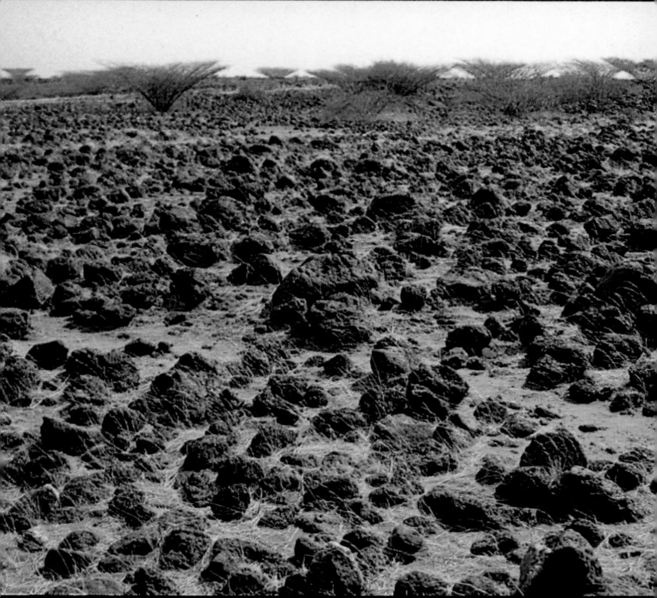

19 Semi-arid savanna with volcanic boulders, northern

20 Open grassland, Masai Mara National Reserve, Kenya, *pp. 36, 79*

21 Kopjes in grassy savanna, Serengeti National Park, Tanzania, *pp. 36, 132*

22 Sahara with date palm, southern Algeria, *pp. 34, 38, 43*

23 Saharan sand dunes, southern Morocco, *pp. 34, 38, 96*

24 Namib Desert, Skeleton Coast, northwestern Namibia, *pp. 30, 34, 38, 101*

25 Namib Desert with African Elephants, Namibia, *pp. 34, 38, 101*

26 Subdesert with succulent plants, western Cape Province, South Africa, *pp. 37, 117*

i Desert, Bots

28 Rocky promontory, Cape of Good Hope, South Africa, *pp. 30, 117*

29 Mangroves on tidal estuary, Gambia, *pp. 30, 39, 69*

30 Granitic boulders and sand beach, Seychelles, *pp. 32, 111*

31 Edge of macchia scrub, Cape of Good Hope, South Africa, *pp. 30, 38, 117*

32 Victoria Falls on Zambezi River, at Zimbabwe-Zambia border, *pp. 31, 146, 151*

33 Murchison Falls on Nile River, northwestern Uganda, *pp. 31, 138*

34 Freshwater inlet of Lake Manyara, Tanzania, *pp. 31, 130*

35 Lake Malawi National Park, Malawi, *pp. 31, 88*

36 Shallow soda lake with flamingos, Ngorongoro

37 Lake Nakuru, Kenya, *pp. 31, 79*

38 Lake Shalla, Ethiopia, *pp. 31, 67*

39 Etosha Pan, with water, Namibia, *pp. 31, 99*

40 Etosha Pan, without water, Namibia, *pp. 31, 99*

41 Niger River near Niger-Mali border, *pp. 31, 90, 101*

42 Nile River near Aswan, Egypt, *pp. 31, 63*

43 Riverbed at low water level, Tarangire National Park, Tanzania, *pp. 31, 130*

44 River at medium water level, Masai Mara National Reserve, Kenya, *pp. 31, 79*

45 Seasonal marsh, South Luangwa National Park, Zambia, *pp. 31, 146*

46 Permanent marsh, Okavango Delta, Botswana, *pp. 31, 49*

47 Muddy water hole, Etosha National Park, Namibia, *pp. 32, 99*

48 Deep water hole, Chobe National Park, Botswana

49 Spring-fed shallow water hole, Ngorongoro Crater, Tanzania, *pp. 32, 131*

50 Small water hole, part of river in wet season, Serengeti National Park, Tanzania, *pp. 32, 132*

Key to the Color Plates of Animal Species

The color plates on the following pages are divided into 46 groups that reflect the large taxonomic groupings to which the animals belong: 18 for mammals, 23 for birds, and 5 for reptiles and insects.

Silhouettes and Thumb Tabs

To make it easy to locate a group, a silhouette drawing of a representative animal from each group has been inset as a thumb tab on the color plate pages. A thumb tab appears on all left-hand and a few right-hand pages.

Index of Plate Numbers

The pages that follow present the large taxonomic groups and their silhouette drawings, which are repeated in the thumb tabs. Some large groups are followed by a listing of animals within that category. For all animals, a third column gives the numbers of the color plates on which they are pictured.

Captions

The caption under each photograph gives the common name of the animal; if the animal is of a particular race (subspecies), the caption gives the name of the race or the region where the animal lives. Animals are adult males, or adults when the sexes are alike, unless otherwise noted. Sometimes the caption identifies the animal pictured as male (♂) or female (♀). Photographs known or presumed to have been taken in captivity have been used for animals that are difficult to photograph in the wild; these photographs are indicated with the abbreviation "cap."

Each caption gives the page number for the text section in which the animal is described; likewise, color plate numbers are given at the headings of the accounts in the text.

Silhouette	Group	Plate Numbers
	MAMMALS	
	Swine	51–54
	Hippopotamuses	55–58
	Giraffes	
	Okapi	59
	Giraffe	60–62
	Antelopes and Bovids	
	Duikers	63–67
	Dwarf Antelopes	68–74
	Gazelles	75–80
	Reedbucks and Kob	81–89
	Rhebok	90
	Horse Antelopes	91–97
	Hartebeests and Wildebeests	98–108
	Impala	109–110
	Spiral-horned Antelopes	111–120
	African Buffalo	121–123
	Aoudad	124

Silhouette	Group	Plate Numbers
	Rhinoceroses	125–128
	Zebras and Asses	129–134
	Elephant	135–138
	Hyraxes	139–141
	Aardvark	142

Silhouette	Group	Plate Numbers
	Pangolin	143
	Seals	
	Cape Fur Seal	144
	Carnivores	
	Genets and Civets	145–149
	Mongooses	150–157
	Hyenas	158–161
	Cats	162–174
	Foxes, Jackals, and Dogs	175–182
	Weasels	183–186
	Primates	
	Bushbabies	187–189
	Lemurs	190–198
	Monkeys and Baboons	
	Guenons	199–208
	Mangabeys	209–211
	Baboons	212–220
	Colobus Monkeys	221–222
	Apes	223–230

Silhouette	Group	Plate Numbers
	**Insectivores**	
	Hedgehog	231
	Tenrec	232
	Elephant-Shrews	233–234
	Bats	235–238
	Hares	239–240
	**Rodents**	
	Squirrels	241–244
	Springhare	245
	Porcupine	246
	Rats and Mice	247–250

Silhouette	Group	Plate Numbers
	BIRDS	
	Ostrich	251–254
	Penguin	255–256
	Grebe	257–258
	Albatross	259

Silhouette	Group	Plate Numbers
	**Pelicans and Allies**	
	Tropicbird	260
	Pelicans	261–262
	Gannet	263
	Cormorants	264–266
	Darter	267
	Frigatebird	268
	**Storks and Allies**	
	Herons	269–274, 279
	Egrets	275–278
	Hammerkop	280
	Shoebill	281
	Storks	282–288
	Ibises and Spoonbills	289–292
	Flamingos	293–296
	**Waterfowl**	
	Ducks and Geese	297–304

Silhouette	Group	Plate Numbers
	Hawks and Allies	
	Kites	305–307
	Eagles	308, 317–318, 323–329
	Vultures	309–316
	Bateleur	319
	Chanting-Goshawk	320
	Buzzards	321–322
	Secretarybird	330
	Falcons	331, 334
	Kestrels	332–333
	Partridges and Allies	
	Spurfowl	335–337
	Francolins	338–340
	Guineafowl	341–342
	Cranes and Allies	
	Cranes	343–346
	Crake	347
	Swamphen	348
	Coot	349
	Bustards	350–354

Silhouette	Group	Plate Numbers
	**Gulls and Allies**	
	Jacana	355
	Crabplover	356
	Stilt	357
	Avocet	358
	Thick-knee	359
	Crocodilebird	360
	Coursers	361–362
	Lapwings	363–365
	Plovers	366–367
	Ruff	368
	Gulls	369–370
	Terns	371–374
	Skimmer	375–376
	Sandgrouse	377–379
	Pigeons and Doves	380–386
	**Parrots**	
	Parrots	387–388
	Lovebirds	389

Silhouette	Group	Plate Numbers
	Turacos and Cuckoos	
	Turacos	390, 395–398
	Plantain-eater	391
	Go-away-birds	392–394
	Cuckoos	399–400
	Coucals	401–402
	Owls	403–406
	Nightjars	407–408
	Swift	409

lhouette	Group	Plate Numbers
	Mousebirds	410–411
	Trogon	412
	Kingfishers and Allies	
	Kingfishers	413–418
	Bee-eaters	419–426
	Rollers	427–430
	Hoopoe	431
	Scimitarbill	432
	Wood-Hoopoe	433
	Hornbills	434–442
	Barbets and Woodpeckers	
	Barbets	443–448
	Honeyguide	449
	Woodpecker	450

Silhouette	Group	Plate Numbers
	**Songbirds**	
	Larks	451–452
	Swallows	453–454
	Wagtails	455–456
	Pipits	457, 460
	Longclaws	458–459
	Bulbuls	461–462
	Brubru	463
	Tchagra	464
	Bush-shrikes	465, 468
	Boubous	466–467
	Shrikes	469–470
	Fiscal Shrikes	471–473
	Helmet-shrikes	474–475
	Vanga	476
	Scrub-Robin	477
	Robin-Chat	478
	Chats	479–480
	Wheatear	481
	Thrushes	482–483
	Babbler	484
	Cisticola	485
	Prinia	486
	Silverbird	487
	Flycatchers	488–489, 491
	Batis	490
	Paradise-Flycatchers	492–493
	Penduline-tit	494
	Sunbirds	495–502
	Sugarbird	503
	White-eye	504

Group	Plate Numbers
Bunting	505
Canaries	506–508
Finch	509
Firefinch	510
Cordon-bleu	511
Grenadier	512
Waxbills	513–514
Whydahs	515–517
Buffalo-Weavers	518–519
Weavers	520–525, 531
Quelea	526
Fody	527
Bishop	528
Widowbird	529
Sparrow-Weaver	530
Sparrows	532–533
Starlings	534–542
Oxpeckers	543–544
Oriole	545
Drongo	546
Piapiac	547
Crows	548–549
Raven	550

Silhouette	Group	Plate Numbers
	REPTILES	
	Turtles	551–556
	Crocodiles	557–560
	Lizards	561–566
	Snakes	567–575

Silhouette	Group	Plate Numbers
	INSECTS	
	Dung Beetle	576
	Termite	577

African Mammals

Plates 51–250 depict 161 species of African mammals, arranged in their respective taxonomic groupings, which are reflected in the headings at the top of each page and in the thumb-tab silhouettes at mid-page. Photographs of the animals appear in the same sequence as the text accounts in Part III; the caption for each photograph provides the page number of the corresponding text account. For help in finding photographs of particular animals, please consult the Key to the Color Plates of Animal Species, which follows the African Habitats and Geography plates.

51 Bush Pig, *p. 447*

52 Giant Forest Hogs, *p. 448*

53 Warthog ♂, *p. 449*

55 Common Hippopotamus, *p. 450*

57 Common Hippopotamuses in river, *p. 450*

58 Pygmy Hippopotamus (cap.), *p. 451*

59 Okapi (cap.), *p. 453*

60 Giraffes, Reticulated, *p. 454*

61 Giraffes, Masai race, *p. 454*

oung, *p. 454*

63 Blue Duiker, *p. 459*

64 Natal Red Duiker, *p. 460*

66 Yellow-backed Duiker (cap.), *p. 462*

67 Common Duiker, *p. 462*

69 Steenbok ♂, *p. 465*

70 Sharpe's Grysbok ♀, *p. 466*

72 **Guenther's Dik-Dik ♀, *p. 467***

73 **Klipspringer, *p. 468***

74 **Oribi, *p. 469***

75 Thomson's Gazelle ♂, *p. 470*

76 Dorcas Gazelle (cap.), *p. 471*

77 Grant's Gazelle ♂, *p. 472*

78 Dama Gazelle, Western race (cap.), *p. 473*

79 Springbok, *p. 474*

81 Bohor Reedbuck ♂, *p. 477*

82 Common Reedbuck sub-adult ♂, *p. 477*

84 Kob, Uganda race ♂, *p. 479*

85 Puku ♂, *p. 481*

87 Nile Lechwe ♂ (cap.), *p. 483*

89 **Waterbuck, Defassa race** ♂, *p. 483*

90 **Gray Rhebok** ♀s, *p. 484*

91 Roan ♀, *p. 486*

92 Sable, Roosevelt race ♂, *p. 486*

93 Addax ♀ and young, *p. 488*

94 Oryx, Beisa race, *p. 489*

95 Oryx, Fringe-eared race, *p. 489*

97 Scimitar-horned Oryx, *p. 490*

99 Hartebeest, Red race, *p. 491*

nstein's Harte , *p. 493*

101 Topi, *jimela* race, *p. 493*

103 Blesbok, Blesbok race, *p. 495*

104 Blesbok, Bontebok race young and ♀ *p. 495*

105 **Wildebeest, Western White-bearded race ♂,** ***p. 496***

106 **Wildebeest, Eastern White-bearded race,** ***p. 496***

107 Wildebeest, Blue race, *p. 496*

109 Impala ♂, *p. 498*

111 Bushbuck ♂, *p. 500*

113 Sitatunga ♀ and ♂ (cap.), *p.* 501

115 **Lesser Kudu** ♀, *p. 503*

116 **Greater Kudus**, *p. 504*

117 Mountain Nyalas, *p. 505*

118 Bongo (cap.), *p. 506*

119 Common Eland, *p. 507*

121 African Buffalo, Cape race ♂, *p. 509*

122 African Buffalo, Cape race ♀ and young, *p. 509*

123 African Buffalo, Forest race (cap.), *p. 509*

125 Black Rhinoceros, *p. 512*

127 White Rhinoceros, *p. 513*

129 Plains Zebra, Boehm's race, *p.515*

130 Plains Zebra, Chapman's race, *p. 515*

132 Mountain Zebra, Cape race, *p. 516*

133 Grevy's Zebras, *p. 517*

135 African Elephant, *p. 519*

136 African Elephants bathing, *p. 519*

137 African Elephant, *p. 519*

138 African Elephants eating and drinking, *p. 519*

139 Rock Hyrax, *p. 521*

140 Bush Hyrax, *p. 522*

141 Western Tree Hyrax, *p. 523*

142 Aardvark excavating, *p. 523*

143 Cape Pangolin at termite nest, *p. 525*

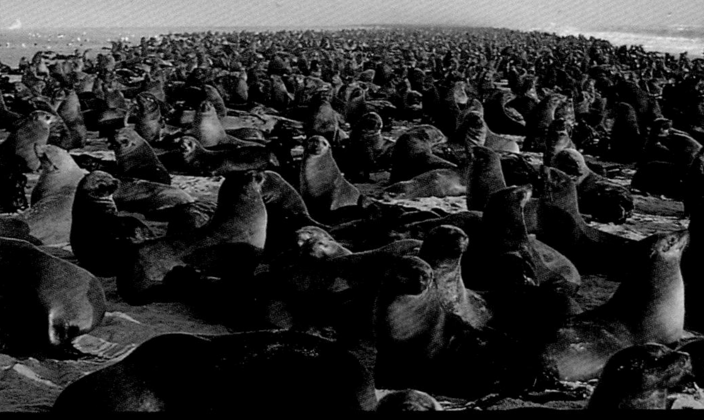

144 Cape Fur Seals at breeding colony, *p.528*

145 Large-spotted Genet, *p. 530*

146 Common Genet, *p. 531*

147 African Civet, *p. 531*

148 Palm Civet (cap.), *p. 532*

149 Fossa (cap.), *p. 533*

150 Slender Mongoose, *p. 534*

151 Marsh Mongoose, *p. 535*

152 White-tailed Mongoose, *p. 536*

154 Dwarf Mongoose, *p. 538*

155 Banded Mongoose, *p. 539*

157 Suricates, *p. 540*

159 Brown Hyena, *p. 543*

161 Aardwolf, *p. 545*

162 African Wildcat, *p. 546*

164 African Golden Cat (cap.), *p. 548*

165 Serval, *p. 548*

166 Caracal (cap.), *p. 549*

167 Leopard, *p. 550*

168 Leopard resting, *p. 550*

169 Cheetah, *p. 552*

170 Cheetah ♀ and young, *p. 552*

171 Lion, *p. 551*

172 Lion ♀ and young, *p. 551*

173 Lion family, *p. 551*

175 Fennec pair (cap.), *p. 554*

177 Bat-eared Foxes, *p.* 555

179 Black-backed Jackal, *p.* 557

181 Ethiopian Wolf, *p. 558*

183 Zorilla (cap.), *p. 561*

184 Ratel, *p. 562*

185 Spotted-necked Otter, *p. 563*

187 Thick-tailed Bushbaby, *p. 566*

188 Lesser Bushbaby, *p. 567*

189 Potto (cap.), *p. 568*

190 Ring-tailed Lemur (cap.), *p. 570*

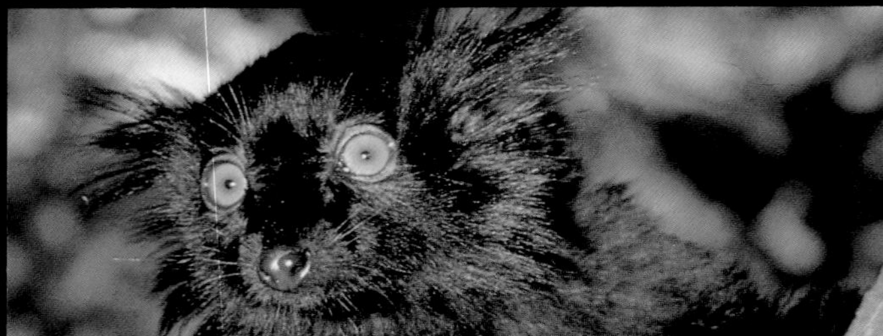

191 Black Lemur (cap.), *p. 571*

192 Mongoose Lemur ♀ and young (cap.), *p. 571*

193 Ruffed Lemur (cap.), *p. 571*

194 Indri, *p. 572*

195 Verreaux's Sifaka, *p.* 573

196 Verreaux's Sifaka, Coquerel's race ♀ (cap.), *p.* 573

197 Diademed Sifaka (cap.), *p. 574*

198 Aye-Aye (cap.), *p. 575*

199 Blue Monkey, Mount Kenya Sykes' race, *p.* 577

200 De Brazza's Monkey (cap.), *p.* 579

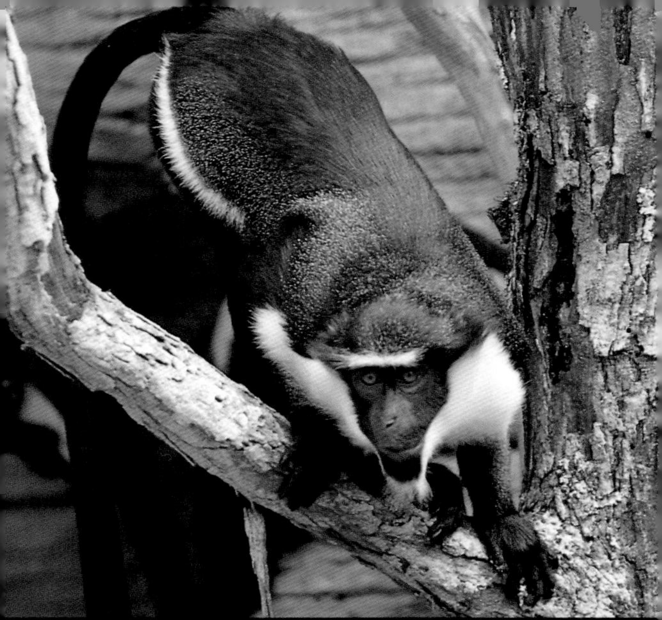

201 Diana Monkey (cap.), *p. 580*

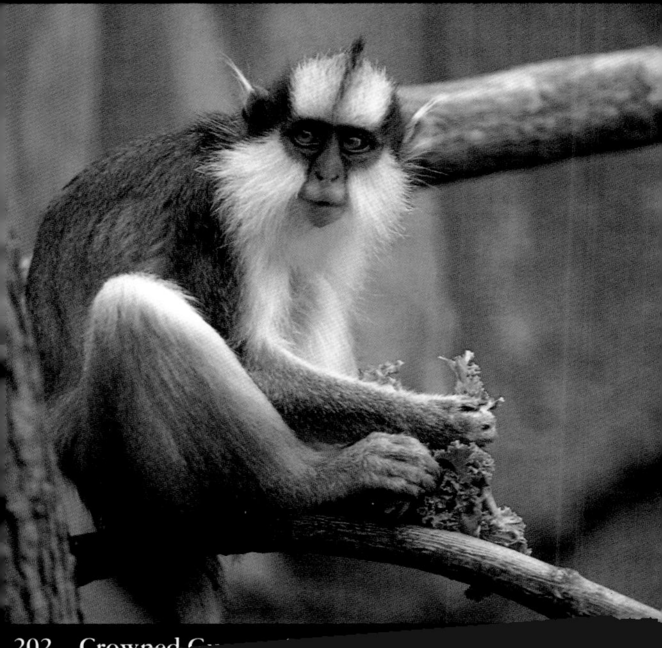

202 Crowned G

203 Mustached Monkey (cap.), *p. 582*

205 Lesser Spot-nosed Monkey (cap.), *p. 583*

206 Vervet Monkeys, East African race, *p. 584*

207 Talapoin Monkey young and ♂ (cap.), *p. 585*

209 Crested Mangabey, Golden-bellied race (cap.), *p. 587*

210 Gray-cheeked Mangabey (cap.), *p. 588*

211 White-collared Mangabey (cap.), *p. 589*

212 Savanna Baboon, Chacma race, *p. 591*

213 Savanna Baboon, Olive race, *p. 591*

215 Savanna Baboon, Yellow race, *p. 591*

216 Savanna Baboons, Yellow race, grooming, *p. 591*

217 Hamadryas Baboon ♂ grooming ♀ (cap.), *p. 593*

219 Drill (cap.), *p. 594*

221 Eastern Black-and-white Colobuses, *p. 597*

222 Red Colobus, Eastern race, *p. 599*

223 Gorilla, Mountain race silverback ♂, *p. 601*

225 Gorilla, Mountain race youngster, *p. 601*

226 Gorilla, Western Lowland race (capt.), *p. 601*

227 Chimpanzee young ♀ (cap.), *p. 603*

228 Chimpanzee ♀ and young (cap.), *p. 603*

229 Chimpanzee family (cap.), *p. 603*

231 Four-toed Hedgehog (cap.), *p. 606*

233 Rufous Elephant-Shrew (cap.), *p. 609*

234 Golden-rumped Elephant-Shrew (cap.), *p. 610*

235 Hammer-headed Bat (cap.), *p. 611*

237 Seychelles Flying Fox, *p. 613*

238 Yellow-winged Bats, *p. 614*

239 Cape Hare, *p. 616*

240 Savanna Hare, *p. 617*

241 Unstriped Ground Squirrel, *p. 619*

242 Cape Ground Squirrel, *p. 620*

243 Southern African Tree Squirrel, *p. 620*

244 Gambian Sun Squirrel, *p. 621*

245 Springhare (cap.), *p. 623*

246 Southern African Crested Porcupine, *p. 624*

247 Naked Mole Rat (cap.), *p. 626*

248 Natal Multimammate Mouse (cap.), *p. 627*

249 Four-striped Grass Mouse, *p. 628*

250 Spectacled Dormouse (cap.), *p. 632*

African Birds

Plates 251–550 depict 283 species of African birds, arranged in their respective taxonomic groupings, which are reflected in the headings at the top of the page and in the thumb-tab silhouettes at mid-page. For birds that acquire a special plumage during the breeding season, breeding birds are shown; if the breeding plumages of the two sexes differ the photo is labeled as ♂ (male) or ♀ (female). Exceptions are noted as "nonbreeding." Photographs of the birds appear in the same sequence as the text accounts in Part III; the caption for each photograph provides the page number of the corresponding text account. For help in finding photographs of particular birds, please consult the Key to the Color Plates of Animal Species, which follows the African Habitat and Geography plates.

251 Ostrich, Somali race ♂, *p. 638*

252 Ostrich, Masai race ♀ and ♂, *p. 638*

253 Ostrich, southern race ♂s, territorial display, *p. 638*

Masai race ♀ ♂s, *p. 638*

255 Jackass Penguins, *p. 639*

257 Little Grebe, *p. 641*

259 Black-browed Albatrosses feeding, *p. 642*

261 Great White Pelicans, *p. 644*

263 Cape Gannets, *p. 646*

264 White-breasted Cormorant on nest, *p. 648*

266 Reed Cormorant, *p. 649*

267 African Darter ♂ drying wings, *p. 650*

r Frigatebird *651*

269 Gray Heron, *p. 653*

270 Black-headed Heron, *p. 654*

272 Purple Heron, *p. 655*

273 Black Heron, *p. 656*

275 Yellow-billed Egret, *p. 656*

276 Little Egret, *p. 657*

278 Cattle Egret, *p. 658*

279 Squacco Heron, *p. 659*

281 Shoebill, *p. 661*

283 African Open-billed Stork, *p. 662*

285 Woolly-necked Stork, *p. 664*

287 Saddle-billed Stork, *p. 665*

289 Sacred Ibis, *p. 667*

291 Hadada Ibis, *p. 669*

293 Lesser Flamingo, *p. 671*

294 Lesser Flamingos, courtship display, *p. 671*

295 Lesser Flamingos, *p. 671*

296 Greater Flamingo, *p. 672*

297 White-faced Whistling-Ducks, *p. 673*

298 Egyptian Goose, *p. 674*

299 Spur-winged Goose, northern race ♂, p. 674

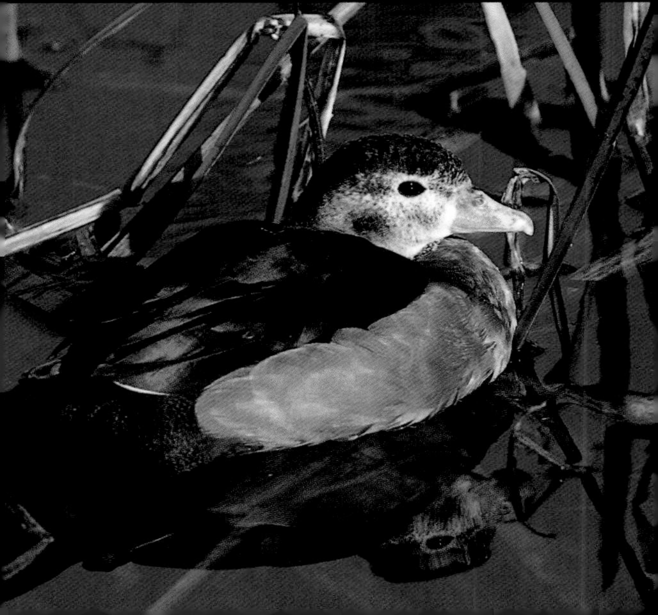

301 Cape Teal, *p. 676*

303 Red-billed Teal, *p. 677*

305 Black-shouldered Kite, *p. 680*

307 Black Kite, yellow-billed race, *p. 680*

308 African Fish-Eagle, *p. 681*

309 Lappet-faced Vultures feeding, *p. 682*

311 Rüppell's Griffon Vulture feeding, *p. 684*

313 White-backed Vulture, *p. 685*

315 Egyptian Vulture, *p. 686*

316 Palm-nut Vulture, *p. 687*

317 Black-breasted Snake-Eagle, *p. 688*

318 Brown Snake-Eagle, *p. 689*

319 Bateleur ♀, *p. 689*

321 Lizard Buzzard, *p. 691*

322 Augur Buzzard ♀, *p. 692*

24 Steppe Eagle, *p. 694*

25 Verreaux's Eagle, *p. 695*

327 Long-crested Eagle, *p. 696*

329 Crowned Eagle, *p. 698*

331 African Pygmy Falcon ♀, *p. 701*

333 Gray Kestrel, *p. 703*

335 Red-necked Spurfowl, East African race, *p. 705*

337 Yellow-necked Spurfowl, *p. 706*

illed Francoli

339 Crested Francolin pair, *p. 708*

341 Helmeted Guineafowl, Namibia race, *p. 710*

343 Wattled Crane, *p. 712*

345 Gray Crowned Crane, *p. 713*

346 Gray Crowned Cranes, courtship display, *p. 713*

347 African Black Crake, *p. 715*

349 Red-knobbed Coot, *p. 716*

351 Kori Bustard, *p. 718*

53 White-bellied Bustard ♂, *p. 719*

54 Black-bellied Bustard ♂, *p. 720*

355 African Jacana, *p. 722*

356 Crabplovers, *p. 723*

357 Black-winged Stilt, *p. 724*

359 Water Thick-knee, *p. 726*

361 Temminck's Courser, *p. 728*

363 Crowned Lapwing, *p. 730*

365 Blacksmith Lapwing, *p. 732*

366 Kittlitz's Plover, *p. 732*

367 Three-banded Plover, *p. 733*

368 Ruffs (nonbreeding), *p. 734*

369 Gray-headed Gull, *p.* 735

371 White-winged Black Tern (nonbreeding), *p.* 737

372 Sooty Tern, *p.* 738

74 White Tern, *p. 739*

75 African Skimmer, *p. 740*

Skimmers, *p.*

377 Chestnut-bellied Sandgrouse ♀, *p. 741*

379 Black-faced Sandgrouse ♂, *p. 743*

380 Speckled Pigeon, *p. 744*

381 Laughing Dove, *p.* 745

382 African Mourning Dove, *p.* 746

384 Red-eyed Dove, *p. 747*

385 Emerald-spotted Wood-Dove, *p. 748*

386 Namaqua Dove ♂, *p. 749*

387 African Gray Parrot, *p. 750*

388 Brown Parrot, brown-crowned phase, *p. 751*

389 Fischer's Lovebirds (cap.), *p. 751*

390 Great Blue Turaco (cap.), *p. 753*

391 Western Gray Plantain-eater, *p. 753*

392 Gray Go-away-bird, *p. 754*

393 Bare-faced Go-away-birds, *p.* 755

395 Purple-crested Turaco, *p. 756*

396 Ross's Turaco (cap.), *p. 757*

397 Green Turaco, West African race (cap.), *p.* 757

398 Hartlaub's Turacos (cap.), *p.* 758

399 Didric Cuckoo immature, *p. 759*

401 Senegal Coucal, *p. 761*

402 White-browed Coucal, *p. 762*

403 African Scops-Owl, *p. 763*

05 Verreaux's Eagle-Owl, *p. 764*

406 Pearl-spotted Owlet, *p. 765*

407 Fiery-necked Nightjar, *p. 766*

408 Gabon Nightjar, *p. 767*

409 Little Swift on nest, *p. 769*

410 Speckled Mousebird, *p. 770*

411 Blue-naped Mousebird, *p. 770*

413 Pied Kingfisher, *p.* 773

414 Malachite Kingfisher, *p.* 773

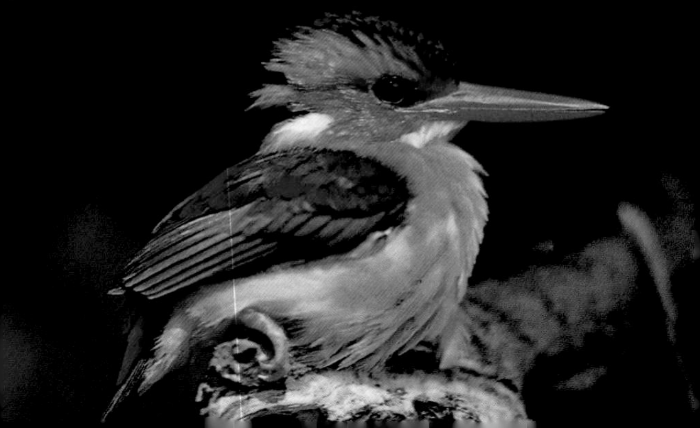

416 Gray-headed Kingfisher, East African race, *p.* 775

417 Woodland Kingfisher, *p.* 775

418 Striped Kingfisher, *p.* 776

419 Red-throated Bee-eater, West African race, *p.* 777

420 White-fronted Bee-eater, *p.* 778

421 Little Bee-eater, East African race, *p.* 779

422 Cinnamon-chested Bee-eater, *p.* 780

423 Swallow-tailed Bee-eaters, *p. 780*

424 White-throated Bee-eater, *p. 781*

425 Carmine Bee-eater, Northern race, *p. 782*

426 Carmine Bee-eater, Southern race, *p. 782*

427 Abyssinian Roller, *p. 783*

428 Purple Roller, *p. 784*

429 Lilac-breasted Roller, *p. 785*

430 Lilac-breasted Roller, *p. 785*

431 Crested Hoopoe, *p. 786*

432 Black-billed Scimitarbill, *p. 787*

433 Red-billed Wood-Hoopoe ♂, *p. 787*

434 Crowned Hornbill ♂, *p. 789*

435 African Gray Hornbill ♂, *p. 789*

437 Southern Yellow-billed Hornbill ♀, *p. 791*

438 Von der Decken's Hornbill ♂, *p. 791*

440 Silvery-cheeked Hornbill ♂, *p. 793*

441 Abyssinian Ground-Hornbill ♀, *p. 794*

442 Southern Ground-Hornbill ♀, *p. 794*

443 Red-fronted Barbet, *p.* 796

444 Black-collared Barbet, *p.* 797

445 Double-toothed Barbet, *p.* 797

447 Red-and-yellow Barbet, *p.* 799

449 Greater Honeyguide ♂, *p. 801*

451 Rufous-naped Lark, south Kenya race, *p. 803*

453 Wire-tailed Swallow, *p. 806*

455 Yellow Wagtail (nonbreeding), *p. 808*

456 African Pied Wagtail, *p. 808*

458 Yellow-throated Longclaw, *p. 810*

459 Rosy-breasted Longclaw ♀, *p. 811*

460 Richard's Pipit, East African race, *p. 811*

461 Garden Bulbul, southern race, *p. 813*

462 African Red-eyed Bulbul, *p. 814*

464 Black-crowned Tchagra, *p. 815*

465 Rosy-patched Bush-shrike, southern race ♂, *p. 816*

467 Crimson Boubou on nest, *p. 817*

468 Gray-headed Bush-shrike, *p. 818*

470 Magpie Shrike ♀, *p. 820*

471 Gray-backed Fiscal Shrike, *p. 821*

472 Long-tailed Fiscal Shrike, *p. 822*

473 Common Fiscal Shrike, *p. 823*

474 White-rumped Helmet-shrike, *p. 824*

475 White Helmet-shrike (cap.), *p. 825*

477 White-browed Scrub-Robin, *p. 827*

479 Stone Chat ♂, *p. 829*

481 Capped Wheatear, *p. 831*

482 Kurrichane Thrush, *p. 832*

484 Arrow-marked Babbler, *p. 834*

485 Rattling Cisticola, *p. 835*

486 Tawny-flanked Prinia, *p. 836*

487 Silverbird, *p. 837*

488 White-eyed Slaty Flycatcher, *p. 837*

489 Southern Black Flycatcher, *p. 838*

491 Blue Flycatcher, *p. 840*

492 African Paradise-Flycatcher ♀ *p. 841*

493 African Paradise-Flycatcher, white phase ♂, *p. 841*

Penduline-ti 342

495 Collared Sunbird ♂, *p. 844*

497 Variable Sunbird ♂, *p. 845*

499 Eastern Double-collared Sunbird ♂, *p. 847*

501 Mariqua Sunbird ♂, *p. 849*

503 Cape Sugarbird ♂, *p. 851*

505 Golden-breasted Bunting, *p. 853*

506 African Citril Canary ♂, *p. 854*

507 Yellow-fronted Canary, *p. 855*

508 Streaky Canary, East African race, *p. 855*

509 Trumpeter Finch ♂, *p. 856*

510 Red-billed Firefinch ♂, *p. 857*

511 Red-cheeked Cordon-bleu ♂, *p. 858*

512 Purple Grenadier ♂, *p. 858*

513 Common Waxbills, *p. 859*

515 Straw-tailed Whydah ♂, *p. 861*

517 Eastern Paradise Whydah ♂, *p. 863*

519 White-headed Buffalo-Weaver, *p. 864*

521 Reichenow's Weaver, eastern race ♂, *p. 866*

522 Spectacled Weaver ♀, *p. 866*

523 Golden Palm Weaver ♂, *p. 867*

525 Village Weaver, southern race ♂, *p. 869*

526 Red-billed Queleas (nonbreeding), *p. 870*

527 Madagascar Red Fody ♂ (molting), *p. 871*

529 Long-tailed Widowbird ♂, *p. 873*

rowed Sparr Veaver, *p. 873*

531 Sociable Weaver, *p. 874*

532 Rufous Sparrow, East African race ♂, *p. 875*

534 Red-winged Starling ♀, *p. 877*

535 Greater Blue-eared Starling, *p. 878*

537 Superb Starling, *p. 880*

539 Hildebrandt's Starling, *p. 880*

540 Golden-breasted Starling, *p. 881*

541 Ashy Starling, *p. 882*

542 Wattled Starling ♂s, *p. 882*

543 Yellow-billed Oxpeckers, *p. 883*

544 Red-billed Oxpeckers on animal's back, *p. 884*

545 African Black-headed Oriole ♂, *p. 885*

546 African Drongo, southern race, *p. 886*

548 African Black Crow, *p. 888*

549 Pied Crow, *p. 888*

550 White-necked Raven, *p. 889*

African Reptiles

Plates 551–575 depict 24 species of African reptiles, arranged in their respective taxonomic groupings, which are reflected in the headings at the top of the page and in the thumb-tab silhouettes at mid-page. Photographs of the reptiles appear in the same sequence as the text accounts in Part III; the caption for each photograph provides the page number of the corresponding text account. For help in finding photographs of particular reptiles, please consult the Key to the Color Plates of Animal Species, which follows the African Habitats and Geography plates.

551 Aldabra Giant Tortoise, *p. 892*

552 Leopard Tortoise, *p. 892*

554 African Pancake Tortoise, *p. 894*

555 Green Sea Turtle, *p. 895*

557 Nile Crocodile resting, *p. 897*

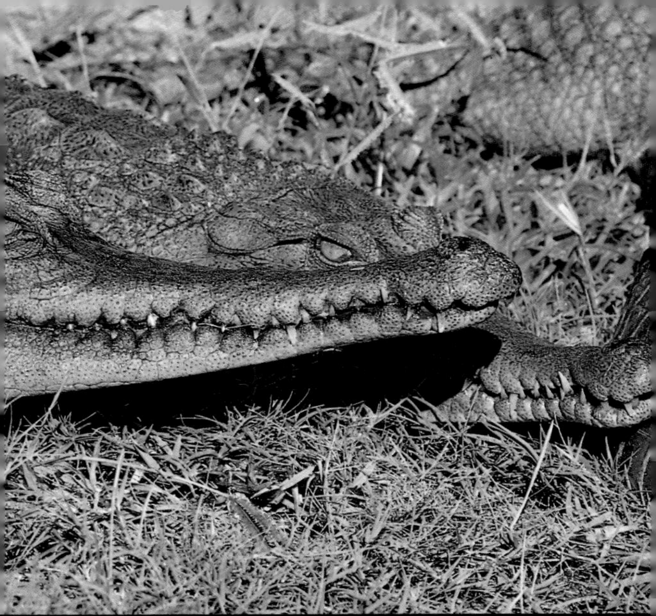

559 Long-snouted Crocodiles (cap.), *p. 898*

561 Red-headed Agama ♂, *p. 900*

562 Jackson's Chameleon ♂, *p. 901*

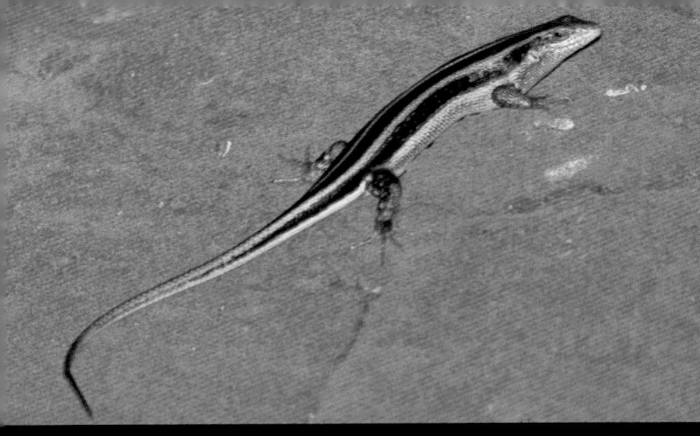

564 Five-lined Skink, *p. 903*

565 Nile Monitor Lizard sub-adult ♂, *p. 904*

p. 905

567 African Rock Python, *p. 906*

568 Madagascar Tree Boa (cap.), *p. 907*

570 Black Mamba, *p. 908*

571 Eastern Green Mamba (cap.), *p. 908*

572 Gabon Viper (cap.), *p. 909*

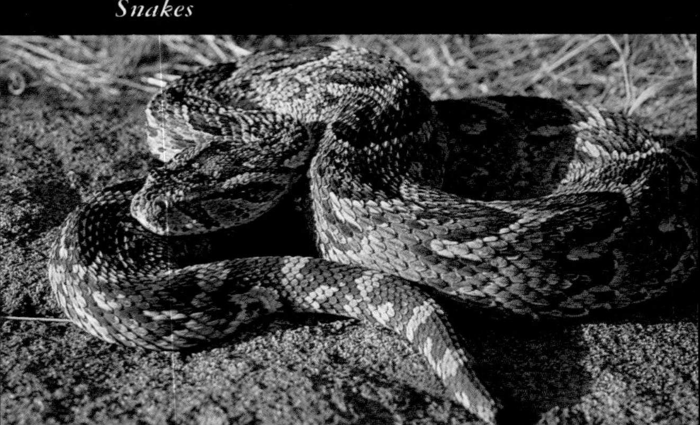

573 Puff Adder, *p. 910*

574 Egyptian Cobra, northeastern race (cap.), *p. 911*

575 Black-necked Spitting-Cobra, *p. 911*

African Insects

Plates 576 and 577 depict two groups of insects. The caption for each photograph provides the page number of the corresponding text account in Part III.

576 Dung Beetle making a dung ball, *p. 914*

577 Termite mound, *p. 915*

Part III
Species Accounts

MAMMALS
Class Mammalia

Primitive mammals arose from the reptiles about 200 million years ago. Mammals are said to be "warm-blooded." Unlike reptiles, they generate their own warmth metabolically, and have hair or blubber for insulation. Mammals lead energy-demanding lives and must eat often; they must chew and quickly digest their food for maximum, rapid energy extraction. Some mammals have highly developed senses of sight and smell, while their relatively large brains allow for superior intelligence. The name "mammal" reflects the production of milk for the young from mammary glands. Mammalian mothers have relatively few babies, but they invest heavily in the survival of each one. Youngsters undergo a long period of learning and physical maturation before they can become independent. Mammals comprise more than 4,600 species worldwide, about 1,125 in Africa.

External Anatomy of a Mammal

The drawing of a Greater Kudu on the following two pages is labeled to show the external parts of a mammal that are mentioned frequently in the order, family, and species accounts in this book. Definitions of other terms that are not in everyday use can be found in the Glossary. Within the species accounts, the measure of a mammal's length is the distance from the tip of the nose to the base of the tail, with neck and head extended. For the tail, a separate measure is provided. Height is measured from the ground to the shoulder. Horns are measured along the curve.

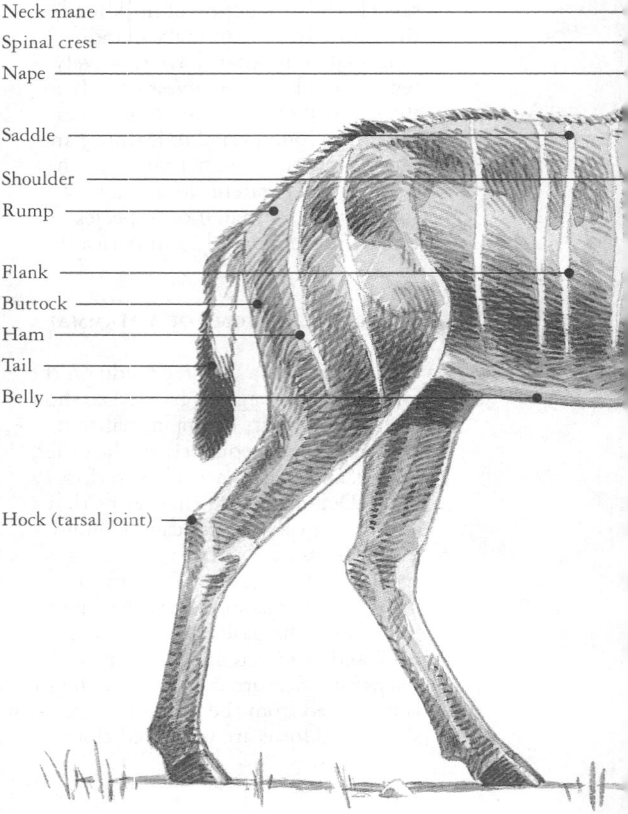

External Anatomy of a Mammal

Neck mane

Spinal crest

Nape

Saddle

Shoulder

Rump

Flank

Buttock

Ham

Tail

Belly

Hock (tarsal joint)

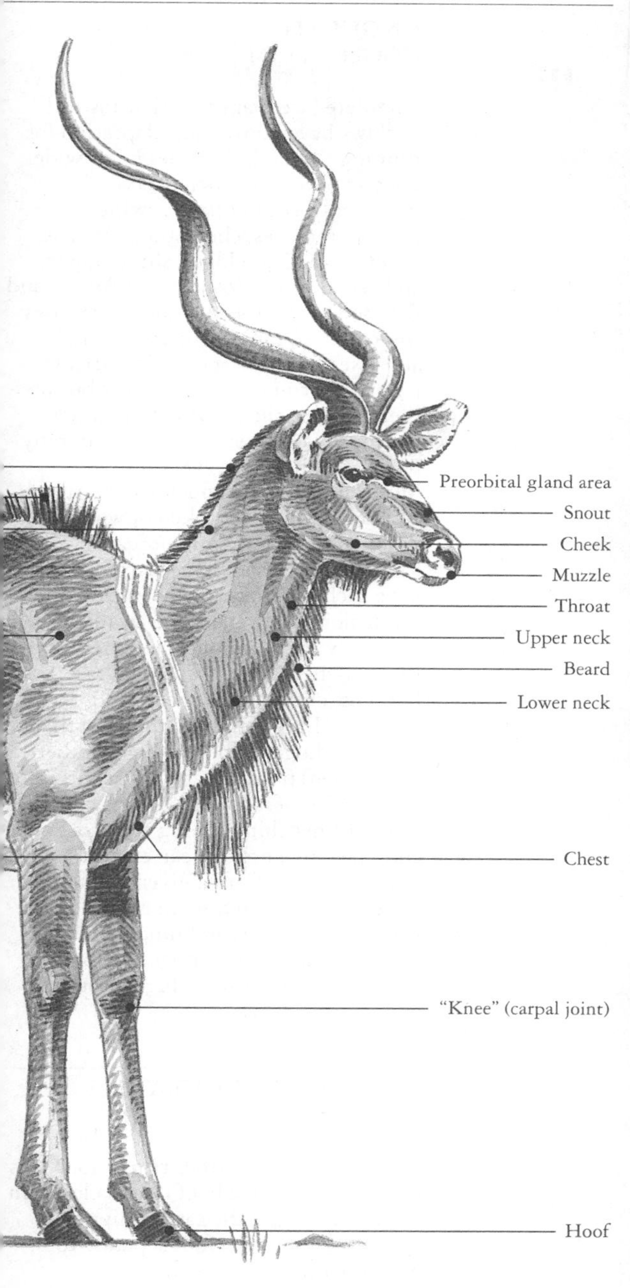
Preorbital gland area
Snout
Cheek
Muzzle
Throat
Upper neck
Beard
Lower neck
Chest
"Knee" (carpal joint)
Hoof

UNGULATES
HOOFED MAMMALS

Ungulates are mammals that instead of claws have hooves, an adaptation for running. With 227 species worldwide, the two orders are Artiodactyla (the even-toed ungulates: swine, hippopotamuses, chevrotains, camels, giraffes, deer, antelopes, sheep, goats, and cattle, with 89 species in Africa) and Perissodactyla (the odd-toed ungulates: rhinoceroses, tapirs, horses, zebras, and asses, with six species in Africa). Ungulates run not on their feet but on their tiptoes; the hazard of predation has made it necessary for them literally to stay on their toes every minute. Most ungulates eat much indigestible cellulose, which is broken down into usable nutrients by microorganisms in the digestive tract. The perissodactyls have such microorganisms in their lower gut (colon); they chew and swallow their food only once. Among the artiodactyls, the cud-chewing (ruminant) giraffes, buffalos, chevrotains, sheep, and antelopes have complex stomachs that include a huge fermentation chamber (the rumen) from which they regurgitate large pieces of food (the cud) to chew again. Other things being equal, a cud-chewing antelope can extract more nutrients from a given amount of vegetation than a zebra can, and thus eats less. Pigs and hippos are nonruminants but compensate for this inefficiency by eating a high-protein and low-fiber diet.

EVEN-TOED UNGULATES
Order Artiodactyla

Artiodactyls have either two or four toes (even-toed), with a hoof that is cloven in the middle or, in the case of hippos, a spreading foot with four separate toes. The order includes the following families: swine, hippopotamuses, chevrotains, camels, giraffes, deer, and bovids (antelopes, sheep, goats, and cattle). Of 210 species worldwide, 89 live in Africa.

SWINE
Family Suidae

Swine are designed as efficient rooting omnivores. Their bodies are compact and powerful, their legs short and sturdy, their necks short, their heads large, their eyes small, and their snouts tipped with a cartilaginous disk. Swine are dangerously armed with lower canine tusks with knife-like edges. Wild pigs do not defend territories. They live in matriarchal sounders composed of one or more generations of related females and their piglets; the mating system is polygynous. There are 16 swine species worldwide, six in Africa.

51 Bush Pig
Savanna Bush Pig
Potamochoerus larvatus

Description: Rounded body on short sturdy legs. Coat shaggy and variably colored, gray-brown to brown-black. *Contrasting white markings on head, ear tassels, and erectile mane.* Tail long and hairless to tufted tip. Male snout has lengthwise bony ridge and warts. Upper tusks barely visible; lower tusks 3″ (7 cm) long and razor sharp. L 3′4″–5′ (1–1.5 m); T 12–17″ (30–43 cm); Ht 22–32″ (55–80 cm); Wt 119–253 lb (54–115 kg).

Similar Species: **Forest Bush Pig** *(P. porcus)* is foxy red, with same white markings; lives in rain forests from Senegal to Zaire. **Giant Forest Hog** is much larger and has conspicuous upper tusks. **Warthog** appears hairless except for dark flowing mane and tail tuft.

Habitat: Montane forests, moist woodlands, grasslands, and swamps.

Breeding: Year-round, with peaks in rainy seasons; produces up to 6 young after 4-month gestation.

Range: Southern Sudan and s Ethiopia south to n Botswana and e South Africa; local in Angola and s South Africa; also Madagascar and Comoros.

The Bush Pig forages mainly at night for roots, bulbs, and fallen fruit. It plows up the ground as it roots for food and is an agricultural pest. Bush Pigs rest in dense thickets by day, and in cold weather make beds in leaves and litter. Highly sociable, they live in sounders of up to 15 females and young, attended by a male.

---

52 **Giant Forest Hog**
Hylochoerus meinertzhageni

Description: The largest of all swine. Broad snout; pointed ear tips. *Eyes of adult male bordered by huge naked cheek pads.* Upper tusks (up to 12"/30 cm long) flare outward. *Shaggy coat unpatterned black or brown-black* against slate-gray skin. L 4'4"–7' (1.3–2.1 m); T 10–14" (25–35 cm); Ht 34–40" (85–100 cm); Wt 286–603 lb (130–274 kg).

Similar Species: Much smaller **Bush Pig** is marked with white and lacks flaring upper tusks. Also much smaller, **Warthog** is lighter gray and appears nearly hairless.

Habitat: Lowland and montane forests and adjacent grasslands; also dense secondary growth.

Breeding: Not strictly seasonal, but birth peak may occur between February and April after gestation of 4–4.5 months.

Range: Congo Basin; w and e Africa.

The Giant Forest Hog is mainly a grazer, with limited ability to root in earth. Sounders comprise a single mature boar and up to five sows and

their offspring. The boar helps defend his offspring against Spotted Hyenas and Leopards. Home ranges include glades with water and wallows, rubbing places, and thickets where the animals bed down in shallow scrapes.

53, 54 **Warthog**
Savanna Warthog
Phacochoerus africanus

Description: A long-legged, level-backed, unpatterned gray hog, with a broad face and white cheek whiskers. *Smooth hairless appearance, except for dark erectile mane and tail tuft.* Paired warts beside eyes are prominent in mature male, all but absent in female. Both sexes have curved upper tusks, much heavier and longer (up to 24″/60 cm) in male. L 3′8″–4′6″ (1.1–1.35 m); T 18″ (45 cm); Ht 24–27″ (60–68 cm); Wt 99–220 lb (45–100 kg).

Hoofprint

Similar Species: **Woodland Warthog** *(P. aethiopicus),* indistinguishable in field, lives in drier scrublands of n Kenya and Somalia. **Bush Pig,** similar in size, has rounded back, inconspicuous upper tusks, and white markings on hairy coat.

Habitat: Moist and arid savannas; floodplains; absent only in rain forests and elevations over 10,000′ (3,000 m).

Breeding: Litter of 2–4 young born toward end of dry season, after gestation of 5.5 months.

Range: Throughout Sahel and south to limits of savanna in South Africa.

The diurnal Warthog uses its sensitive lips to harvest high-protein seeds from the ends of grass stems, and its nose disk is perfectly designed to unearth nutritious culms and rhizomes of grasses; this ability to make the best of scarce food has made the Warthog one of the most abundant and successful herbivores in Africa. Sounders in the same neighborhood are probably related; often sisters or a mother and daughter raise litters together in sounders numbering up to 16 hogs. Alarmed animals trot rapidly with their tails held straight up.

Hippopotamuses
Family Hippopotamidae

This family has only two extant species, both confined to Africa: the Pygmy Hippopotamus and the much larger Common Hippopotamus. The Pygmy Hippo lives in forests and the Common Hippo in grasslands. Both species have naked, sensitive skin that loses water rapidly and must be protected from sun; hippos secrete through pores in the skin a viscous fluid (pigmented red in the Common Hippo, lighter red in the Pygmy) that seems to serve as an antibiotic and sunblock rolled into one. The mating system is polygynous. Hippo tusks inflict terrible wounds during territorial battles between males, even though skin up to 1.75″ (4.5 cm) thick protects their sides.

55–57 Common Hippopotamus
Hippopotamus amphibius

Description: *Huge rotund body on stubby legs.* Ears, nostrils, and protuberant eyes placed high on head. Smooth, purple-brown skin lightening to pink in creases and underparts. Feet have 4 webbed toes. Head has enormously expanded muzzle and wide gape (to 150°). Lower canines up to 18″ (45 cm) long (above gum) in male, sharpened against small upper canines; in prime bulls, middle pair of lower incisors (up to 10″/26 cm long) projects forward like lances. L 11′–12′4″ (3.3–3.7 m); T 14″ (35 cm); Ht 4′4″–5′6″ (1.3–1.65 m); Wt male 3,500–7,000 lb (1,600–3,200 kg), female 1,440–5,160 lb (655–2,344 kg).

Footprint

Similar Species: **Pygmy Hippopotamus** is much smaller.
Habitat: Water deep enough to submerge in, within commuting distance of grassland.
Breeding: Year-round; 1 calf born after gestation of 7.5–8.5 months.
Range: Sub-Saharan Africa in major rivers, lakes, and swamps; common only in protected areas.

The heaviest land mammal after the elephants, the Common Hippopotamus feeds by plucking grass with its wide muscular lips. Hippos forage individually, coming ashore to feed at night, sometimes commuting up to 6 miles (10 km) along well-worn paths. They spend the day digesting and socializing in the water. Hippos form dense aggregations, especially during the dry season when waters recede; herd members often lie in contact with one another. Males compete to monopolize females by defending a stretch of river or lakeshore as an exclusive territory; they assert their dominance and scent-mark by showering urine and dung with their paddle-shaped tails.

---

58 Pygmy Hippopotamus
Hexaprotodon (Choeropsis) liberiensis

Description: Looks like a baby Common Hippopotamus. Glossy, gray-brown skin well-oiled by mucous glands; underparts and cheeks often tinged with pink. *Less amphibious than Common Hippo: eyes placed more to side of head, and toes nearly free of webbing.* L 5′–5′10″ (1.5–1.75 m); T 6–8.5″ (15–21 cm); Ht 28–37″ (70–92 cm); Wt 440–600 lb (200–272 kg).
Similar Species: **Common Hippopotamus** is much larger, with proportionally larger head and shorter legs.
Habitat: Rain-forest swamps and rivers bordered by dense vegetation.
Breeding: Every other year; 1 young, weighing

11–18 lb (5–8 kg), born in June or July, after gestation of 6–7 months.

Range: Mainly Ivory Coast and Liberia; possibly Sierra Leone and Guinea.

The nocturnal Pygmy Hippopotamus feeds on swamp plants, leaves, fallen fruit, roots, and tubers. Unlike the Common Hippo, it spends its days lying up on land. Solitary and territorial, it showers excrement, as its larger relative does.

Chevrotains
Family Tragulidae

The most primitive living ruminants, chevrotains are pig-like in their reliance on scent, in their vocal mating call, and in their practice of lying down by settling first on their hindquarters. Like deer, they have a ruminant digestive system. The mating system is polygynous. Once a major group with worldwide distribution, chevrotains exist today as three Asian and one African species; they inhabit rain forests and are among the smallest hoofed mammals.

Water Chevrotain
Hyemoschus aquaticus

Description: *Thick body on thin legs. Head hornless, with mouse-like, tapering snout and large eyes.* Coat brown to dark red-brown, with *light spots in rows, and white chevrons on throat and chest.* Upper canines dagger-like in male, peg-like in female. L 28–32″ (70–80 cm); T 4–5.5″ (10–14 cm); Ht 13–16″ (32–40 cm); Wt 18–29 lb (8–13 kg).

Similar Species: Small **duikers** lack spotted coat, and have horns or crests.

Habitat: Dense undergrowth close to water, in primary rain forests.

Breeding: Year-round; 1 offspring born after gestation of 4 months.

Range: Western and c African rain forests, from Guinea to Gabon, and east to Central African Republic and n Zaire.

The Water Chevrotain rests and hides by day, and forages at night for foliage and fallen fruit. Except to breed, this animal is solitary. Both males and females defend territories against their own sex. They communicate by calls, and scent-mark with urine and feces impregnated with scent-gland secretions. The oldest, heaviest males' territories overlap the territories of several females.

Giraffes
Family Giraffidae

This family, with only two species, is exclusively African. Giraffes and Okapis share a number of traits: an ambling walk; a very long, prehensile tongue used as a browsing tool; bi-lobed lower canine teeth (coopted into incisor form); an inability to drink or feed at ground level without bending or straddling the forelegs; defensive kicking with the fore- and hindlegs; horns of solid bone, covered by skin; and foreleg-lifting by courting males.

59 Okapi
Okapia johnstoni

Description: Lustrous velvety coat *unpatterned chocolate-brown above (redder in female); black and white transverse stripes on upper legs;* lower legs white, banded at "knee" and "ankle" with dark garters. Vaguely horse-like head; large rounded ears. Long, black, prehensile tongue that can reach into ears. Male only has skin-covered horns no more than 2″ (5 cm) long. L 6′4″–6′8″ (1.9–2 m); T 12–16″ (30–40 cm); Ht to top of head 5′8″–6′ (1.7–1.8 m); Wt 550 lb (250 kg), female slightly heavier than male.

Similar Species: **Bongo,** similar in size, has striped body and prominent horns.

Habitat: Lush undergrowth within rain forests. Avoids swamps and soft ground.

Breeding: Year-round; 1 calf born after gestation of 14–15 months.

Range: Northern Zaire between Ubangi and Uele rivers east to Semliki River and Uganda border.

The Okapi was discovered early in this century. This "forest giraffe" depends on breaks in the canopy (waterways, clearings, regenerating forest) where sunlight penetrates and supports undergrowth. It browses a variety of common rain-forest plants, and eats fruit and fungi, using a trail network that links feeding grounds. The sexes associate only when a female is in estrus.

60–62 **Giraffe**
Giraffa camelopardalis

Description: The tallest mammal in the world, unmistakable for its *very long legs and neck.* All giraffes have a blotchy coat-color pattern, unique to each individual, but see Subspecies, below. Both sexes have horns that are longer (to 5″/13 cm) in male. By middle age, male grows a single medial horn on forehead, and a bump over each eye socket and behind each ear. Prehensile tongue 18″ (45 cm) long; narrow muzzle; short neck mane. Tail has long terminal tuft. Ht to top of horns, male to 18′ (5.5 m), female 2′ (60 cm) shorter; T 30–60″ (75–150 cm); Wt male 2,140–3,070 lb (973–1,395 kg), female 1,540–2,090 lb (700–950 kg).

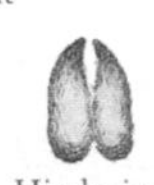

Foreprint

Hindprint

Subspecies: Several subspecies are distinguished by color (pale yellow to black) and size and shape of blotches against white, orange, or buff-colored background. **Reticulated Giraffe** *(G. c. reticulata),* of n Kenya and s Ethiopia, is the most striking, with rich chestnut patches separated by narrow white lines. **Masai Giraffe** *(G. g. tippelskirchi),* of s Kenya and Tanzania, has irregular brown splotches, like jagged leaves, against a buff or ochreous background.

Similar Species: Only the much smaller **Okapi.**

Habitat: Savannas, especially those with acacias and other thorny trees and bushes.

Breeding: Year-round; 1 young (rarely twins) born after gestation of 14–15 months.

Range: South of Sahara to n Namibia, n Botswana, and e Transvaal.

The largest of all ruminants, the Giraffe is a pure browser equipped to reach leaves 19 feet (5.7 m) from the ground. During rainy seasons, Giraffes range widely, browsing mainly deciduous species; in the dry season, they concentrate on evergreen trees growing along watercourses. They drink every few days when water is available. Females and young live in maternal herds. The mating system is polygynous. Males separate from their mothers in their third year to associate in bachelor herds, gradually becoming solitary with maturity. Senior bulls (the darkest males with the most bumps on their heads) monopolize reproduction. Beginning in adolescence, males test one another's fighting potential in regular "necking" contests, pushing against each other and exchanging blows of the head aimed at the opponent's torso or neck. Real fights occur only when the established rank order is challenged.

ANTELOPES AND OTHER BOVIDS
Family Bovidae

Bovids are ruminants with hollow, unbranched, permanently attached horns that are usually present in both sexes. The most familiar members of this family are domestic cattle, sheep, and goats, of which there are many

Antelope Heads

Natal Red Duiker | Kirk's Dik-Dik | Steenbok | Klipspringer

Bohor Reedbuck | Kob | Puku

Roan | Sable | Oryx, Fringe-eared race

Wildebeest | Bushbuck | Greater Kudu

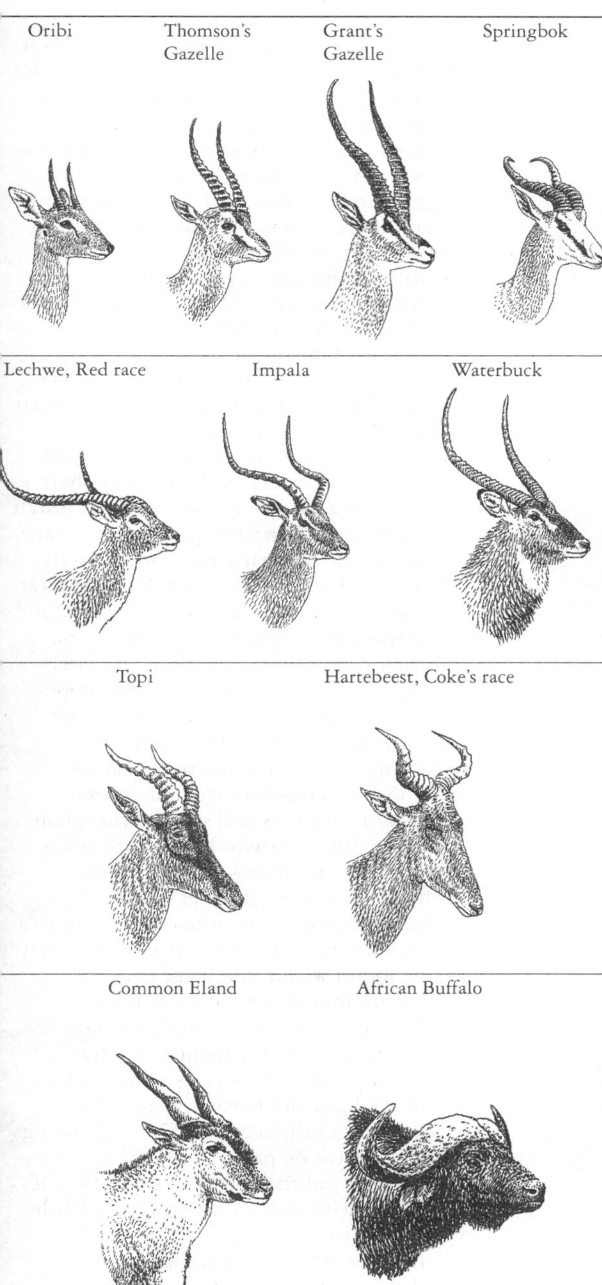
Oribi
Thomson's Gazelle
Grant's Gazelle
Springbok
Lechwe, Red race
Impala
Waterbuck
Topi
Hartebeest, Coke's race
Common Eland
African Buffalo

millions in Africa; however, few of their native wild relatives live there. Far more numerous are the native wild antelopes, and Africa is the place where most of them live: 73 out of 86 antelope species worldwide. Related species of bovids are grouped taxonomically into tribes, each as different from the others as sheep are from cattle. The mating system varies from monogamy to polygyny. Antelopes range in size from the 4-pound (1.8-kg) Royal Antelope *(Neotragus pygmaeus)* to the 2,000-pound (900-kg) Derby Eland, and they live almost everywhere. Antelopes that dwell in forests and bush or other closed habitats tend to have hindquarters that are more developed than forequarters, and relatively short limbs—adaptations for moving through undergrowth and for quick starts, sharp turns, and acrobatic leaps and bounds. To avoid predation, most closed-habitat dwellers—duikers, dwarf antelopes, and reedbucks—hide first, depending on their concealing coloration, and later may make a quick getaway. Antelopes that live in open habitats have either long, equally developed limbs or overdeveloped forequarters that are good for long-distance loping; most rely on alertness and speed rather than concealment to avoid predators; many of these antelopes—such as some wildebeests and gazelles—have conspicuous colors or markings. Up to a dozen different species of antelopes may be found within the space of a few square miles on African savannas.

The size and shape of the horns are key features in the identification of antelopes. For 24 species, drawings of the head and horns appear in the margins of the accounts. These drawings also appear on pages 456–457 in a two-page spread that gives an indication of the relative sizes of the species. (While the drawings of the different heads indicate relative sizes, they are not done to a precise scale.)

Duikers
Tribe Cephalophini

African rain forests are home to 17 species of duikers (pronounced DIKE-ers). Members of this tribe all have overdeveloped hindquarters, a long neck, and short legs—a build well adapted for negotiating forest undergrowth. Other traits include an erectile head crest; spike-like, back-tilted horns in both sexes; small ears; bare nostrils; protective coloration; and preorbital glands (in front of the eyes), with pores opening in a slit. Duikers have a wide gape, mobile lips, and long pointed tongues—adaptations for eating fallen fruit, for which they dig and root in the forest floor. Apparently most species live in monogamous pairs.

63 Blue Duiker
Cephalophus monticola

Description: The smallest duiker and one of the smallest antelopes. Color varies geographically: slate-gray to dark gray-brown, with *bluish sheen on back,* contrasting with whitish underparts, inner legs, and undertail. *Light-colored eyebrow stripe curves to base of horns, framing brown forehead. Curved preorbital gland slit.* Horns strongly ridged and short (2″/5 cm), sometimes absent in female. Head crest short or absent. L 21–29″ (52–72 cm); T 3″ (7–8 cm); Ht 13–14″ (33–36 cm); Wt 8.4–12 lb (3.8–5.4 kg), female slightly larger than male.

Similar Species: **Maxwell's Duiker** *(C. maxwellii)* is larger (Wt to 22 lb/10 kg) and can be reliably distinguished in field only by its range: west of Nigeria's Cross River.

Habitat: Rain and riverine forests; montane forests to 10,000′ (3,000 m); also dense thickets.

Breeding: Year-round; 1 fawn born after

gestation variously estimated as 4 up to 7.5 months. Unhunted rain-forest populations produce 1 offspring a year; those outside rain forest sometimes give birth twice a year.

Range: Widespread east of Nigeria's Cross River, south to c Angola and s Zaire; e Africa from Kenya to South Africa.

By far the most abundant rain-forest antelope, the Blue Duiker, along with its western counterpart, Maxwell's Duiker, is a mainstay of the bushmeat markets of West Africa. Couples maintain visual contact, partly through constant up-and-down movements of their white tails. The Blue Duiker feeds during the day on fallen fruit, foliage, flowers, seedpods, fungi, and occasionally invertebrates.

---

64 Natal Red Duiker

Red Forest Duiker
Cephalophus natalensis

Description: A medium-size duiker, one of several reddish species. *Body bright foxy red; legs orange-red to dark brown;* underparts slightly lighter. Nose bridge dark gray to black; prominent red-and-black (or all-red) erectile head crest often conceals horns (2.5–4″/6–10 cm long). Throat pale; chin and hair inside ears white; nape of neck and feet gray; white tuft on tail. L 28–40″ (70–100 cm); T 4.5″ (11 cm); Ht 14–18″ (35–45 cm); Wt 25–31 lb (11–14 kg).

Similar Species: **Harvey's Red Duiker** *(C. harveyi)* is common red duiker of e African highlands, usually found near water; has narrow, reddish-brown stripe along spine; black nose bridge and center of crest. **Black-fronted Duiker** *(C. nigrifrons)* occurs in lowland and montane forests from Cameroon east to Kenya, and south to Angola; has black blaze that extends from nose to horns. **Peters's Duiker** *(C. callipygus)* and

Bay Duiker *(C. dorsalis)* inhabit dense forests of w and c Africa; median black stripe runs from upper back to tail.

Habitat: Gallery forests, montane forests, dense bush, and coastal forest-savanna transition zones.

Breeding: Year-round; 1 fawn born after gestation variously estimated as 4 up to 7.5 months.

Range: Tanzania south to Natal.

This diurnal species eats the usual duiker diet of fallen fruit, plus foliage and insects. A mated pair apparently jointly defends a territory.

---

65 **Zebra Duiker**
Cephalophus zebra

Description: A medium-size duiker, with short (1.5–2″/3.8–5 cm) conical horns, and short or no head crest. Distinctive color pattern: *light reddish brown with 12–15 black transverse torso stripes.* Brownish-black nose bridge and tail tuft; tail white underneath. Outer limbs, rump, forehead, ear backs, nape, and shoulders darker brown. L 34–36″ (85–90 cm); T 6″ (15 cm); Ht 16–20″ (40–50 cm); Wt 20–33 lb (9–15 kg).

Similar Species: Much bigger **Jentink's Duiker** *(C. jentinki)* is also limited to parts of Sierra Leone, Liberia, and sw Ivory Coast; tri-colored: blackish head and neck are separated from grizzled gray body by wide collar of whitish gray.

Habitat: Dense lowland rain forests and hill forests.

Breeding: Year-round; 1 fawn born after gestation estimated at 7.5 months.

Range: Sierra Leone, Liberia, w Ivory Coast.

Because it is largely dependent on primary forest that is rapidly being cut down, the Zebra Duiker is one of the most endangered antelopes. The Sierra Leone population is already limited to isolated forest patches.

While this species is known to be diurnal, little information is available about it in the wild.

66 Yellow-backed Duiker

Cephalophus silvicultor

Description: The largest duiker. Heavyset, with strong legs. Coat short, glossy, *dark gray-brown to black, with triangular tract of long, erectile, yellow hair* on back; crest on head is red-brown or black. Horns (4–8.5"/10–21 cm long) thin, weakly ridged, with slightly down-curved tips. L 3′10"–4′10" (1.15–1.45 m); Ht 28–35" (70–87 cm); Wt 99–176 lb (45–80 kg).

Habitat: Rain, montane, and riverine forests, and closed woodlands.

Breeding: Year-round; 1 fawn born after gestation variously estimated as 4 up to 7.5 months.

Range: West Africa; Senegal east to Kenya, and south to Zambia and n Angola.

The nocturnal Yellow-backed Duiker has an extensive home range; it eats mainly fruit, seeds, fungi, the bark of shrubs, and foliage. It visits salt licks. During the day, it lies up in undergrowth in a regularly used form (a repeatedly used bed in the vegetation). When excited or alarmed, this duiker erects its yellow dorsal crest and emits a piercing alerting whistle.

67 Common Duiker

Gray Duiker, Bush Duiker

Sylvicapra grimmia

Description: Compared with forest duikers, *has longer, more evenly developed limbs, with less-rounded back,* and longer ears. Color varies geographically (there are as many as 19 subspecies), from chestnut in Angolan woodlands, to grizzled gray in northern savannas, to buff in arid regions. Nostrils and nose bridge black;

Hoofprint

forehead tuft dark. Forelegs have brown or black fronts. Underparts usually white (sometimes tinged with red or gray); underside of tail white. Horns in male only; 3–7″ (7–18 cm) long; round and less tilted than in other duikers. L 32–46″ (80–115 cm); T 4.5–8″ (11–20 cm); Ht 18–28″ (45–70 cm); Wt 33–55 lb (15–25 kg), female 2–3 lb heavier than male.

Habitat: Most habitats with cover adequate for hiding, especially moist savannas, and including edges of settlements; avoids rain forests.

Breeding: Year-round; 1 fawn born after gestation variously estimated at 3 up to 7.5 months.

Range: Sub-Saharan Africa.

The Common Duiker can go without drinking if its diet includes greens. It eats mostly leaves, herbs, fruit, seeds, and flowers. This duiker appears to live in loosely associated, monogamous pairs. Males behave territorially, smearing gland secretions on stems, branches, and rocks, and depositing dung in middens; their preferred resting places (elevated ground, termite mounds) overlook their territory. Females choose deeper cover. Active day and night, Common Duikers become more nocturnal near human settlements.

Dwarf Antelopes
Tribe Neotragini

This wholly African tribe has 13 species. Sizes range from the smallest bovid, the 4-pound (1.8-kg) Royal Antelope *(Neotragus pygmaeus),* to the rare 57-pound (26-kg) Beira *(Dorcatragus megalotis).* Most dwarf antelopes live in dry regions, but the Royal Antelope and the Pygmy Antelope *(N. batesi)* inhabit rain forests. Cover-dependent, dwarf antelopes have protective coloration and high, rounded hindquarters. Males have short, spike-like horns that are more erect and rounder than in duikers. Dwarf antelopes eat high-protein/low-fiber foliage and herbage, and metabolize enough water from food that they don't need to drink. Apparently most species live in monogamous pairs, with both sexes scent-marking the territory with secretions of the preorbital glands and depositing urine and pellets in dung middens.

68 Suni
Neotragus moschatus

Description: A miniature antelope, *slightly freckled reddish brown above;* back darker than flanks and legs; *head and muzzle darker and redder still.* White chin, throat, insides of legs, underside and tip of tail, and small arc over each eye. Legs ringed with black band above hooves. Horns wide-set, back-slanted, ridged most of their length; 2.5–5″ (6.5–13 cm) long. L 23–25″ (58–62 cm); T 3.5–4.5″ (9–11 cm); Ht 14–15″ (36–38 cm); Wt 10–12 lb (4.5–5.4 kg).

Similar Species: **Blue Duiker** is slate gray or gray-brown, with no reddish color; flicks tail up and down. **Natal Red Duiker** is redder, with less white, and has head crest.

Habitat: Coastal forests, scrub, and bushlands with dense undergrowth, especially dry thicket country.

Breeding: Year-round; 1 fawn born after 6- to 7-month gestation.

Range: Eastern Africa, from s Somalia to Natal, extending inland to rift valley in suitable habitat to 9,000′ (2,700 m).

The Suni lies up in thick cover during the hottest hours, and has activity peaks early and late in the day. Sunis are sometimes seen on one of their regular pathways through dense underbrush; watch for their sideways tail-flicking, which shows the tail's white underside. When disturbed, a Suni freezes, then gives a high-pitched *chee-chee* as it bolts in zigzag flight. Typically Sunis live monogamously, but up to four females have been observed with one male.

69 Steenbok
Raphicerus campestris

Description: A small reddish antelope, often seen dashing across open ground between patches of cover. Long legs; *large round ears;* rudimentary tail. *Smooth glossy coat bright rufous-fawn to reddish-brown;* bare, shiny, black nostrils, and *triangular black marking on nose bridge; dark crescent on forehead.* Underparts and insides of ears white. Horns upright straight spikes, without ridges, 3.5–7.5″ (9–19 cm) long. L 28–38″ (70–95 cm); T 2″ (5 cm); Ht 18–24″ (45–60 cm); Wt 20–29 lb (9–13 kg).

Hoofprint

Similar Species: Larger **Oribi** is more slender and longer-necked, with black tail and dark spot below ear. **Common Duiker** is less red; has much smaller ears. **Grysboks** have darker, grizzled coats, rounder backs, and shorter legs.

Habitat: Dry savannas; abandoned fields; edges of settlements. Occurs from sea level to 15,500′ (4,750 m).

Breeding: Year-round; 1 young born after gestation of 5.5–6 months.

Range: East Africa from c Kenya to southern edge of acacia savanna in Tanzania; throughout s Africa from s Angola and Zambezi south.

Although Steenboks are mostly seen singly, evidence suggests that they live in monogamous pairs. Both sexes deposit dung in middens. They are browsers but also dig up roots and tubers in the Kalahari sandveld. Steenboks are water-independent but drink opportunistically.

70 Sharpe's Grysbok
Raphicerus sharpei

Description: Coat *rich reddish brown grizzled with white hairs;* forehead, nose, cheeks, head, and lower limbs yellow-brown. Dark triangle on nose bridge. Underparts, insides of legs, underneck, sides of muzzle, and eye ring whitish. Horns unridged; thick at base, tapering to sharp points; slightly slanted; up to 2.5″ (6 cm) long. L 24–30″ (61–75 cm); T 2–3″ (5–7 cm); Ht 18–20″ (45–50 cm); Wt 16.5 lb (7.5 kg).

Similar Species: Slightly larger **Cape Grysbok** *(R. melanotis)* of s Cape Province has "false," or lateral, hooves. Proportionally longer-legged **Steenbok** has larger ears and eyes.

Habitat: Miombo woodlands, including abandoned cultivated areas, bases of rocky outcrops, and foothills.

Breeding: Year-round; 1 young born after 7-month gestation.

Range: Southeastern Zaire and c Tanzania south through Zambia, Zimbabwe, and Mozambique to ne Transvaal.

Rarely seen because of its nocturnal habits, Sharpe's Grysbok lies up by day in dense vegetation; it dashes from hiding in a crouch and disappears into another thicket, zigzagging when very frightened. Its diet consists of leaves, seedpods, berries, and, in the dry season, coarser fare, including grass. Male and female pair monogamously and jointly defend a territory, but remain apart most of the time.

---

71 Kirk's Dik-Dik
Madoqua kirkii

Description: *A delicate miniature antelope, with very long hindlegs; narrow, mobile, trunk-like snout; erectile head crest.* Large eyes and ears; white eye ring; prominent preorbital glands. Rudimentary tail.

Grizzled gray-brown to gray, with tan flanks and legs; whitish underparts. Horns back-slanted, sharply ridged; 2.5–4.5″ (6–11 cm) long. L 24–29″ (60–72 cm); T 1.2–2.4″ (3–6 cm); Ht 14–17″ (35–43 cm); Wt 8–16 lb (3.8–7.2 kg).

Similar Species: **Salt's Dik-Dik** *(M. saltiana)* occurs in ne Sudan, Somalia, and Ethiopia; most forms have brilliant rufous flanks contrasting with gray back. **Guenther's Dik-Dik** has even more elongated nose than Kirk's Dik-Dik.

Habitat: Arid thornbush interspersed with open glades; avoids tall herbage.

Breeding: Twice per year; 1 fawn born after 6-month gestation.

Range: Namibia and sw Angola; s Somalia south to c Tanzania.

Dik-diks browse forbs, foliage, shoots, berries, and fruit. They are most active at night but often seen by day. Dik-diks never have to drink, and are able to tolerate very high temperatures. All dik-diks live in monogamous pairs. The male defends against intruders of either sex; the female initiates and leads most family movements. The dunging ceremony, in which family members ritualistically urinate and defecate on middens that mark the territorial boundary, is important in maintaining pair and family bonds. High wheezy alarm snorts are given at the sight of prowling predators.

---

72 Guenther's Dik-Dik
Madoqua guentheri

Description: *Resembles Kirk's Dik-Dik, but snout still more elongated and trunk-like.* Upper body and sides grizzled grayish fawn; nose bridge, crest, ear backs, and lower legs rust-red or gray-red; underparts whitish. No eye ring; preorbital glands prominent in both sexes. Tail rudimentary. Horns back-slanted, ridged for half of length; 2.5″ (6 cm) long. L 25–30″ (62–75 cm); T 1.2–2″ (3–5 cm); Ht 14–16″ (35–40 cm); Wt 8–12 lb (3.7–5.5 kg).

Similar Species: **Kirk's Dik-Dik** has white eye ring and shorter snout. **Salt's Dik-Dik** *(M. saltiana)* and **Piacentini's Dik-Dik** *(M. piacentinii),* both of ne Africa, have much shorter snouts.

Habitat: Most types of arid thornbush; gallery forests lining streambeds.

Breeding: Twice per year; 1 young born after 6-month gestation.

Range: Replaces Kirk's in more arid parts of n Kenya, Somalia, s Ethiopia, se Sudan, and ne Uganda.

Guenther's Dik-Dik seems to be more diurnal than Kirk's, but it has a very similar social organization.

73 Klipspringer
Oreotragus oreotragus

Description: *Sturdy build; short neck; overdeveloped hindquarters, giving back bowed appearance. Walks on tips of truncated hooves (as if on tiptoe).* Head wide, tapering to narrow snout. Unique hollow, brittle hair, grizzled gray to yellow-brown, without bold markings except for white linings of large rounded ears, which have conspicuous black borders and networks of dark lines. Horns of males (and some females of e African race) wide-set, upright spikes; ridged at base; 4″ (10 cm) long. L 30–36″ (75–90 cm); T 3–4″ (7–10 cm); Ht 20–22″ (49–54 cm); Wt 20–35 lb (9–16 kg).

Habitat: Steep rocky terrain that provides refuge from predators, with adequate nearby food plants and enough cover to conceal offspring. Tolerates temperature extremes, as in gorges and high mountains, and lives in both arid and humid environments. Occurs to 15,000′ (4,500 m).

Breeding: Twice per year, usually year-round;

1 young born after gestation of about 6 months.

Range: Eastern Africa from Red Sea to Cape of Good Hope, thence north to s Angola. Isolated populations in c Nigeria and Central African Republic.

The water-independent Klipspringer browses a broad range of plants. Monogamous pairs (occasionally two or three females with one male) associate closely in territories, in which they maintain dung middens, mark twigs with preorbital gland secretions, and sound a piercing alarm whistle in duet. The Klipspringer is active during the day and probably at night.

---

74 Oribi
Ourebia ourebi

Description: Resembles a small gazelle. Long neck and limbs; relatively level back; *short tail black on upper surface,* conspicuous against white buttocks. Coat *bright yellow-rufous* (richer in wetter, paler in drier regions), with *contrasting white underparts, buttocks, chin, and eye line. Black glandular spot below ear.* Horns thin, up-standing spikes 3–7.5″ (8–19 cm) long; ridged at base. L 3′1″–4′8″ (92–140 cm); T 2.5–4.5″ (6–11 cm); Ht 20–25″ (51–63 cm); Wt 23–37 lb (10–17 kg).

Similar Species: Smaller **Steenbok** has tail same color as upperparts; no spot below ear.

Habitat: Moist savannas.

Breeding: Births peak in rainy season; 1 calf born after 7-month gestation.

Range: Senegal east to Ethiopia; e Africa; e Angola and w Zambia; c Mozambique to e Cape Province.

Primarily a grazer, the Oribi also browses in the dry season. Usually it forms monogamous pairs. Family members utter soft *phe-phe-phe* whistles to stay in contact; male and female perform a joint dunging ceremony along territorial borders. Two or three males may defend the same territory and share females.

Gazelles
Tribe Antilopini

The gazelle tribe has 22 species worldwide, 12 in Africa, of which half are endangered. The seven that are adapted to subdesert and desert habitats around and in the Sahara suffer from competition with domestic livestock, severe droughts, and hunters who run them down in motor vehicles and aircraft. Gazelles are fleet (top speeds of 50–55 mph/80–88 kph), medium-size antelopes, with long necks, level backs, and long, slender, equally developed limbs. In most species, the sexes are colored alike, and both sexes have horns. All species are polygynous, and gregarious to some extent. In resident populations, territorial males keep females and young separate from bachelor males; during migration and in nonbreeding seasons, the sexes associate in mixed herds.

75 Thomson's Gazelle
Gazella thomsonii

Description: The common small gazelle of the e African plains. *Bright cinnamon with bold black side stripe, facial marks, and tail;* faint to dark vertical lines on hams. Extensive white areas border dark marks on face, underparts, and buttocks. Male horns well developed, nearly parallel, 10–17″ (25–43 cm) long, and strongly ridged; in female, weak spikes 3–6″ (8–15 cm) long, often deformed, broken, or missing. L 28–43″ (70–107 cm); T 7.5–11″ (19–27 cm); Ht 23–28″ (58–70 cm); Wt male 29–64 lb (13–29 kg).

Hoofprint

Similar Species: Stockier **Red-fronted Gazelle**

(*G. rufifrons*) inhabits Sahel and savannas from Senegal east to Sudan. **Grant's Gazelle** is much larger and paler, with less conspicuous (or absent) side stripe; white of rump patch extends over tail.

Habitat: Acacia savannas; open, preferably short-grass plains.

Breeding: Year-round, with 2 peaks 6 months apart in some areas; 1 calf born after gestation of 6 months.

Range: Discontinuous: n Kenya through n and c Tanzania. Subspecies **Mongalla Gazelle** (*G. t. albonotata*) is restricted to s Sudan.

One of the most common antelopes of the East African plains, the "Tommy," in its Serengeti population of more than half a million, migrates seasonally between the short-grass plains and the nearby longer-grass savannas. Smaller resident populations occur in most reserves of Kenya and Tanzania. The Tommy grazes green grass whenever possible, but switches to browse and succulents in the dry season. Tommies drink every day or two in the dry season, making round trips of 10 miles (16 km) or more if necessary. Breeding males establish territories, demarcating the boundaries with dung middens and globs of black preorbital secretions.

---

76 Dorcas Gazelle
Gazella dorcas

Description: The most widely distributed and most common Saharan antelope. A small tan gazelle, with a *broad but poorly defined reddish-brown side stripe and facial blaze;* darker stripe beside snout; dark brown or black tail. White stripe from muzzle over eyes; white underparts and buttocks. Color and markings fade in summer, intensify in winter. Male horns S-shaped, thick, heavily ridged, 10–15″ (25–38 cm) long; in female, thin and weakly ridged, 6–10″ (15–25 cm) long. L 28–43″ (70–107 cm); T 6–8″ (15–20 cm); Ht 22–26″ (55–65 cm); Wt 33–44 lb (15–20 kg).

Similar Species: **Red-fronted Gazelle** *(G. rufifrons),* of Sahel and savannas from Senegal to ne Ethiopia, is redder and has black band on flank. **Slender-horned Gazelle** *(G. leptoceros),* restricted to true deserts from Algeria to Egypt, has longer, more upright horns. **Dama Gazelle,** with its vivid chestnut-and-white coloring, is unmistakable.

Habitat: Deserts and semi-desert shrublands; prefers rocky and sandy terrain.

Breeding: Twice per year in some areas; 1 calf born after 6-month gestation.

Range: Mali to n Sudan, Eritrea, n Ethiopia, and n Somalia, where **Pelzeln's Gazelle** race *(G. d. pelzelni)* occurs in northern coastal zone.

Very adaptable, the Dorcas Gazelle browses the foliage of acacias, desert dates, and shrubs most of the time, but grazes after rains revive pastures, wandering long distances. In the hottest, driest weather, it concentrates in streambeds and wadis that provide shade and browse.

77 Grant's Gazelle
Gazella granti

Description: A large gazelle. Sand- or fawn-colored, with *extensive white underparts; rump patch extends over hips* and is bordered on each side by vertical dark stripe. *Tail white* with black tuft. White throat patch; facial markings lack bold black. Fawn's dark flank stripe often partial or absent in adult female; always absent in adult male. Horns in male very large, thick, and strongly ridged, 20–32″ (50–80 cm) long; in female, thin with weak ridges, 12–18″ (30–45 cm) long. L 3′2″–5′6″ (95–166 cm); T 10–14″ (25–35 cm); Ht 30–36″ (75–90 cm); Wt 84–178 lb (38–81 kg).

Hoofprint

Subspecies: West of rift valley, mature male **Roberts's Gazelle** *(G. g. robertsi)* has widely divergent horns with bent-down tips. Horns of other races less divergent, especially **Peters's Gazelle** (*G. g. petersii)* of e Kenya, which has straighter, close-set horns.

Similar Species: **Thomson's Gazelle** is smaller and lacks white above tail. **Soemmerring's Gazelle** *(G. soemmerringii)* of ne Africa has dark blaze and black stripe from nose through eyes to base of horns; lacks vertical black stripe bordering buttock; smaller horns turn in at tips.

Habitat: Subdeserts and short-grass plains to tall-grass savannas and scrub woodlands.

Breeding: In Tanzania and Kenya, some breeding continues year-round, but with peaks December–February and in August and September; 1 calf born after gestation of nearly 7 months.

Range: Coastal Somalia at equator south to n Tanzania; inland as far as Lake Victoria, thence north to s Sudan and Ethiopia.

Grant's Gazelle lives in areas even after grasses have dried up, subsisting on shrubs and forbs; it also grazes green grass where available. This gazelle is typically distributed in small herds (around nine females and young with one territorial male) and separate bachelor herds averaging five males; groups are smaller in more closed habitats and larger on open plains like the Serengeti, where mixed herds of more than 400 occur in the dry season.

78 Dama Gazelle
Gazella dama

Description: A long-necked, long-limbed gazelle of the Sahel. Color 2-toned: *rich reddish brown above and white below,* the extent of red increasing from eastern to western part of range. *All races have white face, rump, and throat patch.* Horns back-slanting and S-shaped, relatively short (8–17″/20–43 cm long) for this largest of all gazelles; shorter and thinner in female. L 4′10″–5′9″ (1.45–1.72 m); T 10–14″ (25–35 cm); Ht 3–4′ (90–120 cm); Wt 88–165 lb (40–75 kg).

Subspecies: **Western Dama** (Mhorr Gazelle; *G. d. mhorr*) solid red everywhere except face, underparts, and rump; lives in s Morocco. **Red-necked Gazelle** (*G. d. ruficollis*) red only on neck and shoulders; lives in n Sudan.

Similar Species: **Gerenuk** is uniformly red-brown above, including face and rump.

Habitat: Arid zone between true desert and Sahel.

Breeding: 1 calf born after 6-month gestation; births peak at end of wet season.

Range: One of the most endangered antelopes, it is reduced to a few thousand animals in Mali, Niger, Chad, Burkina Faso, and Sudan.

One of the most desert-adapted antelopes, the Dama Gazelle is mainly a browser of acacias, desert dates, and shrubs, especially in temporary watercourses that provide greenery and shade. Formerly aggregations of hundreds migrated into the Sahara during rains, returning to the Sahel in the dry season.

79 Springbok
Springbuck
Antidorcas marsupialis

Description: *Crest of erectile white hair on lower back* (normally concealed in a skin fold). Tan to cinnamon-brown, with extensive areas of *white, including head,* underparts, backs of legs, tail, and rump patch that merges with spinal crest; dark brown side stripe and cheek stripe, and black tail tip. Horns strongly ridged; bowed out with tips hooked inward like stethoscope; 14–20″ (35–49 cm) long. L 3′2″–4′6″ (96–134 cm); T 6–12″

Hoofprint

(15–30 cm); Ht 28–34″ (71–86 cm); Wt 58–106 lb (26–48 kg).

Subspecies: Races of Angola and Namibia are considerably larger, with better developed horns in females, than the South African race.

Habitat: Dry savannas, subdeserts, and deserts.

Breeding: Year-round, with birth peaks in rainy season; 1 calf born after gestation of 6–7 months.

Range: Southwestern Angola, Namibia, Botswana, and South Africa.

The Springbok's name is derived from its "pronking" display, which is the most spectacular form of stotting (high bounding) of any antelope. This sign of excitement is elicited by various stimuli, especially predators. In a complete performance, a Springbok makes stiff-legged jumps to heights of 10 feet (3 m) with its head down, back bowed, and spinal crest fully erected. The Springbok grazes growing grass and herbs, but switches to browse in the dry season. In the Kalahari, it also eats melons, and can go without drinking as long as its food contains more than 10 percent water. It is migratory where there are no fences; aggregations of a few thousand in Botswana and Namibia recall the *trekbokken* of millions that formerly wandered southern Africa in search of food and water.

---

80 Gerenuk
Litocranius walleri

Description: Tall, with *very long neck and legs, narrow head, and big rounded ears.* Color pattern similar to Impala, with 2-tone torso: red-brown saddle delineated by light edging from buff-colored sides and limbs; underparts white; tiny white rump patch. Medium-length tail is chestnut on top surface to black tuft at end. Eye ring, chin, and insides of ears white; ear backs, forehead, and nose bridge brown like saddle. Horns in male only; S-shaped, massive, and heavily ridged; 13–18″ (32–44 cm) long. L 4′8″–5′4″ (1.4–1.6 m); T 9–14″ (23–35 cm); Ht 32–42″ (80–105 cm); Wt 64–114 lb (29–52 kg).

Similar Species: **Dibatag** *(Ammodorcas clarkei)* overlaps with Gerenuk in Horn of Africa; smaller (no more than 70 lb/32 kg), with gray upperparts, stronger facial markings, fluffy white buttocks, long dark tail, and short, forward-curving horns.

Habitat: Woody vegetation in semi-arid zones, especially thornbush below 4,000′ (1,200 m).

Breeding: Year-round; 1 calf born after gestation of 6.5–7 months.

Range: Eastern and c Ethiopia south through Somalia and Kenya to western side of rift valley in n Tanzania.

A pure browser, the Gerenuk selects the tenderest new foliage. Modified lumbar vertebrae, wedge-shaped hooves, and overdeveloped hindlegs enable it to stand erect to reach foliage more than 6 feet (2 m) high. The Gerenuk forms groups that average only two or three females and young, although up to nine may assemble in a temporary herd. Sub-adult males associate in pairs and trios, often attached to an adult female. Males defend territories, scent-marking the borders with preorbital-gland secretions.

Reedbucks and Kob

Tribe Reduncini

This tribe's eight species, all African, are medium-size to large grazers that live in savannas within a few miles of water. The mating system varies. Horns are present in males only: short and hooked forward in reedbucks, long and backswept in lechwes and the Waterbuck. The coat is greasy and strong-smelling. In resident populations, males may occupy the same territories for years.

81 Bohor Reedbuck
Redunca redunca

Description: *Rich yellow-brown upperparts.* Eye ring, lips, chin, and all underparts, including underside of bushy tail, white or grayish white. *Horns short* (8–16″/20–41 cm) *and hooked forward.* Glandular bare patch below ear. L 3′4″–4′4″ (1–1.3 m); T 6–10″ (15–25 cm); Ht 28–36″ (69–89 cm); Wt 79–121 lb (36–55 kg).

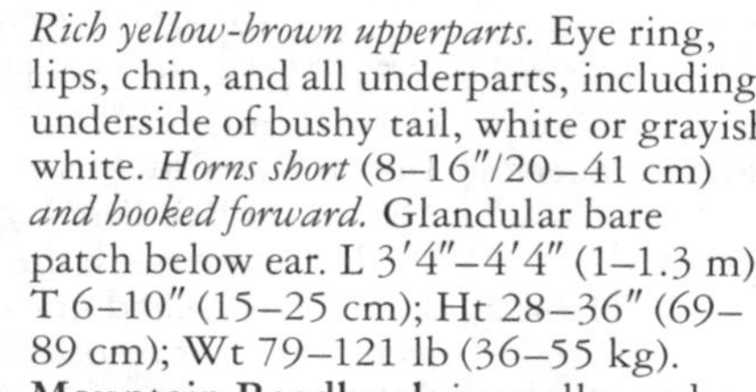

Similar Species: **Mountain Reedbuck** is smaller and grayer. **Common Reedbuck** is larger, less brightly colored, and has longer, less-hooked horns.

Habitat: Floodplain and drainage-line grasslands or reedbeds high enough to hide in.

Breeding: Year-round; 1 calf born after gestation of 7–7.5 months.

Range: Gambia east to Ethiopia, and south to s Tanzania.

In Sudan, floodplain populations of the Bohor Reedbuck concentrate in hundreds on fresh green grasses stimulated by annual fires. Male territories include up to four females, which remain separate with their own offspring as long as cover is available. After the range is burned, females associate in herds of up to ten. Male offspring are driven away beginning at six months, when their horns appear; they associate in small bachelor herds of two or three until they become adult at three years.

82 Common Reedbuck
Southern Reedbuck
Redunca arundinum

Description: The largest reedbuck. Unpatterned light to gray-brown face, head, torso, and outer sides of legs; contrasting white eye ring, insides of ears, chin and throat, belly, and underside of bushy tail. *Most races have dark stripe down front of foreleg.* Glandular bare patch below ear. *Strongly ridged, forward-curving horns form V shape as viewed from front,* typically 12″ (31 cm) long, up to 18″ (46 cm). L 4′6″–5′7″ (1.34–1.67 m); T 7–12″ (18–30 cm); Ht 33–39″ (83–98 cm); Wt 86–176 lb (39–80 kg).

Similar Species: **Bohor Reedbuck** is yellower and **Mountain Reedbuck** grayer; both are smaller and have shorter horns.

Habitat: Valley and upland grasslands close to water; grass or reeds tall enough to hide in.

Breeding: No strict breeding season; 1 young born after gestation of about 7.5 months.

Range: Central Zaire and s Tanzania south to Cape Province.

Common Reedbucks form monogamous pairs. Males defend territories by standing in proud posture, running with high bounds (stotting), and venting whistling alarm calls (also a response to predators). Temporary herds of up to seven females and young, with at most one adult male, form in the dry season, when fresh green grasses or removal of cover tempts or forces the animals into the open. Male offspring are tolerated by their fathers until they are nearly adult (three years old). Though predominantly a grazer, the Common Reedbuck eats herbs and foliage of woody plants when grass is very coarse and non-nutritious; it gets most of its water from forage and dew when pastures are green.

83 Mountain Reedbuck
Redunca fulvorufula

Description: *A small reedbuck, pale gray-tan with white underparts,* including bushy white undertail; *no other contrasting markings.* Horns short, strongly ridged, and forward-curving at tips; average 5–6″ (14 cm) long. Glandular bare spot below ear. L 3′8″–4′6″ (1.1–1.36 m); T 7–10″ (17–26 cm); Ht 26–30″ (65–76 cm); Wt 42–84 lb (19–38 kg).

Subspecies and Similar Species: **Southern Mountain Reedbuck** *(R. f. fulvorufula)* overlaps with **Common Reedbuck** in Swaziland and vicinity, but is scarcely half as big. Eastern African race, **Chanler's Mountain Reedbuck** *(R. f. chanleri),* can overlap with **Bohor Reedbuck,** but is distinguished by smaller size, grayer color, and slender horns that are not as strongly hooked. **Gray Rhebok**'s horns are nearly straight and vertical.

Habitat: Montane grasslands.

Breeding: Year-round; 1 calf born after 8-month gestation.

Range: Discontinuous: hills and mountains of e and s Africa; isolated population in e Nigeria and w Cameroon.

Unlike the other two reedbucks, the Mountain Reedbuck is sociable. Females and young live in herds of two to six (up to eight) animals whose home range includes the territories of several males; immature males associate in small bachelor herds. They are active night and day, but rest during the hottest hours.

---

84 Kob
Kobus kob

Description: Resembles a heavyset Impala. *Smooth shiny coat; golden to chestnut above and on front of neck, with white markings, including conspicuous eye ring,* insides of ears, throat patch, lower chest and belly, insides of legs, and underside of bushy tail. Male darkens with age. Black stripe down front of legs; black tail tip. S-shaped horns bend sharply backward, then curve up; heavily ridged; 16–28″ (40–69 cm) long. L 5′4″–6′ (1.6–1.8 m); T 7–16″ (18–40 cm); Ht 33–40″ (82–100 cm); Wt 132–266 lb (60–121 kg).

Subspecies: **White-eared Kob** *(K. k. leucotis)* ranges from s Sudan floodplains to Ethiopia border; male's blackish-brown coat with white markings and white ears make it among the most conspicuous antelopes. **Buffon's Kob** *(K. k. kob),* which ranges from Senegal to Chad and Central African Republic, is smaller, has shorter horns, and is bright yellow-brown without dark markings. **Uganda Kob** *(K. k. thomasi)* of e Africa is large, with long horns; male is dark tawny with black and white markings described above for species.

Similar Species: Smaller **Puku** occurs farther south and differs in having front of neck all white; lacks broad eye ring; no black on legs or tail.

Habitat: Well-watered areas such as floodplains; avoids hills.

Breeding: Year-round; 1 calf born after 8-month gestation.

Range: Senegal to s Sudan, south to Uganda, w Kenya, e Rwanda, and n Zaire.

The Kob is a pure grazer and is active mainly during the day. Females and young of the year associate in herds of five to 40 animals that frequently exchange members. Bachelor herds include both young and old males. Breeding males either occupy conventional territories or compete for central positions on a lek (breeding ground), where females come to breed. Up to 90 percent of females in a local population visit the leks on their day in estrus and mate with centrally placed males. Leks of Uganda Kobs are permanent fixtures, visible as lawns of short grass or bare ground surrounded by higher vegetation. The White-eared Kob of southern Sudan mates during migration, establishing temporary leks during a defined mating season.

85 Puku
Kobus vardonii

Description: *Similar to Kob, but smaller; golden, without conspicuous markings.* Off-white areas around eyes, cheeks, throat, and underparts, including tail. S-shaped horns shorter and stouter than Kob's; strongly ridged; 18–21″ (45–53 cm) long. L 4′2″–4′9″ (1.26–1.42 m); T 11–13″ (28–32 cm); Ht 31–40″ (78–100 cm); Wt 136–198 lb (62–90 kg).

Similar Species: **Red Lechwe** (see Lechwe) is bright chestnut; has striped legs, and longer, thinner horns. **Common Reedbuck** is browner, with whiter underparts and bushier tail.

Habitat: Floodplain grasslands near water.

Breeding: Year-round; 1 calf born after gestation of 8 months.

Range: Discontinuous: c and w Tanzania, sw and se Zaire, ne Angola, nw and sw Zambia east of Zambezi; Chobe NP, in n Botswana.

The Puku fills the same ecological niche in the southern savanna as the Kob does farther north, and it exhibits the same behavior and social organization, although leks have not been recorded. Herds rarely number more than ten loosely associated females plus their young.

---

86 Lechwe
Southern Lechwe
Kobus leche

Description: A long-bodied antelope, with hindquarters taller than forequarters, and *elongated hooves with wide splay. Coat fairly long, rough, and greasy.* White underparts, neck, chin, mouth, and lips; underside of round, black-tipped tail also white; foreleg has black stripe. Basic color varies according to sex (male darkens with age) and among subspecies

Hoofprint

(see below). Horns long and back-slanted, with upturned tips; ridged but comparatively thin; 18–37″ (45–92 cm) long. L 4′4″–6′ (1.3–1.8 m); T 11–15″ (28–37 cm); Ht 3′–3′9″ (90–112 cm); Wt 136–282 lb (62–128 kg).

Subspecies and Ranges: **Red Lechwe** *(K. l. leche)* is bright chestnut, with black stripe down front side of foreleg; exists in numerous small populations in w Zambia, n Botswana, and se and c Angola. **Kafue Lechwe** *(K. l. kafuensis)* is browner; black foreleg markings extend onto male's shoulders; lives on Kafue Flats, in Zambia. Male **Black Lechwe** *(K. l. smithemani)* turns nearly black; occurs at Lake Bangweulu, in Zambia.

Similar Species: **Puku** is more compact and lacks black stripe on foreleg.

Habitat: Floodplains bordering swamps and marshes.

Breeding: Geographically variable, with peaks at floods or when flooding recedes; 1 calf born after gestation estimated at 7–8 months.

The most aquatic antelope after the Sitatunga, the Lechwe wades to feed on grasses that grow in inundated pastures; when floodwaters recede, it grazes the lush grasses that spring up on the emergent ground, often concentrating in large herds on these greenbelts. A slow, clumsy runner on land, it can outrun its predators in shallow water, thanks to its powerful hindquarters, which propel it in long leaps, and its elongated hooves, which keep it from sinking down in muddy bottoms. Most Red Lechwe males space themselves out in non-overlapping territories, but at high density the fittest mature males of the Kafue and Black races form leks during the rainiest period between November and February.

87 Nile Lechwe
Kobus megaceros

Description: Resembles Lechwe in form, but shaggier, with pronounced short throat mane or beard. *Mature male mahogany or blackish brown;* develops conspicuous white or yellowish nape stripe and shoulder harness. Female and immatures of both sexes yellow-brown, with white or yellowish markings around eyes, muzzle, chin, and throat; whitish ears, underparts, and medium-length, black-tipped tail. Long ridged horns curve back and down, then up; 18–35″ (45–87 cm) long. L 4′6″–5′6″ (1.35–1.65 m); T 18–20″ (45–50 cm); Ht 32–42″ (80–105 cm); Wt 132–264 lb (60–120 kg).

Similar Species: **White-eared Kob** (see Kob) has sleeker coat and shorter, more upright horns.

Habitat: Floodplain and freshwater marshes.

Breeding: Probably year-round, with likely peak in flood months; 1 calf born after gestation of 7–8 months.

Range: Sudd marshes of s Sudan; Machar marshes on w Ethiopia border.

Ecologically and socially similar to the Lechwe, the Nile Lechwe is equally gregarious. Female herds with more than one adult male have been reported, in addition to separate bachelor herds.

88, 89 Waterbuck
Kobus ellipsiprymnus

Description: A *large shaggy antelope,* with a long body and rather short sturdy legs. Reddish brown to grizzled gray, darkening with age; legs black. White markings include eyebrows, insides of ears, muzzle (nostrils bare and black), *throat bib,* and *buttocks or rump ring.* Horns long, strong, heavily ridged; points curve forward; 22–40″ (55–99 cm) long. L 5′11″–7′10″ (1.77–2.35 m); T 13–16″ (33–40 cm); Ht 4′–4′3″ (1.19–1.27 m); Wt 356–574 lb (162–261 kg).

Hoofprint

Subspecies and Ranges: **Defassa Waterbuck** *(K. e. defassa)* is more reddish and has solid white buttocks; occurs west of eastern rift valley, from e Senegal east to w Ethiopia and south to w Zambia. **Common Waterbuck** *(K. e. ellipsiprymnus)* has "bull's-eye" rump ring; occurs east of eastern rift valley, from c Kenya south to n Botswana and e South Africa.

Habitat: Grasslands near woodlands, within a few miles of water.

Breeding: Year-round in e Africa; 1 calf born after gestation of 8–8.5 months; births peak during rainy seasons.

Prime male Waterbucks (seven to nine years old) defend the largest, best territories. Females with a common home range associate casually in small herds of five to ten animals. Bachelor herds often stay near female herds. Some territorial males tolerate adult males on their property as long as they behave submissively; these males help repel other male intruders, sneak occasional matings, and have a good chance of inheriting the territory.

Rhebok
Tribe Peleini

This tribe comprises only one species.

---

90 Gray Rhebok
Pelea capreolus

Description: A rather small-bodied antelope, with long graceful limbs and neck. *Woolly coat gray above, scarcely lighter below, except for white inner thighs and undertail;* fronts of lower legs darker. Dark facial blaze. *Black bulbous nostrils; black inside long narrow ears. Horns, in males only, are upright stilettos rising directly over eyes;* ridged at base; 6–10″ (15–25 cm) long. L 3′6″–4′2″ (1.05–1.25 m); Ht 28–32″ (70–80 cm); Wt 42–66 lb (19–30 kg).

Similar Species: **Mountain Reedbuck** has smaller ears, forward-hooked horns, and bare glandular patch below ears.

Habitat: Slope and plateau grasslands and scrub; avoids tall grasslands.

Breeding: 1 calf born after gestation of 8.7 months; most births occur November–January.

Range: South Africa in highlands above 3,300′ (1,000 m), and near sea level in Cape Province.

The Gray Rhebok grazes the higher slopes during the growing season and browses at lower elevations during the dry season, obtaining sufficient water from herbs, leaves, and green shoots. The mating system is polygynous. Territorial males have exclusive harems, typically of three to five females and their offspring, that live permanently on the territory. Instead of forming bachelor herds, young males remain peripheral until mature enough to claim their own territory.

Horse Antelopes
Tribe Hippotragini

There are six species of horse antelopes worldwide, of which five live in Africa. These are large, powerfully built antelopes of vaguely horse-like appearance and conspicuous coloration. Most have distinctive facial patterns. The sexes are alike, although males are 10 to 20 percent heavier, with thicker horns. All members of this tribe are primarily grazers, but they also browse foliage and herbs when necessary. All species are sociable. Females and young live in herds as small as half a dozen to as large as 60 or more; sometimes hundreds still aggregate on a scarce resource. Unless migratory, males defend large territories and keep bachelor males segregated.

91 **Roan**
Roan Antelope
Hippotragus equinus

Description: A tall, powerfully built antelope. *Upper body gray to roan* (grizzled rufous); legs darker; lower belly, hams, and ruff of longer hair under neck pale gray to white. *Striking black-and-white facial mask; very long ears end in black tassels.* Upstanding mane, with dark-tipped hairs; thin, black-tipped tail. Horns relatively short and thick; deeply ridged; curved backward in an arc; 22–40″ (55–99 cm) long. L 6′4″–8′ (1.9–2.4 m); T 24–28″ (60–70 cm); Ht 4′2″–4′10″ (1.26–1.45 m); Wt 488–658 lb (222–299 kg).

Hoofprint

Similar Species: **Sable** male is black, with much larger horns; female is redder. **Waterbuck** has longer neck; male has longer horns that arc forward, while female is hornless.

Habitat: Tall grasslands and miombo woodlands.

Breeding: Year-round; 1 calf born after gestation of 9–9.5 months.

Range: Senegal east to w Ethiopia, and south to Transvaal, n Botswana, and Namibia.

Female and young Roans live in stable herds of six to 35 animals. Males associate in bachelor herds until they are mature enough to defend territories at age five; females remain in their mothers' home ranges. As water-dependent grazers, Roans disperse during rains but aggregate within a few miles of water during the dry season. Before the Roan's decline, temporary aggregations of more than 100 of these animals were not uncommon in West Africa.

---

92 **Sable**
Sable Antelope
Hippotragus niger

Description: One of the handsomest antelopes. Heavyset, with sturdy limbs and thick

neck enhanced by upstanding mane; *long, scimitar-shaped horns.* Short glossy coat, *jet-black in mature male, sorrel to rich chestnut in female and young* (except southern race). Both sexes have *conspicuous white on head, lower belly, inner thighs, and buttocks.* Male darkens and gains maximum horn development by 5 years. Male horns 32–66″ (80–165 cm) long; female 24–40″ (60–100 cm) long. L 6′7″–7′ (1.97–2.1 m); Ht 3′10″–4′8″ (1.15–1.4 m); Wt 450–580 lb (204–263 kg).

Hoofprint

Subspecies and Ranges: **Roosevelt Sable** *(H. n. roosevelti),* now found in Kenya's Shimba Hills NR (fewer than 200 animals) and Tanzania's Selous GR, has smallest horns: maximum 3′4″ (1 m) long. **Kirk's Sable** *(H. n. kirkii),* which ranges from nw Tanzania through Mozambique, Zambia, Zimbabwe, se Zaire, and e Angola to Zambezi, is most widely distributed and abundant race. **Southern Sable** (Black Black Sable; *H. n. niger*) lives south of Zambezi into n Botswana and e Transvaal; both sexes turn dark; hooked, longer horns of adult male (average 3′5″/1.03 m) are most obvious gender difference. **Giant Sable** *(H. n. variani)* is "giant" only because male horns average a foot longer than in other Sables; endangered population lives in c Angola, in a large reserve (Luando) and a small park (Kangandala).

Similar Species: Female Sable is readily distinguishable from female **Roan** by browner, glossier coat, more extensive white markings, and shorter ears without tassels.

Habitat: Broad-leafed, deciduous woodlands, interspersed with floodplain grasslands. Dependent on drinking holes and perhaps on mineral licks; associated with termite mounds.

Breeding: Annual, with births usually at end of rains; 1 calf born after gestation of about 9 months.

Sable herds typically number from 30 to 75 females and young that share a large home range of 4 to 10 square miles (10–25 sq km) in nutritionally poor miombo woodlands. A cow herd's range overlaps the territories of up to five bulls. Males leave the cow herds in their fourth year and either join together in small bachelor herds (ten animals or fewer) or stay alone until mature.

93 Addax
Addax nasomaculatus

Description: The "Sahara caribou." Short body and neck; legs knock-kneed, with large rounded hooves. *Horns an open spiral;* male 24–44″ (60–109 cm) long, female 22–32″ (55–80 cm) long. Summer coat grayish white; winter coat gray to gray-brown; older individuals lighter. Underparts, rump, limbs, chin, lips, and insides of ears pure white. Forehead has mat of dark brown hair bordering white, X-shaped facial blaze; longer hairs on throat make scraggly beard. L 4′–4′4″ (1.2–1.3 m); T 10–14″ (25–35 cm); Ht 3′2″–3′10″ (95–115 cm); Wt 180–275 lb (82–125 kg).

Habitat: Sandy and stony deserts.

Breeding: 1 calf born after 8.6-month gestation, in September and October and January–April.

Range: Formerly on both sides of Sahara; reduced to a few hundred survivors in remotest reaches of Niger and Chad.

Next to the camel, the Addax is probably the most perfectly desert-adapted large mammal, able to extract the water it needs from the plants it eats: sparse desert tussock-grasses, herbs, and the ephemeral grasses that spring up after rare thunderstorms. This species formerly migrated seasonally between the Sahara and the Sahel, sometimes forming aggregations as large as 1,000 animals. Granted effective protection, the Addax might yet be restored as a wild animal through captive breeding and reintroduction of some of the 1,400 or more individuals currently in zoos.

94–96 **Oryx**
Gemsbok
Oryx gazella

Description: *A large antelope with very long straight or slightly curved horns.* Built rather like a polo pony: compact body with sturdy limbs; short stiff neck mane; small dewlap at jaw/throat intersection. *Black flank stripe; black-and-white facial pattern;* narrow black stripe on spine and chin to chest; black garter on foreleg; *long black tail.* Male heavier, with thicker neck and horns, but female horns equally long: 3′6″–4′ (1.05–1.2 m). L 5′1″–5′8″ (1.53–1.7 m); T 18–36″ (45–90 cm); Ht 3′10″–4′2″ (1.15–1.25 m); Wt 255–460 lb (116–209 kg).

Hoofprint

Subspecies and Ranges: **Beisa Oryx** *(O. g. beisa)* is grayish tan, with very conspicuous black markings; ranges from Ethiopia to Tana River, in e Kenya. **Fringe-eared Oryx** *(O. g. callotis)* is browner, with tuft of black hair growing from ear tips; markings similar to Beisa but less contrasting; ranges from Tana River, in Kenya, to c Tanzania. **Gemsbok** *(O. g. gazella)* is pale gray, with large black patches on rump and on upper hindlegs; ranges from sw Zimbabwe and sw Angola through Botswana and Namibia to n Cape Province.

Habitat: Acacia savannas to deserts. Stony plains, sand dunes, and mountains.

Breeding: Year-round; 1 calf born after gestation of 8.5 months.

The Oryx's ability to survive in waterless areas is second only to that of the Addax among African antelopes. It subsists on coarse desert grasses, browses to some extent, and digs up tubers, roots, and bulbs, filling its water needs with these, along with melons and wild cucumbers in the Kalahari and other sandy soils. The Oryx forms mixed herds, each dominated by an alpha bull who treats subordinate males like unreceptive females. While it is highly nomadic in the desert, where conditions permit (i.e., where there are water holes or water-bearing vegetation) herds may remain year-round in smaller home ranges, within which bulls defend territories.

---

97 Scimitar-horned Oryx
Scimitar Oryx, White Oryx
Oryx dammah

Description: A large antelope, with *scimitar- or sickle-shaped horns* 3′4″–4′2″ (1–1.25 m) long in both sexes. *Coat white with deep russet neck and chest,* washed lighter over flanks and thighs; faint ruddy flank stripe. Outer half of long-haired tail dark brown. Ht 3′11″ (1.17 m); Wt 450 lb (204 kg).

Similar Species: Similar in color to **Dama Gazelle,** an otherwise very different and much smaller animal with short, S-shaped horns.

Habitat: Grassy steppes, rolling dunes, and wooded depressions between dunes in arid grasslands.

Breeding: 1 calf born after gestation of 8–8.5 months.

Range: Persisted in Sahel of Niger and Chad until recent years; now possibly extinct in the wild.

A nomadic, sociable grazer, this oryx traveled in mixed herds of a dozen to 70 animals, grazing at the desert edge when it rained and retreating southward to green patches in otherwise drought-stricken country for the other nine months of the year. Conceivably the Scimitar-horned Oryx, like the Addax, may one day be reintroduced to its former range, as more than 1,000 animals currently live in zoos.

Hartebeests and Wildebeests
Tribe Alcelaphini

The seven species in this tribe, which all live in Africa, are nomadic or migratory grazers that formerly ranged in huge herds over grasslands in many areas of Africa; today just a few populations of wildebeests and Topis survive in anything approaching their former numbers. They are mainly large and conspicuous, with long, narrow faces; their long legs and overdeveloped forequarters are adapted for loping long distances during migration. Both sexes have horns and look much alike, although adult males are 10 to 20 percent heavier than females. The mating system is polygynous. Three members of this tribe, the Blesbok and two wildebeests, are unlike all other antelopes in having follower young that never hide—another adaptation to a migratory existence.

98, 99 **Hartebeest**
Alcelaphus buselaphus

Description: A tall, narrow, high-shouldered antelope with a long narrow head; *forehead elongated to form bony pedicle that supports thick, ridged horns,* 18–28″ (45–70 cm) long. Pedicle height and horn length and shape vary with race, as do color and markings of short glossy coat. Tail black. L 5′10″–8′2″ (1.75–2.45 m); T 18–28″ (45–70 cm); Ht 3′7″–4′9″ (1.07–1.43 m); Wt 284–502 lb (129–228 kg).

Hoofprint

Subspecies and Ranges: **Western Hartebeest** *(A. b. major),* which ranges from Senegal to Central African Republic, is largest race; plain tan, with dark shadows on leg fronts; horns U-form when viewed from front. **Lelwel Hartebeest** *(A. b. lelwel),* which lives from Chad to s Sudan and in n and w Uganda, is uniformly reddish brown; has V-form horns on very high pedicle.

Virtually indistinguishable from Lelwel is reddish **Jackson's Hartebeest** *(A. b. jacksoni),* of Uganda and w Kenya; probably a hybrid of Lelwel and Coke's Hartebeest. **Swayne's Hartebeest** *(A. b. swaynei),* of Somalia, and **Coke's Hartebeest** *(A. b. cokii),* of s Kenya to c Tanzania, are smallest races, with less-developed pedicle; Swayne's is chocolate-brown, with black snout, forehead, and upper forelegs; Coke's is tan relieved only by white rump; both races have horns diverging almost horizontally at base, forming bracket shape. **Red Hartebeest** *(A. b. caama)* occurs in Botswana, Namibia, and n Cape Province, and has been widely introduced in other South African provinces; coat is rich reddish brown, contrasting with white rump; has black snout and forehead, and black blotches on upper legs. Like Lelwel, Red Hartebeest has V-form horns on greatly elongated pedicle.

Similar Species: **Lichtenstein's Hartebeest** has ruddy saddle extending to base of tail, only slightly developed pedicle, and shorter, O-form horns. **Topi** has simpler horns and normal forehead.

Habitat: Medium and tall grasslands, including savannas; montane grasslands.

Breeding: Seasonal in s Africa; year-round in e Africa, where females may be accompanied by 3 or 4 offspring born 9–10 months apart. 1 calf born after 8-month gestation.

All Hartebeest subspecies have the ability to tolerate high-fiber/low-protein grass. A long narrow muzzle enables Hartebeests to graze very selectively. Red Hartebeests living in the semi-arid Kalahari still form large aggregations and migrate, subsisting in waterless areas by eating melons, roots, and tubers. But most populations are resident, with a male territorial network containing small herds of females and young; herds of bachelor males occupy marginal habitats.

100 **Lichtenstein's Hartebeest**
Alcelaphus lichtensteinii

Description: In many ways, looks and behaves like another Hartebeest subspecies. *Frontal pedicle (base for horns) not well developed. Horns thick and strongly ridged at base forming O when viewed from front; tips curve back at acute angle;* 20–24″ (50–60 cm) long. Reddish-brown saddle extends to base of tail, contrasting with white buttocks and grading into pale flanks and underparts; chin, tail tip, and stripe down foreleg black. L 5′4″–6′8″ (1.6–2 m); T 16–20″ (40–50 cm); Ht 4′–4′6″ (1.19–1.36 m); Wt 275–449 lb (125–204 kg).

Similar Species: **Coke's Hartebeest** (see Hartebeest), possibly overlapping in c Tanzania, is paler, with bracket-shaped horns.

Habitat: Miombo woodlands.

Breeding: 1 calf born after 8-month gestation; most births late in dry season (around September).

Range: Southeastern Zaire and c Tanzania south to ne Angola, ne Zimbabwe, and c Mozambique.

More of a woodland dweller than other hartebeests, Lichtenstein's is an "edge" species that favors the grassland strips that dissect the woodlands. Males defend sizable territories within which small herds of related females and young may reside semi-permanently.

101, 102 **Topi**
Tsessebe, Korrigum, Tiang
Damaliscus lunatus

Description: Built for speed and endurance, with high shoulders, deep chest, and long trim legs. Basic color varies geographically from light tan to chestnut, hue intensifying from south to north and west to east; *most races exhibit pronounced sheen and conspicuous*

Hoofprint

purple blotches or wash on forehead, snout, and upper limbs. Coloring lighter on back and rump than on underparts, increasing conspicuousness. Horns strong and deeply ridged; variable in size and shape in different subspecies (see below). L 5–6′ (1.5–1.8 m); T 16–21″ (40–53 cm); Ht 3′6″–4′2″ (1.04–1.26 m); Wt 198–323 lb (90–147 kg), to 500 lb (227 kg) in Korrigum.

Subspecies and Ranges: **Korrigum** *(D. l. korrigum),* which ranges from Senegal to Nile in Sudan, is bright reddish; has longest horns (18–24″/45–60 cm). **Tiang** *(D. l. tiang),* which lives from s Sudan floodplains to Ethiopia, is smaller and redder, with slender horns; has most numerous remaining population (estimated 750,000 in 1980s). **Topi** *(D. l. jimela),* of e Africa west of eastern rift valley in Kenya, Uganda, Rwanda, and Tanzania, is dark reddish brown with strong purple wash, and has small horns. **Topi** *(D. l. topi)* has isolated population in e Kenya north of Tana River; dark ruddy brown like *jimela.* **Tsessebe** *(D. l. lunatus)* occurs from ne Zambia to Angola and ne Botswana, and south to ne Transvaal; reddish like Korrigum and Tiang; horns have uniform, weak outward curve and are relatively short (12–16″/30–40 cm).

Similar Species: **Hirola** *(D. hunteri),* which ranges from ne Kenya to s Somalia, has white chevron between eyes; unpatterned and lighter reddish coat, without purple; white tail with black tip. **Hartebeest** has elongated forehead.

Habitat: Medium grasslands, from lightly wooded savannas to broad floodplains; rarely above 4,500′ (1,400 m).

Breeding: 1 calf born after gestation of 7.5–8 months.

The Topi is a pure grazer with the ability to select green leaf within swards of dry grass. Where grassland occurs in small patches, populations are sedentary and dispersed; males occupy sizable permanent territories that are home to closed herds of between two and ten females and young. Male (and some female) offspring join bachelor herds as yearlings until males mature at three years. In denser populations on broad floodplains, Topis move about constantly in search of new growth, and males occupy territories only briefly during stationary intervals. The Topi is one of only three antelopes known to form breeding leks (see Kob and Lechwe). In certain spots where females regularly congregate, males cluster on traditional breeding grounds; most females visit this "lek" on their day of estrus and mate with the fittest males.

103, 104 **Blesbok**
Bontebok
Damaliscus dorcas

Description: The smallest and most colorful member of the tribe. *Plum or purplish brown, shading to light tan on back; pure white facial blaze, underparts, and lower legs.* Horns as in Topi; 14–15″ (35–38 cm) long. L 4′8″–5′4″ (1.4–1.6 m); Ht 3′ (90 cm); Wt 123–189 lb (56–86 kg).

Subspecies and Ranges: **Blesbok** *(D. d. phillipsi),* which occurs from n Cape Province east to n Natal, has less white on rump; tiny dark band interrupts white facial blaze; outer legs brown like upperparts. **Bontebok** *(D. d. dorcas),* of sw Cape Province, has darker coat contrasting with white rump patch that surrounds tail; lower legs are white all around; white facial blaze continuous from nose to base of horns.

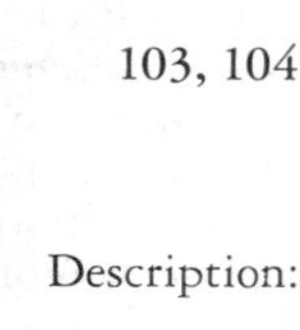

Similar Species: **Topi** lacks white markings.

Habitat: Grasslands of highveld and coastal plains.

Breeding: 1 calf born September–February, after gestation of 8–8.5 months.

This species, like the Topi, can be either resident or migratory. During the breeding season, spacing between territorial Blesbok males is reduced to only 80 yards (meters), compared to 300 yards between territorial Bontebok males. This species was a dominant member of the once-teeming highveld ecosystem; it has been narrowly saved from extinction. Several hundred Bonteboks survive in parks and reserves in southwestern Cape Province; privatization of wildlife led to reintroductions of the Blesbok, which now numbers more than 50,000.

105–107 **Wildebeest**
White-bearded Gnu, Brindled Gnu, Blue Wildebeest
Connochaetes taurinus

Description: An unusual-looking antelope, with a *broad and flattened muzzle; cow-like horns, short neck, and high shoulders.* Blue-gray or brown, lighter above and darker below, with *black vertical stripes of longer hair on forequarters.* Facial blaze, hair of long tail, and mane black; beard may be black or white. Horns unridged, with a knobby boss (raised base of horns) in older animals; horns much thicker and somewhat longer in male (22–32″/55–80 cm) than in female (18–25″/45–63 cm)—both horns measured together from tip to tip along curve. L 6′4″–7′ (1.9–2.1 m); T 24–40″ (60–100 cm); Ht 3′10″–4′10″ (1.15–1.45 m); Wt 350–600 lb (160–272 kg).

Hoofprint

Subspecies and Ranges: **Western White-bearded Wildebeest** *(C. t. mearnsi),* of sw Kenya and n Tanzania west of rift valley, is dark gray; smallest (Wt 350–450 lb/160–205 kg), with shortest horns, but most vociferous (bulls sound like giant bullfrogs). **Eastern White-bearded Wildebeest** *(C. t. albojubatus),* of s Kenya and Tanzania east of eastern rift valley, is light buffy gray, with black mane and whitish beard. **Johnston's Wildebeest** *(C t. johnstoni),* of s Tanzania

south to c Mozambique, usually has fringe of light-colored hair on face. **Cookson's Wildebeest** *(C. t. cooksoni),* of Luangwa Valley in Zambia, has grayish-red coat. **Blue Wildebeest** *(C. t. taurinus),* of s Tanzania to ne South Africa, Botswana, w Zambia, and se Angola, has black beard and upstanding mane, and tan lower legs.

Habitat: Short and medium-length grasslands between savanna and arid biomes.

Breeding: 1 calf born after gestation of 8–8.5 months; births peak in rainy season (February in Tanzania's Serengeti).

The Wildebeest is the dominant plains antelope in the acacia savannas of eastern and southern Africa. Its broad mouth equips it to graze a wide swath in short nutritious grasslands, and it is built to migrate long distances in search of green pastures. The Serengeti population of 1.4 million moves in huge herds, concentrating during the rains on the short-grass plains, and during the dry season circulating through the savanna, where water and green pastures are to be found. Bulls defend temporary territories in migratory populations.

---

108 Black Wildebeest

White-tailed Gnu

Connochaetes gnou

Description: Smaller than the other wildebeest, with nearly level back; *tufts of long hair growing on face* and beady black eyes create bizarre appearance. *Beard and mane also brush-like; long tuft of dark hair on chest. Conspicuous, white, horse-like tail.* Coat very dark brown to black; short and shiny in summer, shaggy in winter. Smooth horns curve downward and point forward and upward like meat hooks; expanded into shield at base, especially in male; 22–31″ (54–78 cm) long in male, 18–24″ (45–60 cm) in female, measured along curve. L 6′2″–7′4″ (1.85–2.2 m); T 32–40″ (80–100 cm); Ht 3′8″–4′ (1.11–1.21 m); Wt 242–352 lb (110–160 kg).

Habitat: Grasslands of highveld; arid shrublands of Karroo region.

Breeding: 1 calf born after 8.5-month gestation; most births in December and January.

Range: Formerly ranged Orange Free State, Transvaal, and Cape Province. Rescued from extinction in late 19th century; increased from 300 in 1938 to more than 10,000 in 1990s, mainly on private farms in South Africa.

In the past, the Black Wildebeest migrated to the Karroo region of South Africa during the rains to graze the short green grass, returning to the taller grasslands and water holes of the highveld to spend the cold dry months. Today virtually all Black Wildebeests are fenced in, fragmented in hundreds of isolated groups. Females and young live in closed herds averaging from 11 to 32 animals. Bulls defend sizable territories; nonbreeding males of all ages associate in bachelor herds.

IMPALA
Tribe Aepycerotini

This tribe comprises one species, described below.

109, 110 **Impala**
Aepyceros melampus

Description: Medium-size; graceful build, with *long neck* and long, evenly developed limbs. Coat short and glossy; *2-tone brown: saddle of rufous-brown over tan torso* and limbs. Black markings include ear tips, forehead patch, *3 vertical lines on rump* (2 on hams, 1 down center of tail), and *hair tufts above rear hooves,* over scent glands. Underside of tail, inner thighs, belly, throat, lips, eye line, and insides of ears white. Male and female colored alike. Horns in male only; wide-spread, S-shaped, prominently ridged; 18–37″ (45–92 cm) long. L 4′3″–4′9″ (1.28–1.42 m); T 9–13″ (23–33 cm); Ht 28–37″ (70–93 cm); Wt 88–167 lb (40–76 kg).

Hoofprint

Subspecies: East African races (*A. m. rendilis* and *A. m. swara*), which range from Kenya and Uganda to c Tanzania, are bright rufous and have the largest horns. **Southern Impala** *(A. m. melampus),* which lives from Zambia and s Tanzania south to Swaziland, is duller, with smaller horns. **Black-faced Impala** *(A. m. petersi),* of s Angola and n Namibia, has black facial blaze and very bushy tail.

Similar Species: **Gerenuk** is similarly colored, but has longer neck, much shorter horns, and broad white eye ring. **Grant's Gazelle** has paler upperparts and extensive white rump patch directly bordered by vertical dark stripes. **Kob** and **Puku** are brighter rufous or golden on upperparts, without rump stripes.

Habitat: Woodland and grassland edges, usually within a few miles of water.

Breeding: 1 calf born after gestation of about 6.5 months; in s Africa, most births occur in November and December, in e Africa year-round.

Range: Kenya, Rwanda, and Uganda south to ne South Africa; isolated black-faced race in nw Namibia.

A grazer during rains that switches to browse in the dry season, the Impala outcompetes pure grazers and browsers within its habitat, reaching high population densities. Herds of females and young often number 50 to 100. Small calves are often seen in groups, guarded by one or more mothers while others go off to feed or drink. The proximity of sizable bachelor herds containing potential rivals puts territorial males to frequent tests of fitness. Impalas are renowned jumpers.

Spiral-horned Antelopes
Tribe Tragelaphini

There are nine species, all confined to Africa. Most are woodland browsers and mixed feeders, built for jumping or careful movement rather than swift running; they are striped and spotted for concealment, and more or less nocturnal. The spiral horns are either tightly wound on their axis or in the form of an open corkscrew; females of most species are hornless. Females and young typically associate peaceably in small herds on small home ranges; males live in small bachelor groups, becoming increasingly solitary with maturity. The mating system is polygynous, but instead of competing for territory, a male of this tribe dominates rivals to mate with a female in heat. This type of sexual competition places a premium on larger size and organs of display and combat in males.

111, 112 Bushbuck
Tragelaphus scriptus

Description: The smallest member of the tribe; a secretive woodland antelope with a narrow, rounded form. *Coat smooth,* except for erectile spinal crest; usually yellowish or reddish tan above (older male dark chestnut, young reddish brown). *6 or 7 thin, white, vertical stripes from shoulder to rump, irregularly spaced; white spots* on cheek, on muzzle between eyes, and on flanks and rump. Bushy tail white underneath. Southern and Ethiopian races are dark, with faint or no stripes. Horns in male only; nearly straight, with 1 tight twist; 10–23″ (26–57 cm) long. L 3′8″–4′10″ (1.1–1.45 m); T 12–14″ (30–35 cm); Ht 26–40″ (65–100 cm); Wt 55–176 lb (25–80 kg).

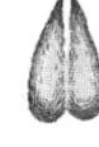

Hoofprint

Similar Species: Female **Nyala** is larger and redder, with 12 or more vertical white stripes, and has prominent white chevron between eyes. Female **Sitatunga** is shaggy; has long hooves and is restricted to marsh habitat.

Habitat: Edges of gallery and rain forests; montane forests with glades; forest-savanna mosaics; bush savannas.

Breeding: Year-round in most areas; 1 young born after gestation of 6–7 months.

Range: Senegal east to Ethiopia, and south through Congo Basin and e Africa to n Botswana and s Cape Province.

The Bushbuck is a mixed feeder on green grass, foliage, herbs, fruit, and flowers, and is often a garden pest; it is active mainly at night. This is the only solitary antelope that is not territorial, although each adult may have an exclusive resting and hiding place. Individuals with overlapping home ranges meet cordially enough, but the biggest male monopolizes females in heat.

---

113 Sitatunga
Tragelaphus spekii

Description: The most amphibious antelope. *Hoof elongated and narrow, with wide splay.* Build similar to Bushbuck's. *Coat shaggy and oily;* longer in male. Female has spots and 2–8 vertical white stripes on body; male's longer hair partially obscures white markings, except for spinal crest, spots on cheeks, *partial chevron between eyes,* and 1 or 2 patches on throat. Male coloring varies from chocolate-brown with conspicuous white spotting and stripes in western race, to gray-brown with no stripes in southern race; female reddish (western) or yellowish (southern). Horns in male only; have 1–1.5 turns, converge at tips; 18–36″ (45–90 cm) long. L 4′6″–5′8″ (1.35–1.7 m); T 7–12″ (18–30 cm); Ht 30–50″ (75–125 cm); Wt 110–275 lb (50–125 kg).

Hoofprint

Similar Species: **Bushbuck** is smaller, with smoother coat, shorter, straighter horns, and small hooves.

Habitat: Swamps with papyrus, bulrushes, or other tall sedges.

Breeding: 1 calf born, usually during dry season, after 7.5-month gestation.

Range: Togo east to sw Kenya, and south to Botswana; isolated populations around Lake Chad, in Senegal, Gambia, s Sudan, and Ethiopia.

The Sitatunga is very difficult to see in the swamps where it spends the daylight hours hiding, resting, and ruminating on islands of vegetation or standing in water. Its movements are slow and stealthy. Most sightings are of a fleeing animal that plunges through the swamp and quickly disappears. Sitatungas come ashore at night along well-defined passageways to browse bushes and other undergrowth.

---

114 Nyala
Tragelaphus angasii

Description: A dryland equivalent of the Sitatunga, with normal hooves. Female and young short-haired; bright rufous-chestnut, with *12 or more vertical white stripes;* white spots on face, throat, lower flanks, and thighs. Male has fewer and less-conspicuous stripes and spots, but conspicuous white dorsal crest; coat turns charcoal gray, except for lower legs; *heavy fringe of dark hair down foreneck, underparts, and hindlegs contrasts with yellowish lower legs.* Both sexes have *white chevron between eyes.* Bushy tail black above, white below. Horns, in male only, have 1–1.5 turns; 24–33″ (60–83 cm) long. L 6–7′ (1.8–2.1 m); T 17″ (43 cm); Ht 3′1″–3′6″ (92–106 cm); Wt 121–275 lb (55–125 kg).

Similar Species: Smaller **Bushbuck** has fewer (in some races no) vertical white stripes and smooth coat; male lacks heavy fringing on underparts. **Sitatunga** female has fewer stripes; male lacks heavy fringe.

Habitat: Dense lowland woodlands and thickets near water, bordering on grasslands.

Breeding: Year-round, with birth peaks in Natal in May and August–December; 1 calf born after 7-month gestation.

Range: Southern Malawi south to Natal.

A mixed feeder, the Nyala comes out to graze floodplain grasslands at night during summer rains; in the dry season, it browses woodland leaves, herbs, pods, and fruit. Females often associate in herds of four or so, although the basic social unit is a female accompanied by her two most recent offspring. Immature males associate in twos and threes.

---

115 **Lesser Kudu**
Tragelaphus imberbis

Description: A smaller, clean-cut version of the Greater Kudu. *Mature male blue-gray,* darkening with age; female and young rufous. *White stripes numerous (up to 14) and striking; white patch on upper and lower throat;* 2 white cheek spots; *chevron between eyes.* Tail short, bushy, black-tipped, white underneath. Legs tawny, with black-and-white patches. Male has short spinal crest that is brown over shoulder, becoming white on back; no beard. Horns, in male only, have 2 spirals; 20–28″ (50–70 cm) long. L 5′4″–5′10″ (1.6–1.75 m); Ht 3′–3′6″ (90–105 cm); Wt 123–238 lb (56–108 kg).

Similar Species: **Greater Kudu** is larger; has fringing beard and fewer body stripes; lacks white patches on foreneck. Female **Bushbuck** spotted on torso; lacks white chevron on snout.

Habitat: Acacia and commiphora thornbush in arid savannas below 4,000′ (1,200 m).

Breeding: Year-round; 1 calf born after gestation of 7.5–8 months.

Range: Ethiopia and Somalia south through much of Kenya to c Tanzania.

The Lesser Kudu is a nearly pure browser; it is active day and night. A great jumper, it easily clears obstacles 8 feet (2.5 m) high. Two or three females with offspring often associate in stable herds. Sub-adult males often live in pairs, whereas adult males avoid one another.

116 Greater Kudu

Tragelaphus strepsiceros

Description: A *very tall, narrow-bodied* antelope, with a small head and *huge cupped ears.* Adult male blue-gray, darkening with age; female and young tan-colored. *White markings* on smooth coat include *6–10 vertical torso stripes, conspicuous chevron between eyes,* 2 cheek spots, underside of black-tipped, bushy tail, and erectile crest on neck and shoulders. Black garters on upper legs. Beard along entire throat, usually in male only. Female may have white fringe on throat. Horns, in male only, have up to 2 full turns; 3′4″–4′8″ (1–1.4 m) long along outer curve. L 6′4″–8′4″ (1.9–2.5 m); T 15–19″ (37–48 cm); Ht 3′4″–5′ (1–1.5 m); Wt 264–693 lb (120–315 kg).

Hoofprint

Similar Species: **Lesser Kudu** lacks shaggy beard, and has 2 distinct white patches on throat.

Habitat: Woodlands and bushlands to 8,000′ (2,450 m).

Breeding: Seasonal in s Africa, with most births in February and March; in equatorial regions, more extended, with most calving during rains. 1 calf born after 9-month gestation.

Range: Discontinuous from s Chad to Red Sea hills of Sudan, south to Cape Province, and west to Namibia and c Angola. Local and uncommon in Kenya and n Tanzania, but common farther south.

Female Greater Kudus form lasting associations (probably mothers and daughters) of two or three cows plus offspring; such small herds may combine temporarily in groups of 20 to 30. Outside of the annual mating peak, bachelor herds of two to 10 males may include mature bulls. Nearly pure browsers that feed on a variety of foliage, herbs, vines, tubers, succulents, flowers, and fallen fruit, Greater Kudus disperse widely during rains; they spend the dry season along rivers and bases of hills where evergreen growth persists.

---

117 Mountain Nyala
Tragelaphus buxtoni

Description: A large antelope more like the Greater Kudu than the Nyala. Sandy gray-brown to dark brown, with *few (2–5) white torso stripes;* white spots on flanks, rump, and cheeks; *white crescent below broad white throat patch; white chevron between eyes;* dark leg garters bordered by white patches. Coat short and glossy, except longer and stiffer on neck, shoulders, and rump of adult male, which also has long spinal crest from nape to tail. Horns, in male only, have 1.5 corkscrew turns; 34–46″ (85–116 cm) long. L 6′4″–8′4″ (1.9–2.5 m); T 8–10″ (20–25 cm); Ht 3′–4′6″ (90–135 cm); Wt 330–550 lb (150–250 kg).

Similar Species: Male **Greater Kudu** has beard and throat fringe. Much smaller female **Bushbuck** lacks nose chevron and has more rounded hindquarters.

Habitat: High-altitude woodlands, bush, grasslands, and moorlands at 10,000–14,000′ (3,000–4,000 m).

Breeding: 1 calf born after 9-month gestation; births peak in late wet season.

Range: Ethiopian highlands; chiefly east of rift valley.

An average group of Mountain Nyalas numbers eight or nine females and young. Males associate in bachelor groups of up to 13 animals, and with females. This "mountain kudu" browses herbs and the foliage of bushes and trees, and avoids cold and heat by resting in woodlands. It uses dense cover such as woodland and heather more in the dry season, feeding in moors and grasslands during rains.

118 Bongo

Tragelaphus (Boocercus) euryceros

Description: The largest forest antelope, built like a giant Bushbuck. Coat short and glossy; *rich chestnut* to brown-black (older male); female yellowish or light red. 12–14 narrow white torso stripes; black and white dorsal crest; whitish crescent under base of neck; *muzzle black, topped by conspicuous white nose chevron,* and flanked by 2 large white spots on cheek. *Legs boldly patterned chestnut, black, and white.* Ears huge, edged inside with black and white. Tail medium-length, white with black tip. Horns in both sexes have 1 turn; 30–40″ (75–99 cm) long; massive and diverging in male; thinner, more parallel, often longer in female. L 5′8″–8′4″ (1.7–2.5 m); T 18–26″ (45–65 cm); Ht 3′8″–4′4″ (1.1–1.3 m); Wt 462–889 lb (210–404 kg).

Similar Species: **Sitatunga** is smaller and shaggy, with fewer white stripes; female is hornless.

Habitat: Rain forest with dense undergrowth.

Breeding: Montane populations have birth peaks during rains; rain-forest populations may breed year-round. 1 calf born after gestation of 9.5 months.

Range: Sierra Leone east to Togo; s Cameroon and Gabon east to sw Sudan and w Uganda. Isolated populations in montane forests of Kenya (Mount Kenya, Mount Elgon, and the Aberdares).

A browser, more active by night than by day, the Bongo is one of the few sociable forest antelopes. Herds of up to 50 have been recorded in Aberdare NP (Kenya), but most groups consist of fewer than a dozen females and young. Adult males sometimes join females to form mixed herds, although bulls are mostly solitary.

119 **Common Eland**
Southern Eland
Tragelaphus (Taurotragus) oryx

Hoofprint

Description: Massive, *ox-like* appearance. Coat *smooth fawn or tan,* with or without narrow, white, vertical body stripes. Tail thin and long, with black terminal tuft; *ears small and narrow.* Male has rug-like patch of brown hair on forehead; darker blue-gray coat; *massive neck and shoulders;* conspicuous *black-tufted dewlap* on lower throat. Horns nearly straight, with 1 or 2 tight twists; generally longer and thinner in female (20–27″/51–68 cm long); male 17–26″ (43–65 cm) long. L 6′8″–11′4″ (2–3.4 m); T 24–36″ (60–90 cm); Ht 4′2″–6′1″ (1.25–1.83 m); Wt 697–2,072 lb (317–942 kg).

Similar Species: **Derby Eland** has large rounded ears and bigger horns; torso always distinctly white-striped.

Habitat: Subdeserts, acacia savannas, and broad-leafed deciduous miombo woodlands.

Breeding: Year-round, though most births occur August–October in s Africa; 1 calf born after 9-month gestation.

Range: East Africa south to Natal and Angola.

The Common Eland is not only the biggest but also the slowest antelope, with a top speed of about 25 mph (40 kph). It is an accomplished high jumper, easily clearing 6.5 feet (2 m). This is one of the most nomadic antelopes; females have home ranges of up to 200 square miles (500 sq km); adult males have far smaller ranges. A mixed feeder, it grazes during the rainy season and browses in the dry season. This eland is the most gregarious species in its tribe; during rains, herds of several hundred form, including both sexes and all ages; however, such groups are open and unstable. Females defend the young cooperatively, even advancing together against Lions.

120 **Derby Eland**
Giant Eland
Tragelaphus (Taurotragus) derbianus

Description: More colorful than the Common Eland, with large rounded ears. *Reddish brown to chestnut, with numerous well-defined, white torso stripes.* Male darkens to blue-gray (female stays brown or chestnut); has black spinal crest; *short dark mane around neck and on top of shoulders, bordered by white patches.* Male has forehead mat of dark brown hair; *extensive dewlap beginning at end of chin.* Horns longer than Common Eland's; *male's horns massive, V-form;* straight shaft with tight twist; 3′–4′1″ (90–122 cm) long. L 7′4″–9′8″ (2.2–2.9 m); T 3′ (90 cm); Ht 5′–5′10″ (1.5–1.75 m); Wt 970–2,000 lb (440-900 kg).

Subspecies and Ranges: 2 isolated populations: *T. d. derbianus,* of Senegal, Guinea, and s Mali, is chestnut-colored, with 15 white stripes. *T. d. gigas* ranges from ne Nigeria to sw Sudan and ne Zaire; paler brown, with 12 white stripes.

Similar Species: **Common Eland** is tan, with stripes less distinct or absent, small ears, less-developed dewlap, and less mane.

Habitat: Broad-leafed savannas, interspersed with glades.

Breeding: Year-round; 1 calf born after 9-month gestation.

Despite the Derby Eland's alternate name, only its much larger, diverging horns justify the adjective "giant." But along with the biggest Common Eland males, prime Derby Eland bulls are the heavyweight champions among antelopes. Eland cows, in contrast, are relatively svelte. Herds of up to 60 Derby Elands have been observed, but groups of 15 to 25 are more usual. They wander widely in search of browse and drink regularly.

Wild Cattle
Tribe Bovini

This tribe has 11 species worldwide but is represented in Africa by just one.

121–123 **African Buffalo**
Cape Buffalo
Syncerus caffer

Description: A massive animal, with a *short neck, ox-like barrel shape,* and short sturdy legs. Coat unpatterned *black or reddish.* Horns in both sexes unridged and more or less flaring to the side. *Head broad; muzzle blunt,* ending in bare moist nostrils. *Ears large, fringed, and drooping;* long tail ends in tuft.

Subspecies and Ranges: **Cape Buffalo** *(S. c. caffer)* is largest race: L 8′–11′4″ (2.4–3.4 m); Ht 4′8″–5′4″ (1.4–1.6 m); Wt 1,100–1,540 lb (500–700 kg); ranges from s Sudan and Ethiopia south through c and e Africa to Angola, Zambia, Zimbabwe, and n and e South Africa. Coat is uniformly brownish black; older male may be grizzled white around eyes. Male horns have up to 3′4″ (1 m) horizontal spread between tips; each horn up to 5′4″ (1.6 m) along outside curve; base broadens into heavy boss; female horns are shorter and thinner, with incomplete boss. **Forest Buffalo** (Red Buffalo; *S. c. nanus*) is smaller: L 6′–7′4″ (1.8–2.2 m); Ht 3′4″–4′4″ (1–1.3 m); Wt 583–704 lb (265–320 kg); westernmost form lives from Senegal east to Benin, and south to nw Zambia. Female and young are red-orange; old

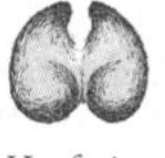

Hoofprint

bulls are darker or even blackish. Crescent-shaped horns curve backward in same plane as face; no frontal boss; 12–16″ (30–40 cm) long in male.

Habitat: Cape Buffalo is primarily a savanna species, while Forest Buffalo lives in primary and second-growth forests. Both races may occur at high elevations and are never far from water.

Breeding: Year-round in some areas; seasonal (wet months) in Uganda and s Africa. 1 calf born after 11- to 11.5-month gestation.

The most sociable of African bovids, the African Buffalo forms herds of up to several thousand animals that pack close together and often lie touching. They cooperatively protect herd members, especially calves, responding to distress calls by charging predators en masse. Large herds are aggregations of distinct clans, each numbering a dozen or more related females and offspring, plus a small number of mature bulls; the mating system is polygynous. Bulls past their prime associate in bachelor groups or become solitary.

Sheep and Goats
Tribe Caprini

This tribe has 17–19 species worldwide, but only two wild caprines—the Ibex *(Capra ibex)* and the Aoudad—occur on the African continent. These stocky animals are adapted for mountainous terrain. Males are much bigger and usually more colorful than females. Horns are thin and short in the female, massive and curving in the male. The sexes live segregated in female and bachelor herds, except during the annual rut. Twin offspring are common.

124 **Aoudad**
Barbary Sheep
Ammotragus lervia

Description: *A reddish-brown, sheep-like bovid,* with thick horns that curve in a semi-circle over the back, up to 22″ (55 cm) long in male; female horns shorter (16″/40 cm) and thinner. Outer coat short and bristly. *Adult male has luxuriant beard extending down chest and forelegs like pantaloons.* L 4′4″–5′6″ (1.3–1.65 m); T 8–10″ (20–25 cm); Ht 30–40″ (75–100 cm); Wt male 220–308 lb (100–140 kg), female 88–121 lb (40–55 kg).

Similar Species: **Ibex** *(Capra ibex)* is a wild goat of ne Sudan and n Ethiopia; has black goatee (male only) and tail; blackish areas on lower flanks and fronts of legs; male horns up to 3′11″ (1.18 m) and heavily ridged.

Habitat: Rocky arid mountains.

Breeding: 1–3 lambs born in March and April; gestation is 5–5.5 months.

Range: Northern Algeria to c Mauritania; thence east to w Egypt and w Sudan.

The Aoudad is a very agile climber and jumper, and stays high in rocky terrain, resting in shade during the heat of the day, descending at night to forage in valleys and plains. It grazes and browses; when feeding on leaves, pods, or fruit, it stands on two feet like goats. The Aoudad gets sufficient water from its food, but comes to water where available.

ODD-TOED UNGULATES

Order Perissodactyla

Perissodactyls have either one or three toes (odd-toed). Horses, zebras, and asses have a single, uncloven hoof; rhinoceroses and tapirs have a spreading foot with three separate toes. Of 17 species worldwide, six live in Africa.

Rhinoceroses
Family Rhinocerotidae

Rhinoceroses are among the largest of the herbivores, with barrel-shaped bodies, thick legs, and three-toed feet. They have heavy heads, with small eyes low on the cheeks; no incisor or canine teeth in the two African species, only massive, serrated cheek teeth for grinding vegetation; two medial horns, which grow from the skin and are unattached to bone; prominent, highly mobile ears; and a thin round tail. The hide is thick, folded at flex points, and hairless apart from ear fringes and tail bristles. The mating system is polygynous. Worldwide all five species are endangered.

125, 126 **Black Rhinoceros**
Hook-lipped Rhinoceros
Diceros bicornis

Description: A wide, powerfully built, dark gray animal. *Upper lip hooked (or pointed) and flexible,* used as selective browsing tool. 2 horns, in both sexes, highly variable in length and shape, the front one typically longer and thicker at base, 12–32″ (30–80 cm) long; rear horn 5–16″ (12–40 cm) long. L 9′6″–10′2″ (2.86–3.05 m); T 24–28″ (60–70 cm); Ht 4′8″–5′4″ (1.4–1.6 m); Wt male 2,191–2,996 lb (996–1,362 kg), female about 440 lb (200 kg) lighter.

Footprint

Similar Species: Larger, wide-mouthed **White Rhino** lacks hooked lip and has neck hump.

Habitat: Many types, but usually dense woody vegetation; sometimes grasslands.

Breeding: Year-round; 1 calf born after gestation of about 15 months; births occur at intervals of 2–4 years.

Range: Formerly from Nigeria east to Somalia, and south to South Africa; now extinct outside reserves. Can be seen in well-protected reserves in e and s Africa.

The Black Rhino is a nearly pure browser that eats more than 200 species of shrubs, herbs, and legumes. Noted for unpredictability, it is nearly as likely to charge as to run away when disturbed; when charging, it puffs and snorts like a steam engine, running with its tail erect at speeds of up to 30 mph (50 kph). Both sexes disperse as sub-adults, then settle down permanently in home ranges. Males (but not females) defend their ranges as territories; huge dung piles mark their patrol routes. Some rhinos travel 5 to 15 miles (8–25 km) every day to drink; in hot weather, they regularly lie in mud wallows.

127, 128 **White Rhinoceros**
Square-lipped Rhinoceros
Ceratotherium simum

Description: One of the largest land animals. *Very long head, with wide square mouth; massive hump at top of neck.* Color slate-gray to yellow-brown. Horns in both sexes; front horn averages 24″ (60 cm), record 5′3″ (1.58 m); back horn shorter (6.5–23″/16–57 cm), more triangular. L 11′4″–13′4″ (3.4–4 m); T 3′–3′4″ (90–100 cm); Ht 5′4″–6′2″ (1.6–1.86 m); Wt male to 5,060 lb (2,300 kg), female to 3,740 lb (1,700 kg).

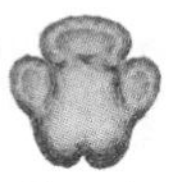

Footprint

Subspecies and Ranges: **Northern White Rhino** *(C. s. cottoni)* survives only in Zaire's Garamba NP. **Southern White Rhino** *(C. s. simum)* was reduced to a few dozen animals by 1904; it is now abundant in Natal reserves (more than 6,400 animals), with several hundred more in Kenya, Zambia, Zimbabwe, Botswana, and Namibia.

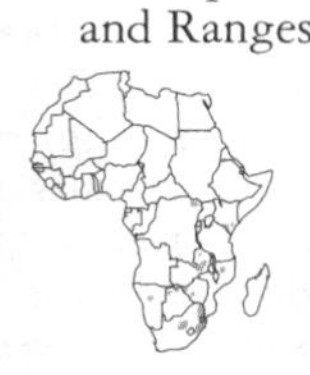

Similar Species: Smaller **Black Rhino** lacks neck hump and has prehensile, triangular upper lip. Skin color, which varies by soil type, does not distinguish the 2 species.

Habitat: Savannas with shade trees, water holes, and mud wallows.

Breeding: 1 calf born in March or April, after gestation of 16 months; births occur at intervals of 2–4 years.

A nearly pure grazer, the White Rhino uses its wide, muscular lips to pluck grass, as hippos do. Cows have overlapping home ranges and are rarely alone. Mothers are accompanied by their latest calf; calfless cows associate in pairs; and juveniles of two to three years, rejected when their mothers calve again, form peer groups that often associate with female pairs in stable groups of up to six rhinos. Bulls defend territories, but tolerate the presence of subordinate males; the dominant bull marks boundaries by spraying urine and renewing dung middens. White Rhinos are rather docile and unlikely to charge.

Zebras and Asses
Family Equidae

Equids are large and long-lived, built for swift locomotion, and have teeth specially adapted for cropping and grinding grass. There are seven extant species worldwide; the African Wild Ass and three species of zebra are African species. No two individual zebras are marked exactly alike. Males and females look alike, although males have triangular upper canine teeth used in fighting. Groupings are as in sociable, polygynous antelopes: herds of females and young, and herds of nonbreeding males that are denied access to females by a small class of mature breeding males. The Plains Zebra dominates the more productive savannas and thus lives at high density, while Grevy's Zebra and the Mountain Zebra live in small, isolated populations in danger of extinction by overhunting, overgrazing by livestock, and periodic drought.

129–131 **Plains Zebra**
Common Zebra, Burchell's Zebra
Equus burchellii

Description: Built like a sturdy fat pony. Short sleek coat *white to buff, with black or brown stripes extending onto belly;* extent, shade, and width of stripes vary among subspecies, becoming progressively less pronounced going south from equator. L 7′8″ (2.3 m); Ht 4′3″–4′8″ (1.27–1.4 m); Wt male average 550 lb (250 kg), female average 484 lb (220 kg).

Footprint

Subspecies and Ranges: **Boehm's Zebra** (Grant's Zebra; *E. b. boehmi*), which ranges from s Sudan and Somalia south to w Zambia, is boldly striped black on white, with wide bands separated by wide spaces. **Selous' Zebra** *(E. b. selousi),* of e Zambia, Malawi, and Mozambique to se Zimbabwe, has numerous narrow black stripes on white ground. **Chapman's Zebra** *(E. b. antiquorum),* of Angola and Namibia southeast to Transvaal and Natal, has dark brown stripes on buff ground; stripes less distinct on hindquarters, often alternating with pale brown shadow stripes; legs only partly striped.

Similar Species: **Grevy's Zebra,** sometimes in mixed herds with Boehm's Zebra, is larger, with many more and narrower black stripes, and unpatterned white belly. **Hartmann's Mountain Zebra** (see Mountain Zebra) overlaps Chapman's Zebra at edge of Namib Desert; Hartmann's has distinct, unshadowed, black stripes, and unpatterned buff belly; stripes on top of rump are perpendicular to hindleg stripes.

Habitat: Grasslands and woodlands.

Breeding: 1 foal born during rainy season, after 12-month gestation.

The Plains Zebra is one of the most nomadic of grazers, ceaselessly in search of green pastures. It can subsist on coarse dry grass, but dependence on water keeps it within 20 miles (32 km) of water holes during the dry season. Social units consist of stable harems or family herds, each shepherded by a mature stallion, and bachelor herds of adolescent to young-adult males. Stallions almost always acquire harems by abducting fillies in heat, in competition with other males. Females remain permanently in the herd where they first become pregnant and foal.

132 Mountain Zebra
Equus zebra

Description: A trimmer version of the Plains Zebra. Variably white or buff background, depending on race, with *distinct black stripes ending at belly, which is unpatterned. Transverse stripes on lower back to base of tail form "gridiron."* Small but distinct *dewlap* on upper throat. L 7′2″ (2.15 m); Ht 4′10″ (1.45 m); Wt male average 656 lb (298 kg; Hartmann's race), female average 607 lb (276 kg).

Subspecies and Ranges: **Cape Mountain Zebra** ("True" Mountain Zebra; *E. z. zebra*), of Mountain Zebra NP and other reserves in s Cape Province, is vivid black and white, with relatively broad stripes. **Hartmann's Mountain Zebra** *(E. z. hartmannae),* of s Angola and n Namibia, is larger race; has creamy or buff ground color, narrower and more numerous black stripes.

Similar Species: **Chapman's Zebra** (see Plains Zebra) has buff background color, but is stockier, with brown stripes that extend over belly, and some shadow striping.

Habitat: Rocky uplands and subdesert plains.

Breeding: 1 foal born after 1-year gestation; most births November–April, during rains.

Hartmann's Mountain Zebra descends to the plains as the rains begin, in search of tender new grasses, and penetrates the Namib Desert to the coastal dunes, but its preferred habitat is the grassy mountain slopes, and it returns as soon as forage there improves. Where the range is still unfenced, bands migrate up to 60 miles (100 km) or more. This zebra must have water, drinking daily from springs or from pits it digs in streambeds. Social organization is very similar to that of the Plains Zebra: harems of one to four mares, and separate bachelor herds.

133 Grevy's Zebra
Equus grevyi

Description: *The largest member of the family.* Head large; thick neck accentuated by upstanding mane; big rounded ears. Narrow stripes in complex patterns, especially *concentric lines on rump bordering white patch over tail, both bisected by broad black spinal stripe.* Belly unpatterned white. L 8′4″–9′2″ (2.5–2.75 m); T 28–30″ (70–75 cm); Ht 4′8″–5′4″ (1.4–1.6 m); Wt 770–990 lb (350–450 kg).

Similar Species: **Boehm's Zebra** (see Plains Zebra) is easily distinguished by its lighter build and wider stripes extending onto belly.

Habitat: Arid grasslands and acacia savannas, within commuting distance of water.

Breeding: 1 foal born after gestation of 13 months. Matings and births occur mostly during rainy seasons: July/August, and October/November.

Range: Northern Kenya, s and e Ethiopia, and s Somalia.

In ecology and social organization, and even in the loud bray of territorial males, Grevy's Zebra is a striped ass. The best grazing and water holes and the approaches to them are occupied as year-round territories by the fittest stallions, even though the rest of the population migrates to distant, greener pastures. Stallions patrol and mark their boundaries with dung middens, at which they often meet and interact with one another. Mares associate and share the same home range with relatives, although clan members often separate into subgroups.

134 African Wild Ass
Equus africanus

Description: Head large, with *long ears.* Coat *gray or buff above, contrasting with white chest, belly, legs, and buttocks;* white muzzle and eye ring. Darker brown spinal stripe; short brown mane; tail medium length, dark-tufted. L 6′8″ (2 m); Ht 3′10″–4′2″ (1.15–1.25 m); Wt 605 lb (275 kg).

Subspecies and Ranges: **Nubian Wild Ass** *(E. a. africanus),* of n Eritrea, has well-defined dark band crossing shoulders that forms a vertical stripe on each side. **Somali Wild Ass** *(E. a. somalicus),* of e Ethiopia and Somalia, is more reddish; shoulder band faint or absent; has well-defined dark transverse stripes on lower legs. Domesticated **Donkey** (*E. asinus* in old usage) is descended from a Nubian-like form and is very difficult to distinguish; is not so sure-footed in rocky terrain, and generally less wary of humans.

Habitat: Mountainous and rocky deserts and semi-deserts; arid grasslands.

Breeding: 1 foal born after 1-year gestation.

The adult male of this species defends territory throughout the year, except during extreme drought, marking boundaries with dung middens. He tolerates bachelor males if they do not attempt to breed with females. The African Wild Ass is mainly a grazer but will also browse during drought, drinking daily when able but at least every three days. Herds typically number six to 12 animals, and are unstable and changeable.

ELEPHANTS

Order Proboscidea
Family Elephantidae

Within this order, which comprises one family, there are two elephant species in the world, one living in Asia and the other in Africa. Imagine a creature as big as a truck, with a nose as long as its legs that functions as siphon, snorkel (on deep-water crossings), squirt-gun, trumpet, and feeding tool powerful enough to rip branches from trees but delicate enough, with finger-like projections at the tip, to pick up a pea. Elephants are mixed feeders, eating grass when they can get it but also browsing all kinds of trees, bushes, reeds, fruit, and bark, reaching up to 20 feet (6 m) to pluck fruit or pull down branches; some bulls are also adept at pushing over trees. Such a bulky, compact body is subject to overheating, so elephants must have shade or water holes at midday; the huge, sail-like ears also dissipate heat from veins lying just under the skin. The tusks, which occur in both sexes, are modified upper incisors that never stop growing.

135–138 African Elephant

Loxodonta africana

Description: *Body rotund; skin nearly hairless, gray or brownish, and wrinkled; nose and upper lip elongated to the ground and prehensile; ears huge, fan-like.*

Subspecies: **Savanna Elephant** (Bush Elephant; *L. a. africana*), of e, c, and s Africa, is the largest land mammal; L male 25′ (7.5 m), female 22′8″ (6.8 m) [lengths include outstretched trunk]; Ht 8′4″–11′ (2.5–3.3 m); Wt male average 11,000 lb (5,000 kg), to 13,200 lb (6,000 kg), female to 6,600 lb (3,000 kg). Tusks diverge and curve forward.

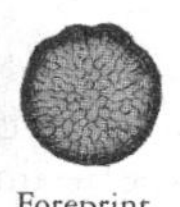
Foreprint

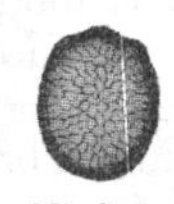
Hindprint

Today tusks rarely exceed 100 lb (45 kg) apiece, due to selective culling, but a male reaching 60 years old has tusks about 130 lb (60 kg) apiece (record 286 lb/130 kg; 11′/3.4 m long); female tusks are much smaller. Huge ears, up to 6′8″ × 5′ (2 m × 1.5 m), with pointed lower lobe. **Forest Elephant** *(L. a. cyclotis),* of w and c Africa, is smaller: Ht 8–9′ (2.4–2.7 m); Wt 4,000–7,000 lb (1,800–3,200 kg). Proportionally smaller, rounded ears; parallel, downward-directed tusks. The two subspecies meet and interbreed at edges of lowland rain forests in w and c Africa.

Habitat: Rain forests to subdeserts, swamps, seashores, and limits of montane forests.

Breeding: Most matings and births occur during rainy season; 1 calf born after gestation of 22 months, the longest in mammals.

Range: Small pockets of Forest Elephants persist from Mauritania to e Zaire; Savanna Elephants occur widely in sub-Saharan Africa and are most commonly seen in reserves of Kenya, Tanzania, Zimbabwe, Botswana, Namibia, and South Africa.

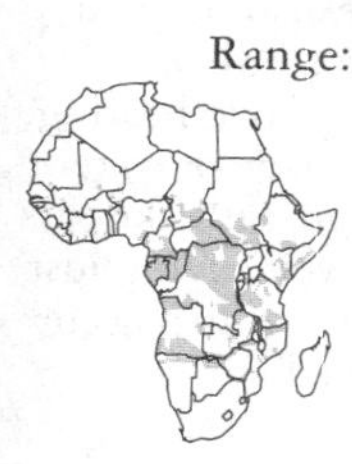

Nearly all that is known about elephant behavior in the wild refers to the Savanna Elephant. A cohesive herd of nine to 11 females and their calves is the basic social unit, led by the biggest, oldest cow. Groups that grow larger tend to split into two or three family units, but they stay in the same vicinity and often associate. Males leave the cow herds at puberty, when they are about 12 years old, and spend the rest of their lives alternately associating with other males and wandering alone. Polygynous, at around 25 years they begin competing reproductively; most matings are monopolized by bigger bulls over age 35. Elephants are rare outside reserves because of excessive hunting for tusks.

HYRAXES
Order Hyracoidea
Family Procaviidae

There are six species of hyraxes, all of which occur in Africa. Hyrax species are grouped into three genera: the Rock Hyrax, bush hyraxes, and tree hyraxes. Hyraxes look like big guinea pigs and live in rock piles, cliffs, and trees; their rubbery-soled feet are specially adapted for climbing. The characteristic dorsal spot is a scent gland ringed with erectile hairs. The sexes are largely alike. Males of all species are territorial. The Rock Hyrax and the bush hyraxes are diurnal and sociable; a clan of related females is monopolized as a harem by a male who defends an exclusive territory. Where they overlap, colonies of the two genera live together communally.

---

139 Rock Hyrax
Procavia capensis

Description: *Coat harsh; yellow-brown to dark brown, with dorsal spot black, brown, or yellowish. Snout blunt;* nose relatively broad. L 16–23″ (40–57 cm); Ht 12″ (30 cm); Wt 4–12 lb (1.8–5.4 kg).

Footprint

Similar Species: Often lives in association with smaller **bush hyraxes,** which have soft gray or grayish-brown fur and white underparts. **Tree hyraxes,** usually nocturnal, overlap with the Rock Hyrax on some high mountains; have thick, soft, light gray to dark brown fur.

Habitat: Rocks of all kinds, from small kopjes to mountain peaks and gorges. Locations must offer vegetation, sunning places, and cavities for shelter and refuge.

Breeding: Most births are in rainy season; 1–6 young born after 7-month gestation.

Range: Senegal to Somalia; ne Africa; south to Cape Province and west to Namibia and s Angola; isolated mountains in Algeria and Libya.

The Rock Hyrax is the most arid-adapted hyrax. These animals minimize exposure to predators by visiting pastures as a group and eating rapidly for only an hour each morning and afternoon. When grass is unpalatable, they browse on bushes, trees, fruit, and succulents. Rock Hyraxes are polygynous. The number of females in a harem depends on the size of the home range and available resources; it can vary from two to 26 females and young.

140 **Bush Hyrax**
Yellow-spotted Bush Hyrax
Heterohyrax brucei

Description: A small hyrax with *soft gray or grayish-brown fur and whitish underparts.* Dorsal patch white or yellowish, depending on race. Head small; *conspicuous white spot over eye; snout pointed,* with small nose. L 13–19″ (33–47 cm); Ht 6–10″ (15–25 cm); Wt 3–5.3 lb (1.3–2.4 kg).

Similar Species: **Rock Hyrax** and **tree hyraxes** are larger, usually browner, and have less-pointed snout.

Habitat: Any vegetation type as long as rocky refuges available, to 11,000′ (3,300 m).

Breeding: Births occur year-round; 1–3 young born after 7-month gestation.

Range: Northeastern and e Africa to n Transvaal, with a band extending north of sandveld to wc Angola.

Predominantly browsers, bush hyraxes spend much of their foraging time in trees, where their smaller size enables them to crop leaves beyond the reach of the Rock Hyrax. Bush hyraxes also graze fresh green grass. Social behavior is similar to that of the Rock Hyrax; clans range in size from five to 34 females and offspring.

141 **Western Tree Hyrax**
Dendrohyrax dorsalis

Description: About the size of a Rock Hyrax, but coat longer, dense, and soft; *grizzled dark brown above,* lighter or ochreous below; dorsal patch elongated and *ringed with long white or yellow hairs;* eye patches light but indistinct in most races. *Large head darker than body;* snout rather blunt. L 13–24″ (32–60 cm); Ht 12″ (30 cm); Wt 3.7–11 lb (1.7–5 kg).

Similar Species: **Rock Hyrax** has rougher brown coats and smaller heads. **Bush hyraxes** have pointed nose, and more conspicuous white patches above eyes.

Habitat: Rain forest and forest-savanna mosaic.

Breeding: In e Africa, 1 or 2 (rarely 3) young born mainly in March and April. In rain forest, may breed year-round. Gestation is 7–8 months.

Range: Gambia to n Angola; Bioko; c and ne Zaire; n Uganda.

Tree hyraxes live in pairs where resources are scarce, in larger families where habitat is favorable (males are in any case territorial). In the best forest habitats, there may be several hundred tree hyraxes per square mile. Seldom seen but often heard at night, these animals utter unearthly cracks, creaks, and screams.

AARDVARK

Order Tubulidentata
Family Orycteropodidae

This order has only one species, described below.

142 **Aardvark**
Orycteropus afer

Description: Rounded back; *massive hindquarters;* short, thick, powerful limbs, with 4 spade-shaped nails on forefoot, 5 on

Hindprint

hindfoot. *Tail muscular and thick,* tapering to a point. Head widest at eye level; *long tubular snout ends in flexible, pig-like disk.* Very large ears fold back and close while tunneling. Coat dull gray-brown; coarse and short on upper body and tail, longer and blackish on limbs. Thin tongue, made sticky by enlarged salivary glands, extends 12″ (30 cm). L 3′5″–4′4″ (1.03–1.3 m); T 18–25″ (45–63 cm); Ht 24–26″ (60–65 cm); Wt 88–143 lb (40–65 kg).

Habitat: Wherever termites are abundant, from arid savannas to rain forests; avoids rocky soils.

Breeding: 1 offspring born, probably during dry season; gestation is 7 months.

Range: Widespread south of Sahara, except Namib Desert.

The Aardvark is strictly nocturnal, solitary, and very rarely seen, although it is common wherever termites and ants are abundant. It feeds almost exclusively on termites during rainy months, switching to ants in the dry season. Aardvarks often dig narrow exploratory trenches with their foreclaws, then use their remarkably sensitive noses to detect insects. They dig short tunnels for overnight use after foraging, as well as long, deep, many-chambered burrows that they use as dens; some permanent refuge-burrows, where young are born, may be up to 43 feet (13 m) long, with many branches.

PANGOLINS

Order Pholidota
Family Manidae

This order comprises one family. Consumers of ants and termites, pangolins have tubular heads and long, narrow, sticky tongues (up to 28″/70 cm in the largest pangolins).

Pangolins have short powerful legs equipped with strong curved claws. Their upper and outer surfaces are armored with a unique covering of horny plates that overlap like roof shingles; the plates are shed and renewed periodically. Rolling into a ball when in danger renders pangolins nearly impregnable. There are seven species of pangolins worldwide. All four African species are solitary and mainly nocturnal.

---

143 **Cape Pangolin**
Temminck's Pangolin
Manis temminckii

Description: A *medium-size, ground-dwelling pangolin.* Tail shorter than head and body, with rounded tip. Covered with *large brown scales,* except face and underside of body, which are almost naked and whitish gray. L 20–24″ (50–60 cm); T 16–20″ (40–50 cm); Wt 33–40 lb (15–18 kg).

Similar Species: Larger (L 30–34″/75–85 cm; Wt 55–73 lb/25–33 kg) and more powerfully built **Giant Pangolin** *(M. gigantea)* has darker brown scales; is also a ground dweller, ranging from Senegal to Gabon, and east to w Kenya, south to c Zaire and sw Angola. Tree-dwelling **Small-scaled Tree Pangolin** *(M. tricuspis)* and **Long-tailed Pangolin** *(M. tetradactyla)* have long prehensile tails; inhabit rain forests from Senegal east to rift valley.

Habitat: Dry and moist savannas and bushlands with sandy soil, below 6,000′ (1,800 m).

Breeding: Produces 1 young that looks like a miniature adult; gestation is estimated at 4–5 months.

Range: Southern Chad and Sudan through e Africa to n South Africa and c Angola.

The Cape Pangolin sniffs out most of its termite and ant prey on or near the surface, rarely digging into mounds or underground nests. It uses burrows dug by other animals as daytime resting

Foreprint

Hindprint

places and refuges for its offspring. Foraging at night, it feeds selectively on the juvenile stages of certain termites and ants, and also spends much time investigating dung and rotting wood that contains termites.

MANATEES AND DUGONGS

Order Sirenia
Families Trichechidae and Dugongidae

Manatees and dugongs are blimp-like, with very tiny eyes and ear openings, valvular nostrils, and flippers instead of forelegs. Like other marine mammals, they propel themselves through the water with up-and-down paddling of the tail rather than with the side-to-side movements of fish. Unlike seals and whales, sirenians are vegetarians. There are three species of manatees, all confined to estuaries and rivers of the Atlantic, and only one species of dugong, in Indian and Pacific ocean coastal waters.

West African Manatee

Trichechus senegalensis

Description: *Rudimentary nails on flippers; tail round and paddle-like;* naked except for scattered hairs and bristles on upper lip. Muddy brown to dark gray; lighter underneath. L 8′4″–12′ (2.5–3.6 m); Wt 770–1,000 lb (350–450 kg).

Similar Species: **Atlantic Hump-backed Dolphin** *(Sousa teuszii),* which enters w African rivers, has dorsal fin and sleeker head.

Habitat: Warm coastal waters and connecting freshwater rivers and lakes.

Breeding: Gestation is 12 months.

Range: Senegal to Angola, as far inland as tributaries of Lake Chad and 1,250 miles (2,000 km) up Niger River.

A completely aquatic herbivore, the West African Manatee subsists on

grasses and other plants that grow in fresh and brackish water, grasping vegetation with two muscular projections of the upper lip. Manatees are essentially solitary, with ephemeral groups occurring when individuals are attracted to a limited resource, or when several males converge to compete for a cow in heat. Manatees are among the most endangered aquatic mammals.

Dugong
Dugong dugon

Description: Similar to West African Manatee, except *tail is forked as in whales; flippers are shorter, with no nails;* scattered fine hairs over body. Brownish gray above; gray flanks, pinkish or whitish underside. *Snout bends downward,* ending in horseshoe-shaped, muscular disk overhanging slit-like mouth; short thick bristles on muzzle and lower lip. L 8′4″–10′8″ (2.5–3.2 m); Wt 770–1,100 lb (350–500 kg).

Habitat: Salt water: shallow bays and estuaries with abundant sea grasses.

Breeding: Year-round; 1 calf born after 11-month gestation.

Range: Red Sea south to s Mozambique; coasts of Madagascar and other islands.

The Dugong does not linger in shallows or extend upriver as the West African Manatee does; it returns to deeper ocean water when it is not feeding or when pursued by hunters. The Dugong prefers the rootstocks of sea grasses it digs from the bottom, rasping its food mainly between rough horny plates that cover its upper and lower palates. Dugongs are gregarious, sometimes forming groups that number in the hundreds, but mother plus calf may be the basic social unit. They have no vocal chords but communicate with high-pitched chirps and squeaks of mysterious origin.

SEALS
Order Pinnipedia

There are 34 pinnipeds worldwide, but only six live or stray onto African coasts. Seals and sea lions haul out of the water for mating and birthing, but they feed in the sea, and it is there that the advantage of their tube-like, neckless form and "winged feet" (*pinnipedia,* or flippers) is apparent. The true seals (family Phocidae), which lack external ears, use their paddle-like hindlimbs for propulsion underwater; on land they rely primarily on the forelimbs to drag or hump themselves along.

Eared Sea Lions and Fur Seals
Family Otariidae

Worldwide this family includes five sea lions and nine fur seals. Its members are distinguished by vestigial external ears; their mode of swimming, in which they are propelled by the forelimbs; and their hindflippers, which can turn forward to function as feet, making eared seals more mobile on land than the true seals. The Cape Fur Seal is the only member of the family likely to be seen in African waters.

144 Cape Fur Seal
Arctocephalus pusillus

Description: *Spindle shape; round head, with huge convex forehead, pointed snout,* and long whiskers; *tiny pointed ears;* stumpy tail. Coat has dense insulating undercoat stiffened by longer guard hairs. Male in breeding condition nearly *black, with reddish-brown mane* emphasizing thick neck; female brownish gray to yellow-brown, with lighter underside. L male 7′4″–8′ (2.2–2.4 m), female 5–6′ (1.5–1.8 m); Wt (varies seasonally) male 440–770 lb (200–350 kg), up to

1,540 lb (700 kg), female 198–253 lb (90–115 kg).

Habitat: Coastal waters, beaches, and offshore islands.

Breeding: Extremely polygynous: Bulls establish breeding territories on beaches in mid-October, several weeks before females come ashore to give birth; within a week of giving birth, they mate and conceive again. Birth and mating finish by end of December, when the females, pregnant with next year's calves, disperse with their newborn young.

Range: Southern Africa from s Angola to Port Elizabeth in se Cape Province.

The wealth of pilchards, sardines, and mackerels, squids, crabs, and other invertebrates associated with the cold Benguela Current, which flows north along the Atlantic coast, has supported a population estimated at more than 1 million Cape Fur Seals. There are 24 established breeding colonies and 10 known colonies of nonbreeders. Unfortunately, unregulated commercial fishing now threatens to destroy the ecosystem of which the seals are an integral part.

CARNIVORES

Order Carnivora

There are 235 carnivore species in the world; about 77 live in Africa. There are two suborders: the Feliformia, which comprises the civets, mongooses, cats, genets, and hyenas; and the Caniformia, which comprises dogs, weasels, raccoons, and bears. Africa has representatives of each group except the latter two. For carnivores (the word means "meat-eating"), food ranges from insects to antelopes, but during evolution many species became omnivorous, a very few even totally vegetarian. Parenting, which includes teaching the young how to hunt, extends for at least a year in many species.

Genets and Civets
Family Viverridae

This family has 33 species worldwide, of which 15 live in Africa. The genets are small, long, and narrow, with bowed backs, short legs, long tails, and claws that are retractile or semi-retractile—adaptations for arboreal habits. Civets are primarily terrestrial, with nonretractile claws. The snouts of both groups are long and pointed, their ears oval and cat-like, set high on the head. Most genets and civets are spotted and/or striped blackish against a pale ground color, and have ringed tails.

145 Large-spotted Genet
Rusty-spotted Genet, Forest Genet
Genetta tigrina (includes *maculata,* considered a separate species by some)

Description: Fur short and soft; yellow-gray (in drier regions) to red-brown above; gray-white or yellowish brown below; brown-black spinal stripe, *without distinct crest. Spots large and elongated,* but not closely spaced; *rust-colored* to dark brown or black; *in 2 rows on each side of spine;* dot-like and scattered lower and on forelegs. Indistinct dark patch on face between inner corner of eye and outer corner of mouth, bordered by whitish patch under eye and next to nose. *Tail has 7–9 black rings and wide black tip.* L 17–22″ (43–54 cm); T 16–22″ (41–54 cm); Wt 3–7 lb (1.4–3.2 kg).

Similar Species: **Common Genet** has more distinct facial mask; smaller blackish spots in rows; conspicuous spinal crest of longer black hair; tail with 9 or 10 dark rings and usually white tip.

Habitat: Moist savannas, forests, secondary growth.

Breeding: Usually bears 2–4 young; gestation is about 10 weeks.

Range: Senegal east to Eritrea, and south to Cape Province.

Though as solitary and nocturnal as other genets, the Large-spotted is more likely to be seen because its habitat preferences bring it into contact with people.

146 **Common Genet**
Feline Genet, Small-spotted Genet
Genetta genetta (includes *felina, senegalensis,* and *dongolana*)

Description: Fur rather long and coarse; light gray to brownish gray, lighter on underside; dark spinal stripe with *distinct crest. Spots round or elongated,* black or brown, on neck, upper thighs, and forelimbs, and in *5 rows on each side of spine.* Dark mask on white face between eyes and nose. *Tail has 9 or 10 black rings and usually a white tip.* L 16–20″ (40–50 cm); T 15–19″ (37–47 cm); Wt 3.3–5 lb (1.5–2.3 kg).

Footprint

Similar Species: **Servaline Genet** *(G. servalina)* of equatorial forests is also called Small-spotted Genet locally; lacks spinal crest. **Abyssinian Genet** *(G. abyssinica)* replaces Common in mountains of Ethiopia and Somalia; coat pale gray; spots black, narrow, elongated as stripes; spinal crest not well developed.

Habitat: Dry savannas and subdeserts.

Breeding: May breed twice a year; 2 or 3 kittens born after gestation of 10–11 weeks.

Range: Drier parts of sub-Saharan Africa.

The Common Genet is an active, semi-arboreal, solitary predator that eats fruit, nectar, and insects as well as small vertebrates. Nocturnal, it tends to be most active in the early part of the night.

147 **African Civet**
Civettictis civetta

Description: A striking, sturdily built, raccoon-like carnivore, with a *black eye mask* above a white muzzle. Coat rough; whitish ground color, heavily spotted and barred with black (in some races brownish); black-ringed tail, with black end. *Prominent erectile crest of black-tipped hair from neck to tip of tail.* Legs longish; nails blunt and nonretractile; tail shorter than body. L 27–36″ (68–89 cm); T 16–20″ (40–50 cm); Ht 14–16″ (35–40 cm); Wt 15–44 lb (7–20 kg).

Similar Species: Smaller **Palm Civet** has yellow-brown coat with indistinct dark spots and narrow brownish rings on tail.

Habitat: Dense undergrowth in forests, savannas, and farmlands, near water; needs holes or other secure daytime resting places.

Breeding: Year-round in tropical Africa, seasonal elsewhere; 1–4 young born after gestation of 60–72 days.

Range: South of Sahara to Natal.

This terrestrial carnivore is omnivorous. Nocturnal, solitary, and possibly territorial, civets follow regular pathways, along which they scent-mark with urine, dung, and anal-gland secretions.

---

148 Palm Civet
Nandinia binotata

Description: A rarely seen arboreal carnivore. *Tail longer than head and body.* Rounded head; short rounded ears; *short powerful jaws.* Thick short legs; big feet with naked moist pads and 5 retractile claws. Coloration subdued: *yellow-brown, with indistinct dark spots* and blotches on torso; narrow brownish rings on tail; *2 light spots on shoulders.* L 17–22″ (42–54 cm); T 20–24″ (49–60 cm); Wt 5–10 lb (2.3–4.7 kg).

Habitat: Forests that produce fruit year-round, up to 6,500′ (2,000 m) elevation, with rainfall of at least 40″ (1,000 mm); riverine forests in savannas.

Breeding: Up to 4 young born in a tree hollow after 9-week gestation; possible birth peak during rainy season.

Range: Western and c Africa; isolated subpopulations in e Africa, Mozambique, and Zimbabwe.

The Palm Civet is a fruit-eater in carnivore clothing; it eats only a few insects and small vertebrates. It is solitary and nocturnal. Both sexes are territorial; the ranges of the fittest mature males include several female ranges. The Palm Civet has a unique hooting call.

---

149 **Fossa**
Cryptoprocta ferox

Description: Cat-like; long and slender, with short thick neck and short legs (hindlegs longer); curved and retractile claws; *tail as long as body. Rounded head and short jaws* (but longer than a cat's); long stiff whiskers; big eyes; round ears. Coat short and thick; *unpatterned red-brown;* darker above, lighter below. L 24–30″ (60–75 cm); T 24–30″ (60–75 cm); Ht 14–16″ (36–40 cm); Wt 15–26 lb (7–12 kg).

Habitat: Wetter forests.

Breeding: 2–4 young born in December or January, after 3-month gestation.

Range: Madagascar, mainly coastal regions.

A nocturnal predator equally at home in trees and on the ground, and probably territorial, the Fossa marks upright objects with its scent glands. The dominant predator in Madagascar, it feeds heavily on lemurs.

Mongooses
Family Herpestidae

The mongoose family has 37 species worldwide, of which 30 live in Africa. Mongooses have narrow feet and nonretractile claws that are good for digging. Their ears are usually low-set and can be folded while burrowing. Mongooses come in two foraging models: The long, low *Herpestes* species (seven in Africa) are well suited for stalking and seizing birds, rodents, and snakes. The other 23 African species are wide-bodied diggers that eat mostly insects and other invertebrate prey.

---

150 Slender Mongoose
Black-tipped Mongoose
Herpestes sanguineus

Description: A sinuous, long-bodied, short-legged predator, with sharp, curved claws adapted for climbing. Very long tapered tail, with *black tassel at end; tail usually held curled up slightly.* Head narrow; snout pointed. Coat short and finely grizzled; varies from grayish fawn (lightest in arid regions) to chestnut. L 13″ (32 cm); T 13″ (32 cm); Wt 13–28 oz (373–789 g).

Similar Species: **Ichneumon** is also diurnal and has black-tipped tail, but is much larger and very long-haired. **Cape Gray Mongoose** *(H. pulverulenta)* of South Africa is similar in size and is semi-diurnal; shaggier coat grizzled gray, darker above (sometimes brownish); uniformly gray tail grizzled and bushy.

Habitat: Prefers dense cover near water, but widespread from rain forests to subdeserts.

Breeding: Up to 3 times a year; produces 2–4 young, after gestation of 8–9 weeks.

Range: Sub-Saharan Africa.

The Slender Mongoose is frequently glimpsed, as it is diurnal. A versatile

predator, it combines terrestrial with arboreal habits and takes all kinds of prey, from rodents and reptiles to beetles and grasshoppers; it also eats fruit.

Ichneumon
Egyptian Mongoose, Large Gray Mongoose
Herpestes ichneumon

Description: A stretch model of the Slender Mongoose. Lithe, *long-haired, and short-legged;* long claws adapted for digging, not climbing. Coat grizzled gray over light brown in arid zones to dark reddish brown in wetter areas; legs darker. Tail long-haired at base but tapered toward end; *black tuft at tip.* L 19–24″ (48–60 cm); T 18–23″ (45–58 cm); Wt 5.3–9 lb (2.4–4.1 kg).

Similar Species: **Slender Mongoose** is smaller, shorter-haired, usually redder. Nocturnal **White-tailed Mongoose** has longer black legs and white tail.

Habitat: Moist and dry savannas; forest-savanna mosaic; Cape macchia scrub.

Breeding: 2–3 young born, usually once a year, after 60-day gestation.

Range: Pan-African, except for deserts and rain forests.

This active, solitary, territorial, diurnal hunter takes mammals, birds, fish, frogs, reptiles, crayfish, crabs, and large insects.

151 **Marsh Mongoose**
Water Mongoose
Atilax paludinosus

Description: A *heavy-set, very dark* mongoose, with a relatively *broad head, short face, and short thick tail.* Shaggy coat varies: dark brown without markings to lighter speckled brown and red-brown. L 18–24″ (45–60 cm); T 10–16″ (25–40 cm); Wt 4.5–9 lb (2–4 kg).

Similar Species: **Bushy-tailed Mongoose** *(Bdeogale crassicauda),* in its darker forms in

Mozambique, Malawi, and Zambia, might be mistaken for Marsh Mongoose, but is smaller (L 17″/43 cm), with long fluffy tail. **Meller's Mongoose** *(Rhynchogale melleri),* a reddish-brown southern savanna species of s Zaire to c Mozambique, has crest-like parting of hairs on each side of neck.

Habitat: Streams and wetlands with concealing vegetation.

Breeding: Year-round in w Africa; births peak August–December in s Africa; 1–3 young born after gestation estimated at 9–10 weeks.

Range: Senegal east to Somalia, below Sahel, and south to Cape Province.

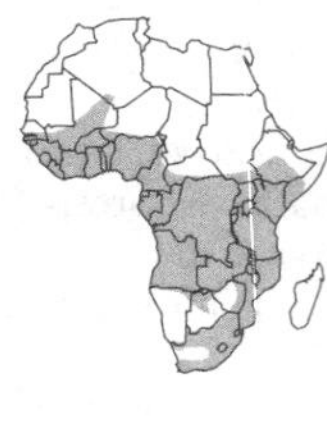

This semi-aquatic mongoose has long hands with naked palms adapted for feeling concealed prey rather than digging. Like an American Raccoon *(Procyon lotor),* it wades and feels under rocks, sifting sediments in search of crayfish, mussels, snails, frogs, and insects. It also takes marsh birds and eggs. It opens shellfish by standing erect and dashing them down onto rocks. The Marsh Mongoose's swimming motion is otter-like, with undulations of its body. It is solitary and mostly nocturnal.

---

152 White-tailed Mongoose
Ichneumia albicauda

Description: A large shaggy mongoose. *Long-haired tail dark at base, but otherwise white* (in some individuals entirely black). Grizzled gray to gray-brown guard hairs over paler undercoat; face light, with *end of snout blackish; legs black.* L 19–28″ (47–69 cm); T 14–20″ (36–50 cm); Wt 6.6–11 lb (3–5 kg).

Similar Species: **Bushy-tailed Mongoose** *(Bdeogale crassicauda),* a woodland species that lives from Kenya south to Mozambique, Malawi, and Zambia, has Kenyan form that is pale with dark legs; smaller (L 17″/43 cm); yellowish rather than gray; tail dark brown or black. **Black-legged Mongoose** *(Bdeogale nigripes),* a tall rain-forest and forest-savanna species that lives from Nigeria south to n Angola and east to sw Kenya, also has long-haired white tail, but rest of coat is short; Kenyan form has yellow throat.

Habitat: Savannas and forest-savanna mosaic to 8,000′ (2,500 m), with daytime refuges (termite mounds, rock piles, burrows).

Breeding: 2 or 3 young born after 2-month gestation; births year-round in tropics, seasonal in s Africa.

Range: South of Sahara, except for coastal w and c Africa.

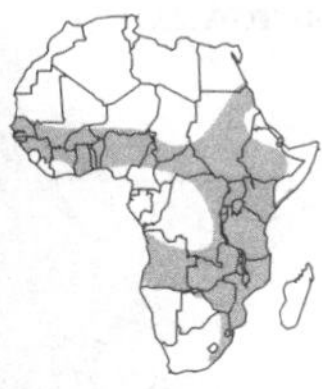

The White-tailed Mongoose is a solitary, nocturnal insect-eater of the open grasslands. It is unable to outrun most predators and relies instead on a noxious chemical spray for defense; it erects and flares its conspicuous tail hairs as a warning. Female and male territories overlap; mothers tolerate grown daughters in their territory.

153 Yellow Mongoose
Cynictis penicillata

Description: *Fox-like,* with broad head, pointed snout, and *large, upstanding ears.* Coat long; tawny to reddish yellow, with *white-tipped, bushy tail* (without white on tail in n Botswana). All forms have white chin, inner legs, and underparts. L 12″ (31 cm); T 9″ (22 cm); Wt 1.75 lb (0.8 kg).

Similar Species: **Selous' Mongoose** *(Paracynictis selousi)* is also a sandy-soil burrower with long soft fur and white-tipped, bushy tail; speckled buff and brown, with contrasting blackish hands and feet; ranges mostly north (Zambia, Malawi) of Yellow Mongoose but may overlap in ne Transvaal and s Zimbabwe.

Habitat: Arid savannas and open plains, preferably with sandy soil.

Breeding: After estimated gestation of 10–11

weeks, alpha female produces 2–4 young early in rainy season.

Range: Southern Angola and Botswana, and south to Cape Province.

This diurnal insectivore forages individually, but dens communally in colonies that include a dominant pair (the only breeders), their offspring, and one or two young adults. The alpha male marks and defends territorial boundaries, aided by the alpha female. Colony members sunbathe around the den at the start and finish of their foraging day. The Suricate and the Cape Ground Squirrel share burrows with the Yellow Mongoose.

---

154 Dwarf Mongoose
Helogale parvula

Description: The smallest African carnivore. *Coat short and glossy; more or less reddish brown,* and finely grizzled. *Eyes red;* nostrils pink. *Stocky build:* head broad, with domed forehead and short face; legs short; tail short and tapered. L 9.5″ (24 cm); T 5.5–7.5″ (14–19 cm); Wt 8–14 oz (225–400 g).

Habitat: Savannas with termite mounds or rock piles.

Breeding: 2–6 young born after gestation of 50–54 days. Alpha female may have 2 or 3 litters per year, during rainy season.

Range: Southern Sudan and Ethiopia south to ne Natal and Angola; also Gambia.

Diurnal, sociable, and territorial, the Dwarf Mongoose lives in packs of 10 to 40 animals and is often seen foraging around lodges and campsites for insects and other invertebrates, the occasional snake or lizard, and small rodents. A single dominant pair monopolizes breeding, and other pack members help rear their offspring by tending, grooming, carrying, and provisioning them. Dwarf

Mongoose packs often include unrelated helpers who have transferred from another pack.

155 **Banded Mongoose**
Mungos mungo

Description: Shaggy, with prominent transverse stripes. Broad head, with pointed snout; low broad ears. Comparatively long legs; 5 toes equipped with long curved digging claws. Coat grizzled *gray to gray-brown, with 10–12 dark brown or black bands;* underparts lighter; lower legs and tail tip black. L 13–16″ (33–41 cm); T 6–11″ (15–28 cm); Wt 2.2–4.4 lb (1–2 kg).

Footprint

Similar Species: **Suricate,** which replaces Banded Mongoose in Namib and Kalahari deserts, is paler, with indistinct bands on back; has dark ears and eye patches.

Habitat: Moist and dry savannas with termite mounds and patches of undergrowth.

Breeding: Up to 4 litters per year, with birth peak in rainy season. 2–8 young born after gestation of 2 months.

Range: Senegal east to s Sudan; Eritrea, Somalia, and e Africa south to Natal; also Angola and n Namibia east to Malawi.

Diurnal, territorial, and highly sociable, Banded Mongooses live in packs of up to 40 animals; they are often seen foraging busily in open grassland and around lodge and camp garbage dumps. In addition to invertebrates, which they dig out of their hiding places, these mongooses occasionally catch mice, snakes, lizards, toads, and ground-nesting birds, and eat eggs.

156 **Cusimanse**
Crossarchus obscurus

Description: A small, dark brown, wide-bodied mongoose. *Very long, mobile snout; short tapering tail; short legs;* 5 toes, tipped with very long claws. Coat shaggy, brown, more or less speckled with yellow. L 12–16″ (30–40 cm); T 6–10″ (15–25 cm); Wt 2.2–3.3 lb (1–1.5 kg).

Similar Species: **Gambian Mongoose** *(Mungos gambianus),* which inhabits moist savannas from Gambia to Nigeria, is unbanded; has conspicuous black stripe on whitish throat. **Alexander's Cusimanse** (Alexander's Mongoose; *C. alexandri*) is larger (L 16″/40 cm) and has black feet; occurs in rain forests of Zaire, Congo, Uganda, and Central African Republic. Smaller **Ansorge's Cusimanse** (Angolan Mongoose; *C. ansorgei*) is lighter brown, with black legs and tail tip and a shorter face; found in se Zaire and n Angola.

Habitat: Rain forests away from populous and disturbed areas.

Breeding: Up to 3 litters a year, with average of 4 young per litter; estimated gestation is 10 weeks.

Range: Sierra Leone east to w Central African Republic.

Diurnal and sociable, Cusimanses range the forest floor in packs of a dozen or more animals, searching busily and noisily for insects and other invertebrates, which they dig out from the litter, rotten trees, and undersides of rocks; they also use their long snouts as probes. Cusimanses have been known to enter shallow water and fling crabs and frogs ashore.

157 Suricate
Suricata suricatta

Description: A pale little mongoose, with a pointed snout widening to a domed forehead; *contrasting dark eye patches and ears.* Legs thin, with 4 long-clawed toes. Coat coarse, with thin undercoat; nearly hairless lower chest/belly looks dark; grizzled gray or tan above, with dark *broken transverse bands over back;* legs more yellowish. Tail thinnest of any mongoose; tip black. L 11″ (28 cm); T 7.5–9″ (19–23 cm); Wt 1.4–2 lb (620–969 g).

Similar Species: **Banded Mongoose** lacks black ears and eye patches; is more boldly banded. **Yellow Mongoose** is soft-haired, with taller ears rising above forehead; lacks contrasting dark markings.

Habitat: Drier, more open country than other mongooses, especially hardpan rather than sandy soil.

Breeding: May have up to 3 litters a year, with birth peak October–April. Typically 3 young born after gestation of 11 weeks.

Range: Southern Africa, including s Angola, Namibia, Botswana, and Karroo and highveld of South Africa.

One of the most engaging of all the African animals, this small creature scratches a living in a harsh land (mainly by unearthing invertebrates) where danger from birds of prey, jackals, and other larger predators is ever present. Packs number from five to 30 animals. Certain members take turns performing sentry duty, standing on their hindlegs atop a mound or bush. All pack members help rear the young.

Hyenas
Family Hyaenidae

This family contains three hyena (also spelled hyaena) species, plus the Aardwolf, all of which range in Africa. They look dog-like but are more closely related to civets and mongooses than to the Canidae. Predators and scavengers of large animals, hyenas eat the whole carcass, or try to—hide, hooves, bones, and all. What they cannot digest is regurgitated later as a dense, tangled packet; bone is digested, its inorganic residue making hyena latrines look like piles of crumbled chalk. The amount of bone in their diets may explain the unusual ability of hyenas to suckle their offspring for a year and up to a year and a half. Hyenas have massive jaws, and backs that slope downward from a well-developed neck and forequarters; the insect-eating Aardwolf is small, lightly built, and narrow-muzzled. Hyenas associate in matriarchal clans and den communally. Brown Hyena mothers suckle one another's cubs; both Striped and Brown hyenas carry food to cubs not their own. Females remain in the clan, whereas males disperse. Aardwolves live in monogamous pairs. All species defend territories and scent-mark with secretions of a large anal pouch.

---

158 **Striped Hyena**
Hyaena hyaena

Description: Shaggy coat tan or gray, with *bold black transverse stripes* on body and legs. Muzzle, cheek stripes, and *underside of throat black.* Light-colored *mane from nape to tail* enlarges silhouette by 8″ (20 cm) when erected in defensive threat. Black pointed ears. Bushy tail uniformly tan or grayish. L 3′4″–4′ (1–1.2 m); T 10–14″ (25–35 cm); Ht 26–32″ (65–80 cm); Wt 77–99 lb (35–45 kg).

Similar Species: Much smaller **Aardwolf** has more pointed snout and black-tipped tail. **Spotted Hyena** is spotted rather than striped; tail has black brushy end.

Habitat: Arid savannas to desert margins.

Breeding: Year-round; 1–6 (usually 2–4) cubs born after 3-month gestation.

Range: Northern and e Africa: south to Senegal and east to Red Sea, thence south through Kenya to c Tanzania.

The Striped Hyena forages alone, ranging about 12 miles (19 km) per night, looking for fruit, insects, carrion, and prey up to the size of antelope fawns. Surplus food is cached and retrieved later; all clan members carry food home to the cubs.

159 Brown Hyena
Hyaena brunnea

Description: A long-legged, *very shaggy* hyena, with a *mantle of straw-colored hair* overlying *dark brown torso;* mantle obscures black transverse stripes on body; dark leg stripes remain conspicuous. Bushy *tail entirely black; ears pointed,* long, and narrow; face blackish. L 3′8″–4′4″ (1.1–1.3 m); T 8–10″ (20–25 cm); Ht 28–35″ (71–87 cm); Wt 77–110 lb (35–50 kg).

Similar Species: **Spotted Hyena** is distinctly dark-spotted and less shaggy. **Aardwolf** is much smaller, with distinct transverse stripes.

Habitat: Arid savannas, subdeserts, and deserts.

Breeding: Year-round; 1–4 young born after gestation of about 90 days.

Range: South of Zambezi in Zimbabwe, Botswana, sw Angola, and Namibia; also n Cape Province, n Transvaal, and Orange Free State.

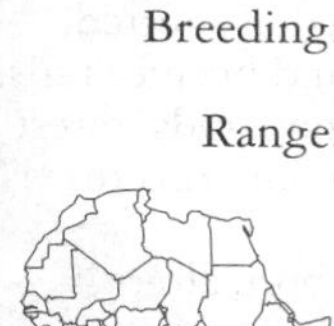

The Brown Hyena is the southern version of the Striped Hyena. Clans of four to 14 animals live in large territories. Much less predatory than the Spotted Hyena, the Brown Hyena eats large ungulates only when it can find carrion or appropriate carcasses from other predators; otherwise it subsists on occasional small vertebrates, fruit, vegetables, and insects. When a Brown Hyena finds more than it can eat at once, it caches the rest and returns to it later. All clan members take food to the cubs. Breeding males are transients who provide no parental care.

160 Spotted Hyena
Laughing Hyena
Crocuta crocuta

Description: The second-largest African carnivore, after the Lion. Solid build, with high shoulders sloping to hindquarters; short mane ends behind shoulders. Long legs. *Short tail brown, with black brushy end.* Broad head, with prominent *rounded ears; heavy muzzle* armed with big teeth. Coat coarse and relatively short. Color uniformly seal-gray at birth, becoming tan to reddish in adult; *solid black spots,* most pronounced in sub-adults, fade with age. L 3′8″–4′8″ (1.1–1.4 m); T 10–12″ (25–30 cm); Ht 32–36″ (79–89 cm); Wt 88–176 lb (40–80 kg), females up to 14 percent heavier than males.

Footprint

Similar Species: Shaggier **Brown Hyena** and **Striped Hyena** are striped instead of spotted, with long pointed ears and bushier tails.

Habitat: Savannas, grasslands, woodlands, forest edges, subdeserts, and mountains to 13,000′ (4,000 m).

Breeding: Year-round; 1 or 2 cubs born after gestation of 4 months. Both sexes appear to have male genitalia. Normal vaginal entrance walled off by facsimile of male's scrotum; copulation and birth occur through female's phallus.

Range: Sahel to s Africa, except equatorial w and c Africa; exterminated from most of South Africa.

The Spotted Hyena adult is capable of running down and killing a bull wildebeest, and hyenas in packs kill zebras and even larger prey. Females produce hormones that make them as aggressive as males, or more so, and that may account for the development in females of a phallus. The alpha female is the biggest and best-fed member of the clan, which may number from three to 12 animals and up to 80 in reserves. Males play no parental role.

161 **Aardwolf**
Proteles cristatus

Footprint

Description: In appearance a miniature Striped Hyena, but with *slender build, long neck, and narrow pointed snout.* Buff to reddish brown, grading to lighter underparts; *dark brown transverse stripes* on torso and limbs, becoming blacker toward feet. Black feet, muzzle, spinal stripe, tail tip, and backs of ears. *Erectile mane from nape to tail* 8″ (20 cm) long. L 26–32″ (65–80 cm); T 8–10″ (20–25 cm); Ht 16–20″ (40–50 cm); Wt 18–26 lb (8–12 kg).

Similar Species: **Striped Hyena** is much more robust.

Habitat: Arid grasslands and dry savannas.

Breeding: Typical litter has 2–3 cubs; most births occur during rainy season after gestation of 90–100 days.

Range: Discontinuous: ne Sudan south to c Tanzania; s Angola and s Zambia through s Africa.

The Aardwolf licks up as many as 200,000 harvester termites per night on its broad, sticky tongue, moving from patch to patch of the insects as they emerge above ground after dark. The termites constitute about 90 percent of this species' food intake; other insects and occasional mice, birds, and carrion make up the rest. Aardwolves apparently live in monogamous pairs. Males guard small cubs at the den while the mother forages.

Cats
Family Felidae

The 36 species of the cat family (ten in Africa) are superbly designed as ambush predators equipped to stalk, capture, kill, and eat prey of any size, including animals larger than themselves. They have camouflaging coloration; muscular limbs with large padded feet; retractile claws used as meat hooks; broad heads with large eyes frontally placed for superior binocular vision; and short, powerful jaws with long, stabbing canines, chisel-like incisors, and sharp-edged cheek teeth designed as meat shears. This design is so efficient and adaptable that most cats are very much alike, differing mainly in size. Cats have quick reflexes, rapid acceleration, and great jumping and climbing ability, but they are notoriously short-winded and rely on ambush; even Cheetahs must sneak up on prey. Most cats are solitary and nocturnal. Females have more or less exclusive home ranges; males compete for territories that overlap several female ranges. Males are larger, but otherwise, except for the Lion, the sexes look alike.

162 African Wildcat
Felis libyca

Description: Wild form of the domestic tabby, but longer-legged, with more upright seated posture. Gray to buff, occasionally black or orange (paler in dry, darker in wet regions), with *indistinct brownish tabby barring or grizzling on face and upperparts. Ears unmarked, thin, and translucent,* backs a rich rufous color. Conspicuous double garters on upper legs; tail distinctly ringed toward end and black-tipped; underparts white to cream. L 20–25″ (50–63 cm); T 11–15″ (28–37 cm); Ht 14″ (35 cm); Wt 7–14 lb (3–6.4 kg).

Similar Species: Much smaller **Black-footed Cat** has large dark spots. **Sand Cat** *(F. margarita),* of n Africa and Sahara, is smaller (Ht 10″/25 cm; Wt 5.5 lb/2.5 kg), with stocky build; uniformly pale buff above, with dark brown bars only on upper legs, and rings or spotting along entire length of tail.

Habitat: Grasslands and woodlands.

Breeding: 2–5 kittens annually, usually during rainy season; gestation is 56–60 days.

Range: Morocco east to Egypt; Senegal east to Somalia; e Africa; c Zaire south to s Africa.

The most common wild cat in Africa, this species eats mammals up to the size of hares, as well as birds, reptiles, and frogs. It is a little larger and has longer legs than a domestic cat. The female defends a core area as her exclusive territory but shares more distant parts of her home range with neighboring cats. The breeding male defends a territory large enough to include up to three females' ranges. The African Wildcat is sometimes included in the same species as the European Wildcat and the domestic cat *(F. silvestris).*

---

163 **Black-footed Cat**
Small-spotted Cat
Felis nigripes

Description: The smallest cat. Short body; relatively long legs; tail less than half of head-body length. Pale cinnamon-yellow in southern part of range to tawny in Kalahari, with *large dark spots on upperparts* elongated into stripes over shoulders; fainter spots on white underparts. *3 broad black transverse bands encircle upper limbs,* narrow short bars lower; black fur on bottom of feet. Tail spotted for entire length, with black tip. L 15–17″ (37–43 cm); T 5–7″ (13–17 cm); Ht 10″ (25 cm); Wt 2.2–4.4 lb (1–2 kg).

Similar Species: **African Wildcat** is larger, without distinct spotting on torso.

Habitat: Arid savannas with termite mounds and burrows dug by other animals.

Breeding: 1–3 kittens born December–March, after gestation of 63–68 days.

Range: Southern Angola and w Zambia south to w South Africa.

Nocturnal and very secretive, the Black-footed Cat preys on rodents, birds, small reptiles, and invertebrates. It derives sufficient water from its prey to subsist without drinking.

164 African Golden Cat
Felis (Profelis) aurata

Description: A *powerfully built* cat with large paws; well-developed hindquarters; *heavy muzzle.* Underparts and cheeks whitish; upperparts vary from shades of red to slate-gray (even black) ground color. *Spots* may be single dots or rosettes, sometimes only on belly and legs. *Small ears* are black on back; tail more or less distinctly ringed or spotted for entire length. L 28–38″ (70–95 cm); T 11–15″ (28–37 cm); Ht 20″ (50 cm); Wt 31–40 lb (14–18 kg).

Similar Species: **Caracal** is tan, nearly spotless; has longer ears with black tufts.

Habitat: Very dense, moist undergrowth of lowland rain and montane forests.

Breeding: Not studied in the wild.

Range: Gambia through s Zaire, Rwanda, and Burundi; mountains of e Zaire, w Uganda, and w Kenya.

Often active by day, the African Golden Cat is a formidable predator with remarkable springing and climbing ability. It takes rodents, duikers, monkeys, tree hyraxes, guineafowl, francolins, chickens, sheep, and goats.

165 Serval
Felis (Leptailurus) serval

Description: A slender, long-legged, spotted cat, with *big, oval, upstanding ears* with black and white markings. Tawny to russet (occasionally black) above, pale below, with *dark longitudinal stripes on neck and shoulders breaking up into spots over back,* flanks, underparts, and legs; some forms have uniformly small dots over entire body. *Tail less than half of head-body*

Footprint

length; ringed for entire length, with black tip. L 27–40″ (67–100 cm); T 14–16″ (35–40 cm); Ht 22″ (55 cm); Wt 19–42 lb (8.7–19 kg).

Similar Species: **Caracal** has unpatterned tawny coat, long tufted ears, and tail only one-third of head-body length. **Leopard,** much heavier and shorter-legged, has rosette-like clusters of dots and much longer tail.

Habitat: Moist savannas, gallery forests, and secondary growth.

Breeding: Reproduces annually, year-round in tropics, December–March in s Africa; 1–5 kittens born after gestation of 65–75 days.

Range: Senegal to Eritrea, thence south through e Africa to Natal, and west to Angola and Namibia.

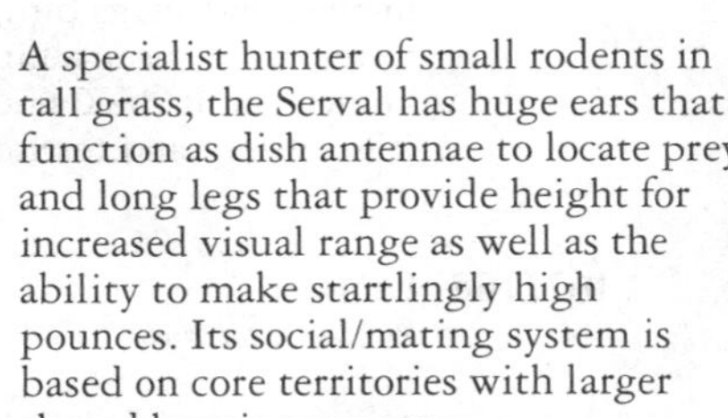

A specialist hunter of small rodents in tall grass, the Serval has huge ears that function as dish antennae to locate prey, and long legs that provide height for increased visual range as well as the ability to make startlingly high pounces. Its social/mating system is based on core territories with larger shared hunting ranges.

---

166 Caracal
Felis (Caracal) caracal

Description: A strongly built cat. *Ears tall and pointed;* white inside, black on backs, with *long black tuft at tips.* Coat unpatterned tawny to rufous (occasionally blackish) above; whitish with faint rufous spots on underparts and insides of legs. Heavily built, like a Canada Lynx *(Lynx canadensis): legs long* and powerful, especially hindquarters; *short tail* about one-third of head-body length. Small head and short muzzle, with black and white markings. L 25–36″ (62–91 cm); T 9″ (22–23 cm); Ht 18″ (45 cm); Wt 22–40 lb (10–18 kg).

Footprint

Similar Species: **African Golden Cat** has small rounded

ears, proportionally shorter legs, and longer tail. Smaller **African Wildcat** has longer tail, ringed toward end; short untufted ears.

Habitat: Savannas, mountains, and rocky hills with some cover.

Breeding: 1–4 kittens born year-round, with peak during rainy season; gestation is 62–81 days.

Range: Pan-African apart from deserts and rain forests.

The most formidable of Africa's small cats, the Caracal regularly kills antelopes its own size and larger (such as the Mountain Reedbuck and the Springbok), suffocating them with a grip on the throat or muzzle. It is such an accomplished jumper that it catches hyraxes and snags birds (sandgrouse, doves) from the air. Little more is known about the Caracal except that it is solitary and territorial.

167, 168 **Leopard**
Panthera pardus

Description: A large *spotted* cat, with *short powerful limbs, heavy torso, thick neck, and long tail.* Short sleek coat tawny yellow to reddish brown; darker (sometimes black) in wetter forested habitats. *Spots grouped into rosettes* on torso and upper limbs; smaller scattered spots on lower limbs and head. L 3′4″–4′2″ (1–1.25 m); T 27–32″ (68–80 cm); Ht 23–28″ (58–70 cm); Wt 62–143 lb (28–65 kg).

Footprint

Similar Species: **Cheetah** has long slender legs, thin waist, and small head with "tear stains" on face.

Habitat: Every type except interior of large deserts; the only large predator in rain forests.

Breeding: 1–4 cubs born year-round, but birth peak occurs during rainy season; gestation is 90–105 days.

Range: Rare in Morocco. Widespread south of Sahara to s Cape Province.

The Leopard eats whatever form of animal protein is available, from termites to a Waterbuck. Where humans have depleted prey, the Leopard turns readily to livestock and domestic dogs. This flexibility and its secretive nocturnal habits have made the Leopard likely to persist near human settlements long after the Lion and Cheetah have been extirpated. It caches kills in trees to prevent Lions and hyenas from taking its food. The Leopard is solitary and territorial but sometimes shares hunting ranges. The black phase of this species is called a black panther.

171–174 **Lion**
Panthera leo

Description: A *very large, robust* cat, with a longish heavy muzzle. Smooth tawny coat with whitish underparts; ears white inside, marked black on backs. *Tail long, with black tassel at tip.* Male develops mane beginning in third year; varies individually from blond to black; fuller in open plains, most sparse in thornbush. Cub has brownish spots that fade by 3 months but may persist on belly as adult. L 8–11′ (2.4–3.3 m); T 24–40″ (60–100 cm); Ht 3′8″–4′ (1.1–1.2 m); Wt 268–528 lb (122–240 kg), record 572 lb (260 kg).

Footprint

Habitat: Grasslands and savannas; woodlands and dense bush.

Breeding: Year-round, with peaks in rainy season; 1–4 (up to 6) cubs born after 3.5-month gestation.

Range: Senegal east to Somalia; e Africa; Angola, n Namibia, and Kalahari east to Mozambique and n Natal.

Lions eat everything from tortoises to giraffes, but tend to hunt the prey they grew up eating, and customs differ among prides. Lions are the only truly sociable cats; related females share a traditional home range, tend to reproduce in synchrony, and cross-suckle their offspring. Prides include anywhere from two or three to 40 lions. Pride members perform a greeting ritual upon meeting; they rub their heads and sides together, with tails looped high, while making friendly moaning sounds. Females are lifelong residents of their mothers' territories, unless food is too scarce, in which case extras emigrate. Adolescent males are forced to depart when their fathers begin to treat them as potential rivals; they spend two or three years as nomads until they mature, then begin seeking a pride to take over. Success depends mainly on numbers. A coalition of two males is the minimum; their tenure is seldom longer than two and a half years—just long enough for one set of cubs to reach the age of independence. Trios and quartets have longer tenures. Most coalitions are made up of brothers, but unrelated nomads also join forces.

169, 170 **Cheetah**
Acinonyx jubatus

Description: Swaybacked, with *"wasp" waist; long, relatively thin limbs.* Dog-like feet with blunt, unsheathed claws. *Head rounded and small,* with very short muzzle; unique "tear stain" below each eye. Coat tawny with white underparts; *heavily spotted with solid round and oval black dots.* Long tail spotted, with several closely spaced black rings near end; tip white. L 3′9″–5′ (1.12–1.5 m); T 26–34″ (66–84 cm); Ht 28–36″ (70–90 cm); Wt 77–143 lb (35–65 kg).

Footprint

Similar Species: **Leopard** has shorter legs; spots arranged in rosettes; lacks "tear stain" under eye.

Habitat: Open and partially open savannas. Absent from rain forests and wet coastal areas.

Breeding: Year-round; litters of 1–6 (average 3) cubs born after gestation of 90–95 days.

Range: Southern Algeria south to n Benin;

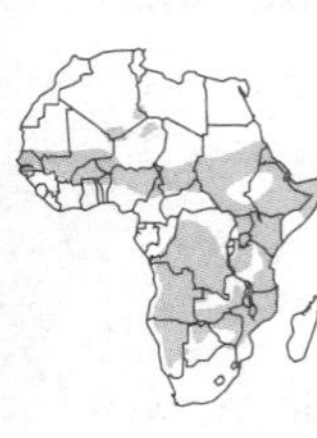

Senegal east to Somalia and thence south and southwest through Tanzania to Namibia and n South Africa. Very rare north of Sahara.

This most specialized cat runs faster than the fleetest prey (top sprinting speed of 70 mph/112 kph) but lacks the staying power of true coursing predators like wild dogs; it must run down the quarry within a distance of 300 yards (meters). So, like other cats, Cheetahs have to stalk their prey and get as close as they can before making an all-out sprint. Unlike other cats, they hunt almost entirely in daytime. A success rate of about 40 percent indicates the Cheetah is a skillful hunter. Male Cheetahs defend territories and, as Lions do, form male coalitions of up to three or four males. They sometimes kill male intruders, and they try to detain and mate with solitary females, whose home ranges are much larger.

Foxes, Jackals, and Dogs
Family Canidae

There are 33 canid species worldwide, and 11 living in Africa. While most experts agree that the Wolf *(Canis lupus)* of Europe is the progenitor of the domestic dog, Africa's canines are familiarly dog-like, with straight and level backs, long and slender legs, large and upstanding ears, and long muzzles. Their coats are usually long, with erectile hackles on the neck, and their tails are bushy. The sexes look alike. Canids are built to run, but stealth and pouncing play important roles in the capture of birds and small mammals; nearly all canids also eat fruit and insects, and most cache food they are not able to eat at once. Unique among carnivores, canids regurgitate meat to feed pups and other nonhunting family members. The basic unit is the monogamous pair, which defends a territory.

175 **Fennec**
Fennec Fox
Vulpes (Fennecus) zerda

Description: The smallest African canid. A *tiny,* short-bodied, cream-colored fox, with *enormous ears* that sit above a tiny face with a *short pointed snout.* Insides of ears, sides of face, underparts, and feet are white; backs and outsides of ears have reddish-brown tinge. *Tail is long,* three-fourths the head-body length; *black-tipped,* with dark hairs over gland on top of tail. L 10–16″ (24–41 cm); T 7–12″ (18–31 cm); Wt 2.2–3.3 lb (1–1.5 kg); ears up to 6″ (15 cm) long.

Similar Species: Larger **Sand Fox** (Pale Fox; *V. pallida*), which lives in Sahara, has proportionally smaller ears and longer muzzle.

Habitat: Sand deserts.

Breeding: 1–5 offspring born March–May, after gestation of 49–52 days.

Range: Sahara, from Mauritania to n Sudan.

Like other small desert creatures, the Fennec goes underground by day and forages by night. Its diet consists of insects, snails, lizards, rodents, ground-nesting birds and their eggs, dates, and berries. It uses its extraordinary ears to locate underground prey. At night it utters a shuddering, descending contact howl and a shrill greeting cry. Fennecs live in monogamous pairs.

176 **Cape Fox**
Vulpes chama

Description: A densely furred fox, with a *long, black-tipped tail two-thirds the head-body length.* Coat pale fawn grizzled with silver-gray over the back; head and backs of ears reddish; small black patch on side of muzzle; legs reddish brown; *dark brown patch on back of upper hindleg;* underparts buff to white. L 18–24″ (45–61 cm); T 12–16″ (30–39 cm); Ht 12″ (30 cm); Wt 8–10 lb (3.6–4.5 kg).

Similar Species: **Bat-eared Fox** has enormous, black-edged ears, black mask, and black legs. **Black-backed Jackal** is longer-bodied and longer-legged, with silver-grizzled black saddle contrasting sharply with rufous flanks.

Habitat: Grasslands, scrub, and subdeserts.

Breeding: 1–5 cubs whelped August–October, after gestation of 50–52 days.

Range: Southern Angola, Namibia, Botswana, and most of South Africa.

This nocturnal fox forages alone, mainly for mice and invertebrate prey, but it dens in monogamous pairs, with core areas urine-marked and defended by the pair. Helpers have been seen at some dens, and occasionally two females reproduce communally with the same male.

---

177 Bat-eared Fox
Otocyon megalotis

Description: Unmistakable. A *masked* fox with *enormous, black-edged, oval ears.* Coat gray-buff, grizzled with black-tipped white hairs over back and flanks; *black legs and tail tip.* Body and tail rather short for a fox; hindquarters well developed. Forefeet equipped with very long nails for digging. L 20–28″ (50–70 cm); T 9–14″ (23–34 cm); Ht 12″ (30 cm); Wt 6.6–10 lb (3–4.5 kg).

Footprint

Similar Species: **Cape Fox** has normal fox-like proportions; lacks facial mask.

Habitat: Grasslands and light woodlands, especially arid savannas with short grass.

Breeding: 3–6 cubs born early in rainy season, after gestation of 60–70 days.

Range: Ethiopia south to c Tanzania; s Angola and Zambia south through South Africa.

The Bat-eared Fox's enormous ears are specialized to detect insects by sound. Harvester termites and dung beetles make up 80 percent of the animal's diet, with other invertebrates, small vertebrates, and fruit making up the rest. Because their insect prey is patchy and ephemeral, Bat-eared Foxes don't defend territories.

---

178 **Golden Jackal**
Common Jackal, Asiatic Jackal
Canis aureus

Description: A typical jackal, with long legs, long pointed muzzle, and tail shorter than a fox's. Coat shaggy and coarse above; yellow or grayish *without distinct saddle,* although *long hackles on shoulders and back are black-brown or yellow-tipped.* Tail has black tip and dark spot over gland. L 3′6″ (1.05 m); T 8–12″ (20–30 cm); Ht 15–20″ (38–50 cm); Wt 15–33 lb (7–15 kg).

Similar Species: **Black-backed Jackal** has prominent blackish saddle; tail is darker for entire length. **Side-striped Jackal** has narrow white stripe on flank (indistinct from afar) and white-tipped tail.

Habitat: Arid grasslands, open savannas, and deserts.

Breeding: Produces 2–9 pups after gestation of 60 days.

Range: Northern Africa south to s Mali, n Zaire, and n Tanzania.

The Golden Jackal is widely distributed as a result of its ability to glean a living in deserts and subdeserts. It eats fruit, carrion, and small prey from insects to infant antelopes. Pairs mate for life, scent-marking and defending a territory. Often male and female offspring of the previous litter remain in the family territory and help rear younger siblings. The Golden Jackal's howl is a high-pitched wail, often given in chorus at sundown.

179 Black-backed Jackal
Silver-backed Jackal
Canis mesomelas

Description: A handsome, soft-haired, rufous to tan jackal with a prominent *black-and-silver saddle.* Tail peppered with black, ending in black tip. Flanks and legs redder than upperparts; underparts, chin, and lips white or creamy. Coat varies seasonally; male breeding coat is most colorful. L 28–40″ (70–100 cm); T 12–14″ (30–35 cm); Ht 15–18″ (38–45 cm); Wt 20–30 lb (9–13.5 kg).

Footprint

Similar Species: **Golden Jackal** lacks saddle contrasting with rufous flanks; tail is black only at tip and gland spot. **Side-striped Jackal** has indistinct diagonal white stripe and white-tipped tail.

Habitat: Savannas and woodlands.

Breeding: Produces 2–9 pups late in dry season, after gestation of 60–65 days.

Range: Northern Ethiopia to Horn of Africa, thence south through c Tanzania; sw Angola and Zimbabwe, and south through South Africa.

The diet and foraging habits of this jackal are very similar to those of the Golden Jackal, though Black-backs are usually more in evidence at hyena and Lion kills. Like Goldens, Black-backs pair for life and jointly defend their territory; young adults often help rear their parents' next litter. The contact call is an abrupt, raucous yell, followed by shorter yelps; in South Africa this jackal also howls.

180 Side-striped Jackal
Canis adustus

Description: A dull grayish jackal. *Blackish tail usually has conspicuous white tip.* Flank has *diagonal white or buffy stripe* edged with black, indistinct at a distance. Muzzle relatively blunt; ears short and rounded. L 28–32″ (70–80 cm);

T 14–18″ (35–45 cm); Ht 16″ (40 cm); Wt 16–31 lb (7.3–14 kg).

Similar Species: **Golden Jackal** is more yellowish, with black-tipped tail. **Black-backed Jackal** is distinctly rufous below saddle; tail is blackish to tip.

Habitat: Moist savannas, bushlands, marshes, abandoned cultivation, and mountains up to 9,000′ (2,700 m).

Breeding: Whelps 3–6 pups just before or during rainy season, after gestation of 57–70 days.

Range: Northern Nigeria to Ethiopia; s Gabon, s Zaire, and s Kenya south to n Namibia and Natal.

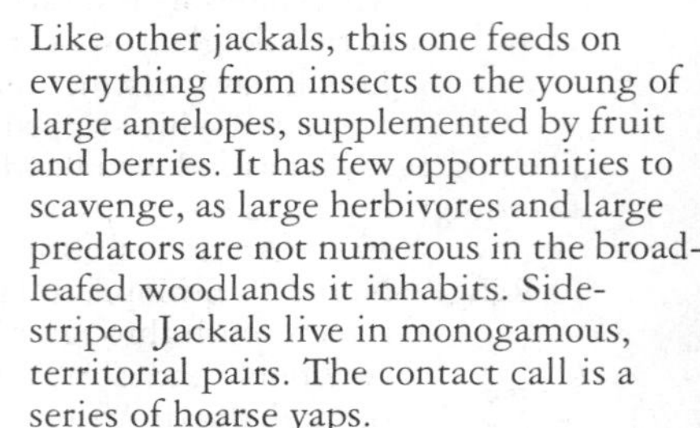

Like other jackals, this one feeds on everything from insects to the young of large antelopes, supplemented by fruit and berries. It has few opportunities to scavenge, as large herbivores and large predators are not numerous in the broad-leafed woodlands it inhabits. Side-striped Jackals live in monogamous, territorial pairs. The contact call is a series of hoarse yaps.

181 Ethiopian Wolf

Simien Jackal, Simien Fox
Canis simensis

Description: The largest African canine, with a *very elongated muzzle. Foxy red* head, torso, outsides of legs, and face; *2 collars of red encircling throat.* Insides of ears, small spot on cheek, chin, all other underparts, and *feet white.* Red tail suffused with black at gland spot and tip; *conspicuous white patch* on underside near base. L 32–40″ (80–100 cm); T 11–16″ (27–40 cm); Ht 21–25″ (53–62 cm); Wt 24–42 lb (11–19 kg), males about 20 percent heavier than females.

Similar Species: Smaller **Side-striped Jackal** is grayish; tail has white tip.

Habitat: Montane grasslands and moors, including bogs and heaths, at 10,000–15,000′ (3,000–4,500 m).

Breeding: 2–6 pups born October–February, after gestation of 8–9 weeks.

Range: Only Ethiopian Plateau, and rare and highly vulnerable there; found in Bale Mountain NP and Simen Mountains.

Recently found to have DNA close to that of the Wolf *(C. lupus)* of Europe, and able to interbreed with domestic dogs, this animal looks, sounds, and behaves like a jackal. It lives in pairs or "helper" family groups rather than in packs, and subsists on small mammals, pouncing on swamp rats and mole rats as they emerge from their grassy tunnel entrances. It also takes hares, hyraxes, and birds. The contact call is a high-pitched wail.

---

182 **African Wild Dog**
Cape Hunting Dog
Lycaon pictus

Description: A lean, lanky canid, with short sparse fur that is a *patchwork of black, white, and varying shades of ocher.* Face black, with tan forehead; tail short-haired and ocher at base, then black, and finally long-haired and white. Hyena-like head, with heavy blunt muzzle; huge rounded ears. L 30–40″ (75–100 cm); T 12–16″ (30–40 cm); Ht 24–30″ (60–75 cm); Wt 44–55 lb (20–25 kg).

Footprint

Habitat: Semi-deserts, moist and dry savannas, montane grasslands, and moorlands to 9,000′ (2,700 m).

Breeding: After gestation of 70–75 days, whelps an average of 10 pups (up to 19), but mortality is around 90 percent.

Range: Patchily distributed from n Nigeria and s Niger east through Horn, south to ne South Africa, and northwest through Angola to s Congo.

The African Wild Dog runs down antelopes under 100 pounds (45 kg); large packs have been known to take zebras and even elands routinely. Packs usually number six to ten adults. Only the dominant male and female successfully reproduce. Subordinate females usually defer breeding; if they do breed, their pups are usually destroyed by the dominant female. Thus subordinate females emigrate (and often perish), while related males more often stay in the pack, waiting to inherit the breeding position.

Weasels
Family Mustelidae

This is the most diverse family of carnivores: about 65 species in 25 genera and six subfamilies. Only seven mustelids occur in sub-Saharan Africa. Members of this family vary from tiny terrestrial weasels to heavy aquatic otters. Most species have long heads and short, vise-like jaws; the ears are round or triangular, set low on the head, and closeable. The skin is tough and loose-fitting in many species, and covered with dense soft fur. Nearly all mustelids are solitary and territorial, with females defending resources needed to rear young and males competing for space containing female territories. Fierceness toward enemies is a family trait.

Striped Weasel
White-naped Weasel
Poecilogale albinucha

Description: The smallest African mustelid, very lightly built. A *long, sinuous,* typical weasel in form, but colored like an American skunk: *jet black, with forehead to nape white; 4 white or yellowish longitudinal stripes on back;* tail white and fluffy. Coat short and sleek. Elongated head, with blunt muzzle, powerful jaws, wide gape; small ears. L 10–14″ (25–35 cm); T 6–9″ (15–23 cm); Ht 3″ (8 cm); Wt 5.6–12.4 oz (160–350 g).

Similar Species: **Libyan Striped Weasel** *(Ictonyx libyca)* of n Africa and **Zorilla** have much longer hair, wide skulls, and faces marked with white patches.

Habitat: Moist savannas, montane grasslands, and agricultural lands.

Breeding: 1–3 minute offspring born during rainy months, after gestation of 32 days.

Range: Zaire east to Kenya west of rift valley; south to s Angola, Botswana, Zimbabwe, e South Africa, and Mozambique.

The nocturnal Striped Weasel feeds mostly on rodents. It locates its prey mainly by scent, then pursues it relentlessly, even into holes and tunnels. It is so flexible it can turn around in any space wide enough to admit its head. It is almost wholly terrestrial.

---

183 **Zorilla**
Striped Polecat
Ictonyx striatus

Description: A shaggy, long-haired, skunk-like mustelid. *Jet black, with 4 wide white stripes from nape to tail;* broad blunt head, with *individualized pattern of white spots between eyes and a spot or stripe on each cheek;* white-backed ears; *bushy tail typically all white,* but varies to all black. L 11–15″ (28–38 cm); T 10–12″ (25–30 cm); Ht 4″ (10 cm); Wt 1.3–3.3 lb (0.6–1.5 kg).

Similar Species: **Libyan Striped Weasel** *(Ictonyx libyca)* of n Africa overlaps with Zorilla in Sahel; is much smaller and slighter.

Habitat: Short grasslands, woodlands, and subdeserts, including sand dunes, to 7,300′ (2,200 m).

Breeding: 1–3 young born during wetter warmer months, after 36-day gestation.

Range: Senegal east to Eritrea, and south to Cape of Good Hope, including all of s Africa north to Angola.

Strictly nocturnal and solitary, the Zorilla tends to be most active after 10 P.M. and

returns to its burrow, pile of stones, or other secure resting place before dawn. Much of its foraging time is spent digging or sniffing out concealed insects, rodents, reptiles, and mammals up to the size of a small hare. The Zorilla does not eat fruit or vegetables but derives enough water from its prey to live in waterless areas. If necessary, it backs up its striking warning coloration by discharging an offensive fluid from its well-developed stink glands, similar to that of a Striped Skunk (*Mephitis mephitis*) of North America.

---

184 **Ratel**
Honey Badger
Mellivora capensis

Description: Badger-like, but more mobile, with longer legs; wide flat feet armed with bear-like, curved claws. Coarse *jet-black fur, with contrasting white or gray mantle from crown to tip of short tapered tail.* Head broad; ears inconspicuous, mere ridges of thickened skin; jaws powerful. L 24–30″ (60–75 cm); T 7–10″ (18–25 cm); Ht 9–11″ (23–28 cm); Wt 18–35 lb (8–16 kg).

Footprint

Habitat: Semi-deserts to moist savannas and montane forests to 5,600′ (1,700 m); rare in lowland rain forests.

Breeding: 1–4 young born after long gestation estimated at 6 months.

Range: Sub-Saharan Africa; also occurs in Mauritania and Morocco.

The warning coloration of this fearless and powerful small animal is more than justified. The Ratel has great strength and formidable jaws and claws, and its loose skin is nearly impenetrable. It is unable to outrun larger carnivores, but as a last resort it will eject a stinking fluid from its anal sacs. It can trot long distances, as far as 22 miles (35 km) in a night. A digger ranking second only to the Aardvark and Giant Pangolin

(Manis gigantea), it is an opportunistic omnivore. Among its favorite foods are bee larvae and honey. The bird called the Greater Honeyguide *(Indicator indicator)* sometimes leads Ratels to hives, with mutual benefit if the Ratel succeeds in gaining access.

185 Spotted-necked Otter
Lutra maculicollis

Description: A small otter, with a broad head and blunt muzzle; very short legs and toes webbed to the tips, each with a short, well-developed claw. Short coat with dense underfur; *reddish to dark chocolate-brown;* cheeks, chin, throat, and upper chest cream to buff, with *irregular reddish or brown blotches.* Long tail flattened on upper and lower surfaces. L 23–28″ (58–69 cm); T 13–18″ (33–45 cm); Ht 12″ (30 cm); Wt 9–14 lb (4–6.5 kg).

Similar Species: Much larger **Cape Clawless Otter** lacks brown neck spots. Much smaller **Marsh Mongoose** has shaggy coat.

Habitat: Usually lakes, rivers, and swamps; sometimes small mountain streams.

Breeding: 2 or 3 young born November–February, after gestation of 2 months.

Range: Sierra Leone to wc Ethiopia; south through Zaire to e South Africa and s Angola.

The Spotted-necked Otter preys mainly on fish, but where frogs and shellfish predominate, they may make up the bulk of its diet. It is active by day and often near dusk, and also on moonlit nights. Despite its fully webbed hands, this Otter has considerable manual dexterity. It is a rather slow, short-winded swimmer. Home ranges feature a network of regularly used trails; sleeping places and dens in the form of holes in banks or logs, and crevices in rock piles; and latrine and musking places.

186 Cape Clawless Otter
Clawless Otter
Aonyx capensis

Description: A *very large otter.* Massive head with wide flat skull and powerful jaws. Sleek coat tan to dark chocolate-brown above; lighter below, with unspotted *white or buff patches on chin, throat, and chest extending onto neck and face* below eyes; belly white. Silvery mantle of white-tipped hairs may occur from forehead to shoulders. Relatively long-legged; forefeet resemble hands, with opposable thumb; hindfeet webbed to outer joints. L 29–36″ (72–91 cm); T 16–28″ (40–71 cm); Ht 14″ (35 cm); Wt 26–46 lb (12–21 kg).

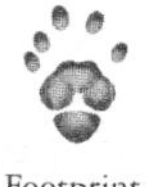
Footprint

Similar Species: **Congo Clawless Otter** *(A. congicus)* inhabits swamps of lowland rain forests in Congo Basin; has more pronounced frosting of head and neck, ears fringed with white, and distinct dark patch in white area ahead of eye.

Habitat: Freshwater streams and lakes to 10,000′ (3,000 m); also salt water along rocky coasts and mangrove swamps.

Breeding: Year-round; 2 or 3 young born after 2-month gestation.

Range: Senegal east to Chad; w Sudan and e Ethiopia south to Cape Province, and west through Angola.

More mobile than the river otters (*Lutra* species), the Cape Clawless Otter travels considerable distances overland. Superior manual dexterity, enlarged molars, and an awesome bite indicate a varied diet of aquatic organisms groped from bottom sediments, holes, and under rocks. This species is more sociable than the river otters.

PRIMATES
Order Primates

Primates comprise the prosimians (lower primates) and the monkeys and apes (higher primates), totaling 225 species worldwide, with 86 in Africa and Madagascar. In general, primates have a rounded skull with a relatively large brain; forward-directed eyes for stereoscopic vision; and hands and feet adapted for grasping. Most primates are arboreal and diurnal, and eat fruit, leaves, and insects. Prosimians (bushbabies and lemurs) have large eyes and relatively simple jaws and teeth. Apes are tailless, and their arms (except in humans) are longer than their legs. Monkey and ape social systems are diverse and complex.

BUSHBABIES
Family Galagonidae

Bushbabies are an exclusively African family of up to 11 species of small nocturnal creatures that strikingly resemble the earliest primates. They bounce through the trees like miniature kangaroos, propelled by overdeveloped hindlegs; a furry tail longer than the head and body functions as a balancing organ. Their hands and feet have long slender digits, with an opposable thumb and big toe. They have rounded heads and short, pointed faces. Their eyes, adapted to see in the faintest light, are frontally placed, reflective, and immobile in their sockets; like owls, bushbabies can rotate their heads 180 degrees. The lower incisor and canine teeth are modified as a scraping/grooming comb. The powerful call of the Thick-tailed Bushbaby, reminiscent of a baby's wail, is what earned these animals their common name.

187 **Thick-tailed Bushbaby**
Large-eared Greater Bushbaby, Greater Galago
Galago (Otolemur) crassicaudatus

Description: A heavyweight bushbaby *the size of a small cat,* with a *thick bushy tail longer than its head and body.* Pointed snout; large reflective eyes; *large rounded ears.* Coat thick, soft, and woolly. Color varies from pale gray to brownish (occasionally black), with tops of hands and feet dark in some races; tail may also be darker toward tip; underparts lighter; face like body or paler, with darker areas around eyes and on forehead. L 13–14″ (32–35 cm); T 14–18″ (36–45 cm); Wt 2.2–3.1 lb (1–1.4 kg).

Similar Species: **Greater Bushbaby** *(G. {O.} garnettii)* ranges from s Somalia to se Tanzania and Zanzibar; smaller (L 11″/27 cm), with shorter rounded ears; forehead same color as face. **Lesser Bushbaby** is less than half the size; has thinner tail.

Habitat: Dense evergreen forests and bush, including plantations of exotic trees and suburban gardens. Fruit must be abundant for at least half the year.

Breeding: Reproduces annually, after gestation of 18 weeks; 1–3 offspring.

Range: Southern Kenya, Tanzania, and Rwanda south to Natal and west to Angola, from sea level to 6,000′ (1,800 m).

The Thick-tailed Bushbaby runs and walks along tree limbs like a monkey, following regular pathways to eat fruit and gum deposits; it also eats insects and small birds and mammals. On the ground, it either walks with hindquarters and tail elevated, hops like a kangaroo with forelegs dangling, or jump-runs, landing alternately on its hind- and forelegs. This bushbaby also sometimes moves in a slow, stealthy manner, like a potto. Several related females and their young share a home range. Infants ride on their mothers' broad backs after spending their first ten days in a leafy nest.

188 **Lesser Bushbaby**
Senegal Bushbaby, Lesser Galago
Galago (Galago) senegalensis

Description: Smaller than most squirrels. Rounded head; pointed snout; very large, pointed, *bat-like ears. Tail thin,* becoming bushier toward tip. Short, soft, woolly coat; light gray to bluish gray, shading into yellowish arms and thighs; white to cream underparts; face gray, with dark cheek and *eye patches;* white streak along nose. L 7″ (17 cm); T 9″ (23 cm); Wt 5.3–8.8 oz (150–250 g).

Similar Species: **Eastern Lesser Galago** *(G. zanzibaricus),* from Kenya's Tana River to s Mozambique and Zanzibar, has cinnamon upperparts. **Eastern Needle-clawed Bushbaby** *(G. matschiei),* of e Zaire, is dark brown, with black ring around each eye. **Thick-tailed Bushbaby** is twice as large; has bushier tail.

Habitat: Acacia savannas, gallery forests, and forest edges.

Breeding: Litters of 1 or 2 young born after gestation of about 21 weeks.

Range: Widespread throughout sub-Saharan Africa to 5,000′ (1,500 m).

Lesser Bushbabies can number as many as 1,300 per square mile (500 per sq km). They subsist almost entirely on acacia gum, insects, and spiders, without drinking. Clan members forage independently but return before daybreak to their leaf nest or tree hole to socialize before retiring for the day, huddled together.

Pottos
Family Loridae

The two African pottos and three lorises of southeast Asia have in common with bushbabies the tooth comb, a rounded head, and large, frontally placed eyes; otherwise they are very different. Instead of bouncing through the trees, they move in slow motion and freeze at the slightest disturbance. Fore- and hindlimbs are nearly equal in length, and hands and feet are adapted for gripping branches securely; the tail is reduced or absent. Pottos do not make birth nests; babies cling to the mother's belly fur.

189 **Potto**
Perodicticus potto

Description: Shaped like a teddy bear: *chunky body and sturdy limbs; rounded head with blunt muzzle;* big eyes and *small ears; stumpy tail.* Hands and feet modified for gripping branches: thick opposable thumb and big toe open to 180°; *2nd finger reduced to stump,* increasing hand span; 2nd toe has grooming claw. Nape and shoulders shielded by thickened skin through which horny extensions of 4 vertebrae project. Dense, soft coat varies from reddish brown to nearly black, with darker spinal stripe; underparts pale to beige or slate-gray. L 13″ (32 cm); T 2″ (5 cm); Wt 2.4 lb (1.1 kg).

Similar Species: **Angwantibo** (Golden Potto; *Arctocebus calabarensis*), which inhabits understory of c African rain forests, is smaller (Wt 1.1 lb/500 g), more delicate, and lighter-colored.

Habitat: Lowland rain forests, isolated forest patches in savannas, coastal scrublands, and secondary forests.

Breeding: 1 (rarely 2) young born annually, after gestation of 6–6.5 months.

Range: Guinea to w Kenya, south to s Zaire, and west to n Angola.

The Potto normally moves very slowly. However, it is capable of sudden, vigorous movements that can startle or dislodge an enemy. Putting its head between its legs and presenting its armored neck, it holds onto a branch with a vise-like grip, or it may rush forward and knock into its adversary. Fighting males also joust with the neck shield. Pottos are solitary, foraging alone for fruit, tree gum, leaves, flowers, and invertebrate prey.

Lemurs

Lemurs are the descendants of bushbaby ancestors that diversified on the island of Madagascar over the last 50 million years. Small, nocturnal, solitary prosimians very similar to the existing dwarf lemurs (family Cheirogaleidae) evolved into larger, diurnal, sociable lemurs like the Ring-tailed Lemur and the Black Lemur, and finally into large forms, as presently represented by the Indri and the sifakas. Species on Madagascar even included several giant ground dwellers the size of gorillas. However, like island animals the world over, lemurs were ill-equipped to cope with the arrival of humans and their livestock two millennia ago. Since then at least 14 species have become extinct; as many as 30 species remain, but all have one or all of their races in danger of extinction. Lemurs preserve their bushbaby ancestry in long, strong hindlegs employed for vertical clinging and leaping; a long tail; the tooth comb, used to scrape tree gum as well as for grooming; forward-facing, parallel eyes with good binocular and night vision; and a grooming claw on the second toe, while other digits have nails.

Typical Lemurs
Family Lemuridae

This family includes ten lemurs with color patterns that range from gray-brown to conspicuous black-and-white or black-and-red. Muzzles are black and pointed, with bare, moist nostrils. Members of this family are vegetarian.

They live at high densities in favorable habitats over most of the island. Although able to reach any part of a tree, they rarely use their hands in feeding except to pull foliage within biting distance. They groom themselves with their teeth and scratch with their grooming claws. Family members use scent marks and calls to preserve spacing between groups. Some species use loud calls to advertise their presence or warn of danger.

190 Ring-tailed Lemur

Lemur catta

Description: Hindquarters higher than forequarters; small head with long pointed muzzle below front-facing eyes. Brilliant pearl gray above; whitish below. Long furry *tail with about 14 black and white rings. Face a black and white mask, with amber-colored eyes.* Bare skin of nose, palms, soles, and genitals black. Male's large pendulous scrotum is obvious. L 16–18″ (39–46 cm); T 22–25″ (56–63 cm); Wt 5–8 lb (2.3–3.7 kg).

Similar Species: **Black Lemur** lacks rings on tail; male is black, female dark reddish brown to light golden-brown.

Habitat: Dry woodlands, gallery forests, and dry transition forests.

Breeding: 1 or 2 young born after 4.5-month gestation; births occur mainly in August.

Range: Southern and sw Madagascar.

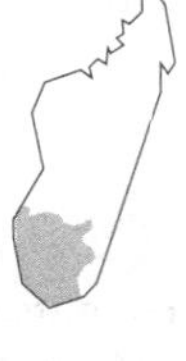

This is the only primate in Madagascar that regularly forages on the ground, for tamarind fruit or grasses and herbs. Aloft, it springs with agility through the branches. The Ring-tailed Lemur lives in groups that average 15 animals. Females remain in their birthplace; males transfer at least once to another troop. Males are most active in maintaining territories, scent-marking and giving hooting calls. The sexes have separate dominance hierarchies, and females dominate males.

191 Black Lemur
Eulemur (Lemur) macaco

Description: Similar in general form and proportions to Ring-tailed Lemur. Muzzle pointed and foxy-looking. Large, amber-colored eyes; small ears. Coat dense and soft. *Male entirely jet black,* including long ear fringes. Female dark reddish brown to light golden-brown, with *darker face and conspicuous white ear fringes.* L 15–18″ (38–45 cm); T 20–25″ (51–63 cm); Wt 4.4–6.4 lb (2–2.9 kg).

Similar Species: **Brown Lemur** *(E. fulvus)* is grayish to dark brown above, with white or orange whiskers; lives on all but extreme s coast. **Mongoose Lemur** (*E. mongoz;* **Plate 192**), of nw Madagascar and Comoros, is grayish, with reddish-brown back, thighs, and arms; female has white throat and underparts.

Habitat: Wet mountain rain forests, with annual rainfall up to 120″ (3,000 mm).

Breeding: 1 offspring (sometimes 2, rarely 3) born August–October, after gestation of 17–19 weeks.

Range: Northwestern Madagascar and neighboring island of Nosy Komba.

Foraging groups of five to 15 Black Lemurs often merge and sleep together at night. These lemurs respond to disturbances with long rattling coughs. For the first few weeks after birth, the young clings to its mother's belly, then begins riding on her back. Destruction of its habitat has caused a drastic decline in this species' numbers.

193 Ruffed Lemur
Varecia variegata

Description: The largest family member. Long dense fur, except on long narrow muzzle; *white ruff begins above ears and encircles face.* Color variable: conspicuous black and white, brownish black and white, or fox-red and white; ruff, lower arms, and legs white; hands, feet, underside, tail, and face colored. L 24″ (60 cm); T 24″ (60 cm); Wt 9–11 lb (4–5 kg).

Habitat: Rain forests.

Breeding: 1–3 young born in November after 14-week gestation.

Range: East coast of Madagascar.

This little-known species may live in monogamous family units of two to five animals. Almost wholly arboreal, it is an agile leaper and climber, and apparently feeds mostly on fruit. Largely inactive by day, it rouses at dusk and remains active through the first half of the night. It often sunbathes early in the morning. Ruffed Lemurs advertise their presence with loud howling in chorus that stimulates other groups to answer.

Leaping Lemurs
Family Indriidae

These large arboreal lemurs move beneath the tree canopy by leaping from trunk to trunk like giant bushbabies. Although the family was once extensive, only four or five species remain, all severely threatened by habitat destruction. Three typify the family in being large, foliage-eating lemurs that are active during the day and live in small groups. The head is rounded, with large eyes, fairly large ears, and a short or medium-length naked muzzle. These lemurs subsist entirely on fruit and leaves; they can feed while hanging head-down.

194 Indri
Indri indri

Description: The largest prosimian in the world. Wide-bodied, with overdeveloped hindlegs; extremely long hands and feet. Face has naked, black-gray muzzle framed by whitish-gray fur; *rounded ears, fringed with longer hair.* Thick silky coat black and white in variable proportions, with black predominating. *Tail a mere stub.* L 23–28″ (57–70 cm); T 2″ (5 cm); Wt 15.4–22 lb (7–10 kg).

Similar Species: Black and white form of **Ruffed Lemur** has much longer tail, as do **sifakas.**

Habitat: Rain forests.

Breeding: 1 young born in May or June, after gestation of 4–5 months.

Range: East coast of Madagascar.

The Indri makes prodigious leaps of up to 33 feet (10 m) between trees. It comes to the ground only to negotiate larger gaps, or to eat bark or earth (a digestion aid); there it moves like a kangaroo, hopping on its hindlegs, with arms held above shoulder level and torso inclined backward. Its diet is predominantly shoots and young leaves, followed by fruit and seeds, and some flowers and mature foliage. Highly vocal, Indris have several long-distance calls and howls.

195, 196 **Verreaux's Sifaka**
Propithecus verreauxi

Description: *A large lemur, with a tail longer than the head and body.* Overdeveloped hindlegs; large hands and feet, with long wide thumb and big toe. Square head with pointed snout; yellow eyes; ears ringed with white fur. Thick silky *coat mainly white,* but extremely variable in the 4 races, from all white or pearl gray to mostly brown to black or maroon, with intermediate forms. Some races have *dark brown cap* behind broad white brow, covering back of head and neck (often bleached gray or reddish in old males). White fur contrasts with black skin on palms and soles, genitalia, and heart-shaped face. Tail hangs down or coils up like a spring. L 16–19″ (39–48 cm); T 20–24″ (50–60 cm); Wt 7.7–9.5 lb (3.5–4.3 kg).

Subspecies: **Coquerel's Sifaka** *(P. v. coquereli)* of

nw Madagascar is white, except for brown arms and brown inner thighs.

Similar Species: Tail of **Indri** is a 2″ (5-cm) stub. Larger **Diademed Sifaka** has tail barely as long as head and body.

Habitat: Gallery and dry deciduous forests.

Breeding: Produces 1 young in June or July after 23-week gestation.

Range: North-central to sw Madagascar.

This large lemur spends between a quarter and a third of its day feeding, mostly on new and old foliage and fruit, as well as flowers, bark, and dead wood. Mixed-sex groups average six animals; unlike most other primates, males apparently outnumber females. Mating is highly synchronized within and among groups.

---

197 **Diademed Sifaka**
Propithecus diadema

Description: Larger than Verreaux's Sifaka, with silkier fur, and *proportionally shorter tail.* Rounded head; ears largely hidden in fur. Coat thick, glossy; varies from *all white to all black, with patches of gold,* gray, or brown; some races have white or yellowish forehead band contrasting with black crown. L 20–22″ (50–55 cm); T 18–20″ (45–51 cm); Wt 13–17.6 lb (6–8 kg).

Similar Species: Smaller **Verreaux's Sifaka** has small ears ringed by white fur; tail longer than head and body. **Woolly Lemur** (Avahi; *Avahi laniger*), of rain forests of e coast of Madagascar, is much smaller (Wt 2 lb/0.9 kg); light to medium gray, with short woolly fur.

Habitat: Evergreen forests.

Breeding: 1 young born after 4- to 5-month gestation; most births in September.

Range: Eastern Madagascar.

Groups of two to five of these sifakas live in large territories. Both sexes engage in scent-marking. Group

members occasionally emit very loud, rattling calls to warn of aerial predators and "kiss-sneeze" alarm calls in response to ground predators.

Aye-Aye

Family Daubentoniidae

The Aye-aye is descended from the same stock as lemurs, but is unique and has been placed alone in its family.

198 Aye-aye

Daubentonia madagascariensis

Description: Big round eyes; *naked, bat-like ears;* cat-like whiskers on upper lip; bare nostrils. Coat long, thick, and coarse; hairs white at base, black on ends, giving flecked effect; *big bushy tail* of same color; underparts pale to white. *3rd and 4th fingers twice as long as others, 3rd especially thin;* fingers and toes have very long claws. L 14–18" (36–44 cm); T 20–24" (50–60 cm); Wt 4.4–6.6 lb (2–3 kg).

Habitat: Rain forests.

Breeding: 1 young.

Range: Madagascar, nw and ne regions.

Moving through the trees, the Aye-aye uses its claws to cling to branches or as hooks to hang upside down by its feet while it feeds. It uses its powerful, beveled incisors (which, like those of rodents, keep growing) to scrape away the outer covering from the fruit it eats and to gnaw away the bark of trees to reach insect grubs and larvae, which it first detects by hearing. The Aye-aye then extracts the fruit pulp or grubs with its thin, elongated middle finger. Rain forest destruction and persecution by humans (superstitious people consider them creatures of ill omen) have brought this unique animal, the largest nocturnal primate, to the verge of extinction.

Monkeys and Baboons
Family Cercopithecidae

Old World monkeys total about 74 species. About half (39 species) are African, including the forest monkeys known as guenons; the mangabeys; a macaque; the baboons; and some of the world's leaf-eating monkeys, represented in Africa by the colobus monkeys. The other 35 species are Asian, including the baboon-like macaques and the majority of the leaf-eating monkeys. The members of this family are dog-shaped primates with narrow bodies, deep chests, and "wasp" waists. They usually move and stand on all fours, and sit and sleep on behinds padded with a pair of calluses. Their hands and feet have five digits protected by nails, not claws. Their heads have a projecting muzzle and a partially naked face. A pair of cheek pouches extends beneath the neck skin (absent in colobus monkeys). The tail is used for balance, not for grasping as in many New World primates. All Old World monkeys are diurnal and sociable, have excellent binocular color vision similar to humans', acute hearing, and a somewhat less acute sense of smell (but a lot better than ours). African monkeys mostly live in the concealing rain forests of the Congo Basin and West Africa.

Guenons
Forest Monkeys
Genera *Cercopithecus, Miopithecus, Erythrocebus, Allenopithecus*

Guenons are graceful monkeys with long tails and silky coats in various shades of brown, gray, red, black, and green; their coats are often grizzled-looking because of hairs banded alternately light and dark. Originally applied only to the spot-nosed monkeys, "guenon" is now used for several genera with distinctive "mustaches," light nose spots, striped sideburns, and rump and body colors and markings. All are basically arboreal quadrupeds that run in trees like squirrels, but some often come to the ground, and one, the Patas Monkey, lives in wooded savannas and is a swift runner overland; most are good leapers. Guenons are omnivorous; competition for fruit is intense, with big species taking precedence over smaller ones. Nearly all guenons live in one-male troops; a number regularly associate in multi-species troops. Africa is home to 23 guenons.

---

199 **Blue Monkey**
Sykes' Monkey, Diademed Monkey, Samango Monkey
Cercopithecus mitis

Description: *A large dark monkey with an unusually long tail.* Coat dense and thick; color varies with subspecies and elevation (see below); face blue-black (in some races), framed by wide, bushy, grizzled cheek whiskers. Forehead hairs point forward in *bristly diadem* in some forms. L 20–26" (49–66 cm); T 22–44" (55–109 cm); Wt male 16.3 lb (7.4 kg), female 9.2 lb (4.2 kg).

Subspecies: 20–25, many in isolated populations, including: **Sykes' Monkey** *(C. m. albogularis),* found in highlands east of e rift valley in e Kenya, lacks diadem; has white throat, greenish to reddish upperparts, black forelimbs, and no black on shoulders, nape, or crown. **Mount Kenya Sykes' Monkey** *(C. m. kolbi),* of Mount Kenya and Aberdare Mountains, has most striking coloration: broad, snow-white collar set off by black shoulders and dark red back; long ear tufts. **Blue Monkey** *(C. m. stuhlmanni),* found from e Congo to w Kenya and n Tanzania, has grizzled blue-gray back, with intensely black arms and black cap that contrasts with pale, grizzled brow patch. **Samango Monkey** *(C. m. labiatus),* which ranges from e Zimbabwe and Mozambique to e Cape Province, has dark brown face, with white limited to lips and chin; grizzled gray-brown upperparts and dirty white underparts; black legs, shoulders, and outer two-thirds of tail.

Habitat: Forests of all kinds to 10,000′ (3,000 m).

Breeding: 1 young born after gestation of 20 weeks; births peak during rainy season.

Range: Congo Basin; Ethiopia; sw Somalia to nw Angola and south in all countries but Namibia and Botswana.

The Blue Monkey eats fruit, leaves, and slow-moving insects, as well as occasional birds and small mammals. Group size, dependent on habitat and resources, varies from two to 70, but typically numbers between 12 and 20 animals. There is intense reproductive competition among males, who give deep booming calls.

Greater Spot-nosed Monkey

Greater White-nosed Monkey
Cercopithecus nictitans

Description: A large dark monkey with a *pure white patch on the nose.* Slaty-black face and underparts; black limbs and tail; grizzled dark olive-green cheeks and upperparts. L 17–28″ (43–70 cm); T 22–40″ (56–100 cm); Wt 9.2–14.5 lb (4.2–6.6 kg).

Similar Species: Smaller **Lesser Spot-nosed Monkey** has white whiskers and brown-over-white tail. **Red-tailed Monkey** has red tail and white cheeks underlined with conspicuous black stripe. **Blue Monkey** lacks nose spot.

Habitat: Rain forests; secondary and riverine forests.

Breeding: 1 young.

Range: Sierra Leone to n Angola, and east to ne Zaire.

This monkey's diet is mainly fruit, leaves, and insects. Troops of up to 60 animals have been reported. Resident males advertise their status and presence with deep, resonant, booming calls.

---

200 **De Brazza's Monkey**
Cercopithecus neglectus

Description: Medium-size; chunky build. Hindquarters higher than forequarters; while walking, holds thick tail in loop or hanging. Colorful coat of soft fur: upperparts and cheeks grizzled olive-gray; underparts, lower limbs, and tail black; *bright orange forehead band* bordered by jet-black band connected to black forearm by stripe down upper arm; upper face black, bordering *white muzzle and goatee; white diagonal thigh stripe;* white buttocks. L 16–24″ (40–60 cm); T 21–34″ (53–85 cm); Wt 8.8–16.5 lb (4–7.5 kg).

Habitat: Humid forests, especially swamp forests, usually near rivers and streams up to 7,000′ (2,100 m).

Breeding: Year-round; 1 young born after 6-month gestation.

Range: Central Africa from Sanaga River in Cameroon south to n Angola, and northeast through Zaire to sw Ethiopia and Sudan.

De Brazza's is a slow-moving, semi-terrestrial monkey that eats mainly fruit, along with small amounts of leaves, animal matter, and mushrooms. In Gabon, groups number four to six animals, and most groups are monogamous family units. The sexes forage independently and deal with predators differently: The female and young hide in the undergrowth, while the male climbs a tree and makes noises at the disturber. Elsewhere, groups of up to 35 animals, presumably polygynous, have been reported.

Owl-faced Monkey
Hamlyn's Monkey
Cercopithecus hamlyni

Description: A robust guenon. *Large round head and black triangular face bisected by vertical white stripe.* Large eyes ringed with wrinkles complete its barn-owlish look. Coat densely furred, especially head region, where *mantle of long, backwardly directed hair* conceals ears. Upperparts dark olive green; underparts and limbs black; face purple-black. Ash-gray tail thick and round at root; ends in black tassel. Rear end and scrotum bright blue. L 22″ (55 cm); T 23″ (57 cm).

Habitat: Montane forests and bamboo stands between 3,000′ and 10,000′ (900–3,000 m), to 15,000′ (4,600 m); also lowland rain forests.

Breeding: Probably year-round; 1 young born after gestation of about 6 months.

Range: Very small area just on and south of equator in e Zaire and nw Rwanda.

The Owl-faced Monkey is usually encountered in groups of ten or fewer. Virtually nothing is known about it—even whether it is nocturnal, as suggested by its unusually large eyes. It may be largely terrestrial, as seems to be the case in montane forests, where it has been observed eating bamboo shoots.

---

201 Diana Monkey
Cercopithecus diana

Description: A medium-size guenon, with a rangy build and long legs; tail often carried in question-mark curve. *Black face framed by white cheeks, beard, and brow line; white continues down throat onto chest and along inner arms;* outer limbs, tail, and belly pure black. Rusty saddle from mid-back to tail root, shading into speckled gray flanks and back; crown nearly black. *Conspicuous white diagonal stripe* on outer thighs and cream or red inner thighs and buttocks distinctive from rear. L 16–23″ (40–57 cm); T 22–33″ (54–82 cm); Wt 11 lb (5 kg).

Similar Species: **Mona Monkey** *(C. mona)* ranges from Ghana to Cameroon; lacks beard and has pinkish muzzle.

Habitat: Undisturbed primary and semi-deciduous forests and gallery forests.

Breeding: Probably year-round; 1 young born after gestation of about 6 months.

Range: Sierra Leone to Ghana.

The Diana is one of the most threatened and little-known African monkeys. Its diet is mainly fruit, supplemented by insects and leaves. It lives in fairly large groups of 14 to 40 animals.

---

202 Crowned Guenon
Cercopithecus pogonias

Description: Grizzled brown, with black lower limbs and outer tail; belly and insides of legs golden. Head and framing whiskers buff-white; blue-gray face, with contrasting pink muzzle; *black band from eye widens at ear; black median stripe from brow to nape forms short crest.* Scrotum blue. L 15–26″ (38–66 cm); T 24–35″ (60–87 cm); Wt 6.6–10 lb (3–4.5 kg).

Similar Species: **Mona Monkey** *(C. mona)* ranges from Ghana to Cameroon; lacks black crest, and has white underparts and sometimes red upperparts.

Habitat: Moist high primary forests and secondary forests.

Breeding: Probably year-round; 1 young born after gestation of about 5 months.

Range: Northeastern Nigeria through Cameroon and Gabon to w Zaire.

The Crowned Guenon eats mainly fruit, followed by insects and other invertebrates, and very little foliage. Northern populations travel long distances to seasonally concentrated food sources; the species is one of the few guenons known to migrate. Groups average 14 monkeys. The Crowned Guenon often associates with Mona *(C. mona),* Mustached, and Greater Spot-nosed monkeys.

203 Mustached Monkey
Cercopithecus cephus

Description: A small monkey, with a blue mask; "mustache" formed by *white chevron on upper lip; bushy yellow cheeks* separated from ash-gray throat by narrow black patch. Ears have yellow fringe. Upperparts and limbs brindled reddish brown; outer tail red or grayish; underparts ash-gray. L 18–23″ (44–58 cm); T 26–40″ (66–99 cm); Wt 6.4–11 lb (2.9–5 kg).

Similar Species: **Red-eared Monkey** *(C. erythrotis)* lives in s and e Nigeria, w Cameroon, and Bioko; has reddish nose and ears, and lacks "mustache."

Habitat: Rain forests, including primary, gallery, and secondary forests.

Breeding: 1 young born after gestation of about 6 months; in Gabon, births peak December–February.

Range: Southern Cameroon to n Angola; east perhaps to n Zaire.

The most abundant monkey in Gabon and Congo, the Mustached Monkey eats primarily fruit, the balance of its diet consisting of insects and leaves. It lives in groups of up to 30 to 35, and often associates with Greater Spot-nosed and Mona *(C. mona)* monkeys. Threatening males flash their white "mustaches" by rotating the head from side to side.

204 Red-tailed Monkey
Black-cheeked White-nosed Monkey
Cercopithecus ascanius

Description: A small monkey, with a brownish upper body and pale undersides; *tail almost orange-red* in good light. *White nose spot* on dark face; clearly defined horizontal black stripe in *white cheek whiskers.* L 14–25″ (34–63 cm); T 22–37″ (54–92 cm); Wt 6.6–9 lb (3–4 kg).

Similar Species: **Lesser Spot-nosed Monkey** has white along underside of tail. **Greater Spot-nosed Monkey** has all-black tail and dark cheeks.

Habitat: Rain forests and savannas.

Breeding: Probably year-round; 1 young born after gestation of about 6 months.

Range: Congo Basin from Central African Republic and w Kenya south to n Zambia, and west to n Angola.

This monkey eats fruit, invertebrates, and leaves. Groups average up to 35 members. There is typically one male per territorial group, and the whole group joins in repelling intruding troops. This species often associates with others, notably with Blue and Mustached monkeys.

---

205 **Lesser Spot-nosed Monkey**
Lesser White-nosed Monkey
Cercopithecus petaurista

Description: A smallish monkey, with a dark slate-blue to blackish face surrounding a distinctive *white nose patch.* Black forehead band runs from ear to ear; white whiskers crossed by black stripe from eye to below ear. Upperparts dark greenish brown, contrasting with white underparts; lower legs gray. *Tail brown at root, darkening to black tip;* whitish underneath. L 16–19″ (40–48 cm); T 23–27″ (57–68 cm); Wt 4.4–7.7 lb (2–3.5 kg).

Similar Species: **Red-tailed Monkey** has orange-red tail. **Greater Spot-nosed Monkey** has entirely black tail and black limbs.

Habitat: Rain forests, riverine forests, and coastal scrub; also secondary forests, gardens, and mature cacao plantations.

Breeding: Probably year-round; 1 young born after gestation of about 6 months.

Range: Gambia to Benin along southern coast of w Africa.

Very little information is available about this species, which is capable of adapting to many forested and wooded habitats. Groups of 12 to 15 animals have been reported.

206 **Vervet Monkey**
Grivet, Green Monkey
Cercopithecus aethiops

Description: A medium-size, light-colored guenon. Coat silky. Color varies geographically, from silver-gray to yellow-, reddish-, or olive-green, with white to yellow-white underparts. *Black face* usually bordered by white brow band; framed by bristling whiskers; pale pink eyelids. Ears, hands, feet, and calluses usually black. Adult male has pale blue scrotum and bright red penis. L 18–33″ (45–83 cm); T 22–46″ (55–114 cm); Wt 9–12 lb, up to 20 lb (4.1–5.5 kg, up to 9 kg).

Handprint

Subspecies: 21 described, with several distinctive forms: **Vervets** occur from s Ethiopia and Somalia to South Africa; have white or whitish forehead band merging with side whiskers similar in color to crown and other upperparts; usually black face, hands, and feet; tuft of reddish hair under tail root; black tail tip; coat color grades from pale yellow-green in e Africa to reddish-green in Mozambique to dark green in s Africa. **Grivets,** with races in Sudan and Ethiopia, have long-tufted, pure white sideburns, contrasting with crown and other upperparts; tuft of white or reddish-brown hairs below tail root; whitish tail tip. **Green monkeys** range from Senegal to Ghana, have yellow whiskers and yellow-tinged back; lack white forehead band.

Habitat: All types of wooded habitats except rain forest; moist and arid savannas, dry montane forests, and alpine moorlands to 15,000′ (4,500 m); primarily a woodland-edge species.

Breeding: 1 young born after average gestation of 5.5 months.

Range: Senegal to Ethiopia, and south to South Africa.

The common monkey of the African savanna, the Vervet Monkey eats grass, herbs, seeds and seedpods, buds, flowers, and various fruit and berries, supplemented with tree products, insects, and small vertebrates. Vervets live in strongly territorial, multi-male troops, which can be as large as 140 animals but generally number between eight and 46. Females and young form the basic social unit; all males emigrate at least once. A strict male dominance hierarchy is enforced by performance of the "red, white, and blue" display, in which dominant males exhibit their colorful genitalia to subordinates.

---

207 **Talapoin Monkey**
Miopithecus talapoin

Description: A *very small* monkey, with relatively *big head and ears;* large eyes; short snout. Yellow-gray, with paler underparts and face; dark hairs on muzzle; yellow whiskers in front of ears. Female has large pink sexual swelling. L 14″ (35 cm); T 17″ (43 cm); Wt 1.5–3 lb (0.7–1.4 kg).

Habitat: Mangroves and any forests or bushlands near water.

Breeding: 1 young born November–March, after 5.5-month gestation.

Range: Equatorial w Africa from s Cameroon south to c Angola; eastern limit unknown.

The smallest of all African monkeys, the Talapoin sleeps in trees over water at river edges or in seasonally flooded forests. When approached by nocturnal predators, it drops into water and swims away. It subsists mainly on insects and fruit. Typical groups usually number 60 to 70, and up to 125 members, with an adult ratio of one male to two females. Near settlements, Talapoins are numerous and forage in same-sex subgroups.

208 Patas Monkey
Erythrocebus patas

Description: *Greyhound build.* Narrow hands and feet, with short digits, and reduced thumb and big toe. *Coarse, shaggy, red-brown coat;* white to yellowish-white underparts and limbs. Face mostly white but variable; nose spot black in w Africa, white in e Africa; white "mustache"; yellowish side whiskers. Dark head band formed by bushy eyebrows; white ears. Male much larger than female, with pale blue scrotum. L 20–30″ (49–75 cm); T 20–30″ (50–74 cm); Wt 9–29 lb (4–13 kg).

Habitat: Savannas. Able to go without water for long periods, but during drought must have access to water.

Breeding: Produces 1 young early in dry season, after gestation of nearly 6 months.

Range: Senegal east to Ethiopia, and south to n Tanzania. Isolated populations in Aïr mountains of Niger and on Ennedi Plateau in Chad.

The home range of the Patas Monkey is the largest known for any nonhuman primate (up to 30 sq miles/80 sq km). A typical troop of 20 monkeys includes one adult male and six to eight adult females who stay together all their lives, and their young; surplus males travel in bachelor groups. Patas Monkeys climb trees to feed, sleep, and for surveillance, but descend and flee from danger (they can sprint up to 35 mph/55 kph). Troop members often stand on two feet to see over grass. The diet is mostly grass seeds, new shoots, and acacia gums, but also includes fruit, berries, and seedpods, as well as insects and other invertebrates, lizards, and birds' eggs.

MANGABEYS
Genus *Cercocebus*

Mangabeys are large monkeys closely related to baboons. The three species all live in tropical African rain forests. While mangabeys don't look much like baboons, they move, act, and sound a lot like them as they sit on their haunches or strut and walk along branches, and the multi-male, nonterritorial social/mating systems of the two groups are also similar. Males are larger than females, but color patterns are the same; genitals are bare and pinkish. Females have prominent, doughnut-shaped sexual swellings. As they forage, mangabey troops frequently emit shrieks, screams, chuckles, barks, grunts, and roars. The distinctive whoop-gobble call of the adult male advertises his presence and individual identity.

209 Crested Mangabey
Cercocebus galeritus (includes *agilis*)

Description: Long legs. Coat rather rough; *usually olive or yellow-brown above,* brown or black on lower legs, lighter on underparts. Cheek whiskers yellowish; sometimes a whorl of longer hair on crown, forming a fringe (crest); face and ears blue-black. L 18–26″ (44–65 cm); T 16–32″ (40–79 cm); Wt 12.1–22 lb (5.5–10.2 kg).

Subspecies and Ranges: **Tana River Mangabey** *(C. g. galeritus),* of lower Tana River in Kenya, has crown fringe that almost conceals ears. **Agile Mangabey** *(C. g. agilis),* which ranges from Bioko east through Zaire, has black ears and face; fringe only above face; short whiskers. **Golden-bellied Mangabey** *(C. g. chrysogaster),* which ranges south of Congo River in Zaire, lacks fringe above face; underside

bright gold; tail held stiffly out behind in downward arc. **Sanje Crested Mangabey** *(C. g. sanje)* is restricted to s Tanzania's Uzungwa Mountains.

Similar Species: **White-collared Mangabey** lacks fringe and is grayer.

Habitat: Rain forests, swamp forests, and gallery forests in savannas.

Breeding: 1 young born after gestation of nearly 6 months.

This mangabey's diet consists of fruit, nuts, seeds, shoots, leaves, and insects. The typical rain-forest group of 10 to 20 monkeys is larger in Kenya, where the available habitat is limited and population density is high. The Tana River and Sanje races are very much at risk, with 500 to 1,500 individuals in each.

---

210 Gray-cheeked Mangabey
Cercocebus (Lophocebus) albigena

Description: A large, long-limbed monkey, with an *exceptionally long, semi-prehensile tail.* Head has either 2 "horns" in form of tufts of long hair (western races) or single crest (eastern races). Coat black, with *mantle of lighter-colored, longer hair on neck and shoulders* to mid-forearms. Tail black; long-haired at base; tapers to a point. Cheeks gray; pale eyelids accentuate facial expressions; *deep hollows below eyes; sloping chin.* Genitals pink. L 18–29″ (45–73 cm); T 29–40″ (73–100 cm); Wt 14–19.8 lb (6.4–9 kg).

Similar Species: **Black Mangabey** *(C. aterrimus),* of Zaire and n Angola, has pointed head crest and no lighter-colored mantle; considered by some to be a race of Gray-cheeked.

Habitat: Rain forests, riverine forests, and montane forests to 5,600′ (1,700 m). Never far from water.

Breeding: 1 young born after gestation of nearly 6 months.

Range: Equatorial Africa, from Cameroon coast east to c Uganda.

This mangabey opens the hardest nuts and seeds, and chews bark and rotten wood from which it extracts hidden insects. It is almost entirely arboreal. Population densities are low and home ranges large. Troops typically number about 15, and have an adult female to adult male ratio of nearly two to one. The loud, whoop-gobble call of adult males, which sounds like a turkey with a "frog in its throat," announces a group's location.

211 **White-collared Mangabey**
Red-capped Mangabey, Sooty Mangabey, Collared Mangabey
Cercocebus torquatus

Description: A large slender monkey. Long legs; *semi-prehensile tail held forward stiffly over back* (often twined around branch while monkey is seated in tree). Deeply hollowed cheeks; deep-set eyes; naked face and ears. Coat relatively short, silky, thin on underside. Color is varying shade of gray, depending on subspecies. L 18–27″ (46–67 cm); T 16–32″ (40–79 cm); Wt 12.1–17.6 lb (5.5–8 kg).

Subspecies and Ranges: **Sooty Mangabey** *(C. t. atys)* ranges from Guinea southeast to Sassandra River in Ivory Coast; entirely slate-gray above, lightening on underside, darker on lower arms, fronts of thighs, and upperside of tail; has grayish to pinkish face; white upper eyelids; light gray whiskers. **White-crowned Mangabey** *(C. t. lunulatus)* is found from Sassandra River in Ivory Coast east to Ghana; has light slate-gray upperparts bisected by dark spinal stripe; white underparts; sharply drawn dividing line on flanks; white crescent on nape, bordering blackish-brown crown. **Red-capped Mangabey** *(C. t. torquatus)* occurs in Nigeria to Congo River; smoky gray above, with bright chestnut crown, and pure white nape, underparts, and tail tip.

Similar Species: **Crested Mangabey,** the other semi-terrestrial mangabey, is yellowish brown above, with fringe of hair on crown.

Habitat: Moist forests, notably mangrove, coastal, and riverine; secondary forests, moist savannas, and plantations.

Breeding: Year-round; 1 young born after gestation of six months.

This semi-terrestrial species forages both in trees and on the ground, using its massive incisors to husk coconuts, and crack oil palm nuts, hard fruit, and seeds; it also eats leaves and shoots, especially field crops and garden vegetables. Troops of 12 to 20 are typical and include a few adult males. Very noisy and vociferous while foraging, these mangabeys often associate with forest guenons.

Baboons

Genera *Papio* and *Theropithecus*

There are five species of baboons, all occurring in Africa, with one also in southern Arabia. Very large monkeys with long, equally developed limbs and shorter tails than their forest-dwelling cousins, baboons spend most of their days foraging on the ground; at night they roost in trees or on cliffs. These dog-headed monkeys have short fingers, but the fully opposable thumb and forefinger provide a good precision grip. The eyes are close together, deep-set under a prominent brow ridge. Females have colorful sexual swellings that balloon grotesquely during full estrus. Males are up to twice the size of females, powerfully built with long fangs. Baboons are highly gregarious, living in large troops that contain a number of adult males. Except for the Hamadryas Baboon, females remain in their natal troop for life; all males emigrate at least once to seek their reproductive fortunes in another troop.

As baboons are nonterritorial, the ranges of different troops overlap widely; however, usually different troops are mutually antagonistic.

212–216 **Savanna Baboon**
Yellow Baboon, Chacma Baboon, Olive Baboon, Common Baboon
Papio cynocephalus

Description: The largest baboon. Sturdy build, with shoulders higher than hindquarters, but almost equally developed limbs; hands and feet short, wide, with stubby digits. *Tail slightly shorter than body, erect at base, then kinked or curved* downward. Coat coarse and grizzled, varying among subspecies in various features (see below). Bare skin of face, ears, hands, feet, and posterior black; eyelids pale; calluses shiny and typically tinged purple. Female sexual swelling the largest of all monkeys; bottom unswollen but scarlet in pregnant and lactating females. L 20–32″ (50–79 cm); T 14–30″ (35–75 cm); Wt male 46–57 lb (21–26 kg) up to 96 lb (43.5 kg), female 26–31 lb (12–14 kg).

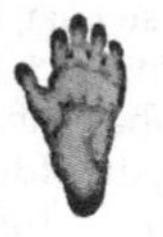

Footprint

Subspecies and Ranges: (Some taxonomists give each of the following races species status.) **Western Baboon** (Guinea Baboon; *P. c. papio*) ranges from Mauritania to Sierra Leone. The largest race, with the biggest mane; short hair on rump and limbs; very thick, dense cheek whiskers; tail carried in curve, not kinked; coat brindled reddish brown; calluses reddish or purplish. **Olive Baboon** (Anubis Baboon; *P. c. anubis*) occurs from Mauritania to Somalia, south to n Tanzania; isolated populations on mountains in Sahara. Heavyset; mane and whiskers as in Western Baboon, making head and shoulders look more massive; tail kinked at sharp angle; coat brindled olive-brown, with bare areas blackish; calluses shiny purple-black. **Yellow Baboon** *(P. c. cynocephalus)*

ranges from Somalia to Mozambique and Zimbabwe; sc Africa from Angolan coast to Indian Ocean; in se Kenya, occupies hot arid lowlands, leaving uplands to Olive Baboon. Rangy build; relatively short-haired with little or no mane; light-colored; upper body brindled yellow-brown to gray, with creamy white underparts and whiskers. **Chacma Baboon** *(P. c. ursinus)* lives from c Angola to tip of Cape of Good Hope, northeast to Zambezi in Mozambique, and north to e Zambia. Slender but large race; coarse coat light gray to dark greenish brown, with blackish lower limbs; male has short blackish mane on neck and shoulders.

Similar Species: Smaller **Hamadryas Baboon** is lighter-colored, male with shocking-pink muzzle and rump.

Habitat: Savannas, semi-desert grasslands and scrub, and forest edges from sea level to 10,000′ (3,000 m) or higher. Requires water and tall trees or cliffs as night roosts.

Breeding: 1 (rarely 2) young born after gestation of about 6 months.

The Savanna Baboon forages with equal ease in trees and on the ground. All races have the same nonterritorial, multi-male social organization. Troops, which range in size from seven to around 200 animals, are aggregations of family groups of females and their offspring, with a small number of mature males. Relations between such groups are competitive, as baboons of high rank enjoy priority access to food, water, and sleeping sites. Male baboons compete for dominance status: High-ranking males tend to obtain first matings with the troop's estrous females; however, lower-ranking males often form alliances that enable them to dominate rivals. Males can also achieve reproductive success by ingratiating themselves with particular female groups or individuals, staying with and helping to protect them and their offspring. Such friends are often preferred as mates over the highest-ranking males. Troops avoid one another but often have to share sleeping trees or cliffs and water holes.

217 **Hamadryas Baboon**
Papio hamadryas

Description: The smallest of the baboons. Pronounced slope from shoulders to rump; tail, not sharply kinked and carried in downward arc, has tufted tip. *Male has heavy cape and bushy cheek tufts* (like a poodle cut); massive, naked, *shocking-pink muzzle* armed with dagger-like upper canines; bare pink behind. Male coat ash-gray; female gray- to olive-brown, with dark brown facial skin and calluses; has pink sexual swellings. L 20–30″ (50–75 cm); T 15–24″ (37–60 cm); Wt 21–47 lb (9.4–21.5 kg).

Similar Species: **Savanna Baboon** is larger, with black face.

Habitat: Acacia savannas; short-grass plains; hilly areas and alpine meadows to at least 7,500′ (2,300 m) in Ethiopia.

Breeding: Year-round, with birth peaks May–July; 1 (rarely 2) young born after 5.7-month gestation.

Range: Northeastern Sudan to sc Somalia.

The Hamadryas forms the largest baboon troops, perhaps because safe sleeping cliffs are scarce and the animals must aggregate. Such sleeping aggregations of up to 750 baboons (average 136) consist of distinct bands, each composed of a cohesive harem of one to ten females controlled by an adult male. Unlike any other monkey, the female Hamadryas is abducted or lured from her mother's group as a two-year-old juvenile by an adult or adolescent male, who guards and rears her for two or three years until she is ready to breed. Harem members come from many troops and bond only to the harem male; they compete to groom and stay close to this male, who dictates his band's movements.

218 **Mandrill**
Mandrill Baboon
Papio (Mandrillus) sphinx

Description: *The most colorful mammal.* Stout build, with very short tail; *elongated muzzle marked with deep longitudinal ridges.* Coat densely furred, with mane on head and neck. Upperparts olive-brown, with black-brown crest; underparts gray tinged with yellow. Muzzle of adult female dusky; adult male's approximates color patterns of rear end: *nose bridge and nostrils lacquer-red* (like penis); *nasal swelling electric blue,* framed by yellow to orange hair fringe; ears pink. Skin around anus and penis scarlet; calluses pale pink to violet; scrotum lilac. Buttocks of female and young dark, except for pinkish calluses. L 22–38″ (55–95 cm); T 3″ (8 cm); Wt male 55 lb (25 kg), female 25 lb (11.5 kg).

Similar Species: Closely related and endangered **Drill** (*P. {Mandrillus} leucophaeus;* **Plate 219**) lives in rain forests and coastal and riverine forests of e Nigeria and w Cameroon south to Sanaga River, and on Bioko. Somewhat smaller (L 18–35″/ 45–88 cm), with shorter muzzle; short brown coat has grayish tinge; ears and face jet black, framed by white ruff; adult male has scarlet lower lip and buttocks colored blue, red, and violet; female has slaty black buttocks except during estrus, when pink sexual swelling develops.

Habitat: Rain forests and plantations; flat, plateau, and mountainous terrain.

Breeding: 1 young born after gestation of nearly 6 months.

Range: South of Sanaga River in Cameroon, south to Gabon and Congo, west to

Atlantic coast; southern and eastern limits unknown.

Mandrill society seems to revolve around adult males, as typically a huge, vividly colored male, shining like a beacon in the forest gloom, is found in the middle of his group of 15 to 30 (up to 50) females and young. Sometimes several one-male units band together. Foraging troops are quite noisy; apart from the sounds of feeding, troop members make conversational sounds, punctuated by deep grunts, high-pitched crowing, and the squeals and shrieks of juveniles. Adult males without groups are apparently peripheral. Great effort is needed to glean sufficient food items: fruit, foliage, ground plants, ants, termites, manioc and oil palm nuts in the lowest, least-productive stratum of the rain forest. The species is mainly terrestrial, though females and young sometimes climb short trees to harvest fruit; all troop members sleep in trees. Often hunted, the Mandrill is a threatened species.

---

220 Gelada Baboon
Theropithecus gelada

Description: An unusual-looking baboon, with a deep rounded muzzle; *small upturned nostrils on top of snout;* hollow cheeks; overhanging brows. Very short index finger permits precise tweezer grip with thumb. Body grayish to dark brown; face reddish to dark brown or black; eyelids white. Male has *leonine mane and back-flaring whiskers* that vary from black to straw-colored, matched by tufted tail. Both sexes have throat patch and large *chest patch of naked pink skin;* female chest patch lined with necklace of fleshy white vesicles (small fluid-filled sacs), mimicked by white fur in male; vesicles swell during full estrus and become bright pink, matching similar structures on rear. L 22–28″ (55–70 cm); T 19–20″ (47–51 cm); Wt 30–45 lb (13.5–20 kg).

Similar Species: **Hamadryas Baboon** is lighter-colored, with longer snout and nostrils at nose tip.

Habitat: Montane grasslands interspersed with alpine forest, within about a mile (2 km) of gorges.

Breeding: 1 young born, usually February–April, after gestation of about 6 months.

Range: Northern and c Ethiopia at elevations of 4,600–15,000′ (1,400–4,500 m).

Next to the human, the Gelada is the most terrestrial primate. Wholly vegetarian, Geladas spend their days seated, plucking grass and digging up grass roots and rhizomes with a rapid, two-handed scooping. They move very little, shuffling on their padded bottoms from clump to clump of vegetation. Geladas use gorges as refuges from predators and for secure overnight sleeping places. This baboon lives in large troops consisting of 20 to 30 one-male harems (each averaging 7 to 14 members) and bachelor groups. The Gelada harem system is very different from the Hamadryas Baboon's. Females are closely related and bonded, and are not herded or bullied by the harem male; a lactating female is usually the group leader. A male must take a harem from another male, or ingratiate himself with the younger females; he then either inherits the whole band or goes off with some young females.

Colobus Monkeys
Leaf-eating Monkeys
African genera *Colobus* and *Procolobus*

Colobus monkeys have complex, chambered stomachs and digestive microflora that enable them to live mainly on leaves and (preferably) unripe fruit that other monkeys carefully avoid because of their toxic chemicals. This specialized diet enables colobines to subsist in a small area, traveling on average only 500 to 600 yards (meters) a day, at much higher densities than fruit- and insect-dependent monkeys. More arboreal than guenons and mangabeys, and rather sluggish much of the time, colobus monkeys can be spectacular leapers. Their hindquarters are longer and stronger than their forequarters. Their absent or reduced thumb gave them their name: *Colobus* is Greek for "mutilated." Fruit is grasped between the palm and fingers; foliage is often eaten directly by bending branches in and biting off leaves. There are 27 species of leaf-eating monkeys worldwide, with seven in Africa.

---

221 **Eastern Black-and-white Colobus**
Abyssinian Black-and-white Colobus, Guereza
Colobus guereza

Description: A large sturdy monkey. *U-shaped cape of long white hair extends from shoulders and meets across lower back.* Short white hair encircles face; black bonnet of erect hairs on crown. Nose bends over upper lip. Black tail ends in white brush. L 25″ (63 cm); T 32″ (80 cm); Wt 14.3–32 lb (6.5–14.5 kg).

Similar Species: **Western Black-and-white Colobus** (King Colobus; *C. polykomos*), which ranges from Senegal to w Nigeria along southern coast of w Africa, has white on shoulders, but body and legs are entirely black; tail is white for entire length. **Angolan Black-and-white Colobus** has very long white hairs on shoulders only, and flaring white sideburns.

Habitat: All types of closed forests, gallery forests, and montane forests to 15,000′ (4,500 m); also acacia woodlands, bamboo stands, and thickets.

Breeding: Year-round; 1 young born after gestation of 5–6 months.

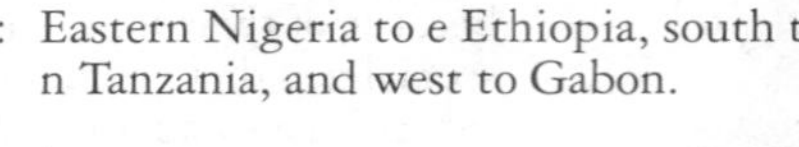

Range: Eastern Nigeria to e Ethiopia, south to n Tanzania, and west to Gabon.

In the East African highlands there may be as many as 700 of these colobus monkeys per square mile (300 per sq km). A typical group of eight includes an adult male, three adult females, and four young. At some seasons, troops may be virtually sedentary, spending whole days feeding in a single grove of trees. Territories are usually well defined and defended. Troop males advertise their status with croaking roars amplified by an enlarged larynx. Troops display themselves to their neighbors during morning sunbathing sessions on tall trees.

Angolan Black-and-white Colobus
Colobus angolensis

Description: A large sturdy monkey. *Long white whiskers* begin at temples and surround face; forehead black. Coat glossy and black, with *long white epaulets.* Tail usually black and short-haired for half to two-thirds of its length, white toward end, and sometimes fluffy or tufted at end. Racial variations include differences in development of epaulets, facial fringe, amount of white in tail and presence of terminal tuft, and white patch or band on buttocks. L 18–26″ (45–65 cm); T 24–36″ (60–90 cm); Wt 13.2–24 lb (6–11 kg).

Similar Species: **Western Black-and-white Colobus** (King Colobus; *C. polykomos*), which ranges from Senegal to w Nigeria along southern coast of w Africa, has shorter white fur encircling face; tail is entirely white and never tufted. **Eastern Black-and-white Colobus** has U-shaped cape of long white hair extending from shoulders to lower back.

Habitat: Lowland, riverine, and montane rain forests, including bamboo stands, to 10,000′ (3,000 m).

Breeding: Year-round; 1 young born after gestation of 5–6 months.

Range: Northern Angola northeast through Zaire to Rwanda and Burundi; se Kenya south to ne Zimbabwe and n Malawi.

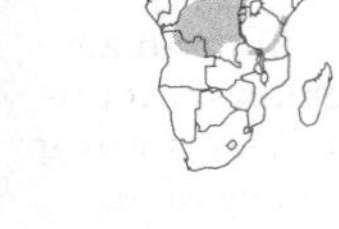

Groups of the Angolan Black-and-white Colobus average five animals. Twenty is an unusually large group, but in Rwanda's Myungwe Forest aggregations of up to 400 have been counted.

---

222 Red Colobus
Procolobus badius

Description: A large slender monkey. Rounded back slopes from shoulders to hindquarters; long legs. Small round head; short muzzle. Coat medium-long and silky; tail long and untufted. *Face slaty, often with pinkish areas.* L 23″ (57 cm); T 26″ (66 cm); Wt 17.6–26 lb (8–12 kg).

Subspecies and Ranges: **Western Red Colobus** *(P. b. badius),* of Senegal to Ghana, has turned-up nose, pinkish eye ring, red whiskers, black or dark gray crown to tail tip, and maroon or orange flanks, underparts, and limbs. **Zanzibar Red Colobus** *(P. b. kirkii)* of Zanzibar has long white forehead tuft, black shoulders and forelimbs, chestnut back, and white underparts. **Eastern Red Colobus** *(P. b. pennantii),* of Bioko and Congo to w Uganda and parts of Tanzania, is reddish or brown above, with black shoulders; flanks and underparts yellowish, gray, or white; whiskers white. **Tana River Red Colobus** *(P. b. rufomitratus),* restricted to e Kenya's Tana River, has reddish-brown crown, black back and tail, gray whiskers, and white underparts.

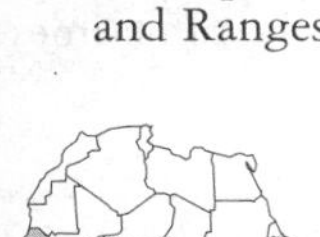

Similar Species: **Olive Colobus** *(P. verus),* which ranges from Sierra Leone to Ghana-Togo border (northern and western limits unclear), is smallest (L 19″/48 cm); light olive above, scarcely contrasting with gray underparts; small crest on crown.

Habitat: Forests, especially moist lowland or gallery forests; some races inhabit acacia woodlands and secondary-growth forests.

Breeding: Year-round; births peak during rainy seasons; 1 young born after gestation of 5–5.5 months.

The Red Colobus lives in multi-male troops of eight to 40 monkeys; groups are usually larger at lower elevations in extensive forest patches. They often associate with Red-tailed and Blue monkeys, and with black-and-white colobus monkeys. Females change troops, often more than once. Within the troop, adult males live in a cooperative clique, with an established rank order, and handle encounters with other troops. Maturing males must either join a clique or transfer to another troop. Transferring is difficult, if not downright dangerous, as females have been known to gang up on and even kill strange males, who sometimes commit infanticide.

Great Apes
Family Pongidae

The great apes are large, broad-chested, hairy primates with no tail, long arms and short legs, long hands with an opposable thumb, and feet with an opposable toe capable of grasping. There are three African species; a fourth, the Orangutan *(Pongo pygmaeus),* lives in Sumatra and Borneo. The pongid head is rounded, with a vaulted cranium housing a large brain, and a prominent brow ridge. The bare, flat face has a small nose, wide mouth, powerful jaws, and a receding chin. The facial features of apes are as individualistic and expressive as humans'. All pongids walk on all fours in the same way—on the whole back foot and on the knuckles of the hands—and all can also walk fairly well bipedally. They climb much better than people but still cautiously, using all four limbs to secure their weighty bodies. Although the three African species all live in forests, they are as different ecologically and socially as they can be. The Gorilla is a terrestrial herbivore, while the Chimpanzee spends half its time in the trees eating fruit; the Bonobo is still more arboreal than the Chimpanzee. Although female Gorillas and Chimpanzees reach puberty as early as eight years, they have monthly menstrual cycles for several years before conceiving. They reproduce at intervals of three to five years. Males rarely have opportunities to father offspring before their mid-teens and become prime only in their twenties. Apes are born with a thin coat and are able to cling to their mothers' front unaided within a few days. They can walk and climb at six months, yet weaning is seldom complete before age five; until then, apes remain dependent on their mothers for guidance and protection. The genes of human beings and apes are 98 to 99 percent the same; in fact, some taxonomists have proposed putting all five species in the same family: Hominidae.

223–226 Gorilla
Gorilla gorilla

Description: *Massive, sway-backed frame;* pot belly; long thick arms; short legs; wide hands and feet, with thick fingers and toes. Head proportionally large, crowned in male with conical mass of muscle. Powerful jaws and large teeth; adult male has formidable canines. Eyes deep-set under prominent brow ridge; *ears small.* Coat short and sparse in lowland populations, long and silky in mountain race. Face, chest, and other bare skin

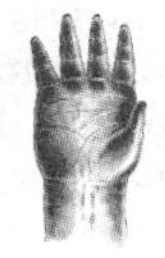
Hand

areas black; fur blue-black to brownish gray; mature male "silverback" has *conspicuous silvery-gray saddle.* Standing Ht 4′8″–6′ (1.4–1.8 m); Wt male 352–462 (160–210 kg), female 150–250 lb (68–114 kg).

Subspecies and Ranges: **Western Lowland Gorilla** *(G. g. gorilla),* the smallest and most abundant race, numbers about 40,000 in lowland rain forests of Cameroon, Central African Republic, Equatorial Guinea, Gabon, and Congo; Wt male 308 lb (140 kg), female 165 lb (75 kg); has relatively small jaws and teeth, but broad face; mature male has large, nearly white saddle covering rump and thighs.

Eastern Lowland Gorilla *(G. g. graueri)* is the largest race (males average 5′10″/1.75 m and 363 lb/165 kg); 4,000–8,000 remain in isolated patches of rain forest in e Zaire and adjacent border regions of Rwanda and Uganda; has narrowest face, and short black fur. Highly endangered **Mountain Gorilla** *(G. g. beringei)* numbers about 450 in Virunga range of volcanos of Rwanda-Zaire-Uganda border; the longest-haired race, with the most massive jaws and broadest face; males average 352 lb (160 kg), females 187 lb (85 kg).

Habitat: Lush undergrowth, as along watercourses and forest edges bordering wetlands, glades, and other openings in lowland rain forest; also regenerating secondary forests. Mountain Gorillas live at altitudes of 9,000–11,000′ (2,700–3,400 m) in the Virunga volcanoes, in moss- and lichen-shrouded cloud forests, where night temperatures are often near freezing and dense undergrowth is usually soaking wet. Some of the forests occupied by Eastern Lowland Gorillas are also montane, as in Kahuzi-Biega NP west of Lake Kivu (Zaire-Rwanda border), where they are found at 6,500–8,200′ (2,000–2,500 m), below and sometimes in the alpine-bamboo zone.

Breeding: Year-round; 1 young born after gestation of 8.5 months.

Female Gorillas live in harems guarded and strictly controlled by a silverback male; often there is a young-adult blackback son (8–12 years old) in the group. Life in a Gorilla harem is usually peaceful and relaxed. Mountain Gorillas need spend only about a third of their day feeding; they spend 40 percent of the day resting and sunning. Gorillas build nests in trees or on the ground to sleep in at night, and most make cruder nests for midday siestas. The silverback leader dictates where his group goes, what it does, and when. Each of his mates is bonded only to him and their offspring, and not to one another; the females are unrelated, acquired usually one at a time as adolescents from their parental group. Male competition for females is intense; the attempts of silverbacks to lure or abduct females in heat from a harem can lead to ferocious battles involving not only the father but his sons and sometimes his mates. Gorillas are not territorial; however, groups normally avoid one another.

227–229 **Chimpanzee**
Pan troglodytes

Description: *Robust build;* long hands and fingers, with short thumb; large prehensile feet. *Round or flat-topped skull;* expressive face, with reduced brow ridge; small nose and nostril holes; *big mouth, with long upper lip; prominent ears.* Teeth larger than humans'; adult male has formidable canines. *Coat usually black,* but varies to brown or ginger. Skin black to yellow, often freckled, darkening with age. Female sexual skin inflates to massive pink swelling in full estrus. Ht 3′4″–5′8″ (1–1.7 m); Wt male 88–121 lb (40–55 kg), female 66 lb (30 kg).

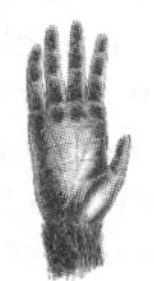
Hand

Similar Species: **Bonobo** is more slender.

Habitat: Rain forests, including montane forests to 6,600′ (2,000 m); also moist savanna and occasionally acacia savannas.

Breeding: Year-round; 1 young born after gestation of 7.7–8 months.
Range: Guinea and Sierra Leone east to Uganda and w Tanzania, north of Congo River.

The Chimpanzee and Bonobo are more closely related to humans than to any other ape, a fact confirmed by DNA studies. These apes are omnivores whose diets vary regionally and seasonally, depending on availability and local tradition. Chimpanzee communities number from 20 to 105 apes; members of large communities may never assemble all together because Chimpanzees are self-sufficient. They wander alone or in small parties searching for edibles, traveling on the ground between food trees, bedding down wherever darkness overtakes them. When they do assemble in larger parties, it is to share bonanzas like a fig tree in fruit. Social relations within a Chimpanzee community are complex. High rank has its privileges, whether priority access to choice food or to mates. A male may become alpha through his own strength or with the support of a brother or two. In Chimpanzee society, females emigrate during adolescence (9–11 years) and eventually settle in other communities. As adult community females are mostly unrelated, they do not associate closely and are not necessarily even on friendly terms. By contrast, males, who remain in the community, share kinship ties and cooperate to defend their territory and females against incursions by their neighbors, with whom they engage in the equivalent of tribal warfare. Chimpanzees make tools out of grass stems to "fish" for termites, and fashion hammers and anvils to crack nuts.

230 Bonobo
Pygmy Chimpanzee
Pan paniscus

Description: Same height as Chimpanzee, but more slender, with narrower chest and *longer hindlegs.* Coat length and color similar, but *face completely black;* hair on crown grows sideways, making fringe; infantile white tail tuft persists in adult. Ht 3′4″–5′8″ (1–1.7 m); Wt male 86 lb (39 kg), female 68 lb (31 kg).

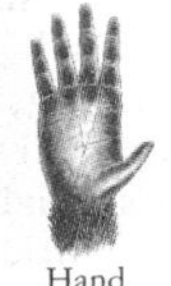
Hand

Similar Species: **Chimpanzee** is more robust, sometimes with lighter skin on face and ears.

Habitat: Lowland rain forests and swamp forests.

Breeding: Year-round; 1 young born after gestation of 7.7–8 months.

Range: Zaire south of Congo River between Yekokora and Lomako rivers.

The Bonobo's diet consists mainly of fruit; when fruit is scarce, ground plants—stems, pith, shoots, and herbs—may be more important. This species also eats a variety of invertebrates, including earthworms and millipedes. More arboreal and acrobatic than Chimpanzees, Bonobos often leap and dive from tree to tree. Bonobo communities number from 50 to 120 animals. The basic unit is a mother with her offspring, including grown sons. Large parties consist of aggregations of maternal units, together with small, all-male groups. In Chimpanzee society, males are the more sociable and interactive sex; in Bonobos, strong bonds also exist between females and males, and between females. The only singles are decrepit old males and young immigrant females.

INSECTIVORES

Order Insectivora

African insectivores comprise 188 species in four families (of 428 species in six families worldwide). They are small, and usually solitary and nocturnal. The order's name notwithstanding, Hedgehogs eat anything from fruit to snakes, while certain tenrecs specialize in crustaceans. Shrews (family Soricidae) have high energy requirements and big appetites; they eat frequent meals of insects, earthworms, and some nuts and seeds; some kill rodents and reptiles as large as themselves. Golden moles (family Chrysochloridae) have lost eyesight but sniff and feel out invertebrates with the bare snout as they tunnel with spade-like claws.

HEDGEHOGS

Family Erinaceidae

In Africa, all hedgehogs have a dense covering of spines. When rolled up in a ball, the entire body fits nicely in the bag formed by the spiny dorsal coat. African hedgehogs, solitary and nocturnal, are often glimpsed ambling along city streets searching for insects and other small animals. Worldwide there are about 21 species, with six in Africa.

231 Four-toed Hedgehog

African Hedgehog
Atelerix albiventris

Description: *Spines white, with dark brown band, absent on center of forehead; belly and legs white.* Muzzle brown, framed by white forehead and cheeks; ears short, hidden by spines. Hindfeet have 4 toes, lack "big toe." L 7–9″ (17–23 cm); T 0.8–2″ (2–5 cm); Wt 9.5–25 oz (270–700 g).

Similar Species: **Desert Hedgehog** *(Hemiechinus aethiopicus)* of Sahara has blackish legs;

ears show above spines. **Long-eared Hedgehog** *(H. auritus),* of n Libya and Egypt, has white underparts; face suffused light brown; lacks "part" in the crown spines. **Algerian Hedgehog** *(A. algirus)* is larger (Wt to 3.5 lb/ 1.6 kg) and paler; sold along roadsides and frequently seen at night; lives from coast of s Morocco to n Libya. **South African Hedgehog** *(A. frontalis)* has blackish muzzle and underparts; ranges from e Botswana and w Zimbabwe to Cape Province, and from sw Angola to Namibia.

Habitat: Sandy, well-drained soils in dry and wet savannas with termite nests, rock piles, or woody and leafy litter for shelter.

Breeding: Year-round in tropics; produces an average of 4–7 young, after gestation of 5–6 weeks.

Range: Senegal east to Somalia, thence south to Zambezi.

Hunting by scent and hearing, this hedgehog consumes one-third its weight each day in insects, earthworms, snails, slugs, small vertebrates, eggs, fruit, roots, fungi, and nuts. Protected by its spines and a high tolerance to animal venoms, it even can kill small venomous snakes.

Tenrecs
Family Tenrecidae

This family is found exclusively in Africa and Madagascar; the family has 24 species in three subfamilies. The spiny tenrecs (subfamily Tenrecinae) resemble hedgehogs, including the ability of some to roll into a ball. Furred tenrecs (subfamily Oryzoryctinae) include the stout, burrowing rice tenrecs; shrew-like, long-tailed forms; and one web-toed swimmer, the Aquatic Tenrec *(Limnogale mergulus),* all living on Madagascar. The mainland tenrecs are otter-shrews (subfamily

Potamogalinae) of western and central Africa; they have a sleek form, thick insulating fur, and a tail adapted for propulsion through water.

232 **Streaked Tenrec**
Hemicentetes semispinosus

Description: *A small spiny tenrec with a long-tufted crown.* Barbed quills on crown and upperparts; *coat is black with contrasting yellow or white streaks;* crown yellowish or whitish. Nose elongated; eyes small. *Lacks tail;* middle of back has group of specialized quills used as noise-making organ. L 5–7″ (12–18 cm); Wt 3–10 oz (80–285 g).

Similar Species: **Tail-less Tenrec** (Common Tenrec; *Tenrec ecaudatus*), widespread on Madagascar, is much larger (L 15″/ 38 cm); coarse hair lacks contrasting streaks. **Giant Hedgehog-Tenrec** (Greater Hedgehog Tenrec; *Setifer setosus*), of Madagascar's central plateau, also lacks streaks; dense spines are short and slender; short, spiny, conical tail.

Habitat: Wooded grasslands and forest edges.

Breeding: Up to 8 young born after gestation of about 8 weeks.

Range: Central and e Madagascar.

The Streaked Tenrec has barbed quills that are loosely attached to its skin. It is unable to roll into a ball but advances with bristles erect and mouth gaping in defense. The noise made by the quills as they move across one another probably functions to keep mothers and young together. The diet is mainly earthworms and insects.

ELEPHANT-SHREWS

Order Macroscelidea
Family Macroscelididae

The 15 species of elephant-shrews are confined to mainland Africa but are widespread, represented everywhere but western Africa and the Sahara. The eyes and ears are large; the snout elongated and mobile; the tail long and sparsely haired; the legs long and slender; the hindquarters well developed. Primarily diurnal and extremely keen-eyed, elephant-shrews sniff out small invertebrates, gathering them with the tongue. When agitated, they drum with their hindfeet or thump the ground with the tail.

233 **Rufous Elephant-Shrew**
Spectacled Elephant-Shrew
Elephantulus rufescens

Description: A small elephant-shrew. Coat fine-textured; upperparts yellowish, reddish, or dark grayish, varying with soil coloration; underparts lighter. *Conspicuous white "spectacles" with white "earpiece" underlined by black bar from outer corner of eye to below ear.* L 4–6" (10–15 cm); T 4–5" (10–13 cm); Wt 0.9–1.8 oz (25–50 g).

Similar Species: **Short-snouted Elephant-Shrew** *(E. brachyrhynchus)* ranges from Uganda and w Kenya south to ne Namibia and Transvaal; lacks white eye ring; has short nose and short thick tail. **Dusky-footed Elephant-Shrew** *(E. fuscipes)* lives in s Sudan, ne Zaire, and Uganda; has dark brown upperparts.

Habitat: Dry acacia bushlands, with well-drained soil; clumps of fire-resistant vegetation important for shelter.

Breeding: 2 young born after gestation of about 60 days; up to 6 litters may be reared each year.

Range: Southern Sudan, Ethiopia, Somalia, Kenya, ne Uganda, and Tanzania.

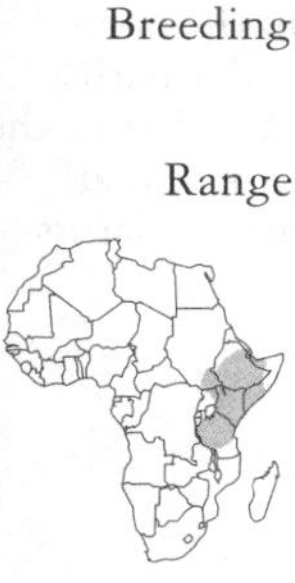

In East Africa, this animal is frequently glimpsed in the daytime running along trails between clumps of grass and thickets. One of the few species that never use burrows or nests, the Rufous

Elephant-Shrew lives exposed on its trails, which it carefully clears of twigs and debris.

234 Golden-rumped Elephant-Shrew
Rhynchocyon chrysopygus

Description: *A large elephant-shrew.* Long, nearly naked brown tail, with the end third white. Coat coarse and grizzled; *upperparts and underparts dark reddish brown with admixture of black; contrasting rump patch yellowish to rich golden.* L 9–10″ (23–26 cm); T 8.5–9″ (21–23 cm); Wt 1.2 lb (540 g).

Similar Species: Larger (L 12″/30 cm) **Chequered Elephant-Shrew** *(R. cirnei)* ranges from Zaire, Uganda, and Tanzania south to Mozambique; has contrasting dark and light squares in rows along back. **Black-and-rufous Elephant-Shrew** *(R. petersi)* lives in se Kenya and e Tanzania; has black rump and rufous head and shoulders. **Four-toed Elephant-Shrew** *(Petrodromus tetradactylus)* ranges from e Africa to Angola and e South Africa; has grayish-buff dorsal coat and 4 toes on forefeet and hindfeet.

Habitat: Fragmented patches of coastal forest.

Breeding: 1 young born at a time, after 6-week gestation; produces up to 5 young each year.

Range: Eastern Kenya from near Mombasa to Somalia border.

These sharp-eyed and fleet-footed elephant-shrews forage in the open. They typically follow regular paths through the forests, and are alert to the movements of snakes, hawks, small carnivores, owls, and other predators.

BATS
Order Chiroptera

At least 925 bat species exist worldwide, with about 211 in Africa; more are being added to the list. Bats are the only mammals that actively fly, as opposed to glide. The "wing" is a membrane supported from the arm and elongated finger bones to the hindleg; in most species, an interfemoral membrane encloses the tail. Old World fruit bats find food by sight and smell, although *Rousettus* species tongue-click to echolocate inside dark caves. Insect-eaters echolocate utilizing ultrasound pulses produced in the larynx: the families with a noseleaf (a fleshy, pointed appendage on the nose) aim beams of sound through the nose, while plain-nosed families emit pulses through the mouth. (In the size measurements below, FA stands for "forearm.")

Old World Fruit Bats
Family Pteropodidae

This large family, which includes 166 species worldwide (36 in Africa), contains the largest bats. With a diet rich in fruit, flowers, nectar and pollen, and leaves, these bats are important pollinators of flowers and dispensers of seeds. They are found in the Old World tropics and subtropics, primarily in forests, but also in savannas and deserts. Although some species roost in colonies in caves, many hang in the open in tall trees.

235 **Hammer-headed Bat**
Hypsignathus monstrosus

Description: This largest African bat exhibits extreme sexual variation: male larger, with *inflated, camel-like snout. Dorsal coat short and sepia in color, becoming reddish brown toward rump. Head and shoulders pale brown, with woolly mantle.* Lacks tail. L 7–11″ (17–28 cm); FA 5–5.5″ (12–14 cm); Wt 8–16 oz (218–450 g).

Similar Species: Various **epauletted fruit bats** (*Epomophorus* species) and **Rousette bats** (*Rousettus* species) are smaller and have thick brown coats. **Straw-colored Fruit Bat** is smaller and has yellowish dorsal coat.

Habitat: Lowland rain forests, remnant or fringing forests in Guinea savannas, swamp forests, and mangrove and brackish swamps along coasts.

Breeding: Female rears 1 young while pregnant with the next, producing 2 per year; estimated gestation is 15 weeks.

Range: Tropical w and c Africa to w Kenya, south to Zambia and Angola.

Hammer-headed Bats usually rest singly or in closely clumped groups of up to 25 individuals that hang on a shaded limb 100 feet (30 meters) above the ground; the sexes live apart. During the breeding season, males set up calling stations, seeking females; the honking and bell-like calls can be heard frequently during the night.

236 Straw-colored Fruit Bat
Eidolon helvum

Description: A large fruit bat. *Long pointed wings and close-cropped hair give it a naked appearance. Coat, basically pale golden-yellow, covers head, shoulders, mid-line of back, throat, and chest;* becomes brown on stomach and lower back. Wings, interfemoral membranes, and tail dark blackish brown. L 6–8.5″ (15–21 cm); T 0.25–0.8″ (6–20 mm); FA 4.5–5.5″ (11–14 cm); Wt 9–11 oz (250–311 g).

Similar Species: **Hammer-headed Bat** is larger and sepia-colored. **Wahlberg's Epauletted Fruit Bat** *(Epomophorus wahlbergi)* ranges from Cameroon east to Somalia, and south to South Africa and Angola, plus

Pemba and Zanzibar islands; smaller (L 5–6″/13–15 cm), with white patch at base of ear.

Habitat: Forests from sea level to over 6,600′ (2,000 m) and savannas.

Breeding: In Uganda, female gives birth to 1 young in February or March, mates in April–May, then disperses with her baby. She carries the newly fertilized egg that does not implant until after her February baby is independent and she returns to her main colony in September or October.

Range: Sub-Saharan Africa and islands.

Colonies of Straw-colored Fruit Bats roost in tall trees in many African cities and towns. The colonies' noise and the movement of individuals flying between trees is noticeable for some distance. The larger colonies number hundreds of thousands of individuals. Strong fliers, they forage up to 18 miles (30 km) from their roosts.

237 Seychelles Flying Fox
Pteropus seychellensis

Description: *A medium-size flying fox, with short, moderately pointed ears and short legs. Golden ocher-buff to golden ocher mantle, crown, and sides of head and neck* contrast with dark brown back and blackish muzzle and chin; *upperparts suffused with glossy silvery hairs.* Breast and belly covered with short, dark brown hair tipped with ocher-buff. Lacks tail. L 9″ (22–23 cm); FA 5–6.5″ (13–16 cm); Wt estimated at 14–21 oz (400–600 g).

Habitat: Colonies roost in tall trees on larger islands.

Breeding: 1 or 2 young born after 5-month gestation.

Range: Seychelles, Aldabra, Comoros, and Mafia islands.

In Seychelles, this bat seems to roost mostly on north- and west-facing slopes

from May through October, the period of the southeast trade winds; it shifts to other sheltered sites from November through April, during the northwest monsoon season. They disperse from roosts at dusk to forage; all the bats return before sunrise. On the Comoros, individuals can be seen "sea dipping" at dusk; they fly out to sea, dip their feet or bellies into the water, then return above an incoming wave. A colony of up to 3,000 individuals lives in Morne Seychellois NP on Mahé.

False Vampire Bats
Family Megadermatidae

Of five species, two are found in Africa. These big bats have very large ears that are joined at the base and have a lengthened tragus. They have unusually large eyes and a noseleaf. Echolocation is of a low-intensity type, and eyesight may be just as important in hunting. All lack tails. Although one species is insectivorous, the others are carnivorous, feeding on small vertebrates. These bats may roost among branches, or in hollow trees, caves, or buildings, singly or in small groups, but never in large colonies.

238 Yellow-winged Bat
Lavia frons

Description: A medium-size bat, with *a long wide noseleaf* and long ears. *Yellow to orange wing, ear, and tail membranes* contrast markedly with bluish-gray fur of body. Lacks tail. L 2.4–3.2″ (6–8 cm); FA 2–2.5″ (5.5–6.5 cm); Wt 1–1.25 oz (28–36 g).

Similar Species: **Heart-nosed Bat** *(Cardioderma cor)* ranges from e Sudan to Somalia, south to Tanzania and Zanzibar; lacks contrasting yellow coloration. 2 yellow bats of family Vespertilionidae have similar ranges to Yellow-winged: **Butterfly Bat** *(Glauconycteris variegata)* is very small (L 2.5"/6.3 cm), with short ears and yellow fur; wings have dark reticulated pattern that resembles leaves. **African Yellow House Bat** *(Scotophilus dinganii)* is similar in size, with variably red or yellowish underparts; brown upperparts; brown wings and muzzle.

Habitat: Grasslands and woodlands; never far from water.

Breeding: Year-round; 1 young born after gestation of 3 months.

Range: Senegal east to Somalia, and south to c Angola and c Mozambique; also islands off coast of e Africa.

This bat often hangs in trees and bushes in direct sunlight and may change roosts during the day. Thought to be entirely insectivorous, it may begin to hunt before sunset, but feeding takes place primarily after dusk.

HARES, RABBITS, AND PIKAS
Order Lagomorpha

Lagomorphs have a large pair of ever-growing gnawing teeth on the upper and lower jaws, just as rodents do; however, they are not closely related to the rodents. The 78 lagomorph species worldwide comprise the hares and rabbits (Leporidae family), with just 12 species in Africa, and the pikas (Ochotonidae), which do not occur in Africa. Lagomorphs are entirely herbivorous.

HARES AND RABBITS
Family Leporidae

Hares and rabbits are small, stocky, short-tailed mammals with thick, usually soft fur. Of 53 species worldwide, 12 occur in Africa. Both groups have long hindlegs for sprinting, and long mobile ears and large eyes for detecting nighttime predators. Most hares rely on cryptic coloration as they lie up in shallow forms in grass and under bushes; when pursued, they can run 30 mph (50 kph) or faster. Rabbits, in contrast, bolt into burrows or thickets.

---

239 **Cape Hare**
African Hare
Lepus capensis

Description: A medium-size hare with a *blunt muzzle.* Hair very soft and straight; *pale buff to grizzled gray-brown above; underparts white, separated from upperparts by ocher-buff lateral band. Nape brownish pink to grayish buff; ears relatively short and black-tipped.* Tail black-tipped. L 16–22″ (40–55 cm); T 3–6″ (7–15 cm); Wt 2.9–6.6 lb (1.3–3 kg), females generally heavier than males.

Similar Species: Field identification may be impossible due to geographic and species variability. **Scrub Hare** *(L. saxatilis),* of Namibia, South Africa, and c Mozambique, lacks ocher-buff lateral band; **Greater Red Rock Rabbit** *(Pronolagus crassicaudatus)* ranges se South Africa and s Mozambique; **Jameson's Red Rock Rabbit** *(P. randensis)* lives in ne South Africa, e Botswana to w Mozambique, Zimbabwe, and w Namibia; **Smith's Red Rock Rabbit** *(P. rupestris)* has disjunct populations in s and e Africa; all four have uniformly brown or reddish-brown tail and short ears. **Bunyoro Rabbit** *(Poelagus marjorita)* occurs in s Chad to w Kenya, and Angola; has tail brownish yellow above and white below, short ears and hindlegs, and coarse coat. **Ethiopian Highland Hare** *(L. starcki),* common around Addis Ababa, has top of tail black in most populations.

Habitat: Dry open savannas and deserts; sometimes moist savannas; never forests.

Breeding: 1–3 young born after 6-week gestation; up to 8 litters per year.

Range: North and most of e Africa; also s Africa.

The Cape Hare is strictly nocturnal and very solitary. It prefers to eat short green grasses, but sometimes eats shrubs. It digs short burrows to escape intense sun, and the young typically use bolt holes to escape from predators.

240 **Savanna Hare**
Crawshay's Hare, Whyte's Hare
Lepus victoriae (includes *crawshayi* and *whytei*)

Description: A small to medium-size hare, with a *pointed muzzle;* ears relatively long and black-tipped; coat often richly colored; *darkly grizzled drab gray to brown above,* white below, *the 2 areas separated by a buff, rufous, or chestnut breast and lateral band.* Nape and legs rufous. Usually has white forehead spot. L 16–20″ (40–49 cm); T 3–5″ (7–13 cm); Wt 2.2–6.6 lb (1–3 kg).

Similar Species: Very similar to **Cape Hare.**

Habitat: Moist savannas and cultivated areas; sometimes dry savannas.

Breeding: 1 or 2 young born after 6-week gestation.

Range: Algeria and Morocco south to Sierra Leone; most of sub-Saharan Africa south to Natal.

The Savanna Hare is usually solitary, although sometimes several are seen feeding together. It co-occurs with the Cape Hare throughout most of its range, but prefers scrubbier, highland habitats rather than open, drier country. The Savanna Hare sprints for cover when disturbed, in contrast with other open-country hares, which run and freeze motionless in the open.

RODENTS
Order Rodentia

Rodents, the most numerous mammalian order, with the list growing and presently more than 2,000 species worldwide (nearly 400 in Africa), more than make up in numbers and rapid reproduction what they lack in size. They feed many predators, and in turn consume vast amounts of vegetation, as well as insects and some vertebrate prey. Rodents are diverse, ranging from quill-covered porcupines to the hairless Naked Mole Rat. What they have in common is two pairs of ever-growing incisor teeth, one in the top jaw and one in the bottom; the cheek teeth are set well back, out of the way of the gnawing action. The 11 families represented in Africa include tiny, kangaroo-like desert jerboas (Dipodidae family); robust cane rats inhabiting watery reedbeds (Thryonomyidae); rock-dwelling dassie rats and gundis (Petromuridae and Ctenodactylidae); scaly-tailed, gliding forms that live in trees (the "flying squirrels" of the Anomaluridae family); as well as the squirrels, mice, gerbils, and other small animals described below.

SQUIRRELS
Family Sciuridae

Squirrels are bushy-tailed rodents with an ability to break open the hardest seeds. The family has 273 species worldwide, and squirrels live in a wide range of habitats. There are two subfamilies. The flying squirrels (Petauristinae), which glide rather than fly, are not represented in Africa. There are 36 species of true squirrels (Sciurinae) in Africa, all diurnal, ranging from the lightly built, needle-clawed African Pygmy Squirrel *(Myosciurus pumilio)* which weighs as little as a third of an ounce (10 grams), to robust burrowing ground squirrels that weigh up to 2.2 pounds (1 kg). Tree squirrels live alone or as small family groups in leaf-lined holes in trees, while ground squirrels may live in large colonies with extensive underground warrens. The African "scaly-tailed flying squirrels" of the Anomaluridae family are not squirrels at all; most have tails that are thin or scaly near the base and brush-like toward the end.

241 Unstriped Ground Squirrel
Xerus rutilus

Description: A small ground squirrel, with a stocky body and a long flattened tail. Coat bristly. Upperparts and tail light yellowish to dark reddish brown, flecked with white; belly yellowish beige. Legs robust, ending in long feet with long pointed claws. Ears small; eyes large and black. *Lacks white longitudinal line on flank.* L 8–10″ (20–26 cm); T 7–9″ (18–23 cm); Wt 10.5–12 oz (300–335 g).

Similar Species: **Geoffroy's Ground Squirrel** *(X. erythropus)* is larger (L 16″/40 cm), with conspicuous white longitudinal stripe from shoulder to hindquarters; ranges from se Morocco and Senegal east to w Ethiopia and n Tanzania.

Habitat: Dry savannas and semi-deserts to over 6,600′ (2,000 m).

Breeding: Year-round, with a single litter of 1–3 each year; gestation is 6–7 weeks.

Range: Southeastern Sudan through Horn of Africa to n Tanzania and ne Uganda.

The Unstriped Ground Squirrel's diet consists of seeds, fruit, leaves, roots, flowers, and even some insects. Although burrow systems may be numerous in suitable habitats, this is not a colonial animal.

242 **Cape Ground Squirrel**
Xerus inauris

Description: A large ground squirrel with a long bristly tail. Coat short and bristly; upperparts cinnamon-brown; sides of neck, underparts, and lower parts of limbs white; conspicuous white lateral stripe from shoulder to hindquarters. *Individual hairs of tail white, with 2 black bands.* Legs robust, ending in long feet with long pointed claws. Ears small; eyes large, each surrounded by white ring. L 9–10″ (23–26 cm); T 7–10″ (18–25 cm); Wt 18–36 oz (511–1,022 g).

Similar Species **Mountain Ground Squirrel** *(X. princepes)* lives in s Angola and w Namibia; lighter-colored, with white speckling; long hairs of tail have 3 black bands.

Habitat: Open country with hard, stony, compacted soils; also fringes of floodplains and pans, along dry riverbeds, and scrub woodlands.

Breeding: Year-round, with a single litter of 1–3 each year; gestation is 6–7 weeks.

Range: Southern Angola, Namibia, Botswana, w Zimbabwe, and South Africa.

This diurnal and gregarious animal lives in colonies of up to 30 individuals in areas of sparse vegetation. It prefers strong sunshine, shading its head and back with its bent tail. The diet consists of insects, seeds, leaves, and stems of grass, plus other vegetation, including crops.

243 **Southern African Tree Squirrel**
Mopane "Ground" Squirrel, Smith's Bush Squirrel
Paraxerus cepapi

Description: *A small tree squirrel with soft short fur,* varying regionally from pale gray to reddish brown, with grizzled appearance; underparts pale yellowish or white. *Eyes large, each surrounded by white ring.* Toes have short, sharp, curved claws. *Tail hairs long, with 2 or 3 black bands contrasting with buff.* L 6.5–15″ (16–37 cm); T 5–9″ (12–22 cm); Wt 3–9 oz (76–265 g).

Similar Species: **Red Squirrel** *(P. palliatus)* ranges from s Somalia to e South Africa; has reddish or yellowish underparts, and red-tipped tail hairs; lacks white eye ring. **Kenyan Tree Squirrel** *(P. ochraceus)* lives in s Sudan, Kenya, and Tanzania; has very long, thin, grizzled tail; some forms also have pale stripe on flank behind shoulder.

Habitat: Moist savannas, especially mopane and riverine woodlands; wooded valleys along watercourses where mature trees provide suitable holes.

Breeding: Year-round, but most young born during rainy months; 1–3 young born after gestation of 7.5–8 weeks.

Range: Southeastern Zaire, sw Tanzania, and Malawi; s Angola east to Mozambique, and south to e South Africa.

This small diurnal squirrel lives in small family groups in part of its range. Its food includes berries, seeds and pods, gums, fruit, flowers, leaves, bark, and lichens, and insects at times of abundance. It often forages on the ground; when disturbed, it races into a nearby tree and hugs a horizontal branch.

---

244 Gambian Sun Squirrel
Heliosciurus gambianus

Description: *Upperparts vary regionally from dark olive speckled with yellow or gray, to grayish brown.* Underparts whitish to orangish, with white breast patch. Tail has conspicuous black rings; hairs long but not dense. Each eye surrounded by incomplete white ring. L 7–8.5″ (17–21 cm); T 7.5–9″ (19–22 cm); Wt 9–12 oz (250–340 g).

Similar Species: **Red-legged Sun Squirrel** *(H. rufobrachium)* ranges from Senegal through tropics to se Sudan, thence south to se Zimbabwe and Mozambique; has red legs in only parts of its range, but always lacks eye ring. **Mountain Sun Squirrel** *(H. ruwenzorii)* occurs at 5,300–9,000′ (1,600–2,700 m) in Rwanda, Burundi, e Zaire, and sw Uganda; thick-furred and gray. **Giant Forest Squirrel** *(Protoxerus stangeri)* lives in rain forests of wc Africa to Lake Victoria; also nearly naked on belly; largest tree squirrel (L 12″/31 cm), with long, densely furred tail barred black and white. Light-colored, unstriped squirrels of **genus *Paraxerus*** range from se Zaire and sw Tanzania to Natal, thence to Angola; considerably smaller. Gambian Sun Squirrel could be confused with some nocturnal "flying squirrels" (Anomaluridae family), which occasionally sun themselves on trees, such as: **Lord Derby's Flying Squirrel** *(Anomalurus derbianus),* which ranges from Sierra Leone to w Kenya, and from Angola to n Mozambique; quite large (up to 15″/38 cm long), with dark gray fur grizzled with silver. **Striped tree squirrels** (*Funisciurus* species) inhabit forest floors from s Senegal to Uganda and southwest through Zaire to Namibia; usually yellowish or olive-brown with 1–4 longitudinal stripes, sometimes indistinct; tail is ringed more or less distinctly in a darker shade. **Splendid-tailed squirrels** (*Epixerus* species) live in lowland rain forests of w Africa; head and outsides of legs rufous.

Habitat: Northern savannas and rain-forest/savanna transition zones.

Breeding: Up to 4 young born after 8.5-week gestation.

Range: Senegal east to Ethiopia, thence southwest to Angola.

Sun squirrels often rest in sunny spots on exposed upper branches of the tallest trees. They occur singly or in pairs,

feeding by day on fruit, nuts, seeds, and acacia pods, as well as some insects, eggs, and small vertebrates. They nest in tree holes.

SPRINGHARE
Family Pedetidae

This exclusively African family has only one species, described below.

---

245 **Springhare**
Pedetes capensis

Description: *A large rodent with reduced forelegs, and paws ending in long, sharp, curved claws; elongated powerful hindlegs end in digits with broad, sharp-edged claws.* Large eyes; *long ears and tail.* Fur long and soft; upperparts cinnamon-buff to yellowish gold, with admixture of black-tipped hairs; back colors continue onto tail, which ends in black tip; underparts white to yellowish white; vibrissae (stiff tactile nasal whiskers) long and black. L 14–18″ (35–45 cm); T 15–19″ (37–48 cm); Wt 5.3–8.6 lb (2.4–3.9 kg).

Foreprint

Hindprint

Habitat: Sandy but firm soils in open scrub savannas, along riverbeds, and in overgrazed agricultural lands.

Breeding: Year-round; 1 large young born 3 or 4 times per year; gestation estimated at 8.5–12 weeks.

Range: Southern Kenya and nw Tanzania; s Zaire, w Zambia, and Angola south to s Mozambique and South Africa.

With its powerful hindlegs and hopping form of locomotion, the Springhare resembles a kangaroo. Strictly nocturnal, this large rodent uses the claws of its forefeet to clear the ground as it consumes leaves, seeds, and underground roots of grasses. When panicked, it hops on its hindlegs up to several yards (meters) per bound, using its long tail as a balancing organ, whipping it up and down or from side to side, depending on speed and surface features. It digs burrow systems, creating numerous escape holes and entrances, the latter surrounded by crescent-shaped mounds. The Springhare gets its water from rain and dewdrops, and from the moisture within plants.

Old World Porcupines
Family Hystricidae

This family of porcupines is confined to Africa, southern Europe, and Asia. Of 11 species worldwide, three live in Africa. There are two groups: the terrestrial crested porcupines, which occur in deserts and savannas, and the arboreal brush-tailed porcupines, found in tropical forests. They are not closely related to the New World porcupines. Both Old World groups have hairs modified as flattened spines or cylindrical quills. In the *Hystrix* species, some quills have become long and wiry, forming a conspicuous crest on the nape. These rodents eat a variety of plants. They excavate large burrows that may be used by a variety of other animals.

246 Southern African Crested Porcupine
Hystrix africaeaustralis

Description: *A large stout rodent, with small eyes and a blunt rounded head. Erectile spines and quills covering crown, back, and flanks.* Quills banded blackish and white; nape crest spines have broad band of white to ends; rest of body covered with coarse, blackish-brown hair. *Area of shorter, all-white quills on rump above tail and on mid-back. Inconspicuous tail.* L 25–29″ (63–73 cm); T 3.5–5″ (9–13 cm); Wt 18–51 lb (8–23 kg).

Footprint

Similar Species: **Northern African Crested Porcupine** *(H. cristata)* ranges from Morocco to nw Libya, and from Senegal through Cameroon east to Ethiopia, and south to Tanzania; has mottled black-and-white rump quills. **African Brush-tailed Porcupine** *(Atherurus africanus)* lives in rain forests from Gambia and Sierra Leone through Congo Basin to w Kenya; much smaller (Wt 9 lb/4 kg), with uniformly blackish-brown upperparts, only a few quills on back, and very long tail with bristly brush at end.

Habitat: Hilly, rocky, and broken country providing burrows or other daytime shelter, to 6,600′ (2,000 m), including agricultural areas; sometimes forested regions.

Breeding: Litters of 1–3 born during wet season, after 3.7-month gestation.

Range: Southern Kenya, s Uganda, and Tanzania to mouth of Congo, and throughout s Africa.

Porcupines are nocturnal but conspicuous because of their large size and red eye shine. When cornered by large cats or hyenas, they raise their quills and charge backward, lodging their loosely attached quills into the attacker. The quills may cause deep festering wounds and in time may even prove fatal. Because they damage garden crops, porcupines are actively hunted and trapped.

African Mole Rats
Family Bathyergidae

This group of 12 burrowing rodents occurs only in Africa. They are cylinder-shaped, short-legged, short-tailed creatures with tiny eyes, no external ears, and enormous protruding incisors. The dune mole rats live in soft, sandy soils and use their front feet to dig burrows. All other genera use the front incisors to chisel through the soil, which may be hard even though the digging season is during the wet months. Roots and tubers are located as the animal tunnels, and whole plants may be pulled underground. Some species cache plant parts in food-storage chambers, while others farm them; they eat only part of the root or tuber, and the plant continues to grow.

247 Naked Mole Rat
Heterocephalus glaber

Description: A small, *nearly hairless rodent, with pink wrinkled skin. Short stubby legs* end in spatulate feet with short claws. Tail short. A few solitary sensory hairs are scattered over body; numerous long vibrissae (stiff, tactile, nasal whiskers) border mouth. Eyes small and black. Long, thin, white incisors protrude from skin around mouth. L 3–4″ (7–10 cm); T 1–2″ (28–44 mm); Wt 0.75–2.5 oz (21–70 g).

Similar Species: **Southern African Common Mole Rat** *(Cryptomys hottentotus)* ranges from sw Tanzania to s Zaire, Namibia, and South Africa; has cinnamon, tan, or grayish velvety fur. **Damara Mole Rat** *(C. damarensis)* ranges from s Angola and e Namibia to s Zambia and w Zimbabwe; furred buffy or black, with white forehead patch. **Cape Mole Rat** *(Georychus capensis)* ranges in sw tip of Cape Province and points in Natal and Transvaal; has black head with white muzzle and areas around eyes and ears. Much larger **dune mole rats** (*Bathyergus* species) range in s and sw Africa. **African root rats** *(Tachyoryctes* species) range from Ethiopia to e Zaire and n Tanzania; have soft, thick, russet-hued fur and bright orange incisors.

Habitat: Semi-deserts and dry savannas to 4,300′ (1,300 m); avoids rocky soil.

Breeding: Year-round, but usually peaks during rainy season; average of 12 young produced by dominant breeding female after 10.5-week gestation.

Range: Eastern and s Ethiopia, Somalia, and e and c Kenya.

This mole rat forms colonies of up to 300 individuals, the largest cooperative breeding groups known for mammals. Burrow systems 2 miles (3 km) long have been recorded. Individuals dig burrows with their incisors, pushing soil along the tunnel with their hindfeet and evacuating it in volcano-shaped cones. Naked Mole Rat colonies comprise overlapping generations; one or a few individuals produce all of the offspring, while the rest of the functionally sterile inhabitants rear juveniles and protect the colony.

Rats and Mice
Family Muridae

The true rats and mice are the largest family of living mammals; worldwide there are some 1,350 species, with at least 313 species living in Africa, and the list is growing. Rats and mice exist in a diverse array of life forms, sizes, and habits. They range from granivores to insectivores to carnivores to generalists who eat anything. Some occur in the driest habitats, with little free water, while others are aquatic, with burrows in stream banks. Most are nocturnal, secretive, and rarely noticed; others are diurnal and easily seen.

248 Natal Multimammate Mouse
Mastomys natalensis

Description: *A large mouse. Upperparts vary from pale to dark gray to brown, occasionally black.* Underparts whitish to buff, with tips of hairs lighter, sometimes separated from dorsal fur by lateral yellowish stripe. *Tail nearly naked, with large scales in circular rows.* Ears naked; feet slender. L 5–5.5″ (12–14 cm); T 4–5.5″ (10–14 cm); Wt 1.7–3 oz (47–81 g).

Similar Species: 8 species of multimammate mice resemble one another closely and can be identified only by specialists. **Forest rats** and **meadow rats** (*Praomys* species) range throughout sub-Saharan Africa, and **climbing wood mice** (*Hylomyscus* species) live in forested regions of w and c Africa east to w Kenya; have long smooth tails with small scales, and long dense fur. Larger **Black Rat** *(Rattus rattus),* introduced throughout the continent, is grayish brown to black on upperparts, with coarse fur and long, coarsely scaled tail.

Habitat: Dry and moist savannas, woodlands, and forests associated with villages and cultivated areas, from sea level to about 7,000′ (2,100 m).

Breeding: Year-round, with litters of 6–12 born after gestation of 23 days.

Range: Southern Africa except s Namibia, s Botswana, and w South Africa; also Senegal.

This mouse is widespread and occurs in many houses in remote villages, where it is a reservoir of human diseases and consumes field crops and stored grain. Where food is ample, these rodents reach epidemic numbers and literally get underfoot. The common name reflects the high number of nipples found in some females—12 pairs. Seeds form the major part of the diet, but other plant parts, insects, and small mammals may be eaten.

249 Four-striped Grass Mouse
Rhabdomys pumilio

Description: A small dark mouse. Upperparts vary from sandy to rich chocolate-brown; *4 blackish-brown stripes run length of back.* Haired tail black to brown above, light brown below. Underparts lighter. Ears small and rounded, varying from buff to reddish brown to orange. L 3.5–5″ (9–13 cm); T 3–5″ (8–13 cm); Wt 1.1–2 oz (32–55 g).

Similar Species: **Striped grass rats** (*Lemniscomys* species) are also striped dorsally, but have pale stripes bordering a central dark one or a single central dark stripe; genus is widespread in savannas north and south of Sahara. **Unstriped grass rats** (*Arvicanthis* species) are common diurnal and nocturnal rats of w, c, and e African grasslands; have similar habits but lack stripes or have a single mid-dorsal stripe.

Habitat: In southern parts of range, grasslands or grassy edges bordering scrub, riverine forests, or drainage pans. In e Africa, restricted to grassy uplands, moorlands, and sub-alpine zones at 5,600–12,000′ (1,700–3,500 m).

Breeding: Litters of 2–9 born in wet summer months after gestation of 25 days.

Range: Uganda and Kenya; s Tanzania and w Mozambique; South Africa northwest to s Angola.

This mouse is frequently seen foraging from sunrise to mid-morning and from mid-afternoon to just after dark. An opportunist, it changes its diet with the season and the availability of foods, consuming seeds, flowers, fruit, green plants, eggs, nestling birds, earthworms, and other invertebrates. It transfers pollen among protea flowers.

Gambian Pouched Rat

Giant Gambian Rat, Savanna Giant Pouched Rat

Cricetomys gambianus

Description: A very large rat. Fur coarse and long, varying from grayish brown to brown; underside light gray. Scaleless, naked *tail longer than head and body; black, with outer third white.* Ears large and blackish; head long, ending in blunt broad nose; *large black eyes surrounded*

by blackish mask. L 14–15″ (34–38 cm); T 15–18″ (37–46 cm); Wt 2.2–6.2 oz (1–2.8 kg).

Similar Species: Unrelated, but a large and frequent agricultural pest also hunted by humans for its succulent meat, is **Greater Cane Rat** (*Thryonomys swinderianus;* family Thryonomyidae, the Cane Rats), widespread south of Sahara; has blunt, guinea-pig-like face, and tail about one-quarter head-body length.

Habitat: Wet and dry savannas, forest edges, and uplands to 7,000′ (2,100 m) or more.

Breeding: Probably year-round where food is abundant; 1–4 young born after gestation of 28 days.

Range: Senegal to e Africa, and south (excluding Horn) to s Angola and n Transvaal.

The Gambian Pouched Rat stuffs its cheek pouches with food for transport to a pantry in its burrow. It digs a temporary burrow and "camps" near abundant food. Its chief predators are humans, who regard it as a pest; the meat is also prized for its taste.

Bushveld Gerbil
Savanna Woodland Gerbil
Tatera leucogaster

Description: A large gerbil with long soft fur: upperparts reddish brown to orangish buff; underparts, including feet, pure white. *Long tail has dark line down top surface, terminating in sparse tuft of dark hairs.* Eyes have white spots above and behind. Hindlegs especially long; feet long and slender, with toes ending in sharp claws. L 3.5–6.5″ (9–16 cm); T 5–7″ (12–18 cm); Wt 1.1–4 oz (32–114 g).

Similar Species: **Robust Gerbil** *(T. robusta)* ranges from Burkina Faso to Somalia; long-haired tail is black at end. **Bocage's Gerbil** *(T. valida)* lives in Chad and Central African Republic to Ethiopia and south to Zambia and Angola; tail is short-haired and pale to end. **Black-tailed Gerbil** *(T. nigricauda),* restricted to e Africa, has long black tail. Ranging from Angola to s Africa: **Highveld Gerbil** *(T. brantsii)* ranges from s Angola to South Africa; **Boehm's Gerbil** *(T. boehmii)* ranges from Uganda to Tanzania and Angola; both have tail with white tassel. **Gorongoza Gerbil** *(T. inclusa),* restricted to ne Tanzania, c Mozambique, and e Zimbabwe, is very large; dark from forehead to base of tail, with dark spot on side of muzzle; tail has dark line down dorsal surface, sometimes with white tip. **Cape Gerbil** *(T. afra),* restricted to macchia zone of sw South Africa, has gray fur and short untufted tail. ***Taterillus* species**, which inhabit savannas from Senegal to Horn of Africa and n Tanzania, are small, slender, and very long tailed.

Habitat: Light sandy soils or sandy alluvium, in open grasslands to savanna woodlands, from sea level to 5,300′ (1,600 m).

Breeding: Year-round, with birth peak in rainy season; litters have 2–9 young.

Range: Southwestern Tanzania, s Zaire, and s Angola south to c Namibia and Orange River in Cape Province.

This nocturnal rodent excavates extensive interconnected warrens. It does not dig in heavy red clay soils, in such areas using holes in termite mounds or under tree roots. Omnivorous, it feeds on insects, seeds, leaves, bulbs, corms, grasses, and stems.

Dormice

Family Myoxidae

Dormice are an Old World family, with 26 species, 15 in Africa. They are large-eyed animals with soft, dense, usually gray fur. Most have squirrel-like, bushy tails that may come off when they are attacked. African dormice are speedy, agile climbers living primarily in hollow trees, crevices in rocky outcrops and cliff faces, and human dwellings. They are omnivorous, but tend to be more carnivorous. They attack and eat lizards, frogs, and young birds when insects and fruit are not in season; they even cannibalize one another under certain circumstances.

250 Spectacled Dormouse
Graphiurus ocularis

Description: A small rodent with a bushy tail. Gray above, with hairs silver-tipped, contrasting with broadly white-tipped fur on lower flanks; sides of face, chin, throat, and feet white. *Above white cheek, black band extends from upper lip and widens to enclose eye and base of ears, giving spectacled appearance.* White tufts above ears. L 5–6″ (12–15 cm); T 4–5″ (10–13 cm); Wt 3 oz (81–85 g).

Similar Species: **Cape Woodland Dormouse** *(G. murinus)* lives in Sudan and Ethiopia south to South Africa; smaller and buffy-gray, with tail very long-haired toward end; has grayish eye ring. **East African Pygmy Dormouse** *(G. parvus)* ranges from Sierra Leone to Tanzania; **Lesser Savanna Dormouse** *(G. kelleni)* lives in Angola, Zambia, Malawi, and Zimbabwe; both are even smaller (L 3–3.5″/7–9 cm) and have short gray fur. All lack striking black spectacles. **Eastern Rock Dormouse** *(G. platyops),* of s Zaire to South Africa, and **Western Rock Dormouse** *(G. rupicola),* from Namibia to nw South Africa, are lighter gray, with more whitish color in dorsal fur; have inconspicuous grayish spectacles.

Habitat: Mountains with many cracks and fissures, especially in sandstone; also hollow trees.

Breeding: Litters of 4–6 born after gestation of about 1 month, probably in wet months.

Range: Cape Province and sw Transvaal.

The Spectacled Dormouse feeds primarily on ants, beetles, crickets, and grasshoppers. It is adapted for climbing rapidly on sandstone, even vertical faces; its feet have large nodules on the soles, and sharp claws. This animal is primarily nocturnal but is sometimes active in the daytime; during cold spells, it may go into torpor.

BIRDS
Class Aves

Birds are the most conspicuous form of animal life. They share with their reptile ancestors (lizards or dinosaurs) similarities in bones, ears, eyes, red blood cells, and eggs, and a multi-boned lower mandible (mammals have a single-boned lower mandible). They are warm-blooded and have soft feathers, and most can fly well. The bird skeleton has evolved toward flight, while the hindlimbs have been modified for bipedal locomotion. In addition to facilitating flight, the feathers of birds retain body heat better than mammalian hair. Worldwide there are more than 9,000 species of birds, about twice the number of mammal species. Some 2,000 species of birds have been recorded in Africa. While most eco-tourists visit Africa to see and photograph mammals, many become fascinated by the continent's highly visible and often spectacular birds.

External Anatomy of a Bird

The drawing of a Yellow-fronted Canary on the following two pages is labeled to show most of the common external parts of a bird that are mentioned in the order, family, and species accounts in this book. Definitions of other terms that are not in everyday use can be found in the Glossary. Within the species accounts, the measure of a bird's length is from the tip of the bill to the end of the tail.

External Anatomy of a Bird

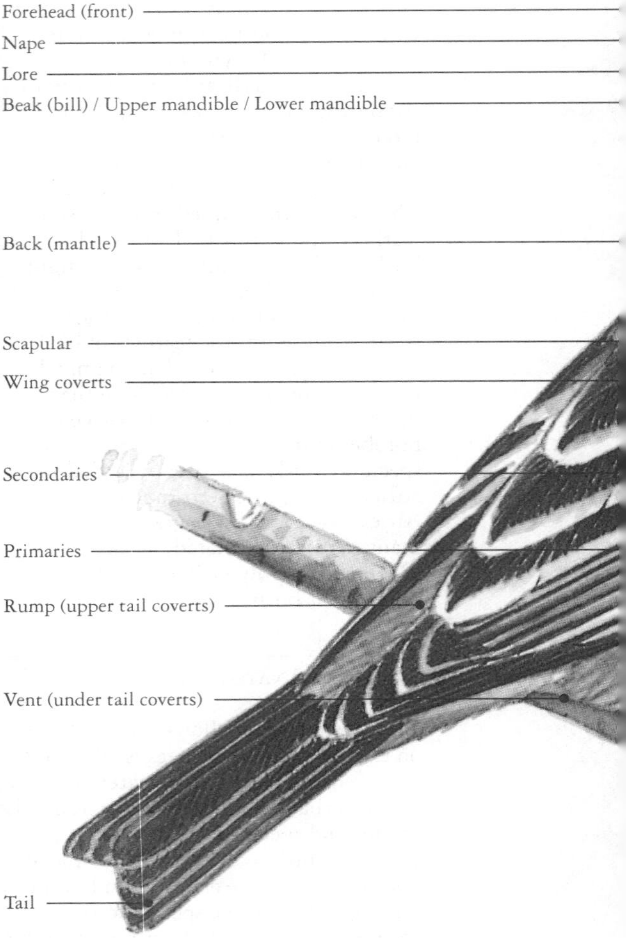

Forehead (front)
Nape
Lore
Beak (bill) / Upper mandible / Lower mandible

Back (mantle)

Scapular
Wing coverts

Secondaries

Primaries
Rump (upper tail coverts)

Vent (under tail coverts)

Tail

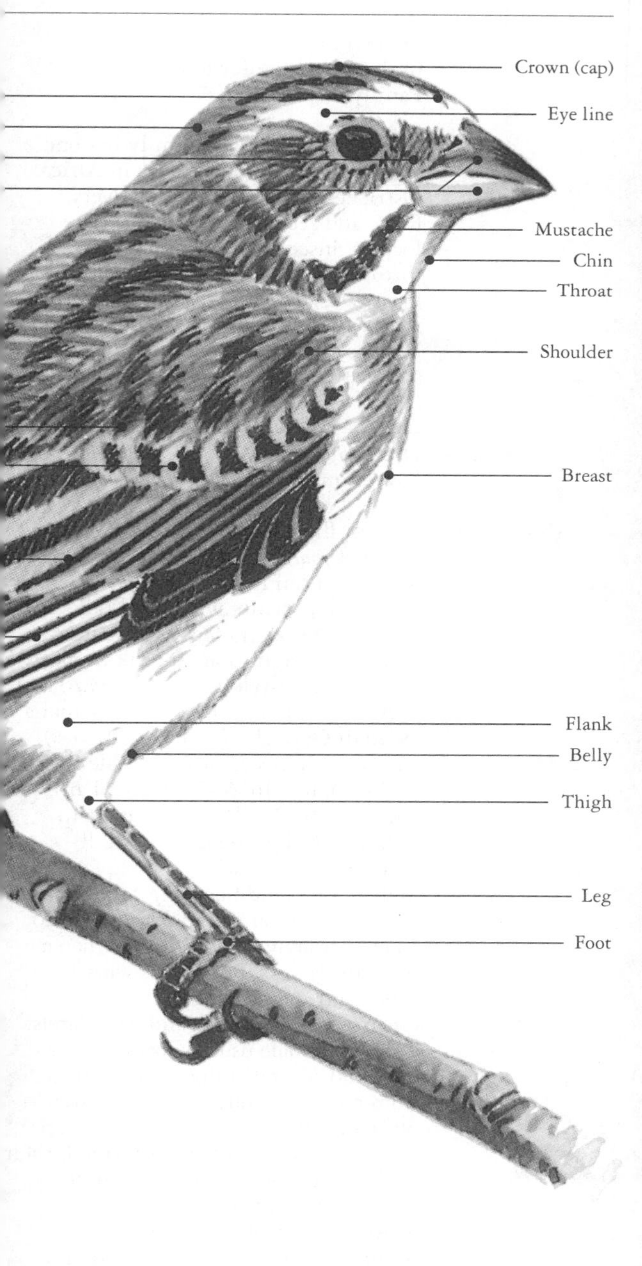
Crown (cap)
Eye line
Mustache
Chin
Throat
Shoulder
Breast
Flank
Belly
Thigh
Leg
Foot

OSTRICH
Order Struthioniformes
Family Struthionidae

The ostrich order and family has one species, which survives only in Africa. Ostriches eat roots, leaves, flowers, fruit, and seeds; they will also take locusts, insects, lizards, and small tortoises. Ostriches sometimes join groups of antelopes and zebras; with the mammals' sense of smell and the birds' eyesight, these groups are often successful at detecting predators.

251–254 **Ostrich**
Struthio camelus

Description: A giant flightless bird with *very long bare neck and legs. Male black,* with white wings and tail feathers. *Female brown,* with "dirty" white wings and tail feathers. Neck and legs of breeding male turn bright orange-pink in most of e (**Masai Ostrich,** *S. c. massaicus*) and w Africa, blue in n Kenya and Somalia (**Somali Ostrich,** *S. c. molybdophanes*), and reddish in s Africa. Ht male to 9′ (2.75 m), usually 6–7′ (1.8–2.1 m), female to 6′3″ (1.9 m); Wt male to 286 lb (130 kg), female to 242 lb (110 kg).

Voice: Male makes loud booming calls, *boo-boo-booo-hooo* (similar to the roar of a Lion), when displaying and at night when a predator is near. Both sexes whistle, snort, and snap their bills.

Habitat: Open semi-arid plains and woodlands.

Nesting: Territorial male usually has a "major hen" and several "minor hens." Eggs from more than one female are often placed in the same nest, a mere scrape in the open plain. Ostriches stretch their necks along the ground at the nest to protect eggs or young.

Range: Southern edge of Sahara and Sahel (rare), east through much of e Africa (common in high plains). Southern race

widespread from s Angola and Zambezi river valley to South Africa.

Footprint

The Ostrich is the largest and heaviest living bird, and the only one with just two toes (footprint is shown at left). The inner toe is thick and strong, and it is on this that the bird runs. The fastest-running bird, the Ostrich can maintain speeds of up to 30 mph (50 kph) for up to 30 minutes. In short sprints it can reach 45 mph (70 kph), with strides of 11 feet (3.5 m).

PENGUINS

Order Sphenisciformes
Family Spheniscidae

The penguin family is the only one in the penguin order. Penguins are the only family of birds in which all species are both aquatic and flightless. Their bodies are uniformly covered with feathers that are thick, dense, and hard, providing insulation and waterproofing. Their long, flat, flipper-like wings are superb for "flying" through the water (most other diving birds propel themselves with their feet). Penguins have short legs set far back on the body, but are able to hop and shuffle on land to and from their nests and chicks. The 17 species of penguins are strictly Southern Hemisphere birds. One endemic species nests in southern Africa, with other Antarctic and subantarctic penguins wandering up at times.

255, 256 Jackass Penguin

Spheniscus demersus

Description: Black above, white below; black *"horseshoe" on chest.* Black face and *pink bare skin* from base of upper mandible to eye area; white eyebrow; compressed black bill. Black legs; long flippers black above, mottled below. Juvenile plain gray-brown, with white belly; lacks white eyebrow. L 28″ (70 cm).

Voice: A loud, donkey-like bray.

Habitat: Breeds on inshore islands. Feeds strictly at sea, foraging regularly out 9 miles (15 km), rarely to 60 miles (100 km).

Nesting: Nests in small colonies. Digs nest in a sandy area or guano deposit under a boulder or bush, or in a burrow. Lays 2 eggs, which hatch in 38 days. Both parents incubate.

Range: Benguela Current off western coast of South Africa and w Namibia. Some wander north to s Angola or east to Natal and s Mozambique. Restricted to Africa.

Jackass Penguins breed on 18 inshore islands and a few mainland spots. They are best seen at Bird Island, reached on foot over a causeway at Lambert's Bay, north of Cape Town. A protected colony can be viewed on the southern side of Simon's Town, south of Cape Town.

GREBES
Order Podicipediformes
Family Podicipedidae

The grebe family is the only one in the grebe order. Grebes are small to medium-size diving birds with very short tails. They nest on inland freshwater and saltwater lagoons and ponds; some species winter on the ocean. Their bills are often long and pointed. Their legs are set far back, inhibiting walking. They have lobed toes rather than the webbed feet of most diving birds. The 21 species are found on all continents but Antarctica; three species breed in sub-Saharan Africa, and Madagascar has two endemic species.

257, 258 **Little Grebe**
Tachybaptus ruficollis

Description: Smaller than any duck. In breeding months, both sexes black, with bright *chestnut face and throat,* and bright yellow or white gape (at base of bill). Eye brown; bill black with pale tip. Juvenile and nonbreeding adult duller, with pale brown face and throat. L 12″ (29 cm).

Similar Species: **Black-necked Grebe** (Eared Grebe; *Podiceps nigricollis*) of e and s Africa has longer neck, pointed head, and thinner upturned bill; in breeding season, has black neck and yellow cheek plumes.

Voice: Courtship whinny given year-round near equator, in summer in south.

Habitat: Shallow marshes and lakes with emergent vegetation.

Nesting: Nest is a partly submerged pad built of soft rushes, weeds, and algae. Lays 2–8 eggs. On hatching, young leave nest at once, swimming near adults and often riding on their backs.

Range: Resident in sub-Saharan Africa and n Africa.

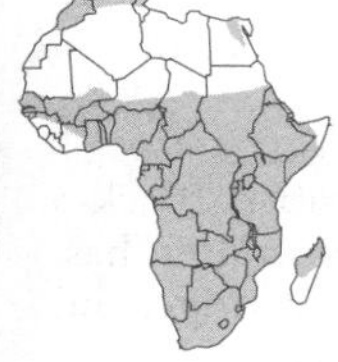

The Little Grebe is usually found in pairs or small groups but will flock in the nonbreeding season at favored sites. The birds feed on water insects and larvae, tadpoles, frogs, and small fish.

TUBENOSES
Order Procellariiformes

This diverse order of seabirds includes the enormous albatrosses, the medium-size shearwaters and petrels, and the tiny storm-petrels and diving-petrels. All have hooked beaks, webbed feet, and long narrow wings. They remain at sea except when breeding on remote islands. They are able to distill fresh water from salt water, excreting the salt via the tubular nostrils on their bills. Africa has 35 of the world's 93 species.

Albatrosses
Family Diomedeidae

These large seabirds are found chiefly in southern oceans. Their wings are very long and narrow. Albatrosses are expert at using the wind, rising against it and descending downwind to wave level at great speed. They feed on squid and cuttlefish that come to the surface at night, and on dead fish, seals, and whales by day. There are 14 species, eight of which occur off southern African coasts.

259 Black-browed Albatross
Diomedea melanophris

Description: Like a large gull, but with a thicker neck, longer yellow-orange bill, and much longer wings. *Long black "teardrop" stripe through eye.* White head, underparts, and rump; black back, tail, and wings. *Underwing black, with thin white central stripe.* Immature has gray-brown hood. L 3′1″ (93 cm); W 7′10″ (2.4 m); Wt to 11 lb (5 kg).

Similar Species: **Yellow-nosed Albatross** *(D. chlororhychos)* outnumbers Black-browed off Natal coast in winter; has black bill with thin yellow ridge, and much more white on underwings. Much larger **Wandering Albatross** *(D. exulans),* with wingspread up to 11′ (3.3 m), is regular off Cape Province and Namibian coasts in winter; adult has pink bill and all-white back.

Voice: A loud *waaahh.*

Habitat: Open ocean, at times close to land.

Nesting: Nests on mud mounds in colonies on many subantarctic islands.

Range: Common nonbreeding visitor in waters off Cape Province and Namibia; rarer east to s Mozambique. Found all year, but most abundant in winter.

The Black-browed is the most common albatross in the world. The young spend about five years at sea before returning to the island of their birth.

PELICANS AND THEIR ALLIES

Order Pelicaniformes

This order is a diverse group of large waterbirds that feed chiefly on fish. All have four forward toes, with three webs connecting them; other orders of waterbirds with webbed feet have two webs connecting three forward toes. Of the world's 61 species, 23 are found in Africa.

TROPICBIRDS

Family Phaethontidae

These beautiful white seabirds, which have very long tail streamers, dive from the air for fish and squid in tropical oceans. Superficially tropicbirds resemble terns, but differ in their foot structure, short legs, and elongated central tail feathers. The world's three species, all of which occur off Africa, have heavy, slightly down-curved bills.

260 White-tailed Tropicbird

Phaethon lepturus

Description: A large white seabird with *white tail streamers* (rarely yellow) equal to half its total length. Black patches at tip and base of each wing above. Black line through eye, as in all tropicbirds; *yellow bill.* L 33″ (82 cm).

Similar Species: Other 2 species have red bills. **Red-tailed Tropicbird** *(P. rubricauda)* of Indian Ocean (Aldabra) is essentially all white with red tail streamers. **Red-billed Tropicbird** *(P. aethereus)* has black and white barring over back and base of wings, black patch on outer flight feathers, and white tail streamers;

found in Red Sea out to Socotra, and on Saint Helena and Ascension.

Voice: A raucous *kirrick-kirrick-kirrick* while flying near nesting cavities.

Habitat: Warm tropical oceans, sometimes far from nesting islets.

Nesting: Prefers shaded crevices on rocks facing the sea; sometimes in tree cavities. Raises 1 chick.

Range: Breeds in Atlantic on Ascension, Cape Verde, and Gulf of Guinea islands. Widespread breeder on Indian Ocean islands, including Aldabra and Seychelles.

The White-tailed Tropicbird feeds on squid, flying fish, and other fish. A rare golden form can be seen flying over uplands on São Tomé island.

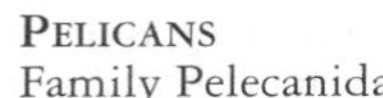

Pelicans
Family Pelecanidae

These enormous waterbirds are among the largest flying birds. They have very long bills, with an upper mandible that is rigid and hooked at the tip; the flexible lower mandible contains a muscular extensible "pouch." Their necks and wings are long, with the head resting back on the neck in flight. Their short legs are placed far to the rear, making the birds awkward waddlers on land. Pelicans' enormous webbed feet (footprint shown at left) allow them to swim well. Their bare facial skin and pouches are colorful, particularly in the breeding season. Worldwide there are seven or eight species; two live in sub-Saharan Africa.

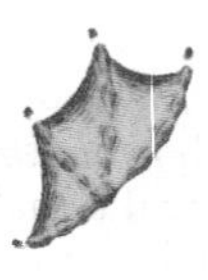

261 Great White Pelican
White Pelican
Pelecanus onocrotalus

Description: *An enormous white waterbird* washed with pink and yellow in breeding season.

Flight feathers all black. Pouch bright yellow; bare facial skin varies from pink to orange to yellow. Red nail at hook of beak. Both sexes develop white crest and swollen forehead when breeding. L 5′9″ (1.75 m); W 12′ (3.6 m); Wt to 33 lb (15 kg).

Similar Species: Smaller **Pink-backed Pelican** is silver-gray.

Voice: Various moos and deep grunts at nesting colonies.

Habitat: Both freshwater and salt lakes, plus seacoasts in Mauritania and South Africa.

Nesting: Nests on the ground in vast colonies of up to 30,000 pairs at select permanent and temporary sites, often only one or two in an entire country.

Range: Nile Valley and much of sub-Saharan Africa.

Usually fishing in groups of a few dozen, Great White Pelicans swim forward in a horseshoe formation with their bills open underwater. They move from lake to lake at midday, using warm air thermals for lift.

---

262 **Pink-backed Pelican**
Pelecanus rufescens

Description: *Silver-gray, with dark gray flight feathers;* somewhat paler whitish on face and underparts. Bill, pouch, and small patch of bare facial skin pink or gray. Nail at tip of beak pink or yellow. Breeding adult develops black patch around eye; yellow pouch; red feet. Trace of pink on back. L 4′4″ (1.3 m); W 9′8″ (2.9 m); Wt to 15 lb (7 kg).

Similar Species: **Great White Pelican** is larger, whiter, and more colorful, with more contrasting wing pattern.

Voice: Usually silent.

Habitat: Mainly freshwater lakes, rivers, and dams, but also salt lakes and lagoons; not on ocean. Often roosts in trees.

Nesting: Usually nests in trees, even in towns,

in groups of 20 to 500 pairs. Also shares colonies with storks, herons, and ibises, as in Nigeria and port of Ziguinchor, in s Senegal.

Range: Widespread south of Sahara, except for most of Namibia and w South Africa.

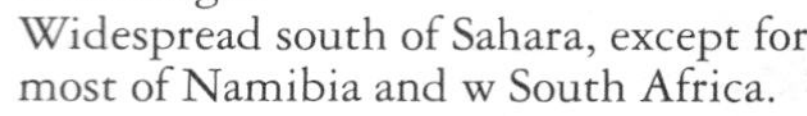

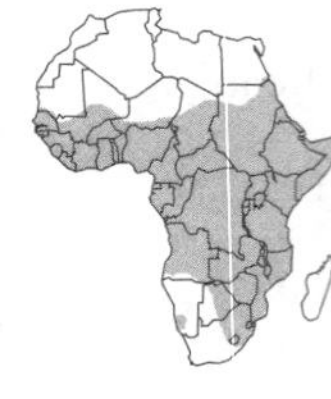

This pelican usually fishes singly, capturing its prey in sudden strikes while swimming on the surface. It occasionally fishes in groups, going for more fry and smaller fish than the Great White Pelican.

Boobies and Gannets
Family Sulidae

These medium to large marine birds have long pointed wings and wedge-shaped tails. Their thick, pointed, unhooked bills have serrated edges for seizing fish. In this family, the eyes face forward, giving the birds binocular vision. They plunge-dive for fish at high speeds, often from a great height. They incubate their eggs using their large feet. The family comprises two groups: the boobies of warm seas and the gannets of cooler seas. Africa is home to three of the world's six boobies, and two of the three gannets.

---

263 Cape Gannet
Sula (Morus) capensis

Description: *Adult white, with black flight feathers, tail, and feet;* gray bill outlined in black. Head and upper neck bright buffy orange in breeding season. Juvenile dark brown. L 3′ (90 cm); Wt to 5.7 lb (2.6 kg).

Similar Species: **North Atlantic Gannet** *(S. bassana)* winters off nw Africa; adult has white tail, and black on primaries only. **Masked Booby** *(S. dactylatra)* has yellow bill and black face and tail. **Red-footed Booby** *(S. sula)* nests in trees and occurs in both white and brown phases. **Brown Booby** *(S. leucogaster)* is dark brown, with clearly demarcated white belly. All 3 boobies live on Indian Ocean islets and on Ascension; Brown Booby also found on Cape Verde Islands and east along w African coast to mouth of Congo.

Voice: A rasping *warra-warra;* female has a deeper voice.

Habitat: Feeds strictly over the ocean.

Nesting: Builds a pedestal nest of guano in tightly spaced colonies. High nest-site and mate fidelity from year to year.

Range: Breeds at only 6 colonies: 3 islets off Namibia and 3 spots in Cape Province—Bird Island at Lambert's Bay (accessible without a permit), Malgas Island, and Bird Island in Algoa Bay. Some young birds wander up to Gulf of Guinea and Mozambique.

Tuna fishermen follow gannets, which feed on shoaling fish forced up by the tuna.

Cormorants

Family Phalacrocoracidae

Medium to large aquatic birds of both coastal and inland waters, cormorants resemble ducks with long necks and long, thin beaks that are hooked at the tip. The sexes are similar. Coloration is usually black, with an iridescent sheen, or black and white. There is a small gular (throat) pouch below the base of the bill. Cormorants flap their relatively short wings almost continuously in flight, with few glides; they fly with the neck outstretched, in lines or in Vs. They scamper with both feet and wings for a distance in order to get airborne from the water. Their short legs, located far back on the body, make them awkward waddlers on land. As their plumage is not fully waterproof, cormorants must leave the water for long periods to dry out, often with outstretched wings. Of 32 species worldwide, eight occur in Africa.

264 White-breasted Cormorant
Phalacrocorax lucidus

Description: The largest cormorant. Chiefly black, with *white face, throat, and upper breast.* Back bronzy with black edges, appearing scaled. Eye blue, with bare yellow skin below. In breeding season, develops white flank patch and thin, lacy, white plumes on upper neck. L 3′4″ (1 m); W 5′4″ (1.6 m).

Similar Species: **Great Cormorant** *(P. carbo)* breeds in nw Africa and winters along Mediterranean shores and lower Nile. Breeding adult is glossy blackish, with white thigh patch. White-breasted Cormorant may be a race of the Great.

Voice: Usually silent, but utters deep guttural calls in courtship.

Habitat: Any open water, fresh or salt.

Nesting: Nests in colonies, often with other cormorants, herons, and ibises. Builds nest of sticks, reeds, or seaweed in a tree or reedbed, or on the ground.

Range: Highland and rift valley lakes of e Africa, most areas south of Zambezi; local elsewhere around Lake Chad and in Senegal.

The shyest cormorant, the White-breasted will desert its nest readily, leaving its eggs or young vulnerable to predators. It usually feeds alone, but flies about and dries its wings with others of its kind.

265 Cape Cormorant
Phalacrocorax capensis

Description: Breeding adult entirely glossy greenish black, without white patches. Eye blue, with blue beads forming eye ring; lacks crest; *brilliant orange, bare gular (throat) pouch and base of bill,* duller at other seasons. L 26″ (64 cm).

Similar Species: **Bank Cormorant** *(P. neglectus),* a rarer black cormorant of w Cape Province and Namibian seas, has black bill and pouch, yellow eye, and usually a white rump, visible in flight.

Voice: A soft *cluck* in flight and at nest.

Habitat: Coastal and marine habitats up to 45 miles (70 km) from mainland.

Nesting: Builds nest of seaweed in densely packed colonies on fairly flat offshore islands. Also on cliffs at Cape Point and on man-made guano platforms along Namibian coast.

Range: Chiefly Benguela Current off w Cape Province and Namibia. Also along coasts of Angola and Natal.

This is the only southern African sea cormorant that feeds in flocks of up to many thousands. It jumps clear of the water before diving.

---

266 **Reed Cormorant**
Long-tailed Cormorant
Phalacrocorax africanus

Description: *A small, short-necked, slender cormorant with a long tail.* Bright red eye. When breeding, glossy black with *short frontal crest and white plumes over eyes.* At other seasons browner, with scaly-looking back feathers. L 21″ (52 cm); W 3′ (90 cm).

Similar Species: Closely related **Crowned Cormorant** *(P. coronatus),* of w Cape Province and Namibian seacoasts, has shorter tail and retains frontal crest year-round.

Voice: Croaks and hisses at nest.

Habitat: Freshwater inland lakes, rivers, and ponds; also mangrove swamps and estuaries. Seacoast of Senegal and Mauritania.

Nesting: Builds nest of twigs or reeds, in colonies in trees and reedbeds, and on rocky ledges.

Range: Most of sub-Saharan Africa and Madagascar.

The Reed Cormorant feeds singly or in small groups, sometimes with other waterbirds. It eats small fish and frogs.

DARTERS
Family Anhingidae

A darter looks like a large cormorant with the head, bill, neck, and wings of a heron. When feeding, it "darts" the closed bill forward like a harpoon into the side of a fish. A darter's wings are long and broad, allowing it to sail between flaps and to soar on the midday thermals. The tail is longer than a cormorant's, and when soaring the bird resembles a flying cross. Because their plumage absorbs moisture, darters ride low in the water and spend much time drying out, with wings and tail spread. Of four species worldwide, there is only one in Africa.

267 African Darter
Anhinga rufa (melanogaster)

Description: A large, blackish, *long-tailed* bird, with a *long kinked neck, small head, and needle-like bill.* Breeding male has white neck stripe and rich rufous throat and foreneck; long, white-centered plumes on back. Female has paler brown neck. L 3′3″ (97 cm); W 4′4″ (1.3 m).

Similar Species: **Cormorants** have strong hook on end of beak, and are less elongated.

Voice: A harsh croak, rarely heard.

Habitat: Freshwater lakes, dams, and rivers with fringing vegetation; also estuaries and mangrove creeks.

Nesting: Builds a bulky nest of twigs and reeds in a tree, usually in colonies with herons and cormorants. Nestlings are white (cormorants are black).

Range: Sub-Saharan Africa and Madagascar.

The African Darter is a highly specialized bird that is great fun to

watch. After spearing a fish with its "twin needles," it flips its prey up in the air, catches it, and swallows it headfirst.

FRIGATEBIRDS
Family Fregatidae

Enormous aerial seabirds that cannot swim or walk, frigatebirds glean fish from the water's surface, catch flying fish in the air, and rob other seabirds of their food. They have very long wings, with a sharp bend at the carpal joint of the forewing. Their tails are long and forked but usually held together in a long spike. Their bills are exceedingly long and hooked at the end. Their very short legs and their partially webbed feet are suitable only for perching. They do not rest on the water due to a lack of waterproofing and an inability to get airborne from the surface. African species are restricted to remote oceanic islands. Four of the five worldwide species occur off African shores.

268 Greater Frigatebird
Fregata minor

Description: *Adult male mainly black, with greenish gloss on crown and back;* pale bar on upper wing. Adult female black, with contrasting white throat, inverted black V in center of breast, and red eye ring. Immature has white on head and breast, separated by *rusty breast band.* L 3′6″ (1.05 m); W 7′8″ (2.3 m).

Similar Species: Larger **Magnificent Frigatebird** *(F. magnificens)* barely survives on Cape Verde Islands; adult male has purple sheen above; female has black head and throat; white breast and flanks; lacks red eye ring. **Ascension Frigatebird** *(F. aquila)* nests only on Ascension; adult male is all black, with green gloss; female has rusty collar. **Lesser Frigatebird** *(F. ariel)* nests on Aldabra and is found north to s Red Sea; adult male has all black underwing, and all stages have white patch from side of breast onto underwing.

Voice: Bill-clattering and a variety of rattles and whinnies at rest.

Habitat: Warm seas near uninhabited islets.

Nesting: Nests in colonies, building a stick nest in a bush. Incubates 1 egg about 50 days.

Range: Islets of w Indian Ocean, with 4,000 pairs on Aldabra. Some cruise to coasts of Mozambique and e Africa.

The adult male's inflatable red throat pouch is usually seen only at the breeding islands during courtship.

STORKS AND THEIR ALLIES
Order Ciconiiformes

These long-legged waders include the herons, egrets, and bitterns; the storks; the ibises and spoonbills; the flamingos; and two chiefly African families with one species each: the Hammerkop and the Shoebill. While a few species are solitary, most are gregarious, feeding, roosting, and nesting in groups. In breeding plumage, many develop bright colors on the bill, face, or legs; some develop long plumes. All have three long toes forward on their feet, one toe behind. Of the world's 117 species, 43 live in Africa.

Herons
Family Ardeidae

Slim, medium to large wading birds, herons have long kinked necks and long legs. Their bills are long, straight, and pointed. When breeding, many species sport beautiful ornamental plumes on the crown, back, and/or chest. All have long wings; they fly with slow, graceful wingbeats, and with the neck folded in an S curve (most storks, ibises and spoonbills, and cranes fly with the head and neck outstretched). Herons' eyes face forward, and the face between the eye and the bill (the lores) is bare. The term "egret" is used for some (usually white) herons. In addition to the well-known day-feeding herons of most waterways, this family includes the shy bitterns, which stalk the interior of marshes, and the night-herons, which feed at night. Worldwide the family has 61 species, 21 of them in Africa.

269 **Gray Heron**
Ardea cinerea

Description: *A large gray heron, with a long yellow bill and legs.* Crown white, with long black eyebrow extending onto trailing occipital crest. Black and white stripes down underside of pale gray neck; black shoulders; *uniformly dark gray underwings.* In breeding season, bill and legs become orange-red, and back and neck develop long white lanceolate plumes. Immature grayer, with black crown. L 3′1″ (93 cm); W to 6′6″ (1.95 m).

Similar Species: Very similar to pink-necked **Great Blue Heron** *(A. herodias)* of North America. In Africa, adult **Black-headed Heron** has uniformly black crown and neck (with white throat), and white underwing linings.

Voice: A harsh *quaarnk* when disturbed.

Habitat: Riversides, lakes, and ponds; also coastal marshes, lagoons, and beaches.

Nesting: Builds a platform nest of twigs in a tree, often in colonies with other large waders. Incubates 3 or 4 eggs for 25 days.

Range: Breeds widely in s Africa, locally in e and w Africa, and in Madagascar. Eurasian breeders winter widely throughout Africa.

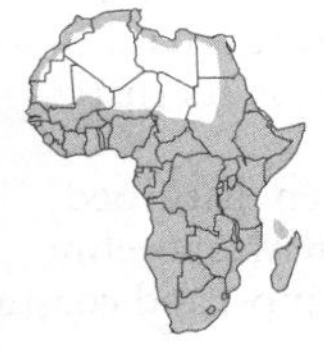

Usually a patient solitary feeder, the Gray Heron catches fish, eels, amphibians, crustaceans, snakes, rodents, and birds such as grebes, ducks, and rails.

270 **Black-headed Heron**
Ardea melanocephala

Description: A large dark heron, with a *black crown and neck,* dark gray body and wings, and long *black legs;* conspicuous white throat; black and white stripes on foreneck. *Very distinct white wing linings contrast with black flight feathers.* Bill varies from black to gray and yellow. Immature shows rusty on foreneck. L 3′2″ (96 cm).
Similar Species: **Gray Heron** has white on crown and yellow legs.
Voice: A raucous croak and a nasal *kuark.*
Habitat: Open grasslands, farms, and savannas; also forest clearings and near water.
Nesting: Colonies of up to 200 pairs build stick nests in eucalyptus, baobab, fig, and palm trees, even in cities; also on papyrus islands.
Range: All of sub-Saharan Africa.

Frequently found far from water, the Black-headed Heron specializes in catching rodents, grasshoppers and other insects, bird nestlings, and lizards. At water holes it will stalk doves and songbirds coming to drink.

---

271 **Goliath Heron**
Ardea goliath

Description: The world's largest heron, with very long *black legs and bill.* Eye yellow; *most of head and neck uniformly rusty orange;* chin and throat white; black and white stripes down foreneck; back and upperwings solid gray. Flight feathers gray; rich chestnut belly, shoulders, thighs, and underwings. L 4′8″ (1.4 m).
Similar Species: Much smaller **Purple Heron** has black lines that form a pattern on its rusty head and sides of neck.
Voice: A harsh *kraak-kraak* when disturbed.
Habitat: Inland lakes and rivers with shoreline vegetation, papyrus swamps, and coastal creeks and mangrove swamps.

Nesting: Builds a large platform nest of sticks or reeds usually less than 10′ (3 m) above water in a tree. Often a solitary nester, but will join mixed heronries.

Range: Sub-Saharan Africa south to n Botswana and Natal. Wanders and breeds irregularly north to Sinai.

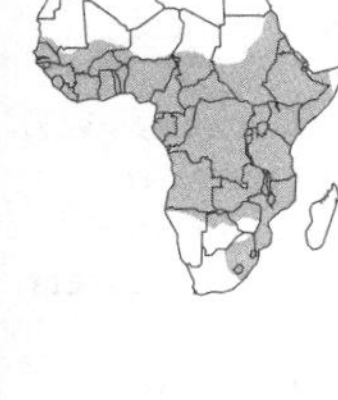

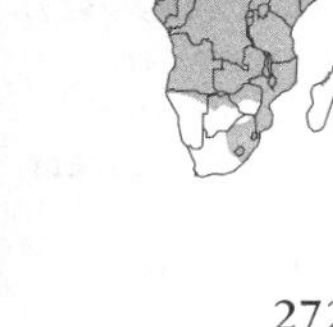

The Goliath Heron normally hunts alone or in pairs, standing still or walking slowly. It hunts large fish, frogs, lizards, snakes, and crabs, often wading out into quite deep water.

---

272 **Purple Heron**
Ardea purpurea

Description: A medium-size gray and rufous (not purple) heron. *Neck and face rusty orange, with black crown, hindneck stripe, and side-neck stripe.* Very long, thin, yellow beak and legs. Belly and underwing linings chestnut. L 3′ (90 cm).

Similar Species: **Goliath Heron** is much larger, with black bill and no black stripes on its rusty head and hindneck.

Voice: Usually silent, but utters a *kwash* in flight. As other herons do, gives various squawks and performs bill-clattering at nest.

Habitat: Vast reedy marshes; also lake margins, mangroves, and coastal mudflats.

Nesting: Builds a reed and stick nest low in a reedbed or tree, alone or in colonies with other wading birds.

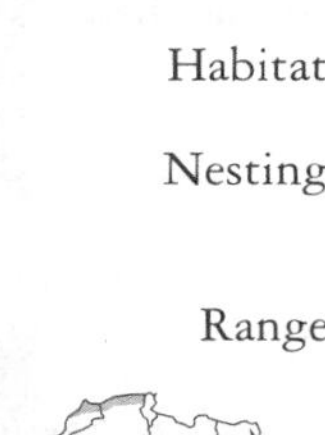

Range: Breeds locally in s, e, and w Africa, and in Madagascar and n Africa. Eurasian migrants winter widely in sub-Saharan Africa. Distinct pale race *(A. p. bournei)* in Cape Verde Islands.

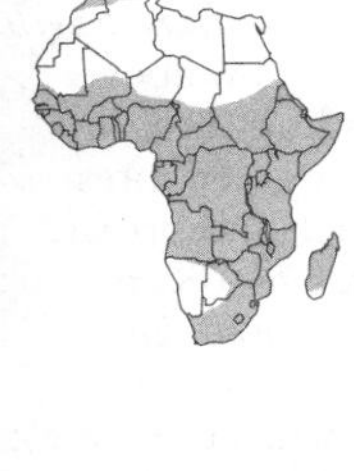

The Purple Heron is a solitary and often secretive denizen of dense marshes, where it feeds on fish, frogs, insects, and ducklings. Its long toes help it walk well on floating vegetation. This heron "freezes" when approached. The birds gather in communal roosts, flying back and forth in groups.

273, 274 Black Heron
Black Egret
Egretta ardesiaca

Description: The blackest heron, with *black plumage, bill, and legs.* Only feet and eyes yellow. In breeding season, develops red feet and black neck and breast plumes. L 26″ (66 cm).

Similar Species: Highly local **Slaty Egret** (*E. vinaceigula),* of n Botswana's Okavango Delta to sw Zambia, has yellow legs, and does not "canopy-feed" (see below). **Western Reef-Egret** (see Little Egret) has longer, thinner neck, white throat, and longer bill.

Voice: Harsh squawks at nest.

Habitat: Shallow lakes, marshes, flooded plains, mangroves, and tidal flats.

Nesting: Builds a stick nest in a bush or reedbed, often with other herons, ibises, cormorants, and darters.

Range: Much of sub-Saharan Africa and Madagascar.

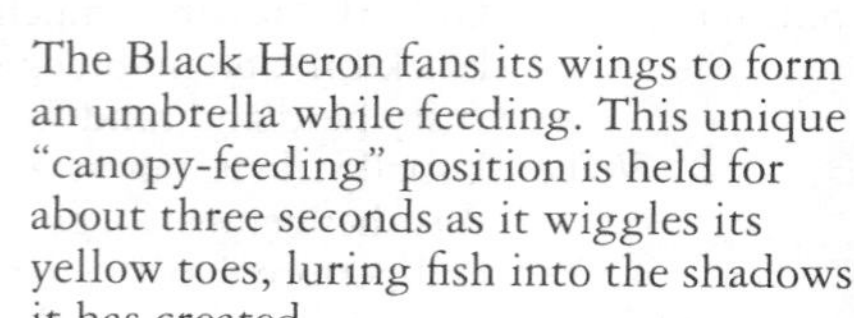

The Black Heron fans its wings to form an umbrella while feeding. This unique "canopy-feeding" position is held for about three seconds as it wiggles its yellow toes, luring fish into the shadows it has created.

---

275 Yellow-billed Egret
Intermediate Egret
Egretta intermedia

Description: An all-white heron, with a *medium-length yellow bill. Legs bicolored,* yellow above knee, black below, including toes. In breeding season, develops green lores, long white plumes on back and breast, and orange upper legs. L 27″ (68 cm).

Similar Species: Larger **Great Egret** *(E. {Casmerodius} alba)* has longer, all-black legs and longer yellow bill (black when breeding); African form (widespread south of Sahara) has black gape line running under and behind eye. Smaller **Cattle**

Egret has short orange bill and legs, and buffy plumes when breeding; nonbreeder has entirely yellow legs.

Voice: A harsh croak, but usually silent. At nest, gives a faint, hoarse, buzzing call.

Habitat: Fresh and salt lakes, streams, and grasslands near water.

Nesting: Builds a stick nest in tree colonies of 50 to 1,000 pairs, mixed with other fish-eating birds.

Range: Widespread in sub-Saharan Africa.

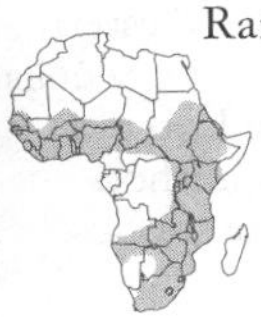

This bird feeds alone or in small groups of its own kind or of other egrets. At night it roosts in a tree.

276, 277 **Little Egret**
Egretta garzetta

Description: *Variable.* Typical bird all white, with *very long, thin, black bill;* yellow lores; long, spindly, black legs; contrasting *yellow feet.* In breeding season, develops green lores, 2 occipital plumes, and showy breast and back plumes. Black-phase birds occur on coasts of w and e Africa, and on Indian Ocean islands; plumage all black, except for *white throat;* bill and legs black; feet yellow. White-phase coastal birds from e Africa and Red Sea have *yellow bill.* L 26″ (64 cm).

Similar Species: Smaller **Cattle Egret** has yellow bill and legs. **Yellow-billed Egret** has medium-length yellow bill and bicolored legs. **Great Egret** *(E. {Casmerodius} alba),* which occurs south of Sahara, has long yellow bill. **Black Heron** canopy-feeds, has shorter legs, and lacks white throat of black-phase Little Egret.

Voice: Chatters and claps its bill at nest.

Habitat: Lakes, marshes, coasts, and reefs.

Nesting: Builds a stick nest on the ground or in reeds, bushes, or trees; nests in large colonies, often with other fish eaters.

Range: Widespread south of Sahara, and along all coasts. Eurasian migrants winter widely in Africa. **Western Reef-Egret**

(E. g. gularis) is common on coasts from Mauritania to Gabon in west, and Red Sea south through Tanzania in east. **Dimorphic Egret** *(E. g. dimorpha)* is widespread on Madagascar and other Indian Ocean islands. These two races occur in both black and white phases.

The Little Egret, the Old World equivalent of the Snowy Egret *(E. thula)* of the Americas, includes the Western Reef-Egret of tropical shores from Senegal to India, and the Dimorphic Egret of Indian Ocean islands. Many authors have treated these as separate species.

---

278 Cattle Egret
Bubulcus ibis

Description: A small, stocky, white heron, with a short yellow bill and relatively short yellow legs. Breeding adult develops orange bill and legs, and *buffy plumes on crown, chest, and back.* Juvenile white, with black bill, legs, and feet. L 22″ (54 cm).

Similar Species: Smaller than other egrets. Breeding **Squacco Heron** is darker brown above than breeding-plumage Cattle Egret.

Voice: Generally quiet, but gives a low *krok* alarm call.

Habitat: Open grassy areas, freshwater swamps, farms, rice fields, and towns.

Nesting: Builds a stick nest in tree colonies of up to 10,000 pairs, often with other large waders. Sometimes nests in cities and far from water.

Range: Virtually all of mainland Africa, except driest deserts. Also Madagascar and smaller Indian Ocean islands.

The Cattle Egret originally followed large wild herbivores for the insects they stirred up. With rapid deforestation and the expansion of cattle herds, this bird has increased greatly in range and numbers. Cattle Egrets are often seen sitting on the heads and backs of grazing mammals. Great lines of the birds fly out of and into communal roosting sites each dawn and dusk.

279 **Squacco Heron**
Squacco Pond-Heron
Ardeola ralloides

Description: A small heron, roughly the size and shape of the Cattle Egret. Brownish, with *dark brown stripes* on head and neck; short, *pure-white wings contrast with brown body in flight.* Short yellowish bill with dark tip; yellowish legs. In breeding season, bill blue with dark tip; neck and back rich rufous; legs reddish. L 17″ (43 cm).

Similar Species: **Malagasy Pond-Heron** *(A. idae)* breeds in Madagascar and Aldabra and migrates to e and se Africa from May through September; when breeding, is all white with pink legs. **Green-backed Heron** *(Butorides striatus)* has bronzy-green back and wings; gray neck and underparts; black crown and mustache; yellow or brown legs; lives in much of sub-Saharan Africa, Madagascar, and most Indian Ocean islands.

Voice: A low staccato squack.

Habitat: Freshwater marshes and watersides with reedy vegetation, and rice fields.

Nesting: Builds a reed nest in reeds or a stick nest in a low tree, often with other herons.

Range: Resident in much of sub-Saharan Africa and Madagascar. Birds breeding in s Europe and sw Asia winter widely south of Sahara.

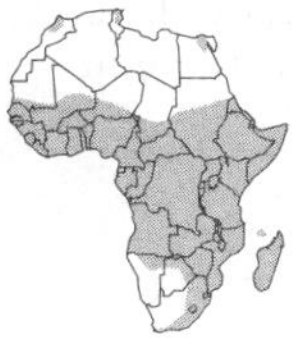

This bird is rather bittern-like and will "freeze" like one when approached. It usually forages alone or in very small groups. Often seen along the Chobe River (in northern Botswana) and on East African rift valley lakes, it will also invade and breed in areas with unusually good rains.

Hammerkop
Family Scopidae

This family comprises one species, described below.

280 Hammerkop
Scopus umbretta

Description: *Brown,* with massive, hammer-shaped head; *thick, rear-facing plumage sweeps back behind head.* Thick, straight, black bill; black, medium-length legs. L 22″ (56 cm).

Voice: In flight, gives a high-pitched *yeep.* Utters a loud nasal *wik-wik-wik-warrk* when displaying at nest.

Habitat: Ponds, marshes, rivers, fishponds, and rock pools.

Nesting: Builds an extraordinary, massive, enclosed "tree house" of strong sticks and reeds with a downward-facing entrance hall on one side. Snakes, bees, owls, raptors, geese, and other creatures breed in or atop the abandoned nests.

Range: Sub-Saharan Africa, Madagascar, and Yemen.

Also called the "Hammerhead," the Hammerkop feeds chiefly on frogs and tadpoles that it captures as it shuffles in shallow water; while in flight, it snatches food from the water's surface. In courtship two, three, or more birds dance, call, hop on each other's backs, stretch their wings, and raise their crests. The Hammerkop is thought by indigenous people to have supernatural powers.

Shoebill
Family Balaenicipitidae

This exclusively African family comprises one species, described below.

281 **Shoebill**
Whale-headed Stork
Balaeniceps rex

Description: Looks like a large, silver-gray stork. *Massive head;* thick neck; large yellow eye. *Distinctive thick, wide, hooked bill;* upper mandible strongly ridged; sides have sharp edges for cutting vegetation. In flight, head and neck retracted like a heron's, not outstretched like a stork's. Long legs; very long toes. L 4′ (1.2 m).

Voice: Bill-clapping at nest.

Habitat: Reedy swamps, marshy lakesides, and especially papyrus beds; prefers floating vegetation.

Nesting: Nest is a flat mound of plant matter on a floating reed island. Usually fledges 2 young.

Range: Central Africa: s Sudan (chiefly Sudd marshes), w Ethiopia, Uganda, w Tanzania, se Zaire, and n Zambia. Scattered records from n Botswana to Central African Republic.

The Shoebill is a slow-moving, solitary feeder in dense swamps but will perch in trees. It feeds on fish (especially lungfish), snakes, frogs, monitor lizards, turtles, and young crocodiles. Its usual hunting mode is to stand erect and wait with its bill pointed down; then it often collapses on bended knees to take its prey. DNA studies indicate the Shoebill's closest relatives may be the pelicans, not the storks.

Storks
Family Ciconiidae

Storks are large to very large wading birds, somewhat heavier-bodied than herons, with long sturdy bills and long necks. The sexes are alike. The bill shape varies from slightly upturned to straight to drooping, depending on the genus. The legs are long, with unwebbed toes. Most storks fly and soar easily, with the neck outstretched and the legs extending beyond the tail. Some species direct their excrement to their legs; when it dries it helps keep the birds cool and often makes their legs appear white. There are 19 species of storks worldwide, eight in Africa.

282 **Yellow-billed Stork**
Mycteria ibis

Description: White plumage (with *rosy wash* in breeding season) and contrasting glossy black flight feathers and tail. *Long, drooping, yellow bill, and naked red face; orangy-red legs.* Immature duller, dirty, pale brown. L 3′6″ (1.05 m).
Similar Species: **White Stork** has straight red bill, and white face and tail. **Egrets** and **spoonbills** have straight bills and lack black on wings.
Voice: Usually silent, but claps bill and gives harsh cries at nest.
Habitat: Salt and freshwater shores and marshes.
Nesting: Builds a platform stick nest in tree colonies, sometimes in towns in w Africa.
Range: Most of sub-Saharan Africa and Madagascar. Nonbreeding summer migrant in s Africa.

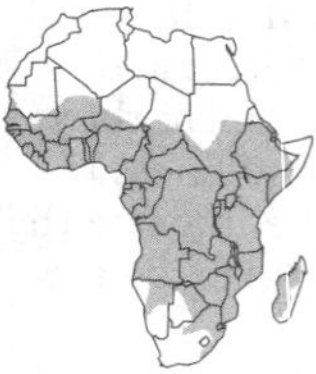

As this stork probes into muddy waters with its beak, searching for frogs, fish, and other food, its head may be underwater for long periods. The birds often rest in groups on exposed sandbanks in rivers and along coasts.

283 **African Open-billed Stork**
Anastomus lamelligerus

Description: Appears *entirely black,* but in breeding season develops a glossy sheen that is variably green, bronzy, and purplish. Heavy bill is dusky, with pale base; *closed bill shows wide gap* toward end before tip. Chick is born with normal stork bill and doesn't develop gap for several years. L 3′1″ (92 cm).

Similar Species: Both **Black Stork** (*Ciconia nigra)* and **Abdim's Stork** have distinct white bellies; the former winters in Africa from Eurasia and breeds in s Africa.

Voice: Bill-rattling, and loud, raucous croaks.

Habitat: Extensive freshwater wetlands of lakes, rivers, paddyfields, and floodplains.

Nesting: Builds a small stick nest in tree colonies and reedbeds.

Range: Sub-Saharan Africa (except in southwest) and Madagascar.

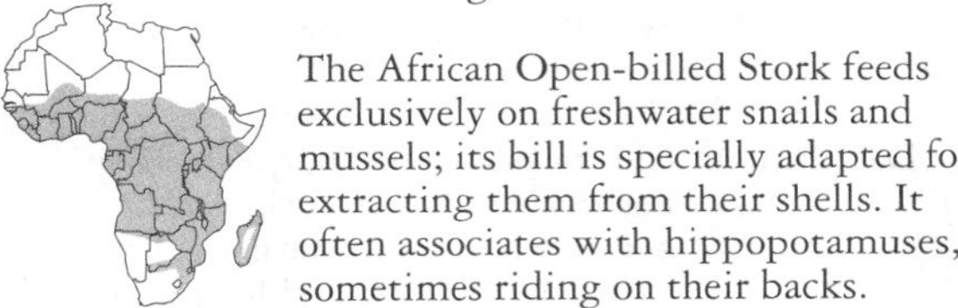

The African Open-billed Stork feeds exclusively on freshwater snails and mussels; its bill is specially adapted for extracting them from their shells. It often associates with hippopotamuses, sometimes riding on their backs.

---

284 Abdim's Stork
Ciconia abdimii

Description: The smallest stork. Black head, neck, back, wings, and tail, with contrasting *white rump, belly, thighs, and part of underwings.* Relatively short straight bill. Gray legs, with *red knees and feet.* In breeding season, *bright red bare skin in front of eye,* and bright blue at base of gray bill. L 30″ (75 cm).

Similar Species: Solitary, larger, and generally uncommon **Black Stork** *(C. nigra)* is also white-bellied, but has long red bill and red legs; winters in Africa from Eurasia, and also breeds in s Africa.

Voice: Claps bill and squawks at roost.

Habitat: Open grasslands, semi-deserts, and cultivated areas. Roosts on trees and cliffs, and rests near water.

Nesting: Builds a stick nest in colonies of up to 20 pairs in tall trees and even on houses in villages. Nests on cliffs on an island in Lake Shalla, Ethiopia.

Range: Breeds north of equator from Senegal to Somalia during rains from May through September. Present south of equator

November–March to feast on large insects abundant during rainy season. Found in e Africa on migration only.

Abdim's Stork is welcomed by many Africans as a harbinger of rain. It specializes in catching grasshoppers, locusts, crickets, and armyworm caterpillars. During migration, this bird travels on thermals in restless flocks of hundreds or thousands.

285 Woolly-necked Stork

Ciconia episcopus

Description: Chiefly black with purplish sheen. Forehead and face black; *back of head and neck white.* Bill slaty, with red tip. White lower belly and long undertail coverts visible in flight and when "sunning" with underwings exposed. Legs vary from reddish to slaty. L 3′2″ (95 cm).

Voice: Claps bill and makes guttural noises at nest.

Habitat: Flooded grasslands, irrigated fields, and stream banks.

Nesting: Builds an enormous platform of twigs in a tall tree; will reuse same nest from year to year. Does not nest in colonies.

Range: Most of sub-Saharan Africa, except southwest.

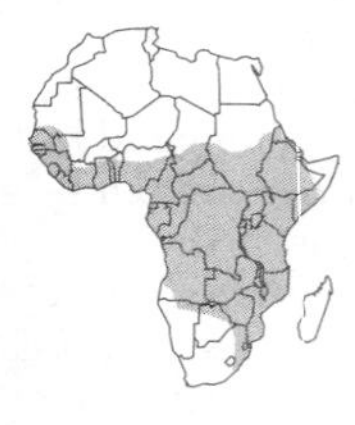

The Woolly-necked Stork is usually encountered singly or in small parties. On sunny days it soars on thermals with other storks and vultures. Rarely seen in the water, it stalks the shores for insects, reptiles, frogs, crabs, and fish trapped in evaporating pools.

286 White Stork

Ciconia ciconia

Description: All white, with black flight feathers. Heavy, straight, *red bill;* long red legs. L 3′5″ (1.02 m); W 5′6″ (1.65 m).

Similar Species: **Yellow-billed Stork** has bare red face and drooping yellow bill. **Egrets** lack black flight feathers.

Voice: Bill-clattering, squawking, and hissing at nest and roost.

Habitat: Open grasslands, savannas, lakesides, and farms.

Nesting: Builds a stick nest on a church, house, or tree, either alone or in small clusters. Usually lays 4 eggs.

Range: Breeds in Europe, sw Asia, and n Africa, migrating via Gibraltar and w African coast to Sahel, and via Bosporus and Suez to follow Nile Valley into e and s Africa. Flocks extend south to Cape Province, where it is a rare breeder.

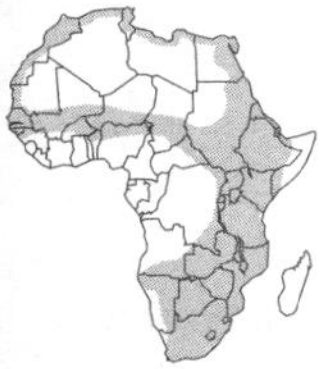

Large numbers of White Storks congregate at grass fires and locust swarms. They also feed opportunistically on rodents, frogs, reptiles, earthworms, and fish. This bird is declining in number due to widespread pesticide use, as well as hunting and trapping.

---

287 Saddle-billed Stork

Ephippiorhynchus senegalensis

Description: One of Africa's most attractive birds. An enormous black and white stork, with a black head and neck. Wings appear all black at rest, but shoulders and *flight feathers white,* with broad black band along middle of wing. Heavy, *upturned, red bill with wide black band in middle,* and brilliant *yellow "saddle" (frontal shield). Female has yellow eye,* while larger *male has black eye* and small yellow throat wattle. May show bare red "medal" on white breast. Long slaty legs, with red knees and feet. L 5′ (1.5 m); W 9′ (2.7 m).

Voice: Usually silent, but will clap bill.

Habitat: Vast marshlands and edges of fresh and salt lakes. Not in forests.

Nesting: Builds a solitary nest of sticks in a tree, preferring isolated trees free from disturbance. May take over nest of Secretarybird. Lays 1 egg.

Range: Sub-Saharan Africa, except southwest.

Only the Ostrich stands taller. This stork walks slowly and deliberately through weedy shorelines searching for fish. It will break the spines off a fish, wash it, and throw it up in the air to swallow it headfirst. It also takes locusts, mollusks, frogs, and lizards, and will probe the mud for lungfish. To maintain the pair-bond, the male will run about in front of the female with his wings spread.

---

288 Marabou Stork
Leptoptilos crumeniferus

Description: An enormous, *ugly* bird. Slaty gray on back and wings, with white "stripes" on wings at rest; white collar and underparts. *Naked red head* with black mottling; naked pink neck with a few wispy feathers. *Legs usually white with excrement.* L 5′ (1.5 m); W to 10′8″ (3.2 m); Wt to 19.6 lb (8.9 kg).

Voice: Cow-like bellows, sighs, and rattles at nest. Wings make loud squeaking noises during takeoff and landing.

Habitat: Savannas, shorelines, and towns.

Nesting: Builds a stick nest in colonies of from 20 to several thousand birds, including other species. Nests in trees or cliffs, sometimes in towns. Lays 2 or 3 eggs.

Range: Sub-Saharan Africa from Senegal to Natal; avoids rain forests and driest deserts.

The wingspread of the Marabou Stork is only slightly exceeded by that of the two condors and the largest albatross. This bird frequents dumps, slaughterhouses, and fishing villages for discarded scraps. It also eats carrion, dominating vultures at carcasses.

Ibises and Spoonbills
Family Threskiornithidae

Medium to large wading birds with long necks and legs, ibises and spoonbills have more or less featherless areas somewhere on the face, throat, head, or neck. During pair formation the bare parts, and sometimes the bill and legs, develop intense colors. The wings are long and broad, providing powerful, rapid flight. Despite their long legs, these birds are agile on tree limbs. There are two distinct subfamilies. Eight of the world's 23 ibis species live in Africa. They resemble herons, but feature heavily down-curved bills. They probe mud for prey with a motion like that of a sewing machine. Two of the world's six spoonbill species live in Africa. They have straight bills, widened into a spoon shape at the end. While wading in shallow water, they sweep their bills from side to side through water and silt.

289 Sacred Ibis
Threskiornis aethiopica

Description: White body and wings, with black tips on flight feathers. *Thick, strongly down-curved, black bill; naked black head and neck.* Dark brown eye. Lacy, black, elongated scapular feathers cover rump and tail at rest. In breeding season, scapular feathers glossed with purple; plumes over legs buffy; bare skin of underwing scarlet. Immature white, with feathered black head. L 3′ (90 cm).

Voice: Infrequent croaking in flight; great variety of calls at nest.

Habitat: Freshwater margins, coastal lagoons, farms, and dumps. Often far from water, especially recently burned areas.

Nesting: Builds a large platform of sticks, in a tree or dense shrubbery, in colonies of 50 to 2,000 pairs, often with other species.

Range: Sub-Saharan Africa to Cape Town;

Madagascar and Aldabra (blue-eyed race). Formerly Egypt.

The Sacred Ibis feeds on worms, mollusks, crustaceans, fish, and aquatic beetles in water, and on grasshoppers, locusts, eggs, and offal on dry land. Many migrate north and south of the equator, following the rains. Flight, in lines or Vs, is of the flap-flap-flap-sail mode. In ancient Egypt, Sacred Ibises were the symbol of Thoth, the god of writing and wisdom.

---

290 Waldrapp Ibis
Geronticus eremita

Description: A large, dark, metallic-green ibis, with purple shoulders. *Naked red vulturine head,* with dull red bill; orange eye. *Long black plumes* on nape and neck form a distinct ruff. Legs and feet dull red. L 32″ (80 cm).

Similar Species: Shorter **Glossy Ibis** *(Plegadis falcinellus)* has feathered head without plumes; nests locally in Mali, e Africa, Zambia, and s Africa, dispersing widely after breeding. **Bald Ibis** *(G. calvus)* lacks long neck feathers; has red crown, and white face and throat; lives in high-elevation grasslands between Lesotho and Swaziland.

Voice: Silent when feeding; variety of calls at nest.

Habitat: Semi-arid plains, rocky escarpments, farms, pond edges, and meadows.

Nesting: Colonies of 3 to 40 pairs build loose stick nests on ledges and in caves, often near humans.

Range: About 220 birds in 6 breeding colonies in s Morocco. Occurs away from colonies, within Morocco in nonbreeding season, some as far south as Senegal. Near-extinct Turkish population winters south to Ethiopia and n Somalia.

Pictured in Egyptian hieroglyphs 5,000 years ago, the Waldrapp Ibis was said to have been released by Noah as a symbol of fertility, and was protected by villagers. Today the bird is endangered due to human hunting and disturbance, pesticides, and the conversion of its habitat to farmland. This ibis pecks on the ground and probes fissures and under stones for locusts, beetles, lizards, spiders, scorpions, and snails.

291 Hadada Ibis

Bostrychia (Hagedashia) hagedash

Description: *A dark brown ibis,* with *glossy greenish purple on wings.* Distinct *white "mustache"* at base of fully feathered head. Swollen black bill, with red stripe on upper mandible. Legs blackish. Immature paler gray-brown on head and neck. L 30″ (75 cm).

Similar Species: **Wattled Ibis** *(B. carunculata)* of Ethiopian highlands is dark, with white shoulder feathers and red wattle hanging from throat. Thin-billed and longer-legged **Glossy Ibis** *(Plegadis falcinellus)* lacks white "mustache"; nests locally in Mali, e Africa, Zambia, and s Africa, dispersing widely after breeding.

Voice: A distinctive, loud *haa-haa-haa-de-dah,* last notes lower. Calls often when flying to and from roost.

Habitat: Grasslands, open woodlands, shores, farms, gardens, and lawns.

Nesting: A solitary nester, unlike most large waders. Builds a flimsy stick nest in a tree often just 10–20′ (3–6 m) above ground.

Range: Widespread in sub-Saharan Africa, south to Cape Town. Absent from much of Angola and southwest.

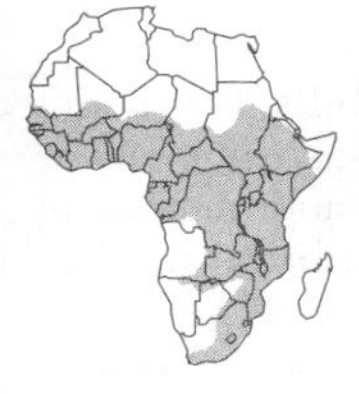

Scanning along the ground and probing in mud, this ibis picks up invertebrates and small reptiles. It is increasing in number; its dawn and dusk calls are heard over many towns and cities.

292 African Spoonbill
Platalea alba

Description: A large, *all-white,* egret-like bird. *Bare red face,* with white eye. Long gray *bill, flattened into spoon shape. Red legs.* Immature has yellow bill and black legs. L 3′ (90 cm).

Similar Species: **Egrets** have pointed yellow or black beaks, and much slower wingbeats. **Eurasian Spoonbill** *(P. leucorodia)* breeds in w Africa from Mauritania to Guinea-Bissau and along Red Sea south to n Somalia, and winters across Sahel; adult has black legs and bill, and lacks bare red face.

Voice: Quiet, but has *uunk-uunk* flight call.

Habitat: Chiefly freshwater shorelines in shallow water; also some coastal lagoons.

Nesting: Builds an oval stick platform in a tree or reeds. Nests in colonies of up to 250 pairs, often with other large waders.

Range: Sub-Saharan Africa and Madagascar. Nomadic and migratory in many areas.

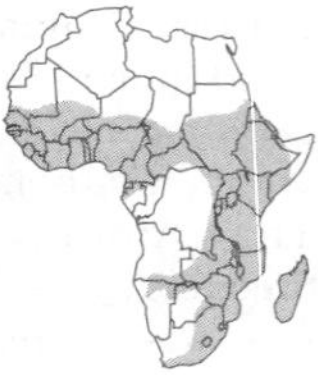

The African Spoonbill sweeps its bill from side to side, straining small items from the water and snapping at frogs and fish; sometimes it probes in the mud. Rather shy and quick to fly off, these birds fly with their necks outstretched, often in a V formation.

Flamingos
Family Phoenicopteridae

Flamingos have the longest necks and legs, relative to body size, of any family of birds. They can wade into very deep water and still feed on the bottom. In shallows they sweep their bills from side to side like spoonbills. Flamingos feed like baleen whales, sifting tiny organisms out of water and mud using filters at the edge of the beak and the tongue. Their diet includes brine shrimp, insect and snail larvae, and algae. They occur in large flocks and fly with their necks fully extended and their long legs trailing. In addition to the two African flamingos, there are three or four species in Latin America.

293–295 Lesser Flamingo
Phoeniconaias minor

Description: Breeding adult *deep rose-pink;* nonbreeding adult white, with slight pink tinge. *Bill dark red with black tip (appears all black).* Flight feathers black; shoulders bright red; *legs dark red.* Immature brown. L 3′ (90 cm); Wt to 4.4 lb (2 kg).

Similar Species: Much larger **Greater Flamingo** has pale pink bill with black tip, and paler pink legs; lacks deep rose-pink breeding plumage.

Voice: A high-pitched *chissick,* and a slow *murr-err* bleat. Constant low murmuring when feeding in flocks.

Habitat: Inland salt lakes, as well as coastal lagoons. Can feed in much saltier lakes than Greater Flamingo.

Nesting: Erratic and irregular breeder in colonies of up to 1,200,000 pairs. Builds mud nest far out in inaccessible salt flats and mudflats to deter humans and carnivores.

Range: Chiefly in rift valley lakes from Ethiopia to s Tanzania. Fewer in coastal and inland s Africa, moving among locales on Namibian coast, Etosha area of Namibia, Botswana, and South Africa. 800 pairs in coastal w Africa, breeding in Mauritania, dispersing to Nigeria.

Lesser Flamingos feed near the surface in calm waters on microscopic blue-green algae and diatoms. When the air is breezy, they create a patch of calm water at the center of a flock. They also swim out into deeper water to feed on the surface.

296 **Greater Flamingo**
Phoenicopterus ruber (roseus)

Description: A huge *white* or pale pink bird, with a long, S-shaped neck, and very long, *pale pink legs.* Contrasting *red shoulders* visible at rest; black flight feathers. Short, thick, *drooping bill chiefly pale pink,* with black tip. L 4′10″ (1.45 m); W 5′6″ (1.65 m); Wt to 9 lb (4.1 kg).

Similar Species: **Lesser Flamingo** is often deeper pink, with dark bill and darker red legs.

Voice: A goose-like, honking *ka-haunk.*

Habitat: Salt lakes, estuaries, and lagoons; sometimes on open beaches.

Nesting: Builds a tall mud nest in which it makes a depression for 1 egg. Also builds nests of stones on rocky ground, lined with grass, twigs, and feathers. Breeds in colonies.

Range: Breeds in Mauritania, Tunisia, e African rift-valley lakes, and s Africa. Visitor to lagoons along most African coasts.

The Greater Flamingo walks steadily along when feeding, keeping its head submerged for up to 25 seconds. It stirs up bottom mud with its feet and, using bristles in its bill, filters the mud for aquatic insects, crustaceans, and mollusks. The Greater Flamingo and the Lesser often mix.

WATERFOWL
Order Anseriformes

These mostly web-footed birds occur in two families: the South American screamers and the familiar ducks, geese, and swans. Worldwide there are 151 species, with 52 in Africa.

DUCKS AND GEESE
Family Anatidae

These medium-size waterbirds have long necks, blunt beaks (with a small hook), and short legs. Their plumage is waterproofed with an underlying coat of down. Their wings are broad and pointed, and their flight rather swift. Their tails are short and usually rounded or pointed. Members of this family are mainly solitary breeders; nests are lined with down from the female breast. Pair-bonds are usually strong. Many Eurasian breeders migrate to winter in northern Africa, the Nile Valley, and sub-Saharan Africa, chiefly north of the equator. Fifty-two of the world's 148 species have been recorded in Africa.

297 White-faced Whistling-Duck
Dendrocygna viduata

Description: A large, long-necked, goose-like duck. *White head and throat;* face often dirty white. Dark eye. Nape and back of neck black, like bill. *Lower neck and chest rich chestnut.* Wings black, with chestnut shoulders. Barred black and white below. L 19″ (48 cm).

Similar Species: **Fulvous Whistling-Duck** *(D. bicolor)* lives in flocks in much of sub-Saharan Africa, avoiding rain-forest areas; orange, with distinct white rump.

Voice: Very characteristic 3-note, whistled *swee-swee-sweeoo,* often given in flight.

Habitat: Wide variety of freshwater wetlands.

Nesting: Nests in small colonies in reedbeds or long grass.

Range: Widespread south of Sahara to Natal, plus Comoros and Madagascar. Most common resident duck in lowlands of w Africa. Less common in highland lakes.

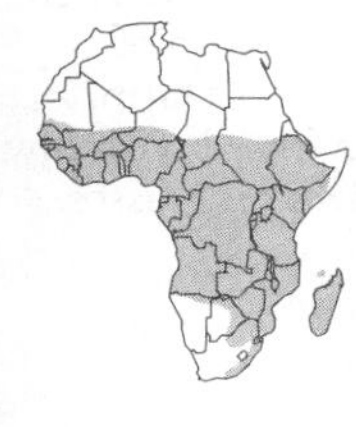

The White-faced Whistling-Duck feeds mainly at night but is diurnal in cooler months. It dabbles, wades, and dives for grass, seeds, rice, and aquatic invertebrates. This duck is most often seen in large, nervous flocks, roosting in marshes by day. At such times certain "bullying" individuals force others to jump up, whistle, and fly to another spot in the flock.

298 Egyptian Goose
Alopochen aegyptiacus

Description: A large, pale gray and brown goose. *Large, oval, chestnut patch around orange eye.* Pale breast often has dark spot. Back and folded wings rich chestnut; *white shoulders* and green secondaries conspicuous in flight. Bill and legs pinkish orange. L 29″ (73 cm).

Similar Species: No other large waterfowl has dark "spectacles" around eyes. **Blue-winged Goose** *(Cyanochen cyanopterus)* of Ethiopian highlands is gray-brown, with powder-blue shoulders.

Voice: Rather quiet. During interactions male utters a husky wheeze, while female gives a nasal, high-pitched *hur-hur-hur-hur.*

Habitat: All manner of wetlands, inland shores, and meadows; also high moorlands of Ethiopia to 13,000′ (4,000 m). Avoids heavily forested areas and most coasts.

Nesting: Forms lifelong pair-bonds. Solitary pairs nest on the ground and in tree holes and abandoned nests of other large birds. Courtship involves ceremonial drinking, flashing yellow undertail coverts, and neck stretching.

Range: Sub-Saharan Africa, and Nile Valley north to Luxor, Egypt. Formerly Nile Delta, n Africa, and s Europe.

The Egyptian Goose is the most often seen member of the family in Africa. Once sacred in Egypt, it has been hunted to extinction in most areas there. Its numbers are increasing south of Egypt due to a proliferation of farm ponds and reservoirs combined with low hunting pressure. It grazes on grasses, sedges, herbs, and grain crops.

299 Spur-winged Goose
Plectropterus gambensis

Description: *The largest African waterfowl,* approaching swans in size. Variable plumage, but most adults *dark, glossy, greenish brown-*

black, with *white face and belly.* Some northern birds have clear white foreneck and underparts. Birds south of Zambezi much darker, with little or no white on face and belly. Most show white shoulders in flight. Long pinkish bill, male with swollen knob. *Long, thick, pink legs.* L 3′4″ (1 m); Wt to 15 lb (6.8 kg).

Similar Species: **Comb Duck** (*Sarkidiornis melanotos;* L male 32″/80 cm) has black wattle over beak, which smaller female lacks; both sexes dark bronzy green above, white below. Ranges widely in sub-Saharan Africa and Madagascar.

Voice: Weak whistles and high-pitched bubbling.

Habitat: Marshes, rivers, and lakes surrounded by open grasslands, farms, and few trees.

Nesting: Isolated pairs nest in reeds, trees, and abandoned nests of large birds.

Range: Sub-Saharan Africa from Abu Simbel, in Egypt, south to Cape Town.

Seasonally common on most large bodies of water, the Spur-winged Goose holds its rear end very high when swimming. Grazing mostly on land, it varies its diet with grain, groundnuts, fruit, and vegetable tubers.

---

300 African Pygmy-Goose
Nettapus auritus

Description: A small colorful duck. *Adult male has clean white face* and collar; *lime-green neck patch* bordered with black. Crown, nape, back, wings, and tail darker green. *Underparts bright orange. Bill clear yellow.* Female lacks face pattern and has plain dusky head. Both sexes show slanted white wing patch on secondaries in flight. L 13″ (33 cm).

Voice: Male gives a soft twittering *choo-choo,* female a weak quack.

Habitat: Swamps, marshes, and shallow waters with reeds and water lilies.

Nesting: Solitary pair builds nest of grasses and leaves in a tree hollow.

Range: Much of sub-Saharan Africa south to Natal, plus Madagascar. Common in some places, such as Lake Tana in Ethiopia and Okavango Delta of n Botswana. Scarce in e Africa and much of w Africa.

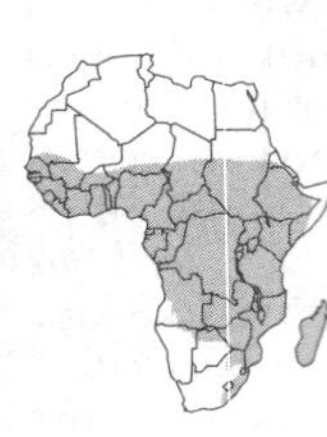

This perching duck is one of the smallest ducks in the world. Its pair-bond is strong. It climbs well and is very agile in trees while inspecting nest sites.

---

301 **Cape Teal**
Cape Wigeon
Anas capensis

Description: A smallish, *light gray* duck, with *dark brown spots below;* pale buff fringes on dark brown back. Entire head pale gray. *Coral-pink bill* with black base and pale blue tip. Flight reveals white secondaries with small emerald patch. L 19″ (48 cm).

Similar Species: **Red-billed Teal** and **Hottentot Teal** have dark cap.

Voice: Quiet. Male has a nasal squeak; female has a low quack.

Habitat: Chiefly salt lakes and brackish waters, including coastal lagoons.

Nesting: Nests singly on the ground on islands.

Range: Ghana to Lake Chad. Ethiopia and Sudan south through interior of e Africa. Most common in s Africa south to Cape Town.

The most common duck at many salt lakes, the Cape Teal forms small groups or flocks. It upends, stirs up mud in shallows, and dives, unlike most *Anas* ducks. The birds feed chiefly in the afternoon, often near flamingos. Couples breed when food (crustaceans, insects, tadpoles, and plants) is abundant.

302 Yellow-billed Duck
Anas undulata

Description: A brown duck, with a *distinct, long, yellow bill* with a black "saddle." Thin neck and head. Green speculum on secondaries, with white line above and below. Darker north of equator, paler south. L 23″ (58 cm).

Similar Species: **Cape Teal** has pink bill and much paler gray head. **African Black Duck** *(A. sparsa)* is darker, with large pale spots on back; bill is slaty in south, yellow with large black "saddle" in north; legs and feet are orange; lives in rivers from Ethiopia south to Cape Province, plus Cameroon highlands.

Voice: Male whistles quietly; female has a variety of calls, including loud quacks in flight.

Habitat: Freshwater lakes, marshes, and slow rivers. In some areas, coastal lagoons.

Nesting: Builds a solitary nest of reeds and grass, lined with down, among rank vegetation.

Range: Eritrea and Ethiopia (to 13,000′/3,900 m) south through e Africa to Cape Town.

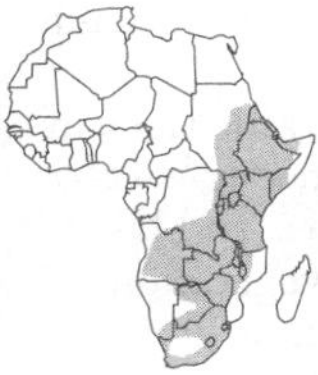

The Yellow-billed Duck is usually the most common duck in its range. Adapted to farms and grainfields with nearby reservoirs, it feeds on seeds, roots, and leaves, as well as insects, mollusks, and crustaceans. It dabbles, upends, dives, and grazes on land.

303 Red-billed Teal
Red-billed Duck
Anas erythrorhyncha

Description: A small brown duck, with a *dark brown cap above clear, buffy-white cheek and throat. Red bill.* L 19″ (48 cm).

Similar Species: Blue-billed **Hottentot Teal** has large dark spot below ear. Others, such as pale-headed **Cape Teal,** lack Red-billed Teal's dark cap with clear cheek.

Voice: Quiet. Male gives a soft *whizz-zet,* female a loud quack and variety of calls.

Habitat: Shallow standing fresh water with abundant duckweed and reeds.
Nesting: Nests singly in reeds or under dense bushes.
Range: Eritrea and c Sudan south through e Africa and e Zaire to Cape Town. Common in Madagascar.

The Red-billed Teal is abundant in southern Africa. It feeds on aquatic plants and invertebrates by dabbling, dipping its head, and upending in water. It also visits farm fields.

304 Hottentot Teal
Anas hottentota

Description: A very small, buffy-brown duck; sexes are alike. *Dark cap* contrasts with pale buffy face and throat. *Blackish ear patch* extends down side of neck. *Bright blue bill.* Black-bordered green speculum, with white trailing edge. L 14″ (35 cm).
Similar Species: **Red-billed Teal** lacks dark ear patch and has bright red bill.
Voice: Both sexes give 3–5 metallic ticks in rapid succession, and a harsh *ke-ke-ke.*
Habitat: Shallow swamps, marshes, and lakes with abundant aquatic vegetation.
Nesting: Builds a grass and reed nest in a reedbed, alone or in small groups.
Range: Eritrea south through e Africa to Cape Town. Also Lake Chad area of nc Africa, and Madagascar.

A rather inconspicuous duck, the Hottentot Teal associates with the Red-billed Teal in pairs and sometimes flocks. It feeds on aquatic insects and plants by dabbling on the surface and by upending, but not diving.

HAWKS AND THEIR ALLIES
Order Falconiformes

Often known as raptors, the hawk order includes the hawk, eagle, and Old World vulture family; the falcon family; the New World vulture family; and two families with a single species each: the Secretarybird and the Osprey. All have hooked beaks, strong feet with curved talons, and large eyes. A fleshy-looking, featherless area called a cere surrounds the nostrils at the base of the bill. Of the world's 289 species, 96 live in Africa.

Hawks, Eagles, and Old World Vultures
Family Accipitridae

This family includes all the familiar hawks, eagles, kites, harriers, and vultures that are familiar features of Africa's skies, poles, and dead tree limbs. Of the world's 220 species, 72 live in Africa. About 15 of these species flood into Africa from Europe and Asia during the northern winter. Old World vultures are actually divergent eagles, with weaker feet and rather naked heads; they feed on large dead mammals in the plains and are tolerated around most towns for their clean-up work. Likewise hawks are respected for their majesty and "vermin" control; the birds are valuable in controlling pests such as rodents and locusts. On a given day in varied habitats in Africa, visitors can often see one or two dozen species of raptors. These birds of prey keep small mammals, birds, reptiles, amphibians, fish, and larger insects constantly alert as they relentlessly hunt them. Females are larger than males by an average of 20 to 30 percent. Juvenile and immature raptors are usually paler or heavily striped below.

305 **Black-shouldered Kite**
Elanus caeruleus

Description: Entirely *white below,* including *all-white tail.* Soft pale gray on crown and back; *black shoulder patch.* In flight, all white below (gull-like), with contrasting *black primaries.* Large, owl-like, *red eyes,* outlined in black. Small black bill with yellow cere. Yellow feet. L 13″ (33 cm); W 34″ (85 cm).

Similar Species: **Scissor-tailed Kite** *(Chelictinia riocourii)* lives in Sahel from Senegal east to Ethiopia, and south into w Kenya; pale gray and white, with long, forked, gray tail; lacks black shoulders.

Voice: A clear piping whistle, *pii-uu,* along with harsher alarm notes. Usually quiet.

Habitat: Open agricultural areas (particularly grainfields), savannas, semi-arid scrub, and forest edges; also edges of towns.

Nesting: Builds a flimsy stick nest lined with grass in an isolated tree in grasslands. Raises several broods per year if rodents are abundant.

Range: Widespread south of Sahara to Cape Town. Also greener areas of nw Africa and Nile Valley of Egypt.

This "white angel" often perches on telephone poles and roadside treetops. When the air is breezy, it is seen facing the wind hovering up to 150 feet (50 m) over grassland. On spotting a mouse or rat, it drops straight down with wings angled upward and talons extended; it also feeds on locusts.

306, 307 **Black Kite**
Yellow-billed Kite
Milvus migrans (parasitus)

Description: Several distinct races, of which none is black. *Yellow-billed resident* sub-Saharan and Madagascar birds are soft brown, with *rusty streaked underparts. Black-billed "winterers"* are darker brown with *paler head.* All have short yellow legs and feet. In flight, long wings are angled back at bend, and primaries appear to be "open-fingered"; *long, deeply notched tail* is often turned like a rudder. L 22″ (55 cm); W 5′ (1.5 m).

Similar Species: No other brown raptor has a long notched tail.

Voice: Quite noisy, uttering a series of harsh *kew-kew-kee-kee-kee* calls and whistles.

Habitat: Cities, villages, and watersides; also savannas, where it is attracted to bush fires for fleeing prey.

Nesting: Builds a stick nest about 100′ (30 m) up in a tree; lines nest with cloth and dung.

Range: Yellow-billed race is widespread south of Sahara, but is intra-African migrant found in s Africa chiefly in southern summer. Migrant black-billed race crosses Sahara from nw Africa, s Europe, and parts of w Asia to winter widely in Africa. Most abundant north of equator.

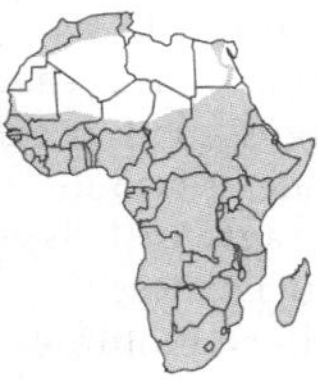

Often common along coasts, rivers, and near humans, the Black Kite feeds on rats, lizards, small birds, fish, and large insects. It frequents highways (for roadkills), dumps, and meat and fish operations, and will take chickens. This bird will even snatch food from baskets carried on the heads of Africans and steal sandwiches from the hands of picnicking tourists.

308 African Fish-Eagle

Haliaeetus vocifer

Description: Adult rich *chestnut on underparts, thighs, and shoulders. Head, neck, chest, back, and short tail white.* Flight feathers black; long beak black with yellow base and cere; large feet bright yellow. Immature heavily striped brown, with black band at tip of white tail. L to 33″ (83 cm); W 7′ (2.1 m).

Similar Species: **Osprey** *(Pandion haliaetus),* which winters widely in Africa, has dark line through eye, white belly, and long banded tail. **Palm-nut Vulture** has white shoulders and belly.

Voice: Loud, piercing, cheerful yelp, freely given, is characteristic sound of many African watersides. Often calls in duets, initiated by female. When perched and calling, throws head way back.

Habitat: Lakes and rivers; also creeks along seashores and man-made reservoirs.

Nesting: Builds a large stick nest in a tree or on a cliff and uses it for many years. Defends territory by calling and chasing. Pairs soar over territory most mornings.

Range: Sub-Saharan Africa.

The African Fish-Eagle hunts from perches over water, gliding down with its feet extended far forward. It feeds chiefly on large fish that swim near the surface. When the fishing is good, it can catch its daily quota of one or two in about ten minutes. This eagle will also take young flamingos, ducks, nestling waders, crocodile hatchlings, monitor lizards, and turtles. A pirate, it will snatch fish from herons, pelicans, storks, and even kingfishers.

309 Lappet-faced Vulture
Aegypius tracheliotus

Description: *The largest African vulture,* with the largest beak of any bird of prey. Naked pink head and neck with *ear-like lappets.* Beak may be dusky or yellow. Short brown ruff; dark brown back, wings, and *short, wedge-shaped tail.* Chest has dark stripes; sides and long *thighs pure white.* Flight reveals black underwings, with thin white line under leading edge. L 3′4″ (1 m); W 9′4″ (2.8 m).

Similar Species: Size and lappets distinguish it on the ground. At distance in flight, differs from **Hooded Vulture** by its distinct long white thighs and sides of breast.

Voice: Normally silent, but can growl and grunt.

Habitat: Semi-arid desert scrub, deserts, savannas, and thorn scrub.

Nesting: Usually a solitary nester, building a massive stick nest up to 10′ (3 m) wide atop a tree, open to the sun. Will use same nest for years. Lays 1 egg.

Range: Sahel from Senegal east to Ethiopia, most of e Africa, and south to Namibia and Natal. A few wander the Sahara, and nest north to Morocco and Tunisia.

This is the strongest, most dominant vulture at kills. At "clean" carcasses, other vultures wait for a Lappet-faced to arrive. With its massive bill and great strength it opens the hide, enabling all to feed. Feeding, it rips off large muscles while holding the carcass with its feet. This very large bird kills adult and young flamingos, and takes locusts and termites on the ground. It is thought to kill hares and gazelle calves.

310 White-headed Vulture

Aegypius (Trigonoceps) occipitalis

Description: *Africa's most colorful vulture.* Adult has downy white head, bare pink skin on face, and *bright orange-red bill with peacock-blue base.* Black body, tail, and wings; white belly, crop patch, and thighs; pink legs. Flight reveals black chest and white belly, *white secondaries,* and white line along middle of wing. Head appears pointed at back. L 33″ (82 cm); W 6′8″ (2 m).

Voice: Usually silent, but chatters at kills.

Habitat: Wooded savannas, plains, and semi-deserts.

Nesting: Widely spaced solitary pairs build large stick nests atop thorny acacias or baobabs; raise 1 young.

Range: Senegal east across Sahel to Ethiopia, south through e Africa to Namibia and Natal. Avoids rain forests and southern temperate zones.

Known as the "Searcher," the White-headed flies out earlier in the day than other vultures, feeding alone at carcasses until other vultures arrive and force it to eat scraps, sinew, and skin. This bird also kills flamingos, hares, and small gazelles.

311, 312 **Rüppell's Griffon Vulture**
Rüppell's Griffon
Gyps rueppelli

Description: A large vulture. Adult blackish brown, with creamy white scaling at tip of breast and wing feathers, giving *spotted effect. Bill and eye yellow.* Head and neck covered with *fine white down.* In flight, *underwings show 3 white lines.* L 3′4″ (1 m); W 8′4″ (2.5 m).

Similar Species: **White-backed Vulture** has black bill and eye, and is darker, without scaly effect; adult has uniformly white underwing linings.

Voice: Hisses, grunts, and shrieks at carcasses.

Habitat: Mountains of Ethiopia up to 14,800′ (4,500 m), and open savannas of Sahel and e Africa. Restricted to areas it can reach from cliffs and inselbergs.

Nesting: Builds a rather small, slight stick nest on a remote cliff ledge in colonies of up to 1,000 pairs. Raises 1 young.

Range: Senegal east to Somalia, and south to n Tanzania.

This vulture feeds only on carrion, focusing on the soft flesh and intestines. It can go many days between meals but will gorge itself with more than 3 pounds (1.5 kg) of food. This bird will forage out to 90 miles (150 km) from communal roosting cliffs, riding on thermals. On arriving at carcasses, it lands outside the mob scene, then bounds forward with wings spread and neck outstretched.

313 White-backed Vulture
Gyps africanus

Description: *Africa's most common large vulture.* Adult pale brown, with *white lower back and rump. Bill and eye black;* dark face and throat contrast with pale crown and hindneck. In flight, adult shows uniformly white underwing linings, contrasting with black flight feathers. Immature dark brown, heavily streaked below, and lacks white rump; neck ruff long and dark, becoming compact and white in adult. L 3′2″ (95 cm); W 7′10″ (2.35 m).

Similar Species: Scaly-appearing **Rüppell's Griffon Vulture** is larger, paler, and longer-necked, with yellow eye and bill. **Cape Vulture** *(G. coprotheres),* of s Africa south of Zambezi, is larger and paler (sandy or light rufous), with yellow eye and grayish flight feathers below.

Voice: Grunts and goose-like hisses and cackles.

Habitat: Open plains and wooded country with game animals and livestock.

Nesting: Builds a flimsy stick nest atop a tree. Incubates 1 egg for 56 days.

Range: Senegal east to s Red Sea, and south through e Africa to Namibia and Natal.

At some carcasses up to 200 of these vultures may gather, while elephant carcasses may attract a thousand. Ferocious fights ensue for shares, and many shy, well-mannered youngsters get nothing and die of starvation. The White-backed will gorge itself on more than 2 pounds (1 kg) of food, then rest with its wings spread and its back to the sun.

314 Hooded Vulture
Necrosyrtes monachus

Description: *The smallest African vulture,* with a small head and *very thin, black-tipped bill.* Face and foreneck pink, with downy white

feathering on crown and hindneck, and around crop; facial skin turns bright red when excited. In flight, appears all dark except for white underwing line at base of secondaries. Long legs and weak feet adapted for walking, not grasping. L 30″ (75 cm); W 5′8″ (1.7 m).

Similar Species: Immature **Egyptian Vulture,** also dark brown, has long nape feathers forming head ruff, and longer, wedge-shaped tail.

Voice: Usually silent, but squeals when excited.

Habitat: Towns, savannas, farmlands, semi-deserts, and clearings in forests.

Nesting: Builds a small, well-cupped stick nest high up in a well-foliated tree. Raises 1 young.

Range: Mauritania and Ghana east to Somalia, and south to Angola and Natal. Absent in wetter areas of w and c Africa.

The Hooded Vulture is a common town scavenger in western and northeastern Africa south to Uganda. In Kenya and southward it is rarer in towns but follows cattle and goat herders. The bird waits patiently for scraps but becomes aggressive when food appears. Unable to compete with larger vultures at carcasses, it stays later, using its long bill to reach into difficult cavities. This vulture also extracts larvae from dung beetle balls.

---

315 Egyptian Vulture
Neophron percnopterus

Description: A smallish, mostly *white* vulture, with a *long, pure-white, wedge-shaped tail; black flight feathers;* white underwing coverts. Fully feathered head with long, shaggy, *white or buffy ruff.* Bright *orange-yellow bare face and base of bill.* Immature dark brown, with shaggy ruff and dusky-pink face. L 26″ (65 cm); W 6′ (1.8 m).

Similar Species: **Palm-nut Vulture** has black tail and red facial skin. **Lammergeier** (*Gypaetus barbatus;* L 3′10″/1.15 m), an enormous, orange, bone-eating mountain vulture of Ethiopia, e Africa, and Drakensberg Mountains of s Africa, has long, narrow, black wings and very long, black, wedge-shaped tail.

Voice: Usually silent.

Habitat: Dry plains, savannas, deserts, and mountains.

Nesting: Builds a small stick nest, lined with mammal skin, hair, and dung. Nests in cliffs, caves, steep riverbanks, and buildings. Raises 2 young.

Range: Canary Islands and Morocco east to Egypt (rare), south locally through Sahara to Sahel, and e Africa south to n Tanzania. Rare and local south to South Africa.

In northern Africa and Ethiopia, the Egyptian Vulture is a common scavenger in towns. Elsewhere it frequents cattle enclosures, flying early in the day and finding many carcasses before other vultures have arrived. This bird kills downy flamingo chicks and eats flamingo eggs. It will grasp a hard rock and fling it repeatedly at a stray Ostrich egg until it breaks.

---

316 Palm-nut Vulture
Gypohierax angolensis

Description: A *large, white,* partly vegetarian vulture. Head, back, underparts, thighs, and wing coverts white. Flight feathers black, but white under primaries. *Short black tail has white terminal band. Bare pink or red skin around yellow eye;* long, strongly hooked yellow beak. Brown juvenile has bare gray facial skin. L 25″ (62 cm); W 5′ (1.5 m).

Similar Species: **Egyptian Vulture** prefers drier areas and has long, white, wedge-shaped tail. **African Fish-Eagle** has rich chestnut body and short white tail.

Voice: Duck-like quacking at roost.

Habitat: In w Africa, mixed forest and cultivated land where oil palms are common. Elsewhere along shorelines, mangrove creeks, and waterways.

Nesting: Each pair defends a territory around its stick nest high in a tall ceiba, palm, or euphorbia tree. Raises 1 young.

Range: Wet tropics from Senegal south to Angola, rarer at e African lakes and along coast from Kenya to Natal.

In West Africa this bird feeds chiefly on oil palm fruits as it perches at the base of the fronds. It also eats other palm fruits, wild dates, crabs, mollusks, frogs, dying birds, and fish. The Palm-nut Vulture soars relatively little as it goes directly to fruiting palms or walks about mangrove creeks.

317 Black-breasted Snake-Eagle

Black-chested Harrier-Eagle
Circaetus pectoralis

Description: *Blackish-brown breast,* head, and upperparts, contrasting with *clear white belly.* Large, owl-like head, with orange eye and small black bill. In flight, long narrow wings feature pale underwing linings and *3 rows of black lines on flight feathers.* Long banded tail. Immature rufous. L 26″ (65 cm); W 6′2″ (1.85 m).

Similar Species: **Martial Eagle** has black underwing linings, spotted belly, and shorter tail. **Beaudouin's Snake-Eagle** *(C. beaudouini),* which ranges from Senegal to nw Kenya, is paler brown, with narrow bars on belly.

Voice: Normally silent. Whistles a harsh *shreee-ee-ee* in courtship flight.

Habitat: Open grass plains, lightly wooded savannas, thornveld, and true deserts.

Nesting: Builds a small nest of thin sticks in the crown of a euphorbia or thorny, flat-topped acacia. Female incubates 1 egg.

Range: Southern Zaire and Eritrea south to sw Cape Province.

Snake-eagles have short toes and small beaks. The largest raptors that hover regularly, they feed chiefly on snakes.

Smaller snakes are swallowed headfirst, with the unconsumed length dangling from the bill for hours. This eagle also feeds on hares and guineafowl.

318 **Brown Snake-Eagle**
Circaetus cinereus

Description: Rich brown, with large square head; large, yellow, owl-like eyes; short black bill. *Tail has 3 narrow gray bands.* In flight, *pale gray underwing flight feathers* contrast with dark brown underwing coverts. Bare gray legs and feet. Immature has white streaks and spots on head and underparts. L 30″ (75 cm); W 6′4″ (1.9 m).

Similar Species: **Tawny Eagle** and **Black Kite** have brown flight feathers below. **Black Kite** has deeply notched tail.

Voice: A deep *hok-hok-hok-hok-hok.*

Habitat: Woodlands and dense thornbush; less often in open plains or arid areas.

Nesting: Builds a very small stick nest lined with fresh green leaves atop a small tree on a hillside. Raises 1 young.

Range: Sahel from Senegal east to Red Sea, and south to Angola and South Africa.

The Brown Snake-Eagle hunts chiefly from treetops and euphorbias, intently scanning the ground for the movements of snakes. This eagle kills cobras, mambas up to 10 feet (3 m) long, Puff Adders, monitor lizards, and francolins.

319 **Bateleur**
Terathopius ecaudatus

Description: The world's most attractive raptor. *Enormous head;* extremely long, pointed wings that hang down well below *extremely short, chestnut tail* when bird is perched. Adult jet black, with yellow bill and *brilliant bare red face and base of bill;* large gray or brown shoulders; *chestnut back.* Short, bright red legs.

Flight reveals white underwing, male with broader black trailing edge. Immature brown, with very short tail. L 24″ (60 cm); W 6′ (1.8 m).

Voice: Usually silent, but gives raucous screams when excited.

Habitat: Open, broad-leafed woodlands with long grass, dense thornbush, acacia savannas, semi-deserts, and open grassy plains.

Nesting: Performs spectacular aerial displays in courtship. Builds or reuses a large stick nest hidden in the canopy of a tall tree. Raises 1 young.

Range: Widespread from Senegal east to Eritrea, and south to ne Namibia and Natal, except for rain-forest belt.

Its canting, side-to-side motion in flight gave this bird its name, which is the French term for a tightrope walker who uses a balancing pole. The Bateleur may fly for most of the day, covering up to 250 miles (400 km). It feeds on hares, dik-diks, guineafowl, bustards, doves, rollers, monitor lizards, and insects, as well as carrion. It perches in trees and on the ground, and is often seen at water holes drinking and preening.

---

320 Pale Chanting-Goshawk
Melierax canorus

Description: *Adult pearly gray on head, breast, and back. Eye dark red; base of bill brilliant red.* Belly and thighs finely gray-barred, with very long red legs. In flight, underwing pale with black tip; rump white. L 22″ (55 cm).

Similar Species: **Dark Chanting-Goshawk** *(M. metabates)* replaces Pale from Senegal to Ethiopia, between rift valleys in e Africa, and in most of Zambezi Valley south to Kruger NP, in Transvaal. While the former is darker and has a barred rump, the two birds are not easily distinguished in areas of overlap. Smaller **Gabar Goshawk** *(Micronisus gabar)* and a variety of small to medium-size, short-winged, bird-eating hawks of the genus *Accipiter* are also found in Africa.

Voice: In courtship, a chanted, fast *klu-klu-klu-klu.* Usually silent rest of year.

Habitat: Treetops in open subdeserts, arid thornbush, and grasslands.

Nesting: Builds a shallow twig saucer atop a thorn tree; raises 1 young.

Range: In e Africa and Somalia, from eastern rift valley eastward. Abundant in Namibia, Botswana, and w South Africa.

This goshawk perches conspicuously on trees and roadside fences and poles. When walking along like a small Secretarybird, this long-legged bird keeps its tail off the ground. It feeds chiefly on lizards, less commonly on snakes, francolins, doves, rodents, and dung beetles.

---

321 Lizard Buzzard

Kaupifalco monogrammicus

Description: A fairly small gray hawk, with a distinct *black line on a white throat.* Appears large-headed; *base of bill and legs bright red.* Belly heavily barred black and white. Flight reveals white rump and boldly banded black and white tail. L 14″ (35 cm); W 3′ (90 cm).

Similar Species: Larger **chanting-goshawks** lack distinct black throat stripe and heavily banded tail. Much larger **African Harrier-Hawk** *(Polyboroides typus),* of sub-Saharan Africa, is also gray, but has bare, bright yellow or red face.

Voice: A loud *pee-oh* repeated for up to 15 seconds from perch. Voice imitated by robin-chats.

Habitat: Wet broad-leafed woodlands with tall grasses in lowlands. Also gallery forests and wooded farmlands.

Nesting: Builds a small stick nest hidden in a

fork well below the canopy of a leafy tree. Usually lays 2 eggs.

Range: Common in wetter zones from Senegal east to s Sudan; less common from Kenya south to Natal and Angola.

Often seen perched in a dead tree or on a pole, staring down into dense grass, the Lizard Buzzard swoops down to catch lizards, skinks, small snakes, grasshoppers, and small birds.

322 Augur Buzzard
Buteo augur

Description: A spectacular highland raptor, black above, *white below.* Male has black on throat. Barred white flight feathers form patch when at rest. In flight, from below appears all white, except for black outline at wing edges and *short red tail.* Some 10 percent of adults in wet forest areas are all black. Immature brown, with streaks and spots. L 21″ (53 cm); W 4′4″ (1.3 m).

Similar Species: **Jackal Buzzard** *(B. rufofuscus),* of South Africa, Lesotho, Swaziland, and s Namibia, is black and chestnut below, with thin white "bow tie" on upper chest; call resembles bark of a jackal.

Voice: Frequent, crowing *ah-aow, ah-aow.*

Habitat: Mountains and plains with isolated hills. Chiefly above 3,300′ (1,000 m). Sometimes hunts in forests, but mainly in grasslands below forests and moors.

Nesting: Pairs intensely defend territories. Stick nest placed on a cliff or in a tree. Will use 1 of 3 nests for a few years, then return to one of the others.

Range: Eritrea south through e African highlands to Zimbabwe. Isolated populations in w Angola and c Namibia.

A fairly common hawk that sits on fences, poles, and exotic trees in highland and plateau farming country, the Augur Buzzard is particularly common in the rift valleys and along routes to major national parks from Nairobi (Kenya), Arusha (Tanzania), and Addis Ababa (Ethiopia). Often seen hovering over fields with its head to the wind, it gracefully descends with its wings held up in a "parachute." It preys on rodents, hares, hyraxes, birds, snakes, lizards, frogs, and grasshoppers.

---

323 **Tawny Eagle**
Aquila rapax

Description: A large, variably colored, dry-country eagle, with heavily feathered "boots" covering legs. Many adults and immatures (particularly in south) are *pale buff,* including shoulders. Others are *clear tawny orange,* some with black-spotted shoulders; others are *dark chestnut brown,* with black striping. Flight feathers and rounded tail dark brown; large feet yellow; cere and gape yellow. Immature shows thin white lines at base of flight feathers, on trailing edge of wings, and on rump. L 29″ (72 cm); W 8′ (2.4 m).

Similar Species: Smaller **Wahlberg's Eagle** *(A. wahlbergi)* is usually dark brown, with small crest and square tail; breeds in rainy seasons from Ethiopia south to Natal, migrating through e Africa to live from Senegal to Ethiopia in summer rainy season north of equator. Closely related **Steppe Eagle** has longer gape; immature has broad white bands on wing.

Voice: Generally silent, but gives a *kwuk-kwuk* when defending territory.

Habitat: Dry lowlands and plateaus to 8,200′ (2,500 m). Prefers open plains, thornbush, semi-deserts, acacia savannas, and water holes.

Nesting: Builds a broad shallow stick nest atop a tree or utility pole.

Range: Northern Africa; Senegal and n Ivory Coast east to Somalia; much of e Africa south to Kalahari Desert and Natal. Some movement into drier areas during rainy season.

The common brown eagle of Africa, the Tawny Eagle may be seen in dead trees, at watersides, and circling in the sky. A powerful killing machine, it takes live mongooses, dik-diks, hares, baby gazelles, rodents, high-flying flamingos, bustards, lizards, snakes, locusts, and flying termites. Ever hungry, it also scavenges roadkills and chases vultures from carcasses. A compulsive thief, it snatches prey from larger eagles and storks. The northern and western African race lives with man in villages, camps, and livestock pens.

324 Steppe Eagle
Aquila nipalensis

Description: A common migrant eagle from Eurasian steppes. Adult dark brown, with long, *orange-yellow gape extending to rear of eye.* Immature more distinctive; paler brown, with *2 wide white bands on secondaries* merging into large white patch at base of primaries; white rump. L 30″ (75 cm); W 8′8″ (2.6 m).

Similar Species: **Tawny Eagle** has shorter gape; immature has far less white on wings. **Lesser Spotted Eagle** *(A. pomarina),* of se Europe and Turkey, migrates via Sinai to spend summer months from Tanzania south to Okavango Delta and Natal; adult is dark brown, with "boots" covering part of legs.

Voice: Usually silent in Africa.

Habitat: Open grassy plains, thorn scrub, mountains, and forest edges.

Nesting: Breeds in steppes from Ukraine east into c Asia.

Range: Migrates through Egypt and Ethiopia in October. Flocks (chiefly of immatures) continue south through plains of e Africa to Kalahari Desert.

Any flocks of eagles from October through April are likely to be this species, which will join Black Kites and other birds to feed on irruptions of winged termites. They flock, along with Tawny Eagles, to nesting swarms of Red-billed Queleas to snatch nestlings.

---

325 **Verreaux's Eagle**
Black Eagle
Aquila verreauxii

Description: A very large, *jet-black* eagle of open rocky mountains. Black adult plumage accented by *large white rump patch extending to white lines on shoulders.* Large white patch at base of primaries visible in flight. Bare yellow lores, eye ring, and cere. Heavy black "boots" and yellow feet. Immature has rufous crown and nape, black chest, and spotted white "boots." L 34″ (85 cm); W 8′2″ (2.45 m).

Similar Species: Most other eagles are dark or light brown, with smaller white rump patches. **Long-crested Eagle** has long crest and white bands on tail.

Voice: Alarm calls include a loud *kok-kok-kok* and a ringing *whaee-whaee-whaee.*

Habitat: Open mountainsides, gorges, and inselbergs to 16,000′ (5,000 m).

Nesting: Performs spectacular aerial courtship displays with deep dives and upward swoops. Builds an enormous stick nest up to 10′ (3 m) wide on a cliff. Older chick usually kills sibling.

Range: Resident in Sinai, Sahara (locally), and widely from Red Sea south through e African highlands to coasts of Namibia and South Africa.

A magnificent flyer, soaring by cliffs and ridges with wings held up in a dihedral, this bird seizes hyraxes (98 percent of its diet in some areas) and will also take dik-diks, Klipspringers, hares, francolins, and guineafowl.

326 **African Hawk-Eagle**
Hieraaetus spilogaster

Description: Black above, white below, *with heavy black streaks on chest.* In flight, *black underwing linings* contrast with white flight feathers and black wing edging. Long gray tail with thin gray bands and wide black terminal band. Juvenile rusty on head, breast, and underwing linings. L 26″ (65 cm); W 5′ (1.5 m).

Similar Species: A sister species, **Bonelli's Eagle** *(H. fasciatus),* resident in nw Africa, is much less streaked below. **Booted Eagle** *(H. pennatus)* breeds in nw Africa and Cape Province, with Eurasian birds wintering widely south of Sahara; typical bird has white underparts and underwing linings, with black flight feathers.

Voice: Usually silent, but will give a *klu-klu-klu-kluuee.*

Habitat: Isolated forested mountains in open country, dense thornbush, savannas, and riverine forests. Not rain forests.

Nesting: Pairs mate for life. Rebuild and reuse a massive, shaded stick nest in a tree or on a cliff, raising 1 young per year.

Range: Senegal east to Ethiopia, and south to Namibia and Swaziland.

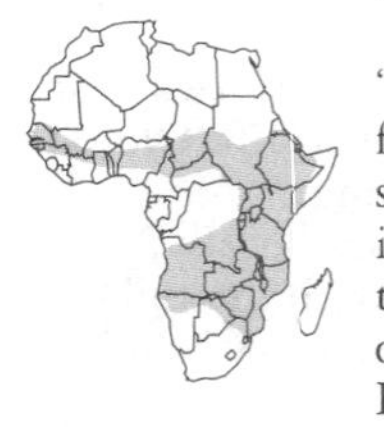

"A big eagle in a small package," this fierce hunter is a fast flier that on sighting prey pursues it to the end, even if forced to run on foot. Pairs often hunt together, one flushing, the other seizing on the other side of a tree. The African Hawk-Eagle feeds chiefly on birds, plus dik-diks, hyraxes, hares, mongooses, and ground squirrels.

327 **Long-crested Eagle**
Spizaetus (Lophaetus) occipitalis

Description: *All-black body, with long waving crest on head.* White bands on fairly long tail, and extensive white under primaries. "Boots" over yellow feet may be white or black. Eye, cere, and gape bright yellow. L 22″ (56 cm); W 4′ (1.2 m).

Similar Species: Long-crested is only African eagle with a long crest. **Bateleur** has bare red face and extremely short tail.

Voice: Quite vocal; gives a high-pitched scream, and a long series of *kik* notes.

Habitat: Woodlands, forest edges, tree plantations, gardens, and swampy grasslands with tall trees. Most common in lowlands; spotty in highlands.

Nesting: Builds a small stick nest (which may be hidden in clumps of mistletoe) in a tall tree. Usually raises 2 young.

Range: Gambia and Ethiopia south to Angola and Zambezi Valley. Also coasts of Indian Ocean from s Somalia to e Cape Province.

The attractive Long-crested Eagle usually perches on a roadside pole or dead tree while searching for rodents. To draw less attention to its nest, it carries its prey in its crop, not in its feet. If rodents are scarce, it either does not breed or moves elsewhere.

328 Martial Eagle
Polemaetus bellicosus

Description: The largest eagle of Africa's savannas. Adult sooty black on head, upper breast, back, and wings. *Breast sharply demarcated from white belly, which is covered with many black spots,* continuing on to "boots." Eyes and feet yellow. Medium-size, black bill with gray cere; small nape crest. Flight reveals *mainly dark underwings.* Small banded tail. Immature (below, at left) has clear white face, underparts, and underwing linings, but black flight feathers. L 32″ (80 cm); W 6′4″ (1.9 m).

Similar Species: Smaller **Black-breasted Snake-Eagle** has pale underwing linings and thinner wings, and lacks breast spots.

Voice: Utters a low whistled *keeeor* from perch.

Both adults and young also give a loud clear *klee-klee-klee-kluee-kluee-kuleee.*

Habitat: Grasslands, arid thornbush, wooded savannas, and cultivated areas. Mainly lowlands below 8,000′ (2,400 m).

Nesting: Builds a stick nest up to 20′ (6 m) wide atop a tall isolated tree, utility pole, or hill. Raises 1 young.

Range: Relatively rare in savanna belt from Senegal east to Ethiopia. More common in its vast e and s African range.

The Martial Eagle spends most of the day soaring at great altitudes with its wings held steady. It can spot prey from great heights and dives down in a long slant. When perched on a tall tree or hilltop boulder, it is often scanning for prey: mammals like dik-diks, Impala calves, mongooses, hares, hyraxes, and ground squirrels, as well as game birds, Egyptian Geese, and monitor lizards.

---

329 Crowned Eagle
Spizaetus (Stephanoaetus) coronatus

Description: The largest and fiercest eagle of Africa's forests. Dark brown head, back, and wings. Head (sometimes), *upper breast, and underwing linings chestnut. Spotty black blotches and barring on breast and thighs ("boots").* Yellow cere and eye; massive yellow feet. Flight reveals white flight feathers with 3 black bands, and banded tail. Juvenile has fairly clear buffy-white head and underparts. *All ages show a laid-back crest on crown.* L 34″ (85 cm); W 5′2″ (1.55 m).

Similar Species: Smaller **Long-crested Eagle** is mainly black and has much longer crest that is usually raised (Crowned Eagle rarely raises its crest); lacks strongly barred underparts.

Voice: Quite vocal. Male utters a far-carrying *keeoowee-keeoowee-keeoowee* in undulating display flight. Female screams *khoi-khoi-khoi,* often from nest.

Habitat: Primarily evergreen forests in both

lowlands and highlands. Less often, but regularly, in riverine forests of savanna country, remnant forests on hills, and miombo woodlands.

Nesting: May perform aerial displays year-round over its territory. Builds an enormous stick nest in a shaded fork of a large forest tree, which may be used for many decades. Raises 1 young.

Range: Guinea east to Togo in w Africa, Nigeria through Zaire to e Africa, and south to e Cape Province.

The Crowned Eagle takes primarily mammals from a quiet forest perch or in aggressive aerial pursuit. When this eagle drops down on forest antelopes, such as duikers, that are heavier than it is, it caches what it can't consume in nearby trees.

SECRETARYBIRD
Family Sagittariidae

This exclusively African family comprises one species, described below.

---

330 **Secretarybird**
Sagittarius serpentarius

Description: A fascinating, long-legged "eagle" of the savannas; a very large, *pearly-gray* raptor, with long, *black, erectile nape feathers.* Yellow cere on typical hooked raptor beak. Bare facial skin may be red, orange, or yellow. Long black "boots" above *very long reddish legs,* with short toes. Pale gray tail with *2 extremely long central tail feathers;* all tail feathers tipped in black and white. Flight reveals pale gray underwings and black flight feathers. L 4′8″ (1.4 m); W 7′ (2.1 m).

Similar Species: **Cranes, herons,** and **bustards** have long straight bills, not short hooked ones.

Voice: Usually silent. Gives a hoarse *grok-grok* at nest and in courtship displays.

Habitat: Grasslands, wooded savannas, and semi-deserts; short and tall grass; grainfields.

Nesting: Up to 6 of these birds may dance like cranes with their wings upheld; pairs defend their territories aggressively. Performs vocal aerial displays. Builds a large stick nest in an isolated, short, thorny tree. Often raises 2 young.

Range: Widespread south of Sahara from Senegal east to Red Sea, where uncommon. More common in e and s Africa, south to Cape Province.

Named for its erectile nape feathers in an era when secretaries stuck quill pens in their wigs, the Secretarybird resembles a crane. Singly or in pairs, it walks randomly and majestically in grasslands, up to 12 miles (20 km) a day. If disturbed, it runs and glides on open wings. It specializes in catching snakes, pelting them with violent blows from its "fisted" feet. The Secretarybird also eats grasshoppers, lizards, rodents, and nestling birds, and uses its crop to carry food back to the nest.

Falcons
Family Falconidae

With their hooked beaks, long talons, and keen eyesight, these raptors resemble hawks and eagles. They differ in internal details, in the appearance of their eggs, in their habit of appropriating the nests of other birds, and in their frequent head-bobbing. Most African species are in the genus *Falco,* and have very pointed wings and fairly long tails. Typical falcons fly very fast, striking birds with "fisted" feet in power-dives. The weaker-footed kestrels are often seen hovering or perched on the lookout for large insects. Of 60 species worldwide, 22 species of falcons are known in Africa and its islands.

331 African Pygmy Falcon
Polihierax semitorquatus

Description: A tiny, shrike-like falcon of thorn scrub. Both sexes grayish above, white below, with red cere, eye ring, and legs. *White face surrounds beady eye.* Thin white banding on black wings and tail. *Female more colorful than male, with rich chestnut patch on back.* Both sexes have white rump and relatively short rounded wings visible in flight. Immature has buffy underparts and nape, but white face. L 8″ (20 cm); W 13″ (33 cm).

Similar Species: Most **shrikes** are slim and show black cap or mask.

Voice: Silent, except in breeding season, when it gives a high-pitched *ki-ki-keek.*

Habitat: Arid thornbush, dry acacia savannas, and plains with scattered trees.

Nesting: Takes over nests of certain weavers. Raises 2 or 3 young.

Range: East Africa from s Ethiopia to c Tanzania. Disjunct paler race in Namibia and Kalahari Desert.

The African Pygmy Falcon is regularly noted at Samburu (Kenya), Serengeti (Tanzania), Etosha (Namibia), and other drier parks, its range tied to that of certain weavers whose nests it takes over. In East Africa, it uses the thorny nest of the White-headed Buffalo-Weaver. In southwestern Africa, it will take over a cavity in the massive communal nests of the Sociable Weaver. This bird typically drops on lizards, insects, small birds, and rodents from an exposed perch over a bare area.

332 Rock Kestrel
Common Kestrel
Falco tinnunculus

Description: The most widespread hovering falcon in Africa. Adult males resident in n Africa and Eurasian winterers in sub-Saharan Africa have *pale gray head, pale rufous back spotted with black,* and *plain gray tail* with black terminal band. Females entirely rufous above, with fine black banding. Both sexes have black "teardrop" line below eye. *Resident sub-Saharan African races much darker,* with dark slaty crown, richer chestnut plumage, heavier black spots above, and heavier streaking below. L 14″ (35 cm); W 32″ (80 cm).

Similar Species: **Lesser Kestrel** *(F. naumanni)* is similar, but male has unspotted rufous back, and lacks black "teardrop" stripe below eye; these gregarious birds breed in nw Africa and s Europe, and spend October to March in semi-arid plains and savannas south of Sahara to South Africa. **Greater Kestrel** *(F. rupicoloides),* of semi-arid grasslands of e and s Africa, has white eye and is buffy with fine black stripes on head, while flanks and back are heavily barred with black.

Voice: A shrill rasping *kree-kree-kree-kree.*

Habitat: Open areas, grasslands, farms, and towns, particularly with rocky areas, scattered trees, and buildings. Adapts well to plantations, highways, and gardens.

Nesting: Does not build nest. Lays 3 or 4 eggs on an earth scrape in a cliff hollow, riverbank, building nook, or nest abandoned by another bird.

Range: Resident races in nw Africa, Canary Islands, Egypt, and most of sub-Saharan Africa to Cape of Good Hope.

Usually seen flying fairly low to the ground in open and lightly wooded areas, Rock Kestrels are gregarious at their wintertime roosts, which are usually on cliffs. Some feed at night by moonlight. When flying they often turn into the wind, hovering with tail spread and wings fanning. These birds specialize in grasshoppers and also feed on swarming termites, small mammals, birds, and lizards.

333 **Gray Kestrel**
Falco ardosiaceus

Description: *Entirely slaty gray, with bright yellow eye ring, legs, and feet.* Indistinct pale bars on flight feathers and tail visible in flight. Yellow cere covers base of black bill. L 13″ (33 cm); W 32″ (80 cm).

Similar Species: **Dickinson's Kestrel** *(F. dickinsoni)* lives in Zambezi Valley, e Tanzania, and south to Swaziland; often found near palms; features white rump and nearly white head.

Voice: Usually silent, but gives a *keek-keek-keek* at nest; sometimes a whistling scream.

Habitat: Lowland tropical savannas, farms, and fields, often near granite kopjes; also clearings in rain forests.

Nesting: Takes over occupied and abandoned Hammerkop nests. Also uses tree holes.

Range: Senegal and much of coastal w Africa east to Eritrea and eastern rift valley of Tanzania, and south to n Zambia and northernmost Namibia.

A shy, solitary species, the Gray Kestrel hunts from high perches, swooping down on grasshoppers and lizards. It does not hover as a typical kestrel does, but pursues birds like cisticolas and longclaws in swift low flight, and also eats rodents, bats, and oil palm fruit.

---

334 **Lanner Falcon**
Falco biarmicus

Description: A fast, powerful falcon with a *rufous crown* on a black head; slaty upperparts. Long black "teardrop" below eye. *Underparts white or buffy, with weak striping in some individuals* (never barred). *Eye ring, cere, and large feet bright yellow.* Juvenile brown above, striped below, with dull rufous crown. L 18″ (45 cm); W 3′10″ (1.15 m).

Similar Species: **Red-necked Falcon** *(F. chicquera)*, widespread in wooded savannas of sub-Saharan Africa, is finely barred above and below in silver; more rufous on hindneck. **Peregrine Falcon** *(F. peregrinus)* has wider "teardrop" below eye, and has solid black crown (without rufous), gray upperparts, and barred underparts; rarer than Lanner as a resident, but others from Eurasia winter throughout Africa. Peregrines have been estimated to fly at up to 200 mph (300 kph) in power dives.

Voice: At breeding sites, gives a loud metallic *chack-chack-chack* and a piercing scream.

Habitat: All types of open country from deserts to wet montane forest edges. Most common in open savannas and grasslands. Also cliffs in forests and up to mountain summits (reaching 15,000′/4,500 m in Ethiopia).

Nesting: Performs spectacular, swift, and noisy aerobatics over nest site, usually a scrape on a cliff ledge. Also uses stick nests abandoned by crows, eagles, or storks. Fledges 2–4 young.

Range: All of Africa, except rain-forest zones. Found even in arid wastes of Sahara and Namib Desert. Resident in some areas, but in w Africa moves north during summer rains.

Some have been lost to falconers, but the Lanner Falcon may be increasing in number due to many new nest sites available on pylons along roads, in eucalyptus plantations, and on city buildings. This raptor seizes birds in flight, sometimes taking them head on; it also flies low to the ground, snatching lizards and rodents, and takes prey on the ground.

PARTRIDGES AND THEIR ALLIES

Order Galliformes

Because of the nutritional and sporting value of some species in this order, they are often termed game birds. Most are stocky, with small heads, plump bodies, and short rounded wings. When flushed, they fly fast and low. There are 264 species worldwide, of which 49 live in Africa.

Partridges
Family Phasianidae

This family includes the partridges, francolins, spurfowl, and quail. Most are small to medium-size, and brownish or grayish. Their short broad bills are adapted for pecking on the ground. They feed on seeds, fruit, and insects and other invertebrates. Large clutches of eggs are laid in ground nests. While the tiny quail are difficult to see, the larger francolins and spurfowl are often conspicuous early and late in the day. These birds prefer to run from danger rather than fly. Of 179 species of partridges worldwide, 43 live in Africa.

335 Red-necked Spurfowl
Francolinus afer

Description: A large spurfowl, with *naked red skin on face, around eye, and on throat; red bill and legs.* Back, wings, and tail solid brown. *Neck and underparts slaty,* with fine white barring in inland northern races. Coastal and southern races heavily striped with black and white on neck and underparts. L 14″ (36 cm).

Similar Species: **Yellow-necked Spurfowl** has yellow throat patch; in flight shows pale rufous wing patch. **Gray-breasted Spurfowl** has pinkish-orange throat patch and gray breast. **Swainson's Francolin** *(F. swainsoni),* common in s Africa, has black legs and is uniformly brown below.

Voice: A loud, repeated *ka-raack* at dawn and dusk.

Habitat: Wooded savannas, thickets, forest edges, streamsides, and gardens.

Nesting: Male courts female with wings lowered

to the ground. Lays up to 9 eggs in a simple scrape at the base of a tree.

Range: Congo east to s Kenya, and south to n Namibia and coastal South Africa.

This bird is usually seen calling from a dead snag or termite mound, or while dust-bathing. It feeds on tubers, shoots, berries, seeds, grain, insects, and ticks, and pecks the dung of buffalos, rhinos, and elephants.

336 Gray-breasted Spurfowl
Francolinus rufopictus

Description: *Naked throat and bare skin around eye pinkish orange. Body gray* with black streaks. Dark brown forehead and crown stripe; white "mustache." *Bill orange;* legs brownish black. L 15″ (37 cm).

Similar Species: **Yellow-necked Spurfowl** has black bill and yellow skin on throat. **Red-necked Spurfowl** has red legs, bill, and throat skin.

Voice: A series of loud, grating *ka-waark* notes. A high-pitched cackle when alarmed.

Habitat: Open grasslands and thickets.

Nesting: Lays up to 5 eggs in a scrape in long grass.

Range: Restricted to n Tanzania, chiefly in s Serengeti NP and w Ngorongoro Conservation Area.

This spurfowl feeds on sedge tubers, seeds, grasshoppers, and termites. It is regularly seen near lodges and camps in Serengeti in mixed grasslands and acacia woodlands.

337 Yellow-necked Spurfowl
Francolinus leucoscepus

Description: Bare skin around eye orange; *bare throat patch bright yellow.* Bill black with red base; legs yellowish brown. Body dark brown above, buffy brown below, with pale buffy streaks. Pale buffy wing patch visible in flight. L 14″ (35 cm).

Similar Species: Only spurfowl with a yellow throat.

Voice: A series of loud, grating *ko-waark* notes. Vocal after dawn and before dusk from ground or open perches.

Habitat: Variety of bushed grasslands in both semi-arid and moist areas, but not tall grasslands. Also riverine thickets, forest edges, and some cultivated areas.

Nesting: Courting male runs around female with open wings and lowered head. Lays 5 eggs in a nest scrape on the ground.

Range: Southern Eritrea and n Somalia south through Ethiopia and Kenya to Tarangire NP area of ne Tanzania.

This bird feeds on sedge tubers in dry months, seeds and insects in wet periods. It joins other birds in chasing flying termites as they leave their nest hole. As the Yellow-necked Spurfowl is snared for its meat near many villages, it is more common in wilder areas.

---

338 Red-billed Francolin
Francolinus adspersus

Description: Brownish gray, with numerous fine white bars on neck and underparts. *Bill bright red. Skin around eye bare yellow,* intensified by black lores and forehead. *Legs red.* L 14″ (35 cm).

Similar Species: **Swainson's Francolin** *(F. swainsoni)* of s Africa has black bill, bare red skin around eye and on front of neck, and black legs. Southern **Red-necked Spurfowl** has white stripes (not bars) on body, and has bare red skin around eye.

Voice: Gives a hoarse cackle, *ka-waark,* up to 10 times at dawn and dusk.

Habitat: Most common near watercourses. Inhabits floodplains, mixed woodlands, thickets, and open areas near cover.

Nesting: Males call to attract females to their territory. Nest is a scraped hollow under a bush, where around 6 eggs are laid.

Range: Most of Namibia and Botswana, s Angola, sw Zambia, and w Zimbabwe.

Less furtive than other francolins, the Red-billed may be seen any time of day in dirt tracks and open areas. It is common in the Okavango Delta and the Chobe (Botswana) and Etosha (Namibia) areas.

---

339 Crested Francolin
Francolinus sephaena

Description: *Rounded solid black or brown crown, contrasting with clear white line over eye and dark line through eye.* Rufous neck and upperparts, with heavy white streaks; underparts buff with dark brown spots. Small blackish bill; red legs (male has spurs). L 14″ (34 cm).

Similar Species: **Stone Partridge** *(Ptilopachus petrosus)* is entirely gray, without eye stripe; has longer black tail, often cocked up over its back; inhabits brush-covered rocky hills from Senegal to nw Kenya.

Voice: A high cackling *kerra-kreek,* repeated about 8 times. If one calls, all neighbors join in.

Habitat: Thickets, woodlands, streambeds, sparse grass, and cultivated areas.

Nesting: Usually lays 6 eggs in a shallow nest lined with grass under a shrub.

Range: Widespread in e and s Africa, from Ethiopia south to Natal, and west to n Namibia.

This francolin does not show a crest. It is often seen along dirt tracks in national parks, walking slowly with its tail cocked up at a 45-degree angle.

---

340 Coqui Francolin
Francolinus coqui

Description: *A small francolin, with a small, yellow-based, black bill and bright yellow legs. Male has plain, buffy-orange head,* with chestnut crown; underparts barred black and white. Distinctive female has white eye line, and white throat bordered with black. L 11″ (28 cm).

Similar Species: In s Africa, several francolins have orange on head like male Coqui, but are much larger, with different white patterns on head. Both sexes of **Common Quail** *(Coturnix coturnix)* have harlequin face patterns like female Coqui, though are much smaller.

Voice: Repeats its name, a loud *co-qui.* Also gives harsher calls like other francolins.

Habitat: Open grasslands and acacia savannas with scattered bushes or small trees. Prefers sandy areas without rocks.

Nesting: Usually lays 4 or 5 eggs in a shallow, grass-lined scrape under a tuft of grass.

Range: 3 disjunct areas: widely south of equator from c Kenya south to Natal and up to mouth of Congo; s Ethiopia; and Sahel grasslands from s Mauritania east to Lake Chad.

The Coqui Francolin is rare in the Sahel due to extreme overgrazing of grasslands by domestic animals, but it is fairly common in many reserves of eastern and southern Africa. It feeds on seeds, young leaves, beetles, ticks, and ants. These birds are usually seen in pairs or coveys.

Guineafowl
Family Numididae

These fairly large birds have black and white spotted plumage. Many have feathered crests or prominent bony casques on the head, which is small, bare, and often brightly colored. The sexes are alike. Outside the breeding season, they wander around in large flocks. The six species of guineafowl are restricted to Africa.

341 Helmeted Guineafowl
Numida meleagris

Description: *Blackish, with abundant white spots over entire plumage. Bright blue, white, and/or red bare skin on head, with bony casque on crown.* Face color, shape of throat wattle, and shape and color of casque vary widely around Africa. L 22″ (56 cm).

Similar Species: Much shier **Crested Guineafowl** *(Guttera pucherani)* has tufts of curly black feathers on crown; neck color varies from bare blue skin with blue spots (e Africa) to solid black with white face wattles (s Africa). Lives in wetter forests and dense thickets from Guinea east to Kenya, and south to Natal.

Voice: A grating, staccato *krak-krak-krak-krak, kridi-kridi-kridi-kridi.* In tall grass, male gives a soft *cheeng-cheeng;* female answers with a 2-note *buck-wheat.*

Habitat: All types of open and wooded grasslands, from moist to semi-arid; some forests, but not rain forests. Also cultivated areas where water and cover are available.

Nesting: Males viciously fight each other over females. Female makes a scrape in dense cover and lines it with feathers and grass. Lays up to 12 eggs, but some communal nests have up to 50 eggs.

Range: Most of sub-Saharan Africa, except rain forests and Horn of Africa. Local in Morocco. Introduced into w Cape Province, Comoros, and Madagascar.

At night these birds roost in groups in trees, at dawn flying down to walk toward water. They feed on seeds, sedge tubers, and insects, especially grasshoppers and termites. Helmeted Guineafowl eat maize kernels and strip seedheads of sorghum and millet.

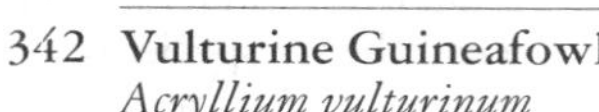

342 Vulturine Guineafowl
Acryllium vulturinum

Description: *A large, long-tailed guineafowl. Bare black head has chestnut nape feathers and no casque. Brilliant blue upper back and breast overlaid with long narrow blue, black, and white plumes.* Rest of body and wings black with white spots. L 24″ (60 cm).

Similar Species: **Helmeted Guineafowl** has colorful face and casque, but lacks blue on back and breast.

Voice: Usually silent, though will give a metallic *kak-kak-kak-kak-kak-kak-kak.*

Habitat: Semi-arid scrub and grasslands.

Nesting: Lays up to 15 eggs in a scrape on the ground under thick grass or a bush.

Range: Most of Somalia, s Ethiopia, n and ne Kenya, and ne Tanzania.

Vulturine Guineafowl roam about in flocks of up to several dozen birds in the dry season, roosting communally in trees at night. This bird does not need to drink water, obtaining it from its diet of seeds, leaves, berries, fruit, shoots, insects, scorpions, and spiders. It is fairly common and tame in such Kenyan parks as Tsavo, Meru, and Samburu.

CRANES AND THEIR ALLIES

Order Gruiformes

This order is a highly diverse "mixed bag" of 12 seemingly unrelated families that share common skeletal characteristics. In addition to the crane, rail, and bustard families presented below, Africa is home to the Mesites (Mesitornithidae family, three species restricted to Madagascar), five species of buttonquail (Turnicidae), and the African Finfoot *(Podica senegalensis)* of the finfoot family (Heliornithidae). Of the world's 198 species, 59 live in Africa.

CRANES

Family Gruidae

Cranes are very large, long-legged birds with relatively short straight bills. They inhabit grasslands, marshes, and riverbeds, sometimes in large flocks in the nonbreeding season. They pair for life, and perform elaborate dancing displays. Their calls include loud trumpeting and honking. Their wingbeats are slow and stiff as they fly in lines or Vs with their necks extended. Of 15 species worldwide, six live in Africa.

343 **Wattled Crane**
Bugeranus carunculatus

Description: *Large, with a long white neck, black cap, bare red facial skin, and white, feathered, pendant wattle on the throat.* Pale gray wings and back; black belly and legs. Elongated inner secondary wing feathers look like a long tail. L 4′ (1.2 m).

Similar Species: **Blue Crane** has white crown and is uniformly blue-gray elsewhere. **Woolly-necked Stork** has longer beak and black wings, and lacks wattle.

Voice: In courtship, both sexes give a shrill call in unison, coiling the head over the back and extending the head and bill upward.

Habitat: Extensive open wetlands and grasslands.

Nesting: Performs a wild courtship dance, with high jumps in the air, bowing, tossing grass into the air, and calling in unison. Builds an enormous grass nest low in a marsh. In s Africa, breeds in winter. Raises 1 or 2 young.

Range: Isolated populations in Ethiopian highlands, s Tanzania, Angola, Zambia, nw Botswana, s Transvaal, and uplands of Natal.

The Wattled Crane is a threatened species, with only several thousand pairs left. It will form flocks, often preferring to join other birds and grazing mammals, and is nomadic in response to flood and drought cycles. When feeding, it often places its head and neck in the water. It eats sedge tubers, rhizomes, seeds, insects, and frogs.

344 **Blue Crane**
Anthropoides paradisea

Description: *A uniformly blue-gray crane, with a white cap on an oversized head.* Beady brown eye and fairly short pink bill; legs and feet dusky. Adult has greatly elongated, black, inner secondary wing feathers that arch over a short tail and often drag on the ground. Immature has brown crown and white head. L 3′4″ (1 m).

Similar Species: **Other cranes** have head ornamentation. **Gray Heron** has longer beak, and black eyebrow and stripes on head.

Voice: Raspy calls and a loud nasal *kraaank.*

Habitat: Grainfields and open grasslands, often far from water; also marshes, river edges, and shallow waters.

Nesting: Performs an elaborate courtship dance: running in circles, jumping with wings flapping, calling, and tossing grass in the air. Usually lays 2 eggs in a simple nest lined with reeds or stones in a shallow marsh or dry field.

Range: Western Transvaal, upland Natal, s Orange Free State, e and s Cape Province, and Etosha NP, in n Namibia.

The national bird of South Africa, the Blue Crane has recently begun living in grainfields, but its numbers are decreasing slowly. It strips seedheads from grasses, digs for tubers, and takes locusts, grasshoppers, crabs, worms, and frogs. These birds fly and soar well, forming flocks in the nonbreeding season.

345, 346 **Gray Crowned Crane**
Southern Crowned Crane
Balearica regulorum

Description: *Golden bonnet of straw-colored feathers on crown. Large patch of bare white skin on head, with red spot above. Large red throat wattle; pale gray neck.* Black forecrown and chin. Back and underparts sooty gray; large white and straw-colored wing patches. Legs and feet black. L 3′6″ (1.05 m).

Similar Species: **Black Crowned Crane** *(B. pavonina)* has black neck; naked area on head is white above, pink below; ranges in a band from Senegal east to Ethiopia, and south to n Uganda.

Voice: Alarm call is *ya-oo-goo-lung.* Unison calls include a low-pitched booming.

Habitat: Grasslands, flooded plains, marshes, grainfields, and watersides.

Nesting: Performs a wonderful courtship dance: bowing, jumping, and tossing objects into the air while calling and circling. Lays 2 or 3 eggs in a bulky sedge nest in a marsh.

Range: Much of Uganda and Kenya south to Natal, and west to n Namibia.

This is one of Africa's most spectacular birds. It strips seedheads from grasses, stamps its feet to attract insects, and often joins grazing mammals for flushed insects.

Rails
Family Rallidae

This is a family of small to medium-size, secretive birds of marshes and shallow lakes. Most are drab gray, brown, or slaty, and many have colorful beaks and legs. Their bodies are laterally compressed (thus "thin as a rail"). Most have distinctive calls. This large family comprises birds with varied group names: Rails usually run from danger with the tail raised, rather than fly; they have longer, thinner beaks than crakes. Coots, which resemble ducks by swimming in open water, are slaty with white beaks. Gallinules and swamphens are purplish or slaty, and walk in open marshland. Of 132 species worldwide, 26 have been recorded in Africa.

347 African Black Crake
Black Crake
Amaurornis (Porzana) flavirostris

Description: Adult dark slaty black, *with bright yellow beak; bright red eye ring; pink legs and feet.* Immature olive-brown above, slaty below, with white throat and blackish beak. L 8″ (20 cm).

Similar Species: Larger **Common Moorhen** *(Gallinula chloropus)* has red bill and distinct white stripes on flanks; swims frequently and ranges widely in African waterways. **Red-knobbed Coot** has white bill.

Voice: Typically a duet: one bird gives a *krrok-krraa-krrok-krraa,* while its mate joins in with loud *krooo* calls.

Habitat: Swampy habitats such as reedbeds, papyrus beds, wooded streamsides, and ponds with water lilies.

Nesting: Lays 3 eggs in a woven nest of reeds and sedges. Young are tended by both parents.

Range: Widely in sub-Saharan Africa south to Cape Town.

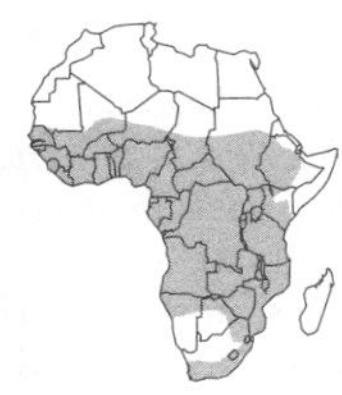

This attractive crake is regularly seen walking on open muddy shores at any time of day and on lawns surrounding resort lakes. The African Black Crake feeds on insects, snails, frogs, worms, and seeds, sometimes from the backs of hippos and warthogs. It swims well and can escape danger by diving.

348 Purple Swamphen
Purple Gallinule
Porphyrio porphyrio

Description: A large, chicken-like marsh bird. *Adult bluish purple, except for olive-brown back. Heavy forehead shield, bill, legs, and long toes all bright red.* Contrasting white undertail coverts. Sub-adult mixed gray and blue. L 18″ (45 cm).

Similar Species: Much smaller and shyer **Allen's Gallinule** *(P. alleni)* is similar, but both sexes have greenish-blue frontal shield; ranges south of Sahara except driest areas.

Voice: A wide variety of harsh shrieks, rattles, trumpets, and wails.

Habitat: Permanent freshwater swamps, lakes, and rivers with dense vegetation.

Nesting: Courting male presents a reed to female while bowing and flapping wings. Lays 3 eggs in a bulky reed nest with a roof of bent-over stems, built in a marsh.

Range: Spotty in n and w Africa. Widespread from Kenya south to Cape Town; also Madagascar.

The largest rail in Africa, the Purple Swamphen feeds on shoots and tubers of water lilies and other water plants, grasping with the feet while stripping with the bill. It also feeds on leaves, seeds, leeches, snails, and frogs.

---

349 **Red-knobbed Coot**
Crested Coot
Fulica cristata

Description: *A slaty-black, duck-like bird. Forehead shield and bill white, with pale blue bill tip. Red eye and 2 small, bulbous, red "bubbles" on crown above shield.* Undertail coverts slaty. Feet lobed along toes, not webbed (see below). In nonbreeding season, red "bubbles" may be absent. L 18″ (44 cm).

Similar Species: **Eurasian Coot** *(F. atra)* breeds in n Africa and Egypt, and winters from Senegal east to Sudan; never shows red "bubbles," and has white leading and trailing edges on wings in flight.

Voice: A harsh metallic *klaak,* along with other sharp shrill notes.

Habitat: Still freshwater ponds, lakes, and dams, plus reed and papyrus swamps.

Nesting: A solitary nester, aggressively charging rivals in water. Lays 4–6 eggs in an unconcealed, floating, bulky reed nest lined with finer grass. Builds false nests.

Range: Certain rift valley lakes and dams in e and s Africa. Local in Morocco, Ethiopian highlands, and Madagascar.

Unlike other rails, coots spend much time swimming on the water surface and diving frequently. If you observe them walking on mudflats, note the unusual lobes around, but not between, each of their toes (grebes also have lobed feet). The Red-knobbed Coot feeds on waterweeds, algae, leaves, stems, flowers, seeds, insects, and snails.

Bustards
Family Otididae

These medium to very large, long-legged birds resemble short-tailed turkeys or giant chickens. Bustards have short straight bills and long necks. They walk grasslands with the head and neck waving forward and back like a cobra in a basket. When flushed they fly with slow jerky wingbeats, low to the ground. Smaller bustards are called *korhaans* in southern Africa. Eighteen of the world's 22 bustards live in Africa, with a few other species in Europe, Asia, and Australia.

350 **Denham's Bustard**
Stanley's Bustard, Jackson's Bustard
Neotis denhami

Description: A large uncrested bustard, *with black and white stripes on head. Foreneck gray, contrasting with rich orange hindneck.* Back brown; underparts white; wings heavily spotted in black and white. Legs yellow. L 3′6″ (1.04 m).

Similar Species: Larger **Kori Bustard** has black crest and thick gray neck.

Voice: Displaying male gives loud booming and barking sounds; otherwise silent.

Habitat: Grasslands with or without scattered trees, shrublands, dry marshes, arid plains, croplands, and burned areas.

Nesting: In courtship, male fluffs out extensive white breast feathers and struts about. Lays 1 or 2 eggs in a scrape on the ground.

Range: Sahel area of w Africa from Senegal east to Ethiopia; local from Kenya south to vicinity of Cape Town. Range contracting due to hunting pressure.

Often solitary, Denham's Bustard will flock during migration and when food is abundant. It pecks ungulate droppings for dung beetles, and feeds on insects, skinks, small snakes, rodents, bird nestlings, and plants. This bird migrates into and out of areas with erratic rainfall.

351 **Kori Bustard**
Ardeotis kori

Description: An enormous, turkey-like bird. *Face and thick neck gray, with black horizontal crest; black patch at base of neck.* Brown back; white underparts; black and white speckling on shoulders. Long yellow legs. Wings appear chiefly gray in flight. L 4′6″ (1.35 m).

Similar Species: **Arabian Bustard** *(A. arabs),* of Sahel from Senegal to Eritrea, lacks black patch at base of neck.

Voice: Male gives a deep, Lion-like *oom-oom-oom.*

Habitat: Open grasslands, savannas with scattered trees, bushveld, and semi-deserts.

Nesting: In courtship, male raises crest, fluffs out long neck feathers, and erects tail above fluffy white vent plumage, then struts around vibrating and clucking. Female lays 1 or 2 eggs in a bare scrape on the ground.

Range: 2 separate populations: e Africa from s Ethiopia to n Tanzania, and s Africa south of Zambezi. Overhunted and eliminated from many unprotected areas.

One of the world's heaviest flying birds (along with condors, swans, and turkeys), the Kori Bustard flies rarely. It feeds chiefly on grasshoppers, dung beetles, small reptiles, rodents, seeds, roots, and wild melons, though it loves eating small animals toasted in grass fires. Its range coincides with many major reserves, such as Tsavo and Amboseli (Kenya), Ngorongoro and Serengeti (Tanzania), Hwange (Zimbabwe), and Etosha (Namibia).

352 **Black Bustard**
Black Korhaan
Eupodotis afra (afroides)

Description: *Adult male has black head, neck, and underparts; brown back barred with black. Eye ring and bill bright red; large white patch behind eye.* Extensive white on wings. Female brown with black belly. Both sexes have yellow legs. Northern birds smaller, with white in primaries. L 21″ (52 cm).

Similar Species: Male **Black-bellied Bustard** has white stripe on side of neck, and sandy-brown hindneck.

Voice: Male noisy in breeding season, giving loud *ka-raack* notes.

Habitat: Open grasslands and grainfields, scrublands, and dunes.

Nesting: In courtship, male flies over territory in circles, calling loudly; descends to ground in fluttering glide. Female lays 1 egg in a scrape on the ground.

Range: Restricted to s Africa: Botswana, w Transvaal, Orange Free State, Cape Province, Namibia, and sw Angola.

The Black Bustard feeds on insects and other invertebrates, grainheads, and shoots. Males draw attention to themselves; females are difficult to find and flush. These birds are common at Etosha NP in Namibia.

353 **White-bellied Bustard**
White-bellied Korhaan
Eupodotis senegalensis

Description: *Male has white face outlined in black, blue neck and chest, bright red base of bill, and white belly.* Female chiefly buffy orange on head and neck, with red bill and white belly. L 21″ (52 cm).

Similar Species: Male **Blue Bustard** *(E. caerulescens),* of highveld grasslands of South Africa, is dark blue on neck and entire underparts.

Voice: Gives a loud, frog-like *tak-warat.*

Habitat: Lightly wooded savannas, open grasslands, clearings, farmlands, and streamsides.

Nesting: Forms pairs, unlike many other bustards. Male raises crown and throat feathers in a ruff when courting. Female lays 2 eggs in a shallow scrape on the ground.

Range: Disjunct: Sahel from Senegal to Sudan; s Ethiopia south to c Tanzania; Gabon to w Zambia; and e South Africa.

This beautiful, small, blue-necked bustard migrates north when it's raining on the southern edge of the Sahara, and moves to lower elevations during cold periods in South Africa.

---

354 **Black-bellied Bustard**
Black-bellied Korhaan
Eupodotis melanogaster

Description: *In male, underparts and line on foreneck black.* White face and white line down side of neck; black line behind eye. Crown and hindneck sandy brown; heavy black spots and blotches on brown back. Wings largely black and white. Female has grayish head, pale buffy-orange neck, and white belly. Both sexes have black and yellow bill, reddish eyes, and yellow legs. L 26″ (64 cm).

Similar Species: Female **White-bellied Bustard** has buffy-orange head and red bill. Male **Hartlaub's Bustard** *(E. hartlaubii)* of e African highlands is grayer, with black rump in flight, more black and white on back, and black line encircling gray chin. Male **Buff-crested Bustard** (Red-crested Korhaan; *E. ruficrista*) has no black on head or neck; nape is buffy and foreneck gray; Buff-crested ranges widely in semi-deserts and savannas from Senegal east to Somalia, and south to Natal.

Voice: Male gives a loud *quick . . . pop,* with its head retracted into its back before the *pop.*

Habitat: Open and partly treed savannas, tall grasslands, farms, and marsh edges.

Nesting: Courting male advertises by flying with jerky wingbeats, showing off white primary feathers. Female lays 1 or 2 eggs in a shallow scrape.

Range: Widespread in tropical and upland savannas from Senegal east to Ethiopia, and south to Natal.

This bird often allows close approach by vehicles in parks. It feeds on beetles, caterpillars, centipedes, grasshoppers, seeds, and fruit.

GULLS AND THEIR ALLIES
Order Charadriiformes

This order is a collection of diverse waterbird families. Most are small to medium-size, with long legs and long thin bills. Worldwide there are 326 species, with 151 in Africa.

JACANAS
Family Jacanidae

Rufous, black, and white marsh birds, jacanas are also known as "lily-trotters," as their extremely long toes allow them to wade across water lilies. In flight, they flap and glide low to the water, with their long legs and toes trailing behind. The family is pantropical, with eight species worldwide, and three in Africa and Madagascar.

355 **African Jacana**
Actophilornis africana

Description: *Adult bright rufous on back, wings, and underparts; shield on forecrown and straight bill pale blue.* Black line extends from eye, down nape, and onto back. White throat and foreneck ends with golden semi-collar on upper breast. Long gray legs, and long claws on all toes. Immature is all white below. L 11″ (28 cm).

Similar Species: **Lesser Jacana** *(Microparra capensis),* found locally in similar areas, is much smaller (L 6″/15 cm), shyer, and rarer; has rufous crown, white line above eye, and white underparts. **Madagascar Jacana** *(A. albinucha)* has white nape and hindneck behind black face and foreneck.

Voice: A rattling screech on taking off, ending with *kaa-ka-ka-ka* on alighting.

Habitat: Lakes, riversides, marshes, muddy shorelines, and swamps with floating water lilies and water hyacinths.

Nesting: Sex roles reversed. Some females pursue a single male, with male incubating eggs and caring for young. Other females may gather several males and provide eggs for each of their nests. Male's underwing brood pouch allows him to carry all 4 young long distances over lilies; their outsized legs and feet can be seen dangling down under the wing (a ten-legged bird!).

Range: Resident in most of sub-Saharan Africa from Senegal east to Ethiopia, and south to Natal. Lives to 6,600′ (2,000 m) on highland lakes.

This bird turns over the undersides of water plants for small clinging insects and mollusks, and takes bees, flies, spiders, and other invertebrates in reeds and from the backs of hippos.

Crabplover
Family Dromadidae

This family comprises one species, described below.

356 Crabplover
Dromas ardeola

Description: *A largely white wader of Indian Ocean shores, with largely white wings. Black back and primaries; large white head set off by large black eye; heavy, dagger-like bill.* Long gray legs trail behind tail in flight. Immature has gray crown and hindneck. L 15″ (38 cm).

Similar Species: **Black-capped Avocet** has black cap and thin upturned bill. **Black-winged Stilt** is solid black on back and wings, and has thin straight bill and long red legs.

Voice: A loud barking *kwa-how* on mudflats. A loud *chuck-chuck* at breeding dunes. Young beg with whistles and wheezing, like young gulls.

Habitat: Indian Ocean and island sandbanks, beaches, mudflats, and mangroves.

Nesting: Nests in colonies, building honeycombed burrows in remote coastal sand dunes. Digs down and then upward to a cool dark nest chamber, where 1 egg is laid.

Range: Breeds chiefly in Somalia, and north along Red Sea to Sudan. Ranges southward along coasts of Kenya, Tanzania, and Mozambique, plus Seychelles, Comoros, and w Madagascar outside breeding season.

Crabplovers, which resemble thick-knees (see below) in shape, fly in tight flocks low to the water. Communal groups roost and feed together, at low tide dining on crabs, other crustaceans, mollusks, and marine worms. A classic spot to see them is Mida Creek, south of the town of Malindi, Kenya.

STILTS
Family Recurvirostridae

Fairly large black and white waders with long thin legs and bills, the members of this family wade about shorelines and salty shallow waters with long strides, looking for aquatic invertebrates. Stilts have straight bills, while avocets have sharply upturned bills. Taxonomists argue about the number of stilt species in the world—there are between two and seven, with one in Africa. There are four species of avocets worldwide, one in Africa.

357 Black-winged Stilt
Himantopus himantopus

Description: *Breeding adult has white head, neck, and underparts, contrasting with solid black back and wings.* Straight black beak fairly long and thin; eye red. *In flight, extremely long red legs trail beyond tail.* In nonbreeding season, gray on crown and nape. Immature duller, with pinkish-gray legs. L 15″ (38 cm).

Similar Species: **Black-capped Avocet** has black cap, strongly upturned bill, white on wings, and dull blue legs.

Voice: Call is an excited *kik-kik-kik-kik-kik.*

Habitat: Shallow marshes, estuaries, mudflats, and edges of salt lakes.

Nesting: Courtship involves fluttering in the air and dancing about. Pairs may nest alone or in loose colonies. Nest is a scrape on dry ground, or a mat of grasses floating in shallow water. Incubates 4 eggs.

Range: Widespread in coastal n Africa, Nile Valley, most of sub-Saharan Africa (except desert and rain-forest areas), and Madagascar.

This stilt is usually seen in small parties, probing mud with its bill or wading in shallows up to its knees or belly. It feeds on flies, water beetles, dragonflies, worms, crustaceans, spiders, tadpoles, frog spawn, and minnows, and sleeps standing on one leg or on its knees.

---

358 **Black-capped Avocet**
Pied Avocet
Recurvirostra avosetta

Description: *A large pied wader, with a black cap that continues down the hindneck. Long, thin, strongly up-curved bill.* Throat, neck, back, and underparts snowy white; wings are mix of black and white. Long legs dull blue. Immature has gray on crown, back, and wings. L 17″ (42 cm).

Similar Species: **Black-winged Stilt** has red legs, straight bill, and uniformly black back.

Voice: Calls include *kooit-kooit* and *kik-kik.*

Habitat: Though often seen with stilts, avocets prefer saltier lakes and estuaries devoid of marsh grass.

Nesting: In a marvelous group courtship, up to 20 birds form a circle facing inward. There they bow and bob, sweep bills from side to side, peck at the water, and shake heads while calling. Lays 3 or 4 eggs in scrape nest, in loose colonies of 10–200 birds.

Range: Resident in coastal salt lagoons of n Africa, Sahel from Senegal east to Somalia, and south through e and c Africa to Cape Town.

The Black-capped Avocet regularly swims, like a duck, with its breast low in the water. It also walks in shallow water, swinging its head from side to side as it locates its prey by touch. Feeding chiefly on larval and adult midges and brine flies, beetles, crustaceans, and worms, the bird also takes large minnows.

Thick-knees
Family Burhinidae

These large brownish or gray-speckled, lapwing-like birds have stout straight bills and long legs. Their knees are swollen, and they have three forward toes, but no hind toe. Thick-knees often rest under a bush or in thick grass by day. Their large yellow eyes are adapted for their nocturnal habits; at night, they walk around catching invertebrates. In South Africa, a thick-knee is called a *dikkop* (thick-head). Of the world's nine species, four live in Africa.

359 **Water Thick-knee**
Burhinus vermiculatus

Description: *A large, long-tailed, brown bird, with long, greenish-yellow legs; short black bill; large yellow eyes. Large gray wing patch outlined by horizontal black and white band.* White throat, and white stripes above and below eye. Fine black stripes, with thin blackish crossbars, overlie brown back and buffy breast; belly white. 16″ (40 cm).

Similar Species: **Senegal Thick-knee** *(B. senegalensis)* is very similar, but has longer, heavier bill with more yellow at base, and whiter wing patch; widespread near waters north of equator from Senegal east to nw Kenya and Ethiopia, and north along Nile through Egypt. **Spotted Thick-knee** *(B. capensis)* avoids watersides, preferring barren, sandy or stony areas and grasslands with scattered trees in sub-Saharan Africa; also brown, it is heavily peppered with large black spots on back and wings, with no pale wing patch.

Voice: A single harsh *wheee,* or a 3-note *whee-you-ee,* given at night.

Habitat: Watersides: muddy and grassy shores of permanent rivers and lakes with bush or forest cover nearby; also mangroves, beaches, and exposed rocks in rivers.

Nesting: Lays 2 eggs in an exposed, scraped-out hollow in sand, usually near driftwood or a bush. Nests in dry season.

Range: Widespread south of equator from Congo River and c Kenya south to n Namibia, Okavango Delta of n Botswana, and coastal South Africa. Also local north of equator from Liberia to Gabon, and in Somalia.

This serious-looking bird, found in small groups near most hippopotamus sites, is reluctant to fly. When flushed, it runs with its head low, or flies off after a running start, using rapid shallow wingbeats. It feeds at night on insects, crustaceans, and mollusks.

Coursers and Pratincoles
Family Glareolidae

These small to medium-size birds of open country have short arched bills, wide gapes, and dark patches or collars on the head, neck, or belly. The 17 species are restricted to the Eastern Hemisphere, with 12 species found in Africa. Coursers run over grasslands and then stand upright like a thrush. Some species are nocturnal. Pratincoles have long pointed wings; they fly by day over waterways and grasslands, hawking aerial insects.

360 Crocodilebird
Egyptian Courser, Egyptian Plover
Pluvianus aegyptius

Description: *White eyebrow and throat contrast with black crown, hindneck, midback, and collar on chest. Rich buffy underparts and silver wings.* Flight reveals white wing feathers with broad black stripe. Short arched bill black; rather short legs blue-gray. L 8″ (20 cm).

Voice: When alarmed, gives a series of high-pitched, harsh *cherk* notes, or a single *wheep.*

Habitat: Riverbeds with sand and gravel bars; sometimes lake edges in wet seasons.

Nesting: Solitary pairs breed in dry season on riverine sandbank islands. Lays 2 or 3 eggs in a scrape made in sand. Often covers eggs with layer of sand, letting sun keep them warm. During heat of day, exposes eggs and stands over them to provide shade, often with dripping-wet breast feathers. Sits on eggs the normal way at night and during periods of cooler temperature.

Range: Widely south of Sahara in Sahel and Guinea savanna zones from Senegal east to Ethiopia and nw Kenya. South of equator only in w Congo Basin. Formerly along Nile in Egypt.

This attractive bird feeds on insects and pieces of dead fish along rivers. Often found with crocodiles, it is said to clean food items from around their teeth, but this has not been proved. The flight of the Crocodilebird is low and jerky. It may be seen in flocks of up to 50 birds outside the breeding season, and is rather comfortable around humans, which results in many being shot.

361 Temminck's Courser
Cursorius temminckii

Description: Unspeckled sandy brown, with thin neck and white, medium-length legs. *Rufous crown and nape; white stripe above large black eye, heavy black line behind. Lower breast chestnut, grading into black V on clear white vent.* Flight feathers black. L 8" (20 cm).

Similar Species: **Cream-colored Courser** *(C. cursor),* of n Africa and southern fringes of Sahara (south to c Kenya), is paler, with gray nape and no dark breast patch. **Burchell's Courser** *(C. rufus),* of Namibia, s Botswana, and w South Africa, has gray nape, thin black line behind eye, and white secondaries visible in flight.

Voice: Contact note is a sharp *perr-perr.*

Habitat: Short grasslands and burned areas.

Nesting: Solitary pair breeds in dry season. Lays 2 eggs on bare ground, standing over them to provide shade in midday heat.

Range: Sahel and Guinea savanna zones of w Africa from Senegal east to Chad. Ethiopia south through e Africa to c Namibia and e South Africa.

Pairs or flocks of this courser can be seen running and stopping in short grass and areas burned by recent fires. They raise and lower their bodies while keeping the head level.

---

362 **Two-banded Courser**
Double-banded Courser
Rhinoptilus (Cursorius) africanus

Description: *A small, short-billed courser, with a pale scaly pattern covering the wings and back.* Body color varies widely from pale sandy to almost rufous; matches local soil color. *2 black "necklaces" around base of neck.* Trailing edge of wings rufous; rump white in flight; legs whitish. L 9″ (22 cm).

Voice: A thin *pee-uu-weet* and a fast *peter-peter-peter-peter-pete.*

Habitat: Open flat semi-deserts, open grasslands with scattered shrubs, and dry riverbeds.

Nesting: In courtship, male walks and dances in semi-circles around female, and stands straight up with head raised. Makes a nest scrape on bare ground, adding antelope droppings and small stones nearby for camouflage. Lays 1 egg.

Range: 3 disjunct populations: Ethiopia and n Somalia; s Kenya and n Tanzania; and Botswana, Namibia, and w South Africa.

This delightful bird often allows close approach by vehicles in reserves. Active by day and on moonlit nights, it runs after harvester termites and other insects on the ground.

PLOVERS
Family Charadriidae

These shorebirds have short straight bills that are flat at the base and have a hard swollen tip. Most have strongly patterned black and/or white patches on the head, neck, or wings. Parents often feign injury to divert a predator from the young. The family comprises two main groups. Typical plovers are small; they run about mudflats and grasslands, stopping every few steps to look about. The much larger lapwings have pied patterns, noisy calls, and a cheeky demeanor; many have wing spurs. Of 64 species worldwide, 27 occur in Africa, including a dozen species that winter here from Eurasian breeding grounds.

---

363 **Crowned Lapwing**
Crowned Plover
Vanellus coronatus

Description: Grayish brown, with white *ring on head bordered by black. Yellow eye;* black-tipped red bill; *long, bright red legs.* Belly, wing stripe, and base of tail white. L 12″ (30 cm).

Similar Species: **Black-winged Lapwing** *(V. melanopterus)* occurs in flocks in short grasslands in Ethiopia, e Africa, and e South Africa; has all-black bill, solid gray head and neck, and white forehead and eye line.

Voice: A loud grating *keer-reet,* given both day and night.

Habitat: Open grasslands, burned areas, lawns, and roadsides; not tied to water.

Nesting: A semi-colonial nester. Lays 2–4 eggs in a scrape on the ground.

Range: Widespread from Ethiopia south through e Africa to all of s Africa.

This commonly seen species tolerates close approach by humans and their vehicles. When a threat is perceived,

it screeches and runs or flies about, warning all birds and game mammals in the vicinity. The Crowned Lapwing is a nomadic breeder, avoiding extreme droughts and the tall grass of wet seasons. It typically takes a number of steps, then stops to seize a cricket, grasshopper, termite, or ant.

364 Wattled Lapwing

Wattled Plover
Vanellus senegallus

Description: Brown body and wings, with *finely striped head and neck. Short yellow wattles (below small red knob) hang from base of chiefly yellow bill.* White forehead, edged in black. Long yellow legs. L 14″ (35 cm).

Similar Species: **White-crowned Lapwing** *(V. albiceps)* has white crown on gray head and neck, and white underparts; inhabits riversides from Senegal south to Transvaal, but absent in most of e Africa.

Voice: A sharp *keep-keep* and a *yip-yip;* harsher shrieks when attacking intruders.

Habitat: Marshes, damp grasslands, and edges of rivers and ponds. Fallow fields and burned areas.

Nesting: Pairs actively defend territories from other lapwings and predators. Lays 3 or 4 eggs in a scrape in mud near water.

Range: Guinea savanna and Sahel zone of w Africa east to Ethiopia. Uganda, sw Kenya, and w Tanzania south to Natal and n Namibia.

The Wattled Lapwing walks slowly, often freezing with one leg raised. It spends much time preening, fluffing up, bathing, and scratching. It feeds on grasshoppers, locusts, dung beetles, crickets, various aquatic insects, and seeds.

365 Blacksmith Lapwing
Blacksmith Plover
Vanellus armatus

Description: Black, white, and gray, without bright colors or wattles. *Snowy white crown, hindneck, and belly. Black nape, face, foreneck, chest, and back.* Black bill and legs. Wings appear mostly gray at rest. Ruby-red eye. L 12″ (30 cm).

Similar Species: **Spur-winged Lapwing** *(V. spinosus)* has black crown, white cheek, and pale brown back; occurs along watersides from Senegal east to Somalia, and from Egypt south to Lake Manyara, in ne Tanzania.

Voice: A long series of *klink* notes, resembling a blacksmith's hammer hitting an anvil.

Habitat: Most open freshwater shorelines, in sand, mud, gravel, or short grasslands.

Nesting: Courtship involves hyperactive running, pecking, flying about in unison, and calling. Lays 2–6 eggs in a small hollow close to shoreline or on an island.

Range: Central Kenya and c Angola south to Cape Town vicinity.

Well known in southern Africa and in the rift valley lakes of East Africa, this noisy and nervous bird warns all the animals about intruders to the wetlands. It forages for insects, worms, mollusks, and small crustaceans by running, stopping, and quickly stabbing in the mud. It also works over the droppings of cattle and other mammals for larvae.

366 Kittlitz's Plover
Charadrius pecuarius

Description: Adult dark sandy brown on crown and back. *Long white eyebrow stripes meet on nape; 3 black bands radiate from eye. Breast washed with robin orange.* Bill and legs black. L 6.5″ (16 cm).

Similar Species: **Chestnut-banded Plover** *(C. pallidus)* is found beside inland salt lakes and coastlines in e and s Africa; adult male has single chestnut band on breast.

Voice: Gives a *tu-wit* in flight.

Habitat: Open sandy and muddy areas and short grasslands far from water.

Nesting: Lays 2 eggs in a scrape in very open area either near or well away from water. Covers eggs with sand when away from nest. Parents walk young out of nesting area 2 days after hatching.

Range: Entire Nile Valley from Egypt southward; sub-Saharan Africa, except rain forests and high mountains; Madagascar; Saint Helena island.

This small plover and its chicks usually freeze on approach of a vehicle, so take care. Kittlitz's Plover feeds on tiny invertebrates, running a few steps and stopping to peck at prey.

---

367 **Three-banded Plover**
Charadrius tricollaris

Description: Upperparts and crown dark, "wet sand" brown. *White band runs from forehead over eye to nape; 2 black chest bands on white underparts. Face and neck gray, with conspicuous red eye ring and red base of bill.* Long, brown, white-bordered tail; pink legs. L 7″ (18 cm).

Similar Species: **Forbes's Plover** *(C. forbesi),* of w Africa from Senegal east through Congo Basin, is very similar, but has brown forehead and is darker above. **Caspian Plover** *(C. asiaticus)* winters in short grasslands of highland Kenya and Serengeti south through Botswana; usually brown with pale eye stripe, it develops wide chestnut breast bands of breeding plumage by February.

Voice: A rising *peeuu-eet,* and a shrill *wick-wick.*

Habitat: Hard rock, gravel, and muddy areas of rivers, streams, lakes, and coastlines. Tolerates shade of trees along waterways more than other plovers.

Nesting: Nest is a scrape located near water in dry mud, in sand, or on hard rock. Usually raises 2 chicks.

Range: Eastern and s Africa from Gabon and

Eritrea south to Cape Town. Also Lake Chad area and Madagascar.

Proliferating due to its use of small dams built in many rural areas, this plover uses its long tail in a variety of courtship displays and threats. The bird calls and flies about at night, and may feed on moonlit nights.

SANDPIPERS
Family Scolopacidae

Sandpipers are a diverse family of small to fairly large, drab-colored birds of coasts, mudflats, and marshes. Larger species, such as curlews and godwits, have longer necks and bills than plovers. Sandpipers are identified by their proportions, patterns, and bill peculiarities more than by color. Many have long thin bills, some strongly downturned or upturned. They often occur in flocks in wet open areas, performing amazing aerobatics in group flights. Of 83 species worldwide, 42 have been found in Africa, but only the African Snipe *(Gallinago nigripennis)* breeds in sub-Saharan Africa. The rest migrate from northern Europe, Asia, and even North America to spend August through May in Africa; a number of first-year and injured individuals remain all year.

368 Ruff
Philomachus pugnax

Description: In nonbreeding plumage, has pale edges on dark brown back feathers. *Thin neck; small head; relatively short black bill with slight droop. Short legs may be yellowish or bright orange.* 2 white oval patches on rump. L male 12″ (30 cm), female 9″ (23 cm).

Similar Species: This is but one of dozens of species of sandpipers that winter widely in both coastal and inland waterways of Africa.

Voice: Usually silent, but may give a *tu-whit* in flight.

Habitat: Mudflats, salt and freshwater lakeshores, riverbeds, and open grasslands.

Nesting: Breeds from w Europe east to e Siberia.

Range: Winters widely in Africa south to Cape Town; rare on Indian Ocean islands.

An estimated 3 million Ruffs winter in Africa, many of them nomadic, given local conditions. Those that breed in eastern Siberia and winter in southern Africa may fly up to 25,000 miles (40,000 km) a year. Often seen in compact flocks, this bird will wade into deep water, sometimes swimming like a phalarope or duck. It feeds on insects, mollusks, crustaceans, and worms.

GULLS
Family Laridae

Gulls are short-legged waterbirds with webbed feet and long pointed wings. There is a wide variety of brownish and grayish immature and sub-adult plumages. Gulls nest in colonies and have harsh calls. Of the 48 species worldwide, 21 are found in Africa. Most breed in Eurasia and winter chiefly north of the equator.

369 Gray-headed Gull
Larus cirrocephalus

Description: *Breeding adult has gray hood and bright red bill and legs;* white eye. Neck, underparts, and tail white; back and wings gray, with white stripe and spot on primaries. Gray head turns white in nonbreeder. L 17″ (42 cm).

Similar Species: **Black-headed Gull** *(L. ridibundus)* winters south to Nigeria and e Africa, on coasts, and on inland lakes and rivers; has black spot behind eye (in winter), white leading edge to primaries above, and black patch under primaries.

Hartlaub's Gull has brown eye; in breeding season, has reddish-black bill and legs, and faint gray hood.

Voice: A harsh *karr.*

Habitat: Coasts, estuaries, marshes, larger lakes (including salt lakes), and open rivers.

Nesting: Undertakes group flights in wide noisy circles around breeding islands in lakes. Lays 2 or 3 eggs on a ground scrape lined with dry grass and sticks, or builds a floating nest of water weeds.

Range: Widespread on Atlantic coast from Banc d'Arguin, Mauritania, south to Ghana; Niger Valley, s Nile, highland lakes of e Africa, and s Africa. Also Madagascar.

Flocks of this gull dip to the water to feed on surface fish. It feeds on mollusks and insect larvae in quiet waters, robs other birds of their fish, scavenges harbors, and preys on the eggs and young of such waterbirds as cormorants, terns, and other gulls.

---

370 Hartlaub's Gull
Larus hartlaubii

Description: *Nonbreeding adult has clear white head, neck, and underparts, with slim black bill and legs.* In breeding season, faint trace of gray hood, and bill and legs become dark reddish black. All adults have brown eyes, gray on back and wings. L 15″ (38 cm).

Similar Species: **Gray-headed Gull** has white eye, bright red legs and bill, and in breeding season distinct gray hood. Much larger **Kelp Gull** *(L. dominicanus)* lives chiefly on South African and Namibian coasts; adult has yellow bill, and black back and wings, with white trailing edge.

Voice: A harsh *kwaarck* and a *kek-kek-kek.*

Habitat: Inshore ocean waters, beaches, intertidal areas, harbors, lawns, and cities.

Nesting: Nests in colonies on islands. Lays 2 or 3 eggs in a nest placed under tall grass or bushes.

Range: Western Cape Province and s Namibia.

Despite its limited distribution, this gull is common on the cool-water coasts of its range. It feeds on fish caught at the sea surface, on shoreline invertebrates, and on offal. This adaptable bird follows tractors in inland fields for worms, catches insects attracted to streetlights, and breeds on buildings in Cape Town.

Terns
Family Sternidae

Terns look like gulls but are usually smaller, with very short and thin pointed bills. Most species are gray and white, with some black on the head, and have forked tails. They hover and then dive headfirst into the water for fish or catch insects in the air. Of 43 species worldwide, 24 are known in Africa. Various localized species breed on African coastlines and offshore islands, and others visit from Eurasia.

371 White-winged Black Tern
Chlidonias leucopterus

Description: *Nonbreeder has black spot behind eye connecting to back of crown;* otherwise is gray above and white below, with white rump, black bill, and reddish legs. L 9″ (23 cm).

Similar Species: Nonbreeding **Whiskered Tern** *(C. hybridus)* has black streak (not spot) behind eye, gray rump, and red at base of bill; in breeding plumage, has black cap, white cheeks, and sooty underparts; breeds in marshes of n Africa, e African highlands, and s Africa.

Voice: A harsh *keck* and *kerr.*

Habitat: Fresh and saltwater lakes, marshes, and inland rivers. Rare on coast.

Nesting: Breeds from se Europe to Ukraine and s Russia east to Pacific Ocean.

Range: Migrates through n Africa and along

Nile Valley to winter widely in sub-Saharan Africa.

This short-tailed tern winters in large flocks at many inland lakes, including rift valley lakes in East Africa. Tight flocks rest on lakeside mudflats or on dead trees in reservoirs. When feeding, the bird gleans insects from the surface of water and land, and from the air.

---

372 **Sooty Tern**
Sterna fuscata

Description: *Adult has jet black cap, eye line, back, wings, and tail,* contrasting with white forehead, underparts, and outer tail streamers. Bill and legs black. L 16″ (41 cm).

Similar Species: **Bridled Tern** *(S. anaethetus)* has longer white eyebrow and is sooty gray on back, wings, and rump; breeds in Gulf of Guinea islands, Mauritania area, Red Sea south to Somalia, and many Indian Ocean islands.

Voice: On breeding islands, air rings day and night with its *ker-wacky-wack* call.

Habitat: Oceanic islands and tropical seas.

Nesting: Breeds in colonies of up to 1 million pairs on remote tropical islands. Lays 1 egg in a shallow unlined scrape.

Range: Breeds on Gulf of Guinea islands, Ascension, and islets off Somalia, Kenya, and Tanzania, plus many islands in Indian Ocean.

The largest colonies of Sooty Terns are at Bird Island in northern Seychelles, with 250,000 pairs, and at Desnoufs island (western Seychelles), with 1 million pairs. The birds arrive in May and desert the islands by October, spending the rest of the year at sea. This tern may sleep on the wing, as it rarely is seen resting on the sea. It catches most of its prey at or just above the surface.

373 **Swift Tern**
Greater Crested Tern
Sterna bergii

Description: *Long, heavy, yellow bill; white forehead; black crown.* Gray above, including forked tail; white below, with black legs. In breeding season, has black crest. L 18″ (46 cm).

Similar Species: **Lesser Crested Tern** *(S. bengalensis)* breeds in e Libya, Red Sea, and Somalia, and winters south to Senegal and Natal; smaller (L 15″/38 cm), with thinner orange bill, and breeder has black forehead and crown. **Royal Tern** *(S. maxima),* of w African coasts, has heavier orange bill. **Sandwich Tern** *(S. sandvicensis)* has black bill with yellow tip; breeds in n Africa, and is common nonbreeder on most coastlines south to Cape Town area.

Voice: Gives a loud *kreee-kreee* at nest.

Habitat: Open ocean, coastlines and coral reefs.

Nesting: Pairs perform elaborate aerial displays in courtship. Breeds in dense colonies, alongside other terns, boobies, and/or gulls. Lays 1 egg in a shallow scrape.

Range: Red Sea, Indian Ocean coast and islands, and around South Africa north to c Namibia.

This tern dives heavily into the ocean to seize fish. It has recently emulated gulls in scavenging for discarded food around boats and beaches. Small groups rest on beaches and rocky headlands.

374 **White Tern**
Fairy Tern
Gygis alba

Description: *Pure white,* with semi-rounded wings and notched tail. *Black eye ring makes black eye appear large.* Long, slightly upturned bill is blue at base. L 12″ (30 cm).

Similar Species: No other tern is pure white. **Gull-**

billed Tern *(Sterna nilotica)* is nearly pure white in nonbreeding plumage, but has pearl-gray back; hawks insects over grasslands, such as Serengeti Plains, and coastlines and rivers of n, w, and e Africa.

Voice: Gives a series of harsh *grrich* notes.

Habitat: Oceanic islands and surrounding seas.

Nesting: A solitary breeder, unlike most terns. Makes no nest, but lays 1 egg in the fork of a tree or on a rock. Long incubation period of 35 days.

Range: Tropical islets in Atlantic, Indian, and Pacific oceans. Off Africa, nests on Ascension, Saint Helena, Seychelles, and Aldabra, and off Mauritius.

Abundant on Cousin Island in Seychelles and on small islets, the White Tern is tolerant of humans. Buoyant and graceful in flight, it has translucent wings that give it an ethereal quality. Adults are often seen with two or three fish held crosswise in the bill.

Skimmers
Family Rynchopidae

Large black and white, tern-like birds with very short legs, skimmers have a longer lower mandible that is narrow and flexible. There are three species worldwide, the other two living in the Americas and in India.

375, 376 African Skimmer
Rynchops flavirostris

Description: *Very long wings, back, hindneck, and crown jet black;* forehead and underparts white. *Long, bright orange bill, with yellow tip.* Short forked tail white; short legs bright red. 15″ (38 cm).

Voice: A sharp *kip-kip-kip.*

Habitat: Wide tropical rivers with sandbanks, lakeshores, and coastal lagoons.

Nesting: Pairs nest in loose colonies on vast

sandbanks. Lays 1–4 eggs in a large scrape. Often dampens breast feathers and returns to nest to wet and cool eggs or young.

Range: Senegal through Niger River system to n Congo River and s Nile Valley; s Tanzania south through Zambezi Valley to Natal and Angola.

Feeding African Skimmers fly in lines over calm waters, their long lower mandibles dipping into the water. This bird flies with slow wingbeats, the body rising with each downstroke. It feeds mainly at dawn and dusk, and at night, resting during the warmer day, when prey is less likely to be at the surface of the water. It is rare or absent in most eastern and southern African parks.

SANDGROUSE

Order Pteroclidiformes
Family Pteroclidae

The sandgrouse order has one family. A sandgrouse looks like a hybrid between a pigeon and a grouse. Chunky or elongated in shape, all species in the family have small heads and short feathered legs. They live on the ground in deserts and grasslands; their long pointed wings carry them daily to distant water sources, where thousands may gather. Males are more colorful, with bands or patches of color on the head or breast, while females are more cryptically spotted, striped, or barred. There are 16 species worldwide, with 12 living in Africa.

377 Chestnut-bellied Sandgrouse

Pterocles exustus

Description: Male buffy brownish on head, chest, and back; buffy-yellow wings have 5 narrow black wing bars; *lower chest has single black breast band, while belly is dark chestnut; central tail feathers are long and*

narrow. Female buffy, heavily barred and striped with black. L 12″ (30 cm).

Similar Species: Male **Namaqua Sandgrouse** *(P. namaqua)* has plain, dull orange head, gray neck, heavy creamy spots above, and white and chestnut breast band; lives in Namibia, Botswana, and w South Africa.

Voice: A deep pleasant *gutter-gutter* in flight.

Habitat: Short-grass plains; barren semi-deserts.

Nesting: Lays 3 eggs in a scrape on the ground.

Range: Egypt west of Nile, Sahel from Senegal east through Chad to Ethiopia, thence south through Kenya to Serengeti and Tarangire areas of n Tanzania.

Large flocks of the Chestnut-bellied Sandgrouse fly fairly high to and from water two to three hours after sunrise, and on some afternoons. This bird feeds on seeds and the young shoots of legumes and grains, and on insects.

---

378 Yellow-throated Sandgrouse
Pterocles gutturalis

Description: A large sandgrouse with a short tail. *Male has bright yellow face and throat above wide black neck band;* body gray-brown, with rufous wings. Female also has yellow face and throat, but is otherwise heavily spotted with black, white, and brown. L 12″ (30 cm).

Similar Species: **Burchell's Sandgrouse** *(P. burchelli),* common in Kalahari area of sw Africa, has numerous white spots on reddish-brown body; male has silver face and throat, and yellow eye ring.

Voice: Several harsh *glock* notes on being flushed; rising *wha-ha* notes overhead.

Habitat: Open short-grass plains; burned ground and fields.

Nesting: Nest consists of a scrape in open stubble or a bare area. Usually lays 3 eggs, and both parents incubate.

Range: Ethiopia, Kenya, and Tanzania south to Transvaal, and west to n Namibia.

Small groups of these chunky birds are commonly seen in open plains, near gazelles and wildebeests. They often crouch in tire tracks on dirt roads. This sandgrouse feeds on wild seeds, plus the fallen grains of cereal crops.

379 Black-faced Sandgrouse
Pterocles decoratus

Description: A short-tailed sandgrouse. Male buffy above with fine black bars; *narrow black ring around base of bill and black throat;* long black and white eyebrow; wide white chest band, with buffy neck and black belly. Female buffy, with fine black barring. L 10″ (25 cm).

Similar Species: Male **Four-banded Sandgrouse** *(P. quadricinctus),* of Sahel from Senegal to Ethiopia, has 2 white bands on black forehead, 1 black and 1 chestnut band fringing wide white chest band. **Double-banded Sandgrouse** *(P. bicinctus)* lives in s Africa from Namibia east to Mozambique; male has pied forehead; yellow bill and eye ring; double black and white breast band.

Voice: A series of short *quit* notes; also guttural *chucker* notes.

Habitat: Dry thornbush country, semi-desert scrublands, and sand dunes.

Nesting: A solitary nester, laying 2 or 3 eggs in an unlined scrape near rocks or trees.

Range: Ethiopia, s Somalia, ne Uganda, Kenya, and n and e Tanzania below 5,200′ (1,600 m).

This bird spends the daytime in the shade of a bush or rock. It feeds on seeds and flies low to water sources at night, when flocks can be heard overhead. When approached in daytime, it either freezes or slowly walks about.

PIGEONS AND DOVES

Order Columbiformes
Family Columbidae

This order has one family. These familiar plump birds have tiny heads, short straight bills, short necks, and short legs. Most have fairly long tails that are somewhat rounded or fan-shaped. The sexes are alike, and there is no seasonal plumage variation. They feed on seeds and small fruit, swallowing their food whole and grinding it up in their powerful gizzards. Monotonous cooing calls are given all day long and at night. Their flight is fast and strong, with much movement to and from roosts, water, and feeding areas. There are about 290 species worldwide, with 37 species known in Africa, 26 of them endemic.

---

380 Speckled Pigeon

Rock Pigeon
Columba guinea

Description: Slaty head and belly, with rusty streaks on neck. Back and wing coverts broadly rufous; *wings heavily speckled with white. Yellow eye surrounded by large oval of bare red skin edged in white. Pale gray rump and pale gray band on blackish tail.* Black bill. L 13″ (33 cm).

Similar Species: **Rameron Pigeon** (Olive Pigeon; *C. arquatrix*) is dark slaty purple, with small white spots and yellow legs, bill, and eye ring; feeds in canopy of tall montane forests from Ethiopia south through e Africa and Malawi to Cape Town. Wild populations of **Rock Pigeon** (Rock Dove, Feral Pigeon; *C. livia*) reside in n Africa, Sahara, and Sahel east to Ethiopia, with semi-wild birds found in most African towns; typically slaty blue, with 2 black wing bars.

Voice: 2 slow muffled *whoor* notes, followed by a series of louder and faster *cooo* notes.

Habitat: Rocks, cliffs, cities, towns, farms, grasslands, and savannas.

Nesting: Performs a circular aerial display with loud wing-claps, or a ground display with fanned tail and quick head-bobbing. Lays 2 eggs in a stick nest on a cliff, tree, or building ledge.

Range: Western Africa north of rain-forest zone from Senegal east to Ethiopia, and thence south to s Tanzania in highlands. Widespread in s Africa.

These birds walk on the ground, feeding on seeds, cultivated grains, and groundnuts, and may form large flocks when not breeding. The Speckled Pigeon has adapted well to man, fearlessly nesting in many towns.

---

381 **Laughing Dove**
Streptopelia senegalensis

Description: Pale pinkish head and underparts; *cinnamon back; bluish forward edge of wings. Tiny black spots in patch on foreneck.* L 10″ (25 cm).

Similar Species: Most other members of the genus are larger and have a distinct black ring on neck. **European Turtle-Dove** *(S. turtur)* breeds in nw Africa and winters in Sahel south to Cameroon; has heavy black spots on buffy shoulders.

Voice: A relatively soft, hurried, rising series of 4–8 *coo* notes, the last one highest and most emphatic. Sings all day, from hour before dawn well into night.

Habitat: Wooded acacia savannas, towns, and farms within 6 miles (10 km) of drinking water.

Nesting: Probably pairs for life. Male defends territory by bowing and bobbing, as well as performing towering display flights with noisy wingbeats. Usually lays 2 eggs in a frail stick nest in a small tree. Male selects sticks, female places them; many nests are reused. Pairs average 5 broods a year.

Range: Northern Africa, Egypt, Saharan oases, and all of sub-Saharan Africa, except rain-forest areas, south to Cape Town.

The Laughing Dove is one of the most common birds in Africa, in both rural and urban areas. Except when it flies to water, most of its flights are short and weak. It walks quickly, pecking at seeds of grasses, herbs, and cereals.

382 African Mourning Dove
Streptopelia decipiens

Description: *Ashy gray head* contrasts with brown back and pinkish breast; *wide black hindneck patch. Bare red skin surrounds yellow eye.* L 12″ (30 cm).

Similar Species: Larger **Red-eyed Dove** is darker brown on back, and has red eye. Smaller **Ring-necked Dove** has black eye (without red eye ring).

Voice: Often noisy, with a guttural gargle; also a long series of notes starting with a purr, then a series of *coo-COO-coo* notes.

Habitat: Thorny and streamside woods and thickets in arid, sandy, lowland areas. Often near palms, villages, and lodges.

Nesting: In courtship, engages in towering display flight and bowing on the ground or on a tree limb. Usually lays 2 eggs in a substantial stick nest lined with fine rootlets and well hidden in foliage of tree.

Range: Sahel from Senegal east to Ethiopia, thence south through e Africa to Okavango Delta, in n Botswana, and Kruger NP, in Transvaal.

The African Mourning Dove forages alone or in groups on the ground for grass seeds, cereals, beans, berries, fallen fruit, and termites. A tame bird on the ground, when roosting it often flies high into trees. It drinks twice daily and will fly 6 miles (10 km) to rivers and ponds.

383 **Ring-necked Dove**
Cape Turtle-Dove
Streptopelia capicola

Description: *Beady black eye.* Pale gray head and underparts, sometimes with pinkish or buffy wash. *Narrow black hindneck patch;* pale brown back. *Extensive white on outer tail.* L 11″ (28 cm).

Similar Species: **Red-eyed Dove** and **African Mourning Dove** are larger and darker. **Laughing Dove** lacks black hindneck patch. **Vinaceous Dove** *(S. vinacea)* replaces Ring-necked in w Africa and Sahel from Senegal east to Ethiopia and n Uganda; has pink forehead and paler gray underwings.

Voice: A monotonous *work HARD-er,* and a harsh *koorr* on alighting.

Habitat: Woodlands, treed savannas, villages, tree plantations, and farms.

Nesting: Pairs for life; paired birds preen each other. Male flies up and claps wings over its territory, which it may defend for 8 years. Lays 1 or 2 eggs in a frail stick tree nest, which thickens with reuse. May raise up to 10 broods a year when food is plentiful.

Range: Eastern and s Africa from Ethiopia and s Zaire south to Cape Town area.

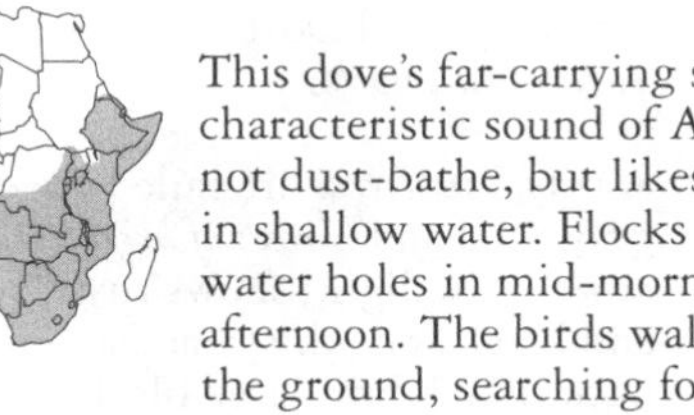

This dove's far-carrying song is a characteristic sound of Africa. It does not dust-bathe, but likes to splash itself in shallow water. Flocks converge on water holes in mid-morning and late afternoon. The birds walk erratically on the ground, searching for grass, cereal, and tree seeds, plus sedge bulbs, aloe nectar, fruit, earthworms, and insects.

---

384 **Red-eyed Dove**
Streptopelia semitorquata

Description: *Bare red skin around red eye; pale grayish face;* heavy black hindneck patch. *Dark brown above;* gray wing coverts; pinkish-gray nape and underparts. In flight, tail brown, with black ring at base. L 14″ (35 cm).

Similar Species: Smaller **Dusky Turtle-Dove** *(S. lugens)* is all slaty, with rufous wings, and black patch on side of neck; feeds in montane grasslands near forests ranging from Ethiopia south to Malawi; common around Ngorongoro Crater in n Tanzania.

Voice: Chief call is 6 notes, *coo-coo-coo-COOK-coo-coo.*

Habitat: Edges of forests, and towns and farms with tall trees.

Nesting: Pairs for life. Engages in towering courtship flight and bowing displays. Builds a substantial stick nest lined with grass or pine needles in a tree over water. Will use old nests of other birds.

Range: Sub-Saharan Africa from Senegal and Ethiopia south to Cape Town.

This bird's range is expanding as tall trees follow farms and towns into former grasslands. The Red-eyed Dove sometimes searches in trees for berries, but forages chiefly on the ground for a wide variety of seeds, flowers, fruit pulp, termites, and millipedes.

---

385 Emerald-spotted Wood-Dove

Green-spotted Dove
Turtur chalcospilos

Description: A tiny, brown, short-tailed dove, with a gray head and *2 rows of bright green spots on wing.* In flight, shows rusty primaries, and black and white bands on lower back. Black bill; large black eye; short pink legs. L 8″ (20 cm).

Similar Species: **Blue-spotted Wood-Dove** *(T. afer)* has red and yellow bill; inhabits wetter rain and montane forests from Senegal east to Ethiopia, and south to n Transvaal. **Tambourine Dove** *(T. tympanistra)* is dark brown above, snowy white below, with white eyebrow; lives in wet forests from Sierra Leone and Ethiopia south to s Cape Province; call series accelerates at the end.

Voice: A long descending series of *du* notes, running together and trailing off at the end; commonly heard in the bush.
Habitat: Dry woodlands, riverine thickets, coastal scrub, and gardens.
Nesting: Lays 2 eggs in a small platform of twigs in a shrub, usually below 7′ (2 m).
Range: Ethiopia south through Kenya and Tanzania to n Namibia and Natal.

Emerald-spotted Wood-Doves usually are found alone or in pairs foraging in the shade of trees. This bird disperses into dry areas when rains arrive, and retreats to areas with water during droughts. It feeds on tiny seeds, and rarely on invertebrates.

---

386 **Namaqua Dove**
Long-tailed Dove
Oena capensis

Description: A tiny dove, with a *very long, thin tail* and bright rufous flight feathers. *Male has black patch extending from face down onto breast;* yellow-tipped red bill; pale gray nape and underparts; brown back. Female is pale gray or pale brown. Both sexes have metallic blue wing spots and small black and white bands on lower back. L 11″ (28 cm).
Similar Species: **Wood-doves** have much shorter tails.
Voice: A low *TWOO-hoooo.*
Habitat: Acacia savannas, desert scrub, and farms.
Nesting: Lays 1–6 eggs in a frail stick nest in a low bush often exposed to sun.
Range: Widespread in all arid areas of sub-Saharan Africa from Mauritania and Sudan southward. Also Madagascar.

This dove is often seen drinking from puddles in dirt tracks at midday. On alighting, it raises its long tail, then lowers it slowly. The Namaqua Dove forages on the ground for minute seeds.

PARROTS
Order Psittaciformes
Family Psittacidae

This order has only one family. Birds of the tropics and Southern Hemisphere, parrots have a blunt, down-curved upper mandible over a broad, up-curved lower mandible. They have short legs but strong feet, with two toes forward, two back; these are used to clamber about in trees and to bring seeds and fruit to the beak. Most parrots nest in tree cavities. The young are born blind and naked, and stay in the nest for many weeks or months. Worldwide there are 330 species, with 23 in Africa.

387 African Gray Parrot
Psittacus erithacus

Description: Chiefly *sooty gray, with pale gray rump and bright red tail.* Black bill; extensive white area around yellow eye. L 13″ (33 cm).
Voice: High-pitched screams and whistles.
Habitat: Rain forests, riverine forests, mangroves, and oil palm plantations to 7,200′ (2,200 m).
Nesting: Nests alone or in loose colonies. Droops wings in mating dance and engages in display flights around nest hole. Lays 1–4 eggs directly in wood dust in a cavity in a large tree.
Range: Bijagós Archipelago of Guinea-Bissau east through forest belt of w Africa to Congo Basin, Uganda, and Kakamega Forest, in sw Kenya.

The largest African parrot, this bird is famous as perhaps the greatest talking parrot. It is declining fast in some forest areas. The African Gray Parrot wanders about, according to which trees are in fruit; it also raids crops such as oil-nut palms and maize.

388 **Brown Parrot**
Meyer's Parrot
Poicephalus meyeri

Description: Dark *brown head,* back, and wings, accented with yellow bend of wings. Blue-green belly; *blue rump.* Some individuals have *yellow crown patch.* L 9″ (23 cm).

Similar Species: **Yellow-bellied Parrot** *(P. senegalus),* of w African savanna woodlands from Senegal east to Lake Chad, is bright green, with gray head and yellow (tending to orange in eastern races) belly. **Orange-bellied Parrot** *(P. rufiventris)* ranges from Ethiopia south to Tarangire NP, in n Tanzania; male has brown head and back, green rump and vent, and orange belly; female has green belly. **Rüppell's Parrot** *(P. rueppelli)* of n Namibia has gray head (without yellow patch); both sexes have blue belly, female a blue rump.

Voice: A shrieking *klee-klee,* plus clinking notes.

Habitat: Wooded savannas and riverine woodlands.

Nesting: In courtship, spins in circles, walks up and down branches, and raises its wings; nests in solitary pairs. Lays 1–4 eggs in tree cavities.

Range: Northern Cameroon east to w Ethiopia, and Uganda and w Kenya south to n Namibia and n Transvaal.

The Brown Parrot breaks open hard seedpods, and also feeds on other nuts, seeds, figs, and flowers. Pairs fly about rapidly, with shallow wingbeats; on arriving at a destination, they drop down suddenly and then swoop up into a tree.

389 **Fischer's Lovebird**
Agapornis fischeri

Description: A tiny, short-tailed parrot, with a white line separating red bill and forehead. *Orange head* shades into yellow above bright green body. Fleshy white ring around eye. Blue rump. L 6″ (15 cm).

Similar Species: **Yellow-collared Lovebird** (Masked Lovebird; *A. personata*), of eastern rift valley and eastward in n Tanzania, has dark brown head and wide yellow collar on neck and upper breast. **Lilian's Lovebird** *(A. lilianae),* with red head and green rump, lives in s Tanzania, Malawi, e Zambia, and n Zimbabwe. **Rosy-faced Lovebird** *(A. roseicollis)* of Namibia has pink throat and green up to crown. **Red-headed Lovebird** *(A. pullaria)* is chiefly green, with red crown and throat; ranges from Guinea east to Uganda and Rwanda.

Voice: A high-pitched twitter.

Habitat: Savannas studded with trees.

Nesting: Nests in colonies; lays 3–8 eggs in a tree hole or wall cavity.

Range: Rwanda, Burundi, and n Tanzania west of eastern rift valley.

Large flocks of Fischer's Lovebirds are a feature attraction around Olduvai Gorge, and at Ndutu Lake and Seronera in Serengeti NP, in Tanzania. They are attracted to birdbaths and scattered seed. They feed on the ground in the open, but within easy flight to a thorny bush.

CUCKOOS AND THEIR ALLIES
Order Cuculiformes

The turacos and cuckoos are two very distinct bird families. They are placed in the same order chiefly due to their similar feet, egg-white proteins, loose plumage, and tender skin. Of the world's 150 species, 56 live in Africa.

TURACOS
Family Musophagidae

A family of 20 species entirely restricted to sub-Saharan Africa, turacos are crow-size birds with short rounded wings, small heads (usually crested), short stout bills, and long necks and tails. Small groups fly from tree to tree in slow, labored, undulating flight. While the wet-forest species are very colorful, those living in dry savanna woodlands are drab, but with colorful personalities. All southern African species are locally called "louries."

390 **Great Blue Turaco**
Corythaeola cristata

Description: Swollen yellow bill with red tip. *Enormous fluffy black crest over entire crown; blue head, neck, back, and wings. Green chest; yellow belly; chestnut vent.* Blue tail green on sides and yellow below, with broad black terminal band. L 30″ (75 cm).

Voice: A deep gobble, followed by up to 50 *kok* notes running for about 10 seconds.

Habitat: Lowland and montane forests, riverine forests, tall trees left standing in felled forests, and old tree plantations.

Nesting: Courtship involves calling noisily, flying about, and flapping wings while perched. Lays 2 eggs in a platform nest, usually built in a clump of leaves on a branch over water.

Range: Guinea east through Congo Basin to w Uganda; also sw Kenya.

The Great Blue is the largest turaco, and a most thrilling sight to see. A poor flier, it often glides downward; upon landing, it hops upward. It is usually seen in parties of a half dozen, though several groups may converge on fruiting trees; it feeds on a wide variety of fruits, leaves, buds, and flowers.

391 **Western Gray Plantain-eater**
Crinifer piscator

Description: *Swollen yellow bill; dark brown head and neck; long spiky feathers on back of head and neck.* Underparts white, with *heavy black streaks;* blue-gray above, with white patch on black primaries; blackish tail. L 20″ (50 cm).

Similar Species: **Eastern Gray Plantain-eater** *(C. zonurus)* is browner, with plainer breast, white tips to neck feathers, and white bases to outer tail feathers; common in savannas from Ethiopia south through Uganda, w Kenya, and nw Tanzania to Burundi.

Voice: Chief call is a series of yelping *cow* notes.

Habitat: Wooded savannas, acacia woodlands, mango groves, and rain-forest edges.

Nesting: Courting bird flies up noisily and then tumbles in a dive. Lays 2 or 3 eggs in a stick nest up to 33′ (10 m) high in a leafy tree.

Range: West Africa from Senegal east to Central African Republic; also s Congo and w Zaire.

Small parties of two to four birds roost in treetops, often perching in the open on a dead branch. Flight consists of alternate flapping and gliding. This bird often cocks its tail over its back when balancing. It feeds on fruit, including figs, dates, oil palm fruit, mangoes, and guavas.

---

392 **Gray Go-away-bird**
Gray Lourie
Corythaixoides concolor

Description: *Entirely smoky gray, with long fluffy crest* and long tail. Black bill. L 19″ (48 cm).

Similar Species: **Bare-faced Go-away-bird** has black face and white neck.

Voice: Main call is a nasal, drawn-out *g' waay;* also other cat-like growls and shrieks.

Habitat: Dry open acacia, miombo, and mopane woodlands, often near water; also farms.

Nesting: A solitary nester, but with helpers from previous broods. Usually lays 3 eggs in a flimsy nest in a thorny tree.

Range: Angola and Namibia east to Selous GR, in s Tanzania, and south to ne Natal; also e Kenya.

The Gray Go-away-bird often perches on treetops, saying its name. Members of this species feed in the bush on pods, fruit, flowers, leaf buds, and termites. They are garden pests in places.

393 Bare-faced Go-away-bird
Corythaixoides personata

Description: *Bare black skin on face;* black bill; long, fluffy, brown crest. *White neck;* pale brownish-gray underparts; gray back, wings, and tail. L 20″ (50 cm).
Similar Species: **Gray Go-away-bird** is uniformly gray.
Voice: A loud bleating *go-way;* also wild laughing calls.
Habitat: Dry acacia woodlands, riverine thickets, evergreen scrub, and farmland with trees.
Nesting: Lays 2 or 3 eggs in a shallow stick nest near the top of an acacia tree.
Range: East Africa from Ethiopia south through w Kenya, Uganda, and c and w Tanzania to n Malawi.

This rather tame and inquisitive bird is locally common in parks such as Masai Mara, in Kenya, and Serengeti and Tarangire, in Tanzania. It feeds on acacia seeds and flowers. The Bare-faced replaces the Gray Go-away-bird north of the Selous GR in southern Tanzania.

394 White-bellied Go-away-bird
Corythaixoides leucogaster

Description: *Long black crest* can be laid back or raised over black bill. Gray head, neck, and back, with *sharply demarcated white belly.* Rows of black bars on wing coverts and white band on primaries. *Broad white band at middle of long tail.* L 20″ (50 cm).
Similar Species: **Eastern Gray Plantain-eater** *(Crinifer zonurus)* has yellow bill and plain brown wings; ranges farther west and south from Ethiopia to Burundi.

Voice: A loud, sheep-like *go-awaay* or *moo-wah.*
Habitat: Acacia woodlands and thorny scrub, chiefly below 4,300′ (1,300 m).
Nesting: Lays 2 or 3 eggs in an untidy twig nest in a dense thorny tree.
Range: East Africa in se Sudan, Ethiopia, Somalia, ne Uganda, n and e Kenya, and e Tanzania south to Ruaha NP.

This attractive, dry-country turaco feeds on fruit and the flowers of acacias and aloes. It often calls while flying from tree to tree.

---

395 **Purple-crested Turaco**
Musophaga porphyreolopha

Description: *Dark purple crest* above glossy green head; *red eye ring; black bill.* Neck and chest green in north, chestnut in south. Rest of body and wings glossy purple, with bright red flight feathers. L 19″ (47 cm).
Similar Species: **Ruwenzori Turaco** *(M. johnstoni)* lives in Mountain Gorilla country of Rwanda, e Zaire, and sw Uganda to 13,000′ (4,000 m); has red patches on nape, chest, and wings.
Voice: A series of up to 25 loud, barking *crook* notes that rise in intensity.
Habitat: Evergreen forests, plantations, and towns with mature trees.
Nesting: Lays 2–4 eggs in a flimsy stick nest well concealed in a tall tree.
Range: Southwestern Uganda and w and s Tanzania southwest to Victoria Falls on Zambezi and s to Natal; isolated population in c Kenya.

This turaco calls in groups from treetops at dawn and dusk. An agile walker in canopies of dense trees, it feeds on a variety of fruits.

396 **Ross's Turaco**
Musophaga rossae

Description: *Heavy yellow bill and large area of bare yellow skin around eye; bright red, fluffy crest.* Rest of bird glossy purple, with red primaries. L 20″ (50 cm).

Similar Species: **Violet Turaco** *(M. violacea),* of w Africa from Senegal to n Cameroon, has red bill, yellow frontal shield, much shorter crest, and bare red skin around eye, bordered below by white stripe.

Voice: A series of weird throaty cackles and cooing notes.

Habitat: Wide variety of forests, from rain forests to riverine gallery forests in drier areas.

Nesting: Lays 1 or 2 eggs in a flimsy stick nest in thick foliage of an isolated tree.

Range: Central Cameroon east to w Kenya, south to n Zambia, and west to mouth of Congo. Apparently absent from much of Congo Basin; may be colonizing Okavango Delta, in n Botswana.

A beautiful bird that hops about the canopy of dense trees, this turaco is not easily seen despite being rather tame and noisy.

---

397 **Green Turaco**
includes Knysna, Green-crested, Schalow's, and Livingstone's turacos
Tauraco persa

Description: *Bright red bill* and red eye ring bordered with black and white stripes. *Brilliant green crested head, neck, and underparts.* Wings and tail glossy purple and green, with red flight feathers. L 18″ (45 cm).

Subspecies: West African **Green-crested Turaco** *(T. p. persa)* has entirely green crest and is heavily purple on back, wings, and tail. **Livingstone's Turaco** *(T. p. livingstonei)* lives from Ngorongoro Crater, in n Tanzania, south to Natal; has white tips (blue in north) on long pointed crest, and green tail. **Schalow's Turaco** *(T. p. schalowi)* lives from sw Kenya south and west to Victoria Falls and Angola; has extremely long, white-tipped crest and purple tail. **Knysna Turaco** *(T. p. corythaix)* inhabits coastal forests from Natal west to Knysna, in s Cape Province; has shorter rounded crest that is also white-tipped.

Similar Species: Other turacos have red, white, or black on head, or have black bills. **White-crested Turaco** *(T. leucolophus)* ranges from ne Nigeria east through Uganda to Lake Baringo, in Kenya; crest and neck area white.

Voice: 2 introductory notes followed by a long series of guttural notes usually described as "barks": *pu-cook, kaarrr-kaarrr-kaarrr-kaarrr.*

Habitat: Middle and upper stories of wet lowland and montane forests and riverine forests.

Nesting: Courtship involves shaking head and flashing red wings. Lays 2 or 3 eggs in a large stick nest hidden in a thick tangle of dense bush or an isolated tree.

Range: Senegal to Angola in west, and sw Kenya south to coastal Cape Province.

The Green Turaco runs along and leaps about tree branches and the tangles of creepers in tall leafy trees. It eats a wide variety of wild and cultivated fruits, seeds, and leaf buds, consuming some seeds that are poisonous to mammals. This bird is seen only in flashes as it flies from one dark tree to another.

---

398 Hartlaub's Turaco
Tauraco hartlaubi

Description: Olive green with iridescent, blue-black crown. *Large white spot in front of red eye ring; long white streak below eye.* Wings and tail glossy purple, with red flight feathers. L 16″ (40 cm).

Similar Species: **Green Turaco** has pointed green crest. In coastal Kenya and ne Tanzania, Hartlaub's is replaced by red-crested **Fischer's Turaco** *(T. fischeri).*

Voice: A series of about 12 *kwok* notes.

Habitat: Highland evergreen forests and gardens.
Nesting: Active and noisy courtship behavior: fans tail, flashes wings, and runs along tree limbs. Lays 2 eggs in a frail stick nest hidden high in a tree.
Range: Kenya, n Tanzania, and e Uganda.

This bird is common, and usually the only turaco, in the wet mountain forests above the popular East African safari routes. It may be glimpsed in Kenya on Mount Kenya, in the Aberdare Mountains, and around Nairobi, and in Tanzania on Mount Meru and Mount Kilimanjaro. Its food and habits are like those of the Green Turaco.

Cuckoos
Family Cuculidae

Cuckoos are small to medium-size, often furtive birds, many with bare eye rings and long tails. They have two toes forward and two toes back. Most species (except coucals) lay eggs in other birds' nests; in some species, the cuckoo eggs match those of the host species. The young cuckoos eject the eggs or young of the host, and the foster parents then feed the young cuckoos. The black-and-rufous coucals are large, slow-moving grassland birds that build their own nests and raise their own young. Worldwide there are 130 cuckoo species, with 25 known in continental Africa, and another 11 restricted to Madagascar.

---

399 **Didric Cuckoo**
Diederik Cuckoo
Chrysococcyx caprius

Description: Male dark green above, white below, with *heavy barring on sides. Conspicuous red eye ring. White stripes on crown, lores, wings, and outer tail feathers, and behind eye.* Female similar but more bronzed. L 7″ (18 cm).

Similar Species: Male **Klaas's Cuckoo** *(C. klaas),* with similar range, is emerald green above, white below, with single white spot behind eye; calls out 2-note *ooeee-jeeuu.*

Voice: Male gives a repetitious *dee-dee-dee-deedereek.*

Habitat: Forest edges, wooded savannas, grasslands, gardens, and desert scrub.

Nesting: Male attracts female with calls from singing perch; he fans tail, bows head, and presents her with caterpillars before mating. Builds no nest. Female lays eggs chiefly in nest of a weaver, bishop, or sparrow.

Range: All of sub-Saharan Africa, except true deserts. Resident in equatorial regions from Sierra Leone east to n Tanzania. Fans out northward from Senegal east to Sudan in northern summer rains; present in s Africa only during its wet summers.

This cuckoo forages both in trees and on the ground, taking hairy and hairless caterpillars, grasshoppers, termites, and moths, even bad-tasting caterpillars avoided by other birds. It sometimes eats the eggs of its host.

400 African Emerald Cuckoo
Chrysococcyx cupreus

Description: Male bright metallic green; *yellow lower breast and belly;* white bars on vent and undertail feathers. Female brown above, with greenish reflections; metallic green bars on white underparts. L 8″ (20 cm).

Voice: Clear, 4-note *pret-ty george-eee,* repeated at 5-second intervals.

Habitat: Forests, woodlands, and thickets.

Nesting: Lays single eggs in several nests of warblers and small thrushes.

Range: Senegal east to s Ethiopia; south to s Angola, n Zimbabwe, and wetter areas of South Africa, to e Cape Province coast. Resident on Gulf of Guinea islands.

This bird's distinctive call is heard often at the forest edge, while the singer itself is hard to see. It calls chiefly during rainy periods. An intra-Africa migrant, the African Emerald Cuckoo is present in many areas only in the wet season.

401 Senegal Coucal
Centropus senegalensis

Description: *Black crown and hindneck; bright rufous back and wings; black tail. Clear white underparts,* sometimes with light buffy wash. Heavy black bill; red eye. L 16″ (41 cm).

Similar Species: **Burchell's Coucal** *(C. burchelli)* replaces Senegal Coucal from e Tanzania south to Cape Town; has white and rufous barring on rump and tail; sometimes considered subspecies of White-browed Coucal. Larger **Coppery-tailed Coucal** *(C. cupreicaudus)* has long, deep copper-colored tail; resides from s Zaire south through Zambia to Okavango Delta, in n Botswana.

Voice: Bubbling notes that run down and then up the scale.

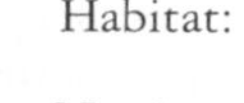

Habitat: Long rank grass in savannas, swamps, forest edges, sugarcane, and palm groves.

Nesting: Lays 3 eggs in a domed nest made of grass, roots, and thin twigs, with an entrance high up on one side.

Range: 3 subspecies occupy 3 disjunct areas: Nile Delta in Egypt; Senegal east to Ethiopia, and south to c Zaire, n Uganda, and Kakamega area of w Kenya; and sc Africa from s Tanzania to Okavango Delta, in n Botswana.

Coucals act like feathered lizards; they are rather slow and spend most of their time creeping about on the ground. In flight, they flap heavily and tire easily, and usually crash in a heap in the grass. They are often seen sunning themselves with wings and tail spread. They feed on insects, crabs, frogs, small snakes, rodents, and small birds.

402 **White-browed Coucal**
Centropus superciliosus

Description: Dark brown face and crown, with *long white eyebrow and red eye. Nape, chest, and upper back dusky, with numerous fine black and white streaks.* White belly. Rufous wings; finely barred rump and vent; black tail. L 18″ (44 cm).

Similar Species: **Black Coucal** *(C. bengalensis)* also has rufous wings but is smaller, with black head and underparts; lives in open wet grasslands over much of sub-Saharan Africa south to Natal.

Voice: A typical gurgling coucal call, like water being poured out of a large bottle.

Habitat: Grassy bush country, rank undergrowth, thornbush savannas, and watersides.

Nesting: Builds a large, untidy, domed nest in a thick bush, where 4 eggs are incubated.

Range: Ethiopia south through most of e Africa to Malawi, Zambezi River, and Angola.

Not as shy as other coucals, the White-browed is often seen. While agile when walking in tangled vegetation, it walks clumsily on open ground and is a poor flier. It feeds on insects, spiders, snails, lizards, and nestling birds.

OWLS
Order Strigiformes

These chiefly nocturnal birds of prey have large heads with no visible neck. They fly noiselessly. In addition to the typical owls of the family Strigidae, Africa is home to three species of "barn owls" of the Tytonidae family. Of 132 species worldwide, 38 live in Africa.

Owls
Family Strigidae

Owls have large eyes on flat faces. They have incredible night vision and hearing, and their strong feet, claws, and hooked beaks are ideal for grasping and tearing at small animals. Their soft plumage is drab brown or gray to camouflage them at their daytime roosting sites. Most other birds hate owls, which include sleeping birds in their diet; owls are mobbed when other birds discover them in daylight. Females are larger than males. Worldwide there are 120 species, with 30 in Africa and another four on Indian Ocean islands.

403 African Scops-Owl
Otus senegalensis

Description: A small gray owl sprinkled with white and black spots. *Yellow eyes on gray face topped by long feathered "ear" tufts,* which may be flat or erect. L 8″ (20 cm).

Similar Species: Pale brown **Malagasy Scops-Owl** *(O. rutilus)* is widespread on Comoros and Madagascar.

Voice: A frog-like *kurr-uup,* repeated at intervals of 5–8 seconds.

Habitat: Savanna woodlands, riverine gallery forests, gardens, and towns.

Nesting: Lays 2 or 3 eggs in a tree cavity.

Range: Senegal east to Somalia, north of rain-forest belt, and south through e Africa to n Nambia and e South Africa.

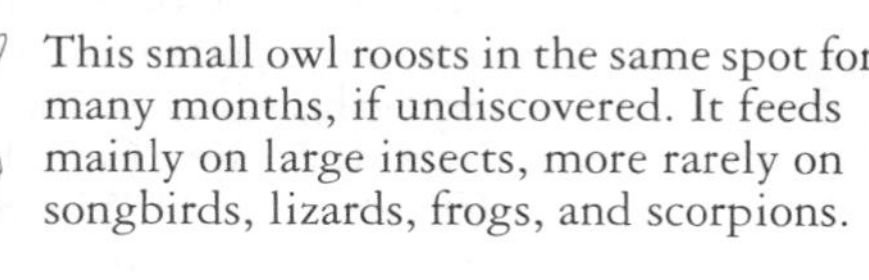

This small owl roosts in the same spot for many months, if undiscovered. It feeds mainly on large insects, more rarely on songbirds, lizards, frogs, and scorpions.

404 White-faced Scops-Owl
Otus leucotis

Description: Gray-brown, with *yellow eyes on white face rimmed in black;* blackish ear tufts. Long, thin, black streaks below. L 10″ (25 cm).

Similar Species: Smaller **African Scops-Owl** has plain gray face.

Voice: Birds that live north and west of n Kenya give a mellow *po-proo* every 4–8 seconds. Those that live south of c Kenya utter a fast bubbling stutter, ending with a rising, flute-like sound.

Habitat: Woodlands of semi-deserts and savannas, and edges of wetter forests.

Nesting: Lays 2 or 3 eggs in an abandoned nest of an eagle, heron, crow, turaco, or pigeon. Sometimes uses a tree hole.

Range: Most of sub-Saharan Africa from Senegal east to Somalia, and south to Orange Free State.

Pairs and, in nonbreeding season, groups of a dozen of these birds may roost together in open view by day. It hunts at night, dropping from a perch onto rodents, birds, and invertebrates.

---

405 **Verreaux's Eagle-Owl**
Giant Eagle-Owl
Bubo lacteus

Description: *Heavy black ring, outlined by white, around face;* large dark eyes and conspicuous *pink eyelids;* fluffy ear tufts. Finely barred plumage appears pale gray below; darker brown above. L 26″ (65 cm).

Similar Species: Much lighter-weight **Spotted Eagle-Owl** (*B. africanus;* L 20″/50 cm) has yellow eyes and long "ears," and is heavily barred below; lives in savanna woodlands, often near rocky areas, from Senegal east to Somalia, and south to Cape Town area. **Cape Eagle-Owl** (*B. capensis;* L 22″/55 cm) is rusty, with heavy dark spots on breast, and has orange eyes; inhabits wet rocky mountains of e and s Africa, and roosts in cities to feed on feral pigeons.

Voice: A series of 2–5 low, grunting, pig-like *huunn* notes that can be heard for 3 miles (5 km).

Habitat: Open wooded savannas, riverine forests, semi-deserts, small forest patches, and tree plantations.

Nesting: Takes over a large nest of a crow, or an abandoned nest of a vulture, eagle, Hammerkop, or Sociable Weaver. Lays

2 eggs. Young may help parents raise next year's brood.

Range: Locally in w Africa from Senegal east to Central African Republic, and from s Congo and Eritrea south to South Africa.

A light sleeper, Verreaux's Eagle-Owl will drop on any prey that wanders below its daytime perching branch. It feeds early at night on small mammals and also takes many birds, as well as snakes, lizards, toads, fish, and insects.

---

406 **Pearl-spotted Owlet**
Glaucidium perlatum

Description: A small, yellow-eyed owl *without ear tufts.* Dark brown above, with many white spots, plus *a pair of black false eyes, rimmed in white, on back of head.* Brownish streaks on pale breast. L 7″ (18 cm).

Similar Species: Larger **Little Owl** *(Athene noctua)* is another earless owl found by day in open country from Morocco east to Red Sea.

Voice: A long series of ascending *tee* notes, followed by a series of louder, descending *teeuu* notes. Calls day and night.

Habitat: Open woodlands and wooded savannas with sparse ground cover.

Nesting: Female locates tree hole, and may evict barbets or woodpeckers using it. Lays 2–4 eggs. Uses artificial nest boxes.

Range: Senegal east to Eritrea, and south to n South Africa.

The Pearl-spotted Owlet hunts frequently by day. Its flight is a fast whir of wings, and the bird glides upward when landing. When the owl is mobbed by small birds, its false eyes help prevent some rear attacks. It feeds on insects, lizards, small birds, and snakes.

NIGHTJARS AND THEIR ALLIES
Order Caprimulgiformes

Nightjars are nocturnal birds with long, narrow wings, small feet, and tiny bills that open into a large, gaping mouth. Four other small families in this order live in Latin America, southern Asia, and Australasia. There are 107 species worldwide.

Nightjars
Family Caprimulgidae

Nightjars are mottled brown and gray birds with long wings and tails, but very short legs. Their muted colors and patterns camouflage them at their nests and roosts by day. At night they fly around catching insects, their loud churring or whistling calls jarring the night air. Most species roost on dead leaves on the ground and look pretty much alike. There are 80 species worldwide, with 23 in Africa, and two more in Madagascar.

407 Fiery-necked Nightjar
Caprimulgus pectoralis

Description: Gray, rufous, and brown, with dark spots above and fine bands below; *rich rufous collar on hindneck.* White tail corners and white primary patch in flight. L 10″ (25 cm).

Similar Species: **Montane Nightjar** *(C. poliocephalus),* dark brown with rufous collar, utters a *peeeoo-peeurr* in montane forest edges of e Africa, such as Ngorongoro's rim, Mount Kilimanjaro, and Mount Kenya.

Voice: A quavering whistle rendered as *Good Lord, deliver us.*

Habitat: Seasonally dry woodlands with continuous canopy and plentiful leaf litter; also edges of wetter forests.

Nesting: Pairs for life and usually lays 1 or 2 eggs

on fallen leaves during full moon.

Range: Southeastern Kenya and s Zaire south to Cape Town area.

This nightjar is commonly heard delivering its sermon from high in a tree in spring and early summer, singing all night when the moon is up. Unlike most nightjars, which cruise about like swallows, it darts out from a tree perch when it spots a beetle or moth.

---

408 **Gabon Nightjar**
Mozambique Nightjar
Scotornis (Caprimulgus) fossii

Description: Brownish gray, with rufous hindneck collar and *many rows of white spots on wing.* Outer tail feathers white in male, pale buff in female. L 9″ (23 cm).

Similar Species: **Fiery-necked Nightjar** is browner and has white corners on outer tail feathers.

Voice: A long series of *churr* notes that alternate between slow and fast cadences.

Habitat: Clearings, bushed grasslands, edges of woodlands, and river sandbanks.

Nesting: Lays 2 eggs in a scrape among leaf litter, usually in sandy areas.

Range: Southern Ghana east to Kenya, and south to n Botswana and Natal.

At night, the Gabon Nightjar is often seen sitting in dirt roads in nonforested areas. Its call is monotonous and frog-like. It is the most common nightjar in most of Tanzania and Zambia.

SWIFTS AND THEIR ALLIES
Order Apodiformes

These birds have tiny feet and fly rapidly. In addition to the swift family, this order includes the Asian tree-swifts (Hemiprocnidae) and the American hummingbirds (Trochilidae). There are 430 species worldwide, with 25 in Africa.

Swifts
Family Apodidae

The most aerial of birds, swifts feed, drink, gather nesting material, and mate in flight. Their bills are tiny but open wide to catch their insect prey. Their feet are small, adapted only for clinging to vertical cliffs and tree hollows. Swifts never perch on twigs, wires, or the ground like swallows. Their wings are long, narrow, and swept back, and they can travel fast and far with few wingbeats; larger species may hit 200 mph (300 kph). There are 85 species of these pied or drab birds worldwide, with 25 species in Africa.

African Palm Swift
Cypsiurus parvus

Description: A small, thin, *pale gray-brown* swift, with a *very long forked tail.* L 7″ (17 cm).

Similar Species: Other swifts are much heavier and darker, with shorter tails.

Voice: High-pitched twittering near nesting palm.

Habitat: Lowland savannas, watercourses in arid areas, clearings in rain forests, and towns—all such areas that have palm trees.

Nesting: Unlike other swifts, these mate at the nest. May nest alone or in colonies of up to 100 pairs. Makes a nest of molted feathers from other birds mixed with plant material; glues it with its sticky saliva to a palm frond hanging downward. Also glues its 2 eggs to the nest.

Range: Sub-Saharan Africa from Senegal east to Somalia, and south to c Namibia and Natal. Also Comoros and Madagascar.

This swift feeds on airborne insects, especially flies, that it catches at treetop level. Its flight is more jerky, with sudden turns, than the long, fast glides of most swifts. The tail streamers can be closed to resemble a long needle.

409 **Little Swift**
Apus affinis

Description: Jet black with white throat, and *wide white band on rump.* Fairly short *tail is square,* not forked. L 6″ (15 cm).
Similar Species: **White-rumped Swift** *(A. caffer)* has narrower white rump stripe and long forked tail; takes over swallow nests in cities and rocky outcrops, and is less colonial; ranges from Morocco and Eritrea south to Cape Town. A wide variety of large dark swifts of this genus is resident or winters in Africa, including the all-dark **European Swift** *(A. apus),* which spends 7 months a year in sub-Saharan Africa.
Voice: Noisy: high-pitched twittering.
Habitat: Common in cities and towns, feeding over fields, gardens, and waters not far from buildings, cliffs, and bridges.
Nesting: Usually nests in small to large colonies. Lays 2 eggs in a nest bag of grass and feathers, glued together with saliva; colonies are located under bridges and overhanging rock ledges, in caves, and on buildings with overhanging roofs.
Range: Northern Africa from Morocco east to Tunisia; sub-Saharan Africa from Mauritania and Eritrea south to Cape Town. Withdraws from much of s Africa in winter.

Large numbers of this swift fly off from colonies, wheeling around and returning together. The bird often does a slow glide with its wings held up in a V. It feeds on aerial insects. The Little Swift is also common in southern Asia, where it is called the House Swift.

MOUSEBIRDS
Order Coliiformes
Family Coliidae

This order comprises one family that lives only in Africa. The long narrow tails of these birds are twice the length of their bodies. Dull in color, they have crests and short, thick, pointed beaks. Unlike other birds, they can direct all four toes forward or move the two outer toes backward. There are six species.

410 Speckled Mousebird
Colius striatus

Description: *A crested, very long-tailed, brown bird.* Face blackish, with silvery cheek in some races; bill often black above, silver below. Some races have fine dark barring on chest. Cinnamon under wings. Legs red or dark purple. L 14″ (35 cm).

Similar Species: Larger, darker, and browner than other mousebirds, with no red or blue on head.

Voice: A harsh *tsik-tsik* when alarmed, and a warbling *tsu-tsu* in flight.

Habitat: Edges of forests, woodlands, scrub, plantations, gardens, and towns.

Nesting: Builds a shallow nest of sticks, grass, leaves, paper, and cloth in a low thick bush. Usually lays 3 eggs. Parents and helpers feed young.

Range: Cameroon east to Eritrea, thence south through e Africa to Cape Province. Ranges to 9,200′ (2,800 m).

This is a common and successful species. When traveling, flock members fly across open areas one at a time, their long tails trailing. The Speckled Mousebird feeds on fruit, buds, and leaves, and may be a nuisance in gardens and orchards. Clusters of up to 20 roost side by side for warmth.

411 Blue-naped Mousebird
Urocolius macrourus

Description: Pale gray (including crest), with long, thin, slightly bluish tail. *Bright red at base of bill and around eye; turquoise-blue on nape.* L 14″ (35 cm).

Similar Species: **Red-faced Mousebird** *(U. indicus)* lives in dry woodlands from sw Tanzania to Cape Town area; pale gray with buffy head; has large patch of bare red skin on face.

Voice: A clear *peeu-peeu,* given often at rest and in flight.

Habitat: Open arid country with thorny trees, watercourses, palm groves, and vicinity of wells and villages.

Nesting: Lays 2 or 3 eggs in an untidy cup nest of twigs, grass, and rootlets, placed in a tree or thorny bush.

Range: Mauritania and Guinea-Bissau east across Sahel to Djibouti, and south to s Tanzania.

The only mousebird in western Africa, the Blue-naped feeds on fruit, berries, leaves, and flowers. This bird flies in flocks; up to 50 birds may gather in one fruiting tree.

TROGONS

Order Trogoniformes
Family Trogonidae

This order comprises one family. Upright-perching forest birds with iridescent plumage, trogons have short broad bills, large eyes, tiny feet, and fairly long, wide tails. Solitary, they sit motionless on branches before flying down to snatch large insects from lower branches. Of the world's 37 species, three live in Africa, the rest in the tropics of Latin America and Asia.

---

412 Narina's Trogon
Apaloderma narina

Description: Male brilliant green on head, chest, and upperparts, with *red belly and vent; thick yellow bill;* white underside of tail. Female duller, with brownish face and chest. L 13″ (33 cm).

Similar Species: Male **Bar-tailed Trogon** *(A. vittatum)* has blue on chest, and tail is heavily barred in black and white; inhabits mountain forests in Cameroon, e Africa, and Malawi.

Voice: A series of up to 14 double notes, *hoo-hoot.*

Habitat: Moist evergreen and riverine forests, forest edges, and gardens with tall trees.

Nesting: Lays 2–4 eggs in a large cavity with a small entrance in a tree within a forest.

Range: Sierra Leone east to Ghana; se Nigeria east to Ethiopia, and south to Zambezi Valley; Indian Ocean slope of s Africa south to se Cape Province.

Narina's Trogon sits quietly on interior branches in forests, where it watches for insects, spiders, and small lizards. It flies down silently in twists and turns, and often returns to the same perch. When calling, it inflates a bare patch of blue skin on its throat.

KINGFISHERS AND THEIR ALLIES
Order Coraciiformes

A diverse group of compact birds, members of this order have large heads and beaks, ample wings, and short legs. Many perch conspicuously on tree limbs or wires, and most are colorful. Africa is home to six families. Worldwide there are 202 species, with 85 in Africa.

KINGFISHERS
Family Alcedinidae

African kingfishers are brightly colored and patterned birds with long, heavy, straight red or black bills, large heads, short necks, tiny feet, and short tails. Some dive headfirst into water for fish, while others hunt large insects, reptiles, and amphibians on land. The smaller species are solitary and quiet, while the larger ones are noisy and conspicuous. There are 87 species worldwide (mostly in southern Asia and Australasia), with 18 species in Africa, plus two in Madagascar.

413 Pied Kingfisher
Ceryle rudis

Description: *Flat-headed, with short black crest; long white eyebrow.* Black above with white spots; white below, male with 2 black breast bands, female with 1 incomplete breast band. L 10″ (25 cm).

Similar Species: **Giant Kingfisher** (*Megaceryle maxima;* L 18″/45 cm), widespread but uncommon in sub-Saharan Africa, is 4 times heavier; has finer black and white speckling above, and rusty on underparts.

Voice: A high *quick-quick* and a *kittle-te-ker.*

Habitat: Freshwater lakes, rivers, rice fields, flooded grasslands, mangroves, and seacoasts.

Nesting: Nests in colonies or singly. Courtship display may involve a dozen birds flying about and perching with wings outspread. Pair digs a burrow into a riverbank up to 8′ (2.5 m) deep, with nest chamber at end. Usually lays 5 eggs.

Range: Nile Delta in Egypt, south into all of sub-Saharan Africa, except deserts.

The Pied Kingfisher perches in the open on dead limbs, the ground, boats, and posts in water. It flies low over water, then rises above it to hover for up to 10 seconds before moving to another site. When it catches a fish, it returns to its perch, holding the fish crosswise and whacking it on a branch until it dies. It also takes some insects.

414 Malachite Kingfisher
Alcedo cristata

Description: *Azure blue above, with orange from eye down through underparts.* White throat and white spot at rear of neck. *Long, thin, red bill;* tiny red feet. Very long, loose, black-spotted crown feathers are often blown sideways. Juvenile has black bill and blackish back. L 6″ (15 cm).

Similar Species: **Half-collared Kingfisher** *(A. semitorquata),* of e and s Africa, has blue face and black bill. **Malagasy Kingfisher** *(A. vintsioides),* which lives in Madagascar and Comoros, has black bill.

Voice: A high-pitched *seek.*

Habitat: Quiet streams, pools, and marshes.

Nesting: Excavates a burrow in earth up to 4′ (1.2 m) long, where it lays 3–6 eggs.

Range: Sub-Saharan Africa from Senegal east to w Ethiopia, and south to Cape Town.

This bird is a feathered jewel that sometimes allows humans to come close. It perches on a reed, twig, or rock low to the water and can turn completely around in a second. Its flight is swift, directly over the water's surface. It dives steeply after prey, entering the water with a little splash, and returns to its perch to kill the fish and swallow it headfirst.

---

415 **African Pygmy Kingfisher**
Ceyx pictus (Ispidina picta)

Description: Tiny, with long red bill; *orange eyebrow* and underparts. Crown blue with fine black dots; white spot near back of neck. Back, wings, and stubby tail dark blue. L 5″ (13 cm).

Similar Species: **Malachite Kingfisher,** found over water, is blue above eye.

Voice: A thin *tseet,* usually given in flight.

Habitat: Understory of rain forests, riverine forests in savannas, elephant-grass glades, dry woodlands, thorny thickets, and gardens. Not tied to water.

Nesting: Excavates a burrow up to 24″ (60 cm) long in an eroded gully, stream bank, or termite mound, where it lays 3–6 eggs.

Range: Resident from Senegal east to s Ethiopia, and south to Malawi. Moves north into Sahel and Eritrea in northern rainy

season, and south to Natal in southern rainy season.

This quiet bird captures large insects, spiders, and small lizards, takes them to its perch, and beats them to death. It does not fish.

416 **Gray-headed Kingfisher**
Gray-hooded Kingfisher
Halcyon leucocephala

Description: Long, heavy, *all-red bill. Dusky gray head,* shading into white throat and chest; *rusty orange belly.* Back and shoulders black; azure-blue flight feathers, rump, and tail. L 8″ (20 cm).

Similar Species: **Woodland Kingfisher** has blue back, white belly, and black-and-red bill.

Voice: A rather weak, descending *jee-jee-jee-jee-jee-chee.*

Habitat: Dry savanna woodlands, forest edges, and sometimes near water.

Nesting: Flashes rusty, black, and white underwings from a treetop in courtship. Excavates a tunnel up to a yard (meter) long in a riverbank, eroded gully, or termite mound, where it lays 3 or 4 eggs.

Range: Cape Verde Islands; also Senegal east to Somalia, and south to n Natal. South of Zambezi it is a summer breeding migrant.

Solitary or in migrant groups, the Gray-headed Kingfisher perches on an open branch and flies down rapidly to snatch up grasshoppers, crickets, beetles, caterpillars, and small lizards, but does not fish.

417 **Woodland Kingfisher**
Halcyon senegalensis

Description: *Strong bill red above, black below;* head gray. Nape, back, tail, and flight feathers blue; shoulders and primary tips black. *Underparts pure white.* L 9″ (23 cm).

Similar Species: Larger **Blue-breasted Kingfisher** *(H. malimbica)* has black on lower back and blue on chest; lives in rain forests, mangrove forests, and wetter savannas from s Senegal east to Lake Victoria.

Voice: A trilling *ki-tirrr* and a harsh *kee-kee-kee-kee.*

Habitat: Wooded savannas and forest edges.

Nesting: Nests in a tree cavity, not in ground. Prefers a large isolated tree with clearing around it. Lays 2–4 eggs.

Range: Senegal east to Ethiopia, and south to n Namibia and Natal. Breeds in northern and southern rainy seasons, retreating from vast areas during dry seasons.

The Woodland Kingfisher perches on a shaded branch, scanning for prey. It feeds chiefly on large insects. It migrates at night and is common in wet months.

---

418 Striped Kingfisher
Halcyon chelicuti

Description: A *drab,* medium-size kingfisher, with a brown back and a black line through the eye. Bill black above, red below. *Fine brown stripes on crown, neck, and underparts.* Bright blue on rump, tail, and wings. L 7″ (18 cm).

Similar Species: Larger **Brown-hooded Kingfisher** *(H. albiventris)* has all-red bill and buff neck; ranges from s Kenya and Zaire south to s Cape Province, in wetter woodlands and gardens with tall trees.

Voice: Varies within range. Calls include a *chee-cheer* and a *cheer-deeoo-deeoo-deeoo.*

Habitat: Wooded savannas, arid thornbush, park-like country, and farmlands.

Nesting: Engages in wing-spreading displays in courtship. Often has helpers at nest. Lays 3–6 eggs in a tree hole.

Range: Southern Mauritania and n Sierra Leone east to Ethiopia, and south to ne Namibia and n Natal.

Regularly seen in most savanna parks, the Striped Kingfisher can be overlooked because of its drab colors, small size, and preference for shaded perches. It feeds on insects and lizards.

Bee-eaters
Family Meropidae

Bright-plumaged birds, bee-eaters specialize in catching large, flying, stinging insects. After banging a bee or wasp dead, they squeeze the venom out and remove the stinger. All bee-eaters have long, thin, arched black bills, as well as small red eyes, pointed wings, and very short legs. Most have a black mark through the eye, and some have long, pointed central tail feathers. The sexes are similar. At night, many roost body to body in a line on a branch. There are 24 species worldwide, with 19 in Africa.

419 Red-throated Bee-eater
Merops bullocki

Description: Green crown, wings, and tail. Black eye mask; *bright red throat;* buffy hindneck and breast. *Deep blue thighs and vent.* Square tail. Eastern birds have turquoise blue above and below eye mask. L 9″ (23 cm).

Similar Species: **White-fronted Bee-eater** has white forehead and white line below eye. 2 small bee-eaters live on rain-forest edges and along rivers in humid w Africa: **Black Bee-eater** *(M. gularis)* is black with blue eyebrow and belly; male has red throat. **Rosy Bee-eater** *(M. malimbicus)* is slaty above, with white line below eye and rosy pink underparts.

Voice: A loud *wip;* also other trilling calls.

Habitat: Open wooded savannas and bushed pastures near rivers and seasonal streams; also gardens and marshes.

Nesting: Nests in colonies. Starts to excavate

burrow, near top of perpendicular cliff, during rains in September. Burrow is 32″ (80 cm) deep. Lays single clutch of 3 or 4 eggs.

Range: West African savannas from Senegal east to Chad; s Nile watershed from w Ethiopia south to nw Uganda.

This bee-eater feeds alone, but within sight and sound of others of its species. It perches on a branch, waiting for a passing bee or beetle. Colonies may have as few as five and as many as 150 pairs.

---

420 White-fronted Bee-eater
Merops bullockoides

Description: *White forehead; black eye mask with wide white line below; bright red lower throat.* Buffy nape and breast; purple-blue rump and vent. Square green tail; green wings and back. L 9″ (23 cm).

Similar Species: Ranges to south of **Red-throated Bee-eater,** which has no white on head. **European Bee-eater** *(M. apiaster)* has yellow throat, black necklace, blue underparts, and brown crown and back; breeds in nw Africa and sw South Africa, wintering or migrating through most of sub-Saharan Africa.

Voice: A nasal *gaah,* and a sharp *waark.*

Habitat: Watercourses, eroded gullies, edges of montane forests, and scrubby hillsides.

Nesting: Excavates a burrow in a vertical cliff in colonies of 10–20, sometimes up to 150, pairs. Clans of up to 5 pairs visit each other's nests, but repel neighbors from other clans. Clan members fly off to distant foraging area, which they vigorously defend from other clans.

Range: Highlands of sw Kenya and n Tanzania; also s Gabon and s Tanzania south to n Botswana and n Natal.

A sentinel feeder that sits on its favorite perch and charges out after passing large insects, the White-fronted Bee-eater conducts elaborate aerial chases or swoops down to herbage.

421 **Little Bee-eater**
Merops pusillus

Description: Green crown, back, wings, and tail. Black eye mask; blue line above eye in e and s Africa. *Bright yellow throat; black-and-rufous necklace;* buffy underparts. *Flight feathers and outer tail feathers rufous, all with black terminal bands;* tail notched. L 6.5″ (16 cm).

Similar Species: **Blue-breasted Bee-eater** *(M. variegatus)* has white at rear of yellow throat and wider blue necklace; inhabits swamps from Cameroon east to Lake Victoria, and south to Zambia, plus Ethiopia. **Somali Bee-eater** *(M. revoilii)* is washed-out green and buff; lives in arid thornscrub north and east of Mount Kenya to Horn of Africa. **Little Green Bee-eater** *(M. orientalis)* is common along Nile from Cairo south to n Uganda, and Sahel from Mauritania east to Eritrea; green with thin black eye mask and necklace, and long thin tail streamers.

Voice: A quiet *slip,* singly or in a series.

Habitat: In dry season: grassy places, usually near streams, marshes, and lakes. In rainy season: wooded savannas, grassy clearings in forests, and plains.

Nesting: Solitary pairs excavate burrows in the lee of a tussock in gently sloping ground, as well as in cliff faces. Lays 4–6 eggs.

Range: Sub-Saharan Africa from Senegal east to Somalia, and south to c Botswana and Natal.

This bird is often seen in pairs perched in tall grass or twiggy bushes below eye level. On safaris to major reserves, many non-naturalists who are looking for cats and antelopes marvel at the sight of the Little Bee-eater.

422 Cinnamon-chested Bee-eater
Merops oreobates

Description: Green crown, wings, and tail. Black eye mask; wide black necklace. *Yellow throat shades into white V on sides of neck. Chest broadly rufous,* shading to buffy on vent. L 8″ (20 cm).

Similar Species: **Little Bee-eater** and **Blue-breasted Bee-eater** (*M. variegatus;* from Cameroon east to Lake Victoria, and south to Zambia, plus Ethiopia) are smaller, with rufous on wings and tail.

Voice: Calls include a long *tzee-ip* and a *tee-si-sip.*

Habitat: Wet montane forest edges, clearings, and gardens. Chiefly from 6,000′ to 8,200′ (1,800–2,500 m).

Nesting: Small colonies of 2–10 pairs excavate burrows in sunny road cuts, quarries, and stream banks. Lays 2 or 3 eggs.

Range: Mountains of e Africa: e Zaire, Uganda, Rwanda, Burundi, Kenya, and n Tanzania.

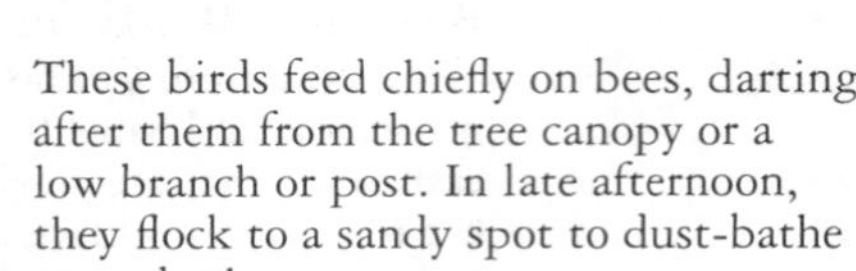

These birds feed chiefly on bees, darting after them from the tree canopy or a low branch or post. In late afternoon, they flock to a sandy spot to dust-bathe or sunbathe.

---

423 Swallow-tailed Bee-eater
Merops hirundinaceus

Description: *Pale green crown, back, wings, and breast;* rufous flight feathers. *Rump and long forked tail blue* (but tail green in w Africa). Black eye mask, with blue line below. *Yellow throat above blue necklace.* L 9″ (22 cm).

Similar Species: **Little Bee-eater** has black-and-rufous necklace, and rufous outer tail feathers on short notched tail.

Voice: Soft twittering notes and a dry *kwit.*

Habitat: Savanna woodlands with tall grass, riverine forests, and semi-deserts.

Nesting: Nests alone or in groups of 2 or 3 pairs. Nest burrow is often in flat sandy ground. Lays 2 or 3 eggs.

Range: Senegal east to n Uganda in savanna belt; also s Tanzania and s Zaire south to n South Africa, chiefly in lowlands.

Many individuals of this species vacate parts of the range during the dry or cooler months. The Swallow-tailed Bee-eater sunbathes with its wings open and its head to the side. When not breeding, up to 30 birds roost side by side on a branch in a leafy tree at night.

---

424 **White-throated Bee-eater**
Merops albicollis

Description: Striking facial pattern: *black crown, eye mask, and necklace, with white eyebrow and throat.* Rusty nape; pale green back, wings, and underparts. Blue tail with very long streamers. L 12″ (30 cm).

Similar Species: **Blue-cheeked Bee-eater** *(M. persicus)* is large, bright green, with turquoise above and below eye mask, and rusty throat; breeds in nw Africa, and breeds and winters in w African savannas; another group breeds from India west to Nile Delta, wintering widely in e and s Africa. **Madagascar Bee-eater** (Olive Bee-eater; *M. superciliosus*) has rufous crown and throat, and white lines above and below black eye mask; breeds in e and sc Africa; Madagascar breeders winter from Ethiopia south to Mozambique.

Voice: A *prueek* note when perched; flocks in flight give a *prreep.*

Habitat: Sparsely wooded subdesert scrub, wadis, and sand dunes during summer rains; wooded savannas during migration; canopy and edges of tall rain forests in northern winter.

Nesting: Nests in colonies of up to hundreds of pairs. Burrows are dug at a steep angle into flat sand. Female lays 6 or 7 eggs; pairs usually have helpers at nest.

Range: Breeds in narrow belt of Sahel from Mauritania east to Eritrea, and arid Kenyan rift valley. Winters chiefly in

tall rain forests of w Africa and Congo Basin east to Uganda. Wanders widely in e Africa and Ethiopia.

Gregarious and vocal at all seasons, this bird darts after flying ants and other insects, eating few bees. It forages from low bushes in summer where there are few trees in its habitat. In winter it may perch 230 feet (70 m) up in a giant rain-forest tree.

425, 426 **Carmine Bee-eater**
Merops nubicus

Description: *Rosy carmine red above and below.* Blue-green crown; black eye mask; pale blue vent and rump. Long, black-tipped central tail streamers. L 15″ (38 cm).

Subspecies and Ranges: **Northern Carmine Bee-eater** *(M. n. nubicus)* has blue-green throat; breeds in savanna belt from Senegal east to Somalia; disperses north into Sahel with rains; winters south to edge of rain forest in west and to coastal Kenya and ne Tanzania in east. **Southern Carmine Bee-eater** *(M. n. nubicoides)* has uniformly carmine throat and underparts; breeds in Zambia, s Malawi, Zimbabwe, and n Botswana; then moves south into South Africa, and later migrates north to s Zaire and s Tanzania.

Voice: A deep throaty *tunk* in flight; a series of *rik* notes when perched.

Habitat: Wooded savannas, grassy plains, swamps with scattered trees, lakeshores, and mangrove forests.

Nesting: Nests in massive colonies of 100–1,000 pairs. Lays 2–5 eggs at the end of a burrow up to 13′ (4 m) long in a steep earthen cliff.

Carmine Bee-eaters do most of their feeding as they sail up to 330 feet (100 m) in the air. Northern birds ride on the backs of large ground birds and large mammals, chasing after flushed insects, and will also fly beside vehicles and herds of animals. They are strongly attracted to bushfires, where they seize flushed insects.

Rollers

Family Coraciidae

Rollers are stocky treetop birds with large heads, heavy hooked beaks, and fairly short legs. Their square tails are mainly short, although some species have long outer tail streamers. Their colors tend to beautiful shades of blue, purple, and russet, and are especially evident on the spread wings and tail. They are named for the aerial rolling that is part of the courtship and territorial display of many species. Worldwide there are 12 species, with eight in Africa.

427 Abyssinian Roller

Coracias abyssinica

Description: Heavy black bill and white face. *Rest of head, entire underparts, wing stripe, and tail turquoise-blue;* back cinnamon rufous. *Very long, blackish-purple tail streamers;* dark purple rump and flight feathers. L 17″ (43 cm).

Similar Species: **Lilac-breasted Roller** has dark purplish lilac on throat and breast, pale blue rump, and shorter tail streamers. **Blue-bellied Roller** *(C. cyanogaster),* of wet savannas from Senegal east to s Sudan, has creamy white head, neck, and breast; dark blue belly and wings; black back; long outer tail feathers.

Voice: A loud *rack* in flight; an explosive, screeching *aaarh* when perched.

Habitat: Dry savanna woodlands, roadsides, farms, gardens, and villages with scattered trees and posts to hunt from.

Nesting: Courtship and territorial flight involves noisy swoops up, diving and gliding, and swooping up again. Lays 4 eggs in a wall cavity, under a building eave, or in a tree or termite mound.

Range: Northern savannas from Senegal east to Ethiopia, and from s Egypt south to n Uganda and nw Kenya.

The Abyssinian Roller is commonly seen along most roadsides north of the rain-forest zone. Intolerant of people near its nest, it flies full speed at their heads, veering off at the last second. This bird feeds on large insects.

---

428 **Purple Roller**
Rufous-crowned Roller
Coracias naevia

Description: *The heaviest and darkest roller.* Crown and nape rufous-brown in north, olive green in south. Heavy black bill and eye mask, with long white eyebrow. *Throat, cheeks, and underparts dull purple, with many fine white stripes.* Back olive-brown. Wings, rump, and short tail are 2 shades of dark purple. L 16″ (40 cm).

Similar Species: **European Roller** *(C. garrulus)* is azure blue, with rufous back; breeds in nw Africa, and winters widely in savannas south of Sahara from Senegal east to Kenya, and south to Cape area. **Broad-billed Roller** (*Eurystomus glaucurus;* L 11″/28 cm) has yellow bill, rufous head and neck, violet throat and underparts; lives in sub-Saharan forest edges.

Voice: A muffled *kaa,* often given in a long series; during display flight, gives harsher *karaa-karaa* notes.

Habitat: Open wooded savannas, tilled farmlands, rocky hillsides, and arid thornbush with large trees or overhead wires for perches.

Nesting: Rolls to left and right in courtship flight. Lays 2–4 eggs in a cavity in a tree, stream bank, cliff, old building, or termite mound.

Range: Senegal east to Somalia, and south to c Tanzania; s Zaire and Zambia south to n South Africa.

A rather sluggish bird that hunts alone, the Purple Roller flies down fast to take insects, small lizards, snakes, and young birds. In many areas, it is nomadic, following the rains.

429, 430 **Lilac-breasted Roller**
Coracias caudata

Description: Heavy black bill; pale green crown and nape; black line through eye; white eyebrow and chin. *Dark purplish-lilac throat and chest with fine white streaks;* turquoise belly, wing patch, rump, and tail. Cinnamon-rufous back; dark purple shoulders. Birds of Ethiopia and Somalia have pale blue chest. L 15″ (38 cm).

Similar Species: **Abyssinian Roller** has turquoise-blue head and throat. **Racquet-tailed Roller** *(C. spatulata)* perches in canopy of woodlands from Angola east to Mozambique; is all turquoise below, and has enlarged tips on tail streamers.

Voice: A loud guttural *rak-rak.*

Habitat: Grasslands, wooded acacia savannas, gallery forests, and cultivated areas.

Nesting: Rolls noisily in flight when courting or defending territory. Lays 2–4 eggs in a cavity in a dead tree or termite mound.

Range: Eritrea south through most of e Africa to ne Namibia and n South Africa.

This bird's range coincides with the great wildlife reserves in Kenya, Tanzania, Zambia, Zimbabwe, Botswana, Namibia, and Transvaal. It scans for large insects from conspicuous low perches and telephone wires, and explodes in a riot of color when giving chase.

Hoopoe
Family Upupidae

This family, found in southern Europe, southern Asia, and Africa, comprises one species, described below.

431 **Crested Hoopoe**
Hoopoe
Upupa epops

Description: *Long, thin, down-curved bill. Buffy-orange head, neck, back, and underparts.* Long, *orange, black-tipped crest feathers* that can be raised or lowered over nape. Black and white bars and spots on wings and tail. Short legs. L 11″ (28 cm).

Voice: A low-pitched *hoop-hoop.*

Habitat: Wooded savannas, open parklands, olive groves (nw Africa), and towns.

Nesting: Finds a cavity in a tree, termite mound, stone wall, the ground, or a crevice in a building. Lays 4–9 eggs.

Range: Resident in nw Africa, along Nile, most of sub-Saharan Africa, and Madagascar. Eurasian breeders winter in savannas from Senegal east to Ethiopia.

An impressive bird, the Crested Hoopoe is usually seen probing in soft earth, leaf litter, or mammal droppings for a wide variety of insects. It flies like a giant butterfly with wide, rounded, pied wings. Individuals cross the Sahara in a broad front when migrating.

Wood-Hoopoes
Family Phoeniculidae

Wood-hoopoes are medium-size birds with long pointed bills (most strongly down-curved) and long tails. Their plumage is glossy blue, green, or black. They fly from tree to tree in forests and savanna woodlands, searching bark and limbs for insects; some are attracted to flowers and fruit. There are eight species in this family, which is restricted to sub-Saharan Africa.

432 **Black-billed Scimitarbill**
Greater Scimitarbill
Rhinopomastus cyanomelas

Description: *Long, thin, highly down-curved black bill;* black legs. Male glossy black, with *single white wing band in flight.* Female similar, but head brownish. L 10″ (26 cm).

Similar Species: **Red-billed Wood-Hoopoe** and **Violet Wood-Hoopoe** (*Phoeniculus damarensis;* lives chiefly in nw Namibia and n and e Kenya) are larger and have red bills and legs. **Lesser Scimitarbill** *(R. aterrimus)* inhabits northern savannas from Senegal to nw Uganda and Ethiopia, plus Angola; smaller, with shorter straight bill, and shorter tail without white spots. **Orange-billed Scimitarbill** (Abyssinian Scimitarbill; *R. minor*) lives in wooded savannas from Ethiopia south to c Tanzania; dark purplish black, with down-curved orange bill and no white on wings.

Voice: A series of up to 25 soft *wha* notes.

Habitat: Dry thorny savanna woodlands.

Nesting: A solitary nester without helpers. Lays 2–4 eggs in a tree cavity.

Range: Central Kenya south to n South Africa.

Usually found in pairs, probing branches and trunks of trees for hidden insects, the Black-billed Scimitarbill rarely gathers in flocks. It will join wandering, mixed-species bird parties in the nonbreeding season. It often hangs upside down and will descend trunks headfirst.

---

433 **Red-billed Wood-Hoopoe**
Green Wood-Hoopoe
Phoeniculus purpureus

Description: *Long, thin, down-curved, red bill; bright red legs.* Body dark glossy green; wings and *very long tail* dark glossy purple. Long and short white bands on outer wings; white spots on outer tail feathers. L 15″ (38 cm).

Similar Species: Larger **Violet Wood-Hoopoe** *(P. damarensis),* which lives chiefly in nw Namibia and n and e Kenya, is glossy purple and has floppier flight.

Voice: A series of *kak* and *kuk* calls.

Habitat: Savanna woodlands, riverine forests in arid areas, gardens, and villages.

Nesting: A cooperative breeder, with 1–10 helpers for the breeding pair; most a pair's recent young. Nests in a rotted cavity in a tree, fence post, or building. Lays 2–5 eggs.

Range: Senegal east to w Ethiopia, and south through e Africa to c Namibia and e South Africa.

Usually seen in territorial flocks of five to eight birds, Red-billed Wood-Hoopoes creep about all sides of trunks and branches, looking for insects and their larvae and pupae. On encountering another flock, they break out in hysterical cackling from a treetop.

Hornbills
Family Bucerotidae

Hornbills are large birds with long, heavy-looking, down-curved bills. Many of the larger species have a casque over the bill (the casque is a very light structure filled with hard, sponge-like tissue). They have long eyelashes, short legs, and long tails. Most species nest in tree cavities that the female seals up (except for a small hole) with her excrement; the female, eggs, and young are enclosed safely inside. The female is incarcerated for a few months in small species and up to five months in larger species; the male brings food to her and the young. There are 50 species worldwide and 23 in sub-Saharan Africa.

434 **Crowned Hornbill**
Tockus alboterminatus

Description: *Sooty brown,* with white belly and tail tip. *Bill red, with yellow band at base* and small casque above. *Yellow eye;* white spotting on long, loose crown feathers. L 21″ (53 cm).

Similar Species: **Bradfield's Hornbill** *(T. bradfieldi)* is paler brown and has orange bill without casque; lives in upper Zambezi Valley and n Botswana. **African Pied Hornbill** *(T. fasciatus)* is black, with white belly; yellow bill has black tip in w African forests, red tip in Congo Basin forests; common from Gambia east to w Uganda.

Voice: A loud *kew,* repeated rapidly when alarmed; also loud, piping calls.

Habitat: Montane, coastal, and riverine forests.

Nesting: Pairs form for life and reuse same nest hole in tree for many years. Female seals herself in before incubating 2–4 eggs for 30 days; breaks out when chicks are 40 days old. Youngsters reseal nest and remain another 2 weeks before their first flight.

Range: Uganda and c Kenya south locally to se Cape Province; also w Ethiopia.

The Crowned Hornbill pursues large insects on the ground, in trees, and in flight, and eats fruit when it is locally available. It may wander around in groups during times of food scarcity.

435 **African Gray Hornbill**
Tockus nasutus

Description: *Gray-brown, with white eyebrow,* belly, and tail tip. Male has black bill with *yellow or white blaze* in middle and small pointed casque. Female bill chiefly yellow above, with *dark red tip.* L 18″ (45 cm).

Similar Species: **Pale-billed Hornbill** *(T. pallidirostris)* has entirely cream-colored bill; lives in tall miombo woodlands from Angola east through Zambia to s Tanzania.

Voice: A long series of mournful whistled *whee* notes, then *whee-wheeu* notes, ending with *whee-whee-wheeu* notes.
Habitat: Savanna and riverine woodlands.
Nesting: Nests in a hollow tree cavity. Female seals herself in, leaving a slit through which male feeds her. Usually lays 2–4 eggs, which are incubated for 25 days.
Range: Senegal east to Ethiopia, and south to n South Africa.

This hornbill forages in leafy trees and on the ground. It takes half its food on the wing as it flutters about the branches, focusing on insects, tree frogs, chameleons, and small rodents. These birds undertake seasonal migrations to find food.

---

436 **Red-billed Hornbill**
Tockus erythrorhynchus

Description: Relatively narrow *red bill* (without casque), with some yellow at base. Face mainly white (grayer in s Africa); white underparts. Black back and tail; large white spots on shoulders. Flight reveals white on secondaries and outer tail feathers. L 18″ (45 cm).
Similar Species: **Von der Decken's Hornbill** has red bill with yellow tip (male) or black bill (female); no spots on shoulders.
Voice: A long series of *wok* notes, at first singly, then accelerating with *wok-wok* notes.
Habitat: Open wooded savannas, wooded streambeds, and thorn scrub.
Nesting: Nests in tree cavities and sealed-up honey logs. Lays 2–7 eggs. Incubation is 24 days.
Range: Savanna belt from Senegal east to Ethiopia, south to n Natal, and west to s Angola and n Namibia.

A social species found in groups of up to a dozen, the Red-billed Hornbill forages chiefly on open ground in areas that have been heavily grazed. It digs in the ground with its pick-ax bill for dung beetle larvae, and also feeds on large insects, scorpions, and centipedes. It raids Red-billed Quelea nesting colonies, taking eggs and young.

437 Southern Yellow-billed Hornbill
Tockus leucomelas

Description: *Bright yellow bill, with black cutting edges;* yellow casque of male merges with upper mandible. *Bare red skin around eye and throat.* Long, wide, white eyebrow, and white underparts; black crown and upperparts, with large white spots on wings. L 22″ (55 cm).

Similar Species: **Eastern Yellow-billed Hornbill** *(T. flavirostris)* lives in arid ne Africa from Eritrea south to ne Tanzania; has lower voice, and female has black patch on side of throat.

Voice: Single clucking notes, and a long series of *kok* notes that increase in intensity.

Habitat: Semi-arid savannas and riverine forests.

Nesting: Male feeds female for a month before she seals herself up in tree cavity. Usually lays 3 or 4 eggs, incubating them for 24 days.

Range: Zambezi Valley west to n Namibia and south to n Cape Province and Natal.

This hornbill is quite omnivorous, feeding on large insects, rodents, centipedes, scorpions, ants, bird eggs, fruit, and seeds. It runs about on open ground between clumps of taller grass, regularly turning over rocks and logs, using its bill as a lever.

438 Von der Decken's Hornbill
Tockus deckeni

Description: *Male has heavy red bill with bright yellow tip; female and immature have all-black bill.* White eyebrow, neck, and underparts; black face, crown, back, wings, and tail. White wing stripe and outer tail feathers. L 20″ (50 cm).

Similar Species: **Red-billed Hornbill** has large white spots on shoulders; both sexes have thinner red bill, without yellow tip.

Voice: A clucking series of *wek-wek-wek-wek* notes.

Habitat: Open savanna woodlands and semi-arid scrublands.

Nesting: Nests in a tree cavity. Female seals most of entrance with droppings and food remains. Usually lays 2 eggs and remains in nest for about 8 weeks.

Range: Central Ethiopia south through n and e Kenya to c Tanzania.

This hornbill forages mainly on the ground for large insects, snails, mice, nestling birds, lizards, seeds, buds, and fruit. It associates with the Dwarf Mongoose, the hornbill eating locusts that the mongoose flushes and in turn warning it of raptors. This bird is attracted to feeders.

---

439 Black-and-white Casqued Hornbill

Ceratogymna (Bycanistes) subcylindricus

Description: Male has *huge, blunt, black casque* (with cream-colored base in east) over thick blackish beak; bill of female smaller, all black. *Glossy black, with white lower breast and belly, secondaries and inner primaries, rump, and tail corners.* L 30″ (75 cm).

Similar Species: **Silvery-cheeked Hornbill** has all-black wings and yellowish casque. **White-crested Hornbill** *(Tockus albocristatus)* is black with fluffy white crest; looks like a giant wood-hoopoe, with white spots on wings and extremely long tail; inhabits wet forests from Sierra Leone east to w Uganda.

Voice: A loud prolonged *hoot,* repeated slowly. Western birds give raucous quacking.

Habitat: Rain forests, forest edges and patches, and towns with huge trees.

Nesting: Courting male gives piece of bark to female. Both help seal nest cavity, 30–100′ (9–30 m) up a tree. Incubates 2 eggs for 42 or more days, with chicks leaving hole in 80 days; thus female spends more than 17 weeks incarcerated.

Range: Ivory Coast east locally to Uganda and sw Kenya; also ne Angola. Ranges to 8,500′ (2,600 m).

These hornbills are a spectacular sight. They are usually seen in pairs, roosting on a dead branch. Sometimes flocks mob a predator. This bird tears off bark looking for large insects, and crashes into foliage when chasing roosting bats and birds.

---

440 **Silvery-cheeked Hornbill**
Ceratogymna (Bycanistes) brevis

Description: *Heavy gray bill with yellow line at base, and large, pointed, all-yellowish casque.* Glossy black, with white lower belly, rump, and tail corners. Silver tips to feathers on face. L 32″ (80 cm).

Similar Species: **Black-and-white Casqued Hornbill** has darker casque, more white on breast and belly, and extensive white on closed wings. Smaller **Trumpeter Hornbill** *(C. {Bycanistes} bucinator)* has bare red skin on face, white on breast and belly, and narrow white band on secondaries; cries like a loud human baby, *waaa-aaa-aaaa-aaaa;* lives in forests from se Kenya to Natal.

Voice: A series of growling *quark* notes; softer grunts and quacks when feeding.

Habitat: Montane and lowland forests, and towns with very large trees.

Nesting: Male swallows lumps of soil and coughs them up as pellets for female to apply to edges of nesting cavity. Incubates 1 or 2 eggs for 40 days.

Range: Mountain forests from Ethiopia south through Kenya (chiefly east of rift valley) to e Zimbabwe; also coastal forests in Kenya and Tanzania. Ranges to 8,500′ (2,600 m).

These hornbills roost communally, in groups of up to 200 birds. They fly off a half hour after sunrise and return before sunset, their wings making a loud whooshing sound. This bird feeds mainly on fruit in the tree canopy, but it also hunts small animals, attacks roosting bats, and eats nestling birds, ranging widely in its searches for food.

441 Abyssinian Ground-Hornbill
Bucorvus abyssinicus

Description: A huge, black, turkey-like bird. Long, down-curved, black bill surmounted by *high, short, sharply angled casque;* base of upper mandible red or yellow. *Bare blue skin around eye.* Large, bare, red and blue inflatable throat pouch. *White primaries.* L 3′7″ (1.08 m).

Similar Species: **Southern Ground-Hornbill** has bare red skin around eye.

Voice: A series of deep booming notes, *uumh-uuh-uuh-uuh-uuh.*

Habitat: Grasslands and wooded savannas.

Nesting: Solitary pair (without helpers) nests in a large tree cavity, beehive log, or a hole dug in an earthen bank. Does not seal hole. Lays 1 or 2 eggs. Male brings food to female, who does all incubating. Nesting period is about 90 days.

Range: Senegal east to nw Kenya and Ethiopia.

These birds walk the savanna in pairs, catching any small mammals, birds, reptiles (including turtles), frogs, and insects in their path, and also eating some fruit, seeds, and peanuts. They rarely fly, preferring to walk away from a disturbance.

442 Southern Ground-Hornbill
Bucorvus cafer

Description: Heavy, down-curved, black bill with *small rounded casque. Bare, bright red skin*

around eye and down foreneck, forming pouch; female pouch has blue center. Plumage dull black, except for *white primaries.* L 3′6″ (1.05 m).

Similar Species: **Abyssinian Ground-Hornbill** has blue facial skin.

Voice: A low-pitched, booming *oom oom oom-oom,* very like a Lion's roar; may be given in duet and in flight.

Habitat: Open woodlands and grasslands.

Nesting: 1 pair, with up to 6 immature and adult helpers, defends a vast territory year-round. All adult males courtship-feed the breeding female, but only dominant male mates with her. Lays 1 or 2 eggs on a bed of leaves in a tree hole, rock face, or earthen bank. Nest is not sealed. Other females may relieve mother for periods of the 40-day incubation.

Range: Central Kenya and s Zaire south to c Botswana and e South Africa. Ranges to 10,000′ (3,000 m).

This hornbill walks up to 7 miles (11 km) a day, but will fly across territory unsuitable for walking. It takes most food on the ground, digging with its bill deep into the soil for prey that run into holes. It eats rodents, hares, snakes, lizards, toads, snails, and large insects, and flies to grass fires in order to capture fleeing creatures.

BARBETS, WOODPECKERS, AND THEIR ALLIES

Order Piciformes

These birds have strong bills, usually nest in cavities, and have two toes forward, two behind. Africa has representatives of the barbet, honeyguide, and woodpecker families. The other three families—the jacamars, puffbirds, and toucans—are restricted to Latin America. Of the world's 376 species, 89 live in Africa.

Barbets
Family Capitonidae

These are tiny (the tinkerbirds) to medium-size, woodpecker-like birds. Strongly patterned or colored, barbets are stocky and have large heads. The sexes are alike. Their bills are thick and pointed, some with notches on the sides to aid in tearing up fruit. Barbets nest and roost in holes they excavate in trees, termite mounds, or the ground. Their voices are loud. They occur from the wettest rain forests to the edges of deserts, with 42 of the world's 75 species found in Africa.

443 Red-fronted Barbet
Tricholaema diademata

Description: A small pied barbet, with a black eye mask; black crown accented by *red forecrown.* Long eyebrow yellow in front, white behind. Upperparts black, with golden spots; throat and underparts white, with *dark spots on flanks.* L 6″ (15 cm).

Similar Species: 2 similar small barbets in e Africa lack red forecrown and have black throats: **Spotted-flanked Barbet** *(T. lachrymosa),* with heavy black flank spots and unspotted black back; and **Black-throated Barbet** (Brown-throated Barbet; *T. melanocephala*), with yellow-spotted black back and clear white underparts. **Pied Barbet** *(T. leucomelaina)* has red forehead and black throat; widespread in acacia woodlands from Zambezi south to Cape Town area.

Voice: A series of up to 15 low *twa* notes.

Habitat: Wooded and bushed grasslands at 2,000–7,000′ (600–2,100 m) elevation.

Nesting: Both sexes excavate a hole on the underside of a dead limb in a tree, or (especially) the giant, cactus-like euphorbia. Lays 3 or 4 eggs.

Range: Ethiopia south to c Tanzania.

This barbet moves slowly through trees, bushes, and tangles, eating fruit and berries. It also feeds on termites and winged ants on the ground.

444 **Black-collared Barbet**
Lybius torquatus

Description: Heavy black bill. *Red forehead, cheeks, and throat; black hindcrown and collar around neck and chest.* Olive-brown back, tail, and wings; wings have yellow edging. Belly yellow. L 8″ (20 cm).

Similar Species: **Vieillot's Barbet** *(L. vieilloti),* common in much of w Africa from Senegal east to Sudan, has red head but lacks black collar. **Brown-breasted Barbet** *(L. melanopterus)* has red head, brown collar, and white belly; lives from Kenya coast south to Mozambique, and inland to Arusha area of n Tanzania.

Voice: A repeated, synchronized duet of *tooo-borra.*

Habitat: Open savanna woodlands, riverine forest edges, and gardens with tall trees.

Nesting: Engages in very active displays of bobbing, wiping bill on branch, and flicking wings and tail; pairs touch bills, as if kissing. Excavates nest hole in a dead branch and may reuse it for years. Adults and helpers share incubation of 2–5 eggs and feeding of young.

Range: Resident from coastal Kenya, se Rwanda, and c Tanzania, south to e South Africa, and west to c Angola.

This barbet's duet is a common sound in the southern bush. The bird feeds chiefly on fruit and berries, but also actively seeks large insects in trees, in the air, and on the ground.

445 **Double-toothed Barbet**
Lybius bidentatus

Description: Large ivory bill with 2 heavy serrations; short black whiskers; large patch of bare yellow skin around eye. Black above, with red stripe on wing; white rump. *Bright red below, with white, fan-shaped flank patch.* L 9″ (23 cm).

Similar Species: **Bearded Barbet** *(L. dubius)* ranges just to north, from Senegal east to Central African Republic; has black breast band and long black whiskers around bill.

Voice: Quiet for a barbet. Calls include a hard *check* and a prolonged buzzing trill.

Habitat: Edges of rain forests, riverine forests, and savanna woodlands.

Nesting: Young of previous year often welcomed as helpers at nest. Lays 2 or 3 eggs in an excavated cavity in a tree or stub.

Range: Guinea-Bissau south to n Angola, and east to Ethiopia and sw Kenya.

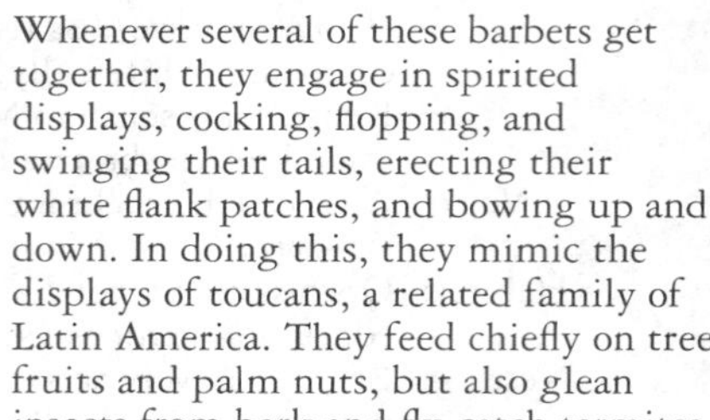

Whenever several of these barbets get together, they engage in spirited displays, cocking, flopping, and swinging their tails, erecting their white flank patches, and bowing up and down. In doing this, they mimic the displays of toucans, a related family of Latin America. They feed chiefly on tree fruits and palm nuts, but also glean insects from bark and fly-catch termites.

---

446 Crested Barbet
Levaillant's Barbet
Trachyphonus (Lybius) vaillantii

Description: Heavy, pointed, ivory bill with dark tip. *Yellow head and underparts all flecked with red;* red forehead; small black crest. Upperparts, necklace, and long tail black, marked with *white, scale-shaped spots.* Red rump. L 9″ (23 cm).

Similar Species: **Red-and-yellow Barbet** has red bill and head, and round white spots.

Voice: Male gives a long *trrrrrrrrrrrrrr,* like a distant alarm clock, and a fast series of *kik* notes; female responds with a series of double notes, *puka-puka-puka.*

Habitat: Open woodlands, thickets, and riverine forests.

Nesting: Pairs stay together and maintain territory

all year, chasing away other hole-nesting birds. Excavates a nest hole or uses a natural hole; lays 3 or 4 eggs.

Range: Spottily distributed from e Rwanda and c Tanzania south to e South Africa.

This bird forages chiefly on the ground, feeding on fruit, berries, seeds, large insects, and worms. It clings to trees like a woodpecker, opening up termite tunnels. The Crested Barbet is not graceful; it hops and lurches about, both on the ground and in its slow, floppy flight.

---

447 **Red-and-yellow Barbet**
Trachyphonus (Lybius) erythrocephalus

Description: *Long red bill; red head with white ear patch. Upperparts and necklace black with round white spots;* underparts bright yellow. Male has black chin stripe. L 9″ (23 cm).

Similar Species: **D'Arnaud's Barbet** has pale yellow belly and lacks red bill and head. **Crested Barbet** has scale-shaped, white spots. **Yellow-billed Barbet** *(T. purpuratus)* lives in forest edges and gardens from Sierra Leone east to sw Kenya; has dark, glossy, purplish head and upperparts, and yellow belly with black spots.

Voice: Duet is a long bubbling medley that sounds like its English name, *red n' yellow,* repeated over and over.

Habitat: Low woodlands, scrubby savannas, and rugged, semi-arid terrain.

Nesting: Pairs often have several sub-adult helpers. Tunnels about 16″ (40 cm) into a termite mound, stream bank, or road cut. Usually lays 4 or 5 eggs.

Range: Ethiopia south to n Tanzania.

The Red-and-yellow Barbet forages on the ground and in thickets for fruit, berries, large insects, centipedes, and nestling birds. It is very tame in areas where humans feed it, such as at the historic overlook of Olduvai Gorge, in northern Tanzania.

448 **D'Arnaud's Barbet**
Trachyphonus (Lybius) darnaudii

Description: Ivory-colored bill (black in Serengeti area); *yellow head with black spots and narrow black forecrown.* White-spotted, black upperparts. *1 large and many small spots on pale yellow underparts;* red vent. L 6.5″ (16.5 cm).

Voice: Duet, often with birds facing each other, can be rendered as *ker-ta-tee-tootle.*

Habitat: Semi-arid desert scrub and wooded savannas below 5,000′ (1,500 m).

Nesting: Pair often has helpers. Digs a vertical hole straight into earth as deep as 3′ (1 m), with a chamber to the side above the bottom. Lays 2–4 eggs.

Range: Southern Ethiopia south to n Tanzania.

This bird's duet, repeated over and over, is a characteristic sound of the eastern African bush. D'Arnaud's Barbet hops on the ground with its head raised, and also forages low in bushes, feeding on insects, fruit, berries, and seeds.

HONEYGUIDES
Family Indicatoridae

Honeyguides are small olive or brown-and-white treetop birds with white outer tail feathers. There are 19 species worldwide, with two in southern Asia; the other 17 live only in Africa. Two of these are known to guide humans and Ratels (Honey Badgers) to beehives, where the birds hope for scraps. All lay their eggs in other birds' nests; the female may puncture or remove the host's eggs. The young are born with a hook on the bill for killing the host's nestlings; the hook then drops off, and the honeyguides are fed by the host.

449 **Greater Honeyguide**
Black-throated Honeyguide
Indicator indicator

Description: Dull brown above, dingy white below. White edging on wing feathers; *white outer tail feathers. Some males have black throat, white cheeks, and pink bill.* Immature buffy yellow below. L 8″ (20 cm).

Similar Species: **Lesser Honeyguide** *(I. minor),* of sub-Saharan Africa, has gray head, dark "mustache," and olive-green wings. **Scaly-throated Honeyguide** *(I. variegatus)* of e and s Africa has spotted head and underparts.

Voice: Male gives a series of up to 11 far-carrying *burr-wit* notes.

Habitat: Forest edges, woodlands, wooded savannas, and pine and eucalyptus plantations.

Nesting: A nest parasite. Male has stud-perch on a treetop, where he sings all day long in breeding season in hopes of mating with many females. Female lays 4–8 eggs, 1 each in nests of hole-nesting birds; unwitting hosts include hoopoes, bee-eaters, kingfishers, barbets, woodpeckers, and swallows.

Range: Senegal east to Ethiopia, and south to Cape Town area.

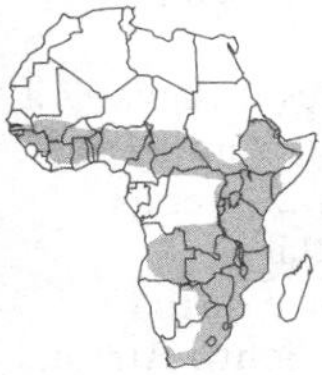

In consciously seeking help from people in opening up bee nests, the Greater Honeyguide may have the most advanced bird/human relationship in the wild. It guides humans and other mammals by flicking its white tail feathers. It eats not only some wax, but the bee larvae and eggs inside. It also forages in trees for termites, ants, beetles, and grubs.

Woodpeckers
Family Picidae

Woodpeckers use their strong toes and stiff tail feathers to hitch up tree trunks, although a few feed chiefly on the ground. Many hammer with powerful, tapered, chisel-like beaks. Their extremely long tongues, some armed with a horny spear at the tip, can follow openings in the wood. There are 212 species worldwide (none in Madagascar or Australasia). The 30 African species are mainly drab, uncommon, and inconspicuous compared to their relatives in the Americas and Eurasia.

---

450 **Bearded Woodpecker**
Thripias (Dendropicos) namaquus

Description: *Long-billed, with black ear patch and "mustache" on white head.* Black crown with white spots on forehead; male has red cap. Body dark olive, *barred above and below with yellowish white.* L 10″ (25 cm).

Similar Species: **Cardinal Woodpecker** *(Dendropicos fuscescens)* is small (L 6″/15 cm), with hindcrown red (male) or black (female), and white face with black mustache; lives in savanna woodlands from Senegal east to Ethiopia, and south to South Africa.

Voice: Loud rattles: *wicka-wicka-wicka.*

Habitat: Dry scrub, wooded savannas, and riverine forests.

Nesting: Maintains large territories. Excavates a hole in a dead or live tree from 7′ to 66′ (2–20 m) high. Lays 2–4 eggs, incubating them for 13 days.

Range: Central African Republic east to Ethiopia, and south to n South Africa.

This bird drums more loudly and more often than other woodpeckers in its range. It forages a long time in one spot if the tree or log has beetle larvae or grubs.

SONGBIRDS
Order Passeriformes

The following families belong to a single order that includes the majority of living birds. These species, called songbirds or passerines, are generally small land birds with pleasing songs. Of about 5,400 species worldwide, 1,276 live in Africa.

LARKS
Family Alaudidae

Small terrestrial birds known for their songs, larks nest on the ground and advertise their territory mainly with song flights, but they also sing from bush tops and posts. Most are cryptically colored; their streaky browns match the soil colors where they live, an adaptation that has created a large number of subspecies. The sexes are alike, except in sparrow-larks. Lark bills are usually short and conical; a few are long and down-curved. Larks walk (rather than hop) on the ground with strong feet, and many have long hind toes. The 80 worldwide species are concentrated in Eurasia and Africa. Of 67 species known from Africa, 52 are restricted to sub-Saharan Africa.

451 Rufous-naped Lark
Mirafra africana

Description: Dark brown upperparts spotted with black. *Rufous wing patch conspicuous in flight.* Sometimes appears crested; *crown and nape brown or rufous.* Pale buffy eyebrow, throat, and underparts; streaked chest. L 7″ (18 cm).

Similar Species: **Red-winged Bush-Lark** *(M. hypermetra)* is larger (L 9″/23 cm), with longer tail and conspicuous patch of black streaks on side of neck; lives in low arid bush country below 4,300′ (1,300 m) from

Ethiopia south to n and e Kenya, n Uganda, and ne Tanzania east of rift valley. **Sabota Lark** *(M. sabota)* is common in arid parts of Namibia, Botswana, and South Africa; heavily striped, with dark cap, white eye line, and no rufous on wing.

Voice: Clear, 2-part whistle with 4 notes, *treelee-truloo;* or 5 notes rendered as *hope you can see me.* Sings year-round in air or from a low bush, rock, or hillock, often endlessly. Also mimics alarm notes and songs of other birds.

Habitat: Highland grasslands, acacia savannas, clearings, and grainfields. Usually above 4,000′ (1,200 m) in tropics, but down to sea level in se Africa.

Nesting: Builds a nest of grass that is partially domed. Lays 1–4 eggs.

Range: Local in w Africa in Mount Nimba (Ivory Coast) and Cameroon areas. Widespread in e African highlands and south to c Namibia and e South Africa.

This is perhaps the most common lark in Africa, and certainly the most conspicuous along many highland roadsides. It likes open ground to run around in, tall grass to hide in, and anthills to sing from.

452 **Red-capped Lark**
Calandrella cinerea

Description: A small lark, with a *white breast and eyebrow. Red crown and red patch on side of chest above wing.* Black tail narrowly edged in white. L 6″ (15 cm).

Similar Species: **Short-toed Lark** *(C. brachydactyla)* breeds in nw Africa and s Eurasia and winters commonly in Sahel from Mauritania east to n Ethiopia; has partial black collar below, and brown crown. **Fischer's Sparrow-Lark** *(Eremopterix leucopareia),* abundant in e African dry grasslands, is tiny, with gray back; male has black eyebrow and black line down throat and chest.

Voice: Utters a *chirrup* when flushed. (See also Nesting.)

Habitat: Short dry grasslands, especially where recently grazed or burned; also plowed and recently harvested fields.

Nesting: Performs display flight 165′ (50 m) or higher in sky; flies into wind, fluttering and gliding in arcs while giving a pleasing jumble of sounds. Dives sharply back to earth. Lays 2 or 3 eggs in a grass cup nest placed in a depression so that the lip of the nest is even with the ground. Usually lays 2 eggs, incubating them for 14 days.

Range: Highland and plateau grasslands from Eritrea south to n Tanzania. Widespread from s Zaire south to Cape Town area.

When not breeding, this bird wanders about in flocks of a dozen, and sometimes of hundreds. If flushed, it takes off in low, dipping flight. It walks and runs about the open ground, catching small insects and eating seeds, and searching mammal droppings for seeds and larvae.

Swallows
Family Hirundinidae

Small birds that hunt insects as they fly low over fields, water, and treetops, swallows and martins all have stubby bills that open wide back to the gape, located below the eye. They have long wings, and some species have long outer tail streamers. The legs are very short. Unlike swifts, members of this family perch in the open on twigs, wires, rocks, and man-made structures. They gather in flocks, and many undergo long migrations. Worldwide there are 74 species, of which 38 occur in Africa; Africa is the winter home of eight species that breed in Eurasia.

453 **Wire-tailed Swallow**
Hirundo smithii

Description: *Rusty cap.* Dark blue face and upperparts; underparts and underwing linings white. *Very long, thin tail streamers.* L 5.5″ (14 cm).

Similar Species: **Mosque Swallow** *(H. senegalensis)* is large (L 10″/25 cm), with long forked tail; dark blue cap, hindneck, and upperparts; orange underparts; rusty patch behind eye; white throat and wing linings; ranges in pairs over savanna woodlands, often near water, baobabs, and villages, from Senegal east to Ethiopia, and south to Transvaal. **Barn Swallow** *(H. rustica)* is locally abundant migrant and winterer from Europe and n Asia south to Cape Town area; dark blue above, with dark necklace on buffy-white underparts.

Voice: Call is a flat *twit;* has a twittering song.

Habitat: Rivers and lakes near towns, villages, and bridges in savanna country.

Nesting: Builds a mud cup lined with straw under an eave, bridge, or overhanging rock.

Range: Senegal east to n Sudan and Somalia, and south through e Africa to Angola and Natal.

This swallow's flight is swift and graceful, with rapid wingbeats. Pairs or small groups cruise low over water and fields or above trees and buildings. The birds perch on bridges, overhead wires, and dead trees.

---

454 **Lesser Striped Swallow**
Hirundo abyssinica

Description: *Rusty head (to below eye), underwing linings, and rump.* Long forked tail; back and wings dark blue-black. Throat and underparts white, with *heavy black stripes throughout.* L 6″ (15 cm).

Similar Species: **Rock Martin** *(H. fuligula),* though not similar, is a commonly seen swallow near buildings and in rocky areas; pale brown in Sahara, dark brown in sub-Saharan Africa; has short notched tail.

Voice: A series of 3–5 descending *zree* notes, often given from perches below nest; quite vocal for a swallow.

Habitat: Savanna woodlands, streambeds, farms, forest edges, and highland grasslands. Often near rocks and man-made structures.

Nesting: Pairs are usually solitary, though they may nest near colonies of other swallows and swifts. Builds a hanging, gourd-shaped mud nest with a tubular entrance, attached to the underside of a large branch, overhanging rock, bridge, or eave of a building.

Range: Gambia east to Eritrea, and south to n Namibia and e South Africa.

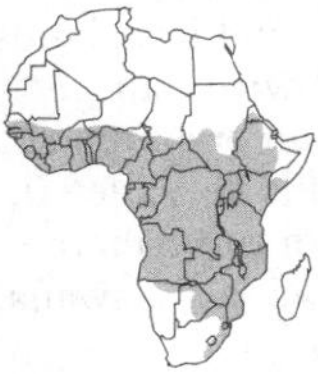

Unlike most swallows, this one feeds on acacia seedpods and some fruit, in addition to flying insects. Groups gather at insect concentrations and during migrations within Africa.

Pipits and Wagtails
Family Motacillidae

Small birds with thin bills, long legs, and long tails (usually with white outer tail feathers), members of this family walk around in grass and along watersides, searching for insects. There are three main groups: The pipits are brownish and streaked above. They resemble larks and have similar flight songs, but have straight thin bills and wag their tails often. The wagtails are very long-tailed and are often tied to watersides. They are gray or black above, with black patterns on white or yellow underparts. The longclaws are streaked brownish above, with bright colors on the throat and/or breast. The family numbers some 55 species worldwide, with 36 known in Africa, including some that winter from Eurasia.

455 Yellow Wagtail
Motacilla flava

Description: A typical fall and winter bird might have a *gray crown* and cheeks, *grayish green on upperparts, and bright yellow underparts;* pale whitish eyebrow and throat; 2 pale wing bars; white outer tail feathers. In spring, colors and patterns on heads of males are various combinations of black, white, blue-gray, and yellow. L 6.5″ (16 cm).

Similar Species: **Cape Wagtail** *(M. capensis),* of marshes and towns in e and s Africa, has brownish-gray necklace and upperparts, with white underparts and eyebrow.

Voice: In sub-Saharan Africa, gives a single loud *tsee* or a *tsee-weep.*

Habitat: Wet meadows, marshes, lawns, open watersides, rice paddies, and grasslands.

Nesting: Makes a cup nest, lined with hair, in a shallow depression in an open marsh.

Range: Breeds in nw Africa and Nile Valley in Egypt. Winters widely in sub-Saharan Africa south to c Namibia, n Botswana, and e and s South Africa.

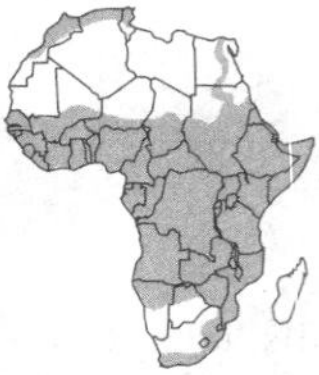

About a dozen subspecies of Yellow Wagtails winter in Africa. Breeding-plumage males look quite different from each other. They often snatch insects flushed by grazing mammals.

456 African Pied Wagtail
Motacilla aguimp

Description: *Black above, with white eyebrow and largely white wings.* Wide black patch on face; black necklace surrounding white throat; rest of underparts white. Long black tail with white outer tail feathers. L 8″ (20 cm).

Similar Species: **Mountain Wagtail** (Long-tailed Wagtail; *M. clara*) inhabits rocky streams in mountains and wet areas from Sierra Leone east to Ethiopia, and south to e South Africa; has gray crown and back, white eyebrow and underparts, and black crescent on chest. **White Wagtail** *(M. alba)* winters widely from n Africa south to upper Niger Valley and Ethiopia; adult has white forehead and face, surrounded in black or gray.

Voice: A melodious, canary-like song, repeating most notes 2 or 3 times. Flight call is a loud *chiz-zit* or *tuu-whee.*

Habitat: All manner of watersides, and cities, villages, farms, and homes.

Nesting: Builds a rough, bulky, cup-shaped nest lined with fine grass, hair, and feathers in a rock cleft or building. Lays 2–7 eggs. Often suffers as host of cuckoos.

Range: Sierra Leone and s Egypt south to n and e South Africa. Ranges to 10,000′ (3,000 m).

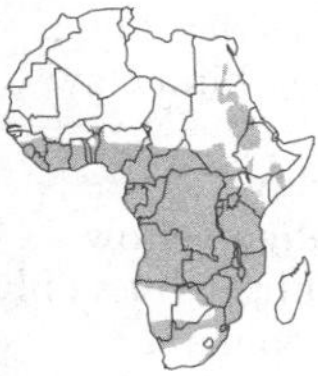

A striking and familiar bird, the African Pied Wagtail shakes its tail up and down upon landing. It then walks about, wagging its tail more slowly and making short dashes for insects. This bird gathers in communal roosts of up to hundreds of individuals in city shade trees or on roofs or boats.

457 Golden Pipit
Tmetothylacus tenellus

Description: *Male has bright yellow eyebrow, underparts, flight feathers, and most tail feathers; outer primaries tipped with black; wide black necklace;* crown and upperparts streaked brown. Female nondescript, with faint yellow on belly. L 6″ (15 cm).

Similar Species: **Longclaws** are larger, with brown wings and white outer tail feathers.

Voice: Male gives soft *djee* notes, interspersed with lower *durr* notes while singing from a bush or in colorful flight song.

Habitat: Semi-arid grasslands with thornbushes; chiefly below 3,300′ (1,000 m).

Nesting: Courting male slowly flutters wings and sings while flying over its territory before gliding down with wings held in a V. Makes a nest of twigs and grasses hidden low in a bush. Lays 2–4 eggs.

Range: Eastern Ethiopia south to ne Tanzania.

The Golden Pipit is a spectacular bird that looks like a giant yellow butterfly as it gently flies up from a thornbush. These pipits become conspicuous after rains in places like Tsavo and Meru national parks, in Kenya.

458 **Yellow-throated Longclaw**
Macronyx croceus

Description: Upperparts striped brown, with white tail corners. *Bright yellow eye line, throat, and belly; black, V-shaped necklace on chest,* with fine black stripes on sides. Long, pale brown legs, with long hind claw. L 8″ (20 cm).

Similar Species: Smaller **Pangani Longclaw** *(M. aurantiigula)* has orange-yellow throat and narrower necklace; lives only in e Africa, from coastal Somalia through s Kenya to Ngorongoro Crater, in n Tanzania. **Sharpe's Longclaw** *(M. sharpei)* is yellow below, without black necklace; common in grasslands above 6,600′ (2,000 m) in Kenya from Mount Elgon east to Mount Kenya.

Voice: Varies widely. One call consists of 4 or 5 *tri* notes, which is likened to *What do I see?* Alarm is a whistled *twe-wee.*

Habitat: Tall grasslands and cultivation.

Nesting: Sings from bushes and in circling display flights before breeding. Male whistles at female while hovering above her. Lays 2–4 eggs in a deep, grassy, cup-shaped nest, with an entrance ramp, built in a grass tussock.

Range: Senegal and Sierra Leone east to s Sudan, and south to n Angola and Natal.

This longclaw walks with long strides, searching for adult and larval insects. It crouches when approached; when discovered, it stands tall and flies off to a bush or drops into tall grass. Its flight is slow and jerky, with its tail fanned or hanging down.

---

459 **Rosy-breasted Longclaw**
Pink-throated Longclaw
Macronyx ameliae

Description: Striped brown head and upperparts; white outer tail feathers. *Male has bright rosy-red throat, wide black necklace, and rosy wash down center of belly.* Female has spotted necklace and rose on throat only. L 8″ (20 cm).

Similar Species: **Orange-throated Longclaw** *(M. capensis)* lives in highlands and coastal districts from Zimbabwe south to Cape Town area; has orange throat and eyebrow, black necklace, and yellow-orange belly.

Voice: A high-pitched, drawn-out *sweeeeee,* and *tee-you* notes given from perch or in flight. Gives *pink* notes when hovering above nestlings.

Habitat: Short tussocky grasslands, with or without low bushes, that are seasonally or permanently wet. Often near marshes on floodplains; likes fairly short grass.

Nesting: Hides a deep compact cup nest in a tussock of grass. Lays 2 or 3 eggs.

Range: Central Kenya south to n Tanzania; Zambia south to n Natal, and west to c Angola.

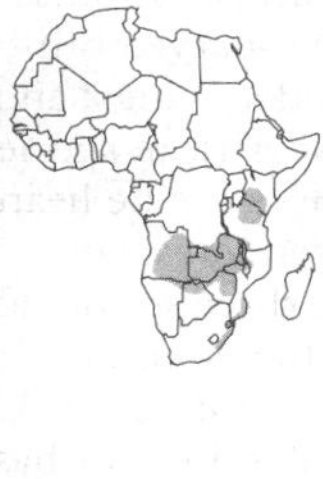

This bird is a real gem that rewards those who pay attention to the many smaller grassland birds. It flies with fast direct flight, like that of a pipit and unlike the jerky flight of other longclaws. It feeds on insects up to grasshopper size, as well as frogs in season.

---

460 **Richard's Pipit**
Grassveld Pipit
Anthus richardi (cinnamomeus)

Description: Upperparts brown and streaked. *Underparts pale buffy white; chest streaked in adult,* spotted in juvenile. White outer tail feathers. Colors are darker in birds found in wet areas, paler in those that live in drier savannas. L 6.5″ (16 cm).

Similar Species: There are 19 species of pipits in Africa, most of which do not greatly differ from Richard's Pipit.

Voice: A loud *chis-sik* on taking flight. In display, it soars overhead, calling *tinkle-tinkle-tinkle-tinkle* before diving to the ground.

Habitat: Open grasslands, short grass, and muddy areas near water; also cultivated fields.

Nesting: Lays 2–4 eggs in a neat, shallow, grass cup placed by a tussock or rock.

Range: Resident from c Sudan east to n Somalia, and south through e Africa to Cape Town; isolated population in Cameroon.

Richard's Pipit is common in grass grazed and trampled by mammals and littered with droppings, which it breaks up for larvae. This bird often forms small flocks and will join larks and wheatears in recently burned areas.

Bulbuls
Family Pycnonotidae

Medium-size, plain, dull olive or brownish birds of the forest canopy and edges, scrublands, and farms, bulbuls have sharp, slightly down-curved bills; crests (some); short rounded wings; and long rounded tails. Most African species are rarely seen; their voices can be heard emanating from evergreen forests or undergrowth. However, three species are among the birds most often seen in African villages and cities. Of 123 species worldwide, mainland Africa has 52; others inhabit nearby islands.

461 **Garden Bulbul**
Yellow-vented Bulbul, Dark-capped Bulbul, Black-eyed Bulbul, Common Bulbul, White-vented Bulbul
Pycnonotus barbatus

Description: *Blackish head, pointed at crown;* black thin bill and eye. Pale brown chest and upperparts. Dingy white belly and vent in w Africa; dingy white belly, with *bright yellow vent,* in e and s Africa. L 9″ (22 cm).

Similar Species: **African Red-eyed Bulbul** has red eye ring, while **Cape Bulbul** *(P. capensis)* of coastal Cape Province has white eye ring. **Mountain Greenbul** *(Andropadus tephrolaemus)* is abundant in montane forests and edges from Mount Cameroon southeast to Malawi; often seen in highlands of e Africa; green, with gray head and white eye ring. **Yellow-whiskered Greenbul** *(A. latirostris),* common in forests from Sierra Leone east to Mount Kenya, is olive, with bright yellow "whisker."

Voice: Calls and songs vary widely by locality. Often heard is an abrupt *quick doc-tor quick,* or a simple *quick.* Vocal all day long; at dawn and dusk, they chatter in choruses.

Habitat: Gardens, yards, villages, farms, orchards, thickets, riverine forests, desert streambeds, and wet forest edges.

Nesting: Builds a thin, fragile-looking cup of twigs, leaves, and plant fibers in a tree fork or bush; often near buildings. Lays 2–5 eggs.

Range: Mediterranean shores south to n Botswana and Natal. Absent in mid-Sahara.

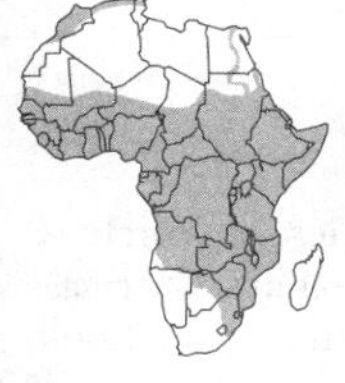

One of the most widespread birds in Africa, the Garden Bulbul, along with the African Red-eyed Bulbul and the Cape Bulbul, lives in virtually every garden, orchard, farm, and urban area, as well as in many wild areas. Noisy family parties, and sometimes flocks, gather at fruiting trees with many other birds. This bird's food also includes a wide variety of insects. Garden Bulbuls often mob hawks, owls, snakes, and small predators. None of its former descriptive names is adequate for all subspecies.

462 African Red-eyed Bulbul
Pycnonotus nigricans

Description: Black head, with *fleshy red eye ring* and black bill. Brownish-gray chest and upperparts; whitish belly; *bright yellow vent.* L 8″ (20 cm).

Similar Species: **Garden Bulbul** lacks red eye ring. **Cape Bulbul** *(P. capensis)* has large white eye ring and grayer body; replaces African Red-eyed in lusher winter rainfall areas of w and s Cape Province.

Voice: Common call has a cadence similar to its name: *red-eyed bul-bul;* harsh alarms and liquid whistles.

Habitat: Streambed woodlands, thickets, parks, and gardens.

Nesting: Lays 2 or 3 eggs in a cup-shaped nest of twigs and grass concealed in a leafy tree.

Range: Southwestern Angola, Namibia, Botswana (except Okavango Delta area), and Hwange NP, in sw Zimbabwe, south to interior Cape Province and Lesotho.

The African Red-eyed is the common bulbul at Etosha NP, in Namibia, and throughout the edges of the Kalahari Desert. It feeds on beetles, aphids, ants, flower pollen and nectar, and wild and cultivated fruit.

Bush-shrikes
Family Malaconotidae

This family has 44 species, of which 43 are confined to sub-Saharan Africa. They have long thick bills with a hook at the end, like true shrikes. Their tails are short to medium-long. Unlike "true" shrikes, bush-shrikes skulk about in foliage and thickets, offering only glimpses of themselves. Poor fliers, they rarely sit out in the open. Many are colorful or strongly patterned and have loud distinctive calls. Their food consists of insects, small invertebrates, and fruit.

463 **Brubru**
Brubru Bush-shrike
Nilaus afer

Description: Black cap, eye, and line through eye. *White eyebrows meet at nape* in most races. Back, wings, and tail black with white patches. *Underparts white, with chestnut on sides.* In female, dark brown replaces black. L 6″ (15 cm).

Voice: Male gives a drawn-out *brrrruuuu,* to which its mate may add a lower *eeeuuu.* Defends territory and calls frequently year-round, even from nest.

Habitat: Savanna trees, deciduous woodlands, and low trees in semi-arid regions.

Nesting: Builds a well-concealed cup nest in a fork of a small, lichen-covered tree. Takes leaf stems to spiderweb, rolls them in it one at a time, and returns to nest site. Finished nest looks like a little bump on the tree. Incubates 1–3 eggs for 18 days.

Range: Southern Mauritania east to Sudan, and south to n South Africa.

This bush-shrike feeds on insects and spiders in the inner branches of small trees in dry areas. When not breeding, it joins mixed-bird feeding parties.

464 **Black-crowned Tchagra**
Tchagra senegala

Description: *Narrow black crown stripe,* and black line through eye; pale buffy eyebrow and cheek. Gray-brown back; *rufous wings.* Long, wedge-shaped tail, with broad white tips. L 9″ (22 cm).

Similar Species: Smaller **Brown-crowned Tchagra**

(Three-streaked Tchagra; *T. australis*) has smaller bill and brown crown edged in black; often occurs with Black-crowned from Sierra Leone east to e Kenya, and south to n South Africa.

Voice: Song is a series of descending whistles, *tcheer-tcharee-tcharoo-tcharee-tcharoo.*

Habitat: Woodlands and lightly bushed country.

Nesting: Builds a sturdy cup nest of grasses and rootlets bound with spiderwebbing, placed low in a fork of a small tree. Lays 2 or 3 eggs.

Range: Morocco east to n Tunisia; sub-Saharan Africa from Senegal east to Somalia, and south to c Namibia and Natal.

The largest of the open-country bush-shrikes, this bird is often seen running on the ground between bushes. It pursues grasshoppers, beetles, and caterpillars, and is relatively fearless of man.

---

465 Rosy-patched Bush-shrike

Rhodophoneus (Tchagra) cruentus

Description: *Pale gray-brown,* with long graduated tail; black outer feathers with white tips. *Rosy patches on rump,* and in line down center of breast. Female has black V surrounding white throat. In s Kenya and n Tanzania, male has black V around rosy throat. L 9.5″ (24 cm).

Voice: Song is a loud *diak-dee-deee;* call a shrill *chirp.*

Habitat: Arid thorn scrub, bushed grasslands, and thickets along normally dry streambeds.

Nesting: Builds a flat nest platform of dry sticks in a low bush. Lays 2 or 3 eggs.

Range: Gebel Elba of se Egypt/ne Sudan south through e Ethiopia to n Tanzania. Usually below 4,300′ (1,300 m).

This bush-shrike often feeds on the ground and is an extremely fast runner, like a little Greater Roadrunner *(Geococcyx californianus)* of American deserts. A cheerful, inquisitive bird, it goes around in small, noisy family parties.

466 Tropical Boubou
Laniarius aethiopicus

Description: Heavy black beak with hooked tip. Black above, with *horizontal white wing band.* White underparts, with *pinkish-buff wash on flanks and vent.* Brown eye. L 9″ (23 cm).

Similar Species: **Southern Boubou** *(L. ferrugineus)* of e and s South Africa has extensive rust color on belly and vent; duet is a *boo boo whee-oo.* **Slate-colored Boubou** *(L. funebris)* is all slaty; lives in semi-arid bushland from n Somalia south to s Tanzania, and is common around kopjes in Serengeti area of Tanzania.

Voice: Highly synchronized duet by male and female sounds as if it is given by a single bird; variations include a bell-like *boo-boo-boo,* immediately followed by a *huuee;* also a *weer-weer-haww.*

Habitat: Rain-forest edges, montane forests, savanna woodlands, riverine gallery forests in drier areas, scrub, and gardens.

Nesting: Builds a saucer-shaped nest of fiber and rootlets in a fork of a bush. Lays 2 eggs.

Range: Sierra Leone east to Eritrea, and south to s Zimbabwe.

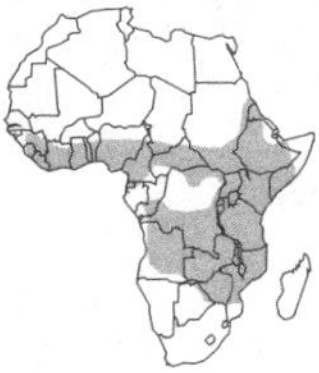

The Tropical Boubou is a skulking bird, commonly heard but rarely seen. It is usually glimpsed in flight as it dives into a thicket. While it rarely stays long in the open, it can be inquisitive. In addition to large insects, it eats the eggs and young of other songbirds. Locals call it the Bellbird or Bell-shrike.

467 Crimson Boubou
Crimson-breasted Shrike
Laniarius atrococcineus

Description: Heavy black beak with hooked tip. Black eye. Black above, with long, horizontal, white wing patch. *Throat and underparts bright red.* L 9″ (23 cm).

Similar Species: There are 3 other black-above/red-below boubous that live farther north:

Western Gonolek *(L. barbarus),* of savannas from Senegal to nc Africa's Lake Chad, has yellow crown. **Black-headed Gonolek** *(L. erythrogaster)* has yellow eye and buffy vent; lives from Lake Chad and Eritrea south to Lake Victoria. **Papyrus Gonolek** *(L. mufumbiri),* of Uganda and Lake Victoria, has orange crown and white wing bars.

Voice: Pairs give a loud, fast, synchronized duet: *turr-quip-quip* or *turr-chew, turr-chew.*

Habitat: Acacia thornveld, often near ranches, water holes, and towns.

Nesting: Takes long strips of bark from acacias to form a neat cup nest in a fork of a thorny tree. Usually lays 3 eggs, incubating for 19 days; chicks fledge 19 days after hatching.

Range: Namibia, sw Angola, and sw Zambia to nw South Africa.

Namibia's national bird, the Crimson Boubou is seen regularly around Windhoek and in Etosha NP. Pairs call often to maintain their territory. This bird is elusive, moving in long hops into dense vegetation. It feeds on beetles, caterpillars, and ants on the ground and in dense trees.

---

468 Gray-headed Bush-shrike
Malaconotus blanchoti

Description: Large, with *massive, black, hooked beak. Large gray head, with white area in front of large yellow eye.* Yellow throat and underparts, with faint orange wash on chest. Rest of upperparts olive green, with *pale tips on wing feathers.* L 11″ (28 cm).

Similar Species: **Sulphur-breasted Bush-shrike** *(Telophorus sulfureopectus)* is smaller (L 7.5″/19 cm) and has yellow eyebrow and black eye; lives in woodland canopy from Senegal east to Ethiopia, and south to e South Africa.

Voice: A haunting, drawn-out, ghost-like *hoooooooooooop* that rises at the end. Also gives other raspy and rattling calls.

Habitat: Dense riverine forests and thickets.

Nesting: Nest is a loose collection of grass, twigs, and rootlets placed in a tree fork 10–16′ (3–5 m) above ground. Usually lays 3 eggs.

Range: Senegal east to Ethiopia, and south to Angola and e South Africa.

The largest bush-shrike, this bird is a formidable predator that takes not only large insects, but mice, young snakes, lizards, chameleons, and songbirds. It has adapted to living in some gardens and around lodges.

"True" Shrikes
Family Laniidae

Medium-size songbirds with weak feet, "true" shrikes have strong, heavy, hooked beaks. Behind the hook is an additional "tooth" that fits into a sharp indentation in the lower mandible. While classified as songbirds, shrikes act like little hawks, killing large insects and smaller reptiles, birds, and mammals with their beaks (rather than with their feet, as hawks do). Many have a black "bandit" mask. Their colors are typically black, white, and gray, though some have buffy or rufous accents. Immatures and some females are brownish. Unlike bush-shrikes, the "true" shrikes sit conspicuously on treetops, dead branches, and overhead wires, flying down to their prey on rapid wingbeats. Worldwide there are 25 species; 16 live in Africa, some wintering from Eurasia.

---

469 Yellow-billed Shrike
Corvinella corvina

Description: Striped brown above, with *rufous primaries* and *very long, graduated, rufous tail. Yellow bill;* white eyebrow above dark brown eye mask. White throat and finely striped, buffy underparts. L 12″ (30 cm).

Voice: One of Africa's noisiest birds, with harsh, rasping cries given in concert. Calls include a *scis-scis,* inspiring the local name "Scissorbird." A longer, shrill call is often rendered as *may-we may-we-wait may-we.*

Habitat: Savanna woodlands and gardens.

Nesting: All members of the group help to defend a territory and feed the nesting female, nestlings, and dependent juveniles. Builds a large nest of sticks and rootlets in an open site in a bush or low tree. Lays 4 or 5 eggs.

Range: Senegal east to Sudan and wc Kenya.

This gregarious species occurs in noisy flocks of six to 15 birds. The "gangs" fly from one tree to another and, on perching, jerk their long tails up and down. They feed on lizards, insects, flying ants, nestling birds, and some fruit.

---

470 **Magpie Shrike**
Long-tailed Shrike
Urolestes (Corvinella) melanoleuca

Description: Head, back, underparts, and *extremely long tail jet black;* tail usually curls downward. White rump, scapulars, and patch on primaries. Female's tail is 3″ (8 cm) shorter than male's. L 20″ (50 cm).

Similar Species: **Long-tailed Fiscal Shrike** has white underparts and shorter stiff tail. **Red-billed Wood-Hoopoe** has dark rump and long, thin, red bill.

Voice: Gives loud melodious whistles rendered as *kee-leeoo,* and a longer *needle boom needle boom come here come here.*

Habitat: Tall acacia woodlands in savannas, and open mixed woodlands along streambeds.

Nesting: Builds a large bulky nest of thorny sticks out on a limb of a thorny tree 10–20′ (3–6 m) up. Lays 3 or 4 eggs. Birds of earlier broods help at nest.

Range: Southern Kenya south to n South Africa. Absent in zone of miombo woodlands from Zambia into s Tanzania.

The Magpie Shrike sits conspicuously on lower branches of large trees, waiting to pounce on large insects. Its flight is straight and high above the grass, but fairly slow. Its long tail may hinder its speed and may account for its inability to catch most small lizards and birds. Groups of this highly social shrike frequent one area for a few months, then move elsewhere.

---

471 **Gray-backed Fiscal Shrike**
Gray-crowned Fiscal Shrike
Lanius excubitoroides

Description: *Black mask from forehead through eyes and down sides of neck.* Crown and back silver-gray; black wing has small white patch. *Half of broad tail near body is white,* the end black. White underparts. L 10″ (25 cm).

Similar Species: The Gray-backed is the only resident fiscal shrike with a gray crown. No migrant shrike is as large or has white basal half of tail.

Voice: Noisy chattering and low musical notes given in a group. Song is a medley of strident metallic notes.

Habitat: Acacia woodlands, bushed savannas, riverine forest edges, farms, and gardens.

Nesting: A cooperative breeder, with several helpers at nest from previous brood. Main pair builds a compact nest of sticks and rootlets in a thorny bush or tree. Lays 2–4 eggs.

Range: Lake Chad east to Ethiopia, and south to sw Tanzania. In e Africa, occurs in and between rift valleys. Most common at 2,000–5,000′ (600–1,500 m), sometimes higher.

This bird is often seen in gardens and parklands, in places such as Kenya's Lake Naivasha and Tanzania's Lake Manyara. (The Long-tailed Fiscal Shrike replaces the Gray-backed to the east of the eastern rift valley.) It is very social, with large family parties sitting about in bushes, chattering and fanning their tails. They will fly off together like a flock of babblers, their flight labored and weak.

472 **Long-tailed Fiscal Shrike**
Long-tailed Fiscal
Lanius cabanisi

Description: Black crown and face; *black back merges into dark gray lower back;* black wings, with small white spot on primaries. White rump and underparts. *Long, stiff, graduated tail is black.* L 12″ (30 cm).

Similar Species: **Taita Fiscal Shrike** *(L. dorsalis)* is smaller (L 8″/20 cm), with pale gray back and adjacent white scapulars, and tail bordered in white; similar range, but also west of rift valley to Serengeti NP in Tanzania, and Mount Elgon, in Uganda. **Common Fiscal Shrike** is black above, with white scapulars. **Gray-backed Fiscal Shrike** has silver-gray crown and white basal half of tail.

Voice: Harsh scolding calls and a whistled *chit-er-row.*

Habitat: Grasslands with trees and bushes, coastal scrub, and cultivated areas.

Nesting: Builds a large nest of coarse grass and rootlets, placed in a low thornbush. Lays 3 or 4 eggs.

Range: Southern Somalia, s Kenya, and ne Tanzania. Western boundary is Meru NP, Mount Kenya, and Nairobi (all in Kenya), and Tanzania's Lake Manyara.

This social bird is usually seen in small parties. The group may gather in one bush, each bird calling wildly and swinging its tail sideways (like a pendulum) or up and down (as if having trouble balancing). It feeds chiefly on grasshoppers and beetles, which it pounces on in grass or on bare ground.

473 **Common Fiscal Shrike**
Lanius collaris

Description: Black above, white below; brown eye; *long white band on scapulars.* White shrike spot on primaries (shows as a narrow band in flight); gray rump. *Medium-long, graduated, black tail, with white outer tail feathers.* Some females have grayish black above and/or rusty on sides. Both sexes have white eyebrow stripe in sw Africa. L 9″ (23 cm).

Similar Species: In e Africa, **Taita Fiscal Shrike** *(L. dorsalis)* has pale gray back, while **Long-tailed Fiscal Shrike** lacks white scapular patch and has longer black tail.

Voice: Calls include clear whistles and a harsh *cheeeeeeeeeee;* song is a pleasing *chirp-chirp-chirp-hurry-chirp-chirp-chirp-hurry.*

Habitat: Cultivated areas, edges of towns, savanna woodlands, and grasslands; also semi-arid scrub in s and w Africa.

Nesting: Each pair nests alone, without helpers. Makes a rough nest of multi-branched rootlets and sticks, and strips of bark, placed in a small solitary tree. Lays 2–4 eggs.

Range: Guinea east to Eritrea, and south to Cape Town area.

In East Africa, this bird is restricted to wetter areas above 5,000 feet (1,500 m), where it is common. It sits in the open on all kinds of perches, and on the ground; it flies down directly to its prey, dispatches it with its strong hooked beak, and often flies back to the original perch. It feeds on insects, frogs, lizards, chameleons, small snakes, and small birds, storing excess kills on thorns.

HELMET-SHRIKES
Family Prionopidae

Small to medium-size birds, helmet-shrikes have hooked beaks and bristled foreheads. Highly social, they go around in flocks of three to 12 birds. The nine species are restricted to sub-Saharan Africa. The seven species of typical helmet-shrikes have shorter tails and actively flit through treetops gleaning insects in woodlands and forests; they have brightly colored eyes, eye rings, and/or bills. The white-crowned helmet-shrikes sit upright in the open on trees in grasslands with their long tails hanging down. They wait to spot prey and then fly down to seize it, like "true" shrikes.

474 **White-rumped Helmet-shrike**
White-crowned Helmet-shrike
Eurocephalus rueppellii

Description: *Flat white crown,* with patch of short bristles over bill. Bill black and tapered, with hook at tip. Black shrike eye mask widens behind eyes, forming *dark "earmuffs."* Dusky brown back, wings, and tail, with *white rump* conspicuous in flight. Underparts white from throat to vent, with light brown on flanks. L 9″ (23 cm).

Similar Species: **White-crowned Helmet-shrike** *(E. anguitimens)* lives south of Zambezi from Namibia east to s Mozambique; has brown rump and light brown belly, flanks, and vent.

Voice: Group flies off with a weak squeak note. Alarm is a sharp *kak-kak-kak.*

Habitat: Open savannas with scattered trees. Ranges from sea level to 7,300′ (2,200 m).

Nesting: Makes a small nest of grass stems tied together with spiderwebbing, placed on an outer branch of a tree. Lays 3 or 4 eggs. May be up to 6 helpers at nest.

Range: Ethiopia south to s Tanzania.

This atypical helmet-shrike is common in most savanna reserves of eastern Africa. It has a curious, direct flight with shallow stiff wingbeats, like that of many parrots. Loose flocks of three to 12 birds sit in the open, feeding chiefly on grasshoppers, caterpillars, and beetles.

475 **White Helmet-shrike**
Long-crested Helmet-shrike
Prionops plumata

Description: All races have mainly black back; white underparts; *white edging to black tail; orange-pink legs;* gray head with fan of bristles over bill; striking, *yellow, sunflower-like wattles encircling yellow eye.* West African birds have long, straight, white crest and long white wing patches. Birds north and east of Mount Kenya lack crest and have black wings. Birds from Mount Kenya south to South Africa also lack crest, but have white wing patches. L 8″ (20 cm).

Similar Species: **Gray-crested Helmet-shrike** *(P. poliolopha)* ranges from Lake Naivasha, Kenya, southwest through w Serengeti to nc Tanzania; lacks sunflower eye ring, and has long gray crest.

Voice: Chattering calls, such as a repeated *isshh-gwee,* interspersed with flute-like notes. Also loud bill-snapping.

Habitat: Savanna woodlands, including miombo woodlands of sc Africa; clearings with crops and scattered clumps of trees.

Nesting: Nest is a compact cup made of grass and strips of bark bound with spiderwebbing, placed in a tree. Usually lays 4 eggs.

Range: Senegal east to Eritrea and Somalia, and south to n Namibia and n Natal.

These attractive pied birds fly silently in flocks from tree to tree, chatter and forage a bit, and then fly on as a group. They are rather hard to observe well, as they seem to be constantly on the move. They feed on insects in branches and sometimes by dropping down to the ground. At the start of the breeding season, a group of brothers departs, interacts with a neighboring group, and convinces a set of sisters to start a new commune. Once they secure a territory away from both parent groups, the dominant brother and sister form a pair, and the rest become helpers.

Vangas
Family Vangidae

This family comprises 14 species of small to medium-size birds that are restricted to Madagascar, except for one that extends to the Comoros. The various vangas resemble wood-hoopoes, barbets, shrikes, nuthatches, honeyeaters, wood-swallows, and birds-of-paradise. Of the 14 vanga species, 12 are distinct enough to be in their own genus. Vangas are forest canopy birds that lead many multi-species flocks. They feed chiefly on insects, spiders, and small vertebrates. Many vangas are restricted to fast-disappearing virgin forests.

476 Sickle-billed Vanga
Falculea palliata

Description: *White head,* underparts, and underwing coverts. Back, wings, and tail black, glossed with dark blue. *Very long, highly curved, light gray bill.* L 13″ (32 cm).

Similar Species: **White-headed Vanga** *(Artamella viridis),* widespread in Madagascar woodlands, has heavy, conical, gray bill with hook at tip. Both sexes have black back, wings, and tail; male has white head and underparts; female is gray.

Voice: A prolonged nasal *waa-ahh,* likened to the crying of a human baby. Also a loud *gaya-gaya-gaya.*

Habitat: Dry thorn forests, wooded savannas, baobab woodlands, patches of rain forests, mangroves, and gardens.

Nesting: Builds a large stick nest in a tree, often a baobab. Both parents incubate the 4 eggs.

Range: Madagascar only. Lives below 3,000′ (900 m), in north, west, and south.

The largest vanga and fairly common in flocks of a dozen or so, this noisy and bold bird works over large branches and trunks, probing rotten wood, peeling bark, and searching cracks. It feeds on insects, spiders, snails, small lizards, and probably the eggs and young of small birds. Up to 40 may congregate at nighttime roosts.

Thrushes
Family Turdidae

Small to medium-size songbirds with slender bills and strong feet, most thrushes are larger and plumper than warblers and flycatchers. Thrushes include some of the finest singers in the world. There is some sort of thrush around most farms, gardens, and homes in Africa. Plumages are usually brown, gray, or rufous, though some have blue, black, or green feathers. There are about 300 species worldwide. Of Africa's 131 species, 13 breed in Eurasia and winter in Africa, while seven are restricted to Madagascar, the Comoros, and Seychelles.

477 White-browed Scrub-Robin
Cercotrichas (Erythropygia) leucophrys

Description: Pale brown above, with distinct *white eyebrow.* White wing bars; *heavily streaked, brownish-white underparts. Rufous rump; black tail with white corners.* Wide range of variation in subspecies: some races have rufous back, more rufous on tail, or more white on wings. L 6″ (15 cm).

Similar Species: **Kalahari Scrub-Robin** *(C. {E.} paena)* lives from Namibia east to Transvaal; has broad black bar at end of tail, and unstriped underparts.

Voice: A high-pitched, whistling song, each phrase repeated several times. Alarm is a scolding rattle.

Habitat: Dense bushy growth in acacia steppes, stream courses, gardens, and clearings in rain forests.

Nesting: Very aggressive in maintaining territory, with combatants tussling on the ground. Builds a grass nest in a bush close to the ground. Lays 2–4 eggs.

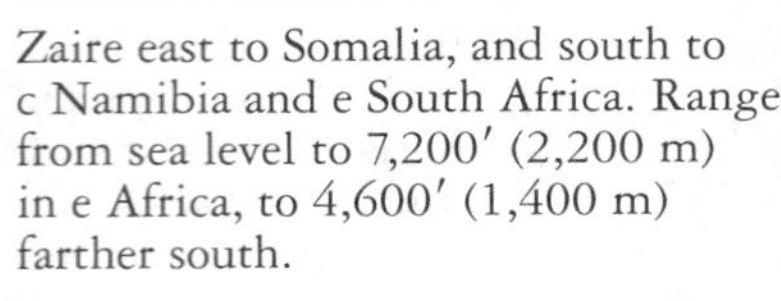

Range: Zaire east to Somalia, and south to c Namibia and e South Africa. Ranges from sea level to 7,200′ (2,200 m) in e Africa, to 4,600′ (1,400 m) farther south.

This bird draws attention to itself with its oft-cocked tail and rattling alarm. It is often seen on an exposed perch or as it runs on open ground, stopping and looking about while raising and lowering its wings and tail. It breaks into termite galleries, searches herbivore droppings for fly larvae and dung beetles, and feeds on fruit and nectar.

---

478 Cape Robin-Chat
Cossypha caffra

Description: *Pale gray crown and upperparts; light orange throat and breast.* Short white eyebrow; black eye mask. Vent and outer tail feathers orange. L 7″ (18 cm).

Similar Species: **White-browed Robin-Chat** *(C. heuglini)* has longer white eyebrow and entirely orange underparts; ranges at low to medium elevations from Lake Chad east to Ethiopia, and south to Natal.

Voice: A melodious song of repeated phrases, often starting with *charoo-weet-weet-weet.* Some individuals mimic other birds. Alarm call is a guttural *wur-de-durr.*

Habitat: In e Africa, moist highland gardens, plantations, and tangles at edges of montane forests. In s Africa, almost anywhere there is dense cover.

Nesting: Builds a nest of grass and twigs lined with moss, placed low down in a bush or stump. Lays 2 or 3 eggs.

Range: Mountains of e Africa from s Sudan and c Kenya south to e Zimbabwe; lowlands and highlands in South Africa.

Called simply the Cape Robin in South Africa, this is a friendly garden bird. It feeds on the ground under shrubs and hedges, going up to the canopy of trees when caterpillars are common. It will visit bird tables, snack from pet food bowls, and enter kitchens.

479 Stone Chat

Saxicola torquata

Description: A large-headed, short-tailed bird with long black legs. *Male has black head* and upperparts, with narrow white line at base of secondaries; white rump; *white patch on side of neck; rufous chest;* white belly. Female dark brown, with white wing spot and light orange wash below. L 5″ (13 cm).

Similar Species: 2 related species with white throat and eye line are restricted to islands off Africa: **Canary Islands Chat** *(S. dacotiae),* in e Canaries, and **Réunion Chat** *(S. borbonensis).*

Voice: Call note is a dry *teck-teck.* Male has a short melodious song, given in low display flight or from a bush.

Habitat: Grassy hillsides, mountain moorlands, rocky areas, low thickets, scrub, and marshes. In e Africa it resides chiefly at 5,000–10,000′ (1,500–3,000 m) elevation.

Nesting: Builds a deep nest of fine grasses, placed under a tussock of grass or a rock. Usually lays 3 or 4 eggs (4–6 in nw Africa).

Range: Resident in nw Africa; mountains of w Africa, Ethiopia, and e Africa; more generally south of equator, including Madagascar. Some Eurasian birds winter in nw and ne Africa.

The Stone Chat perches upright on wires, posts, bush tops, and nearly vertical branches and dead sticks, with one foot much higher than the other. It is commonly seen from vehicles as it looks for insects along roadsides. It darts down to the ground, often returning to the same perch, and chases flies, butterflies, and moths on the wing.

480 Mocking Cliff Chat

Cliff Chat

Thamnolaea cinnamomeiventris

Description: A slim, fairly long-tailed thrush of rocky areas. Male has black head, eye, chest, back, wings, and tail; *white shoulders.* Thin white band below black chest; *rest of underparts and rump rusty orange.* Female paler gray, with darker orange belly and rump. L 9″ (23 cm).

Similar Species: **European Rock-Thrush** *(Monticola saxatilis)* breeds in Moroccan mountains and winters south to Tanzania; breeding male has pale blue head, white rump, and short orange tail; winter male, female, and immature are scaly buff.

Voice: Both sexes sing. Song is a loud, melodious, flute-like warbling. Also imitates other birds. Alarm note is a harsh *krat.*

Habitat: Fig trees, woodlands, and scrublands adjacent to cliffs, rocky hills, valley walls, rocky watersides, villages, and kopjes.

Nesting: Pairs defend large territories; male and female sing a highly synchronized song. Makes an untidy nest of grass, leaves, twigs, and hair, placed in a rock or building crevice. Usually lays 3 eggs. Some pairs forcibly take over a swallow nest, ejecting eggs or young and using it for several broods.

Range: Local in mountains and hills from Senegal east to Sudan; widespread in plateaus and mountains from Eritrea south through e Africa to e South Africa.

Often shy, this bird can become tame when it lives near humans. Excellent fliers, pairs can be seen speedily diving down cliff faces, the male in the lead. On landing on a rock or branch, this chat often raises its tail up and down. It feeds on insects, spiders, and fig fruit.

481 Capped Wheatear
Oenanthe pileata

Description: *Black cap;* dark brown nape, back, and wings. White eyebrow and throat. *Black band from bill through eyes and down sides of neck, forming wide V on breast;* rest of underparts white, with buffy flanks. Like many wheatears, has white rump and white bases to outer tail feathers, forming black T on tail. L 7″ (18 cm).

Similar Species: Numerous other wheatears live in nw and ne Africa, while in winter Africa is full of Eurasian winterers; the latter are most abundant from Ethiopia south to Tanzania.

Voice: Song is a melodious whistle, mixed with imitations of lapwings, coursers, longclaws, and mammals; sometimes sings on the wing. Alarm calls include a thin *weeet.*

Habitat: Short-grass plains, especially where heavily grazed by wild or domestic animals. Flocks into burned areas. Uses cultivated fields when just planted or after harvest.

Nesting: Defends breeding area against wintering Eurasian wheatears and others of its own kind. Male flies low over territory, singing with tail spread. Uses old rodent burrows up to a yard (1 m) long. Lays 3–6 eggs.

Range: Central Kenya south to Cape Town area.

While this species is resident year-round in the highlands of southern Kenya to Tanzania's Serengeti Plains (where it is common), birds that live in other areas undertake long-distance migrations, vacating areas that develop long grass or that become too cold or arid. In South Africa it is present mainly in summer. It feeds on insects. The name "wheatear" evolved from "white-arse" (for its white rump).

482 Kurrichane Thrush
Turdus libonyanus

Description: Gray-brown upperparts; *bright orange bill* and eye ring. *Black "mustache,"* and finer black streaks on white throat. Gray chest; *orange flanks;* white belly. Pale orange legs. L 9″ (23 cm).

Similar Species: **Olive Thrush** *(T. olivaceus)* lives in mountains from Ethiopia south to South Africa, where it also inhabits lowlands; has gray throat and orange belly. **African Thrush** *(T. pelios)* is browner above, has faint striping on throat, and white belly; found from Gambia east to w Kenya and c Zambia.

Voice: Common call is a pleasant, whistled *sitz-seeoo.*

Habitat: Acacia, miombo, and riverine woodlands; also gardens and plantations.

Nesting: Builds a cup nest of grass, rootlets, leaves, and string glued with mud, placed in a tree fork 10–20′ (3–6 m) up. Lays 2 or 3 eggs.

Range: Eastern and s Tanzania and s Zaire south to n Botswana and Natal.

Common in many areas but rather shy in the wild, this thrush becomes bold in gardens and is seen easily in the winter dry season, when it comes out to muddy edges of water holes. It runs on the ground, stops, listens, and may peck into moist ground. It feeds on insects on the ground, as well as berries and wild figs, and takes bread, bananas, cheese, and bone meal from bird tables.

483 Groundscraper Thrush
Psophocichla (Turdus) litsitsirupa

Description: *Long bill black above, yellow below.* Gray-brown crown and upperparts; white face and underparts, with *2 black "crying" lines below eye, and black "teardrop" spots* on white underparts. Long, pale yellow legs; short gray tail. Ethiopian birds have shorter bills and are washed with buffy below. L 9″ (22 cm).

Voice: Pleasing and varied song includes a phrase that became its specific scientific name: *lit-sit-sirupa.* Also has a sharp alarm note and a starling-like murmur.

Habitat: Open woodlands, overgrazed and recently cleared areas with trees, and parks and gardens.

Nesting: Builds a large nest high in a tree fork. Nest is made of grass, rootlets, mud, rags, string, paper, and bits of cloth. Both parents incubate the 2–4 eggs.

Range: Highlands of Ethiopia; sw Tanzania and s Zaire south to c Namibia and Natal.

This thrush scrapes debris and scratches leaves on the ground as it looks for insects and worms. When running across a lawn, it leans forward; when it stops, it raises its head high, and flicks and folds one wing at a time.

Babblers
Family Timaliidae

Medium-size, thrush-like birds with slightly down-curved bills, short rounded wings, fairly long, broad, rounded tails, short legs, and strong feet, babblers usually go about in noisy family parties. They fly one at a time from bush to bush and sometimes hop around on the ground in the open. Near homes and lodges, especially those with bird tables, they have become quite tame, even brash. Unlike most songbirds, they can grip food with their feet (like parrots), and often line up body to body (like mousebirds and bee-eaters). Of 257 species worldwide, about 40 are known in Africa and Madagascar.

484 Arrow-marked Babbler
Turdoides jardineii

Description: All brown, darker on wings and tail, paler on vent. *Feathers of head and underparts have white, arrow-shaped points.* Piercing, tricolored eye: black center surrounded by yellow, then by red around the yellow. Immature has red eye and lacks white arrow spots. L 9.5″ (24 cm).

Similar Species: **Black-lored Babbler** *(T. melanops)* has yellow eye and white feather edges that resemble scales; lives in inland e Africa, nw Botswana, and n Namibia.

Voice: Very noisy. When one gives its cackling, grating *churr,* all others in the family party come over one by one to join in.

Habitat: Savanna woodlands, rank grasslands, forest edges, and riverine thickets.

Nesting: Helpers from previous generations aid breeding pair in raising young. Builds a bulky cup nest of plant materials low in a thick bush. Lays 4 eggs.

Range: Uganda, Lake Naivasha area of Kenya, and s Somalia south to Okavango Delta, in n Botswana, and Natal.

Each group has between three and 12 birds that are related and do everything together. When two groups meet at the edge of a defended territory, there is a skirmish and a wild cacophony on both sides. This babbler hops on the open ground and leaf litter, looking for large insects and small lizards.

Warblers
Family Sylviidae

Small birds with long thin bills that glean insects in grass, weeds, brush, and trees, warblers occur in virtually all habitats, from near desert to the canopy of rain-forest trees. As most have dull colors and skulking habits, they present difficult identification problems. From September through

May, many confusing Eurasian breeders are present that usually are not singing. The 44 resident cisticolas are a particularly challenging group to identify. The colorful American warblers are in a distinct family, the Parulidae. Worldwide there are about 363 species, with about 218 known from Africa and its islands.

485 Rattling Cisticola
Cisticola chiniana

Description: Rusty crown and face; blotched brown back and wings, with rufous primaries. *Long, graduated, rusty tail,* with outer feathers tipped with black and white. White throat; pale buffy breast. *Breeding male has black palate,* quite visible as it sings often. Female smaller. In nonbreeding plumage, both sexes are redder, with more distinct stripes. L 6″ (15 cm).

Similar Species: 1 of 44 species of cisticolas. The grasslands of Africa are home to many species of very small cisticolas with short tails, striped backs, and buffy underparts. In forest edges of highlands of Kenya and n Tanzania, **Hunter's Cisticola** *(C. hunteri)* commonly duets, mixing a *chorry-cheer* with shivering trills that rise and fall; both sexes are brown above, gray below, with rusty cap.

Voice: Song is a rattling, 2-part *jee-jee-jee-jee, tiddliddle,* with considerable variation during the season and by locality. Alarm call is a harsh *chaaaaa.*

Habitat: Savannas with tall grass and many bushes, open woodlands, and overgrown cultivated fields.

Nesting: Builds an oval-shaped ball of dry grass bound with spiderwebbing. Nest is well concealed and placed low in a tangle of grass or in a bush. Lays 3 or 4 eggs.

Range: Congo and Ethiopia south to n Namibia and Natal.

This cheeky bird will approach and scold intruders who invade its space. It is active and conspicuous compared with other cisticolas, and is often seen singing from the tops of bushes.

486 **Tawny-flanked Prinia**
Prinia subflava

Description: A slender plain bird, with a *long thin tail.* Gray-brown above, with rust color on primaries. Narrow, graduated tail indistinctly tipped with dusky and white. White eyebrow; red eye; black lores. Underparts white, with *tawny wash on flanks.* L 5.5″ (14 cm).

Similar Species: **Black-chested Prinia** *(P. flavicans)* of Namibia to Transvaal has white underparts with black chest band when breeding, yellow breast when not. **Spotted Prinia** *(P. maculosa),* abundant in Cape Province, is dark brown above and heavily spotted below.

Voice: A series of high-pitched, buzzy *zertz* notes that may last up to 15 seconds; also high-pitched *chee* notes.

Habitat: Forest edges, tall grass in woodlands, savanna grasslands with bushes, marshes, thickets, and gardens.

Nesting: Builds a domed nest of woven grass in a living tussock or in a large-leafed bush. Lays 3 or 4 eggs.

Range: Senegal east to Eritrea, and south to Victoria Falls, in Zimbabwe, and e South Africa.

This widespread bird occurs in a great variety of habitats. Its tail seems loosely attached and is often wagged high over the head. This species moves around in pairs or family groups in low vegetation. In dry seasons, when undergrowth is grazed or burned, it is often forced to feed in trees.

FLYCATCHERS
Family Muscicapidae

These upright-sitting birds have pointed wings and short legs. Their snapping beaks are pointed and have a small hook at the tip, while the base is wide and surrounded by stiff bristles. Looking out from perches, flycatchers dash out after a flying insect or drop on one spotted on the ground. Most nest in tree holes. There are 147 species, with 35 in Africa. American flycatchers are in a completely different family (Tyrannidae).

487 Silverbird
Empidornis semipartitus

Description: A large slim flycatcher, with a small head and a long graduated tail. *Silver head (to below eye), back, wings, and tail; underparts entirely pumpkin-orange.* L 7″ (18 cm).

Voice: Usually silent, but male has a soft, sweet, warbling song.

Habitat: Grasslands with scattered acacia trees and bushes.

Nesting: Builds a large nest of dry grass with a roof of thorny twigs. Also uses old weaver nests. Lays 2 eggs.

Range: Southern Sudan, w Ethiopia, n Uganda, w Kenya, and nc Tanzania.

A beautiful bird that adorns many an acacia tree around Lake Baringo, in Kenya, and Serengeti NP, in Tanzania, the Silverbird perches on treetops and shaded branches as it scans for flying and walking insects.

488 White-eyed Slaty Flycatcher
Melaenornis (Dioptronis) fischeri

Description: A fairly large, plump, long-tailed flycatcher. *Large white eye ring. Dark gray above,* with darker wings and tail;

paler gray underparts. Immature has white spots above, dark spots below. L 6″ (15 cm).

Similar Species: **Pallid Flycatcher** *(M. pallidus),* of acacia savannas throughout sub-Saharan Africa, is plain gray-brown above, paler below. **Spotted Flycatcher** *(Muscicapa striata),* a common winterer from Eurasia over much of Africa, is small, brown, and (despite its name) striped on crown and chest.

Voice: Rather quiet, but has a sunbird-like *tsssikk* and a descending, chattering trill.

Habitat: Edges of montane forests, woodlands, and gardens. Ranges from 4,600′ to 10,000′ (1,400–3,000 m).

Nesting: Builds a small cup nest of moss, lichens, and plant fibers, anchoring it with spiderwebbing; nest is well hidden in a tall tree. Lays 2 or 3 eggs.

Range: East African mountains from s Sudan south to n Malawi.

This flycatcher gleans insects from foliage, hawks from perches, and hops in shaded paths like a robin-chat. It also eats berries and some small nestling birds. It is commonly seen in gardens of homes and lodges, and along trails in the mountains of East Africa.

489 Southern Black Flycatcher
Melaenornis pammelaina

Description: *All black,* with metallic blue gloss and *dark brown eye.* Medium-length *tail appears square, though has 2 rounded tips.* Immature dark brown, with buffy spots above, barring below. L 9″ (22 cm).

Similar Species: **Northern Black Flycatcher** *(M. edolioides),* of w Africa from Senegal east to sw Kenya, is dull black with more rounded tail. **African Drongo** has red eye and strongly forked tail. Male **Black Cuckoo-shrike** *(Campephaga flava)* has shorter bill with wide orange gape; ranges from s Ethiopia to s South Africa.

Voice: Gives soft wheezy notes. Alarm call is a buzzy *churr.*

Habitat: Savanna woodlands (particularly yellow-bark acacias), riverine forests, thornveld, and evergreen forests.

Nesting: Female builds a nest made of rootlets, placed within a tree crevice, charred tree stump, or clump of aloe or banana leaves. Sometimes uses nests of other birds. Lays 2 or 3 eggs.

Range: Central Kenya and s Zaire south to n Namibia and e South Africa.

This bird sits and waits for passing and crawling insects, gleans insects in foliage, and takes fruit on occasion. Black-Flycatchers are mimics of the much more aggressive drongos. As passing hawks may wish to avoid drongos, they would probably give this look-alike a wide berth as well.

Monarch-Flycatchers
Family Monarchidae

Compared to the previous (Muscicapidae) family, this is a jazzier group of flycatchers, many of which have strong patterns, colors, eye wattles, crests, or tails that may be very short or long. Many have a keeled ridge on the upper mandible. While some will wait for flying insects (although they do not sit in the open), most feeding is done by gleaning on branches and in foliage, as warblers do. Worldwide about 163 species are concentrated mainly in southern Asia and Australasia. Africa and its islands are home to 49 species.

490 Chin-spot Batis
Batis molitor

Description: *A tiny, strongly pied bird,* with a *yellow eye, large head, and short tail.* Both sexes have *wide black eye mask,* with thin white band above; gray crown and back; white wing bar and outer tail feathers. *Female has rusty chin spot and breast band.* Male has clear white throat and black breast band. L 4.5″ (11.5 cm).

Similar Species: The Chin-spot is the most widespread of 16–18 species of batis. **Senegal Batis** *(B. senegalensis)* lives from Senegal to Cameroon; female lacks rusty chin spot. **Cape Batis** *(B. capensis)* lives from e Zimbabwe to sw Cape Province; has rufous wings.

Voice: Descending call, *hick-hack-hock,* sounds like "three blind mice." Also a *chi-cheer,* usually given twice.

Habitat: Riverine forests, savanna woodlands, thickets, and gardens.

Nesting: In courtship, whenever female gives a buzzing call, male catches an insect and brings it to her. Builds a neat cup nest of plant fibers covered with lichens and bound by spiderwebbing, placed on a low tree branch. Usually lays 2 eggs.

Range: Congo and c Kenya south to n Namibia, n Botswana, and e South Africa.

This restless and trusting bird is regularly seen in acacia woodlands around houses, camps, and lodges. It works the bark of larger branches, gleans in the foliage, hovers at leaf clumps, and is rather energetic. The wings are noisy in flight.

---

491 **Blue Flycatcher**
Cerulean Blue Monarch
Elminia longicauda

Description: A slim, *crested* bird, *cerulean-blue* above and below; fine black bill and lores. *Long graduated tail with longer central tail feathers.* L 7″ (18 cm).

Similar Species: **White-tailed Blue Flycatcher** *(E. albicauda)* ranges from Ngorongoro Crater area, in n Tanzania, and w Uganda south to Malawi; pale blue above, white below, with white outer tail feathers.

Voice: A weak, brief, twittering song, like that of some sunbirds.

Habitat: Forest clearings, woodlands, riverine forests, and gardens.

Nesting: Builds a tiny, delicate, shallow cup on a horizontal tree fork; nest is covered with lichens and bound with spiderwebbing. Lays 2 eggs.

Range: Senegal east to w Kenya, and south to w Angola.

When you catch a glimpse of this bird flitting around with its tail fanned in the understory or canopy of a giant tree, you might think you've seen a blue fairy. Highly energetic, it seems to change directions constantly as it searches for flies.

492, 493 **African Paradise-Flycatcher**
Terpsiphone viridis

Description: Black crested head, with *blue bill and eye ring.* Gray breast merges into white lower belly. *Bright rufous back, wings, and tail. Male has 2 extremely long central tail feathers.* Some males in e, c, and w Africa have metallic blue-black head; may be rufous above with long white wing patches, or have entirely white back, wings, and tail. L male 16″ (40 cm), female 8″ (20 cm).

Similar Species: There are several other variable species of paradise-flycatchers in w African rain forests, and 4 species restricted to offshore islands: São Tomé, Madagascar, Réunion/Mauritius, and Seychelles each have their own.

Voice: Song is a pleasing, whistled *twee-dee-dee-twee-dee-dee.* Calls include a *swee-sweer.*

Habitat: Mature trees in rain forests, montane forests, woodlands, riverine forests, and shaded gardens.

Nesting: Builds a small cup nest on a horizontal branch in the lower tree canopy 6–20′ (2–6 m) up. Nest is often placed near buildings or over water, and is adorned with lichens. Lays 2 eggs. Both sexes incubate.

Range: Senegal east to n Somalia, and south

to c Namibia and sw Cape Province. Strongly migratory in many areas, particularly away from equator; in s Africa, birds arrive in September and leave in April.

The male molts its long feathers after breeding. This bird seems to prefer to nest near houses and people.

Penduline-tits
Family Remizidae

These small, tit-like birds have short wings and tails, dull plumage, and straight (not curved) culmens on rather conical bills. They also differ from "true" tits in creating elaborate pouch nests made chiefly of plant down. There are ten species worldwide, seven in Africa. *Note:* The "true" tits of the family Paridae include 15 species in Africa, of 50 worldwide.

494 African Penduline-tit
Gray Penduline-tit
Anthoscopus caroli

Description: *A tiny, stub-tailed, tit-like bird,* with a short slender bill. Pale gray above, with *pale buffy forehead and underparts.* L 3.5" (9 cm).

Similar Species: **Cape Penduline-tit** *(A. minutus)* replaces African in most of Namibia, Botswana, and w South Africa; has yellow wash on belly, and black and white spots on forehead and chin. **Yellow-bellied Eremomela** *(Eremomela icteropygialis)* is a tiny (L 4"/10 cm) warbler with longer bill, gray head with faint eye line, and bright yellow underparts; widespread in bushlands and woodlands from Niger east to Ethiopia, and south to Cape Town.

Voice: Song is squeaky, with second note lower, *tsee-whee;* also a single weak *cheep.*

Habitat: Acacia, mopane, and miombo woodlands and forest edges.

Nesting: Gathers plant down to create a felt-like material that is shaped into a hanging, gourd-shaped pouch; makes an entrance tube that leads into the nesting chamber, and a false entrance that leads into an empty fold. Nest is suspended from an outer branch of a bush or high in the canopy of a tree. Lays 4–6 eggs.

Range: Congo, Uganda, and c Kenya south to c Namibia and e South Africa.

This nondescript little bird has a fascinating home life. When leaving the nest it "zips" the entrance tube shut with its bill and opens the false entrance; nest-raiding snakes or birds find an empty pocket. On returning, the parent opens the real entrance tube. Pairs spend considerable time at this and in general nest repair. They glean insects in leaves, flowers, and fruit.

Sunbirds
Family Nectariniidae

Important pollinators, these small birds feed on nectar and insects attracted to flowers. Most males have very bright iridescent colors, although in some species males typically have a drab nonbreeding plumage. Females are mainly plain brown or olive year-round; most are not described below. Sunbirds are often compared to hummingbirds, which are restricted to the Americas. Sunbirds hover slowly at some flowers, but generally they perch on them with their wings closed while feeding. Their black bills are slender and down-curved (some greatly so). Many males and some females have colorful pectoral tufts that can be displayed or hidden. Songs are high-pitched twitterings, calls abrupt. There are 120 species, all in Africa, Asia, and Australasia. Africa has 81 species, including a number restricted to Gulf of Guinea and Indian Ocean islands.

495 **Collared Sunbird**
Anthreptes collaris

Description: *A tiny sunbird, with a very short, slightly down-curved bill,* and a short tail. Brilliant iridescent green head, throat, and upperparts. Obscure violet collar on chest where green meets *clear yellow belly.* Female also brilliant green above, but entirely yellow below. L 4″ (10 cm).

Similar Species: There are several other short-billed species in this genus with purple head, throat, and upperparts contrasting with pure white underparts. **Eastern Violet-backed Sunbird** *(A. orientalis)* ranges from Ethiopia south through Kenya to c Tanzania in dry thornbush country. Larger and heavier-billed **Common Violet-backed Sunbird** *(A. longuemarei)* ranges from Senegal east to Uganda and Mozambique.

Voice: Male has a weak, cricket-like song. Calls include a brisk *seep-seep.*

Habitat: Most types of forests and woodlands; also some semi-arid areas.

Nesting: Weaves a hanging oval nest with a small roof on a small pendant branch. Nest is made of grass and plant fibers and lined with plant down. Lays 1 or 2 eggs.

Range: Gambia east to Ethiopia, and south to n Botswana and e South Africa. Ranges commonly to 9,200′ (2,800 m).

With its short bill and small size, the Collared Sunbird looks like a bright warbler. The most widespread African sunbird, it is tolerant of highly cut-over habitats. Unlike most sunbirds, it feeds mainly on insects away from flowers and in masses of dead leaves.

---

496 **Scarlet-chested Sunbird**
Nectarinia senegalensis

Description: *Male black,* with heavy, strongly arched bill and short tail; *brilliant scarlet chest.* At some angles, *iridescent green forehead and throat* may be visible. Female brown, with yellowish "mustache" stripe. L 6″ (15 cm).

Similar Species: Male **Hunter's Sunbird** *(N. hunteri)* has purple rump and green "mustache" stripe, but black throat; replaces Scarlet-chested in arid thornbush country of Ethiopia, Somalia, n and se Kenya, and a bit of ne Tanzania. Male **Amethyst Sunbird** (Black Sunbird; *N. amethystina*) appears black, but with a green forecrown and amethyst throat; widespread from e Africa to s Cape Province.

Voice: Male has a rapid *chip-chew-chip-chew-tip-tip-tip* and soft warbling notes. Call note, given by both sexes, is a *ship* or *shup.*

Habitat: Forest edges, woodlands, thornveld, and ornamental trees in gardens.

Nesting: Builds a pear-shaped hanging nest of plant fibers and lichens, hung from a small branch or overhanging roof. Lays 2 eggs.

Range: Senegal east to Eritrea, and south to c Namibia and e South Africa.

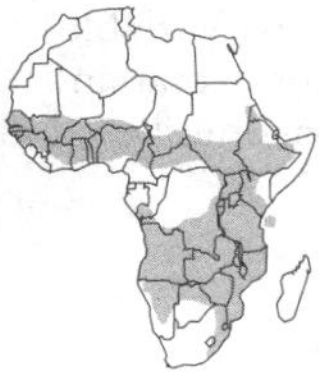

Like many sunbirds, this one moves around locally to wherever flowers are in bloom. It likes native aloes and imported showy trees with large flowers, but varies its diet by taking spiders from their webs, hawking flying termites, and picking up ants from the ground.

---

497 **Variable Sunbird**
Yellow-bellied Sunbird
Nectarinia venusta

Description: Male has iridescent green head and upperparts; *chin and upper breast purple. Belly yellow* in most areas, but white from c Kenya north and east, and orange in Uganda and Zaire. Rarely seen pectoral tuft is red. L 4.5″ (11 cm).

Similar Species: Southern **White-bellied Sunbird** is similar but has white belly. Gorgeous **Orange-breasted Sunbird** *(N. violacea)* inhabits sw Cape Province coastal macchia area; male has elongated central tail feathers, green head and throat, purple chest band, and orange breast shading to yellow. **Collared Sunbird** has much shorter bill.

Voice: Male has a soft warbling chatter, which may include imitations of other birds. Call note is a drawn-out *cheer-cheer.* Gives a clicking note in flight.

Habitat: Forest edges, woodlands, marshy areas, and gardens.

Nesting: Often breeds in dry season or winter. Builds a bulky, oval hanging nest of grass, leaves, and flower heads, often placed a few feet (less than a meter) from the ground. Nest is bound by spiderwebbing and usually contains 2 eggs.

Range: Senegal east to Somalia, and south to e Zimbabwe. Occurs from sea level to 10,000′ (3,000 m).

This is usually one of the more common sunbirds wherever it occurs. Many novice bird-watchers confuse it with the much smaller-billed Collared Sunbird. Little groups of the restless Variable Sunbird work treetops for nectar and spiders, dart out after passing flies, and descend to flowers.

498 White-bellied Sunbird
Nectarinia talatala

Description: Male has iridescent *green upperparts;* green head blends into purple chest band just above *clear white belly.* When breeding, has yellow pectoral tufts near shoulders. L 4.5″ (11 cm).

Similar Species: Male **Variable Sunbird** has yellow belly. Male **Dusky Sunbird** *(N. fusca)* is all slaty, except for white lower belly; ranges from Etosha Pan area of n Namibia south to Cape Town area.

Voice: Call is a sharp *click.* Male gives a few *cheer-y cheer-y* notes, followed by a tinkling warble.

Habitat: Dry acacia and miombo woodlands, and towns at lower elevations.

Nesting: Builds oval nest with side or top entrance,

often near a wasp nest. Camouflages nest exterior with dead leaves and cocoons.

Range: Central Angola and s Tanzania south to c Namibia and Lesotho.

An active bird that searches for insects and visits flowers for nectar, the White-bellied Sunbird has adapted well to gardens, even in cities. It sticks to drier areas than the Variable Sunbird in their zones of overlap, such as Zimbabwe, and flocks to areas with flowering plants.

---

499 **Eastern Double-collared Sunbird**
Nectarinia mediocris

Description: *Brilliant green head and back;* blue rump. Narrow blue line between green throat and *red chest band. Yellow pectoral tufts* at edge of red chest band; white belly. L 4″ (10 cm).

Similar Species: Larger **Greater Double-collared Sunbird** *(N. afra)* has longer bill, longer tail, and wider red breast band; lives in high mountains from w Uganda south to Malawi, and at lower elevations in e and s South Africa. **Lesser Double-collared Sunbird** *(N. chalybea),* the only double-collar around Cape Town, is widespread in sc Africa and coastal regions of South Africa; has shorter bill and narrower breast band.

Voice: Male has a clear warbling song. Call is a sharp *tsip.*

Habitat: High mountain forest edges; brushy areas with bracken, bamboo, and tree-heath; gardens and moorlands.

Nesting: Builds a spherical nest of grass, rootlets, and lichens, lined with plant down. Nest is placed at any level from a low shrub to a high tree. Lays 2 eggs.

Range: Highlands of Kenya south to Malawi. Chiefly found from 4,600′ to 12,000′ (1,400–3,700 m).

The narrow, blue, second breast band is often hard to see. This bird is common in gardens around lodges on Ngorongoro's rim (Tanzania), and is often seen on Mount Kilimanjaro and Mount Kenya.

500 Tacazze Sunbird

Nectarinia tacazze

Description: *Male large and all dark,* with long, down-curved bill, and long central tail streamers. *Back, shoulders, and chest reflect purple,* while head reflects coppery green. Wings and belly black. Short-tailed *female unstriped yellowish below.* L 9″ (23 cm).

Similar Species: **Bronze Sunbird** *(N. kilimensis)* lives in mountains from w Uganda and c Kenya south to e Zimbabwe; male similar to Tacazze, but with coppery-green (bronzy) reflections on head, chest, and upperparts, but no purple; female has dark streaks on yellow chest. Male **Malachite Sunbird** *(N. famosa),* of mountains from Ethiopia south to Cape Town area, is much brighter green and has extremely long central tail streamers. Male **Golden-winged Sunbird** *(N. reichenowi)* appears black, with copper or ruby tones; both sexes have large golden wing patches; lives in montane forest edges and scrublands of e Africa, and is common on rim of Ngorongoro Crater, in Tanzania.

Voice: Male has a warbling song. Call is a single or double *tsssip.*

Habitat: Montane forest edges, glades, shrubbery, gardens, and cultivated areas.

Nesting: Builds a pear-shaped hanging nest of plant fibers and lichen. Lays 1 egg.

Range: Mountains of Eritrea, Ethiopia, s Sudan, e Uganda, s Kenya, and n Tanzania. Chiefly ranges from 7,000′ to 14,000′ (2,100–4,300 m).

This sunbird is often seen around houses and lodges in colder, mountainous areas of Ethiopia and East Africa. Dozens may be present at places where flowers attract other sunbirds.

501 **Mariqua Sunbird**
Marico Sunbird
Nectarinia mariquensis

Description: A medium-size, *dark sunbird,* with a strongly down-curved bill and no long tail streamers. Male is iridescent bronzy green on head and back. Chest has narrow blue band, and *wide, reddish-purple band* above black belly. L 5.5″ (14 cm).

Similar Species: **Purple-banded Sunbird** *(N. bifasciata),* of Zambezi Valley and coastal scrub from Kenya to Natal, has shorter, less down-curved bill. Various **double-collared sunbirds** have white bellies.

Voice: Male rapidly utters a long series of notes, starting with *tseep-tseep-tseep.* Call notes include a *shitz-shitz.*

Habitat: Dry acacia savanna woodlands, riverine forest edges, semi-arid bushlands, and isolated kopje vegetation.

Nesting: Female builds a nest of plant fibers attached to a hanging branch up to 25′ (8 m) high. Lays 2 eggs.

Range: Eritrea and n Somalia south through e Africa to Malawi; Angola and s Zambia south to c Namibia and n Natal.

The aggressive Mariqua Sunbird may chase other birds far from its nest or food source. It often hovers in front of seedheads to pick out insects, and darts upward to snatch a fly or wasp. Its face is sometimes colored bright orange or yellow by pollen. It visits flowering trees and aloes in the savanna parks, such as Masai Mara (Kenya), Serengeti (Tanzania), Etosha (Namibia), and Kruger (Transvaal).

---

502 **Beautiful Sunbird**
Beautiful Long-tailed Sunbird
Nectarinia pulchella

Description: *A tiny sunbird,* with a *short, down-curved bill; male has long tail streamers.* Breeding male dark green, with colorful *"flag" of yellow-red-yellow on chest.* Belly is green north of equator, black to south (s Kenya and Tanzania). Nonbreeding male retains long tail, but plumage resembles female's: brownish above, yellowish below. L 6″ (15 cm).

Similar Species: In 2 other tiny Sahel sunbirds, males have long tail streamers, entirely yellow bellies, and even shorter bills: **Pygmy Sunbird** (Long-tailed Sunbird; *Anthreptes platurus*) ranges from Senegal east to Sudan and extreme nw Kenya. **Nile Valley Sunbird** *(A. metallicus)* ranges from Nile Delta south to c Sudan, Ethiopia, and n Somalia.

Voice: Male has a subdued warbling song. Call is a sharp *tsip.*

Habitat: Drier country, such as bushed and wooded savannas, scrublands, cultivated areas, and semi-deserts.

Nesting: Builds an elongated nest of grass and bark fibers, with entrance near the top, bound by spiderwebbing and attached to a small branch. Lays 2 eggs.

Range: Sahel zone from Mauritania and Guinea-Bissau east to Ethiopia, and south to s Tanzania.

Ranging farther into the Sahel and the Sahara than other sunbirds, yet absent from Somalia, this bird feeds heavily on aloe and acacia blossoms. It is particularly common at Lake Baringo, in Kenya, and around the Serengeti Plains, in Tanzania.

SUGARBIRDS
Family Promeropidae

These are fairly large songbirds with long, down-curved beaks and long graduated tails. The plumage is brown, with a yellow vent. Sugarbirds feed on flower nectar and insects. The two species are restricted to southern Africa.

503 **Cape Sugarbird**
Promerops cafer

Description: *Brown above,* with *dark "mustache"* on white throat; brown chest; streaked belly; *yellow vent. Male's tail is twice as long as the body,* while female's tail is equal to body length. Female has shorter, straighter bill. L male 16″ (40 cm), female 10″ (25 cm).

Similar Species: **Gurney's Sugarbird** *(P. gurneyi)* ranges from e Zimbabwe through Drakensberg Mountains, in s Africa, south to e Cape Province; smaller (L male 12″/29 cm, female 9″/23 cm), with tail of both sexes equal to body length; cap and chest band rusty; throat and breast white.

Voice: Song is a mix of metallic gratings, harsh chirping, and starling-like whistles. Calls include a loud *chink-chink* and a long series of *clack* notes.

Habitat: The unique brushlands (the protea-dominated fynbos) and gardens of the Cape Province "floral kingdom."

Nesting: Male sings during display flight over territory. Breeds during winter rainy season (April–August), and usually raises 2 broods of 2 youngsters. Builds a cup-shaped nest of protea twigs lined with protea down and placed in a protea bush.

Range: Southern Cape Province.

The male Cape Sugarbird is a familiar sight as it sits conspicuously on tops of bushes and telephone wires with its long tail flopping about. As the summer dry season approaches, these birds retreat to the higher mountains or invade gardens to feed on exotic flowers.

White-eyes
Family Zosteropidae

These small, warbler-like birds with brush-tipped tongues feed on nectar, fruit, and small insects. They have short, rounded wings and thin, slightly down-curved beaks; most have a ring of white feathers around the (usually dark) eye. Pairs mate for life, leave their flock to breed, and return later to the same flock. There are no plumage differences due to sex, age, or season. The family has 85 species worldwide. There are 17 species in Africa, the majority restricted to offshore islands in the Gulf of Guinea and southwest Indian Ocean.

504 African Yellow White-eye

Zosterops senegalensis

Description: *Pale yellow-olive above;* bright yellow below. Thin black bill; black lores; *white eye ring* around dark eye. L 4″ (10 cm).

Similar Species: **Cape White-eye** *(Z. pallidus)* replaces African Yellow in most of South Africa and Namibia; darker olive above, with yellow only on throat and vent. **Montane White-eye** (Broad-ringed White-eye; *Z. poliogastra*) is darker green above and has broad white eye ring; inhabits forests and gardens at 5,000–10,000′ (1,500–3,000 m) from Ethiopia south to n Tanzania.

Voice: A series of high warbling notes.

Habitat: Evergreen forest edges, savanna and riverine woodlands, and thickets.

Nesting: Builds a compact, cup-shaped nest of plant fibers, grass, and lichens, bound by spiderwebbing. Nest is suspended from a forked branch in the shady canopy of a tree. Lays 2–4 eggs.

Range: Senegal east to w Ethiopia, and south to ne Namibia and n Natal.

This is the most widespread white-eye in Africa. In areas with no other white-eyes, it may live in wet mountain forests or semi-arid desert scrub.

BUNTINGS
Family Emberizidae

Buntings are sparrow-sized birds with strong, conical, seed-cracking bills and large feet. They perch in trees, but feed on and nest near the ground. This predominantly Western Hemisphere group includes members of just one genus in Africa. Worldwide there are 580 species, with 16 species in Africa.

505 Golden-breasted Bunting
Emberiza flaviventris

Description: Male has zebra-like *black head, with 5 white stripes;* rather long and pointed bill, dark above, paler below. *Yellow throat; golden-orange chest. Rufous back;* 2 white wing bars. White lower belly; gray rump; white outer tail feathers. Female paler. L 6.5″ (16 cm).

Similar Species: **Cabanis's Bunting** *(E. cabanisi)* has solid black face under white eyebrow, and grayer back; ranges from Guinea east to Uganda, and south to Zimbabwe. **Cinnamon-breasted Bunting** *(E. tahapisi)* lives in rocky hills and open areas in woodlands from Senegal east to Somalia, and south to e South Africa; has unstriped cinnamon breast and black head with 7 white stripes.

Voice: Song is *chip-chip-chip-chip teeee tew-tew-tew-tew.* Alarm call is *tsip-tsip-cheeer.*

Habitat: Woodlands, treed savannas, plantations, and gardens.

Nesting: Builds an untidy, frail, shallow, cup-shaped nest of twigs and grass, lined with long hairs from cattle and antelopes, placed in a bush. Lays 2 or 3 eggs.

Range: Northern Mali east to Eritrea; Zaire, Uganda, and Kenya south to c Namibia and e South Africa.

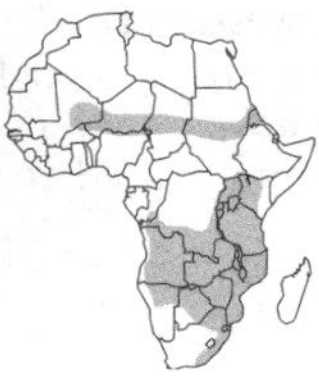

This bunting is usually seen in pairs, feeding on the ground. When flushed, it flies in an undulating, wagtail-like flight, complete with white outer tail feathers.

Finches
Family Fringillidae

These are small, seed-eating birds, many of which have thick bills for cracking seeds in trees, bushes, and flower beds. Most finch species in sub-Saharan Africa belong to the canary genus *Serinus;* many of these are bright yellow or greenish yellow, while others are brownish. Worldwide there are 144 species, with 44 known from Africa.

506 African Citril Canary
African Citril
Serinus citrinelloides

Description: *Green-yellow upperparts;* yellow underparts, with fine dark streaks on crown and back. Males vary geographically: in eastern part of range, blackish forehead, cheek, and throat, with yellow line behind eye; in south, whitish stripes on dusky head; in west, yellow forehead and eye line, black only on lores. L 4.5″ (11.5 cm).

Similar Species: **Island Canary** *(S. canaria),* common in Canary Islands, is yellow, with gray crown, cheeks, and back; is ancestor of diverse domestic varieties.

Voice: Call is loud *cheep* notes; song is long whistling series at low volume.

Habitat: Forest edges, scrublands, and gardens from 3,600′ to 11,000′ (1,100–3,300 m).

Nesting: Builds a neat cup of dry grass and rootlets in the fork of a tree; nest bound by cobwebs and lined with plant down.

Range: Highlands from s Sudan and Eritrea south to Malawi.

Common in the greener mountains flanking the eastern and western rift valleys in East Africa, the African Citril Canary is often found in flower gardens when flower heads are going to seed.

507 **Yellow-fronted Canary**
Yellow-eyed Canary
Serinus mozambicus

Description: Gray crown and head behind brown eye. *Black lores and "mustache."* Bright yellow eyebrow, patch above "mustache," underparts, and rump. L 4.5″ (11 cm).

Similar Species: **White-bellied Canary** *(S. dorsostriatus)* also has "mustache," but belly is white; replaces Yellow-fronted in many dry areas east of Lake Victoria northeast to Somalia. **Black-throated Canary** (Yellow-rumped Canary; *S. atrogularis*) is brown, with black throat and yellow only on rump; lives from Ethiopia south to c South Africa in drier country.

Voice: Cheerful song rises and falls; may be rendered as *yes, yes, I see you.*

Habitat: Open woodlands, scrub, cultivated areas, and gardens from sea level to 7,500′ (2,300 m).

Nesting: Builds a deep cup nest of rootlets and grass. Nest is placed in a tree fork near the shaded end of a branch. Usually lays 3 or 4 eggs.

Range: Senegal east to Ethiopia, and south to n Botswana and e South Africa.

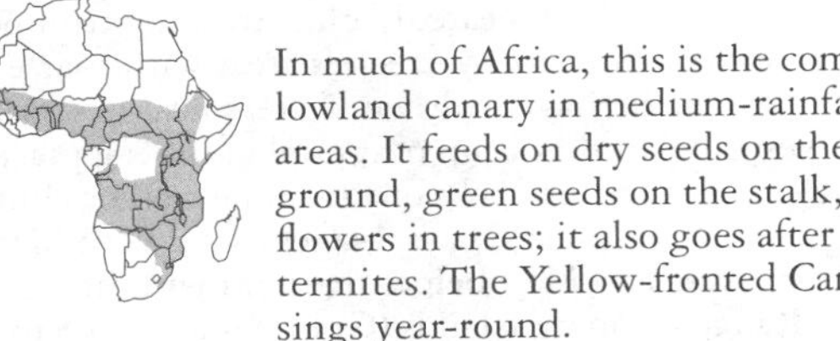

In much of Africa, this is the common lowland canary in medium-rainfall areas. It feeds on dry seeds on the ground, green seeds on the stalk, and flowers in trees; it also goes after flying termites. The Yellow-fronted Canary sings year-round.

508 **Streaky Canary**
Streaky Seedeater
Serinus striolatus

Description: *Dark brown face patch and "mustache," with creamy white eyebrow.* Heavy brown stripes above; 2 narrow wing bars. Dull white below, with fine or bold brown stripes. L 6″ (15 cm).

Voice: Male has a bubbling song. Also a soft, 3-note call, with last 2 notes lower.

Habitat: Montane forest edges, wet bushlands, cultivated areas, and gardens. Ranges from 4,300′ to 14,000′ (1,300–4,300 m).

Nesting: Builds a cup-shaped nest of rootlets, grass, and moss, placed in a creeper, bush, or tree. Lays 3 or 4 eggs.

Range: Mountains from w Eritrea south to Burundi and e Tanzania. Isolated race in s Tanzania and n Malawi has yellow eyebrow and throat.

This is a common roadside and garden bird in the greener country of the highlands. It is usually found in pairs, rather than flocks.

509 **Trumpeter Finch**
Trumpeter Bullfinch
Rhodopechys githaginea

Description: Breeding male pale brown, with *pinkish sheen on face, underparts, wings, and rump;* short, notched, brown tail. Female and winter male pale gray with pinkish tinge. Stubby, conical, pale orange bill. L 5.5″ (14 cm).

Voice: Quick, nasal, trumpeting call, like a child repeatedly blowing a toy trumpet.

Habitat: Arid, rocky, treeless areas with sparse herbage; cultivated areas near deserts.

Nesting: Builds a cup nest of plant fibers, placed among rocks or in a stone wall or clump of plants. Lays 4–6 eggs between March and May, before the summer heat.

Range: Canary Islands (Gran Canaria) east to Red Sea in Egypt and n Sudan.

The Trumpeter Finch is fairly common in the Sahara, where it searches for small seeds and insects and runs along the ground like a lark. Hard to see when stationary, at sundown it flies to the nearest water source to drink.

Waxbills
Family Estrididae

The very small, seed-eating waxbills are popular cage birds. In the wild they feed on the ground and in tall grass. They have short legs and conical (often brightly colored) bills. The plumage often has patches of bright colors or strong patterns. In courtship, most males hop around singing and waving nesting material in front of the female; some also imitate nestlings begging for food. This Old World family has 133 species, 75 in Africa.

510 Red-billed Firefinch
Lagonosticta senegala

Description: *A tiny, pink-billed bird;* thin white eye ring; red rump; black tail; *very short legs.* Male has red crown; brown back, wings, and vent; rest of *head and underparts rosy.* Female has red lores; rest of body soft brown. Both sexes have tiny "dash of salt" speckling on sides. L 4″ (10 cm).

Similar Species: Male **African Firefinch** (Blue-billed Firefinch; *L. rubricata*) has dark slaty bill with pink base to lower mandible, gray crown and nape, darker brown back, and black vent; lives in thickets from Guinea-Bissau to e South Africa.

Voice: A soft warbling song. Call note is a high thin *dwee.*

Habitat: Dry woodlands, acacia savannas, riverine thickets, farms, and towns.

Nesting: Builds a round, grass-and-straw nest with a side entrance. Nest is placed on the ground, in a low bush, or in a cavity on a wall. Lays 3–5 eggs.

Range: Cape Verde Islands; Senegal east to Somalia, and south to South Africa.

This "animated plum" is a familiar sight as it hops about on lawns and walkways, looking for tiny seeds and insects. It is the tamest of birds, often reluctant to fly at the approach of humans.

511 Red-cheeked Cordon-bleu
Uraeginthus bengalus

Description: *Pink bill with dark tip. Brown crown,* back, and wings. Azure-blue face, underparts, rump, and tail. Male has *red cheek.* L 5″ (13 cm).

Similar Species: Male **Blue-capped Cordon-bleu** *(U. cyanocephalus)* has all-blue head, including crown, while female Blue-cap has brighter red bill with black tip; lives in semi-arid acacia country of e Africa from s Somalia to n Tanzania. Both sexes of **Southern Cordon-bleu** (Blue Waxbill; *U. angolensis*), which ranges from Zambezi Valley southward, have blue face and throat, brown crown, and black bill.

Voice: A high-pitched, 3- or 4-note song, *tsee-tsee-see-tchee.* Call is a weak *tsee-tsee.*

Habitat: Acacia woodlands, thorny savannas, semi-deserts, gardens, and farmlands.

Nesting: Builds a round nest of grass tops with a side entrance, lined with feathers and placed in a small tree, sometimes near a hornet nest for protection. Lays 4 or 5 eggs.

Range: Senegal east to Ethiopia, and south to Zambia.

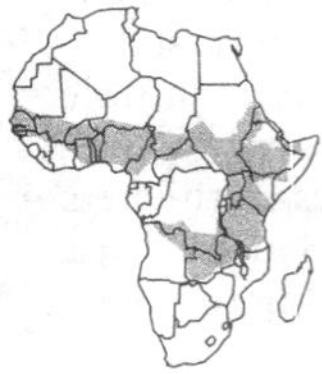

This bird is commonly seen, as it is often tame around homes. A pair or small flock may hop along on lawns, trails, and open ground, searching for grass seeds and insects. It wanders widely when not breeding.

512 Purple Grenadier
Uraeginthus ianthinogaster

Description: *Red bill* and eye ring; long black tail. *Male chestnut, with purple face, chest, and belly.* Female paler rusty, with purple rump and *pale blue circle around eye ring.* L 5.5″ (14 cm).

Similar Species: **Violet-eared Waxbill** *(U. granatina)* ranges from Angola and Zambia south to c South Africa; has large violet face patch, blue forehead, and rusty underparts.

Voice: Both sexes sing a jumbled song that mixes soft notes with buzzes and ends in a trill. Call is a weak *chirp.*

Habitat: Dry thorn scrub, woodland edges, and gardens.

Nesting: Builds a spherical nest of dry grass lined with feathers, placed in a low bush. Lays 3–5 eggs. Sometimes hosts parasitic Straw-tailed Whydah.

Range: Southern Ethiopia south to s Tanzania.

This bird is fairly common and trusting when living near people or bird tables. It feeds on seeds and insects, foraging in pairs and small parties on the ground in shady areas.

513 Common Waxbill
Estrilda astrild

Description: *Red bill and stripe through eye.* Pale brown, with *fine slaty barring on upperparts, rump, tail, and sides.* White throat; pink mid-belly; black vent. L 5″ (13 cm).

Similar Species: **Crimson-rumped Waxbill** *(E. rhodopyga)* has red on wings and rump; lives from Eritrea south to Malawi. **Black-rumped Waxbill** *(E. troglodytes)* ranges widely from Senegal east to w Kenya; has black rump and tail. Another common w African bird is **Orange-cheeked Waxbill** *(E. melpoda);* has unbarred gray body with brown back, red bill, orange face, red rump, and black tail.

Voice: Song is short and unmelodious. Call is a clear *ping-ping.*

Habitat: Grassy areas, marshes, and cultivation from sea level to 10,000′ (3,000 m).

Nesting: Builds an elaborate grass and seedhead nest, placed in the grass or a low bush and with a "walkway" hanging down. Lays 4–6 eggs. Pin-tailed Whydah often adds an egg; its youngster grows up with the waxbill babies.

Range: Sierra Leone and Liberia; widespread from e Nigeria east to Ethiopia, and south to Cape Town area.

This tiny bird with a fairly long tail is rather shy and restless. Small parties move off one bird at a time. In nonbreeding seasons, large flocks travel together and join up with others at communal roosts. The Common Waxbill feeds mainly on seeds, but, like virtually all savanna species, it will fly up to feed on swarms of flying termites.

---

514 **Cut-throat Waxbill**
Cut-throat Finch
Amadina fasciata

Description: Heavy ivory bill. *Buffy,* with fine black barring. Male has *blood-red band from ear coverts down to throat.* L 5″ (12 cm).

Similar Species: **Red-headed Waxbill** (Red-headed Finch; *A. erythrocephala*) ranges widely in arid areas of Namibia, Botswana, Zimbabwe, and inland South Africa; male has all-red head and is boldly scalloped below. **Bronze Mannikin** (*Lonchura cucullata;* L 3.5″/9 cm) is common in flocks in tall grass and towns in most of sub-Saharan Africa; male has black head and throat, and bronze upperparts; white below, with black scalloping on sides.

Voice: Song is low-pitched, buzzy humming, mixed with low warbling notes. In flight, gives a thin *eee-eee-eee.*

Habitat: Arid scrub, acacia savannas, cultivated fields, and mopane woodlands.

Nesting: Builds an untidy, ball-shaped grass nest with a short entrance funnel; may be in a bush, a tree up to 15′ (4.5 m), a metal fence hole, or a building cavity. Sometimes uses an old weaver nest. Lays 4–7 eggs, sometimes 9.

Range: Senegal east to Somalia, and south to Transvaal. Ranges from sea level to 5,000′ (1,500 m).

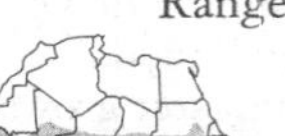

Despite its morbid name, this is a shy, pretty bird. The pair-bond is strong, and pairs will stay together even when joining flocks in the nonbreeding season. They wander widely, feeding on seeds on the ground, but will take flying termites when they see them.

WEAVERS
Family Ploceidae

Small to medium-size, finch-like birds, weavers have stout pointed beaks that are used for a diet that includes seeds of grasses and herbs, buds, and insects. Some species are very colorful, and many weave incredible nests. One occasionally sees trees covered with dozens, or even hundreds, of the little green (new) or yellow (old) straw-bag nests of yellow weavers, and the black buffalo-weavers cover entire branches of giant trees with their "pick-up-sticks" nests. On the other hand, the whydahs and indigobirds weave nothing, laying their eggs in other birds' nests. After the breeding season (usually the rainy season), most male weavers molt out of their finery and come to resemble the drab females. In the dry season, these birds are a nightmare to identify and thus are rarely discussed in detail below; descriptions of males are of breeding males. The weaver family is primarily African, with 142 of the world's 160 species found in Africa. *Note:* The sparrows are sometimes split into their own family, the Passeridae.

515 Straw-tailed Whydah
Fischer's Whydah
Vidua fischeri

Description: Male black, with *golden-yellow crown, breast, and belly; 4 extremely long, thin, straw-colored central tail feathers.* Red bill; pink legs. L male 11″ (28 cm), female 4″ (10 cm).

Similar Species: **Shaft-tailed Whydah** *(V. regia)* lives in Namibia, Botswana, s Zimbabwe, and n South Africa; male has black crown and face, buffy yellow underparts and collar; 4 long tail feathers are thin feather shafts, with "paddles" at tips.

Voice: Song is an oft-repeated 3- or 4-note warbling. Call is a sharp *tssip.*

Habitat: Dry thornbush areas and bushed grasslands in plateau country to 6,000′ (1,800 m). Vagrant down to sea level.

Nesting: In display, male holds on to a twig at the top of a bush, flaps its wings, and swings its tail plumes. Builds no nest. Lays eggs in nest of Purple Grenadier.

Range: Ethiopia and Somalia south through Kenya to c Tanzania.

This very attractive bird adorns many a bush top along roadsides in the rainy seasons. It is most common in brush bordering farms outside the national parks.

---

516 **Pin-tailed Whydah**
Vidua macroura

Description: Male has red bill; *black cap and face; white collar and underparts.* Upperparts black, with *long white wing patch;* white rump; *4 very long, black central tail feathers.* L male 13″ (33 cm), female 4.5″ (11.5 cm).

Voice: Male has a wheezy song. Call is a monotonous series of *tseet* notes.

Habitat: Grassy clearings in forests, wooded savannas, farms, and gardens.

Nesting: Builds no nest. Lays 1 egg in nest of Common Waxbill, other waxbills, firefinches, or mannikins.

Range: Senegal east to Somalia, and south to Cape Town area, including rain-forest belt.

In courtship, the male flops around in circles, calling and showing off his tail; he is usually accompanied by a number of females or young males. The mouth spots of young whydahs are remarkably like those of the young of their hosts. Unlike baby cuckoos, they do not evict or kill the host nestlings.

517 **Eastern Paradise Whydah**
Vidua paradisaea

Description: Male black, with *pale yellow hindneck;* chestnut chest; pale yellow belly. Strange *tail has 2 very long, wide feathers that come to a point and 2 shorter rounded feathers that look like a big bump.* L male 16″ (40 cm), female 5″ (13 cm).

Similar Species: Male **Broad-tailed Paradise Whydah** *(V. obtusa)* ranges from c Kenya south to n Transvaal; 2 longer tail feathers are much thicker, hindneck more orange.

Voice: Call is a sparrow-like *teeet.*

Habitat: Savanna woodlands, bushlands, and acacia thickets.

Nesting: Displaying male flies steeply in the sky, then swoops down in undulating arcs. Builds no nest. Lays 1 egg in several nests of Green-winged Pytilia. Nestlings' mouth markings are exactly like those of young pytilias.

Range: Eritrea south to s Tanzania, thence west to w Angola and south to e South Africa.

The large "bump" near the base of its tail makes the male of this species distinctive in flight. These birds often gather in small flocks of ten or so, rarely up to 100. They search for seeds on the ground by scratching with both legs and then hopping back to see what has been uncovered.

518 **Red-billed Buffalo-Weaver**
Bubalornis niger

Description: *Male black, with sturdy red bill;* white flash on primaries and white speckling on sides under wings. Female has red bill and is dark brown on back; pale-bellied with dark streaks in e Africa; brown-bellied with faint white scaling in s Africa. L 10″ (25 cm).

Similar Species: Male **White-billed Buffalo-Weaver** *(B. albirostris)* is black, with blackish or white bill; ranges from Senegal east to Eritrea, and south to nw Kenya.

Voice: Noisy near nest, with a variety of churrs, chatters, croaks, and creaks.

Habitat: Dry open woodlands, palm groves, acacia savannas, and farms.

Nesting: Builds massive stick nests, with separate entrances underneath leading into domed grass nests; each male has 2 or more females with separate nesting chambers. Up to 20 "harems" may have nests in the same baobab or acacia. Lays 2–4 eggs.

Range: 2 distinct populations: Ethiopia south to c Tanzania; Angola and Namibia east to s Mozambique.

The conspicuous nests of this species are tended year-round, but during drought many colonies are abandoned as the flock searches for food elsewhere. This bird feeds on seeds and large insects on bare ground, often joining starlings and other weavers. Buffalo-weavers have nothing to do with buffalos.

---

519 White-headed Buffalo-Weaver
Dinemellia dinamelli

Description: Thick, grosbeak-like, black bill. *White head* and underparts; black lores and black around eye; blackish-brown back, wings, and tail. *Large white spot on primaries. Bright red rump and vent.* L 9" (23 cm).

Similar Species: **White-headed Barbet** (*Lybius leucocephalus;* L 6"/15 cm) has longer black bill and small white spots on wings; feeds in tall fruiting trees from Nigeria southeast to c Tanzania.

Voice: A loud harsh cry, likened to a parrot, a rusty pump, or a trumpet.

Habitat: Dry bushed and wooded savannas with acacia or baobab trees.

Nesting: Builds a long row of thorny stick nests draped over low solid branches; entrances, from below, lead to grass- and feather-lined nests. Lays 3 or 4 eggs.

Range: Somalia, s Ethiopia, se Sudan, n Uganda, and Kenya south to sc Tanzania. Ranges to 5,000′ (1,500 m).

This bird is usually spotted flying up into a thorny tree, with its red rump, white head, and wing spots clearly visible. It occurs in small groups of three to six, sometimes with starlings. It feeds on the ground and in trees, looking for seeds, fruit, and insects.

---

520 Grosbeak Weaver

Thick-billed Weaver
Amblyospiza albifrons

Description: *Very heavy bill,* black in male, yellowish in female. *Male dark blackish brown, with white forehead and small white wing spot;* head color varies from black (east and upper Zambezi) to rufous (west) to brown (northeast and southeast). Female brown above, with dark streaks on pale underparts. L 7″ (18 cm).

Similar Species: Male **Vieillot's Black Weaver** *(Ploceus nigerrimus)* is all black, with longer, thinner beak and yellow eye in range from Gabon east to sw Kenya; race that lives from Sierra Leone to Nigeria is black, with chestnut on back and belly.

Voice: Male has a brief bubbling song at nest; gives a *tweek* in flight.

Habitat: Breeds in marshes, but forages in nearby forests, brush, and cultivated areas.

Nesting: Nests singly or in colonies of up to 50 pairs. Male connects 2 or 3 reeds or papyrus stalks with a bridge of stems, then tightly weaves a cup, back wall, and roof, with entrance on the side. Lays 2–4 pink eggs.

Range: Sierra Leone east to Ethiopia, and south to e South Africa. Ranges to 10,000′ (3,000 m).

This weaver's superbly made nest can be seen in reeds even in small lily pools in gardens. Abandoned nests are eagerly used by waxbills and mice. Its diet includes hard seeds, fruit stones, sunflower seeds, berries, and a few water snails and insects. The flight is undulating.

521 Reichenow's Weaver

Baglafecht Weaver
Ploceus baglafecht

Description: Races are very variable, but all have yellow eyes. In highlands of Kenya and n Tanzania, has *black upperparts,* with yellow wing edging; entirely yellow underparts. *Male has black ear patch encircled with yellow, and yellow forecrown.* Female has solid black head, except for yellow throat. L 6" (15 cm).

Similar Species: **Speke's Weaver** *(P. spekei),* of highlands of Kenya and n Tanzania, has yellow eye, black face and throat, and black-spotted back; is otherwise yellow, including crown and forehead.

Voice: Song is a short, unmelodious chattering. Alarm call is a sharp *twee-up.*

Habitat: Medium- and high-elevation forest edges, woodlands, farms, gardens, and towns.

Nesting: Does not nest in colonies. Weaves a stout oval nest of green grass, hung from a bough or frond. Lays 2 or 3 eggs.

Range: Eritrea south to n Malawi; also Cameroon mountains.

This very attractive black-and-yellow weaver is found in most highland gardens in eastern Africa. Plumage differs greatly among the subspecies.

522 Spectacled Weaver

Ploceus ocularis

Description: *Yellow head washed with orange;* yellow underparts; olive-yellow upperparts. *Thin black bill; thin black line on face* through piercing yellow eye. *Male has black bib.* L 6" (15 cm).

Similar Species: **Black-necked Weaver** *(P. nigricollis)* ranges from Senegal south to c Angola and east to s Somalia; both sexes have solid black upperparts and yellow underparts; male has yellow-orange head with black line through eye, and black bib; female has black crown and line through eye, with yellow eyebrow.

Voice: Male has a short warbling song. Both sexes have a series of descending *tee* notes. Alarm call is a sharp *shack.*

Habitat: Undergrowth in forests, shrubbery, bushed grasslands, and gardens.

Nesting: Does not nest in colonies. Male builds a finely woven nest of thin fibers, with a long entrance tunnel (up to 12″/30 cm) hanging down to one side. Nests often hang from boughs over water and gullies. Lays 2 or 3 eggs.

Range: Cameroon east to Ethiopia, and south to extreme n Namibia and e South Africa.

This shy and inconspicuous weaver is fairly common and often joins mixed-bird parties. It forages thickets for insects, geckos, soft fruit, berries, and nectar.

---

523 Golden Palm Weaver
Ploceus bojeri

Description: Male has black bill, *dark brown eye, golden-orange head,* yellow breast, yellow-olive upperparts, all without stripes or spots. L 6″ (15 cm).

Similar Species: **Yellow Weaver** *(P. subaureus)* occurs in Indian Ocean lowlands from Kenya to Natal; male is bright yellow, with red eye. Larger **Holub's Golden Weaver** *(P. xanthops)* ranges from Kenya's rift valley west to Angola, and south to Natal; male has heavy black bill, yellow eye. Male **Taveta Golden Weaver** *(P. castaneiceps)* is yellow, with chestnut nape and chest patches; common in limited range centered on Amboseli and Tsavo parks of s Kenya and Arusha area of n Tanzania.

Voice: Low-pitched, hissed chatter at nest.

Habitat: Coconut plantations, cultivated areas,

bushed and wooded grasslands; usually near water.

Nesting: Weaves round or oval nest on palm stem or bush. Nests in pairs or small colonies.

Range: Coast and lowlands to 4,000′ (1,200 m) in s Somalia, Kenya (west to Samburu area), and ne Tanzania.

The Golden Palm Weaver is a conspicuous and common resident throughout the Kenya coast, even near towns and hotels. It is a gregarious and noisy bird.

---

524 **Lesser Masked Weaver**
Masked Weaver
Ploceus intermedius

Description: Male has *pale yellow eye; extensive black mask* on forecrown, throat, and face (to well behind eye); yellow neck and underparts; olive back, with *faint black spots.* L 6″ (15 cm).

Similar Species: **Vitelline Masked Weaver** *(P. vitellinus)* ranges from Senegal east to Somalia, and south to c Tanzania; male has yellow eye, chestnut crown and throat, and black on chin. **Southern Masked Weaver** *(P. velatus)* lives from Zambia south to Cape Town area; male has more yellow on crown (with only narrow black forehead) and red eye. Larger **Village Weaver** has red eye and black-and-yellow-spotted back.

Voice: A persistent wheezy chatter at nest.

Habitat: Bushed and wooded grasslands, often with acacias, riverine forests, and cultivated areas to 6,600′ (2,000 m).

Nesting: Weaves a small grass nest with a short entrance funnel on one side of the base. Forms colonies of a few up to 200 pairs.

Range: Ethiopia south to n Namibia and Natal.

When the females of this species are choosing mates, the colorful males hang from nests with their wings open and fluttering.

525 Village Weaver

Layard's Black-headed Weaver,
Spotted-backed Weaver
Ploceus cucullatus

Description: A large, *red-eyed weaver;* black face and throat; yellow underparts; *black-and-yellow-spotted back.* Heads of males vary geographically. In w Africa, entire head is black, with narrow chestnut band on nape. In Congo Basin, head has wide chestnut nape band. In e Africa and south to Zambezi, entire head is black, without chestnut on nape. In s Africa, entire crown is yellow. Some birds are also washed with chestnut on breast. L 7″ (18 cm).

Similar Species: Village Weaver is somewhat larger and has heavier bill than other masked weavers. **Black-headed Weaver** (Yellow-backed Weaver; *P. melanocephalus*) is common in open wetlands and cultivated areas from Senegal east to Lake Victoria basin; male has black head, brown eye, and unspotted olive back; breast is yellow in w Africa, chestnut in e Africa.

Voice: Song is a loud chatter, ending with a long wheezy note. Alarm call is a loud *chuck.*

Habitat: Rain-forest edges, swampy areas, riverine woodlands in savanna zones, villages, gardens, and farms.

Nesting: Nest is started by building a 360-degree, hanging "belt loop." Each nest is woven of grass or palm fiber with an entrance below (some with funnels). Nests are clustered in colonies of sometimes hundreds in an isolated large tree or in reeds. Lays 2 or 3 eggs.

Range: Senegal east to Ethiopia, and south through Congo Basin and e Africa to Zimbabwe and e South Africa. Yellow-crowned southern race introduced on Réunion and Mauritius.

This is one of the most common weavers, with one or more colonies in many villages. It feeds mainly on seeds of wild and cultivated grains, either on the plant or on the ground. It also takes insects in the air and from bark, as well as some nectar. By nesting in trees in the middle of fields or in villages, Village Weavers reduce predation by forest-inhabiting monkeys and egg-eating snakes that are reluctant to cross open areas or enter villages.

---

526 **Red-billed Quelea**
Quelea quelea

Description: A stocky, short-tailed, waxbill-like weaver. *Thick, waxy, red bill* in most plumages. *Male has black face mask* from forehead around to throat; spotted back and clear breast, the wings edged with yellow; *rosy-red (or buffy-yellow) wash over crown, nape, and breast.* L 5″ (13 cm).

Similar Species: **Cardinal Quelea** *(Q. cardinalis)* and **Red-headed Quelea** *(Q. erythrops)* males have slaty bills, red heads, striped brown backs, and pale underparts. The former has red head and neck, and lives in e Africa; the latter lives in wetter areas from Gambia through Congo Basin to e South Africa.

Voice: Continuous chattering at nests and within flocks; colony noise sounds like a swarm of bees.

Habitat: Wooded and open grasslands, cultivated grainfields and farms. Ranges from sea level to 10,000′ (3,000 m).

Nesting: Mass nestings of 100,000 to 2 million pairs or more are not unusual. Weaves a flimsy, oval, hanging nest close to others in reeds or thorn trees. Some trees have 500 nests. Lays 2–5 eggs.

Range: Senegal east across Sahel to Somalia; s Congo east to e Africa, and south to s Namibia and c South Africa.

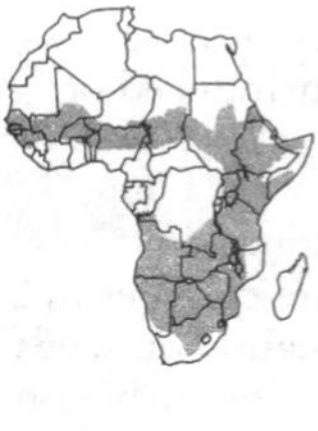

Rains are erratic in the dry country in which the Red-billed Quelea lives. It flocks to areas after they have been drenched and hastily begins nesting. The mass nestings attract many local predators—snakes, small carnivorous mammals, and birds, such as most raptors, storks, hornbills, and wood-hoopoes—that together may consume tens of thousands of quelea eggs and young, but most young fledge. Of greater import is the vast damage that roving flocks of millions of these birds do to local grain crops. Rarely seen alone, this bird generally occurs in groups of 10 to 100 when it is not a member of a massive flock.

527 **Madagascar Red Fody**
Foudia madagascariensis

Description: *Male bright red,* with black bill, *narrow black eye mask,* and black streaks on back. L 5.5″ (14 cm).

Similar Species: **Forest Fody** *(F. omissa)* of Madagascar rain forests and **Comoros Fody** *(F. emintissima)* of Comoros and Aldabra are similar; males have red head and chest, with spotted brown back and white belly. There are 3 insect-eating fodies without red in plumage, all rare: **Seychelles Fody** *(F. sechellarum)* survives only on Cousin, Cousine, and Frigate islands. **Mauritius Fody** *(F. rubra)* numbers 100 at most in native highland forest in southwest. Yellow-breasted **Rodrigues Fody** *(F. flavicans)* numbers less than 100 on its island home east of Mauritius.

Voice: Male's song is a series of *cheet* notes that may rise to a high pitch, becoming insect-like. Alarm is a short shrill *tik-tik.*

Habitat: Open parklands, grasslands, shrubbery, farms, cultivated fields, rice paddies, gardens, and villages. Ranges to 7,500′ (2,300 m).

Nesting: Builds an untidy sphere of grasses, with a short entrance funnel on the side. Nest is placed on a tree bough 3–10′ (1–3 m) above ground. Lays 3 or 4 eggs.

Range: Native to Madagascar. Introduced and common in Seychelles, Mauritius, Réunion, Rodriguez, and all 4 Comoros in Indian Ocean, and on Saint Helena island in Atlantic Ocean.

This beautiful bird sings in the open and feeds on grass seeds, flower nectar, insects, and spiders. It does great damage in rice paddies.

528 **Southern Red Bishop**
Red Bishop
Euplectes orix

Description: *Male has fluffy red nape, neck, back, rump, and undertail coverts; black forehead,* face, throat, and belly; wings and short tail brown. L 5.5″ (14 cm).

Similar Species: **Northern Red Bishop** (Orange Bishop; *E. franciscanus*) ranges from Senegal east to c Kenya; male has black over more of crown, and red or orange plumage covers tail. Male **Red-crowned Bishop** (Black-winged Red Bishop; *E. hordeaceus*) has entirely red crown and black tail and wings; ranges from Gambia east to coastal Kenya, and south to e Zimbabwe.

Voice: Male has a complicated variety of chatters, hisses, rattles, and *zik* notes at nest. Flight call is *cheat-cheat.*

Habitat: Open grasslands, green field crops, marshes, and bushes near water.

Nesting: Nests in colonies in reedbeds. Each male has a territory of a few square yards (meters), where he may build up to a dozen nests and attract up to 7 females. Nest is a tightly woven grass ball suspended between several reeds, with an entrance funnel on the side. Lays 2–4 eggs.

Range: Western Uganda, Lake Victoria, and s Kenya south to Cape Town area.

The male Southern Red Bishop looks like a red tennis ball as he patrols his territory with noisy wingbeats. It feeds on seeds in tall grass or on the ground, chases dragonflies on the wing, and takes other insects on the ground.

529 **Long-tailed Widowbird**
Euplectes progne

Description: Breeding male *black, with red shoulders* above white wing bars; *black tail twice as long as body,* with many variable-length "elastic" feathers. L 24″ (60 cm).
Similar Species: **Jackson's Widowbird** *(E. jacksoni)* lives in highlands of w and c Kenya and Ngorongoro highlands of n Tanzania; male is black, with chestnut on wings, and long, down-curled tail.
Voice: Male has a swizzling song and a slowly repeated series of *chip* notes.
Habitat: Open tall grasslands.
Nesting: Weaves a spherical grass nest with a side entrance, placed near the ground and hidden by growing grass twisted over it. Lays 2–4 eggs.
Range: Highlands of Kenya; parts of Angola, s Zaire, and Zambia; e South Africa.

In their territory, males fight each other off during the day, but come evening they roost together in a reedbed far away from the incubating females. They forage on the ground and in grass for seeds and insects, with their tails dragging on the ground.

530 **White-browed Sparrow-Weaver**
Plocepasser mahali

Description: A large, sparrow-like bird, brown above, white below. *Black crown and "mustache"; white eyebrow and rump, plus 2 white wing bars.* Some show spots on breast. Sexes alike; no seasonal variation. L 7″ (18 cm).
Similar Species: **Rufous-tailed Weaver** (*Histurgops ruficauda;* L 9″/22 cm) replaces White-browed Sparrow-Weaver in wooded savannas from Serengeti east to Tarangire NP in n Tanzania; both sexes are drab scaly brown, with blue eye and rufous outer tail feathers.
Voice: Song is a loud, rambling, and liquid *cheeoo preeeoo-chop-chop,* with variations. Call is a loud *chuk-chuk.*

Habitat: Wooded acacia savannas in semi-arid areas, chiefly from 1,300′ to 4,600′ (400–1,400 m).

Nesting: Builds untidy straw nests with 2 entrance funnels, 1 for each roosting chamber. Builds many nests for practice and to discourage predators. Colony usually has just 1 breeding pair at a time, with helpers bringing food to young of breeding pair. Lays 2 or 3 eggs.

Range: Ethiopia south to Tsavo NP, in Kenya, and Lake Natron, in n Tanzania; s Angola east to s Tanzania, and south to sc South Africa.

This bird is often very common and conspicuous where it occurs, in much of Kenya and in the Zambezi Valley. It is fond of being near humans in villages and around isolated houses and lodges. It feeds by hopping on the ground, searching for seeds and insects, particularly harvester termites.

531 Sociable Weaver
Philetairus socius

Description: A short-tailed, pale brown weaver, with a *black patch on the face from lores to throat.* Hindneck, back, and flanks have dark feathers with pale edges, giving a *scaly appearance.* L 5.5″ (14 cm).

Similar Species: Smaller **Scaly-fronted Weaver** (Scaly-feathered Finch; *Sporopipes squamifrons*) lives in same area; pale brown, with scaly forehead and black "mustache" stripes. Its sister species, **Speckle-fronted Weaver** *(S. frontalis),* lives from Senegal east to Ethiopia, and south to n Tanzania; has tiny white dots on black crown, rusty nape, white face, and black "mustache."

Voice: Gives nasal, clicking *chip* or *klok* notes.

Habitat: Acacia savannas, semi-deserts, and grasslands with some trees.

Nesting: Builds the most elaborate communal nest of any bird in the world. Builds a lattice network of strong twigs over

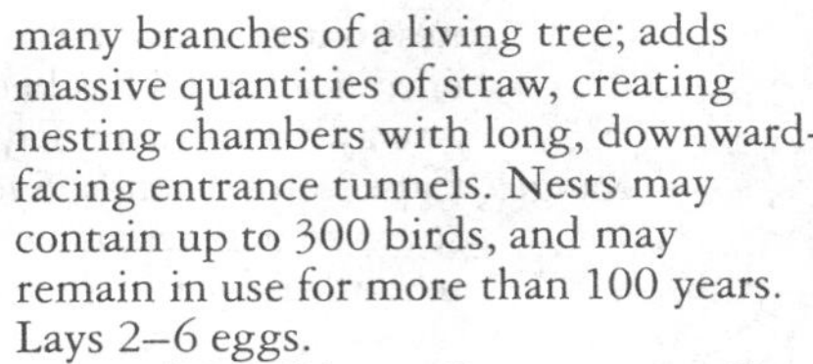

many branches of a living tree; adds massive quantities of straw, creating nesting chambers with long, downward-facing entrance tunnels. Nests may contain up to 300 birds, and may remain in use for more than 100 years. Lays 2–6 eggs.

Range: Most of Namibia, sw Botswana, ne Cape Province, w Transvaal, and w Orange Free State.

Each pair of Sociable Weavers roosts in its own chamber, taking midday siestas inside. On cold desert nights, the birds cram into just a few chambers to conserve body heat. By day, they fly off in groups to feed on grass seeds and insects. Cobras and Boomslangs scale nest trees to take eggs and young. Spotted Eagle-Owls *(Bubo africanus)* sometimes nest atop the colony and may help by eating such snakes. Other birds sometimes take over single chambers.

---

532 **Rufous Sparrow**
Great Sparrow
Passer motitensis (rufocinctus)

Description: Both sexes have narrow gray crown; *rest of upperparts rufous;* white underparts. *Male has narrow black throat patch.* L 6" (15 cm).

Similar Species: **House Sparrow** *(P. domesticus),* native to nw Africa and Egypt (and much of Eurasia), has been introduced in South Africa, from which it has already spread north to the Zambezi; breeding male has extensive gray crown, black extending from chin to upper chest, and gray rump. **Chestnut Sparrow** *(P. eminibey)* wanders in flocks in arid bush country from Ethiopia south to n Tanzania; breeding male is all chestnut, with paler wing edgings.

Voice: A typical sparrow *chirp,* plus a short song.

Habitat: Acacia scrublands, open plains, bushy grasslands, farms, and gardens.

Nesting: In a thorny bush, builds an untidy ball

nest out of straw. Nest's long horizontal entrance funnel has been described as a straw frankfurter. Lays 4–6 eggs.

Range: Cape Verde Islands; Sudan and Ethiopia south to n Tanzania; w Angola south to n South Africa.

The Rufous Sparrow is a tame bird in villages in East Africa, which has no House Sparrows (yet). In southern Africa, where the Rufous has lost out to the expanding House Sparrow or to the Cape Sparrow *(P. melanurus),* it is considered shy.

---

533 Gray-headed Sparrow
Passer griseus

Description: *Plain, gray, unstriped head and underparts; dull rufous back, wings, and rump.* Some races have single or double white wing bars. L 6″ (15 cm).

Similar Species: **Cape Sparrow** *(P. melanurus)* is the only native sparrow in winter rainfall areas of s Africa, but also occurs north to n Namibia and Transvaal; male has black head, broad white crescent from eye onto neck, and chestnut back.

Voice: A typical sparrow *chirp.*

Habitat: Rain-forest edges, woodlands, savannas, semi-deserts, gardens, and towns.

Nesting: Builds an untidy nest of grasses and feathers hidden in a hole in a tree or building. Lays 3–5 eggs.

Range: Senegal east to Somalia and south, including Congo Basin, to c South Africa.

The Gray-headed Sparrow is a familiar bird anywhere the House Sparrow has not invaded, but it is forced to withdraw by that pugnacious bird. The Gray-headed feeds on seeds and insects on the bare ground.

Starlings
Family Sturnidae

Medium-size to large songbirds with slightly arched, pointed bills and strong legs, the starling family includes some highly iridescent and colorful birds. Most nest in holes in trees and form flocks in the nonbreeding season. They feed on insects and fruit, in trees or on the ground. Starlings are good mimics and have pleasing, rambling songs. There are a number of highly localized species and genera in Africa, where it is likely starlings evolved. The two oxpeckers are specialized feeders that travel with wild and domestic herbivores. Of 108 species worldwide, 52 are found in Africa (including two on Madagascar).

---

534 **Red-winged Starling**
Onychognathus morio

Description: Male *glossy black,* with dark purplish tinge; *long, wedge-shaped tail; chestnut primaries.* Female similar, but with *pale gray head.* L 12" (30 cm).

Similar Species: **Slender-billed Chestnut-winged Starling** *(O. tenuirostris)* is smaller, with thinner bill; lives in high mountain forests and moorlands from Ethiopia south to Malawi. **Bristle-crowned Starling** *(O. salvadorii)* is larger and has tuft of longer feathers on forehead; lives from Ethiopia south to Lake Baringo and Samburu NR, both in nc Kenya.

Voice: Song consists of pleasing warbled whistles. Calls include a descending *spreeooo* and a harsh *chore.*

Habitat: Rocky hills and buildings in forests, savannas, and semi-desert areas.

Nesting: Builds a large, platter-shaped nest of sticks and grass plastered with mud and lined with animal hair. Nest is placed under a ledge in a cliff, cave, building, or mine shaft. Usually lays 3 eggs; often has 2 broods.

Range: Eastern Senegal east to Central African

Republic; Eritrea and n Somalia south through e Africa to Cape of Good Hope.

These starlings are usually seen in pairs, as they mate for life. They are vocal, restive, and conspicuous in many areas, such as downtown Cape Town, and are cheeky beggars at picnic sites at Cape Point. They sometimes perch on mammals, such as buffalo and cattle, searching for ticks like Piapiacs or oxpeckers. They are generalist feeders, taking millipedes, caterpillars, worms, termites, and fruit. In flowering season, they go for nectar, and their faces are often dusted with pollen.

535 **Greater Blue-eared Starling**
Lamprotornis chalybaeus

Description: Glossy blue-green, with yellow eye; *large black face patch;* 2 rows of black spots on wings; *blue belly and flanks.* Top of head appears flat. Immature sooty blackish below. L 9″ (23 cm).

Similar Species: **Lesser Blue-eared Starling** *(L. chloropterus)* is smaller, with more compact head, finer bill, and magenta-purple underparts; ranges from Senegal east to c Kenya and from s Tanzania south to n Zimbabwe. **Cape Starling** *(L. nitens)* lacks black ear patch, is entirely green below, and ranges from s Angola to Harare, in Zimbabwe, and south almost to Cape Town.

Voice: Song is a mixture of rattling whistles, chirps, and clicks. Call is a distinctive nasal *squee-aarr.*

Habitat: Open woodlands, savannas, and semi-deserts, provided trees are present.

Nesting: Nests in holes in trees, buildings, and fence posts; lines hole with grass. Lays 3 or 4 eggs.

Range: Senegal across Sahel to Eritrea, and south to n Botswana and n Natal.

This bird hops, rather than runs, on the ground. It feeds on a wide variety of fruit

in trees, and on grains, grasshoppers, and beetles on the ground. In the dry season, it flocks by the hundreds.

536 Burchell's Starling
Lamprotornis australis

Description: A large, *black-eyed starling,* with a *fairly long tail.* Black ear patch; *small head and bill.* Glossed with greenish purple; *wings and tail extensively barred.* L 14" (35 cm).

Similar Species: **Western Long-tailed Starling** *(L. caudatus)* reflects oily green and has tail longer than body; ranges from Senegal east to Nile of Sudan. **Rüppell's Long-tailed Starling** *(L. purpuropterus)* reflects violet-blue and has tail shorter than body; ranges from Sudan, east of Nile, south to c Tanzania. **Southern Long-tailed Starling** *(L. mevesii)* is smaller bodied, with much longer, thinner tail; has more purple than green on body; ranges from n Namibia east to Malawi and e Zimbabwe.

Voice: Calls include a loud *cheer-eet,* and various chuckling notes. Noisy at roosts.

Habitat: Open woodlands with mixture of tall and short grass, within flying distance of water.

Nesting: Takes over a tree cavity, lining it with grass; fights other starlings and Lilac-breasted Rollers for quality holes. Lays 3 or 4 eggs. Both sexes incubate and feed young.

Range: Namibia, Botswana, and lowlands of e and w Transvaal.

This confident and noisy bird perches conspicuously and has a slow, lumbering flight with noisy wingbeats. It is seen in pairs or in flocks of up to 50 birds. It walks around with a cocky gait, searching for insects and seeds. It takes fruit and berries in trees, and is often found near grazing mammals.

537, 538 **Superb Starling**
Spreo superbus

Description: Black head, with large, yellow-orange eye. Glossy blue-green chest and upperparts, with large black spots on wing coverts. *White line above rusty-orange chest; white vent and underwing linings.* L 7″ (18 cm).

Similar Species: **Hildebrandt's Starling** has dark orange underwings and orange or red eye, and lacks white breast band and vent. **Pied Starling** *(S. bicolor)*, of South African grasslands, is all sooty, with white belly and vent.

Voice: Has a long warbling song that includes mimics of other birds. Calls include chattering and a whining alarm.

Habitat: Lightly wooded areas with short grass in semi-arid zones, savannas, farms, and gardens. Chiefly in low- and medium-rainfall areas below 7,200′ (2,200 m).

Nesting: In courtship, jumps about with drooping wings and outstretched head. Nest varies from a large, weaver-like, twig-and-grass ball in a thorny tree to old nests of other birds and holes in trees and cliffs. Usually lays 4 eggs.

Range: Ethiopia south to c Tanzania.

A beautiful bird that is common in East Africa, the Superb Starling is eager to take scraps of food at picnic sites and lodges. Flocks feed on the ground, searching for insects, fruit, and berries.

---

539 **Hildebrandt's Starling**
Spreo hildebrandti

Description: *Orange eye.* Uniformly *deep blue head, neck, upper chest, back, and tail.* Hindneck and flight feathers green, with 2 rows of black spots on wing coverts. Rest of *underparts and underwing lining dark orange* (without white). L 7″ (18 cm).

Similar Species: **Shelley's Starling** *(S. shelleyi)*, of Ethiopia, Somalia, and ne Kenya, is deeper orange below and more purple

above. **Chestnut-bellied Starling** *(S. pulcher)* ranges thorn scrub just south of Sahara from Senegal east to Eritrea; has brown head, large white eye, green chest and upperparts, chestnut belly, and pale cream wing patches visible in flight.
Superb Starling has yellow-orange eye, and white on breast band and vent.

Voice: Song is a low warbling series of *chew-er* notes. Alarm call is *chuu-ee.*

Habitat: Bushed and wooded grasslands, brush, and farmlands below 7,200′ (2,200 m).

Nesting: Nests in tree holes, lining its hollow with hair or plant fibers. Lays 3 or 4 eggs.

Range: Southern Kenya from Nairobi and Tsavo West NP south to c Tanzania, and west to Serengeti NP, in n Tanzania.

Hildebrandt's occurs alongside the Superb Starling in many areas, but is generally shier. It feeds on the ground on seeds, fruit, and insects.

540 Golden-breasted Starling
Cosmopsarus regius

Description: Slender bill and yellow eye on small head. Glossed green, blue, and violet on head, neck, and upperparts. *Underparts bright golden yellow. Very long, wedge-shaped, black tail.* L 14″ (35 cm).

Voice: Whistles and chatters.

Habitat: Grasslands and semi-deserts with small trees or thornbush, to 4,000′ (1,200 m).

Nesting: Lines a tree hole with straw, rootlets, and leaves. Lays 2–6 elongated eggs.

Range: Djibouti, e Ethiopia, Somalia, e Kenya, and ne Tanzania in Mkomazi GR.

This is one of the world's most beautiful birds, isolated in the acacia savannas east of Mount Kenya. It sometimes comes for scraps at lodges in Tsavo NP. Rather shy in the bush, it will perch in the open on a large branch or treetop. It forages on the ground for insects and in trees for various fruits and berries. It also chisels into hard termite mounds and seizes the termites as they panic.

541 **Ashy Starling**
Cosmopsarus unicolor

Description: *Entirely ashy gray, with long, wedge-shaped tail.* Slender bill; yellow eye; faint greenish gloss on wings and tail. L 12″ (30 cm).
Voice: Soft whistles. Rather quiet.
Habitat: Open parklands with scattered tall trees, baobab woodlands, riverine thickets, and flat-topped acacia savannas.
Nesting: Unknown; probably uses tree holes.
Range: Restricted to Tanzania: Ranges from southern side of Lake Victoria and Lake Manyara south to Ruaha NP and Mbeya area near Malawi.

The Ashy Starling occurs in pairs or small parties, searching the ground for insects. It comes to lodges and tented camps for scraps in Tarangire NP.

542 **Wattled Starling**
Creatophora cinerea

Description: Female and nonbreeding male gray-brown, with black wings and tail, and pale bill. Flight reveals *white rump* and short, triangular, pointed wings. Breeding male is creamy white on back and underparts, and loses head feathers; *head skin becomes yellow with contorted black wattles.* Eye dark in all plumages. L 8.5″ (21 cm).
Similar Species: **European Starling** *(Sturnus vulgaris)* winters in n Africa and has been introduced from Cape Town to Durban in South Africa; shaped like Wattled Starling, but is dark greenish purple with pale spots. **Indian Mynah** *(Acridotheres tristis)* is chestnut, with black head, white wing patch, yellow bare patch on face, and yellow bill; introduced, it is common in Natal and

s Transvaal, and islands such as Ascension, Saint Helena, Madagascar, Comoros, Réunion, Mauritius, Rodriguez, and Seychelles.

Voice: Often silent, but has a variety of squeaky whistles, hisses, and cackles.

Habitat: Open grasslands, acacia savannas, open woodlands, and cultivated areas, often with domestic or wild mammals.

Nesting: An opportunistic nester when locusts settle down to breed. Nests in colonies of several hundred or more pairs. Untidy grass and straw nest is placed in a thornbush or on the ground. Lays 2–5 pale blue eggs.

Range: Eritrea south to Cape Town area.

Highly nomadic, the Wattled Starling follows the locust swarms. As the insects breed at varied sites, the starlings must be prepared to nest on short notice. One might see flocks of tens of thousands wheeling about in formation near locust swarms. This bird also walks along with cattle and herds of wild grazers like the Serengeti wildebeests, looking for flushed insects. It will be common for a few days or a month and then vanish, often for several years. It feeds on other insects besides locusts, as well as on fruit.

---

543 **Yellow-billed Oxpecker**
Buphagus africanus

Description: Dark brown head and upperparts. *Buffy-yellow underparts and rump. Swollen yellow bill, with red tip.* Red eye. L 9″ (22 cm).

Similar Species: **Red-billed Oxpecker** has thinner, all-red bill, conspicuous yellow eye ring, and uniformly brown upperparts without pale buffy rump.

Voice: A hissing *chris-chris,* and a harsh rattle.

Habitat: Grasslands, wooded savannas, riverine trees, and forest edges with large wild or domestic grazing animals.

Nesting: Nests in a natural tree cavity, building a

cup of grass, straw, and mammal hair. Lays 2 or 3 eggs.

Range: Senegal east to Ethiopia, and south to n Botswana and Zimbabwe. Ranges to 10,000′ (3,000 m).

Both oxpeckers feed on ticks and flies they find on the bodies of large mammals with short or sparse hair. While they do enlarge some wounds on the animals' bodies, they are beneficial in removing vast numbers of ticks. Hunters, poachers, and predators dislike them, as they are alert and warn their hosts of approaching danger. This species, the western oxpecker, overlaps with the Red-billed in some areas.

---

544 **Red-billed Oxpecker**
Buphagus erythrorhynchus

Description: Dark brown head and upperparts; buffy-yellow underparts. *Long, blood-red bill;* red eye, with *wide yellow eye ring.* L 9″ (22 cm).

Similar Species: **Yellow-billed Oxpecker** has swollen yellow bill with red tip, and pale buffy rump; lacks yellow eye ring.

Voice: A scolding *churrrrrr,* and various hisses and whistles.

Habitat: Grasslands and wooded savannas, with large wild or domestic grazing mammals.

Nesting: Within each flock, only 1 pair will breed, and they may have 3 broods in a year. Nests in natural tree cavities, where it prefers holes as deep as 3′ (1 m). Usually lays 3 eggs.

Range: Eritrea south through e Africa to e South Africa.

Like the Yellow-billed Oxpecker, this bird takes ticks and flies from the bodies of short- or sparse-haired mammals. One oxpecker stomach held the remains of 250 adult and 1,400 larval ticks. The host animals seem pleased with such work, holding still except when the birds are too rough in their nostrils and ears. These bird also feed on grasshoppers and other large insects kicked up by animals, and catch flying termites on the wing.

Orioles
Family Oriolidae

Orioles are medium-size, stocky birds of forest and woodland treetops. Many males are brilliant yellow, black, and/or green, with sturdy red bills and red eyes. The females are duller, and the young often streaked. Oriole songs and calls are loud and melodious, and more birds are heard than seen. There are 26 species, restricted to Eurasia, Africa, and Australasia. Africa has nine species. The American troupials of the genus *Icterus* have been erroneously called orioles but are unrelated.

545 African Black-headed Oriole
Oriolus larvatus

Description: Adult has *black head,* heavy red bill, and red eye. *Yellow collar and underparts;* upperparts and central tail feathers olive green. Black flight feathers, with small white wing bar and white feather edgings. L 9.5″ (24 cm).

Similar Species: **African Golden Oriole** *(O. auratus)* has yellow body, wings, and head, with long black line through eye; widespread in sub-Saharan Africa.

Voice: A loud liquid *phee-ooo* or *pheea-pheeooo.* Will mimic other birds, and has various harsh calls, including a *churr.*

Habitat: Broad-leafed savanna woodlands, eucalyptus forests, evergreen forest edges, and exotic plantations.

Nesting: Weaves a deep cup nest of "old man's beard" lichen and some grass, placed on an outer fork of a branch high in a tree. Lays 3 colorful eggs.

Range: Ethiopia south to e Cape Province.

This oriole is sometimes a conspicuous and noisy bird. It is generally seen in pairs, feeding high in trees or low in aloes. It eats caterpillars, other insects, fruit, berries, nectar, and pollen.

Drongos
Family Dicruridae

Medium-size, glossy black birds with red eyes, drongos have stout pointed bills and short legs; most have forked tails. They perch upright and fly out after insects. Bold and aggressive, they chase raptors and rob other birds of their food in flight. Their calls are harsh and unmusical. There are 23 species in southern Asia, Australasia, and Africa. Mainland Africa has four species, with four others restricted to Indian Ocean islands.

546 African Drongo
Fork-tailed Drongo, Savanna Drongo
Dicrurus adsimilis

Description: An upright, *glossy black bird,* with a red eye and a *long, deeply forked tail.* Pale ashy bases of flight feathers conspicuous in flight. L 10″ (25 cm).

Similar Species: **Square-tailed Drongo** *(D. ludwigii)* is smaller (L 7.5″/19 cm), with only a notch in its tail; lives in humid forests and denser woodlands from Senegal east to s Somalia, and south to Natal.

Voice: Song includes liquid, twangy notes and imitations of the hawks, kites, eagles, and owls it is fond of harassing. Calls are harsh and grating.

Habitat: Savannas with trees and bushes for perches, open woodlands, forest edges, gardens, and cultivated areas.

Nesting: Builds a flat, saucer-shaped nest of twigs and rootlets, placed on a horizontal fork of a low branch. Lays 2–4 eggs.

Range: Senegal east to Somalia, and south through South Africa.

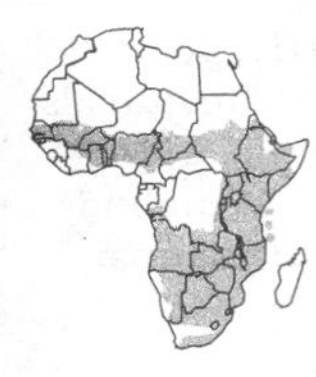

This is a familiar species in all but the wettest and driest areas. It hunts insects from perches, on the wing, by dropping to the ground, or as a member of mixed-bird parties. Known for chasing raptors, it also attacks domestic cats, small wild carnivores, as well as humans near its nest.

Crows
Family Corvidae

Large brash birds, crows and ravens have heavy bills, and strong legs and feet for active foraging on the ground. Omnivorous, they are scavengers near humans and take many baby birds from nests. This family also includes the jays, magpies, and choughs, which are present in northern Africa but not south of the Sahara. Worldwide there are 113 species, with 17 known from Africa.

547 Piapiac
Ptilostomus afer

Description: *Glossy black, with very long, graduated, dark brown tail. Primaries pale brown.* Immature black, with pale blue eye; *pink bill with black tip.* L 16″ (40 cm).

Similar Species: **Western Long-tailed Starling** *(Lamprotornis caudatus)* has thinner beak and yellow eye, and lacks pale primaries in flight; ranges from Senegal east to Nile of Sudan. Male **Red-winged Starling** is black, with chestnut primaries.

Voice: Shrill *peee-ip* or *pia-piac,* plus raspy *kweeer.*

Habitat: Savannas with borassus palms, baobabs, or other scattered trees, cultivated lands, and grasslands with grazing mammals.

Nesting: Builds a large nest of sticks, rootlets, plant fibers, and grasses in a hole or notch of a palm or baobab. Lays 3–7 eggs.

Range: Senegal east to Uganda.

This aberrant crow has no close relatives. It is usually seen in small flocks foraging on the ground, and is tame in some

villages. It perches on cattle, goats, rhinos, elephants, and other mammals to scan for flushed insects and glean ticks. It also feeds on palm-fruit and joins other birds at termite swarms.

548 **African Black Crow**
Cape Rook
Corvus capensis

Description: *Black, with long, thin, slightly drooping bill.* L 20″ (50 cm).
Similar Species: **Pied Crow** has white collar and breast. **House Crow** *(C. splendens)* of India and Sri Lanka, with gray hood and breast, has been introduced widely from Malindi, Kenya, south to Durban; a nuisance, it lives on garbage, and kills other nestling birds.
Voice: A high-pitched *kaaah,* plus croaks and gargles; mimics other species.
Habitat: Open grasslands, wet and arid plains, and pastures. Not in woodlands, but likes scattered trees and poles for perches.
Nesting: Builds a large stick nest on a tree branch, utility pole, or rock ledge.
Range: Patchy distribution from Ethiopia south to n Tanzania, and from Angola and Zimbabwe south to Cape Town area.

The African Black Crow is usually seen in pairs or small groups, feeding on the ground or perching on dead trees or utility poles. In flight it seems to flap only its primaries. It feeds on large insects like grasshoppers, frogs, grain, berries, fruit, and some carrion.

549 **Pied Crow**
Corvus albus

Description: *Black, except for white collar and breast.* L 20″ (50 cm).
Similar Species: **White-necked Raven** has half collar above, and is completely black below.
Voice: A deep guttural croak, a loud *caw,* and gargling notes.

Habitat: Open country, seacoasts, and watersides, as well as farms, villages, and cities.

Nesting: In courtship display, both birds raise heads and gargle, side by side. Builds a large, saucer-shaped stick nest on a high tree, pole, or crag. Lays 3–7 eggs, which are incubated for about 19 days.

Range: Southern Mauritania east to Eritrea, and south to Cape Town area.

The Pied Crow, common and bold in many towns, eats lots of garbage that otherwise would be left to rats. Playful in the air in strong winds, it is mischievous in harassing raptors and vultures. Its food includes large insects, dead fish, chicken eggs, and carrion.

---

550 White-necked Raven
Corvus albicollis

Description: Black, except for *thick white half collar on back of neck.* Short, wedge-shaped tail; *tall flattened bill with white tip.* L 22″ (55 cm).

Similar Species: **Pied Crow** has white breast. **White-naped Raven** (Thick-billed Raven; *C. crassirostris*) of Ethiopia and Eritrea has only a white patch on nape.

Voice: A high-pitched, far-carrying, harsh croak.

Habitat: Usually mountains, whether forest or grassland, from sea level (in s Africa) to 19,000′ (5,800 m) on Mount Kilimanjaro, in n Tanzania.

Nesting: Builds a large stick nest on a rocky crag. Normally lays 4 eggs.

Range: Western Uganda and c Kenya south through Zimbabwe to Cape Town.

Pairs of these ravens remain mated for life and normally travel around together. They feed on carrion, small mammals, baby chickens, turtles, garbage, locusts, and large insects and their larvae. They are often seen around lodges and camps in high country, such as the rim of Ngorongoro Crater in Tanzania.

REPTILES
Class Reptilia

Reptiles, the ancestors of all birds and mammals, have a multi-boned lower jaw. Unlike birds and mammals, reptiles have a variable blood temperature; they move in and out of sun and shade, or seek or avoid heated surfaces as they attempt to reach optimum temperature. The skin of reptiles is dry, not slimy, and is covered with scales or plates that help retain water, allowing reptiles to occupy dry habitats denied the amphibians. Most reptiles lay eggs; some retain them until near the time of hatching. Reptiles neither feed their young nor nurse them. Of 7,000 species of reptiles worldwide, about 1,000 live in Africa, with 400 found south of the Zambezi alone. There are four orders of reptiles: the Rhynchocephalia, with two surviving members, the spiny, four-legged tuataras, found on islands off the coast of New Zealand; the turtles; the crocodiles; and the scaled reptiles.

TURTLES
Order Testudinata

The tortoises of the land, the terrapins of fresh water, and the turtles of the sea are collectively known as turtles. Their distinctive shells may be hard, leathery, or soft in texture, and may have a flat, rounded, knobbed, or hinged structure. In some species, like tortoises and sea turtles, the bony plates on the upper shell (called epidermal scutes) have raised centers. In all turtles, the upper shell is the *carapace,* the lower the *plastron;* the backbone and ribs are fused to the carapace. Most turtles have parrot-like beaks. Their feet may be heavily clawed or modified into flippers. All turtles lay eggs, often in a pit dug with the hindlegs. There are 230 species worldwide, with 50 known from Africa and its islands. In the descriptions that follow, the length given is that of the animal's carapace.

551 **Aldabra Giant Tortoise**
Geochelone (Testudo) gigantea

Description: *An enormous tortoise, with a gray-brown shell;* thick, elongated, domed carapace, upturned at rear; small plastron. Some have upturned fore-carapace that looks like a saddle. *Pointed, wedge-shaped head with convex forehead.* Forelimbs have many round scales that do not overlap. L to 4′8″ (1.4 m); Wt to 560 lb (255 kg).
Habitat: Grasslands, scrub, and mangrove swamps.
Breeding: Digs nest amid grass and shrubbery in dry season. Female lays eggs at night, 4 or 5 in years when population is high, 12–14 when numbers are low. Young hatch after 100–200 days, during rains.
Range: Aldabra. Introduced to Mauritius, Réunion, and Curieuse Island, just north of Praslin Island in Seychelles.

The Aldabra Giant Tortoise feeds on dead land crabs and tortoises, and grazes on woody plants, including fallen leaves of figs, coconut palms, and screw-pines. The grazing of these animals produces a "tortoise turf" of sedges, grasses, and small herbs. Both domed and saddle-backed forms have evolved on Aldabra, the latter stretching its neck higher into shrubs and trees for greenery.

552 **Leopard Tortoise**
Geochelone pardalis

Description: High-domed carapace has *nearly vertical sides* and V-shaped notch in front; dorsal scutes not strongly raised. *Background yellow* or, in some areas, tan, reddish brown, or olive. *Young have dark brown or black patterns; adult has more, but smaller, spots.* Head, limbs, and tail usually brownish yellow. Very old individuals may be an unspotted sandy brown. L 12–18″ (30–45 cm); Wt 15–20 lb (7–9 kg); in e Cape Province, may reach 28″ (70 cm) and 88 lb (40 kg).

Similar Species: There are about a dozen species of African tortoises, most in s Africa and Madagascar; those with the most attractive patterns are greatly endangered. **Geometric Tortoise** *(Psammobates geometricus),* with long yellow stripes on a black background, barely survives in extreme sw Cape Province. **Radiated Tortoise** *(G. radiata)* has yellow triangles and black diamonds on carapace; lives in small area of sw Madagascar.

Habitat: Lightly wooded savannas, open grassy plains, edges of marshes, kopjes, dry woodlands, and thorn scrub. Lives from sea level to 9,500′ (2,900 m).

Breeding: Female digs a flask-shaped burrow up to 12″ (30 cm) deep. Lays 5–30 round white eggs at 3-week intervals for up to 20 weeks. Eggs hatch 1 year later.

Range: Southern Sudan and Ethiopia south to Natal and Cape Province, west to Namibia and s Angola.

The young Leopard Tortoise has a bold, leopard-like pattern on its carapace, and tends to stay in thicker vegetation. These turtles prefer succulent plants with high water content; they feed on fallen fruit, thistles, introduced prickly pear cacti, grasses, fungi, and other wild plants. In the Serengeti Plains, they are regularly seen crossing dirt tracks.

553 **Bell's Hinged Tortoise**
Bell's Hinge-backed Tortoise
Kinixys belliana

Description: Elongated carapace has sloping sides and *movable rear hinge;* color and pattern vary, but often *black with yellow center to each scute.* Small head has nonprojecting snout. Tail has claw-like tip. Adult male faded in color, with concave plastron and very large tail. L 6–9″ (15–22 cm); Wt 2.2–4.4 lb (1–2 kg).

Habitat: Savanna woodlands, open grasslands, coastal plains, and dry brush.

Breeding: Lays clutches of 2–10 elongated eggs at 40-day intervals (up to 45 eggs a season) in wetter months.

Range: Senegal east to Eritrea, and south to n Natal. Introduced in w Madagascar.

The movable hinge allows this tortoise to cover its hindlimbs and tail when threatened by a predator; the four members of the strictly African genus are the only turtles to have such a hinge. Omnivorous, Bell's Hinged Tortoise feeds on insects, snails, fruit and leaves, sugarcane, grasses, sedges, and fungi.

---

554 African Pancake Tortoise
Malacochersus tornieri

Description: *Carapace extremely flat, sometimes concave.* Yellow to tan, with darker and lighter areas; some individuals have dark scute borders, others have radiating yellow stripes. Plastron yellow with brown splotches. Head, limbs, and tail yellow-brown; limbs slender and flexible. L 4–7″ (10–18 cm).

Habitat: Arid scrub and thornbush with abundant rocks in flat savannas and hilly country. Ranges to 6,000′ (1,800 m).

Breeding: Lays 1 hard-shelled egg, maximum 2 eggs per year.

Range: Southern Kenya from Mount Kenya south to se Tanzania, and west to Lake Victoria.

The African Pancake Tortoise's carapace scutes are separated by flexible areas. While most tortoises withdraw into their shells to avoid sun or predators, the Pancake Tortoise wedges itself into a rock crevice and hangs on with its claws. It feeds on various fruits, grasses, and herbs. When the weather is cool, this tortoise basks in the sun, while in the hotter, drier months it estivates beneath flat rocks. A spectacular climber for a turtle, it can scale vertical rock faces.

555 Green Sea Turtle
Chelonia mydas

Description: *Carapace has thin, non-overlapping scutes,* and is greenish brown to black; some adults have spots or streaks. Plastron dirty white to yellow. Adult has large flippers, each with a *single claw.* Jaw serrated. Juvenile dark gray. L to 4′8″ (1.4 m); Wt to 660 lb (300 kg).

Other Species: Rare **Leatherback Sea Turtle** *(Dermochelys coriacea)* breeds in Natal, Madagascar, and Senegal; has thick smooth skin, and 12 long ridges on the body (5 above, 5 below, and 1 on each side) that run from head to tail; the largest sea turtle, with a carapace up to 6′ (1.8 m) long, and a weight of up to 1,500 lb (680 kg); long flippers give it a "wingspread" of up to 9′ (2.7 m).

Habitat: Migrates across open ocean, but feeds in shallow coastal waters and estuaries. Comes ashore to isolated beaches to breed and to rest and bask in the sun.

Breeding: May breed throughout the year in favored sites in shallow coastal waters. Female comes ashore on breeding beaches at night and digs a pit above high-tide line, where she lays 100–200 eggs. May return to do this 2–6 times at intervals of 10–20 days. All eggs in a nest hatch on the same night, after 30–56 days.

Range: Major nesting areas include Cape Verde Islands, Ascension Island, west coast of Africa, Europa Island in Mozambique Channel, Madagascar, Mauritius, Aldabra, and other islands of Seychelles; also Eritrea. Major feeding areas are from Mauritania south and east to Nigeria in Atlantic, and from Somalia south to Natal in Indian Ocean.

The young Green Sea Turtle may drift or migrate long distances, but when ready to mate it usually returns to the beach where it was born. This turtle grazes on sea grasses and algae, pulls up roots, and dines on mangrove leaves.

556 Hawksbill Sea Turtle
Eretmochelys imbricata

Description: A relatively small sea turtle, with a long narrow head ending in a *hawk-like beak. Carapace scutes thick and overlapping,* and pointed toward rear; *translucent amber color, with varying streaks of reddish brown, black, and yellow;* carapace also pointed toward rear. Head and flippers yellowish in Atlantic, blacker in Indian Ocean, with large black scales. L 2–3′ (60–90 cm); Wt usually to 110 lb (50 kg), but can reach 300 lb (135 kg).

Similar Species: Larger **Loggerhead Sea Turtle** *(Caretta caretta)* has much broader head and neck, light yellowish-gray skin, and smoother, plainer carapace; extremely strong jaws are used to crush crabs, sea urchins, jellyfish, and mollusks; uncommon in Canary Islands and tropical w Africa, more common along Indian Ocean shores and islands.

Habitat: Rocky places and coral reefs near islands; also in mangrove swamps and estuaries, and in oceanic waters.

Breeding: Formerly nested in mass influxes in which up to 46,000 females converged on a single beach on a single day. Today most nesting beaches are used by solitary individuals or a few dozen at most. Lays 70–180 eggs in a burrow in coarse sand, perhaps up to 4 clutches at intervals of 15–19 days. Young hatch in about 60 days.

Range: Breeds in Cape Verde Islands, Senegal, and Mauritania in Atlantic; islands in Red Sea off Sudan and Eritrea; and islands of w Indian Ocean off Kenya and Tanzania, and from Seychelles, Comoros, Europa Island in Mozambique Channel,

Réunion, Mauritius, and Rodriguez to north and west coasts of Madagascar. Wanders north into Mediterranean, and south to South Africa.

The scutes on the Hawksbill's carapace are the source of tortoiseshell sold as jewelry and objets d'art. This turtle's diet includes toxic corals, sea urchins, the Portuguese man-of-war, jellyfish, sponges, barnacles, and fish, as well as mangrove fruit, leaves, and bark.

CROCODILES
Order Crocodylia

Ancestors of modern-day crocodiles lived concurrently with the dinosaurs from 135 to 65 million years ago. All species are very much reduced in range, and some are near extinction. Crocodiles are large, lizard-like animals with powerful jaws, many conical teeth, short legs with webbed toes and claws, and long massive tails used for aquatic propulsion. Their dorsal skin is thick and plated, but the belly skin is softer. Of 23 species worldwide, there are three African species.

557, 558 **Nile Crocodile**
Crocodylus niloticus

Description: *Long jaws with prominent teeth;* snout twice as long as it is broad. Body covered with horny plates, many keeled and bony, including 6 enlarged keeled plates behind head; long tail (rectangular in cross section) has *2 raised dorsal keels;* hindfeet webbed. Adult gray or gray-olive, with yellowish belly. Young greenish, with black marks on back and sides, and yellowish below. L 10–12′ (3–3.6 m), max to 21′ (6.3 m); Wt to 2,200 lb (1,000 kg).

Foreprint

Hindprint

Similar Species: **Long-snouted Crocodile** has 4 enlarged keeled plates behind head; snout is 3 times longer than it is broad. **African Dwarf Crocodile** has snout as broad as it is long.

Habitat: Large freshwater lakes, swamps, and rivers, plus coastal estuaries and mangrove swamps.

Breeding: Mating occurs in water. Female digs a hole with her hindlegs, lays 16–90 (usually about 40) hard-shelled eggs, and covers them with sand, then fasts for about 90 days while defending the egg site. When she hears peeping, she opens the nest and gathers the young into her mouth. She washes them in the river, and they then remain in a group for several months.

Range: Senegal east to Ethiopia, and south to Okavango Delta (in n Botswana) and n Natal; also nw Madagascar and Nosy Be, off northwest coast. Eliminated along Nile, Mediterranean coast, and many other areas.

The young Nile Crocodile begins feeding on insects on land, but as a sub-adult moves into swamps and backwaters to take fish, frogs, terrapins, birds, and small mammals. It attains sexual maturity in 12 to 15 years, when it reaches 7 feet (2.1 m) in length. At this stage it feeds chiefly on larger fish, but will ambush antelopes, buffalos, zebras, and domestic animals coming to drink. It approaches its prey underwater or on the surface, camouflaged as a partially submerged log. Nile Crocodiles are surprisingly fast runners on land. You should be aware of their whereabouts whenever walking near water.

---

559 **Long-snouted Crocodile**
African Slender-snouted Crocodile
Crocodylus cataphractus

Description: A narrow-tailed crocodile, with *a long narrow snout (3 times longer than broad) and dark and light blotches along jaws.* Has 4 enlarged keeled plates behind head;

3 or 4 rows of dorsal neck scales join back armor. L 6–8′ (1.8–2.4 m), max to 13′ (4 m).

Similar Species: **Nile Crocodile** has snout twice as long as it is broad; **African Dwarf Crocodile** has snout as broad as it is long.

Habitat: Rivers, streams, and freshwater lakes; also brackish water of coastal lagoons.

Breeding: Builds a mound of vegetable debris along overgrown banks of small streams. Some nests are built while hatchlings are leaving others. Lays 13–27 eggs.

Range: West Africa, from s Mauritania east to Central African Republic, and south to n Angola and w Tanzania.

This crocodile uses its slender snout to catch fish hiding in burrows and among fallen trees and roots, and also feeds on shrimp, crabs, snakes, and frogs. It rarely lies out on open sandbanks, preferring to rest in the shade of trees. The Long-snouted Crocodile is becoming increasingly hunted for food and trade, as the Nile Crocodile has been eliminated in many areas.

---

560 **African Dwarf Crocodile**
Broad-fronted Crocodile
Osteolaemus tetraspis

Description: *Small* crocodile with *short wide snout* that is as broad as it is long. L 5–6′ (1.5–1.8 m).

Habitat: Floor of rain and swamp forests; small quiet streams, ponds, and swamps.

Range: Senegal east to extreme w Uganda; Congo Basin south to Cabinda enclave of Angola and sc Zaire.

Rarely seen or studied in the wild, the African Dwarf Crocodile is a timid, slow-moving crocodile that stalks animals chiefly on land at night.

SCALED REPTILES (LIZARDS AND SNAKES)

Order Squamata

While lizards evolved somewhat earlier than snakes, the two groups share many characteristics. Both have a scaly skin covered with a thin, dry, horny layer that is periodically shed. Male lizards and snakes have two penises (called hemipenes) stored at the base of the tail. Most species lay eggs, but 20 percent give birth to live young.

LIZARDS

Suborder Sauria (Lacertilia)

Lizards are the most frequently seen reptiles; most are essentially harmless creatures as far as humans are concerned. A few species are herbivorous, but most are carnivorous, feeding chiefly on insects and other invertebrates. Most have well-developed limbs, enabling them to run swiftly to take prey or escape danger. All are covered with scales that are usually small and nonoverlapping, and most have external ears and movable eyelids. Most females lay eggs, but some give birth to live young. Geckos, skinks, and some other lizards can shed their tails to a predator's grasp, escape, and grow a new one. There are about 3,850 species of lizards worldwide, with 300 living in Africa.

561 **Red-headed Agama**
Common Agama
Agama agama

Description: *Dominant male has red head and tail, blue body and limbs during day.* Female, subordinate male, and, at night, dominant male brownish. Triangular head; distinct neck; long tapering tail that cannot be regenerated. Spiny appearance due to keeled scales. Round eyes with movable eyelids. L 14″ (35 cm).

Similar Species: There are several dozen species of agamas in Africa. **Tree Agama** (*A. atricollis;* L to 16″/40 cm) lives in trees from Ethiopia south to Natal; male has enormous blue head with swollen cheeks, gold-speckled brown body, and bright orange mouth lining; can inflict a nasty bite if handled.

Habitat: Rocky outcrops, cliffs, savannas, farms, houses, and villages.

Breeding: Dominant male may mate with a half-dozen females. Female has enough protein to produce eggs only after heavy rains, when insects are common. Lays 3–12 soft-shelled eggs in a hole in the ground.

Range: Senegal east to Ethiopia, and south to n Angola and s Tanzania.

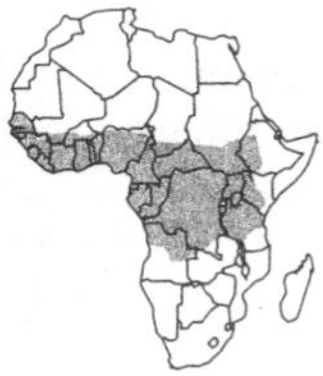

This colorful lizard is well known to villagers in much of equatorial Africa, Kenya, and Tanzania. It speedily chases after ants, termites, and beetles, sometimes running on only its back feet or leaping into the air. It is also able to scamper up vertical walls and rocks, and roosts communally in rock crevices or under the eaves of buildings.

562 Jackson's Chameleon
Kikuyu Three-horned Chameleon
Chamaeleo jacksonii

Description: *Male has 3 forward-facing, spear-like horns* that may measure 1.5″ (3.8 cm); 1 projects from snout, 2 from forehead. Female lacks horns. Green and/or brown body somewhat more elongated than other chameleons. L 7.5″ (19 cm).

Habitat: Highland forests, woodlands, gardens, and scrub.

Breeding: Gives birth to large numbers of live young, who emerge from a membranous sac as perfect miniatures of adult.

Range: Highlands of c and s Kenya from

Mount Kenya south to Mount Meru, in n Tanzania.

Chameleons are a family of distinctive, slow-moving, diurnal lizards, with about 130 species found in Africa and Madagascar. They shoot out their very long, telescopic tongues to capture insects. Each eye operates independently of the other, so that one may look forward, the other back, or one up, the other down. Chameleons vary their patterns from plain to spotted; they are often green or brown, but can add many brighter colors when excited or to match their surroundings. Their prehensile tails, which are often rolled up, can be used as a fifth "limb" for grasping. They are found chiefly in trees, but can be spotted crossing open areas, paths, and roads, usually on tiptoe. Some residents fear the roving eyes of chameleons, dislike touching them, and even club them to death.

---

563 **Tropical Gecko**
House Gecko
Hemidactylus mabouia

Description: A medium-size gecko, with a flattened head and body. *Grayish or gray-brown with numerous darker spots or bands* that fade if exposed to light. Tail stout and flattened below. *Toes, held out in fan,* have strong retractile claws. Belly cream-colored. L 6–7.5″ (15–19 cm).

Voice: Often quiet, but will give a short series of *tchk* notes.

Habitat: Trees, rocky areas, caves, and buildings to 6,000′ (1,800 m).

Breeding: Breeds year-round; lays 1 or 2 hard-shelled eggs, usually in a remote nook. Sometimes lays egg(s) at a communal nesting location.

Range: Sierra Leone east to Somalia, and south to n Namibia and Natal; also Madagascar, Comoros, and Seychelles.

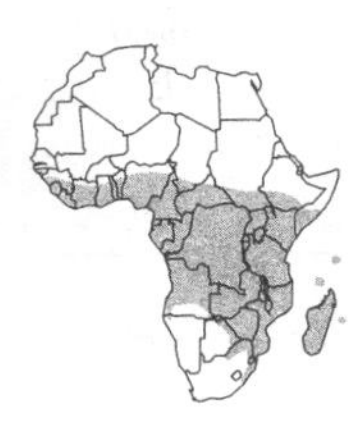

The toes of geckos have scales with minute hairs that act as suction cups on small cracks in cliffs, tree trunks, and walls, allowing them to scamper up vertical surfaces as smooth as glass and even to walk upside down on ceilings. Active at night, they have large, light-gathering eyes without movable lids. Geckos feed on moths, mosquitoes, flies, crickets, ants, cockroaches, and spiders.

564 **Five-lined Skink**
Rainbow-tailed Skink, Blue-tailed Skink
Mabuya quinquetaeniata

Description: Elongated body, with smooth scales, shiny appearance, small legs; head not distinct from body. Adult male lacks distinct stripes; *has fine white spots* on background of buffy olive-brown; tail orange-brown. Female and young male black or dark brown, with *pale blue stripes* on back and sides merging into *brilliant blue tail.* L 7–9.5" (18–24 cm).

Similar Species: **Striped Skink** *(M. striata)* is common in gardens and rocky areas from Ethiopia south to e Cape Province; black or reddish brown, with several pale yellowish stripes.

Habitat: Rocky areas and bases of trees in wet and dry savannas.

Breeding: Adult male (15 months or older) defends territory. Female lays 6–10 eggs under a rock or stone.

Range: Senegal east to Ethiopia; Nile Delta of Egypt south to Natal. May also occur in Algeria.

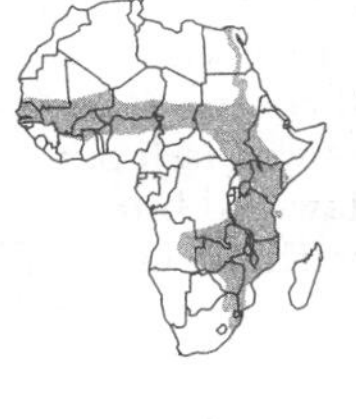

The Five-lined Skink is an active species that scampers swiftly across the ground, the roofs of huts, fallen trunks, and rocks in pursuit of insects. A diurnal lizard, it is one of the most frequently seen species in savanna country. Skinks are smooth-scaled and have streamlined bodies, with reduced limbs, long-tailed lizard shapes, and no head ornaments. Many species have blue tails that can be detached by a predator. The severed limb jerks about, while the skink escapes and grows another tail.

565 **Nile Monitor Lizard**
Water Monitor Lizard
Varanus niloticus

Description: Bead-like scales cover stout body and tough skin; long neck supports elongated head with snake-like, protrusible tongue. Strong limbs and claws. Longer than body, *tail is laterally compressed* (like a crocodile's). *Adult gray or olive-brown, with darker blotches and bands, plus fine yellow spotting.* Sub-adult black, with brighter yellow spots and blotches. L 3′4″–4′8″ (1–1.4 m), max to 6′8″ (2 m).

Fore, hind, and tail print

Similar Species: **Savanna Monitor Lizard** is stockier, with more rounded snout and shorter tail; lives away from permanent water.

Habitat: Rivers, lakes, and marshes, plus adjacent woodlands.

Breeding: Female usually excavates a burrow in a living termite mound during the rainy season. Lays 20–60 eggs; young hatch 1 year later.

Range: Senegal east to s Egypt, and south to Angola and n and e South Africa.

Only three of the 30 species of monitors live in Africa; the rest are confined to Asia and Australasia. Monitors dig up unguarded crocodile and turtle eggs. They swim after crabs, mussels, frogs, fish, and birds. The young feed on insects and frogs in reedbeds, avoiding deep water. If cornered, with no water exit, monitors will lash out with their tails, and claw and bite. They walk sinuously, with the belly off the ground.

566 **Savanna Monitor Lizard**
Rock Monitor Lizard
Varanus exanthematicus

Description: Head has *broad bulbous snout,* and nostrils nearer to eyes than to tip of snout. *Body drab blackish or gray-brown,* with 5 or 6 rows of dull yellow blotches; tail rounded in cross section. Southern race has white throat. Juvenile has more distinct patterning. L 28–44″ (70–110 cm), max to 4′4″ (1.3 m).

Similar Species: Larger **Nile Monitor Lizard** is more elongated, with narrower snout and laterally compressed tail; usually found near water.

Habitat: Savanna grasslands and woodlands, rocky areas, and semi-deserts.

Breeding: May use a termite mound for nest, but more often digs a burrow in soft moist soil during the rainy season. Lays 8–36 eggs, which hatch 1 year later.

Range: Senegal east to Eritrea and Somalia, and south to Namibia and e South Africa.

The Savanna Monitor Lizard is bulkier than the Nile, and can be more dangerous if cornered because of its stronger jaws and serrated tail. Most days it lumbers around alone, looking for carrion, baby tortoises, bird nests, land snails, millipedes, beetles, and grasshoppers.

Snakes
Suborder Serpentes

Snake track

Snakes, creatures without arms, legs, external ears, or eyelids, have existed for at least 100 million years. Except for slow-moving vipers and camouflaged tree snakes, most snakes vanish when they sense humans approaching. Snakes' forked tongues, which can be protruded and retracted, gather scent molecules from the air and transfer these to a sensory organ (called the Jacobson's organ) located in the nasal region above the palate just below the nose. All snakes are carnivorous, feeding on small animals; larger boas and pythons are able to prey on medium-size mammals. Prey is swallowed whole. Some snakes feed by grasping their prey and swallowing it; some constrict in tight coils around their prey until it suffocates; others poison the prey with venom. Of 2,750 snake species worldwide, 450 occur in Africa.

567 African Rock Python
Python sebae

Description: *An enormous stout snake,* with small smooth scales. *Triangular head* has many teeth for holding prey. *Top of head has dark brown triangular "spear-head"* outlined in buffy yellow. Rest of body blotched in *brown, olive, chestnut, and/or buffy yellow.* L 9–15′ (2.75–4.5 m), rarely to 23′ (7 m).

Similar Species: **Ball Python** *(P. regius),* which lives in rain forests of w Africa, can reach 6′4″ (1.9 m) in length and has golden blotches on black background; when threatened, it coils into a ball with its head protected in the center.

Habitat: Savanna woodlands and grasslands, forests, rocky areas, and edges of rivers and lakes.

Breeding: Female lays 20–60 elongated eggs inside a cavity in an old Aardvark burrow, termite mound, or cave, wrapping herself around eggs to protect them. Young hatch in 10–15 weeks.

Range: Senegal east to Ethiopia, and south to c Namibia and Natal.

This python, Africa's largest snake, usually attacks by biting first, hanging on with its many teeth, and then coiling around the victim. The African Rock Python prefers small antelopes, jackals, hares, hyraxes, and monkeys. It also takes waterbirds, monitor lizards, fish, and crocodiles, sometimes in turn falling prey to the last. Engorged pythons have been killed by packs of African Wild Dogs and hyenas.

568 **Madagascar Tree Boa**
Sanzinia madagascariensis
(Boa manditra)

Description: A gray-green snake, with lateral blackish diamonds outlined in cream; *skin has a purplish-blue sheen.* Triangular head; black line behind eye; *bright blue forked tongue.* L 3–5′ (90–150 cm).
Habitat: Lives both in trees and on the ground in humid and dry primary and secondary forests and in deforested areas.
Breeding: Ovoviviparous, carrying 3–16 (or more) young for 6–8 months before birth.
Range: Throughout Madagascar.

Called "manditra" by residents, this common snake probably feeds chiefly on small mammals.

569 **Boomslang**
Dispholidus typus

Description: A fairly thin snake, with the head wider than the body, and *large eyes.* Colors variable: *adult male usually bright green,* but some are light blue, bright red, or bright yellow with black-edged scales. Adult female light brown or olive. Juvenile has brown on top of head, white lower jaw, large green eyes, and blue spots on underside of body. L 4–5′ (1.2–1.5 m), max to 6′8″ (2 m).
Habitat: Open bush, thickets, savanna woodlands, and towns with weaver colonies.
Breeding: Lays 8–25 eggs in an unoccupied tree hollow or, at times, an earthen bank. Eggs hatch in 4–7 months.
Range: Senegal east to Somalia, and south to c Namibia and much of South Africa.

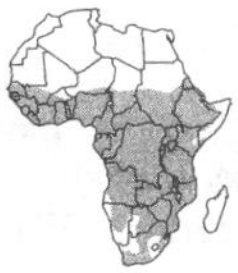

This snake has a highly potent venom—more toxic than a mamba's or cobra's—that prevents clotting and acts on both the nervous and blood systems. Fortunately it is shy, and bites humans only if handled. It glides gracefully through tree limbs during the day. It feeds on a variety of birds, chameleons, and other lizards, and is sometimes cannibalistic. When cornered, it inflates its neck in a defensive posture.

570 **Black Mamba**
Dendroaspis polylepis

Description: A large, slender snake, with a long, rectangular head. *Uniformly olive-brown or gunmetal gray above (not black), distinctly lighter below.* Some individuals have trace of banding. Interior of mouth black. L 6′8″–8′4″ (2–2.5 m), max to 14′ (4.3 m).

Habitat: Bushed savannas, grasslands, woodlands, and coastal scrub.

Breeding: Female lays 6–14 eggs, about 3″ (8 cm) long, in burrows in a termite mound, hollow log, or rock crevice. Young hatch in 11.5–13 weeks.

Range: Spotty in w Africa; widespread from s Sudan and Somalia south to c Namibia and Natal.

This is the largest and most dangerous poisonous snake in Africa, and is considered to be the world's fastest. It glides along rapidly (at up to 7 mph/ 11 kph), its head well off the ground, and chases game birds and small mammals. A Black Mamba will flee from trouble; if cornered, it will raise its hood, hiss, and, if the intruder does not retreat, strike, most likely on the face or neck. Untreated bites are quickly fatal.

571 **Eastern Green Mamba**
Dendroaspis angusticeps

Description: A large, slender, *bright green snake, with large eyes* and a rectangular, coffin-shaped head. Undersides yellow-green; *interior of mouth pink or white.* Juvenile bluish green. L 5–6′ (1.5–1.8 m), max to 10′ (3 m).

Similar Species: Green male **Boomslang** has much shorter head and larger eyes.

Habitat: Trees of montane, riverine, and coastal evergreen forests.

Breeding: Lays 12–14 eggs in a hollow log or leaf litter; young hatch in 10–11.5 weeks.

Range: Central and coastal Kenya south through e Tanzania to coastal Natal.

This mamba inhabits thatched roofs in some coastal areas, but generally goes unnoticed in green trees in wet tropical and montane forests. It feeds on small arboreal mammals, birds and their eggs, and lizards. Its venom attacks the nervous system, and is less potent than that of the Black Mamba. It is also less belligerent, biting only as a last resort. The bite causes mild paralysis, but rarely death.

---

572 **Gabon Viper**
Gaboon Adder
Bitis gabonica

Description: An extremely fat, *short-tailed* snake, with a beautiful *geometric pattern of hourglass and triangle markings* in various shades of dark and light brown, gold, lavender, and buff. *Massive triangular head* clear buff, with 2 dark stripes below eye, and *brown, mid-dorsal line.* 2 small horns on tip of snout. 3–4′ (90–120 cm), max to 6′ (1.8 m).

Habitat: Dead leaves on floor of rain forests, montane forests, and coastal dune forests.

Breeding: Breeds every 2–3 years; 16–60 young are born live about 1 year after mating.

Range: Guinea east to c Kenya, and south to c Angola and Malawi; also coastal Tanzania south to highlands of e Zimbabwe and coastal Natal.

With its superb camouflage and habit of remaining motionless, awaiting the approach of rodents and ground-feeding forest birds, the Gabon Viper is rarely seen. It is good-natured and sluggish, and prefers not to bite humans. Its curved fangs are the longest in the world, up to 1.5″ (4 cm).

573 Puff Adder
Bitis arietans

Description: *A thick-bodied, dark brown or yellow-brown snake, with paler white or yellowish bars and chevrons.* Some are speckled, or striking yellow or orange with black markings. Large rounded head has *pale U flanking dark crown.* Keeled scales give rough appearance. L 3–4′ (90–120 cm), max to 6′3″ (1.9 m).

Similar Species: **Gabon Viper** has buffy top of head, with thin mid-dorsal stripe.

Habitat: Virtually all habitats except pure deserts and highest mountains. Most common in savannas.

Breeding: Gives birth to live litters of 20–40 young.

Range: Southern Mauritania east to Somalia, and south to Cape Town. Isolated populations in Morocco and Algeria.

The Puff Adder's caterpillar-like forward locomotion occurs in a straight line (track shown at left), unlike the twisting locomotion of most snakes. Active chiefly at night, it often lies beside trails and behind rocks and logs, waiting for small mammals, especially rodents, and birds to amble by, and then rapidly injects its venom and follows its prey until it dies. When approached, it gives a loud, prolonged hiss. With its long fangs, which can inject a large dose of blood-destroying venom, the Puff Adder causes the majority of snake-bite deaths in Africa.

Track

574 Egyptian Cobra
Naja haje

Description: A thick snake, with smooth scales and variable coloration. *Often unmarked dull yellow, gray, or brownish above,* sometimes mottled. *Underside of neck has dark blotches.* Banded phase has 9–11 yellowish bands on blackish background. *Like all cobras, can raise umbrella-like hood on neck by elevating anterior ribs.* L 5′–6′8″ (1.5–2 m), max to 8′ (2.4 m).

Similar Species: **Cape Cobra** *(N. nivea)* replaces Egyptian in s Namibia, s Botswana, Orange Free State, and Cape Province; coloring varies from bright yellow to chestnut to black.

Habitat: Arid grasslands, bushed savannas, woodlands, and agricultural country.

Breeding: Lays 8–33 large oval eggs in loose soil or termite mound.

Range: Morocco east to Egypt; Senegal east to Sudan, and south to Natal.

The Egyptian Cobra's image appears on ancient Egyptian headdresses. It rests and suns itself during the day, inhabiting termite mounds, hollow logs, and rocky outcrops; at night it forages, feeding on birds, bird eggs, rodents, toads, and other snakes. It will often fake death when cornered; when forced to strike, it bites the victim's lower leg. Large doses of antivenin are needed to counteract its often fatal neurotoxic venom.

575 Black-necked Spitting-Cobra
Naja nigricollis

Description: A broad-headed cobra with a rounded snout. In most of tropical Africa, *uniformly black or olive-brown above,* with yellow or red underparts, and *broad dark throat band.* In n and c Namibia, banded black and light gray; in s Namibia and w Cape Province, black above, gray below with streaks. L 4–6′ (1.2–1.8 m), max to 9′ (2.7 m).

Similar Species: **Mozambique Spitting-Cobra** *(N. mossambica)* replaces Black-necked from s Tanzania and ne Namibia southeast to Natal; olive-brown with yellow or pink belly; venom destroys blood cells and causes great tissue damage, but is rarely fatal.

Habitat: Most common in grasslands, savannas, and scrub woodlands, but occurs in arid rocky areas of sw Africa.

Breeding: Lays 10–22 eggs.

Range: Senegal east to n Somalia, and south to w Cape Province.

Africa has four species of spitting cobras, all with modified fangs that can spit venom accurately up to 10 feet (3 m) or more. The relatively toxic venom is aimed into the eyes, causing temporary blindness and instant pain, and allowing the cobra to escape. If the spray hits only the skin, there is no reaction. This snake normally feeds on lizards, snakes, rodents, and toads, chiefly at night. A nervous species, it is best avoided.

INSECTS
Class Insecta

Africa may have a million species of insects, though an exact number is impossible to calculate, and the majority are yet to be described. In this section, we cover three of the most prominent groups. Limited space prevents us from discussing others of interest, including the crop-destroying locusts, the mosquitoes, and the lovely butterflies. Insects occupy virtually all habitats on land and fresh water. They have three body parts: a head, with compound eyes and usually a pair of feelers or antennae sensitive to smell; a thorax, or chest; and an abdomen. They have six legs that originate from the thorax. Many also have wings, usually four, though true flies have just two. Insects are not vertebrates; instead of a backbone they have an exoskeleton, or shell, which supports their weight. They breathe through holes and tubes, called spiracles, in the abdomen.

Tsetse Flies
Genus *Glossina*

Description: A large fly, with *large, reddish-brown eyes. Long wings lie folded together over back.* Long proboscis. L 0.25–0.55″ (6.5–14 mm).

Species: There are about 22 species of tsetse flies, which fall into 3 groups: one widespread in savanna woodlands and grasslands; one in wet forests from Guinea-Bissau east to e Zaire; the third along rivers and lakes from Gambia River east to Lake Tanganyika, in Tanzania.

Habitat: Savannas, forests, and watersides. Absent from deserts, most higher mountains, cities, and most of s Africa.

Breeding: While most insects lay massive numbers of eggs, a female tsetse nourishes 1 large larva with milk glands inside her abdomen, then drops it on the ground. It buries itself in the sand to pupate and emerges 1 month later from a black shell. Female bears up to 10 young over 6-month potential life span.

Range: Southern Senegal and Liberia east to sw Ethiopia, and south to c Angola, Okavango Delta (in n Botswana), and s Mozambique.

Through their bites, tsetse flies can transmit to humans the trypanosome parasites that cause African sleeping sickness. If detected early, the disease can be cured by drugs. Most of the insects are not infected with trypanosomes, and they are easily deterred by insect repellent on skin and clothes. (If one enters your vehicle, kill it immediately or flush it out the window with a hat. If one lands on you, slap it at once, as they bite quickly and can leave a welt.) Tsetses also transmit parasites that do not kill native wild animals, because of immunity built up for millions of years, but do kill domestic livestock, recent arrivals on the ecological scene. One trypanosome, called *nagana,* kills about 3 million cattle, goats, and pigs a year. Tsetses have effectively prohibited the colonization of sizable areas of African savanna, woodland, and wetland that have become reserves; if it weren't for these insects, man probably would have taken over those areas and killed off most larger mammals as competitors or predators. Thus the tsetse has made a major contribution to the protection of some of the greatest remaining concentrations of wildlife on the planet.

---

576 **Dung Beetles**
Scarab Beetles
Family Scarabaeidae

Description: *Stout black body* (a few are greenish), with wide thorax. Short clubbed antennae, giving wide head appearance of having 6 points. *Hindlegs trail closer to tip of*

Track in sand

abdomen than to middle legs. L 0.08–2″ (2–50 mm).

Similar Species: There are thousands of species of dung beetles, 1,800 in s Africa alone.

Habitat: Widespread in most habitats.

Breeding: The female carves out a chunk of dung the size of a Ping-Pong ball with the shovel-like, front part of her head, then uses her stout front legs to round it into a ball. Some then build a chamber below the ball, while others roll it away to hastily built underground tunnels. The female may deposit a number of balls in the tunnels, laying a single egg in each ball. The hatched larvae feed on the dung, and then pupate in it.

Range: All of Africa and Madagascar.

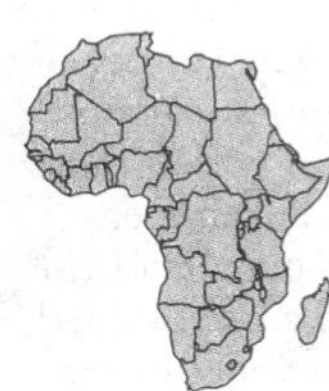

Adult dung beetles fly over Africa's grasslands singly or in groups at sites of recent mammal droppings. They feed on these droppings and bury some for their offspring to eat later. Dung beetle larvae serve as food for a number of birds and small animals.

---

577 **Termites**
Order Isoptera

Description: In the representative species *Macrotermes vitrialatus,* male (soldier) is 0.4–0.6″ (10–15 mm) long, with wingspan of 2.8–3″ (70–75 mm). Single queen often very large, with enormous pale abdomen. Countless small sterile workers resemble ants; larger soldiers have larger pincers. In some species, soldiers have prominent snout or pointed gland on forehead that squirts sticky secretion on enemies. Reproductive males and females born with *2 pairs of clear wings* that are held directly outward from body in flight, and trail behind body at rest.

Species and Habitats: There are hundreds of termite species in Africa. One or another occurs in all habitats except sterile sand deserts and the highest mountaintops.

Nesting: Single queen, who may live for 20 years,

lays all eggs. Mate is male of normal (small) size. Majority of offspring are small, blind, sterile workers that gather food, tend the "garden," and work on construction and repair of the chamber (see below). Winged offspring are reproductively active males and females that swarm into the air to start new colonies. Nests of the harvester termites (Hodotermitidae family) are completely underground, with only scattered heaps of loose soil visible at the tunnel entrances.

Mounds: Termites modify the soil to create their homes, many of which are constructed above ground in mounds that are impressive feats of collective engineering. The mounds of termites in the Termitidae family have a variety of shapes; those of the *Macrotermes* genus are large—up to 20′ (6 m) wide—and rounded, with grasses and even trees growing on top. The hay-makers of the *Trinervitermes* genus build a steep-sided, knee-high mound clear of vegetation, while members of the *Cubitermes* genus build a pagoda-style mound resembling a stack of large mushrooms. Giant, leaning, chimney-shaped mounds, some of which are ingeniously air-conditioned, are made by *Odontotermes* termites and their relatives.

Range: Termites occur throughout all of Africa and nearly worldwide.

Residents and travelers to most parts of Africa, particularly savanna areas, are impressed with the size, shape, variety, and numbers of termite mounds, some of which are extremely substantial and well planned. Termites feed on dead wood, grass, seeds, and dry manure. Some species construct gardens underground to grow a fungus that produces an enzyme that helps them break down the cellulose in plant tissue. Just after heavy downpours, clouds of reproductively active males and females, looking to start new colonies, pour out of openings in the mounds, guarded by soldiers. A wide variety of birds finds these winged termites tasty and nutritious, while Aardvarks, Aardwolves, and pangolins dine on terrestrial termites. Termite mounds, too, are of use to mammals, birds, and reptiles as resting sites, lookout points, scratching areas, and places to hide from enemies. Many trees and shrubs take root in abandoned termite mounds, providing shade, food, and shelter for wildlife.

Part IV
Appendices

CONSERVATION STATUS OF AFRICAN WILDLIFE

Conservation efforts are underway all over Africa, as the unique needs of the continent's animals and ecosystems are assessed by various groups. International and local conservation organizations continue to help focus scarce resources on endangered species and ecosystems. Many African governments have set aside large tracts of land for reserves, with the result that most animal species in successful reserves have adequate habitat and protection to ensure their survival in the coming decades. However, Africa's skyrocketing human population, which is doubling every 20 years, is adversely affecting wildlife outside the reserves. Squatting, hunting, and logging have caused severe degradation even of some reserves.

On the bright side, thanks to habitat protection and enforcement, the great migratory herds of wildebeests, zebras, and gazelles of the Serengeti–Masai Mara ecosystem of East Africa have grown from under a half million in the 1960s to well over 1 million in the 1990s. Likewise, reintroductions of animals from other reserves and zoos have been successful in areas where protection is good.

Habitat Destruction

Africa's population boom has had and will continue to have an adverse effect on the land. With most of the arable land already in production, ever poorer farmers are forced into increasingly marginal land that is too dry or too wet or too infertile for successful farming. There are many areas that are excellent for year-round or nomadic grazing. The problem is that there are too many cattle, goats, and sheep in marginal areas with erratic rainfall, where a plague of domestic animals is contributing to desertification. Late in the dry season, when every blade of grass has been chewed, these animals or their herders knock over trees to get at the leaves. Misguided attempts to introduce windmills and gasoline-powered water pumps in drier savannas and subdeserts exacerbate the problem. At one time, nomadic herders entered the drier areas for a few months and retreated to rivers in the dry season; now, lured by the promise of these new water sources, they have settled year-round in places where, despite technological advances, there still is not enough year-round forage, particularly in drier cycles or years.

Another major threat to Africa's unique habitats is forest clearance. While the Congo (Zaire) Basin and Gabon still have large tracts of forest, more than 90 percent of the forests of the region west of Cameroon have been felled for timber and cleared for farmland. Much of the wildlife in the remaining West African rain forest is highly endangered. Few outsiders visit these forests, so it is unlikely that the enticement of tourism revenue will prompt governments to save them.

Hunting of Wildlife

Over the centuries, hunting has resulted in the elimination of a number of species of African wildlife, particularly larger mammals. Firearms hastened the extinction of many subspecies and eliminated many species from vast portions of their ranges. Most extinctions of entire species have been not on the continent but on surrounding islands; they have been lost to these islands due to a combination of hunting, habitat destruction, and introduced predators and competitors.

During this century, improved weapons, roads, motor vehicles, railroads, and aircraft have facilitated the widespread slaughter of larger mammals by sport hunters. In addition, poaching for bushmeat (usually smaller antelopes but occasionally larger herbivores), with guns, snares, and traps, is widespread. Finally, the worldwide demand for elephant ivory, rhinoceros horn, and spotted cat furs has created a tragic situation for those animals. In most European and North American countries, game laws, with restricted seasons and lists of prohibited species, are constantly refined and strictly enforced. In much of Africa, where funding for such efforts is scarce, there is very little enforcement of any laws that might make it onto the books. Some reserves do have adequate anti-poaching patrols and dedicated staff members who put their lives on the line daily to protect wildlife. Banning sport hunting has not always helped in the conservation effort, however, and it is still allowed in some African countries. A strong argument has been made in favor of sport hunting in Kenya—where it has been banned—because without the responsible parties who monitor hunting areas, poachers move in and quickly exterminate anything of value.

Habitat Preservation

Africa has the greatest assemblage of national parks and game reserves of any continent, most located between Kenya and South Africa in moist or drier savannas, and many well managed by dedicated (and underpaid) staff. Thus most species of larger savanna mammals, as well as the birds and reptiles of those areas, have a fairly secure short-term future. However, this is only part of the story. There are relatively few parks and reserves in rain-forest areas; some of these parks exist on paper only, with little or no protection, and are subject to rampant poaching. Many of the savanna parks of West Africa also are suffering from human encroachment; far too many domestic animal herders, with far more mammals than the land can support, invade these few parks when resources in other areas fail. The large mammals of the Sahara and the Mediterranean countries are in the worst shape; decades of gross overhunting have left very few scattered survivors. The island of Madagascar has lost 95 percent of its moist forest habitat to logging and farming; major conservation efforts are being made to protect the remnants and the highly endangered fauna surviving in them. Throughout the African continent and on the offshore islands, saving samples of entire ecosystems, particularly large blocks, is of critical importance.

Tourism

The foreign exchange earned by a few major wildlife safari countries is substantial and is directly responsible for the creation and funding of many national parks. In those countries, tourism revenue, much of it based on the continued presence of wildlife, supports an increasing number of African businesses and individuals. However, the majority of African countries have little or no wildlife tourism because they lack abundant large mammals, have a poor tourism infrastructure, or have experienced recent periods of civil unrest. For the non-safari countries, where the prime wildlife interest is birds, butterflies, small mammals, or plants, and the number of tourists is fewer, conservation of endangered habitats or species will have to rely on high ideals rather than on the lure of foreign currency.

Concentrated in a tiny fraction of the African landscape, tourists usually stay within a few hours' drive of several hundred game lodges and tented camps in several dozen national parks and game reserves. They have a negative impact on primarily one creature, the cheetah. This cat hunts by day in open savanna and finds it difficult to surprise its prey when surrounded by vehicles. Visitors are encouraged to spend as little time as possible around cheetahs.

Travelers to Africa can also take many steps to ensure that their trip has as little negative impact on the envrionment as possible.

This can begin with trip planning, by researching and choosing tour operators that encourage environmentally responsible travel and that advocate programs that benefit the local ecology. Once in Africa, tourists must obey local and park rules, taking care to stay on trails and in vehicles as instructed. Habitats and vegetation must not be disturbed, and waste and litter must never be left behind. Additionally, travelers should not perpetuate the slaughter of endangered animals by buying such items as ivory and sea turtle products or cat skins. Lastly, travelers should consider themselves guests of the African continent, and should take care to respect the people and cultures of their host countries.

Conservation and Education

While outstanding individuals and local wildlife organizations care deeply about their wildlife and work hard to get their countrymen to learn about it, the vast majority of Africans have never seen a lion or a giraffe or an elephant, and most cannot afford to visit a national park (though many do see a wide variety of birds, which are welcomed or at least tolerated in most villages and towns). It would be wise to allocate a larger proportion of scarce conservation funds to publications and videos on local wildlife in local languages. The safari drivers and naturalist guides who work in the parks are becoming dedicated proponents and teachers of both foreign visitors and their countrymen. The further education of local naturalists will help create the political will to save endangered habitats and species. Dozens of excellent parks and reserves have been created in the last decade; sadly, during the same period some protected areas have been given over to settlers.

The international community owes a debt of gratitude to the many governments, park services, safari and tourist outfitters and their staffs, and to the many organizations that promote the conservation of African wildlife. Those interested in Africa and its people, wildlife, and ecosystems are urged to seek out and join worldwide conservation efforts.

GLOSSARY

Acacias Common, mimosa-like, dry-country trees and shrubs, with tiny, feathery, nutritious leaflets and white or yellow flowers that are ball-shaped or in long clusters; often have heavy thorns.

Alkaline lake See *Soda lake.*

Aloe Succulent plants of the lily family, with clusters of heavy, fleshy, sharply pointed leaves and sprays of red or yellow flowers; common in semi-arid areas of southern and eastern Africa.

Alpha Term applied to the socially dominant individual in a group of animals, usually primates and social carnivores.

Atoll Low-elevation, ring-like coral island encircling the sunken top of a submerged volcano.

Avifauna Bird life of an area.

Baobabs Trees with enormous, wide, gray trunks that bear edible, gourd-like fruit; deciduous in dry seasons; common in interior and coastal savannas of Africa and Madagascar.

Bar Line (usually short) that runs counter to the axis of a body part. *Barring* refers to closely spaced parallel bars.

Basin Area of land drained by a river and its tributaries.

Boots Heavily feathered thighs of raptors.

Boss In certain bovids, a convex, shield-like thickening of the horn at its base that spreads toward the mid-line of the head.

Brachystegia Dominant trees of miombo woodlands, which cover vast areas of south-central Africa; leaves turn orange or brown in the dry season, and most drop off.

Breeding plumage Coat of feathers, sometimes brightly colored, worn by many birds during the breeding season.

Broad-leafed trees Trees of better-watered areas, with larger, wider leaves than the narrow or fine leaves prevalent in vegetation of drier areas.

Browse To eat leaves on bushes and trees, as well as fruits, herbs, and sedges; also used as a noun to describe the vegetation.

Bushmeat Meat from wild animals killed by local people.

Caldera Large, steep-walled basin that remains after the peak of an extinct volcano has collapsed inward; e.g., Ngorongoro Crater, in northern Tanzania.

Call A specific vocalization (usually brief) that communicates location, identity, social status, alarm, or anger.

Canopy In a forest, the uppermost layer of spreading, overlapping branches.

Carapace Upper part of the shell of turtles and crustaceans.

Casque In birds, a bony growth over the bill of some hornbills; its sponge-like center is filled chiefly with air.

Cere Fleshy-looking, featherless area surrounding the nostrils at the base of the bill of raptors, parrots, and other birds.

Chott North African term for vast, usually dry, alkaline (soda) lake beds.

Class In taxonomic classification, a category that ranks above the order and below the phylum (division).

Clutch Set of eggs laid by one bird.

Colonial Living in a colony or group.

Commiphora Tree or shrub genus common in low-rainfall areas such as the Sahel.

Congolese forest Rain forest between the Gulf of Guinea and the western rift valley.

Coniferous Trees and shrubs with naked seeds in cones.

Coverts In birds, small feathers that overlie or cover the bases of the large flight feathers of the wings and tail, or that cover a particular area or structure (e.g., ear coverts).

Covey Mature bird or pair of birds with a brood of young; also, a small flock.

Crèche Group of young birds of several parents that stay together for protection before becoming independent.

Crepuscular Active at twilight (dawn or dusk).

Crest Tuft of long feathers or hairs, often on the crown or nape.

Crop In birds, a pouch in the throat in which food is stored.

Cryptic Serving to conceal; applied to coloration, form, or behavior.

Culmen In birds, ridge on top of the upper beak.

Cycads The most primitive living seed plants; stem is an unbranched column up to 65′ (20 m) tall with a crown of fern-like leaves. Indigenous to the tropics and subtropics.

Deciduous Trees and shrubs that shed their leaves during the hot dry season or the cold season.

Derived savanna Poor grassland with sparse trees and shrubs; the result of forest clearing and erosion.

Dewlap Loose, hanging fold of skin on an animal's lower throat.

Diurnal Active by day.

Dorsal Pertaining to the back or upper surface of the body or a body part.

East Africa Geographical region that encompasses Kenya, Tanzania, and Uganda; sometimes also refers to Rwanda, Burundi, and Somalia.

Echolocation Method in which some animals orient themselves by emitting high-frequency sounds and interpreting reflected sound waves. Bats, toothed whales, tenrecs, shrews, and a few birds navigate and locate prey by this means.

Eclipse plumage In birds, a dull-colored coat of feathers acquired immediately after the breeding season and worn for a few weeks.

Ecology Study of the interrelationships of organisms to one another and to the environment. As applied to species, the study of the individual or its species in relation to the environment.

Ecosystem Ecologically self-sustaining unit in nature defined by interrelationships among animals, plants, and the physical environment.

Endemic Native to an area; restricted or peculiar to a locality or region.

Epiphyte Plant that usually grows on the limbs of trees or on rocks and that derives its moisture and nutrients from the air and rain.

Estivation In animals, dormancy or sluggishness during hot or dry periods; helps conserve water.

Estrus In mammals, a state of sexual attractiveness in the female during which she is capable of conceiving; adjective, *estrous*.

Estuary Intersection of ocean and river, where fresh water and salt water meet.

Euphorbia Plant genus of the spurge family, comprising more than 700 species of trees, shrubs, and herbs, all with irritating white sap; some species in Africa are large or small cactus-like plants of moderate- or low-rainfall areas.

Extirpation Extermination of a species in a particular geographical area; usually the result of deliberate eradication by humans.

Eye line In birds, a line that runs horizontally from the base of the bill through the eye; also called *eye stripe.*

Family In taxonomic classification, a category that ranks above the genus and below the order.

Fauna Assemblage of animals of all species in a particular place at a given time.

Feral Having escaped from domestication and become wild.

Flora Assemblage of plants of all species in a particular place at a given time.

Forb Small, herb-like plant, usually broad-leafed and not woody, that grows in grasslands but is not a grass; sometimes used as a synonym for *herb.*

Form Habitual resting place in grass or ground litter that is shaped to an animal's body.

Frontal shield In birds, a fleshy, featherless, and often brightly colored area on the forehead.

Fynbos South African term for heath-like, shrubby vegetation composed of many species; plants have leathery, stiff, evergreen leaves.

Gallery forest Strips of forest or woodland along rivers in otherwise dry areas that cannot support such vegetation with natural rainfall; also called *riverine forest.*

Gape Corners of the base of a bird's beak where it meets the mouth.

Genus In taxonomic classification, a category that ranks above the species and below the family; a genus is a group of species that share many characteristics. The first word in each species' Latin name is the genus; for the Goliath Heron *(Ardea goliath),* the genus name is *Ardea.*

Graze To eat grasses; compare *Browse.*

Greenbelt Low-lying terrain that has higher water content in its soil than nearby areas and that supports green vegetation longer between rains.

Greenflush Fresh green grasses that sprout in dry grassland after rain or, in areas with sufficient moisture, after fire has removed vegetation.

Grizzled The effect of flecking, created by hairs of some contrasting color (usually gray) against another background color.

Guard hairs Long coarse hairs that form a protective coating over a mammal's underfur.

Guinea savanna Zone of broad-leafed, deciduous woodlands located roughly from Guinea to northeastern Zaire, south of drier Sudan savanna and north of evergreen rain forest.

Gular Of, relating to, or situated on the throat.

Harem In some ungulates and primates, a group of two or more breeding females, plus their young, monopolized and sometimes protected by one male.

Hibernation In animals, dormancy during cold periods; temperature and all bodily processes are greatly reduced to conserve energy.

High sun Months when the sun appears highest in the sky; correlates with rainy season(s).

Highveld South African term for cooler, open grassland of higher elevations.

Home range Familiar area an adult individual uses year-round; extremely large for nomadic or migratory animals. Differs from *territory* in not being defended; the territory lies within the home range.

Hood On a bird's head, color that contrasts with the neck or body color.

Horn of Africa Easternmost wedge of Africa, dominated by Somalia and eastern Ethiopia.

Immature Young animal no longer under parental care but not yet adult in appearance.

Indigenous Native to a given area; not introduced.

Inselberg Isolated, granitic mountain rising above lowlands.

Introduced species Non-native species that has been taken to an area by humans and now successfully occupies it.

Isoberlinia Several species of broad-leafed, deciduous trees that commonly occur in the Guinea savanna zone.

Juvenile In birds, young individual wearing its first coat of feathers. In mammals, offspring still dependent on parent(s).

Kopje Granitic mountaintop or inselberg; granitic outcrop on a plain. (Also *koppie.*)

Lagoon Shallow lake or enclosed water adjacent to an ocean that is nearly isolated by sand dunes or coral.

Lanceolate Shaped like a lance head; i.e., tapering to a point at the apex and sometimes at the base.

Lappet Loosely hanging or folded fleshy part; e.g., a dewlap or earlobe.

Lateral Pertaining to the side.

Lek Breeding ground.

Lobelia Herb that grows up to 30′ (9 m) tall in African montane forests.

Local Occurring in relatively small, restricted areas.

Lore In birds, a small patch, sometimes distinctively colored, between the eye and the base of the bill; generally used in the plural.

Low sun Months when the sun appears lowest in the sky; usually a very dry period.

Lowveld South African term for a wooded grassland of lower elevations.

Macchia Flora of the winter-rainfall areas near the Mediterranean and the southern coast of South Africa; characterized by dense evergreen shrubs and small trees.

Mandible In mammals, the lower jaw. In birds, one of the two parts of a bird's bill, termed the *upper mandible* and the *lower mandible.*

Mangroves Salt-tolerant evergreen trees and shrubs of tropical coastlines.

Mantle In birds, the back, scapulars, and wings, especially when these areas are of one color. In mammals, all or part of dorsal fur that has contrasting color or longer hair.

Massif Dominant central mass of a mountain range.

Midden Dung hill or refuse heap.

Migratory Populations that move seasonally to an area of predictably better availability of food or water. Compare *Nomadic* and *Resident.*

Miombo woodland Woodland dominated by trees of the

Brachystegia genus that covers vast areas of moist savanna in south-central Africa.

Molt Process of shedding and replacing feathers or hair.

Monogamy Mating system in which one male mates with one female; usually correlates with both male and female parental care being essential to survival of the young.

Montane Referring to mountains.

Montane forest Forests of mountainous areas, where frequent clouds and cooler temperatures mean less evaporation than occurs in the surrounding drier lowlands.

Mopane woodland Woodland with trees of several species, including *Colospermum mopane,* covering the drier savannas of south-central Africa.

Morph In birds, one or more distinctive plumages seen in certain species; also called a *phase.*

Mustache In birds, a colored streak running from the base of the bill back along the side of the throat. In monkeys, a horizontal bar of contrasting color below the nose.

Nocturnal Active at night.

Nomadic Populations that move in an irregular, patternless way within a huge range in search of forage. Compare *Resident* and *Migratory.*

North Africa Countries north of the Sahara and bordering the Mediterranean; usually refers to Morocco, Algeria, and Tunisia; sometimes also includes Libya and Egypt.

Northern savanna Broad belt of both moist and drier savannas north of the equator from Senegal east to western Ethiopia.

Noseleaf In bats, a fleshy, variably shaped appendage on the nose.

Nuchal Of, relating to, or lying in the region of the nape.

Omnivorous Feeding on both plant and animal material.

Order In taxonomic classification, a category that ranks above the family and below the class.

Oviparous Producing young by means of eggs that hatch after being laid.

Ovoviviparous Producing young by means of membranous eggs retained within the body of the female that hatch either within the body or immediately after laying.

Oxbow lake Semi-circular lake formed when a bow in a river becomes separated from the main river when the channel shifts.

Pan Shallow depression that fills temporarily with water during wetter months or years; salts dissolved from the soil become concentrated as a result of evaporation in the dry season.

Papyrus Tall marsh plants of the sedge family with triangular stems and large clumps of drooping rays.

Pedicle Stalk-like base or support for horns; looks like a raised forehead.

Pelagic Of or inhabiting the open ocean.

Phase See *Morph.*

Plastron Lower part of a turtle's shell; the flat skeletal plate on a turtle's underside.

Plume Feather that is larger, longer, or of a different color than the feathers around it; generally used in display behavior.

Podocarpus Genus of large, ancient, coniferous trees of moister montane forests.

Polyandry Extremely rare mating system in which a female is bonded with more than one male.

Polygyny Common mating system among mammals in which relatively few males inseminate all the females, or in which a male mates with more than one female; usually the female raises the young with little direct help from the father.

Prehensile Adapted for seizing or grasping, especially by wrapping around.

Preorbital In front of the eyes.

Primaries Outermost and longest flight feathers on a bird's wing.

Prime Fully mature.

Protea Large evergreen shrub genus of South Africa; plants have enormous showy flowers.

Race Portion of a species that usually differs in appearance (and is usually geographically isolated), but whose individuals can still interbreed and produce viable offspring with other members of the species; also called a *subspecies.*

Rain forest Evergreen forest with a short dry season and high precipitation; can be either lowland or montane.

Rain shadow Drier area that occurs on the leeward side of mountains; moisture-laden clouds on the windward side drop rain as they rise over the mountains, leaving no moisture to deposit on the rain-shadow side.

Range Geographical area or areas normally inhabited by a species or subspecies.

Raptor Bird of prey.

Reintroduce To release individuals from zoos or other wild populations into an area in which the species was extirpated in former times.

Relict Tiny fragments of habitat or small populations of animals and plants that were once more widespread.

Resident Populations that remain in one place all year; nonmigratory. Compare *Migratory* and *Nomadic.*

Rift valley Descending valley forming where the continental plate that supports Africa's eastern sixth is drifting eastward; splits into two valleys (eastern and western) in eastern Africa.

Riparian Of or inhabiting the banks of rivers or streams.

Riverine forest See *Gallery forest.*

Rostrum In mammals and some invertebrates, any snout-like process at the front of the head. In birds, a central forward-directed process just above the breastbone.

Ruff Longer feathers or fur usually around the face or neck that in some animals may be erected during courtship displays or excitement.

Ruminant Even-toed hoofed mammal that has a complex three- or four-chambered stomach from which partially masticated food, the "cud," is regurgitated into the mouth for chewing to aid more complete digestion.

Rut In mammals, the period during which most conceptions occur; usually applied to ungulate (hoofed) species in which males display and compete vigorously for mates and territory.

Sahel Zone of driest savanna that borders the southern edge of the Sahara from Mauritania east to Sudan.

Savanna Habitat in tropical regions with extended wet and dry seasons dominated by grasses and predominantly leguminous trees of varying density, depending on rainfall; sometimes (imprecisely) used to refer to treeless grassland.

Scapulars In birds, a group of feathers along the side of the back and overlapping the folded wing.

Scutes Large scales; horny shields or plates covering a turtle's shell.

Secondaries Large flight feathers growing from the "forearm" of a bird. In flight, these are closer to the body than primaries; at rest, they overlap the upper sections of the primaries.

Secondary vegetation Vegetation that grows after the primary (virgin) forest or woodland is cleared.

Sedge Marsh plants that differ from the related grasses in having solid triangular stems.

Semi-desert See *Subdesert.*

Shoulder In birds, the point where the wing meets the body; also loosely applied to the bend of the wing when this area is distinctively colored.

Soda lake Arid-region lake or shallow pond without outlet that is subject to periodic drying, which results in a high concentration of mineral salts (chiefly sodium bicarbonates and carbonates) and high alkalinity; also called *alkaline lake* or *salt lake.*

Somali-Masai arid zone Subdesert and dry savanna areas of the Horn of Africa extending south into northern Tanzania.

Song In birds, a vocalization, generally more complex than a call, that is given to advertise ownership of a nesting or feeding territory.

Sourveld South African term for tall grassland that in the dry season becomes unpalatable and lacking in nutrition for herbivores.

Southern savanna Savanna areas south of the equator.

Species In taxonomic classification, the smallest unit of classification to comprise individuals that freely breed among themselves but not with others, even in the same genus (hybrids are rare and usually infertile). Features and behavior differ little within species, although local differences may arise through recent geographical isolation. Each species is designated by a two-part scientific name in which the first word is the genus name, the second the species name.

Spiracle Breathing hole or tube.

Steppe Dry grassland of temperate zones, usually without trees, bordering desert.

Stotting In ungulates, series of high bounds in which all four feet leave the ground at once; tail or rump hairs are often erected.

Strandveld Grassland in sandy areas of the coastal plain of Cape Province.

Stripe Line of variable width, in a color contrasting with background; may be longitudinal or transverse.

Subdesert Dry vegetation zone that receives erratic annual rainfall of 6–12″ (150–300 mm) and supports sparse vegetation (small shrubs and grass); also called *semi-desert* and *semi-arid desert.*

Subspecies See *Race.*

Sudan savanna Vegetation zone south of the Sahel stretching from Senegal east to eastern Sudan that is drier and has fewer trees than Guinea savanna to the south.

Taxonomic classification In biology, the systematic categorization of organisms. From large to small, the categories, with the Blue Monkey *(Cercopithecus mitis)* as an example, are: kingdom Animal, phylum or division Chordata, class Mammalia, order Primates, family Cercopithecidae, genus *Cercopithecus,* and species *mitis.*

Termitarium Mound constructed by termites; aboveground earthen dome or underground chambers housing massive termite colonies; plural, *termitaria.*

Territory Area claimed and defended by an animal or group of animals (e.g., a pride of lions); holder may patrol, scent-mark, vocalize, and even fight to keep intruders away.

Thornveld Acacia-dominated, bushed savanna in the low hot country of southern Africa; most thornveld plants have copious thorns.

Torpor Temporary loss of all or part of the power of sensation or motion, resulting from the reduction of body temperature and the slowing of bodily processes; adjective, *torpid.*

Tragus Cartilaginous prominence in front of the external opening of the ear.

Veld South African term for a natural grassland. See also *Highveld, Lowveld, Sourveld, Strandveld,* and *Thornveld.*

Ventral Pertaining to the belly or underside of the body or a body part.

Vibrissae Long, stiff hairs that serve as touch receptors, most commonly around the nose or mouth of certain mammals ("whiskers"), but also on the limbs and body of some species.

Vlei South African term for a marsh or pan, often with water only in the wet season.

Wadi North African term for a streambed that may or may not have regular water.

Wattle Fleshy, wrinkled, sometimes colorful appendage, often paired, hanging from the chin or throat of a bird.

West Africa Countries south of the Sahara from southern Mauritania to Cameroon.

Woodland Growth of trees that is drier and less dense than a forest, with shorter and often deciduous trees.

PICTURE CREDITS

1 Stan Osolinski
2 Y. Arthus-Bertrand/Altitude/Peter Arnold, Inc.
3 Y. Arthus-Bertrand/Altitude/Peter Arnold, Inc.
4 Helga Lade/Peter Arnold, Inc.
5 Gavin Thomson/ABPL
6 Gavin Thomson/ABPL
7 Diane Blell/Peter Arnold, Inc.
8 Alan Binks/ABPL
9 Y. Arthus-Bertrand/Altitude/Peter Arnold, Inc.
10 Alan Binks/ABPL
11 Kazuyoshi Nomachi/PPS/Photo Researchers, Inc.
12 Bob Burch
13 Walt Anderson
14 Brendan Ryan/ABPL
15 Daryl Balfour/ABPL
16 Gavin Thomson/ABPL
17 Jason Laure/ABPL
18 Jason Laure/ABPL
19 Mary M. Thacher/Photo Researchers, Inc.
20 Hans Reinhard/Okapia/Photo Researchers, Inc.
21 Anthony Bannister/ABPL
22 Kazuyoshi Nomachi/PPS/Photo Researchers, Inc.
23 Noboru Komine/Photo Researchers, Inc.
24 Anthony Bannister/ABPL
25 Gavin Thomson/ABPL
26 Peter Alden
27 Nigel J. Dennis/Photo Researchers, Inc.
28 H. R. Bramaz/Peter Arnold, Inc.
29 Roger Tidman
30 Kevin Schafer
31 Peter Alden
32 Roger De la Harpe/ABPL
33 James F. Parnell
34 Stephen G. Maka
35 Anthony Bannister/ABPL
36 Beverly Joubert/ABPL
37 Walt Anderson
38 Gavin Thomson/ABPL
39 Daryl Balfour/ABPL
40 Carol Hughes/ABPL
41 D. Waugh/Peter Arnold, Inc.
42 Will & Deni McIntyre/Photo Researchers, Inc.
43 R. D. Estes/Photo Researchers, Inc.
44 Alan Binks/ABPL
45 Brendan Ryan/ABPL

46 Anthony Bannister/ABPL
47 Charles G. Summers, Jr.
48 Clem Haagner/ABPL
49 Alan Binks/ABPL
50 Bildarchiv Okapia/Photo Researchers, Inc.
51 Roland Seitre/Peter Arnold, Inc.
52 Alan Shoemaker
53 Peter Alden
54 Daniel J. Cox/DJC & Associates
55 Larry Sansone
56 Kevin Schafer
57 Joe McDonald
58 Tom McHugh/Photo Researchers, Inc.
59 Rita Summers
60 Walt Anderson
61 Walt Anderson
62 Anup Shah/ABPL
63 Nigel J. Dennis/ABPL
64 Nigel J. Dennis/ABPL
65 Ron Austing
66 Ron Garrison/Zoological Society of San Diego
67 Anthony Bannister/ABPL
68 Clem Haagner/ABPL
69 Stan Osolinski
70 Nigel J. Dennis/ABPL
71 Richard J. Chandler
72 Kenneth W. Fink/Photo Researchers, Inc.
73 Doug Cheeseman
74 M. P. Kahl/Photo Researchers, Inc.
75 Daniel J. Cox/DJC & Associates
76 Zoological Society of San Diego
77 Stan Osolinski/Dembinsky Photo Associates
78 Ron Austing
79 G. C. Kelley
80 Stan Osolinski
81 Doug Cheeseman/Peter Arnold, Inc.
82 Gavin Thomson/ABPL
83 Anup Shah/ABPL
84 Larry Sansone
85 Peter Alden
86 Art Wolfe
87 Zoological Society of San Diego
88 Peter Alden
89 Fritz Polking/Peter Arnold, Inc.
90 Nigel J. Dennis/Photo Researchers, Inc.
91 Charles G. Summers, Jr.
92 Richard E. Webster
93 Jeffrey L. Rotman/Peter Arnold, Inc.
94 Richard J. Chandler
95 Stan Osolinski
96 Daniel J. Cox/DJC & Associates
97 Jeffrey L. Rotman/Peter Arnold, Inc.
98 Daniel J. Cox/DJC & Associates
99 Charles G. Summers, Jr.
100 Roland Seitre/Peter Arnold, Inc.
101 Dale & Marian Zimmerman
102 Rita Summers
103 Charles G. Summers, Jr.
104 Steve Bentsen
105 R. D. Estes
106 James F. Parnell
107 Rita Summers
108 Charles G. Summers, Jr.
109 Mark J. Thomas/ Dembinsky Photo Associates
110 Stephen G. Maka/Photo/ Nats
111 G. C. Kelley
112 Peter Alden
113 Richard Weiss/Peter Arnold, Inc.
114 Roger Tidman
115 Dale & Marian Zimmerman
116 Clem Haagner/ABPL
117 William Campbell/Peter Arnold, Inc.

118 Michael W. Dulaney
119 Joe McDonald
120 Eric Reisinger/ABPL
121 Mark Newman/Photo Researchers, Inc.
122 Stephen G.Maka
123 Tom McHugh/Photo Researchers, Inc.
124 Jeanne White/Photo Researchers, Inc.
125 Stan Osolinski
126 Daniel J. Cox/DJC & Associates
127 Charles G. Summers, Jr.
128 Kevin Schafer
129 Peter Alden
130 Roger Tidman
131 Clem Haagner/ABPL
132 Peter Alden
133 Steve Kaufman/Peter Arnold, Inc.
134 Eric & David Hosking/Photo Researchers, Inc.
135 Stan Osolinski
136 Clem Haagner/ABPL
137 Mark Newman/Photo Researchers, Inc.
138 Anup Shah/ABPL
139 Steve Kaufman/Peter Arnold, Inc.
140 Dale & Marian Zimmerman
141 John Visser
142 Lorna Stanton/ABPL
143 Lorna Stanton/ABPL
144 Fred Bruemmer
145 Nigel J. Dennis/ABPL
146 Dale & Marian Zimmerman
147 Nigel J. Dennis/ABPL
148 Tom McHugh/Photo Researchers, Inc.
149 Zoological Society of San Diego
150 G. C. Kelley
151 John Visser
152 Dale & Marian Zimmerman
153 Daniel J. Cox/DJC & Associates
154 Rita Summers
155 P. Morris Photographics
156 John Visser
157 Charles G. Summers, Jr.
158 Michael W. Dulaney
159 Charles G. Summers, Jr.
160 Rita Summers
161 Mitch Reardon/Photo Researchers, Inc.
162 Daryl Balfour/ABPL
163 John Visser
164 Art Wolfe
165 Fritz Polking/Peter Arnold, Inc.
166 Ron Austing
167 C&M Denis-Huot/Peter Arnold, Inc.
168 Joe McDonald
169 Fritz Polking/Peter Arnold, Inc.
170 Alan Binks/ABPL
171 Daniel J. Cox/DJC & Associates
172 Daniel J. Cox/DJC & Associates
173 Joan Ryder/ABPL
174 Paul Funston/ABPL
175 John Visser
176 Stan Osolinski
177 Stephen J. Kraseman/ Peter Arnold, Inc.
178 Joe McDonald
179 Rita Summers
180 Beverly Joubert/ABPL
181 William Campbell/Peter Arnold, Inc.
182 Rita Summers
183 Zoological Society of San Diego
184 Charles G. Summers, Jr.
185 Dale & Marian Zimmerman
186 Tom McHugh/Photo Researchers, Inc.
187 Anthony Bannister/ABPL
188 Dave Hamman/ABPL

189 Michael W. Dulaney/ Cincinnati Zoo & Botanical Gardens
190 Ron Austing
191 David Haring/Duke University Primate Center
192 David Haring/Duke University Primate Center
193 David Haring/Duke University Primate Center
194 Art Wolfe
195 Art Wolfe
196 David Haring/Duke University Primate Center
197 D. Halleux/BIOS/Peter Arnold, Inc.
198 David Haring/Duke University Primate Center
199 Dale & Marian Zimmerman
200 Art Wolfe
201 Emily Short/Riverbanks Zoo and Garden
202 Ron Austing
203 Art Wolfe
204 Lysa Leland
205 Art Wolfe
206 Joe McDonald
207 Zoological Society of San Diego
208 Art Wolfe
209 John Mitchell/Zoological Society of San Diego
210 Zoological Society of San Diego
211 Art Wolfe
212 Charles G. Summers, Jr.
213 Klaus Paysan/Peter Arnold, Inc.
214 Mark J. Thomas/ Dembinsky Photo Associates
215 Dale & Marian Zimmerman
216 Steve Bentsen
217 Larry Cameron/ Riverbanks Zoo and Garden
218 Michael P. Turco
219 Art Wolfe
220 Klaus Paysan/Peter Arnold, Inc.
221 Ron Austing
222 Lysa Leland
223 Larry Sansone
224 Lysa Leland
225 Alan Binks/ABPL
226 Art Wolfe
227 Lawrence Migdale/ Photo Researchers, Inc.
228 Tom McHugh/Photo Researchers, Inc.
229 Art Wolfe
230 Ron Austing
231 Ken Kelley/Zoological Society of San Diego
232 Ian C. Tait
233 Zoological Society of San Diego
234 P. Morris Photographics
235 Merlin D. Tuttle/Bat Conservation Int'l
236 Merlin D. Tuttle/Bat Conservation Int'l
237 Art Wolfe
238 Merlin D. Tuttle/Bat Conservation Int'l
239 Doug Cheeseman
240 Mark J. Thomas/ Dembinsky Photo Associates
241 G. Ziesler/Peter Arnold, Inc.
242 G .C. Kelley
243 Doug Cheeseman
244 George W. Frame
245 P. Morris Photographics
246 John Visser
247 R. Andrew Odum/Peter Arnold, Inc.
248 Tom McHugh/Photo Researchers, Inc.

249 Charles G. Summers, Jr.
250 John Visser
251 Walt Anderson
252 Stan Osolinski
253 Nigel J. Dennis/ABPL
254 R. D. Estes/Photo Researchers, Inc.
255 Ian C. Tait
256 Charles G. Summers, Jr.
257 Roger Tidman
258 Roger Tidman
259 J.W. Enticott
260 Roland Seitre/Peter Arnold, Inc.
261 Stan Osolinski
262 Dale & Marian Zimmerman
263 Fred Bruemmer/Peter Arnold, Inc.
264 Charles G. Summers, Jr.
265 Charles G. Summers, Jr.
266 Roger Tidman
267 Charles G. Summers, Jr.
268 Roland Seitre/Peter Arnold, Inc.
269 Steve Bentsen
270 Roger Tidman
271 Dale & Marian Zimmerman
272 James F. Parnell
273 Roger Tidman
274 Dale & Marian Zimmerman
275 Charles G. Summers, Jr.
276 Dale & Marian Zimmerman
277 Roger Tidman
278 Doug Cheeseman/ Peter Arnold, Inc.
279 Richard J. Chandler
280 Joe McDonald
281 G. C. Kelley
282 Stephen G. Maka
283 Roger Tidman
284 Charles G. Summers, Jr.
285 Charles G. Summers, Jr.
286 Mark J. Thomas/ Dembinsky Photo Associates
287 Joe McDonald
288 Rita Summers
289 Charles G. Summers, Jr.
290 Ron Austing
291 Charles G. Summers, Jr.
292 Rita Summers
293 Fritz Polking/Peter Arnold, Inc.
294 Art Wolfe
295 Ron Austing
296 Charles G. Summers, Jr.
297 Roger Tidman
298 Peter Alden
299 Peter Alden
300 Roger Tidman
301 Herbert Clarke
302 Roger Tidman
303 Roger Tidman
304 Roger Tidman
305 Joe McDonald
306 Dale & Marian Zimmerman
307 Peter Alden
308 Doug Cheeseman
309 Roger Tidman
310 Joe McDonald
311 Joe McDonald
312 Joe McDonald
313 Charles G. Summers, Jr.
314 Roger Tidman
315 Fritz Polking/Peter Arnold, Inc.
316 Roger Tidman
317 Daniel J. Cox/DJC & Associates
318 Richard J. Chandler
319 Charles G. Summers, Jr.
320 G. Ziesler/Peter Arnold, Inc.
321 Roger Tidman
322 Doug Cheeseman/Peter Arnold, Inc.
323 Daniel J. Cox/DJC & Associates
324 Peter Alden
325 Ian C. Tait
326 Peter Alden
327 Roger Tidman
328 Daniel J. Cox/DJC & Associates

329 Dale & Marian Zimmerman
330 Charles G. Summers, Jr.
331 Rita Summers
332 Stan Osolinski
333 Joe McDonald
334 Roger Tidman
335 David Hosking/ Dembinsky Photo Associates
336 Stephen J. Krasemann/ Peter Arnold, Inc.
337 Richard J. Chandler
338 Doug Cheeseman
339 Richard E. Webster
340 Arnold Small
341 Charles G. Summers, Jr.
342 Joe McDonald
343 Doug Cheeseman
344 Charles G. Summers, Jr.
345 Gregory G. Dimijian/ Photo Researchers, Inc.
346 G. Ziesler/Peter Arnold, Inc.
347 Roger Tidman
348 Roger Tidman
349 Roger Tidman
350 Joe McDonald
351 G. C. Kelley
352 G. C. Kelley
353 Joe McDonald
354 Charles G. Summers, Jr.
355 Rita Summers
356 Dale & Marian Zimmerman
357 Charles G. Summers, Jr.
358 Doug Cheeseman
359 Roger Tidman
360 Roger Tidman
361 Richard J. Chandler
362 Dale & Marian Zimmerman
363 Joe McDonald
364 Charles G. Summers, Jr.
365 Steve Bentsen
366 Roger Tidman
367 Charles G. Summers, Jr.
368 Roger Tidman
369 Joan Ryder/ABPL
370 Richard J. Chandler
371 Richard J. Chandler
372 Sam Fried/Photo/Nats
373 Dirk Heinrich/ABPL
374 Arnold Small
375 Gunter Ziesler/Peter Arnold, Inc.
376 Emily Hubbs Scott
377 Joe McDonald
378 Joe McDonald
379 Mike Danzenbaker
380 Dale & Marian Zimmerman
381 Stephen G. Maka
382 Fritz Polking/Peter Arnold, Inc.
383 G. C. Kelley
384 Roger Tidman
385 G. C. Kelley
386 Richard J. Chandler
387 P. Morris Photographics
388 Stan Osolinski
389 Gerald Lacz/Peter Arnold, Inc.
390 Zoological Society of San Diego
391 Roger Tidman
392 G. C. Kelley
393 Joe McDonald
394 Dale & Marian Zimmerman
395 G. C. Kelley
396 Dale & Marian Zimmerman
397 P. Morris Photographics
398 Frederick J. Dodd/Peter Arnold, Inc.
399 Richard J. Chandler
400 Dale & Marian Zimmerman
401 Shawneen E. Finnegan
402 Lee Hung
403 Doug Cheeseman
404 Larry Sansone
405 G. C. Kelley
406 Mike Danzenbaker
407 Herbert Clarke
408 Arnold Small
409 Mike Danzenbaker

410 G. Ziesler/Peter Arnold, Inc.
411 Dale & Marian Zimmerman
412 Anthony Bannister/ ABPL
413 Rita Summers
414 Charles G. Summers, Jr.
415 Dale & Marian Zimmerman
416 Stephen G. Maka
417 Ron Austing
418 Fritz Polking/Dembinsky Photo Associates
419 Shawneen E. Finnegan
420 Charles G. Summers, Jr.
421 Joe McDonald
422 Dale & Marian Zimmerman
423 Charles G. Summers, Jr.
424 Stephen G. Maka
425 Ron Austing
426 Gunter Ziesler/Peter Arnold, Inc.
427 Shawneen E. Finnegan
428 Kevin Schafer
429 Kevin Schafer
430 Kevin Schafer
431 Dale & Marian Zimmerman
432 Peter Alden
433 Roger Tidman
434 Mark J. Thomas/ Dembinsky Photo Associates
435 Stephen G. Maka
436 Dale & Marian Zimmerman
437 Charles G. Summers, Jr.
438 Dale & Marian Zimmerman
439 Dale & Marian Zimmerman
440 Doug Cheeseman
441 Mary Clay/Photo/Nats
442 Fritz Polking/Peter Arnold, Inc.
443 Dale & Marian Zimmerman
444 G. C. Kelley
445 Dale & Marian Zimmerman
446 Roger Tidman
447 Richard J. Chandler
448 Mike Danzenbaker
449 Nigel J. Dennis/ABPL
450 Dale & Marian Zimmerman/VIREO
451 Dale & Marian Zimmerman
452 Ian C. Tait
453 Dale & Marian Zimmerman
454 Roger Tidman
455 Roger Tidman
456 Mike Danzenbaker
457 Dale & Marian Zimmerman
458 Joe McDonald
459 Steve Bentsen
460 Dale & Marian Zimmerman
461 G. C. Kelley
462 Richard J. Chandler
463 Dale & Marian Zimmerman
464 Roger Tidman
465 Ron Austing
466 Dale & Marian Zimmerman
467 Clem Haagner/ABPL
468 Shawneen E. Finnegan
469 Roger Tidman
470 Roger Tidman
471 Dale & Marian Zimmerman
472 Peter Alden
473 Kevin Schafer & Martha Hill
474 Dale & Marian Zimmerman
475 C. H. Greenewalt/ VIREO
476 Doug Cheeseman
477 Doug Cheeseman/ Peter Arnold, Inc.
478 Roger Tidman
479 Roger Tidman

480 Dale & Marian Zimmerman
481 Dale & Marian Zimmerman
482 Roger Tidman
483 Roger Tidman
484 Dale & Marian Zimmerman
485 Dale & Marian Zimmerman
486 Dale & Marian Zimmerman
487 Ron Austing
488 Mike Danzenbaker
489 Dale & Marian Zimmerman
490 Roger Tidman
491 Richard J. Chandler
492 Ian C. Tait
493 Dale & Marian Zimmerman
494 Dale & Marian Zimmerman
495 G. C. Kelley
496 Peter Alden
497 Peter Alden
498 G. C. Kelley
499 Dale & Marian Zimmerman
500 Dale & Marian Zimmerman
501 Joe McDonald
502 Mark J. Thomas/ Dembinsky Photo Associates
503 Nigel J. Dennis/ABPL
504 Tim Davis/Photo Researchers, Inc.
505 Roger Tidman
506 Peter Alden
507 Dale & Marian Zimmerman
508 Dale & Marian Zimmerman
509 Roger Tidman
510 Johan Van Jaarsveld/ABPL
511 Daniel J. Cox/DJC & Associates
512 Richard E. Webster
513 Nigel J. Dennis/ABPL
514 Dale & Marian Zimmerman
515 Richard J. Chandler
516 Dale & Marian Zimmerman
517 Doug Cheeseman
518 Roger Tidman
519 Ron Austing
520 Walt Anderson
521 Dale & Marian Zimmerman
522 Dale & Marian Zimmerman
523 Fritz Polking/Peter Arnold, Inc.
524 Charles G. Summers, Jr.
525 Roland Seitre/Peter Arnold, Inc.
526 Rita Summers
527 David Hosking/Photo Researchers, Inc.
528 Roland Seitre/Peter Arnold, Inc.
529 Nigel J. Dennis/ABPL
530 Dale & Marian Zimmerman
531 Stan Osolinski
532 Peter Alden
533 Stephen G. Maka
534 Roger Tidman
535 Dale & Marian Zimmerman
536 Peter Alden
537 Stephen G. Maka/Photo/ Nats
538 Dale & Marian Zimmerman
539 Dale & Marian Zimmerman
540 Doug Cheeseman/ Peter Arnold, Inc.
541 Peter Alden
542 Charles G. Summers, Jr.
543 Stan Osolinski
544 Kevin Schafer
545 Carol Hughes/ABPL
546 Charles G. Summers, Jr.
547 Roger Tidman

548 Roger Tidman
549 Dale & Marian Zimmerman
550 Dale & Marian Zimmerman
551 Kevin Schafer
552 Peter Alden
553 Allen Blake Sheldon
554 R. Andrew Odum/Peter Arnold, Inc.
555 Gerard Lacz/Peter Arnold, Inc.
556 Doug Cheeseman
557 Roger Tidman
558 Fritz Polking/Peter Arnold, Inc.
559 Nigel J. Dennis/ABPL
560 Nigel J. Dennis/ABPL
561 Peter Alden
562 Andrew R. Odum/Peter Arnold, Inc.
563 Herbert Clarke
564 Larry Sansone
565 Daniel J. Cox/DJC & Associates
566 Peter Alden
567 Anthony Bannister/ABPL
568 Howard Uible/Photo Researchers, Inc.
569 Anthony Bannister/ABPL
570 Anthony Bannister/ABPL
571 Anthony Bannister/ABPL
572 Joe McDonald
573 Anthony Bannister/ABPL
574 Joe McDonald
575 Anthony Bannister/ABPL
576 Stan Osolinski
577 Jason Laure/ABPL

GEOGRAPHICAL INDEX

Numbers in italic type refer to page numbers. Numbers in boldface type refer to plate numbers.

A

B

C

D

E

I

J

K

L

M

N

T

U

V

W

Y

Z

SPECIES INDEX

Numbers in boldface type refer to plate numbers. Numbers in italic refer to page numbers.

A

E

G

L

M

P

S

T

U

V

W

X

Z

NOTES

NOTES

STAFF

Prepared and produced by
Chanticleer Press, Inc.

Founding Publisher: Paul Steiner
Publisher: Andrew Stewart

Staff for this book:

Managing Editor: Edie Locke
Senior Editor: Amy K. Hughes
Project Editor: Patricia Fogarty
Copyeditor: Lisa Leventer
Editorial Assistant: Kristina Lucenko
Art Director: Areta Buk, Drew Stevens
Design Assistant: Taruna Singh
Production Manager: Susan Schoenfeld
Photo Editor: Giema Tsakuginow
Photo Assistant: Consuelo Tiffany Lee
Publishing Assistant: Alicia Mills
Drawings and Silhouettes:
Barry Van Dusen, Kimio Honda
Range Maps and Maps of Africa:
Paul Singer, Acme Design

Original series design by
Massimo Vignelli.

All editorial inquiries should be
addressed to:
CollinsNatural*History*
HarperCollins*Publishers*
77-85 Fulham Palace Road
London
W6 8JB
UK